GUNI SERIES ON THE SOCIAL COMMITMENT OF UNIVERSITIES 3

HIGHER EDUCATION IN THE WORLD 3

Higher Education: New Challenges and Emerging Roles for Human and Social Development

GUNI
GLOBAL UNIVERSITY
NETWORK FOR INNOVATION

palgrave
macmillan

First published 2008 by
PALGRAVE MACMILLAN
Houndmills, Basingstoke, Hampshire RG21 6XS and
175 Fifth Avenue, New York, N.Y. 10010
Companies and representatives throughout the world

PALGRAVE MACMILLAN is the global academic imprint of the Palgrave
Macmillan division of St. Martin's Press, LLC and of Palgrave Macmillan Ltd.
Macmillan® is a registered trademark in the United States, United Kingdom
and other countries. Palgrave is a registered trademark in the European Union
and other countries.

ISBN-13: 978–0–230–00048–3
ISBN-10: 0–230–00048–7

This book is printed on paper suitable for recycling and made from fully
managed and sustained forest sources. Logging, pulping and manufacturing
processes are expected to conform to the environmental regulations of the
country of origin.

A catalogue record for this book is available from the British Library.

A catalog record for this book is available from the Library of Congress.

10 9   8   7   6   5   4   3   2   1
17 16 15 14 13 12 11 10 09 08

Printed and bound in Great Britain by
Hobbs the Printers, Totton, Hampshire

TEAM INVOLVED IN THE PREPARATION OF THIS REPORT

GUNI PRESIDENT
Antoni Giró Roca

PRINCIPAL EDITOR
GUNI

GUEST EDITOR
Peter Taylor

EDITORIAL TEAM
Yazmín Cruz López
Cristina Escrigas
Josep Lobera
Francisco López Segrera
Joan Mayans
Bikas C. Sanyal
Peter Taylor

AUTHORS OF GLOBAL AND REGIONAL ISSUES
Philip Altbach (USA)
Richard Bawden (Australia)
Anne Corbett (UK)
Axel Didriksson (Mexico)
Cornelia Dragne (Canada)
Budd Hall (Canada)
Federico Mayor-Zaragoza (Spain)
Goolam Mohamedbhai (Mauritius)
Teboho Moja (South Africa)
Deepak Nayyar (India)
Rajesh Tandon (India)
Peter Taylor (UK)
Hebe Vessuri (Venezuela)
Wang Yibing (China)
Mohaya Zaytoun (Egypt)

AUTHORS OF SPECIAL CONTRIBUTIONS AND GOOD PRACTICES
Swami Atmapriyananda (India)
Firdous Azim (Bangladesh)
Miquel Barceló (Spain)
Aziza Bennani (Morocco)
L. David Brown (USA)
Carlos Cortez Ruiz (Mexico)
Yazmín Cruz López (Mexico)
Jean-Marie De Ketele (Belgium)
Gerard Delanty (Ireland)
Cristina Escrigas (Spain)
Didac Ferrer (Spain)

António Fragoso (Portugal)
Georges Haddad (France)
Claudia Harvey (Trinidad and Tobago)
Alma Herrera (Mexico)
Richard Hopper (USA)
Sylvia Hurtado (USA)
Leo Jansen (Netherlands)
Sheila Jasanoff (India)
Andy Johnston (UK)
Josep Lobera (Spain)
Francisco López Segrera (Cuba)
John McArthur (USA)
Roberta Malee Bassett (USA)
Andrei Marga (Romania)
Christine Marrett (Jamaica)
Marcela Mollis (Argentina)
Goolam Mohamedbhai (Mauritius)
Manuel Ramiro Muñoz (Colombia)
Deane Neubauer (USA)
Victor Ordoñez (Philippines)
Imanol Ordorika (Mexico)
Agustí Pérez-Foguet (Spain)
Jeffrey D. Sachs (USA)
Jamil Salmi (Morocco)
Bikas C. Sanyal (India)
Boaventura de Sousa Santos (Portugal)
Mary Stuart (UK)
Charas Suwanwela (Thailand)
Peter Taylor (UK)
José de Val (Mexico)
Josep Xercavins (Spain)
Richard Yelland (UK)
Paul Tiyambe Zeleza (Zimbabwe)

BIBLIOGRAPHY
Sonia Fernández Lauro

MAPS
Jorge Brenner Guillermo

GUNI SECRETARIAT
Miquel Cano (ICT Responsible)
Àngels Cortina (Network Coordinator)
Nuria Crespo (Research Assistant)
Yazmín Cruz López (Report Coordinator)
Cristina Escrigas (Executive Director)
Jacqueline Glarner (Communications Officer)
Josep Lobera (Research Fellow)
Valtencir Maldonado (Observatory Coordinator)
Joan Mayans (Project Manager)
Mariví Ordóñez (Administrator)
External Collaborators
Francisco López Segrera (Academic Adviser)
Bikas C. Sanyal (Executive Coordinator of the Report)

GUNI EXECUTIVE COMMITTEE
Founding Institutions
Georges Haddad (Director, Division of Higher Education, UNESCO)
Konrad Osterwalder (Rector, UNU)
Antoni Giró Roca (Rector, UPC)

GUNI Executive Director
Cristina Escrigas

Regional Offices
Peter Okebukola (Africa)
Juma Shabani (Africa)
Ramzi Salame (Arab States)
Abdel Bagi A.G. Babiker (Arab States)
Yunhe Pan (Asia and the Pacific)
Pornchai Matangkasombut Pan (Asia and the Pacific)
Marianne Frenay (Europe and North America)
Rodolfo Pinto da Luz (Latin America)
Giovanna Valenti (Latin America)

CONTENTS

TEAM INVOLVED IN THE PREPARATION OF
THIS REPORT   iii

LIST OF FIGURES, BOXES, TABLES AND MAPS   vii

LIST OF ABBREVIATIONS USED IN THIS REPORT   ix
Global University Network for Innovation   xiii

ACKNOWLEDGEMENTS   xvi

ABOUT THE AUTHORS   xix

INTRODUCTION   xxiv

FOREWORD   xxviii

OVERVIEW   xxxii

Special Contribution A HIGHER EDUCATION,
AN ACTOR IN HUMAN AND SOCIAL DEVELOPMENT:
UNESCO'S POINT OF VIEW *Georges Haddad*   xxxv

Summary of the World Declaration
on Higher Education   xxxvi

Special Contribution B CONTRIBUTION OF
HIGHER EDUCATION TO THE UN MILLENNIUM
DEVELOPMENT GOALS *Goolam Mohamedbhai*   xxxvii

The UN Millennium Development Goals   xxxix

Special Contribution C TRANSFORMING HIGHER
EDUCATION IN DEVELOPING COUNTRIES: THE ROLE
OF THE WORLD BANK *Richard Hopper, Jamil Salmi
and Roberta Malee Bassett*   xl

Special Contribution D THE OECD'S VIEW OF
THE ROLE OF HIGHER EDUCATION FOR HUMAN
AND SOCIAL DEVELOPMENT *Andy Johnston and
Richard Yelland*   xliv

Special Contribution E KEY INTERNATIONAL
FRAMEWORKS FOR THE ROLE OF HIGHER
EDUCATION IN HUMAN AND SOCIAL DEVELOPMENT
Yazmín Cruz López   xlvi

PART I

GLOBAL ISSUES ON THE ROLE OF HIGHER EDUCATION FOR HUMAN AND SOCIAL DEVELOPMENT   1

A

Present and future challenges for higher education's role in the context of globalization   3

**I.1 THE COMPLEX ROLES OF
UNIVERSITIES IN THE PERIOD OF
GLOBALIZATION** *Philip G. Altbach*   5
Special Contribution I.1 CONTEMPORARY
CHALLENGES FOR PUBLIC RESEARCH UNIVERSITIES
Imanol Ordorika   14

**I.2 THE UNIVERSITY OF THE 21ST
CENTURY: POLITICAL AND SOCIAL
TRENDS OF GLOBALIZATION –
CHALLENGES FOR HIGHER EDUCATION**
Federico Mayor-Zaragoza   20
Special Contribution I.2 THE UNIVERSITY AND
COSMOPOLITAN CITIZENSHIP *Gerard Delanty*   28

Special Contribution I.3 THE CONTRIBUTION OF
HIGHER EDUCATION TO MULTICULTURAL EXISTENCE:
PRESENT AND FUTURE CHALLENGES *Aziza Bennani* 31
Special Contribution I.4 HIGHER EDUCATION
AND ITS INSTITUTIONS AND THE CIVILIZATIONAL
PARADIGM CRISIS: REFLECTIONS, ANALYSIS AND
PROPOSALS FROM THE PERSPECTIVE OF A FORUM
OF INTERNATIONAL CIVIL SOCIETY ORGANIZATIONS
Josep Xercavins i Valls   35

**I.3 GLOBALIZATION AND MARKETS:
CHALLENGES FOR HIGHER
EDUCATION** *Deepak Nayyar*   40
Rethinking human and social development: the
perspective of Gross National Happiness   50
Special Contribution I.5 THE NEW ROLE OF
GLOBALIZED EDUCATION IN A GLOBALIZED WORLD
Deane Neubauer and Victor Ordoñez   51
Special Contribution I.6 THE SOCIAL RELEVANCE
OF HIGHER EDUCATION *Jean-Marie De Ketele*   55

B

The emerging roles of higher education: Implications for education, research, civil engagement and institutional development   63

**I.4 THE EDUCATIVE PURPOSE OF
HIGHER EDUCATION FOR HUMAN
AND SOCIAL DEVELOPMENT IN THE
CONTEXT OF GLOBALIZATION**
Richard Bawden   65
Special Contribution I.7 THE PURPOSE OF
HIGHER EDUCATION: A DISCUSSION BASED ON
EDGAR MORIN'S THINKING *GUNI Secretariat*   73
Special Contribution I.8 ETHICS AND VALUES IN
LEARNING AND TEACHING: CHALLENGES FOR THE
ROLE OF HUMAN AND SOCIAL DEVELOPMENT IN
HIGHER EDUCATION *Swami Atmapriyananda*   75
Special Contribution I.9 THE CONCEPT OF GLOBAL
CITIZENSHIP IN HIGHER EDUCATION *Mary Stuart* 79
Special Contribution I.10 HIGHER EDUCATION'S
CONTRIBUTION TO SUSTAINABLE DEVELOPMENT:
THE WAY FORWARD *Leo Jansen*   83

**I.5 HIGHER EDUCATION CURRICULA
FOR HUMAN AND SOCIAL
DEVELOPMENT** *Peter Taylor*   89
Special Contribution I.11 TRAINING FOR THE
PROFESSION OF SUSTAINABLE DEVELOPMENT:
EDUCATIONAL REQUIREMENTS FOR PRACTICAL
IMPERATIVES *John W. McArthur and Jeffrey D. Sachs* 101
Good Practice I.1 TRAINING PROFESSIONALS IN
SOCIALLY RESPONSIBLE VALUES, ATTITUDES AND
BEHAVIOUR PATTERNS (University of Concepción,
Chile) *GUNI Observatory*   105
Special Contribution I.12 HIGHER EDUCATION
CHALLENGES EMERGING FROM THE INTERCHANGE
BETWEEN SCIENCE AND ANCESTRAL KNOWLEDGE IN

CENTRAL AND SOUTH AMERICA
Manuel Ramiro Muñoz 107

Good Practice I.2 DISCIPLINARY INTEGRATION TO
PROMOTE MODELS OF SUSTAINABILITY (Kingston University,
United Kingdom) *GUNI Observatory* 112

Special Contribution I.13 MULTICULTURALISM,
INTERCULTURALITY AND LEADERSHIP *Andrei Marga* 114

**I.6 THE ROLE OF RESEARCH IN HIGHER
EDUCATION: IMPLICATIONS AND CHALLENGES
FOR AN ACTIVE CONTRIBUTION TO HUMAN
AND SOCIAL DEVELOPMENT** *Hebe Vessuri* 119

Special Contribution I.14 THE POLITICAL AND SOCIAL
CONTRIBUTION OF RESEARCH *Charas Suwanwela* 132

Good Practice 1.3 THE EXPERIENCE OF THE SCIENCE SHOP
AND THE LIVING KNOWLEDGE NETWORK IN EUROPE
GUNI Observatory 135

Special Contribution I.15 ETHICAL, ENVIRONMENTAL AND
SOCIAL IMPLICATIONS OF SCIENCE AND TECHNOLOGY:
CHALLENGES FOR THE FUTURE *Sheila Jasanoff* 137

**I.7 CIVIL ENGAGEMENT IN HIGHER EDUCATION
AND ITS ROLE IN HUMAN AND SOCIAL
DEVELOPMENT** *Rajesh Tandon* 142

Special Contribution I.16 PRACTICE–RESEARCH
ENGAGEMENT FOR HUMAN AND SOCIAL DEVELOPMENT IN
A GLOBALIZING WORLD *L. David Brown* 152

Good Practice I.4 CHALLENGES AND OPPORTUNITIES FOR
UNIVERSITY-BASED CIVIC SERVICE IN LATIN AMERICA
Carlos Cortez Ruiz 156

Good Practice I.5 EDUCATIVE EXPERIENCES THROUGH
COOPERATION FOR DEVELOPMENT ACTIVITIES
(Technical University of Catalonia, Spain) *Agustí Pérez-Foguet* 157

**I.8 INSTITUTIONAL CHALLENGES AND
IMPLICATIONS FOR HEIs: TRANSFORMATION,
MISSION AND VISION FOR THE 21ST CENTURY**
Teboho Moja 161

Special Contribution I.17 THE ROLE OF THE UNIVERSITIES IN
CONSTRUCTING AN ALTERNATIVE GLOBALIZATION
Boaventura de Sousa Santos 169

Good Practice 1.6 INSTITUTIONAL LEARNING: PARTICIPATORY
DESIGN OF THE 2015 UPC SUSTAINABILITY PLAN
(Technical University of Catalonia, Spain) *Miquel Barceló and
Didac Ferrer* 171

Good Practice I.7 FOUR EXPERIENCES OF INCLUDING SOCIAL
COMMITMENTS IN THE ROLE AND ORGANIZATION OF LATIN
AMERICAN UNIVERSITIES *GUNI Observatory* 174

Special Contribution I.18 SOCIAL RESPONSIBILITY OF
UNIVERSITIES *Alma Herrera* 176

**PART II
REGIONAL PERSPECTIVES ON THE
ROLE OF HIGHER EDUCATION FOR
HUMAN AND SOCIAL
DEVELOPMENT** 179

**II.1 AN OVERVIEW OF REGIONAL PERSPECTIVES
ON THE ROLE OF HIGHER EDUCATION IN SOCIAL
AND HUMAN DEVELOPMENT**

Bikas C. Sanyal and Francisco López Segrera 181

**II.2 THE ROLE OF HIGHER EDUCATION FOR
HUMAN AND SOCIAL DEVELOPMENT IN SUB-
SAHARAN AFRICA** *Goolam Mohamedbhai* 191

Special Contribution II.1 SCIENCE AND TECHNOLOGY FOR
HUMAN AND SOCIAL DEVELOPMENT IN AFRICA
Paul Tiyambe Zeleza 202

Good Practice II.1 SETTING UP AN OPENCOURSEWARE
PROJECT (University of the Western Cape, South Africa)
GUNI Observatory 206

Good Practice II.2 ACHIEVING SUSTAINABLE DEVELOPMENT
THROUGH CURRICULUM TRANSFORMATION IN HIGHER
EDUCATION INSTITUTIONS OF SOUTHERN AFRICA
GUNI Observatory 209

**II.3 THE ROLE OF HIGHER EDUCATION FOR
HUMAN AND SOCIAL DEVELOPMENT IN THE
ARAB STATES** *Mohaya Zaytoun* 211

**II.4 HIGHER EDUCATION FOR HUMAN AND
SOCIAL DEVELOPMENT IN ASIA AND THE
PACIFIC: NEW CHALLENGES AND CHANGING
ROLES** *Wang Yibing* 226

Good Practice II.3 BUILDING ON THE LOCAL: THE
APPROACH OF BRAC UNIVERSITY (Bangladesh) *Firdous Azim* 237

**II.5 THE ROLE OF HIGHER EDUCATION FOR
HUMAN AND SOCIAL DEVELOPMENT IN
EUROPE** *Anne Corbett* 240

Special Contribution II.2 HIGHER EDUCATION FOR HUMAN
AND SOCIAL DEVELOPMENT IN PORTUGAL *António Fragoso* 253

Good Practice II.4 THE NATIONAL SYSTEM OF RECOGNITION,
VALIDATION, CERTIFICATION OF COMPETENCES: A DESCRIPTION
OF THE LAGOA CENTRE (University of the Algarve, Portugal)
António Fragoso 255

Good Practice II.5 THE DUTCH NATIONAL NETWORK FOR
SUSTAINABLE DEVELOPMENT IN HIGHER EDUCATION
CURRICULA (Netherlands) *GUNI Observatory* 256

**II.6 THE ROLE OF HIGHER EDUCATION FOR
HUMAN AND SOCIAL DEVELOPMENT IN THE
USA AND CANADA** *Budd L. Hall and Cornelia Dragne* 259

Special Contribution II.3 HIGHER EDUCATION FOR HUMAN
AND SOCIAL DEVELOPMENT IN THE USA *Sylvia Hurtado* 273

Good Practice II.6 TRAINING AND RESEARCH FOR
COMMUNITY-BASED DEVELOPMENT (Coady International
Institute, Canada) *GUNI Observatory* 278

Good Practice II.7 RESEARCH AND SERVICE-LEARNING
MODEL (Duke University, USA) *GUNI Observatory* 280

**II.7 THE ROLE OF HIGHER EDUCATION FOR
HUMAN AND SOCIAL DEVELOPMENT IN LATIN
AMERICA AND THE CARIBBEAN** *Axel Didriksson* 283

Special Contribution II.4 THE SOCIAL RESPONSIBILITY OF
UNIVERSITIES IN LATIN AMERICA *Alma Herrera* 295

Special Contribution II.5 HIGHER EDUCATION IN
ARGENTINA: TAKING STOCK AT THE TURN OF THE MILLENNIUM
Marcela Mollis 297

Special Contribution II.6 HIGHER EDUCATION FOR HUMAN
AND SOCIAL DEVELOPMENT IN THE CARIBBEAN
Claudia Harvey and Christine Marrett 300

Good Practice II.8 DESCRIPTION OF THE MEXICO
MULTICULTURAL NATION UNIVERSITY PROGRAMME
(UNAM, Mexico) *José de Val* 303

PART III
DELPHI POLL   305

III.1 DELPHI POLL – HIGHER EDUCATION FOR
HUMAN AND SOCIAL DEVELOPMENT
Josep Lobera and GUNI Secretariat   307

PART IV
STATISTICAL APPENDIX   333

IV.1 STATISTICAL APPENDIX   335

FURTHER READING: SELECTED
BIBLIOGRAPHY ON HIGHER EDUCATION FOR
HUMAN AND SOCIAL DEVELOPMENT
Sonia Fernández Lauro   365

FIGURES

II.6.1	University enrolment in Canada increased	261
II.6.2	Participation in post-secondary education in the USA increased	262
III.1.1	Participants in the first round by region (%)	309
III.1.2	Participants in the first round by profile (%)	309
III.1.3	Participants in the second round by region (%)	310
III.1.4	Participants in the second round by profile (%)	310

Special Contribution I.10

1	SD research in context	84
2	Areas of SD-related tension in HE	85
3	Demands on graduates	86
4 and 5	Modes of research in HE	87

Special Contribution I.12

| 1 | Classification of higher education experiences from and for indigenous peoples | 109 |

BOXES

I.6.1	Quantifying asymmetry	121
I.7.1	Service-learning in ancient times	146
II.2.1	University of Bakhat Alruda, Sudan: educating rural women	196
II.2.2	University for Development Studies, Ghana	199
II.3.1	The Arab Science and Technology Foundation (ASTF)	221
II.3.2	The March 9 academic group	222
II.6.1	The knowledge to live together	263
II.6.2	Globalization changes our communicative culture	264
II.6.3	Economic inequalities translate into academic inequalities	265
II.6.4	HEIs seek increased participation of minorities both as students and as teachers	266
II.6.5	Knowledge transfer and community involvement – part of a university's mission	266
II.6.6	University presidents about civic engagement	267
II.6.7	'Our' university	267
II.6.8	Community engagement	267
II.6.9	University goes green	268
II.6.10	Sombre self-assessment	269
II.6.11	In Canada, PSE is recognized as crucial to social cohesion	270
II.6.12	An evolving and transparent social contract	270
II.6.13	HE for a vibrant civil society	271

TABLES

II.1.1	Regional average of enrolment, GER and GPI (1999 and 2004)	182
II.2.1	Tertiary enrolment in S&T fields in certain African countries	194
II.2.2	Female enrolment and teaching staff at the tertiary level in sub-Saharan Africa	196
II.2.3	Female enrolment in S&T fields in certain African countries	196
II.3.1	Indicators of HE access in the Arab world (1999–2005)	212
II.5.1	The Europe of higher education: membership of selected international organizations	242
II.5.2	Human Development Index (HDI) ratings in Europe, as it is variously defined	243
II.5.3	The policy agendas of the WCHE and 'Europe of Higher Education' organizations	244
II.5.4	Delivering on a modernization agenda for Europe: The Commission's nine action points	246
II.5.5	The strategy for the European Higher Education Area in a global setting, adopted by European Ministers for Higher Education, London 2007	246
II.5.6	The trajectory of the Bologna Process 1999–2007	247
II.6.1	Current trends in HE and democracy	266
III.1.1	The initial sample of people invited to participate	308

III.1.2	Participants in the first round by region and profile	308
III.1.3	Home country of the participants	309
III.1.4	Participants in the second round by region and profile	310
III.1.5	Reasons why higher education should contribute to human and social development	311
III.1.6	Why should higher education play an active role in human and social development (open response)?	311
III.1.7	Main arguments of the Asia-Pacific participants	312
III.1.8	Main arguments of the European participants	312
III.1.9	Main arguments of the North American participants	312
III.1.10	Main arguments of the African participants	312
III.1.11	Main arguments of the Arab States participants	312
III.1.12	Main arguments of the Latin American and Caribbean participants	313
III.1.13	Most frequently identified challenges for human and social development	313
III.1.14	Priority challenges for African participants	314
III.1.15	Priority challenges for Latin American and Caribbean participants	314
III.1.16	Priority challenges for Asia-Pacific participants	315
III.1.17	Priority challenges for Arab States participants	315
III.1.18	Priority challenges for European participants	315
III.1.19	Priority challenges for North American participants	315
III.1.20	Priority action lines	317
III.1.21	Priority action lines for African experts	317
III.1.22	Priority action lines for Latin American and Caribbean experts	317
III.1.23	Priority action lines for Asia-Pacific experts	317
III.1.24	Priority action lines for Arab States experts	318
III.1.25	Priority action lines for European experts	318
III.1.26	Priority action lines for North American experts	318
III.1.27	A general selection of the attributes that are, will be and should be acquired in HEI (second round)	319
III.1.28	African participants' selection of attributes	320
III.1.29	Latin American and Caribbean participants' selection of attributes	321
III.1.30	Asia-Pacific participants' selection of attributes	322
III.1.31	Arab States participants' selection of attributes	322
III.1.32	European participants' selection of attributes	323
III.1.33	North American participants' selection of attributes	323
III.1.34	Universities in the knowledge society	326
IV.1.1	Adult and youth literacy (2004)	336
IV.1.2	Education expenditure, spending as a percentage of gross domestic product/financial year ending in 2004	342
IV.1.3	Education expenditure, sources as a percentage of gross domestic product/financial year ending in 2004	347
IV.1.4	Tertiary education enrolment and teaching staff	352
IV.1.5	Reseach and development expenditures as a percentage of the GDP and researchers in R&D per million people	357
IV.1.6	Human development rank, index, total population and GDP per capita	360

Special Contribution C

Table 1	Recent higher education studies (2001–2006)	xli
Table 2	New commitments for education by sub-sector (fiscal year 01–06)	xlii

Special Contribution I.8

Table 1	Individual and social development at each layer of the personality	77

Special Contribution II.5

Table 1	New students by management sector, 2005	297
Table 2	Number of students: average annual growth rate (AAGR) by management sector, 2005	298
Table 3	Distribution of students by management sector, 2005	298

Special Contribution II.6

Table 1	Performance of CARICOM countries in respect of the 15% tertiary enrolment target for 2005	301

MAPS

1	Number of GUNI members per country	xiv
2	Higher education gross enrolment ratios (GER) by country and human development index (HDI), 2006	lii
3	Gender parity index in tertiary education	60
4	Number of researchers per million people	130

AAC&U	American Association of Colleges and Universities		CBHE	Cross-border Higher Education
AAGR	Average Annual Growth Rate		CBPR	Community-based Participatory Research
AAOU	Asian Association of Open Universities		CCD	Centre for Development Cooperation
AASCU	American Association of State Colleges and Universities		CDESR	Steering Committee for Higher Education and Research
AAU	Association of African Universities		CEE	Central and Eastern Europe
ACCORD	African Centre for the Constructive Resolution of Disputes		CEGEP	Colleges of General and Vocational Education
ACU	Association of Commonwealth Universities		CEPES	European Centre for Higher Education
ADB	Asian Development Bank		CIDA	Canadian International Development Agency
ADEA	Association for the Development of Education in Africa		CIHR	Canadian Institutes for Health Research
ADF	African Development Fund		CITIES	Sustainability Centre
AECI	Spanish Agency for International Cooperation		CMS	City Montessori School
AIDS	Acquired Immune Deficiency Syndrome		CNDPI	National Committee for the Development of the Indigenous Peoples
AISHE	Auditing Instrument for Sustainability in Higher Education		CONCORD	European NGO Confederation for Relief and Development
AJKU	University of Azad Jammu and Kashmir		C-SCAIPE	Centre for Sustainable Communities Achieved through Integrated Professional Education
ALECSO	Arab League Education, Culture and Science		CSL	Community Service-learning
APQN	Asia-Pacific Quality Network		CSOs	Civil Society Organizations
ARC	Arab Regional Conference		CSPR	Committee on Scientific Planning and Review
ASSWI	Association of Schools of Social Work in India		CSUCA	Higher Council of Latin American Universities
ASTF	Arab Science and Technology Foundation		CURA	Community University Research Alliance
AU	African Union		DAAD	German Academic Exchange Service
AUAP	Association of Universities of Asia and the Pacific		DDT	Dichloro-Diphenyl-Trichloroethane
AUCC	Association of Universities and Colleges of Canada		DHO	Dutch National Network for Sustainable Development in Higher Education Curricula
AVOIR	African Virtual Open Initiative and Resource		DMPA	Depot Medroxyprogesterone Acetate
BA	Bachelor of Arts			
BC	British Columbia		EC	European Commission
BFUG	Bologna Follow-up Group		ECDO	Expertise Centre for Sustainable Development
CARICOM	Caribbean Community			
CAUT	Canadian Association of University Teachers			

ECTS	European Credit Transfer System		HIV	Human Immunodeficiency Virus
EFA	Education for All		HPI	Human Poverty Index
EHEA	European Higher Education Area		IAU	International Association of Universities
EI	Education International		IB	International Baccalaureate Programme
EIT	European Institute of Technology		ICI	Institute of Sciences
ELSI	Ethical, Legal and Social Implications		ICO	Institute of Conurbation
EMAS	Eco-management and Audit Scheme		ICRG	International Council for Risk Governance
ENHR	Essential National Health Research		ICSU	International Council for Science
ENQA	European Association for Quality Assurance in Higher Education		ICT	Information and Communication Technology
ENTS	National School of Social Work		IDB	Inter-American Development Bank
ERA	European Research Area		IDEI	Institute of Industry
ESREA	European Society for Research on the Education of Adults		IDH	Institute of Human Development
ESU	European Student Union		IDRC	International Development Research Centre
EU	European Union		IDS	Institute of Development Studies
EUA	European University Association		IEEE	Institute of Electrical and Electronic Engineers
EURASHE	European Association of Institutions in Higher Education		IESALC	International Institution for Higher Education in Latin America and the Caribbean
EWB	Engineers Without Borders			
FAO	Food and Agriculture Organization of the United Nations		IGNOU	The Indira Gandhi National Open University
FAWE	Forum for African Women Educationalists		IGOs	Inter-governmental Organizations
FLACSO	Latin American Faculty of Social Sciences		IHDP	International Human Development Programme
FTE	Full-time Equivalent		IICBA	International Institute for Capacity Building in Africa
GATS	General Agreement on Trade in Services		IIEP	International Institute for Educational Planning
GATT	General Agreement on Tariffs and Trade		IISUE	Institute for Research on Universities and Education
GCAP	Global Call to Action Against Poverty			
GDI	Gender-related Development Index		ILO	International Labour Organization
GDP	Gross Domestic Product		IMF	International Monetary Fund
GE	General Education		IMHE	Programme on Institutional Management in Higher Education
GER	Gross Enrolment Ratio			
GERD	Gross Expenditure on Research and Development		IPCC	Inter-governmental Panel on Climate Change
GHESP	Global Higher Education for Sustainability Partnership		ISESCO	Islamic Educational, Scientific and Cultural Organization
GNP	Gross National Product		ISSC	International Social Science Council
GPI	Gender Parity Index/Genuine Progress Indicator		ISSNET	International Science Shop Network
GUNI	Global University Network for Innovation		IT	Information Technologies
			ITU	International Telecommunication Union
HD	Human Development		IUAES	International Union of Anthropological and Ethnological Sciences
HDI	Human Development Index			
HE	Higher Education		IVIC	Venezuelan Institute for Scientific Research
HECS	Higher Education Contribution Scheme			
HEFCE	Higher Education Funding Council for England		KU	Kingston University
HE4SD	Higher Education for Sustainable Development		LAC	Latin America and the Caribbean
HEI	Higher Education Institution		LDCs	Less Developed Countries
HESA	Higher Education South Africa			

LEAPS	Learning through Experience, Action, Partnership, and Service	SAUVCA	South African Universities Vice-Chancellors Association
LEED	Leadership in Energy and Environmental Design	SCA	Science Council of Asia
LOM	Learning Object Metadata	SCIPAS	Study and Conference on Improving Public Access to Science through Science Shops
MDGs	(United Nations) Millennium Development Goals	SD	Sustainable Development
MEW	Measure of Economic Welfare	SEAMEO	Southeast Asian Ministers of Education Organization
MIT	Massachusetts Institute of Technology	SELA	The Latin American Economic System
M.Phil.	Master of Philosophy	SGS	Steering Group for Sustainability
NASULGC	National Association of State Universities and Land Grant Colleges	SHD	Social and Human Development
		Sida	Swedish International Development Agency
NCE	Networks of Centres of Excellence	SPU	Argentine Secretariat of University Policies
NCES	National Center for Education Statistics		
NER	Net Enrolment Rate	SRU	Social Responsibility of Universities
NGO	Non-governmental Organization	SSA	Sub-Saharan Africa
NSERC	National Science and Engineering Research Council	SSHRC	Social Sciences and Humanities Research Council
OCW	OpenCourseWare	STD	Dutch Sustainable Technology Development
OCWC	OpenCourseWare Consortium		
ODA	Official Development Assistance	STI	Science, Technology and Innovation
ODCs	Other Developing Countries	TB	Tuberculosis
OECD	Organisation for Economic Cooperation and Development	TCU	University Community Work
		TNCs	Transnational Companies
PANCAP	Pan-Caribbean Partnership Against HIV and AIDS	TRAMS	Training and Mentoring of Science Shops
PD	Participatory Development	TTISSA	Teacher Training Initiative for Sub-Saharan Africa
Ph.D.	Doctor of Philosophy		
PR	Participatory Research	TWAS	Third World Academy of Sciences
PRE	Practice–Research Engagement	UACM	Autonomous University of Mexico City
PRIA	Society for Participatory Research in Asia	UAIN	Intercultural Autonomous University
PSE	Post-secondary Education	UAM	Autonomous University of Mexico
PSU	Portland State University	UASLP	Autonomous University of San Luis Potosí
PUMC	Mexico Multicultural Nation University Programme		
		UBA	University of Buenos Aires
R&D	Research and Development	UBUNTU	World Forum of Civil Society Networks
RCE	Regional Centres of Expertise	UCC	Cooperative University of Colombia
REEP	Regional Environmental Education Programme	UCLA	University of California at Los Angeles
RNCs	Regional Nodal Centres	UDUAL	Union of Latin American Universities
RSL	Research Service-Learning	UIA	Ibero-American University
RVCC	National System of Recognition, Validation and Certification of Competences	UIS	UNESCO Institute for Statistics
		UK	United Kingdom
		ULSF	University Leaders for a Sustainable Future
SAARC	South Asian Association for Regional Cooperation		
		UN	United Nations
SADC	Southern African Development Community	UNAM	National Autonomous University of Mexico
SAP	Structural Adjustment Programme		
SARUA	Southern African Regional Universities Association	UNCED	United Nations Conference on Environment and Development
S&T	Science and Technology	UNCTAD	United Nations Conference on Trade and Development

UNDP	United Nations Development Programme	URACAN	University of the Autonomous Regions of the Nicaraguan Coast
UNEP	United Nations Environment Programme	US	United States
		USA	United States of America
UNESCO	United Nations Educational, Scientific and Cultural Organization	USDLA	United States Distance Learning Association
UNGS	National University of General Sarmiento	UV	University of Veracruz
		UVic	University of Victoria
UNICE	Union of Industrial and Employers' Confederations of Europe	UWC	University of the Western Cape
		UWI	University of the West Indies
UNICORE	Uniform Interface to Computing Resources	WB	World Bank
		WCED	World Commission on Environment and Development
UNITAR	United Nations Institute for Training and Research		
		WCHE	World Conference on Higher Education
UNITWIN	University Twinning and Networking Scheme	WFEO	World Federation of Engineering Organizations
UNPFII	United Nations Permanent Forum on Indigenous Issues	WGHE	Working Group on Higher Education
		WHO	World Health Organization
UNU	United Nations University	WIDER	World Institute for Development Economics Research
UPC	Technical University of Catalonia		
UPEACE	University for Peace	WTO	World Trade Organization
UPN	National Pedagogic University	WWII	World War II

LIST OF ABBREVIATIONS USED IN THIS REPORT

The Global University Network for Innovation (GUNI) was created in 1999 by UNESCO, the United Nations University (UNU) and the Technical University of Catalonia (UPC), the institution that hosts its Secretariat. GUNI is a global network composed of over 120 members from around the world that include the UNESCO Chairs in Higher Education, higher education institutions, research centres and networks related to higher education.

GUNI members are spread worldwide and distributed in five regions that follow specific UNESCO definitions (Africa, the Arab States, Asia and the Pacific, Europe and North America, and Latin America and the Caribbean). In each region GUNI has a regional office with at least one regional representative. One representative from each of the founding institutions (UNESCO, the UNU and the UPC) and a maximum of two representatives from each region constitute the Executive Committee of GUNI. The President of GUNI is the rector of the UPC.

Mission and objectives
GUNI's mission is to contribute to the reinforcement of higher education throughout the world by helping to put into practice the decisions taken at UNESCO's World Conference on Higher Education (WCHE) held in Paris in 1998. Its main objectives are to reflect on and to promote innovation, universities' social commitment and the quality of higher education. Specifically, GUNI aims to:

- Contribute to the implementation of the WCHE's *World Declaration and Framework for Priority Action for Change and Development in Higher Education*, with a view to strengthening local, national and regional development. This includes helping to bridge the growing gap between developed and developing countries in the field of higher education and research
- Follow the lines of the UNESCO/UNU Forum in order to obtain an overall perspective of existing problems and propose potential solutions, and by so doing to consolidate the role of higher education as an essential means of development within knowledge societies
- Contribute to the reform and renewal of higher education policies across the world
- Contribute to research on higher education and to ensure that progress is made, particularly in developing countries
- Promote cooperation between higher education institutions and society.

Lines of Action
Higher Education in the World report
Higher Education in the World is published as part of the GUNI Series on the Social Commitment of Universities. This report is the result of an overall analysis of higher education in the world. A specific subject is chosen for each edition, reflecting on the key issues and challenges facing higher education and its institutions in the 21st century. A Delphi poll, statistical appendix, analytic maps and a detailed bibliography round off the report.

International Barcelona Conference on Higher Education
The GUNI Conference is an international forum for debate on the challenges facing higher education. Held in Barcelona and attended by renowned experts, university leaders, academics, policymakers and practitioners from all over the world, the Conference addresses innovative proposals and the results of the latest research.

Universities and Social Commitment Observatory
The Observatory detects and disseminates good practices in its endeavour to serve as a meeting point between universities. Its purpose is to facilitate the transfer of good practices and to bring about change within higher education institutions. In order to disseminate practices among institutions and broaden their role in the construction of harmonious societies, the Observatory also acts as a resource centre, using the common goal of social commitment as its underlying premise.

Communication and Networking
GUNI uses information and communication technologies intensively to promote debate, creation and exchange of knowledge on higher education worldwide. The website, which has an increasing range of open-access multimedia content, and the monthly newsletter, which is delivered to thousands of subscribers, are cornerstones in the accomplishment of the GUNI mission.

Research Projects
GUNI undertakes research projects on higher education for public and private not-for-profit institutions. Every year a Delphi survey is conducted for the report to gauge the opinions of over 100 participants taken from academics, politicians, civil society members and professionals. To do so, it has a group of researchers who apply GUNI's mission to practical realities.

http://www.guni-rmies.net

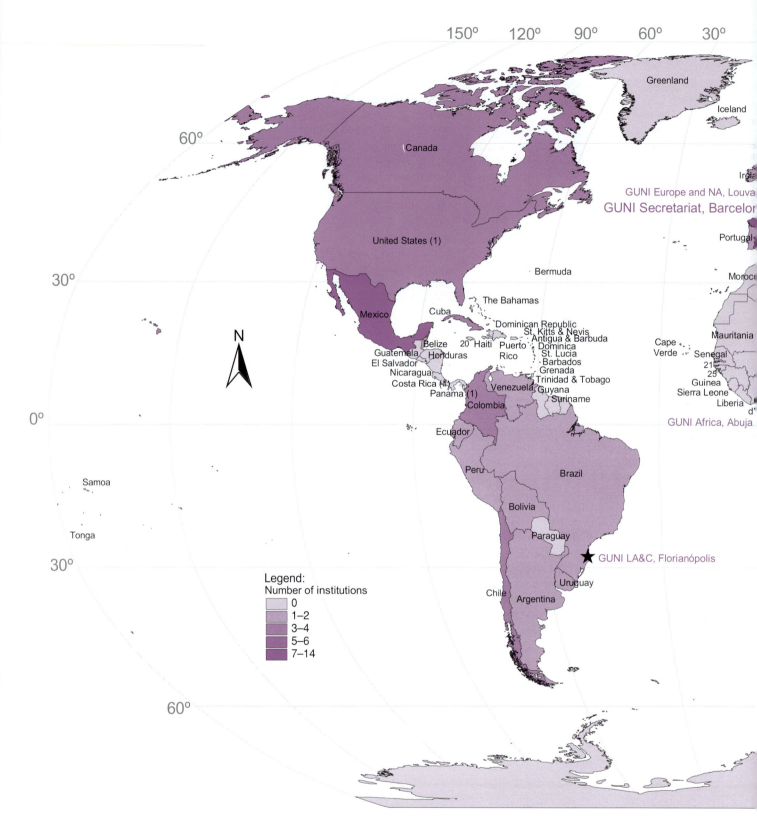

150°   120°   90°   60°   30°

Greenland

Iceland

Canada

Irel

GUNI Europe and NA, Louva

GUNI Secretariat, Barcelor

Portugal

60°

Moroc

United States (1)

30°

Bermuda

The Bahamas

Cuba

Dominican Republic

Mauritania

St. Kitts & Nevis
Antigua & Barbuda
Dominica

N

Mexico

Cape
Verde

Senegal

20 Haiti Puerto St. Lucia
Rico Barbados

21
25

Belize
Guatemala Honduras
El Salvador
Nicaragua
Costa Rica (4)

Guinea
Sierra Leone
Liberia

Grenada
Trinidad & Tobago
Venezuela Guyana

d'

Panama (1)

Suriname

Colombia

GUNI Africa, Abuja

0°

Ecuador

Samoa

Peru

Brazil

Bolivia

Tonga

Paraguay

★ GUNI LA&C, Florianópolis

30°

Legend:
Number of institutions

Uruguay

Chile

Argentina

	0
	1–2
	3–4
	5–6
	7–14

60°

Notes

Members approved in July 2007
Provisional members until October 2007 in brackets
Classification method: natural breaks (Jenks optimization)

MAP 1   **Number of GUNI members per country**

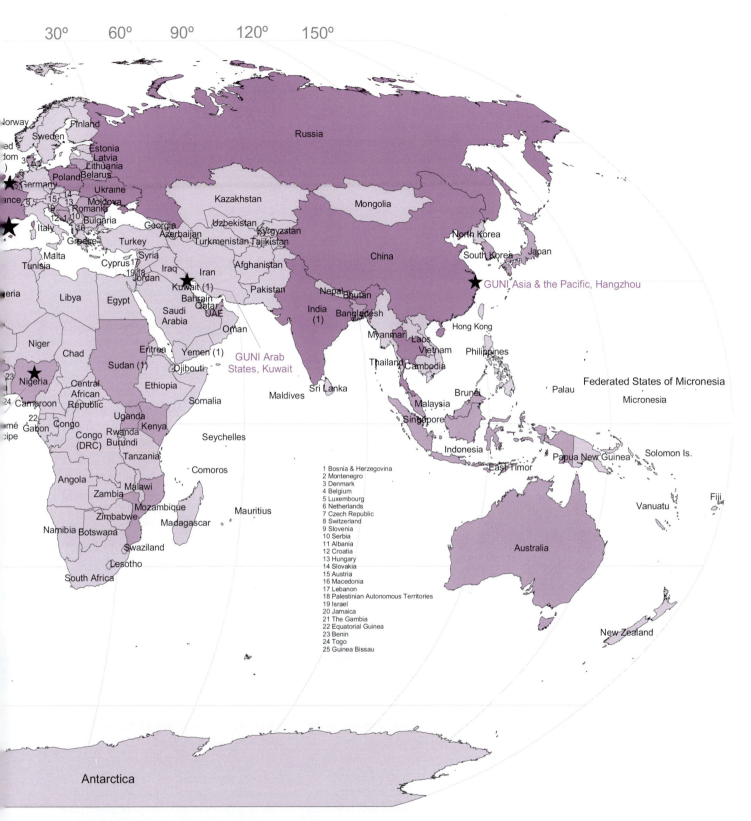

30°　60°　90°　120°　150°

Norway
Sweden
ed
dom 3 43
6
Germany
ance 8
15 14
9 13
12 1 10
Italy 11 16
Greece
Finland
Estonia
Latvia
Lithuania
Poland Belarus
Ukraine
Moldova
Romania
Bulgaria
Georgia
Azerbaijan
Turkey
Cyprus 17
19 18
Jordan
Syria
Iraq
Kuwait (1)
Bahrain
Qatar
UAE
Oman
Malta
Tunisia

Russia

Kazakhstan

Uzbekistan
Turkmenistan Tajikistan
Kyrgyzstan

Mongolia

China

North Korea
South Korea
Japan

GUNI Asia & the Pacific, Hangzhou

Afghanistan

eria
Libya
Egypt
Saudi
Arabia

Niger
Chad
23
Nigeria
24
Cameroon
Central
African
Republic
omé
cipe
Gabon
Congo
Congo
(DRC)
22
Sudan (1)
Eritrea
Yemen (1)
Djibouti
Ethiopia
Somalia

Pakistan
Nepal Bhutan
India
(1)
Bangladesh
Myanmar
Laos
Vietnam
Thailand Cambodia

Hong Kong

Philippines

Federated States of Micronesia
Micronesia

GUNI Arab
States, Kuwait

Sri Lanka
Maldives

Brunei
Malaysia
Singapore

Palau

Uganda
Rwanda Kenya
Burundi
Tanzania

Seychelles

Indonesia

East Timor

Papua New Guinea

Solomon Is.

Angola
Malawi
Zambia
Zimbabwe
Mozambique
Namibia Botswana
Madagascar

Comoros

Mauritius

1 Bosnia & Herzegovina
2 Montenegro
3 Denmark
4 Belgium
5 Luxembourg
6 Netherlands
7 Czech Republic
8 Switzerland
9 Slovenia
10 Serbia
11 Albania
12 Croatia
13 Hungary
14 Slovakia
15 Austria
16 Macedonia
17 Lebanon
18 Palestinian Autonomous Territories
19 Israel
20 Jamaica
21 The Gambia
22 Equatorial Guinea
23 Benin
24 Togo
25 Guinea Bissau

Vanuatu

Fiji

Australia

Swaziland
Lesotho
South Africa

New Zealand

Antarctica

Vector layer source: ESRI Data; Projection: Robinson

MAP 1　XV

ACKNOWLEDGEMENTS

Cristina Escrigas

A report on the new challenges and emerging roles in higher education for human and social development would not have been possible without the participation of a large number of people and institutions. Although previous reports were also the result of a collective effort, the pluralism and diversity of the contributions in this report are especially notable. The report aims to provide ideas and proposals to give direction on the future role of higher education. This is not an easy, or indeed customary, exercise in the academic world, which is more accustomed to providing understanding of what already exists and generating new knowledge than to applying acquired knowledge to planning the future. The GUNI Secretariat asked for this exercise to be based on what should ideally happen in order for higher education to contribute to human and social development, rather than be based on possible future scenarios that might result from the present situation. These ideas were shaped from the excellent academic work and renowned research activities of all the contributors. I would therefore like to express my sincere gratitude to each and every one of the people who have supported this project and who have believed and participated in it.

First, I would like to thank Antoni Giró Roca, President of the Global University Network for Innovation (GUNI) and Rector of the Technical University of Catalonia (UPC), for his constant, unconditional support, his useful suggestions and his complete confidence in the project. His willingness to help was especially important since GUNI's headquarters are located in a technical university, in which there is no department carrying out research on higher education. This is in itself an innovative characteristic, as the incorporation of knowledge across disciplines will be necessary in educational institutions in the future. I would like to point out that the UPC has demonstrated its ability to anticipate events in this way ever since it was founded. In its long history, it has always known how to identify developments that are ahead of their time and apply them in its own setting, thus providing leadership and becoming a reference point in universities' institutional innovation. The Rec-

tor of the UPC also ensured that GUNI and this project could count on the help of all the staff at the UPC Rectorate. For their cooperation and support, I am grateful to Josefina Auladell, UPC Manager; Emilia Bordoy and her team at the Rector's Bureau; and Joan Brunet, the Vice-Manager of Institutional Relations, as well as the units he manages.

I would like to express my gratitude to Banco Santander and its President, Emilio Botín for crucially providing the financial support for GUNI's mission. My thanks also to José Antonio Villasante, José Manuel Moreno, Alfredo Albáizar, Alberto Alciturri, Antonio Pérez-Portabella and David Gutiérrez. GUNI would like to repay their invaluable help with gratitude and tangible results, by producing a report of international scope and academic rigour, and of both institutional and political interest for the professionals around the world involved in analysing and developing higher education. Their help also enabled us to distribute more than 2,000 copies of the report, mostly in developing countries, thus fulfilling part of our objective by contributing to local capacity building in human and social development.

I am deeply grateful to Peter Taylor, the guest editor, for his contribution and his willingness to take part in the project, his dedication, and his ideas, enthusiasm and patience during the whole process. GUNI wishes to show its appreciation and respect for the Institute of Development Studies in Sussex for collaborating with us. I sincerely hope that our experience of cooperation will not end here and that we will have new opportunities to work together in the future. I would like to thank Joaquim Tres, who had the perspicacity and resolve to promote this opportunity in July 2006 before leaving GUNI.

I would also like to express my gratitude for the contribution made to the project by Francisco López Segrera, the Academic Adviser of GUNI, who supported and understood the project and who was always prepared to work whenever necessary; and for the contribution made by Bikas C. Sanyal, the Executive Coordinator of the report, without whose participation the project could not have been accomplished. He put great effort and enthusiasm into carrying out the most difficult tasks in time to meet the deadlines. I extend my gratitude to the rest of the members of the editorial team: to Yazmín Cruz López, the Coordinator of the report, whose professional work and untiring dedication transformed the contributors' work into a publication; to Joan Mayans, who found time to participate, in spite of his many other duties; and to Josep Lobera for enriching the project with his committed vision of reality. Thanks to the whole editorial team, who worked hard even when I could not be present, and whose excellent contribution to the project was essential to its success.

It goes without saying that the personnel of the GUNI Secretariat collaborated constantly in the development of the report. I would especially like to mention the work done by Joan Mayans, the Project Manager, who ensured that GUNI's work was not adversely affected by the magnitude of this one project. Many thanks to Josep Lobera for his dedication, in spite of the limitations of time and resources that he had to battle with; he made a great effort, coordinating the process and integrating the contents of the Delphi poll. He worked with Nuria Crespo, whose dedication and rigour in obtaining and processing the data from numerous participants in different parts of the world I greatly appreciate. Thanks to Montserrat Constans and Valtencir Maldonado for enabling us to include good practices from the Universities and Social Commitment Observatory in this report. Thanks for their support and dedication in the framework of their own tasks, including the academic seminar, to Àngels Cortina, Mariví Ordóñez, Miquel Cano, Manuel Fernández, Jacqueline Glarner and Juan Carlos González.

Thanks also to our editors: José María Hernández, General Manager of Mundi-Prensa Libros, and Alison Jones, Editor of On-line Reference Works at Palgrave Macmillan, along with their respective teams, for all the help that they have given us, their willingness to cooperate and their flexibility in adapting to the needs of everyone involved. My most sincere thanks to Linda Norris and her team at Aardvark Editorial for all their editorial work. I wish to express my gratitude for the cooperation and support of the UPC Language and Terminology Service, and especially to Alan Lounds, Head of the Language Advisory Unit, for the dedication, flexibility and professionalism with which he has, once again, undertaken this project.

When the project was first conceived and throughout the whole process of producing the report we received the wholehearted support of the GUNI Executive Committee. The representatives of the regional GUNI offices – Peter Okebukola and Juma Shabani in Africa; Rodolfo Pinto da Luz and Giovanna Valenti in Latin America; Wei Yang, Pornchai Matangkasombut, Ni Mingjiang and Wang Yibing in Asia and the Pacific; Abdel Bagi, A.G. Babiker and Ramzi Salame in the Arab States; and Marianne Frenay in Europe – have transmitted their ideas, criteria and comments to the Secretariat and participated actively in the academic seminar organized by GUNI (5–6 July 2007).

I wish to extend my gratitude to UNESCO and the United Nations University (UNU). These institutional supports are a great help to GUNI in the task of trying to fulfil in the best way possible its founding mandate. I would therefore like to take this opportunity to thank these institutions for extending GUNI's foundation agreement last November (2006) and thus giving everyone on the project renewed confidence in the future. My most sincere thanks to Georges Haddad, Director of the UNESCO Division of Higher Education, and also to Hans van Ginkel, Rector of UNU until August 2007, for his expert advice, confidence and explicit support of GUNI.

I would like to express my sincere gratitude to Marco Antonio Rodrígues Días for his enduring support, his advice, his ideas and his active participation throughout the process of drawing up the report, and also during the academic seminar; his help was invaluable. I would also like to express my gratitude here to Carmen Piñán, the Programme Specialist at the UNESCO Division of Higher Education, for her active participation in the academic seminar and on the executive committee of GUNI, where she provided support and made valuable proposals.

I am grateful to Víctor Ordoñez, Higher Education Adviser and Senior Education Fellow at the East–West Center (Hawaii), for having agreed once again to help with the process of drawing up the report and with the academic seminar. His contribution is an excellent complement to the report.

Special thanks are due to all those who dedicated their time and knowledge to writing the different parts of this report: the global and regional sections and the special contributions, good practices and appendices. My thanks go to all the writers of the report. Many of them, despite their busy schedules, dedicated time and effort to writing their articles and redrafting them in accordance with the recommendations of the editorial team and the participants in the academic seminar. All of them have put something of themselves into this report and are its true protagonists.

I am grateful for the invaluable contributions of Philip G. Altbach, Richard Bawden, Anne Corbett, Axel Didriksson, Cornelia Dragne, Budd Hall, Federico Mayor-Zaragoza, Goolam Mohamedbhai, Teboho Moja, Deepak Nayyar, Rajesh Tandon, Hebe Vessuri, Wang Yibing and Mohaya Zaytoun. I much appreciate the enthusiasm and willingness of Edgar Morin, to whom I feel close, to participate in this report. I regret that personal circumstances prevented him from doing so this time and I hope that we will work together in the future on another project.

Together with the main authors, another group of experts have presented special contributions, good practices, boxes, bibliographic details, statistical appendices and maps. These all helped to give this report its final shape. I would therefore like to express my most sincere gratitude to all of these people: Swami Atmapriyananda, Firdous Azim, Miquel Barceló, Aziza Bennani, L. David Brown, Carlos Cortez, Yazmín Cruz López, Jean-Marie De Ketele, Gerard Delanty, Didac Ferrer, António Fragoso, Georges Haddad, Claudia Harvey, Alma Herrera, Richard Hopper, Sylvia Hurtado, Leo Jansen, Sheila Jasanoff, Andy Johnston, Josep Lobera, John McArthur, Roberta Malee Bassett, Andrei Marga, Christine Marrett, Goolam Mohamedbhai, Marcela Mollis, Manuel Ramiro Muñoz, Deane Neubauer, Víctor Ordoñez, Imanol Ordorika, Agustí Pérez-Foguet, Jeffrey D. Sachs, Jamil Salmi, Bikas C. Sanyal, Boaventura de Sousa Santos, Mary Stuart, Charas Suwanwela, José de Val, Josep Xercavins, Richard Yelland and Paul Tiyambe Zeleza. Furthermore, I am extremely grateful to Sonia Fernández Lauro, who compiled the bibliography of the report, as she does every year. As for the maps, I would especially like to mention the efforts made by Jorge Brenner Guillermo, who once again did an excellent job.

I would like to thank the 214 experts who took part in the Delphi poll for their time, patience and commitment, and for their opinions. Without their contributions it would not have been possible to provide contents of such high quality. All their names appear in the appendix to the corresponding paper in this report. Their contributions provide new perspectives for thinking and taking decisions about the future of higher education.

We are grateful to the Spanish Ministry of Education and Science (MEC), the Government of Catalonia and Barcelona City Council's Department of Economic Promotion for the unconditional support they gave to this project, especially during the International Barcelona Conferences on Higher Education, in which the different reports were presented.

I also thank Jaume Pagès, the Executive Director of Universia, who always expressed his support for the project. I am especially grateful for his willingness to disseminate our work and to participate actively in it. GUNI will always be grateful to him for being the first president of this project, and enabling it to be set up.

Various organizations and institutions have helped to elaborate this report by providing data, information sources and other research materials. Many thanks to all of them.

Finally I would like to apologize for any omissions and for any inconvenience or difficulties that we may have unintentionally caused during the project.

AUTHORS OF GLOBAL AND REGIONAL ISSUES

Philip G. Altbach

Philip G. Altbach is the J. Donald Monan, S.J., Professor of Higher Education and director of the Center for International Higher Education at the Lynch School of Education, Boston College. He has been a senior associate of the Carnegie Foundation for the Advancement of Teaching and served as editor of *The Review of Higher Education, Comparative Education Review* and *Educational Policy*. He is the author of *Comparative Higher Education, Student Politics in America* and other books. He co-edited the *International Handbook of Higher Education*. Dr Altbach holds BA, MA and Ph.D. degrees from the University of Chicago. He has taught at the University of Wisconsin–Madison and the State University of New York at Buffalo, where he directed the Comparative Education Center and chaired the Department of Educational Organization, Administration and Policy. He was a postdoctoral fellow and lecturer on education at Harvard University. He is a guest professor at the Institute of Higher Education at Peking University in China. He has been a visiting professor at Stanford University, the *Institut de Sciences Politiques* in Paris, and the University of Mumbai in India, and a Fulbright Scholar in India, Malaysia and Singapore. He has received awards from the Japan Society for the Promotion of Science and the German Academic Exchange Service (DAAD). He has been an Onwell Fellow at the University of Hong Kong, and a senior scholar of the Taiwan government. He is listed in *Who's Who in America* and other major biographical volumes. He was the 2004–2006 Distinguished Scholar Leader of the Fulbright New Century Scholars programme.

Richard Bawden

Richard Bawden has been a full-time Visiting Distinguished University Professor at Michigan State University and an occasional visiting professor at the universities of Minnesota and Cornell, KwaZuluNatal University in South Africa, and at the Open University in the UK, for the past eight years. For 20 years prior to that he was Dean of Agriculture and Rural Development and Professor of Systemic Development at the Hawkesbury Agricultural College (incorporated into the University of Western Sydney in 1989). In 2000 he was made a Member of the Order of Australia for his contribution to agriculture and rural development both in Australia and internationally.

Some recent and current research/development initiatives include: The Engagement Interface in a 'Risk Society'; Bio-ethics and Bio-law in Agricultural and Rural Development; Systemic Development as a Paradigm for Sustainability – Learning to Learn Our Way Forward; and Learning to Learn and the 'Essential Learnings'.

Anne Corbett

Anne Corbett is the author of *Universities and the Europe of Knowledge: Ideas, Institutions and Policy Entrepreneurship in European Union Higher Education Policy, 1955–2005* (Palgrave Macmillan, 2005) and co-editor (with Bob Moon) of *Education in France: Continuity and Change in the Mitterrand Years* (Routledge, 1996).

She holds a Ph.D. in political science from the University of London. She is a visiting fellow at the European Institute of the London School of Economics and Political Science, where she studies the politics and policies of the European Higher Education Area, as well as French politics. She is deputy chair of the Franco-British Council (British section) and an active member of the University Association for Contemporary European Studies. As a Paris-based journalist, she wrote extensively on French education and public policy for the *Times Educational Supplement* and other papers in the 1980s and 1990s. In the 1970s, she was an education correspondent for *New Society*, a well-known British weekly of the period. She holds the French state decoration *l'Ordre des Palmes Académiques* with the rank of *Officier*.

Axel Didriksson

Axel Didriksson, holds a bachelor's degree in sociology, a master's degree in Latin American studies and a doctorate in economics. He was the director of the Centre for University Studies at the National Autonomous University of Mexico (UNAM), which became the Institute for Research on Universities and Education (IISUE). He is coordinator-general of the Network of Public Macro-universities of Latin America and the Caribbean and vice-president of the executive committee of the Union of Latin American Universities (UDUAL). He is a Level-2 member of the Mexican National System of Researchers. Since 1995, he has held the UNESCO Chair on Regional Integration and University. He is a regular member of the Mexican Academy of Sciences and has been an educational researcher for 30 years. He has written ten books, the most recent being *The University in the Knowledge Society*, published by UNESCO Mexico in 2006, and has co-authored 30. He is Secretary of Education of the Government of the Federal District in Mexico.

Cornelia Dragne

Cornelia Dragne is a doctoral candidate in Leadership Studies at the Department of Education at the University of Victoria, British Columbia, Canada. She holds a master's degree in computer systems and a bachelor's degree in engineering. Her research interests focus on gender equity issues in technical higher education and the use of information and communication technologies in education.

Budd Lionel Hall

Budd Lionel Hall is the director of the Office of Community-Based Research and a senior fellow at the Centre for Global Studies at the University of Victoria, British Columbia, Canada. His work in higher education administration and lifelong learning research has included roles as dean of a faculty of education, chair of a department of adult education, and secretary-general of the International Council for Adult Education. He has written on participatory research, learning and social movements, adult education and international development, and higher education reform. He is one of the authors of the *Mumbai Statement of Lifelong Learning, Higher Education and Active Citizenship*. He participated in the UNESCO World Conference on Higher Education. He is also a poet.

Federico Mayor-Zaragoza

Federico Mayor-Zaragoza earned a doctorate in pharmacy from the Complutense University of Madrid in 1958. In 1963, he became a professor of biochemistry in the School of Pharmacy at the University of Granada, where he later served as rector (1968–1972). In 1973, he was appointed professor in his specialty at the Complutense University of Madrid.

He has held the following political posts, among others: Undersecretary of Education and Science in the Spanish government (1974–1975), member of the Spanish Congress of Deputies (1977–1978), adviser to the Spanish Prime Minister (1977–1978), Minister of Education and Science (1981–82) and member of the European Parliament (1987). In 1978, he became deputy director-general of UNESCO. In 1987, he was elected director-general of UNESCO, a post he held until 1999, when he created the Foundation for a Culture of Peace, of which he is now president.

In 2005, the secretary-general of the United Nations named him co-chair of the High-Level Group for the Alliance of Civilizations, a post he held until November 2006 when the Group presented its final report in Istanbul. In addition to numerous scientific publications, he has published four collections of poems and several books of essays.

Goolam Mohamedbhai

Goolam Mohamedbhai is currently the president of the International Association of Universities. He was vice-chancellor of the University of Mauritius from 1995 to 2005. He obtained his bachelor's and doctoral degrees in civil engineering at the University of Manchester, UK. He then joined the University of Mauritius as a lecturer in 1972 and was appointed professor in 1978. In 1980, he carried out postdoctoral research at the University of California, Berkeley under a Fulbright-Hays Award. In Mauritius, he has served as chairman or member of a number of national boards and councils. He was also a director of the State Bank of Mauritius (2003–2006).

He has undertaken consultancies and commissioned studies for a number of international organizations, including the International Development Research Centre (IDRC), Canada; the UN Economic Commission for Africa; the UN Centre for Human Settlements (UN Habitat); the UNESCO Regional Office for Education in Africa; and the Association of African Universities. At the regional/international level, he has been a member or chairman of several UNESCO Committees on Higher Education for Africa. He has also been chairman of several university associations, including the Association of Commonwealth Universities (2003–2004), University Mobility in the Indian Ocean Rim (2001–2004) and the University of the Indian Ocean (1998–2005). He is currently chairman of the Regional Scientific Committee for Africa of the UNESCO Forum on Higher Education, Research and Knowledge. He has been conferred honorary doctorates by Mykolas Romeris University, Lithuania and the Institute of Business Management in Karachi, Pakistan.

Teboho Moja

Teboho Moja is a professor of higher education at New York University. She has worked as a policy analyst at the Center for Education Policy Development, where she focused on the South African higher education system, and as an adviser to two South African ministers for education after the first democratic elections in 1994. She served as executive director and commissioner to the National Commission on Higher Education appointed by President Mandela. Her research focuses on the implications of globalization in higher education. She teaches courses on this subject, as well as on leadership in higher education and educational reform. She has published extensively on higher education in South Africa and has served as a board member of the International Institute for Educational Planning (IIEP). She now serves on the UNESCO Scientific Committee for Africa and is a member of the advisory committee of the Global Center on Private Financing of Higher Education, an initiative of the Institute for Higher Education Policy.

Deepak Nayyar

Deepak Nayyar is professor of economics at Jawaharlal Nehru University, New Delhi. He has taught economics at the University of Oxford, the University of Sussex and the Indian Institute of Management, Calcutta. Until recently, he was vice-chancellor of the University of Delhi.

His distinguished career in academia has been interspersed with short periods in government. His first such post was in the Indian Administrative Service. For some time, he worked as an economic adviser in the Ministry of Commerce. Later, he was the chief economic adviser to the Government of India and secretary of the Ministry of Finance.

He was educated at St Stephen's College, University of Delhi. Later, as a Rhodes Scholar, he studied at Balliol College, University of Oxford, where he obtained a B.Phil. and Ph.D. in economics.

He has served as a member of many commissions, committees and boards, both national and international: he is a member of the National Knowledge Commission in India; he was a member of the World Commission on the Social Dimension of Globalization; he was a director on the boards of the State Trading Corporation of India, the State Bank of India, the Export–Import Bank of India and Maruti Udyog (now Maruti Suzuki India Limited). He received the VKRV Rao Award for his contribution to research in economics and was president of the Indian Economic Association. He also sits on the editorial board of several professional journals.

He is an honorary fellow of Balliol College, Oxford. He is chairman of the board of the World Institute for Development Economics Research (UNU-WIDER), Helsinki and he sits on the board of directors of the Social Science Research Council in the United States. He is chairman of the advisory council for the Department of International Development, Queen Elizabeth House, University of Oxford. He is also vice-president of the International Association of Universities, Paris. His current research focuses on globalization and development.

Rajesh Tandon

Rajesh Tandon is an internationally acclaimed leader and practitioner of participatory research and development. In 1982, he founded the Society for Participatory Research in Asia (PRIA), a voluntary organization that provides support to grassroots initiatives in South Asia. He remains the organization's chief official.

He is the holder of a Ph.D. from Case Western Reserve University, a degree in Electronic Engineering (IIT, Kanpur) and a postgraduate degree in Management (IIM, Kolkata) and has specialized in social and organizational change. His contributions to the enhancement of perspectives and capacities of many voluntary activists and organizations revolve around issues of participatory research, advocating for people-centred development, and policy reform and networking in India, South Asia and beyond. He has advocated a self-reliant, autonomous and competent voluntary sector in India and abroad. He is currently promoting local government bodies (*Panchayats* and municipalities) as institutions of local self-governance in South Asia, with a special focus on women and marginalized groups. He is also working to build alliances and partnerships among diverse sectors in societal development. Under his leadership, PRIA has created numerous innovative methodologies for participatory learning and training, participatory bottom-up micro-planning, and participatory monitoring and evaluation. In the past 25 years, he has conducted major research, training and educational work on a wide variety of topics in order to strengthen the capacities and institutional mechanisms of voluntary development organizations in India and other developing countries.

Peter Taylor

Peter Taylor is guest editor of this edition of the report on *Higher Education in the World*. He is a research fellow and leader of the Participation, Power and Social Change Team at the Institute of Development Studies (IDS), Brighton, UK. He has a Ph.D. in agricultural education and is a qualified teacher. He has worked for many years on issues relating to education for agricultural and rural development, as well as participatory approaches and processes in educational arenas. In addition to authoring two books and a number of other publications, he has been involved in a wide range of research and advisory activities, including: participatory curriculum development in agricultural and forestry education; research on the use of contextualized curricula and teaching methodologies in basic education; initiatives supporting the development of educational access for people in rural areas; training of trainers and teachers on participatory approaches and methodologies; engaging in collaborative inquiry into education for community change; research on grassroots democracy and empowerment; and facilitation of distance-learning events and seminars. He directs the MA in Participation, Power and Social Change and the D.Phil. programme at the IDS. He is currently involved in international initiatives on 'Learning and Teaching for Transformation,' 'Facilitating Learning for Social Change,' 'Universities and Participatory Development' and 'University Education for Community Change'. He has lived and worked extensively in Europe, Africa and Central, South and Southeast Asia.

Hebe Vessuri

Hebe Vessuri has a D.Phil. in social anthropology from the University of Oxford. She currently directs the Department of Science Studies and coordinates the graduate programme on Social Studies of Science at the Venezuelan Institute for Scientific Research (IVIC), Caracas.

She has contributed to the emergence and consolidation of the field of social studies of science and technology in Latin America by setting up initiatives at the national, regional and international levels and through research and teaching. She has created graduate programmes in several Latin American countries. Her research focuses on sociology and contemporary history of science in Latin America, science policy, sociology of technology, expertise and democracy, and social participation/exclusion.

She sits on the editorial boards of several international journals, including *Social Studies of Science; Science, Technology & Society; Industry & Higher Education; Interciencia*; and *Redes*, and contributes actively to the growing regional literature on the subject. She is also a member of the board of trustees of the internet science and development network SciDev.Net. She currently chairs the Latin American Scientific Committee of the UNESCO Forum on Higher Education, Research and Knowledge.

She also sits on the scientific committees of the International Human Development Programme (IHDP), the International Council for Risk Governance (ICRG), and the Committee on Scientific Planning and Review (CSPR) of the International Council for Science (ICSU). She is a member of the governing council of the United Nations University (UNU). In the past, she has acted as vice-president of the International Union of Anthropological and Ethnological Sciences (IUAES), representing it at the International Social Science Council (ISSC).

Wang Yibing

After ten years as a specialist in higher and distance education at the UNESCO Regional Education Bureau in Bangkok, Professor Wang Yibing retired in 2003 and became a GUNI-AP adviser based at Zhejiang University, Hangzhou, China.

Before joining UNESCO, he was a senior research fellow of the Chinese Ministry of Education and Chinese National Centre for Education Development Research, which focuses on comparative policy studies (1981–1993). He also served as a research fellow in the Chinese Delegation to UNESCO (Paris 1986–1989) to study the evolution, function and interaction of the Western higher education governance mechanism composed of the state, market, social participation and HEIs since the 1960s.

He graduated from Beijing Foreign Studies University in 1964. He worked there as a lecturer, vice-dean and vice-president before moving to the Chinese Ministry of Education in 1981.

Mohaya Zaytoun

Mohaya Zaytoun is a professor of economics at the faculty of commerce, al Azhar University, women's branch. She holds a Ph.D. in economics from Oxford University. She teaches economic thought, mathematical economics, economic development and research methodology. She is also a member of the Egyptian Society for Political Economy, Statistics and Legislation, a member of the economic research committee, the Egyptian Academy for Scientific Research and Technology, and a member of the Arab Society for Economic Research.

AUTHORS OF SPECIAL CONTRIBUTIONS AND GOOD PRACTICES

Swami Atmapriyananda, Vice-Chancellor, Ramakrishna Mission Vivekananda University.

Firdous Azim, Chairperson, Department of English and Humanities, BRAC University.

Miquel Barceló, Commissioner for Sustainable Development, Technical University of Catalonia.

Aziza Bennani, Ambassador of Morocco to UNESCO.

Jorge Brenner Guillermo, Postdoctoral Research Associate, Harte Research Institute for Gulf of Mexico Studies, Texas A&M University.

L. David Brown, Associate Director for International Programs, The Hauser Center for Nonprofit Organizations, Harvard University.

Carlos Cortez Ruiz, Professor, Metropolitan Autonomous University.

Yazmín Cruz López, Report Coordinator, Global University Network for Innovation.

Jean-Marie De Ketele, Université Catholique de Louvain, School of Psychology and Education Sciences.

Gerard Delanty, Professor, University of Sussex.

Cristina Escrigas, Executive Director, Global University Network for Innovation.

Sonia Fernández Lauro, Former Chief of the Information and Documentation Service of UNESCO, Education Sector.

Didac Ferrer, Technical Director, Sustainability Centre-CITIES, Technical University of Catalonia.

António Fragoso, Professor, Vice-Rector, University of Algarve.

Georges Haddad, Director of the Higher Education Division, UNESCO.

Claudia Harvey, Director of Office, UNESCO Cluster Windhoek Office.

Alma Herrera, Observatory Coordinator, Network of Public Macro-Universities of Latin America and the Caribbean.

Richard Hopper, Education Specialist, World Bank.

Sylvia Hurtado, Director of the Higher Education Research Institute, University of California.

Leo Jansen, Professor Emeritus, Technological University of Delft.

Sheila Jasanoff, Pforzheimer Professor of Science and Technology Studies, Harvard University.

Andy Johnston, Head of Education and Learning, Forum for the Future.

Josep Lobera, Research Fellow, Global University Network for Innovation.

Francisco López Segrera, Academic Adviser, Global University Network for Innovation.

John McArthur, Associate Director of the Earth Institute at Columbia University, Senior Macroeconomic Adviser in the UN Development Program's Africa Bureau.

Roberta Malee Bassett, Centre for Higher Education Management and Policy, University of Southampton.

Andrei Marga, Professor, Babefl-Bolyai University.

Christine Marrett, Senior Programme Officer, Distance Education Centre, University of the West Indies.

Marcela Mollis, Professor, Faculty of Philosophy, University of Buenos Aires.

Manuel Ramiro Muñoz, Consultant, IESALC/UNESCO.

Deane Neubauer, Senior Adviser to the Education Program, East-West Center.

Victor Ordoñez, Adjunct Fellow, East-West Center.

Imanol Ordorika, Professor, Higher Education Seminar, National Autonomous University of Mexico.

Agustí Pérez-Foguet, Professor, Technical University of Catalonia.

Jeffrey D. Sachs, Director of the Earth Institute at Columbia University, Quetelet Professor of Sustainable Development, Professor of Health Policy and Management, Columbia University.

Jamil Salmi, Coordinator of the World Bank's network of tertiary education professionals.

Bikas C. Sanyal, Report Executive Coordinator, Global University Network for Innovation.

Boaventura de Sousa Santos, Director, Centre for Social Studies, School of Economics, University of Coimbra.

Mary Stuart, Deputy Vice-Chancellor, Kingston University.

Charas Suwanwela, Professor Emeritus, Chulalongkorn University.

Peter Taylor, Leader, Participation, Power and Social Change Team, Institute of Development Studies.

José de Val, Director, Programme 'Mexico a multicultural nation', National Autonomous University of Mexico (UNAM).

Josep Xercavins, UBUNTU Coordinator, World Forum of Civil Society Networks.

Richard Yelland, Head of the Education Management and Infrastructure Division, Directorate for Education, OECD.

Paul Tiyambe Zeleza, Department Head, Professor of African American Studies, University of Illinois at Chicago.

INTRODUCTION

Peter Taylor

BRIDGING THE PAST AND THE PRESENT

The role of higher education institutions (HEIs) in today's world is immense, complex and vital. A wide range of challenges and opportunities is emerging, with many political, economic and social implications. Perhaps most significant are the challenges associated with shifting perspectives on knowledge itself, which are strongly influencing the role and the responsibility of universities in society. HEIs have a long history of engagement with the world. As centres of training, knowledge production and knowledge transmission, they are well positioned to link the local (through their proximity to neighbouring communities and sociocultural particularities) and the global (through their association with transnational learning networks and research systems). This gives them considerable access to and influence over change processes in many societies. It may enhance their potential to contribute to human and social development through the promotion and facilitation of citizen participation and involvement in these processes.

This report seeks to explore the challenges that we now see influencing the nature and form of higher education (HE). It aims to provide an opportunity for educators, researchers, policy-makers and members of the wider society to look forward into the future, as a new course is charted that will help to reshape the roles of HE.

GLOBAL TRENDS, INFLUENCES AND CHALLENGES FOR HE

If we are to develop a vision of HE in the future, we need first to consider the key emerging challenges and influences to which it will have to respond. An overarching trend is that of globalization and the move towards a global economy, accompanied by a political transition from national to transnational organizations. Such movement is leading to increasing debate over the notion of development. Hotly debated for decades, and with origins in the field of biology, development has been equated by many with global economic growth that would result in all peoples of the world achieving economic parity with those living in the 'developed' nations. However, over time, 'human development' has acquired more complex meanings. The United Nations Development Programme (UNDP) states:

> Human development is about much more than the rise or fall of national incomes. It is about creating an environment in which people can develop their full potential and lead productive, creative lives in accord with their needs and interests. People are the real wealth of nations. Development is thus about expanding the choices people have to lead lives that they value. And it is thus about much more than economic growth, which is only a means – if a very important one – of enlarging people's choices ... Fundamental to enlarging these choices is building human capabilities – the range of things that people can do or be in life. The most basic capabilities for human development are to lead long and healthy lives, to be knowledgeable, to have access to the resources needed for a decent standard of living and to be able to participate in the life of the community. Without these, many choices are simply not available, and many opportunities in life remain inaccessible. (UNDP website, accessed 2006)

The UNDP statement goes on to note that human development is also a right, and that:

> the goal is human freedom. And in pursuing capabilities and realizing rights, this freedom is vital. People must be free to exercise their choices and to participate in decision-making that affects their lives. Human development and human rights are mutually reinforcing, helping to secure the well-being and dignity of all people, building self-respect and the respect of others.

A number of well-known global frameworks and initiatives aim to support this goal, including the Millennium Development Goals, the Kyoto Protocol, Education for All, Food for All and the UNESCO Decade for Sustainable Development. However, these frameworks do not provide a guarantee of positive change, as evidenced by the slow or nonexistent progress towards some of the targets enshrined within them. Progress is complicated by a wide range of variables that influence the process of human development, regardless of the goals and targets that are set. These include *economic, social, political and environmental* factors; *demographic and climate change;* the emphasis on the need for *sustainable development;* the desire for *peace-building* and *mutual understanding* between peoples to alleviate conflict and violence; *equality based on gender, ethnicity and religious belief;* and even the pursuit of '*happiness*'. All play a part in determining global development pathways in an era in which a prevailing framework of belief in material acquisition is shaped by a dominant neo-liberal economic agenda.

There is also a critical relationship between human development, within which is enshrined a series of freedoms as rights (civil, political and social), and *citizenship*, whereby we assure rights that empower every person to play an active role as a citizen, within a legal framework of participatory or deliberative democracy (Melo, 2006). However, the evolution of the state in many societies has been such that its willingness and ability to support social or citizenship rights is severely limited. How, in different contexts, can the tension between the need for economic growth and the needs for equity, inclusiveness, justice and citizenship be balanced?

Many would agree with the notion of development as 'good' change (Chambers, 2005). However, the ways in which we – individually and collectively – wish to live our lives are affected by challenges and opportunities of an unprecedented nature. Globalizing forces are channelling the voices of the world's citizens into ever-narrower spaces. Many feel that the influence of increasingly powerful economic, cultural, social and political ideologies is becoming the mainstream. Those who think and see the world differently find it harder to make their voices heard. There is a danger that knowledge becomes the currency of the powerful, as a means of legitimating and communicating the acceptable. Knowledge that is seen to be of less worth is thus relegated to the sidelines. In order to look towards the future roles of HE, the role of *knowledge* itself thus becomes inescapable.

THE ROLE OF KNOWLEDGE

We can imagine knowledge becoming an essential ingredient in every part of our lives: for economic production; for the activities, structures and systems of the state and major institutions; and for most of our daily needs as citizens. In effect, we are becoming dependent on knowledge. These trends in information and knowledge have enormous implications for education. From a knowledge society perspective, education will play a vital role in sharing, applying and creating knowledge in a globalizing world (UNESCO, 2005). HE and universities in particular will, it is claimed, 'fuel the driving forces of the transformation towards a global knowledge society' and have 'a certain capacity to steer and eventually to correct the direction of trends within globalisation' (Van Damme, 2002, p. 4).

However, there are other ways of looking at the relationship between HE, knowledge and society. HEIs may be perceived as purveyors of information and propagators of knowledge that fit within existing paradigms, these paradigms themselves having become unreliable and open to question. Universities, whose existence is justified in terms of their contribution to learning, may become weighed down by inertia, unable to learn themselves or to support the learning of others. The emergence of a global knowledge economy exacerbates concern that some academic institutions may be contributing to the *undemocratization* of society by discouraging questioning of meanings and assumptions that constrain or block open and reflective dialogue between individuals.

The optimistic glow arising from the vision of a global flow of knowledge improving the lives of all is tempered by the reality of huge disparities in the resourcing and autonomy of HEIs in the North and South. Differences in capacity (due to infrastructure, information and human resources) are made worse by the 'brain drain' away from Southern institutions to those in the North, as researchers and teachers seek better working conditions. At the same time, many Northern HEIs continue to propagate a deficit model, assuming that those based in the South should adopt Northern practices and ways of working, but without seriously addressing the asymmetrical power relations between them. Additionally, as HEIs play a particular role in training teachers and developing and updating school curricula, their increasing orientation towards the global knowledge market may influence the value system of basic education, having a much greater impact on development and society in the longer term.

CHALLENGES AND OPPORTUNITIES – LOOKING TO THE FUTURE

In this report, we look towards the future. We aim to understand where we have come from and to carefully analyse and consider where we are now. In addition, we fix our eyes, unashamedly, on a different world, in which all people are free from poverty and injustice, and where the voices of those who are currently marginalized are not only heard but make a difference to the world that we all share. What can HEIs contribute? Will they become redundant? Or will they play a crucial role with new responsibilities? In this report, we will consider a number of ways in which this contribution may be made. We will also suggest what needs to happen in order for this contribution to be maximized. Most importantly, perhaps, we will ask questions that we believe require serious engagement and debate by all those who have a stake in the future of HE, and indeed all those with a vision for human and social development.

EDUCATION, CURRICULUM AND PEDAGOGY

To imagine a different world, we need to consider what knowledge is needed and generated for what kind of society. We also need to understand the relationship between scientific knowledge and other forms of knowledge, and the ways in which ethics and values should be addressed and become an inherent force behind the contribution of HE to positive change. How do these concepts of knowledge, values and ethics help shape a curriculum that responds to a new understanding and practice of citizenship? How can this help to establish an education that is grounded in complexity, with an interdisciplinary or transdisciplinary character? How do we create opportunities for learning that are likely to contribute to sustainable human and social development, based on dialogical, co-learning, participatory, problem-oriented and ethical approaches? How can we overcome the factors that constrain such learning approaches at the individual, organizational and societal levels? Finally, what pedagogies are required for such an education, in which power relations are made explicit through the learning and teaching process?

RESEARCH

Research is assumed to be a vital part of the role of HE. However, there is a growing need to question the paradigms of knowledge and innovation that inform the research carried out in various contexts; the relationship between research carried out by HEIs and its application in wider society; and the way that society and human-development needs shape the research agenda itself. There are great differences in the ability of HEIs around the world to engage in research. This is due to a range of constraints, including poor infrastructure and material resources, a lack of human resources, a policy environment that is not conducive to research, and assumptions about the processes by which knowledge is generated. What should be the nature of the policy framework for HEI research, if we are to attend to issues of interdisciplinary research, participatory research, action research and collaborative research? How can we encourage the emergence of international research networks and local research services that are congruent with such policy? How can we achieve shifts in the relationships between the natural sciences, technology, social sciences and transdisciplinarity in the context of human and social development?

UNIVERSITY ENGAGEMENT IN SOCIETY

Education at all levels plays a critical role as a transmitter, reproducer or resistor of a complex weave of knowledge and power relations. However, in recent times, education has itself been transformed through changes in its purposes and priorities, according to new global standards and the transfer of policies, curricula and methods of assessment between countries. HEIs are international in their outlook. Their role as producers and transmitters of knowledge has important repercussions in the context of globalization and in the national contexts in which they operate (Taylor and Fransman, 2004). HE, for all its recognition as a social good and significant contributor to societal transformation, is seen by many as potentially exploitative and manipulative. How would it be possible to resist and challenge exploitative practices of this form of education? How can we work at different levels – including structural levels and different social actors – in order to address and bring about change in the relations of knowledge and power that determine the potential for human and social development? How can we encourage greater social engagement, as well as research and education that support learning about learning (Boothroyd and Freyer, 2004)? How can we challenge ideas about 'dominant knowledge' residing in the hands of experts and engage with the *majority* in ways that make connections between knowledge, action and consciousness?

INSTITUTIONAL CHARACTERISTICS AND CAPACITY

The *capacity* of HEIs to take on new responsibilities and occupy new spaces in the knowledge society, and to become engines of wider societal change, is frequently called into question. HEIs are poised to influence political, economic and social transformation largely because of their comparative advantage and position in relation to the knowledge society. Questions remain, however, over their contextual relevance in research, teaching and community engagement. Do they address local needs and priorities as well as the demands of the global knowledge economy? Do their missions and visions of HE in the 21st century reflect emerging patterns and trends in wider society? To what extent do their governance, leadership, culture, organization and management take account of the need for social values in a context of social change? In a period of new managerialism, target-setting, and increasing involvement of the private and corporate sectors, do HEIs continue to serve the needs of their individual students and the societies in which they are located? How do they capture and utilize new information technologies in order to deliver more flexible and blended learning and teaching programmes? Will a global landscape, in which traditional boundaries become ever more permeable, result in the abandonment by transnational HEIs of the local, from which they are derived? What are the ethical dimensions of future university–society engagement?

STEERING A COURSE FOR THE FUTURE OF HE

If we believe that HEIs are at a critical point in their history as learning institutions, we need to encourage, nourish and support critical debate on the role of HE in a globalizing world. We also need to frame this debate by questioning the ways in which HEIs support and facilitate human and social development. There is no doubt about the urgency of our global realities, which are often mirrored in the catastrophes, conflicts and crises experienced at the local level throughout the world. Problems and challenges continue to emerge; some of these are long-running, others more recent. Through their contribution to the social construction of knowledge, HEIs have the potential to explore these complex problems and to help shape new goals within a context of globalizing economic forces. They need to develop not only their *capability* to articulate a vision of the future and solutions to ongoing problems, but also their *willingness* and *ability* to reach out towards an unknown future by working in concert.

This does not necessarily mean that they should work with one voice or with a single strategy; more important is their ability and willingness to question, to communicate, to draw on different forms of knowledge and to help create and shape spaces for debate and dialogue. A move

in this direction should not be driven purely by managerialism or by financial and technical opportunity. *A vision is needed*, in the context of new global alignments and wider demands, to achieve greater well-being, for example through poverty reduction, inclusion, and a greater voice for those who are marginalized and on the fringes of society. Perhaps more than ever before, HEIs themselves need to learn, and to engage with and encourage dialogue in a wide range of social sectors.

This report aims to contribute to the ongoing debate around these themes by providing evidence from a wide range of contexts. It provides us with a moment to pause, reflect and take a view of a rapidly changing world. It enables us to explore and elaborate on the real potential of HE to contribute constructively and creatively to human and social development. We believe it offers us an opportunity to work together to chart a new course for HE in the future.

BIBLIOGRAPHY

Boothroyd, P. and Freyer, M. (2004) Mainstreaming social engagement in higher education: benefits, challenges and successes. Paper presented at the UNESCO Forum Colloquium on Research and Higher Education Policy, 1–3 December 2004.

Chambers, R. (2005) *Ideas for Development: Reflecting Forwards*. London: Earthscan.

Melo, A. (2006), Is there a right to development? Paper presented at the first European seminar of the European Society for Research on the Education of Adults (ESREA) research network, Between Global and Local: Adult Learning and Development, Human Development and Adult Learning, Faro: University of the Algarve, October.

Taylor, P. and Fransman, J. (2004) Learning and teaching participation: exploring the role of higher learning institutions as agents of development and social change. Working paper 219. Falmer, UK: Institute of Development Studies.

Taylor, P., Pettit, J. and Stackpool-Moore, L. (2006) Learning and teaching for transformation: insights from a collaborative learning initiative. In: Guerstein, P. and Angeles, N. *Learning Civil Societies: Shifting Contexts for Democratic Planning and Governance*. Toronto, ON: Toronto University Press.

UNDP website (2006), www.undp.org.

UNESCO (2005) *Towards Knowledge Societies*. Paris: UNESCO.

Van Damme, D. (2002) Outlooks for the international higher education community in constructing the global knowledge society. Paper presented at the First Global Forum on International Quality Assurance, Accreditation and the Recognition of Qualifications in Higher Education. Paris: UNESCO, 17–18 October.

FOREWORD

Cristina Escrigas

The search for justice may take longer than our lifetimes, but our children will attain it in the future and peace will not be the product of violence but of education.
Rigoberta Menchú

The third *Global University Network for Innovation (GUNI) Report* offers a look into the role of higher education and higher education institutions and their contribution to human and social development in the context of globalization. This is a particularly important subject for GUNI, not only because it has a direct bearing on its commitment to the agreements undertaken in the Framework for Priority Action for Change adopted during the World Conference on Higher Education (WCHE) in 1998 in Paris, but also because it is the backdrop to a reappraisal of the function of higher education in the world regarding its impact on economies, politics, societies, cultures and human development. At GUNI, we aim to share and debate ideas in order to *enrich our vision of the relevant social role that higher education is called upon to play in this increasingly globalized world*. We wish to provide a space for analysis of the role of knowledge in our society, in which we consider *what knowledge for what society* and how universities define their role in this regard.

Universities now are facing one of the most exciting times, since globalization implies the possibility of taking advantage of important opportunities; but it also brings challenges and poses serious problems for the future, by questioning what should be the main value of universities – serving the common good – in an era when what is 'common' and what is 'good' are difficult to define.

Higher education institutions, as well as the societies in which they operate, are currently undergoing a global transformation process in all contexts, although with specific characteristics in different parts of the world. Such changes are evident enough to cause us to reconsider what the *social contract* between both, higher education and society, should be, in the light of this context and institutional changes, and what form it should take. The circumstances are therefore ideal *for a critical and constructive analysis of the role of higher education* in the world.

The world has changed considerably in recent years. In contrast to the better quality of life enjoyed by one sector of humanity, we are becoming increasingly aware of the challenges faced by the remainder and the need for such things as: international justice, global equity and human rights; inter-cultural understanding; peace building, global citizenship and governance; and sustainable development. In short, it is essential to explore solutions to global problems and even to bring about a *paradigm shift for reconstructing society* in answer to these challenges, and to build a better world for future generations.

Changes in higher education are mostly related to internationalization, access, technologies, quality, financing and the diversification of institutions in their nature and their activity and forms of provision, among other things. Some of these topics have been dealt with in previous GUNI reports.

This time we have chosen to analyse the role of higher education and higher education institutions in terms of their contribution to human and social development in the context of globalization. We will look in detail at the concept of development and its scope, with an understanding that *sustainable development is the only possible form of development*. Sustainability is a core principle to our discussions and debates and it underpins our concept of human and social development.

The concept of social commitment is not a new idea for higher education institutions, as they have always played a significant role in civic service and public good. We are proposing, however, the need to review and reconsider the *interchange of values between university and society;* that is to say, we need to *rethink the social relevance* of universities.

THE WORLD WE LIVE IN

At the 2003 International UNU/UNESCO Conference, *Globalization with a Human Face – Benefiting All*, the following statement was made:

> Globalization, broadly conceived, has brought many benefits to humankind: through its economic impact, through its technological impact and through its social and political impact, especially because it reveals our global interdependence and opens up new opportunities for participation, empowerment and communication.

> … A key goal … is to build international consensus on emerging norms and principles in order to respond to new challenges and dilemmas as a result of globalization. The trend towards homogenization of educational, cultural, scientific and communication activities is disquieting and risks bringing about uniformity, of content and perspective, at the expense of the world's creative diversity.

Humanity as a whole is now facing a time of major challenges, not to say *serious and profound problems regarding coexistence and relations with the natural environment*. Unresolved problems include social injustice, marginalization and exclusion; poverty and disparity in wealth distribution; abuse and lack of respect for human rights; illness, HIV/AIDS and major epidemics; corruption, fraud and a lack of democracy; armed conflicts; over-exploitation and exhaustion of natural resources and climate change. These crises are so deep that they raise philosophical questions relating to why we are here, and what is the purpose of existence. The crisis of values in this era, particularly, is undeniable, and this is significant, in the supposedly developed world. This crisis comes alongside a search for new meanings, linked sometimes with new forms of spirituality or beliefs that give some significance to life. Life, which should be a constant celebration of a wonderful gift, is being transformed into a struggle against indifference, depression and anxiety for the more fortunate, and against exclusion, war, poverty, abuse, hunger and illness for those who are less so.

Voices are increasingly being raised, many of them coming from within universities themselves, warning that *the models that have guided development* over the past century, *are now exhausted*. There is a demand to rethink the current development paradigm and our *collective social values*. There is a growing need to articulate a sustainable development model that should not only embrace environmental issues but also consider economic, human, cultural and social aspects. This implies a new regard for reality itself, in which *complexity and interdependence*

are key concepts of a *new perception of what exists*, that has major implications for the entire education system.

Therefore, we have adopted a broad definition of human and social development for this report that includes and recognizes the essential nature of economic growth but is not reduced solely to it. We could not assimilate economic growth with development, if we limited this last concept.

As Peter Taylor notes in the Introduction to this report, several global frameworks are being introduced, including the Millennium Development Goals, the Kyoto Protocol, Education for All, Food for All, the UN Decade of Education for Sustainable Development, the High-level Group Report on the Alliance of Civilizations, and others. As he mentions, these frameworks do not provide a guarantee of positive change in themselves, however Higher Education could ask what its contribution could be, regarding its mission and the social commitment of knowledge.

THE WORLD WE TEACH – THE WORLD WE BUILD

At this point in history, *education and knowledge resources are more accessible than ever before*. Science and technology have seen spectacular advances and education attainment rates worldwide at all age levels have reached historic highs. Therefore the *knowledge society is truly starting* to take shape.

The university is still the main institution for communicating and disseminating knowledge and has a direct impact, therefore, on nations' economic and social development. Higher education is responsible for *training the professionals* who, in the course of their careers, will attain the *positions of greatest responsibility* in society and the labour market. Their professional actions are essential to countries' wealth creation and development. The decisions of university-trained professionals throughout the world make a decisive contribution to the way life develops on this planet and their decision-making can have results that are either positive or negative for the global progress of humankind and societies, in both developed and developing countries. Higher education, therefore, plays a decisive and fundamental role in terms of the teaching *content, values and skills* it incorporates.

We should be interested in what education citizens receive and what they give back to the society that provided it for them, particularly when their education is financed with public funds. It should be essential for society to find out how to preserve the common interest implicit in the results of professional activities. Individuals who access higher education do not only obtain personal returns, but also can and should be aware of how their activities can contribute or not to the common good.

Universities today are also the institutions that contribute most to scientific and technological progress, as part of their crucial function of generating new knowledge. The 20th century saw a *massive expansion of science and technology* into every aspect of human life: transportation, communication, education, commerce, agriculture, human reproduction, medicine, energy, space and ocean exploration, and of course war. A pressing task for the 21st century is to foster human capacities to absorb, critically examine and reflect on those earlier developments. How to do this effectively, as well as rigorously, is a looming challenge and a critical responsibility for the world's universities (see Jasanoff in this volume).

If higher education has indeed a role to play in *generating and distributing knowledge with the purpose of serving the whole of humankind* (see Xercavins in this volume), this role – by its own definition – can only aim at contributing to sustainable human development. Therefore, HEIs are designated to play a fundamental role in social construction, from the social commitment perspective.

WHAT'S NEXT?

EDUCATION, THE FIRST SOLUTION

As stated at the Universal Forum of Cultures, 2004:

> Globalisation is not news anymore. Neither is it the future. *Globalisation* is the current state of the world. In times of globalisation, *human rights* are – and will continue to be – the main challenge and the major aim of society and governments worldwide. *And the path to be taken is education.* This is surely the most important assertion that can be taken ... from the debates.

Globalization, which also affects education, is an irreversible phenomenon that is here to stay. But the way it evolves in the long term will depend on the *responses that we are able to articulate* in the present and near future. We, at higher education institutions (HEIs), have a collective responsibility for how we *help to build societies*.

Following this commitment, many higher education institutions worldwide are involved in partial – but essential – innovative experiences in the way they engage with society. Most of these experiences imply *a new way of understanding the value interchange between higher education institutions and society* by providing specific responses to human and social development needs.

Institutions are faced with a *major challenge:* whether to choose between reacting literally to the labour market

demands or anticipating the needs of society. Anticipating the needs means that institutions must identify where to redirect problems and how to do this, where new knowledge is needed and where it has to be disseminated. Anticipating and being proactive are ways of responding to social demands, but perhaps not in the manner that society or the market expects. Such responses involve *coordinating an effective network of relations* with all agents. This is a hard task, but not an entirely new one. We need to overcome the dichotomy between self-absorption and marketization in order to come up with an innovative, socially committed response that anticipates and contributes value for social transformation.

Another challenge is related to the social value of teaching. Teaching can either be focused on just training professionals or on educating citizens who will carry out a profession. The question that needs to be discussed seriously is whether it is possible to choose between the two. Again, the challenge is huge, but also not new.

We need to incorporate *new transversal curriculum contents* that can provide individuals with new tools more fitted to making them actors of positive social transformation through the exercise of their professions. Proposing individual and collective responsibility in professional decision-making within new global *ethical paradigms* will be a subject for the intermediate future. Higher education policies cannot neglect such a demand.

In this global era, being prepared as a citizen who will interact with society through the exercise of a profession implies a complex vision of reality that demands inter- and transdisciplinary education. It also implies the need for abilities and values such as: a deep understanding of human being and life; sustainable development as a collective social process to be learned; a need for common recognition, understanding and respect of different cultures for inter-cultural relationships and support of diversity; the ability to deal with an exponential expansion of technology, without losing the capacity to put it to common human service; and the need to set aside fear in order to confidently cooperate on peace building in any spheres of activity. Any profession has influence and interaction with at least some of these things, if not with all. In addition, we need to break the hegemony of *the single mindset* that seems to be advancing rapidly in globalized society. We therefore need to accept the *complexity of reality* and the interdependence of areas of knowledge in a real interdisciplinary approach to education.

Higher education institutions are responsible also for creating and spreading knowledge, and thus contributing to solutions to global problems. The *relationship between scientific research and social needs*, mainly to support *political decision-making with collective implications,* needs to be explored and analysed. Higher education should also address how to build bridges between research and political decision-making for collective well-being.

To link research agendas with sustainable development needs, with climate change needs and with collective targets such as the Millennium Development Goals needs, could have a great impact in the future, if we give them their due importance at the present. Another challenge is to provide other social agents with access to research, to ensure that HEIs respond to wider social needs. The European Science Shops, for example, could be one way forward. Action-based research and community-based research are other examples. It is also extremely important to find solutions to the problem of brain drain and to facilitate the development of local science and technology capacities.

The contribution of higher education to human and social development could maybe involve a paradigm change in what is expected from universities, in a move from the individual and competitive to the social and cooperative.

From individual and competitive	To social and collective
Focused on content	Focused on content, abilities and values
Focused on training productive professionals	Focused on training citizen-professionals
Oriented to labour market needs	Oriented to the needs of society as a whole
Social use based on individual status and enrichment, and economic growth	Social use based on contributing to the collective good, society building and to human and social development

We should be cautious about *putting higher education institutions under more pressure* than they find themselves already; their work is too important to society as a whole. However, we can guide their path in society, keeping them in the central position that they should occupy.

The speed of change in the past few years has been such that perhaps we now need to consider the way we are taking, and the one we wish to take in the future.

We may envision a university that anticipates social challenges, a university linked to the local that works in global networks, an independent, open, plural, university that integrates society, contributing to the collective good and taking full responsibility for public service.

We do not aspire to include all the proposals to be found in this report. There are many, and it would take numerous pages to describe, develop and share each one for debate. We are grateful for the collaboration of the 52 authors who have made 14 global and regional contributions, 29 special contributions and described 15 good practices. In these papers they present an exciting, and we believe provocative series of ideas, options, visions and specific challenges for the role that higher education has in order to contribute to human and social development.

The aim of this report and its subsquent presentation at the *International Barcelona Conference on Higher Education* at the end of March 2008 is to stimulate debate among all those whose different links with the world of higher education could contribute to enriching the discussion. The report will have met its target if it contains enough ideas to make this debate rich and plural. We do not wish to present a closed view of the future, or only one true mission. We aim to *stimulate serious and profound thought, which will open opportunities* that should be jointly analysed, discussed and hopefully used by academics, university leaders, policymakers and members of civil society and the business community.

This report aims to present more than an analysis of the current situation. It is *proactive*, offering *many ideas and visions* for orienting the future. We are not focusing on potential scenarios extrapolated from the present. We want to reconsider the social function of higher education through an academic analysis based on what higher education *is today and how it should change its role to meet future challenges.*

The main objectives of *Higher Education: New Challenges and Emerging Roles for Human and Social Development*, are to examine the latest knowledge, research, experiences and practices to rethink and propose *new routes* for the interchange of values between higher education institutions (HEIs) and society. We may achieve this through *reconsidering the role that we assign to higher education* (HE), in terms of its *contribution to human and social development* in economic, political, social, environmental and cultural spheres.

The report is structured as follows:

- *Introduction*
- *Part I* Global issues on the role of higher education for human and social development: Main challenges and trends that affect higher education functions, and how they are being and should be handled to contribute to human and social development. This part is divided in two sections:
  - *Section A* – Present and future challenges for higher education's role in the context of globalization
  - *Section B* – The emerging roles of higher education: implications for education, research, civil engagement and institutional development
- *Part II* Regional perspectives on the role of HE for human and social development: Main challenges and trends in each region and how they are being and should be handled, taking into account diversity and avoiding uniformity
- *Part III Delphi Poll:* The views of experts, university rectors and presidents, policy-makers and civil society on higher education's role in human and social development
- *Part IV Statistical appendix*
- *Bibliography:* Useful further reading for studying these issues in more depth.

Along with the main articles we have included institutional frameworks, special contributions and good practices related to the role of higher education for human and social development. The reader will find also four maps that give a graphic view of key issues on the theme.

The **Introduction** of the report includes a box on GUNI, a map of the GUNI members,

the Acknowledgements, a brief profile of the authors, the Introduction, the Foreword and this Overview.

There are two more boxes – the first on the United Nations Millennium Development Goals and how higher education could help to achieve them, and the second is a summary of the World Declaration on Higher Education for the Twenty-first Century and the Framework for Priority Action for Change adopted during the World Conference on Higher Education (WCHE) in 1998.

There are also two special contributions on the contribution of higher education to the UN Millennium Development Goals, and on key international frameworks on higher education's role for human and social development, and three more contributions giving the institutional views of UNESCO, the World Bank and the OECD on the role of higher education for human and social development.

Part I, Global Issues on the Role of Higher Education for Human and Social Development, exposes the present and future challenges for HE's role in the context of globalization and the emerging roles of HEIs, their implications for education, research, civil engagement and institutional development, and how they are being and should be handled to contribute to global harmony. This part is divided into two sections:

Section A. Present and future challenges for higher education's role in the context of globalization: presents a critical analysis of the current worldwide context, taking into account the political, social and economic aspects in which HE plays its role and offers its outcomes. The aim is to define the context, explain the main present and future trends, and discuss how the role of HE should change in response to this situation. It examines a range of challenges or influences that are likely to be critical globally – like cosmopolitism, multicultural coexistence and sustainable development – for the role of higher education in relation to human and social development in the context of globalization.

Additionally, it presents a critical view of HE's and HEIs' roles in the present day, by addressing the idea of where we are now and what we are doing, or not doing, regarding social needs. It also addresses how HE currently interchanges values with society, and the actual functions and responsibilities which enable HEIs to do this.

This section includes:

- Three papers addressing global issues on: the complex roles of universities in the period of globalization; the university of the 21st century, political and social trends of globalization; globalization and markets, challenges for higher education.

- Six special contributions on: contemporary challenges for public research universities; the university and cosmopolitan citizenship; the contribution of higher education to a multicultural co-existence; higher education and its institutions and the civilizational paradigm crisis; the new role of globalized education in a globalized world; and globalization and higher education relevance.

This section provides a strong foundation for further parts of the report that examine where higher education may be heading in the future in relation to human and social development in a globalizing world.

Section B. The emerging roles of higher education: implications for education, research, civil engagement and institutional development: attempts to highlight HE roles and the implications for the educative purpose, curricula transformation, research, civil engagement and the institutional challenges, along with some future visions, strategies and actions in order to achieve human and social development.

This section includes an analysis on the *educative purpose* of HE and the underlying concept of education in terms of a positive vision of human and social development. It also discusses its contribution to building a better future, and the main characteristics that HE should possess in order to achieve this end.

Additionally, this section examines how the *higher education curriculum* can be applied for human and social development in the context of globalization. It invites the reader to rethink the academic curriculum from a complex view of the world, and the teaching and learning process for developing skills that can be useful for addressing current challenges. A range of issues, including inter- and trans-disciplinary work, sustainability and multicultural understanding, education for peace, global citizenship, science and ancient knowledge, and ethics and values in higher education are also discussed.

Along with the educative purpose and the HE curriculum, this section explores *the role of research* in higher education and its relationship with society. The implications and challenges to research for an active contribution to societal and human development needs are also

discussed. Issues such as how research can help to solve global problems while at the same time addressing local needs, ethics, and the environmental and social implications of science and technology are highlighted. Some ways of re-examining the relationship between research and political decision-making at all levels, the nature of the policy framework for HEI research, and issues of interdisciplinary, participatory, action and collaborative research, and the emergence of international research networks and local research services are also examined.

Furthermore, this section includes a discussion on how HE supports human and social development through *civil engagement;* including issues of service learning, practice–research, development cooperation, knowledge and learning from the local to the global and vice versa, and relations and links between HE and civil networking and other actors.

This section presents readers with a specific discussion on what role HEIs should play in human and social development, by exploring the *main institutional challenges and responses* required in order to assume a new proactive role and anticipate social needs. Issues such as how to build a shared vision and mission and what kind of institution should assume this new role are discussed.

This section includes:

- Five global issues on: the educative purpose of higher education; higher education curriculum; the role of research; civil engagement in HE; and the institutional challenges and implications for HEIs

- Twelve special contributions dealing with: the purpose of higher education; ethics and values in learning and teaching; the concept of global citizenship in higher education; higher education's contribution for sustainable development; the educational needs of future development professionals and practitioners in the framework of the MDGs; science and ancient knowledge; multiculturalism, interculturality and leadership; the political and social contribution of research; ethical, environmental and social implications of science and technology; practice–research engagement; democratic reform and emancipation in higher education; and social responsibility of universities.

- Seven good practices on: training professionals in socially responsible values; disciplinary integration in research and teaching to promote sustainability models; the Science Shop and the Living Knowledge Network; an overview on university-based civic service; educative experiences through development cooperation projects; participative process inside the HEIs; and four institutional models.

Part II, Regional perspectives on the role of higher education for human and social development. Regions have a great deal of diversity within them, not only in higher education. However, this section attempts to offer a comparative analysis that readers may find interesting and useful. In doing this we try to maintain the richness and the diversity of each region. It explores, therefore, similarities within the regions by looking at the functions played by HE around the world, the main challenges in each region and possible alternatives for achieving human and social development.

The regional analysis is based on a review of the present situation; an assessment of the outcomes ten years after the WCHE; the main political, social, human, economic, environmental and technological challenges of globalization in the regions; the implications for HE regarding its contribution to human and social development; some visions of the future role of HE in human and social development; and strategies and actions that could be adopted by HEIs in order to achieve a new role in the region.

This section includes:

- An overview of the regional perspectives
- Six articles on the role of higher education for human and social development in: Sub-Saharan Africa, the Arab States, Asia-Pacific, Europe, the USA and Canada, and Latin America and the Caribbean
- Six special contributions: one on science and technology for human and social development in Africa; four illustrating the national situations regarding the higher education role for human and social development in Portugal, the USA, Argentina and the Caribbean; and a contribution on the social responsibility of universities in Latin America
- Eight good practices on: an OpenCourseWare project in Africa; curriculum transformation for sustainable development in Southern Africa; the approach of BRAC University; a system of recognition, valida-

tion and certification of adult education in Portugal; the Dutch National Network for Sustainable Development; community based education and research for development; improving university outreach; and a description of the Mexico Multicultural Nation university programme.

Part III, Delphi poll on higher education for human and social development. This study explores the main trends, emergent opinions and perspectives of 214 higher education experts, university leaders, policymakers and civil society actors from over 80 countries regarding the new challenges and emerging roles for the HE contribution to human and social development in the regions. The reader will find that most of the participants agree that HE should play an active role in human and social development. They also agree on the key challenges posed by human and social development to HE in each region including poverty reduction, sustainable development, critical thinking, ethical values and democracy. However, there are major divergences on the measures for meeting the challenges, ranging from increasing the social dialogue to curricula revision.

Part IV, Statistical appendix, offers information on adult and youth literacy; education expenditure, spending as a percentage of gross domestic product; education expenditure, sources as a percentage of gross domestic product; tertiary education enrolment and teaching staff; research and development expenditures as a percentage of the GDP and researches in R&D per million people; and the human development rank, index, total population and GDP per capita in each country.

Finally, the **bibliography** suggests further literature and websites that could be useful for studying these issues in greater depth.

The opinions put forward on the role of higher education in human and social development are varied and complex, making it difficult to consider this question succinctly and to put forward UNESCO's point of view on this matter.

With the support of its 192 member states, UNESCO must put forward the most objective outlook possible on the realities and prospects of higher education in the world through dialogue and comparison. This vision must draw on three well-defined but closely related time factors: the past, the present and the future.

Since the Middle Ages, higher education's most advanced institutional expression, the university, has asserted itself as a pillar and actor of development in the most diverse ways, through what we would now call a 'social contract'. This contract has quite clearly changed over time in order to adapt to socioeconomic and cultural progress, and indeed to revolutions. Moreover, it has very often allowed universities to anticipate and prepare for the major changes that have arisen in modern history. Indeed, few institutions have been as adept as universities at resisting the uncertainties and ravages of time. Over eight centuries lie between the beginnings of the earliest European universities such as the Universities of Bologna and the Sorbonne, which is clear proof of their commitment to humankind and society. Initially a place for preserving and advancing knowledge at the service of feudal societies, slowly but surely universities have opened up to broader social strata. Following crucial periods such as the Renaissance, the Reformation and, above all, the Enlightenment and the Age of Revolution, universities were able to evolve into their current state at the turn of the 19th century under the Humboldtian paradigm, which met with some opposition from the French model in the shape of the Napoleonic *grandes écoles*. The main features of modern universities and their new 'social contract' can be defined by three pivotal terms: democratization, professionalism and innovation.

These three keywords characterize universities' fundamental missions today, and no doubt will continue to do so in the future. In more general terms, they define a structurally diverse higher education system.

The World Conference on Higher Education, organized by UNESCO in 1998, starkly brought to light the truth of the above statement, which was to serve as a premise for higher education devoted to humankind and the community.

Democratization spread slowly but surely, first in Europe, America and Japan, to the new ruling classes described as middle class in a society that was undergoing profound changes. It now embraces all socioeconomic strata and is particularly apparent in new nations that have freed themselves of the colonial yoke. Within this framework, the circumstances are highly diverse as, prior to their independence, certain countries were able to benefit from higher education systems that had been put in place by the colonial powers, but all too often the necessary structures have had to be set up from scratch.

Through its foresight, which has progressively been refined over the past 60 years, UNESCO has unambiguously promoted the principle of higher education as a 'public good' that is accessible in every country to every individual, in accordance with personal merit and talent. Whatever the ways or the means used to transfer this public good, UNESCO and its partners have been working for a number of years to guarantee its relevance and quality.

Finally, and this point is drawn from hard evidence, a quality education system must be designed on the basis of circular rather than linear geometry, in which higher education takes its legitimate place on a par with primary and secondary education.

The principle of vocational training has progressively taken root and is no doubt here to stay. Modern-day professions, such as engineering, medicine and teaching, have found their fulfilment within the university *alma mater* and the French *grandes écoles*. The modern notion of continuing training and lifelong training in response to the permanent development of professions driven by science and technology is becoming accepted everywhere as the overriding mission of higher education at the service of individuals and communities.

Professionalization can by no means justify the dehumanization of university missions. On the contrary, as heralded by UNESCO, new professions and the new ethical responsibilities that they entail are more than ever in need of humanist support based on interdisciplinarity and multidisciplinarity in order to respond to the foreseeable challenges in this new century. Within the framework of its prerogatives, UNESCO is convinced that the higher education that is necessary in order to prepare professionals and lead students into professional life must also provide a broader training to prepare students to take on the missions and responsibilities of citizens.

Finally, modern higher education must above all justify its mission at the service of development by its active participation in innovation through research. It is unanimously recognized that modern higher education has been built up based on its basic and applied research missions. Moreover, there is absolutely no need to highlight the importance of the contributions made by university research to every facet of development. The permanent contract with research and innovation constitutes the basis of the university world. Specifically, in order to offer relevant, quality education, it is imperative that higher education lecturers abide by this rule.

UNESCO has brought to light the present and future challenges that face all the issues involved in university research. A renewed social contract must be entered into with society that serves to cement partnerships with all socioeconomic and cultural sectors.

Universities no longer have a monopoly on research, but they will continue to hold a privileged position in this field as long as they are able to find the means to open up to a broad array of public and private sectors by fully asserting their entrepreneurial spirit.

Finally, UNESCO gives its unqualified but realistic support to the notion that research cannot be a privilege that is solely enjoyed by the richest countries. Scientific cooperation programmes must be supported to allow each country and each region to take an active part in building the knowledge society. Not only is their progress at stake but also their global dignity and responsibility, which is at the heart of UNESCO's concerns. There is not enough room here to mention all that has been accomplished by UNESCO in this regard. However, one might mention the UNESCO Chair programmes and the UNITWIN networks, which are so effectively represented by GUNI, the Global University Network for Innovation.

By way of conclusion, it is wholly legitimate to state that higher education everywhere has contributed, contributes and will contribute to both social and human development. Furthermore, in the framework of its missions UNESCO relentlessly strives to build a globalization with a human face by slowly but unfailingly establishing a modern humanism that is made harmonious and outstanding thanks to the contribution of higher education.

Summary of the World Declaration on Higher Education

The World Conference on Higher Education (WCHE) was held in UNESCO Headquarters in Paris, from 5–9 October 1998. Over 180 countries, as well as representatives of the academic community, including teachers, students and other stakeholders in higher education took part in this major event. In the conference the participants adopted the World Declaration on Higher Education for the Twenty-first Century and Framework for Priority Action for Change and Development of Higher Education. This document highlights priority actions for the renewal and revitalization of higher education at all levels:

1. Higher education shall be *equally accessible to all* on the basis of merit, in keeping with Article 26.1 of the Universal Declaration of Human Rights. As a consequence, no discrimination can be accepted in granting access to higher education on grounds of race, gender, language, religion or economic, cultural or social distinctions, or physical disabilities.
2. The core missions of higher education systems (to educate, to train, to undertake research and, in particular, to contribute to the sustainable development and improvement of society as a whole) should be preserved, reinforced and further expanded, namely to *educate highly qualified graduates and responsible citizens* and to provide opportunities ('espaces ouverts') *for higher learning and for learning throughout life*. Moreover, higher education has acquired an unprecedented role in present-day society, as a vital component of cultural, social, economic and political development and as a pillar of endogenous capacity-building,

the consolidation of human rights, sustainable development, democracy and peace, in a context of justice. It is the duty of higher education to ensure that the values and ideals of a culture of peace prevail.

3. Higher education institutions and their personnel and students should preserve and develop their crucial functions, through the exercise of ethics and scientific and intellectual rigour in their various activities. They should also enhance their *critical and forward-looking* function, through the ongoing analysis of emerging social, economic, cultural and political trends, providing a focus for forecasting, warning and prevention. For this, they should enjoy *full academic autonomy and freedom*, while being fully responsible and *accountable* to society.
4. *Relevance in higher education should be assessed in terms of the fit between what society expects of institutions and what they do*. For this, institutions and systems, in particular in their reinforced relations with the world of work, should *base their long-term orientations on societal aims and needs, including the respect of cultures and environment protection*. Developing entrepreneurial skills and initiatives should become major concerns of higher education. Special attention should be paid to higher education's role of service to society, especially activities aimed at eliminating poverty, intolerance, violence, illiteracy, hunger, environmental degradation and disease, and to activities aimed at the development of peace, through an interdisciplinary and transdisciplinary approach.
5. Higher education is part of a seamless system, starting with early childhood and primary education and continuing through life. The contribution of higher education to the development of the whole education system and the reordering of *its links with all levels of education, in particular with secondary education, should be a priority*. Secondary education should both prepare for and facilitate access to higher education as well as offer broad training and prepare students for active life.
6. *Diversifying* higher education models and recruitment methods and criteria is essential both to meet demand and to give students the rigorous background and training required by the 21st century. Learners must have an optimal range of choice and the acquisition of knowledge and know-how should be viewed from a *lifelong perspective*, based on flexible entry and exit points within the system.
7. *Quality in higher education is a multidimensional concept*, which should embrace all its functions and activities: teaching and academic programmes, research and scholarship, staffing, students, infrastructure and the academic environment. Particular attention should be paid to the *advancement of knowledge through research*. Higher education institutions in all regions should be committed *to transparent internal and external evaluation*, conducted openly by independent specialists. However, due attention should be paid to specific institutional, national and regional contexts in order to take into account diversity and *to avoid uniformity*. There is a perceived need for a new vision and paradigm of higher education, which should be student-oriented. To achieve this

goal, curricula need to be recast so as to go beyond simple cognitive mastery of disciplines and include the acquisition of skills, competencies and abilities for communication, creative and critical analysis, independent thinking and team work in multicultural contexts.

8. A vigorous policy of *staff development* is an essential element for higher education institutions. Clear policies should be established concerning *higher education teachers*, so as to update and improve their skills, with stimulus for constant innovation in curriculum, teaching and learning methods, and with an appropriate professional and financial status, and for *excellence in research and teaching*, reflecting the corresponding provisions of the Recommendation concerning the Status of Higher-Education Teaching Personnel approved by the General Conference of UNESCO in November 1997.

9. National and institutional decision-makers should place *students* and their needs at the centre of their concerns and should consider them as major partners and responsible stakeholders in the renewal of higher education. Guidance and counselling services should be developed, in co-operation with student organizations, to take account of the needs of ever more diversified categories of learners. Students who do drop out should have suitable opportunities to return to higher education if and when appropriate. Institutions should educate students to become well-informed and deeply motivated citizens, who can think critically, analyse problems of society, look for solutions to the problems of society, apply them and accept social responsibilities.

10. Measures must be taken or reinforced to ensure the *participation of women in higher education*, in particular at the decision-making level and in all disciplines in which they are under-represented. Further efforts are required to eliminate all gender stereotyping in higher education. To overcome obstacles and to enhance the access of women to higher education remains an urgent priority In the renewal process of systems and institutions.

11. The potential of *new information and communication technologies* for the renewal of higher education by extending and diversifying delivery, and by making knowledge and information available to a wider public should be fully utilized. Equitable access to these should be assured through international cooperation and support to countries that lack capacities to acquire such tools. Adapting these technologies to national, regional and local needs and securing technical, educational, management and institutional systems to sustain them should be a priority.

12. Higher education should be considered as a *public service*. While diversified sources of funding, private and public, are necessary, *public support for higher education and research remains essential* to ensure a balanced achievement of its educational and social missions. Management and financing in higher education should be instruments to improve quality and relevance. This requires the development of appropriate planning and policy-analysis capacities and strategies, based on partnerships between higher education institutions and responsible state authorities. Autonomy to manage internal affairs is

necessary, but with clear and transparent accountability to society.

13. The *international dimension* of higher education is an inherent part of its quality. *Networking*, which has emerged as a major means of action, should be based on *sharing, solidarity and equality* among partners. The 'brain drain' has yet to be stemmed, since it continues to deprive the developing countries and those in transition, of the high-level expertise necessary to accelerate their socioeconomic progress. Priority should be given to training programmes in the developing countries, in centres of excellence forming regional and international networks, with short periods of specialized and intensive study abroad.

14. Regional and international normative instruments for the recognition of studies and diplomas should be ratified and implemented, including certification of skills, competencies and abilities of graduates, making it easier for students to change courses, in order to facilitate mobility within and between national systems.

15. Close *partnership* among all stakeholders – national and institutional policy-makers, governments and parliaments, the media, teaching and related staff, researchers, students and their families, the world of work, community groups – is required in order to set in train a movement for the in-depth reform and renewal of higher education.

Source: http://portal.unesco.org/education/en/ev.php-URL_ID=19189&URL_DO=DO_TOPIC&URL_SECTION=201.html.

SPECIAL CONTRIBUTION B

Goolam Mohamedbhai

Contribution of Higher Education to the UN Millennium Development Goals

Whilst participating in an international workshop where I was making a presentation on how higher education can make a contribution to development in Africa, I asked at one point: do you know how many Millennium Development Goals (MDGs) there are and, if so, can you recall at least half of them? I saw a couple of hands hesitatingly go up, a few participants apologetically looked down in front of them and the rest looked dazed. That is the first major problem

with higher education and the MDGs. The vast majority of academics are not aware of them, and cannot therefore even start thinking about how their institutions can contribute to them.

I therefore explained that in 2000, the leaders of all the countries of the world assembled and took stock of the bleak picture of our planet. They formulated a vision of how they want their world to be in the future – a world where there is less poverty and fewer hungry people; a

world free from infectious diseases, where mothers and their babies can expect to live longer, children can have access to education and girls and women have equal opportunities in life as boys and men; a world which cares for its precious environment and one where the haves and have-nots join hands for the betterment of the whole mankind. The leaders then drew up the MDGs and set the target time of 2015 for their achievement.

When I listed the eight MDGs, the next major problem surfaced. Some bewildered faces queried: are these MDGs really the business of higher education? Should not these be the responsibility of our governments? Most academics have difficulty in relating higher education to the MDGs or rather cannot link the work of their institutions to the goals to be achieved. And yet, there is no question that higher education can, indeed does, contribute towards achieving the MDGs.

Let us therefore examine the MDGs in some detail and see how they relate to higher education:

GOAL 1: ERADICATE EXTREME POVERTY AND HUNGER

The regions with the largest proportions of poor people are sub-Saharan Africa and Southern Asia. In countries in these regions the vast majority of the population live in rural areas where poverty is worst, and where agriculture is the main rural activity. Agricultural colleges and universities can therefore play a key role in promoting rural agricultural development through teaching, research and outreach programmes. In fact, rural development should be mainstreamed in all areas of higher education in those regions. In engineering, for example, the students should be apprised of the local building materials, of the water supply and sanitation technologies appropriate to rural areas, of alternative sources of energy and so on. The University of Development Studies in Ghana, created in 1992, is a remarkable example of a pro-poor, rural community-based institution where in all programmes students have to spend one trimester each year over three years doing community-based practical fieldwork.

GOAL 2: ACHIEVE UNIVERSAL PRIMARY EDUCATION

Again it is in rural areas in developing countries that we find the largest numbers of children who do not attend school. Higher education can contribute by researching the causes of non-attendance in specific areas; arranging for literacy programmes for parents who can then be influenced to send their children to school; encouraging their student teachers to give preference to a rural rather than an urban posting and so on. But of course the most important contribution of higher education to the primary education sector is in ensuring that sufficient teachers are trained to meet the needs of the country, and existing ones are re-trained. It has been estimated that sub-Saharan Africa, where about 40% of primary-school age children are out of school, would require an additional 1.6 million teachers to achieve universal primary education by 2015 – a mammoth task.

GOAL 3: PROMOTE GENDER EQUALITY AND EMPOWER WOMEN

Women can play a major role in the development of a country, especially in developing countries. Higher education should first develop appropriate policies to remove gender inequity in education at all levels. There are still many universities where women are grossly under-represented at student or staff level, particularly in science and technology areas. Higher education institutions should also mainstream gender in all their teaching, research and outreach activities. Some universities, for example the University of Makarere in Uganda, have done so by establishing a Gender Institute for that specific purpose. There is also the excellent example of the University of Bakhat Alruda in Sudan which, in 2005, created a Faculty of Community Development with the main mission of promoting the education and training of women in the rural areas of the White Nile.

GOALS 4 AND 5: REDUCE CHILD MORTALITY AND IMPROVE MATERNAL HEALTH

Under-five child mortality is quite high in many countries and it has been found that educating mothers significantly increases the rate of child survival. Higher education institutions should therefore target the education of mothers through their faculties or departments of social work. The other important factor in reducing infant mortality is immunization against measles. Here the faculties of health, in collaboration with the national ministries of health, should assist in the immunization programme. With regard to maternal mortality, evidence shows that maternal death in childbirth is considerably reduced when the mother is assisted by skilled attendants. Higher education institutions should train appropriate skilled personnel, such as nurses and midwives, to provide assistance at childbirth, especially in remote rural areas.

GOAL 6: COMBAT HIV/AIDS, MALARIA AND OTHER DISEASES

HIV/AIDS is perhaps one of the worst health scourges to affect the world in recent times, and sub-Saharan Africa is by far the worst affected region. There are many ways in which higher education institutions can assist in combating HIV/AIDS, but first and foremost they should assess the impact of the pandemic on their own institution. They should have a written policy on HIV/AIDS, if necessary set up a specialized unit to coordinate HIV/AIDS activities in their institution, integrate HIV/AIDS into their curriculum, undertake research and encourage community outreach activities. They should also collaborate with other institutions in their country or even region to adopt a concerted approach to the problem. An interesting example of regional collaboration is in the West Indies, where a Commonwealth Regional Chair in Education and HIV/AIDS was launched in 2004 at the University of West Indies to coordinate the contribution of higher education to HIV/AIDS.

GOAL 7: ENSURE ENVIRONMENTAL SUSTAINABILITY

Promoting sustainable development is a major international challenge in which higher education has a crucial role to play. Higher education institutions must train teachers to be aware of the need for promoting sustainable development in schools, and develop school curricula which incorporate sustainable development. In fact, all higher education programmes, be they in pure or applied sciences, or in social science and humanities, need to be revised, not only to introduce the concept of sustainable development but also to orient the teaching approach and methods (multi- and inter-disciplinary, team work and project-based) necessary for a sustainable future. Higher education institutions can also initiate appropriate programmes for training key professionals such as engineers, architects, economists and so on in relevant aspects of sustainable development, and they are well positioned to undertake research and development in areas of sustainable development. Indeed, higher education must play an important role in the UN Decade of Education for Sustainable Development.

GOAL 8: DEVELOP A GLOBAL PARTNERSHIP FOR DEVELOPMENT

For higher education institutions to be in a position to play a meaningful role in achieving the MDGs, they must first be efficient and effective. In many countries this is not the case. The disparity among higher education institutions, especially between those in the North and the South, is blatant. More than ever, there is need for North–South higher education collaboration and international donor and funding agencies must place higher education high on their list of priorities.

The above list is merely indicative. There must be many, many other examples of possible contributions of higher education to the MDGs.

The UN Millennium Development Goals

The Millennium Development Goals (MDGs) are eight goals to be achieved by 2015 that respond to the world's main development challenges. The MDGs are drawn from the actions and targets contained in the Millennium Declaration that was adopted by 189 nations and signed by 147 heads of state and governments during the UN Millennium Summit in September 2000.

Goal 1. Eradicate extreme poverty and hunger
- Reduce by half the proportion of people living on less than a dollar a day
- Reduce by half the proportion of people who suffer from hunger.

Goal 2. Achieve universal primary education
- Ensure that all boys and girls complete a full course of primary education.

Goal 3. Promote gender equality and empower women
- Eliminate gender disparity in primary and secondary education preferably by 2005, and at all levels by 2015.

Goal 4. Reduce child mortality
- Reduce by two thirds the mortality rate among children under five.

Goal 5. Improve maternal health
- Reduce by three quarters the maternal mortality ratio.

Goal 6. Combat HIV/AIDS, malaria and other diseases
- Halt and begin to reverse the spread of HIV/AIDS
- Halt and begin to reverse the incidence of malaria and other major diseases.

Goal 7. Ensure environmental sustainability
- Integrate the principles of sustainable development into country policies and programmes; reverse loss of environmental resources
- Reduce by half the proportion of people without sustainable access to safe drinking water
- Achieve significant improvement in lives of at least 100 million slum dwellers, by 2020.

Goal 8. Develop a global partnership for development
- Develop further an open trading and financial system that is rule-based, predictable, non-discriminatory, includes a commitment to good governance, development, and poverty reduction – nationally and internationally
- Address the least developed countries' special needs. This includes tariff and quota-free access to their exports; enhanced debt relief for heavily indebted poor countries; cancellation of official bilateral debt; and more generous official development assistance for countries committed to poverty reduction
- Address the special needs of landlocked countries and small island developing states
- Deal comprehensively with developing countries' debt problems through national and international measures to make debt sustainable in the long term
- In cooperation with developing countries, develop decent and productive work for youth
- In cooperation with pharmaceutical companies, provide access to affordable essential drugs in developing countries
- In cooperation with the private sector, make available the benefits of new technologies, especially information and communications.

Source: http://www.un.org/millenniumgoals/goals.html.

Richard Hopper, Jamil Salmi and Roberta Malee Bassett

The contribution of higher education to economic and social development is multifold. It exercises a direct influence on national productivity, which helps to determine living standards and a country's ability to compete in the global economy. Higher education institutions support knowledge-driven economic growth strategies and poverty reduction by (a) training a qualified and adaptable labour force, including high-level scientists, professionals, technicians, teachers in basic and secondary education, and future government, civil service, and business leaders; (b) generating new knowledge; and (c) building the capacity to access existing stores of global knowledge and to adapt that knowledge to local use. Higher education institutions are unique in their ability to integrate and create synergy among these three dimensions. Sustainable transformation and growth throughout the economy are not possible without the capacity-building contribution of an innovative higher education system. This is especially true in low-income countries with weak institutional capacity and limited human capital.

The World Bank has actively supported tertiary education reform efforts in a number of countries. Nevertheless, there is a perception that the Bank has not been fully responsive to the growing demand by clients for tertiary education interventions and that, especially in the poorest countries, lending for the subsector has not matched the importance of tertiary education systems for economic and social development. The Bank is commonly viewed as supporting only basic education; systematically advocating the reallocation of public expenditures from tertiary to basic education; promoting cost recovery and private sector expansion; and discouraging low-income countries from considering any investment in advanced human capital. Given these perceptions, the rapid changes taking place in the global environment, and the persistence of the traditional problems of tertiary education in developing and transition countries, reexamining the World Bank's policies and experiences in tertiary education has become a matter of urgency.

POVERTY REDUCTION THROUGH ECONOMIC GROWTH

Tertiary education exercises a direct influence on national productivity, which largely determines living standards and a country's ability to compete in the global economy. Tertiary education institutions support knowledge-driven economic growth strategies and poverty reduction by (a) training a qualified and adaptable labour force, including high-level scientists, professionals, technicians, teachers in basic and secondary education, and future government, civil service, and business leaders; (b) generating new knowledge; and (c) building the capacity to access existing stores of global knowledge and to adapt that knowledge to local use. Tertiary education institutions are unique in their ability to integrate and create synergy among these three dimensions. Sustainable transformation and growth throughout the economy are not possible without the capacity-building contribution of an innovative tertiary education system. This is especially true in low-income countries with weak institutional capacity and limited human capital.

POVERTY REDUCTION THROUGH REDISTRIBUTION AND EMPOWERMENT

Tertiary education supports the opportunity and empowerment dimensions outlined in the World Bank *World Development Report 2000/2001*. Access to tertiary education can open better employment and income opportunities to underprivileged students, thereby decreasing inequity. The norms, values, attitudes, ethics and knowledge that tertiary institutions can impart to students constitute the social capital necessary to construct healthy civil societies and socially cohesive cultures.

FULFILMENT OF THE MILLENNIUM DEVELOPMENT GOALS

It is doubtful that any developing country could make significant progress towards achieving the United Nations Millennium Development Goals (MDGs) for education – universal enrolment in primary education and the elimination of gender disparities in primary and secondary education – without a strong tertiary education system. Tertiary education supports the rest of the education system through the training of teachers and school principals, the involvement of specialists from tertiary education institutions in curriculum design and educational research, and the establishment of admission criteria that influence the content and methods of teaching and learning at secondary level. A similar argument applies to the contribution of post-secondary medical education – especially the training of medical doctors, epidemiologists, public health specialists, and hospital managers – to meeting the basic health MDGs.

THE STATE AND TERTIARY EDUCATION

Research on the dynamics of knowledge-driven development has identified the converging roles of four contributing factors: a country's macroeconomic incentive and institutional regime, its ICT infrastructure, its national innovation system, and the quality of its human resources. Of these, the contribution of tertiary education is vital to the national innovation system and the development of human resources.

In this context, continued government support of tertiary education is justified by three important considerations: the existence of externalities from tertiary education, equity issues, and the supportive role of tertiary education in the education system as a whole.

EXTERNALITIES

Investments in tertiary education generate major external benefits that are crucial for knowledge-driven economic and social development. Private investment in tertiary education can be sub-optimal because individuals do not capture all the benefits of education. A few examples will illustrate how education yields benefits to society as a whole.

Technological innovations and the dissemination of scientific and technical innovations lead to higher productivity. Such innovations are mainly the product of basic and applied research undertaken in universities. Progress in the agriculture, health and environment sectors, in particular, is heavily dependent on the application of such innovations. In addition, productivity is boosted by higher skill levels in the labour force – an outcome of increased educational levels – and the qualitative improvements that permit workers to use new technology.

Tertiary education facilitates nation building by promoting greater social cohesion; trust in social institutions; democratic participation and open debate; and appreciation of diversity in gender, ethnicity, religion and social class. Furthermore, pluralistic and democratic societies depend on research and analysis fostered through social sciences and humanities programmes. Improved health behaviours and outcomes also yield strong social benefits, and higher education is indispensable for training healthcare professionals.

EQUITY

Imperfections in capital markets limit the ability of individuals to borrow sufficiently for tertiary education, thereby hindering the participation of meritorious but economically disadvantaged groups. Although more than 60 countries have student loan programmes, access to affordable loans frequently remains restricted to a minority of students. Moreover, these loans are not necessarily available to the students with limited resources who most need financial aid. Only a few countries have national programmes that reach more than 10% of the student population. These exceptions are rich countries such as Australia, Canada, Sweden, the United Kingdom and the United States. In addition, where they do exist, student loans are not always available for the whole range of academic programmes and disciplines.

SUPPORT FOR OTHER LEVELS OF THE EDUCATION SYSTEM

Tertiary education plays a key role in supporting basic and secondary education, thereby buttressing the economic externalities produced by these lower levels. Improved tertiary education is necessary for sustainable progress in basic education. The supply of qualified teachers and school leaders, capacity for curriculum design, research on teaching and learning, economic analysis and management – these and many more components of basic education reform are hampered by weak tertiary education systems. A comprehensive approach to the development of the education sector is required, along with a balanced distribution of budgetary resources to ensure that countries invest appropriately in tertiary education, with attention to their progress towards the Millennium Development Goals.

When looking at the public benefits of tertiary education, it is important to note the existence of joint-product effects linked to the complementarity between tertiary education and the lower levels of education, as described above, and between undergraduate and postgraduate education. While many undergraduate and professional education programmes can be offered in separate institutions (business and law are examples), high-cost activities such as basic research and various types of specialized graduate training are more efficiently organized in combination with undergraduate training. Cross-subsidization across educational disciplines, programmes, and levels leads to public-good effects that are valuable but are difficult to quantify. In addition, there are economies of scale that justify public support of expensive programmes such as basic sciences that are almost natural monopolies.

WORLD BANK ACTIVITIES IN HIGHER EDUCATION

Even though the World Bank is known essentially for the loans given to countries in support of their development efforts, an equally significant contribution is the policy dialogue and analytical work conducted by the Bank as a knowledge-sharing institution, to help governments consider options for possible higher education reforms and set the stage for their implementation. Table 1 presents the list of countries in which higher education studies have been prepared in recent years.

Through its projects in various areas of

TABLE 1
Recent higher education studies (2001–2006)

Region	Countries
Eastern Europe and Central Asia	Russia (2002), **Georgia** (2003), **Kazakhstan*** (2006)
East Asia and Pacific	**Vietnam** (2003), **Malaysia** (2006)
Latin America and the Caribbean	**Colombia** (2002), **Venezuela** (2004)
Middle East and North Africa	**Yemen** (2001), **Palestine** (2002), **Morocco** (2004), **Tunisia** (2005), Egypt (2001)
South Asia	Sri Lanka (2004), **Pakistan** (2006)
Sub-Saharan Africa	**Uganda** (2004), Mauritius (2004), Namibia (2004), Niger (2005), Nigeria (2006)
Regional Studies	**Africa** (2004, 2006), South Asia (2006)

Notes: Names in bold indicate studies exclusively dedicated to higher education; in the other cases higher education is part of a sector-wide education study.

* Study carried out jointly with the OECD.

Source: World Bank data.

the four continents, the World Bank has supported countries' efforts to expand higher education and improve its quality and relevance. Even in earlier times when higher education was not officially a priority sub-sector, the Bank financed a significant number of projects in response to specific requests by countries such as China, Kenya and Tunisia. World Bank projects in tertiary education have amounted to approximately one-third of total lending in education in the era since the 1970s. Table 2 details the breakdown of lending for tertiary education within total education lending between 2001 and 2006. It provides important data that highlights fluctuations in education lending as a whole, and tertiary education lending in particular. Specific commitments to tertiary education during this five-year period amount to only 14.5% of new education commitments during this period. It is important to note, however, that commitments in other areas (like lifelong learning initiatives and lending for teacher training for primary and secondary school teaching, for instance) may be classified under a different education sub-sector but are, in fact, specifically tied to tertiary education.

The main types of activities supported by Bank projects come under one or more of the following headings. They are tailored to the needs of the country and the specific requests of the national authorities and the higher education community:

- Vision development, strategic planning, and consensus building at both the national and institutional levels
- Finance reforms (for example allocation of recurrent budget; competitive funding; cost sharing; student loans; scholarships)
- Governance and management reforms (creation of policy bodies; mergers; adoption of academic credit systems; management information systems)
- Quality improvement (strengthening of existing programmes; evaluation and accreditation systems; innovations in programme content and delivery; innovations in academic organization; information and communication infrastructure)
- Institutional diversification (establishment or strengthening of polytechnic or technical institutes)
- Science and technology development (strategy development; capacity for monitoring and evaluation; reform of resource allocation mechanisms; competitive funding; promotion of research in priority areas; joint public–private sector technology development; capacity for metrology, standards, and quality testing; intellectual property rights)

The combination of policy dialogue, analytical work and financial assistance has facilitated the implementation of comprehensive reforms in the higher education sector in countries as diverse as Argentina, Chile, China, Vietnam, Egypt, Tunisia, Ghana and Mozambique. Often, governments use the resources made available through multilateral loans as incentives for institutions willing to break new ground after thorough strategic planning and/or self-evaluation efforts.

The competitive innovation funds that several countries have established with World Bank support have been among the most effective channels for stimulating the participation of higher education institutions in meaningful transformation efforts. Under such funds, institutions are typically invited to formulate project proposals that are reviewed and selected by committees of peers according to transparent procedures and criteria. One of the main benefits of competitive funding mechanisms is that they encourage higher education institutions to adopt a forward-looking strategic planning approach, which helps them formulate well-conceived projects that are consistent with the overall direction of the institution.

Often, the Bank was able to act as a bridge builder, bringing to the discussion table stakeholders who do not routinely talk to each other. In several countries, for example, the Bank was instrumental in initiating a dialogue between public and private universities, between universities and technology institutes, and between universities and employers. Similarly, in countries where the relationship between the government and the university sector is tense or even conflictive, the Bank sometimes manages to facilitate a constructive policy dialogue on key issues. This happened in 2003 in Bolivia, around the themes of quality enhancement and accreditation.

The Bank has also played a convening role at the regional level, as evidenced by the success of the global business school initiative in the Africa region and the launch of several regional quality assur-

TABLE 2
New commitments for education by sub-sector (fiscal year 01–06)

Sub-sector	IBRD+IDA new commitments (millions of current US$)					
	FY01	FY02	FY03	FY04	FY05	FY06
Adult liter./non-formal ed.	56	18	4	11	5	40
General education sector	435	442	639	355	507	457
Pre-primary education	32	32	102	25	88	147
Primary education	315	406	780	883	565	552
Secondary education	124	133	285	250	376	449
Tertiary education	41	268	524	62	361	263
Vocational training	91	85	15	98	50	82
Total	1,095	1,385	2,349	1,684	1,951	1,991

Note: The general education sector includes more than one sub-sector. About 50% of financing under 'general education' is for primary education.

Source: World Bank EdStats. Retrieved April 2, 2007 from http://devdata.worldbank.org/edstats/wbl_A.asp

ance networks (Asia, Latin America). More often than not, the regional policy seminars that the Bank organizes on a regular basis provide an effective forum for South–South knowledge sharing. In 2002–03, for example, a series of seminars in South Asia helped stimulate reform efforts in Sri Lanka and Nepal. In 2005 and 2006, the Bank organized seminars in sub-Saharan Africa that helped disseminate successful reforms in individual countries and/or institutions.

While it is difficult to measure the direct impact of global publications such as *Constructing Knowledge Societies* (World Bank, 2002), sometimes these policy documents can serve as catalysts for initiating reforms. In Pakistan, for instance, after the publication of *Peril and Promise* (World Bank and UNESCO, 2000), the government established its own Higher Education Task Force whose findings and recommendations guided the launch of a comprehensive reform in 2003. In Yemen, the government received a small technical assistance loan (the 'Learning and Innovation Loan') from the Bank in 2004 that facilitated the launch of a nation-wide consultation effort and the preparation of a long-term strategy for higher education reform.

The capacity of the World Bank to play these roles of convenor and facilitator is due to several factors: the institution is able to rely on direct experience across a wide range of countries and situations; it interacts with client countries from a multi-sectoral perspective; it has learned to cooperate with multiple stakeholders and it seeks to integrate its higher education work into the overall economic and social development framework of the concerned countries.

CONCLUSION

In the past two decades, the World Bank has adopted a more holistic view of education. Higher education has become an essential part of the Bank's work in the sector, representing between 15% and 25% of the lending programme in education, depending on the year. Today,

even countries that do not need or want to borrow from the World Bank anymore, such as China, Kazakhstan or Malaysia, actively seek policy advice on various aspects of higher education reform, often guided by their aspiration to become full-fledged knowledge economies.

Second, in accord with a renewed Bank-wide focus on results, the success of higher education reforms will be assessed by looking at outcomes rather than considering only the reform measures themselves. This will require extensive work on the determinants of quality and the effectiveness of various quality assurance mechanisms, progress in measuring actual learning outcomes of students, and impact evaluations of innovative schemes such as the new voucher funding in the US State of Colorado and Kazakhstan or the ProUni programme in Brazil which provides scholarships for low-income students financed through tax exemptions for private higher education institutions.

Third, the World Bank recognizes that, in higher education more than any other area of education development, reform programmes and innovative approaches have little chance of success unless careful attention is paid to the political economy of change. Stakeholder consultation and consensus building are as important as a technically sound design. Mozambique provides a powerful illustration of how a new Minister of Higher Education managed to implement a comprehensive reform based on a strategic vision elaborated after extensive consultations and debates. Bank experience in several countries underscores the need for continuous policy dialogue and vision sharing with all stakeholders to ensure the sustainability of reforms. Increasingly, the preparation of new Bank projects in support of higher education reform includes a social assessment exercise to identify the concerns of key stakeholders and inform the design of the project, as happened for example in Jordan, China and Colombia.

Finally, increased attention is being paid to global public goods that affect higher education in all countries but that are often beyond the control of any one government. For example, the World Bank is supporting efforts to improve connectivity in Africa and to develop distance education opportunities through the African Virtual University. It is also helping establish regional networks of quality assurance agencies in Asia, Latin America and Africa and working towards consolidating these regional initiatives into a global network that would help developing countries enhance the quality and relevance of their tertiary education institutions through capacity-building and experience-sharing activities. In attempting to address these global public goods issues, the World Bank works increasingly in partnership with other multilateral agencies (the OECD, UNESCO, the AUF, and so on) and with international and regional associations of universities (the IAU, the AAU, SADEC and so on).

BIBLIOGRAPHY

Bloom, D., Canning, D., and Chan, K. (2005) *Higher Education and Economic Development in Africa*. Washington, DC: World Bank. Retrieved March 21, 2007, from www.worldbank.org.

Saint, W. (2004) *From Aid to Global Sharing of Knowledge: Research Excellence and Commitment to Development*. Washington, DC: World Bank. Retrieved March 21, 2007, from http://www.daad.de/de/download/entwicklung/ veranstaltungen/2004_dies_saint.pdf.

Salmi, J. (1994) Shaping the higher education study: the dynamics of consultation. *Norrag News*, **16**, pp. 1–6.

World Bank (1994) *Higher Education: The Lessons of Experience*. Development in Practice series. Washington, DC.

World Bank (1999) *World Development Report 1998/1999: Knowledge for Development*. New York: Oxford University Press.

World Bank (2001) *World Development Report 2000/2001: Attacking Poverty*. New York: Oxford University Press.

World Bank (2002) *Constructing Knowledge Societies: New Challenges for Tertiary Education*. Washington, DC.

World Bank (2005) *Education Sector Strategy Update*. Washington, DC.

World Bank and UNESCO (2000) *Higher Education in Developing Countries: Peril and Promise*. Report of the Independent World Bank/UNESCO Task Force on Higher Education and Society. Washington, DC.

NOTE

1 The findings, interpretations, and conclusions expressed in this paper are entirely those of the authors and should not be attributed in any manner to the World Bank, the members of its Board of Executive Directors or the countries they represent.

SPECIAL CONTRIBUTION D

The OECD's view of the role of higher education for human and social development

Andy Johnston and Richard Yelland

Local, national and international policy development in the past 20 years has made it clear that sustainable development is the only strategic framework that facilitates a coordinated approach to problems such as poverty, human rights abuses, corruption, poor physical and mental health, loss of biodiversity and climate change.

Increasingly, higher education institutions (HEIs) across the world recognize that they are key players in their country's efforts to develop sustainably. Some welcome the opportunity to play their part. However, not one country has taken a nationwide strategic and systemic approach to this issue.

In the past, neither public policy nor HEIs themselves focused strategically on the contribution that they can make to the sustainable development of the regions or countries in which they are located. For older, traditional HEIs in particular, the emphasis has often been on the pursuit of knowledge, with little regard for the surrounding environment. There are signs that this is now changing. To be able to play their full role, HEIs must do more than simply educate and research. They must engage with others in their regions, provide opportunities for lifelong learning and contribute to the development of meaningful jobs that will enable graduates to find employment and contribute positively to the development of their countries.

In a recent study by the Programme on Institutional Management in Higher Education (IMHE) of the OECD's Higher Education for Sustainable Development (HE4SD) project, 16 HEIs demonstrated not just a willingness to be involved in the project but a desire to take a leading role. In a series of workshops and questionnaires, staff at every level and students developed views that positioned HEIs as 'tools for the transformation of society', 'deliverers of change', being 'responsive to societal needs' and 'gaining the respect of future generations'. This is ambitious stuff, and the strategies suggested for achieving these goals were a far cry from the traditional explanation of the purpose of an HEI. Many talked of the HEI as a 'social entrepreneur' or a 'community leader' that builds on hard-won integrity and independence to become the main reference point for knowledge. This knowledge helps their countries work through the unprecedented and complex challenges that modern society faces.

It would be easy to dismiss these ambitions as wishful thinking or cynical marketing. However, the partners in HE4SD suggested that their progress should be evaluated through peer review, which would examine the credibility of their action plans and judge the effectiveness of their attempts to integrate sustainability thinking into the practice of the HEI by focusing on the concrete outcomes of their activities. In other words, peer review would analyse whether all the planning and strategizing actually resulted in an increased likelihood of sustainable development locally or globally.

What gives the HE4SD HEIs credibility is their existing record of achievement. They provide real examples of how organizations can contribute to the simultaneous achievement of economic growth, protection of the environment and enhanced social capital.

At Chalmers University of Technology in Sweden, sustainability has been integrated into most of the teaching programmes. Three years ago, all new students were invited to a common lecture on sustainable development as part of the welcoming programme. By 2008, all students will be obliged to take one compulsory course (7.5 ECTS) on the environment and sustainable development.

The Autonomous University of San Luis Potosí (UASLP) in Mexico has a centrally run 'Agenda Ambiental' to promote campus sustainability, work with lecturers on curriculum innovation and act as an incubator for research into sustainability.

At the University of Graz in Austria, the Oikos student group has led efforts to disseminate good practices throughout the university and to the wider community and stakeholders. At the Technical University of Catalonia in Spain, stakeholder engagement to support sustainability is now part of normal practice.

At the University of Veracruz (UV) in Mexico, social service activities are carried out by students in some of the least-developed Mexican towns and communities. The UV pays special attention to generating social consciousness among students, in order to encourage them to participate in activities linked to the eradication of poverty and social inclusion in backward municipalities. Moreover, the University has established four University Houses in four different municipalities so that students can directly apply their knowledge to the solution of local problems.

Contributing to sustainability is enshrined in the core strategies of some HEIs. At the University of the Sunshine Coast in Australia, the HEIs' purpose is 'engagement and sustainability'. The aim of the Tipperary Institute in Ireland is sustainable regeneration of the region.

At Hosei University in Japan, the long-term goal is to be 'open and green'. The Hosei Environmental Management System addresses reducing the extraction and use of natural resources. It focuses on green purchasing (especially green-labelled goods such as paper and electronic appliances), energy and resource conservation in the construction or renovation of buildings, and waste management (the zero-emission approach, using a university-wide recycling system) A separate subcommittee is responsible for setting and reviewing targets and implementing programmes for each of these issues.

At the Turku University of Applied Sciences in Finland, the university strategy is complementary to the town's sustainability strategy.

These significant commitments are serious responses to changes happening in society.

At Portland State University (PSU) in the United States, it has become normal

practice – a state of mind – to think about sustainable development in all university operations. This is partly due to the influence of Portland itself, as it is one of the most sustainable cities in the world. The newest building, the Engineering Tower, is PSU's first LEED Gold building. It showcases how natural systems can be used directly for both research and building operation. The building has a partially visible rainwater harvesting system that collects water for use in the hydraulics laboratory and for flushing toilets on the first floor. The building also pumps both hot and cold groundwater to moderate the indoor temperature. This groundwater heat-pump system saves energy and eliminates the need for a cooling tower.

All these HEIs are making a significant effort, and without exception they recognize that they could do more. However, there are some tough barriers to overcome. The HEIs' own management capacity is one of these barriers. Another major barrier is the poor leadership of governments that have signed up to sustainable development without recognizing the full implications. Such governments do not put implementation mechanisms in place to encourage HEIs to achieve their potential. The next major barrier for some HEIs is the low level of awareness among students and employers. As a result, academics do not receive demands to change the way they teach. Even if teaching methods were changed, another major barrier is the autonomous nature of academic disciplines that do not lend themselves to the wide-ranging character of sustainability. The ability to tackle these issues is hampered by traditionally poor communication channels within HEIs.

However, HEIs have undergone much change in recent years and have shown themselves to be highly adaptable. There are some tried-and-tested ways of supporting the change process that complement rather than antagonize academic culture. Foremost is the power of research to commit, engage and enthuse academics and students. When research

is supported by a proactive unit promoting sustainability, such as those at UASLP or Chalmers, the transfer of good practices into all aspects of university life is accelerated. In particular, the current interest in climate change and a general increased awareness of sustainability are helpful. HEIs operate in many different networks based on their locality or learning. Such networks can be used to spread good practices.

This challenging change agenda requires the support of the formal management structures of the HEIs through the development of strategies, action plans, performance indicators and evaluation processes. However, procedures alone are not enough. They should be complemented by strong messages that interdisciplinary research is valued and sustainability is a subject worthy of study. Staff need to be confident that senior management know what sustainability is and are capable of supporting implementation of the policy.

For some HEIs, this represents a challenging step change in policy direction and staff capacity requirements, but unfortunately this is still not enough. HE4SD partners recognized that every HEI exists within an education system. If HEIs are to meet the strict test of 'contributing to sustainable development', then the whole system must be engaged to support them.

At the highest level, this means that policymakers will have to step up their efforts to promote their own sustainable development policies. This can be achieved by endorsing initiatives such as the UN Decade of Education for Sustainable Development and also by recognizing that policies on poverty alleviation, environmental protection and health services cannot be delivered without key individuals and organizations being 'sustainability literate'. None of the countries in the study were able to demonstrate the joined-up approach to policymaking that will facilitate sustainability.

At the executive level of government, more targeted awareness-raising campaigns will help to confirm the importance of sustainable development. HE4SD partners recognized that significant funding for sustainable development is currently not available. Therefore, funding for small pilot projects, national coordinating activities and support networks for disseminating good practices could accelerate uptake across the higher education sector.

In summary, the higher education systems in the study countries have only begun to recognize the importance and relevance of the sustainable development challenge. The leading HEIs identified by the study have made progress with little support from their higher education systems. These HEIs may not be the only ones with something to show the world, and they are not representative of the higher education sector as a whole. In fact, it would be safe to say that on the basis of this small study, less than 5% of HEIs take sustainable development seriously. The world will not be able to

develop sustainably unless the other 95% join in.

This is where we hope that the IMHE Programme and the OECD in general can make a contribution. Publication of the study report, supported by documentation of best practices in the participating institutions, may inspire more HEIs to take a close look at their policies and at how much more they could be doing. Demonstrating the link between sustainable development and the mission and purpose of universities and other higher education institutions will be an important step. The OECD report of a major project on the contribution of higher education institutions to regional development shows how far there is to go (OECD, 2007). HEIs' role in regional development is too often understood as confined to a narrow model of economic innovation and technology transfer. Teaching and learning are undervalued in a world where the image of institutions is dominated by rankings based on research

activity. Social and cultural development and environmental sustainability are a long way down the agenda.

Progress will only be made if institutions are committed. As a network, the IMHE can only be a catalyst and facilitator of action by organizing workshops, encouraging the sharing of experience and mobilizing expert opinion.

Governments and funding agencies also have a role to play. Moving to a larger scale will only be possible if there is better joined-up policy from government and intelligent, well-resourced support from higher education systems.

What this amounts to is a 'get real' challenge for the whole HE sector. On issues such as poverty, scarce resources and climate change, the clock is already ticking.

REFERENCE

OECD (2007) *Globally Competitive, Locally Engaged – Higher Education and Regions*. Paris, France.

SPECIAL CONTRIBUTION E

Key international frameworks for the role of higher education in human and social development

Yazmín Cruz López

This a selection of international declarations and agreements, in chronological order, that refer to the role of higher education in responding to global challenges directly related to human and social development, such as environmental protection, sustainability and cultural understanding.

For reasons of space it is not possible to provide an exhaustive description of all the documents published to date. The content included here has therefore been selected according to the following criteria: documents, declarations or reports produced by international institutions such as the UN and UNESCO and endorsed by government representatives and university leaders.

1972 Stockholm Declaration, Sweden

This declaration was presented at the United Nations Conference on the Human Environment, held in Stockholm, Sweden, on 5–16 June 1972. The text *proclaims the need to be fully aware of environmental issues and Principles 19 and 20 highlight the importance of education and research*:

Principle 19

Education in environmental matters … is essential in order to broaden the basis for an enlightened opinion and responsible conduct … in protecting and improving the environment in its full human dimension.

Principle 20

Scientific research and development in the context of environmental problems … must be promoted in all countries, especially the developing countries … In this connection, the free flow of up-to-date scientific information and transfer of experience must be supported and assisted …

Source: http://www.unep.org/Documents.Multilingual/Default.asp?DocumentID=97&ArticleID=1503

1990 Talloires Declaration, France

This was the *first joint declaration made by higher education institutions* and signed by university rectors, in which they express a *commitment to sustainability and the environment.* Signatories undertake to design and implement strategies and programmes for achieving the action requirements defined in the programme. Between 1990 and March 2006 the declaration was signed by 328 higher education institutions: 17 in Africa, 130 in Canada and North America, 36 in Asia and the Pacific, 33 in Europe and Russia, 2 in the Middle East and 110 in Latin America. Signatories commit themselves to the following principles, among others:

1. *Increase awareness of environmentally sustainable development*, openly addressing the urgent need to move towards an environmentally sustainable future.
2. *Engage in education, research, policy formation and information exchange* to ensure a sustainable future.
3. *Establish programmmes* to produce expertise and ensure that all university graduates have the awareness and understanding to be *ecologically responsible citizens*.
4. *Develop the capability of university faculty* to teach environmental literacy.
5. Set an *example of environmental responsibility*.
6. Encourage *involvement of government, foundations and industry* in supporting interdisciplinary research, education, policy formation, and information exchange in environmentally sustainable development. Expand *work with non-governmental organizations* to assist in finding solutions to environmental problems.
7. *Develop interdisciplinary approaches to curricula, research initiatives, operations, and outreach activities* that support an environmentally sustainable future.
8. Establish partnerships with *primary and secondary schools* to help develop the capacity for interdisciplinary teaching about population, environment and sustainable development.
9. Work with the United Nations Conference on Environment and Development, the United Nations Environment Programme and other national and international organizations to *promote a worldwide university effort towards a sustainable future*.

Source: http://www.ulsf.org/index.html

1991 Halifax Declaration, Canada

In December 1991, a meeting was held in Halifax, Canada between the presidents and rectors of 33 universities from 10 countries representing all five continents. Their aim was to *define the role of universities* with respect to the *environment and sustainable development*. Also present were representatives of the business and financial world, governmental organizations and NGOs. The meeting was promoted by the International Association of Universities, the United Nations University, the Association of Universities and Colleges of Canada and Dalhousie University, Canada.

The Halifax Declaration, signed by more than 250 institutions from 40 countries, *defines a basic action plan* for designing and implementing practical strategies for sustainable development in universities. The declaration emphasizes the *importance of education, qualification, research and information*, but places the greatest importance on *interdisciplinary work* and stresses the *pro-active attitude* that universities must take towards sustainable development.

Source: http://www.iisd.org/educate/declarat/halifax.htm

1992 Rio Declaration, Brazil

This Declaration was adopted by the governments present at the United Nations Conference on Environment and Development in Rio de Janeiro in June 1992. It reaffirms the commitments expressed in the Declaration of the United Nations Conference on the Human Environment, adopted in Stockholm in 1972. Its objective is to *establish a new and equitable global partnership* through the creation of new levels of cooperation among states, key sectors of society and people, working towards international agreements which respect the interests of all and protect the integrity of the global environmental and developmental system.

Principle 9 declares that:

States should cooperate to *strengthen endogenous capacity-building* for sustainable development by *improving scientific understanding* through *exchanges of scientific and technological knowledge*, and by enhancing the development, adaptation, diffusion and transfer of technologies, including new and innovative technologies.

Source: http://www.unep.org/Documents.Multilingual/Default.asp?DocumentID=78&ArticleID=1163

1992 Agenda 21

Agenda 21 is an *international, national and local action plan* that was adopted by more than 178 governments during the United Nations Conference on Environment and Development, held in Rio de Janeiro, Brazil, in June 1992. This document addresses the pressing environmental and developmental issues and challenges of the 21st century. It reflects an *international consensus and political commitment* at the highest level, but its successful implementation is first and foremost the responsibility of the signatory governments. Agenda 21 is divided into four sections:

1. Social and economic dimensions
2. Conservation and management of resources for development
3. Strengthening the role of major groups
4. Means of implementation.

Chapter 36, in the final section, deals with *promoting education, public awareness and training*, and states that:

> Education is critical for *promoting sustainable development* and improving the capacity of the people to address environment and development issues … It is also *critical for achieving environmental and ethical awareness, values and attitudes, skills and behaviour* consistent with sustainable development and for effective public participation in decision-making.

Source: http://www.un.org/esa/sustdev/documents/agenda21/english/agenda21toc.htm

1993 Swansea Declaration, Wales

In August 1993 the Association of Commonwealth Universities held its Fifteenth Quinquennial Conference in Swansea, Wales. The central theme of the event was People and the Environment – Preserving the Balance. Representatives drawn from over 400 universities in 47 different countries, inspired by the examples of Talloires and Halifax, looked for ways in which the universities, their leaders, professors and students might respond successfully to the challenges facing the environment and sustainable development.

The Swansea Declaration urges universities to *seek, establish and disseminate a clearer understanding of sustainable development, enhance the capacity of the university to teach and undertake research* in sustainable development principles, to *increase environmental literacy*, and enhance the *understanding of environmental ethics*. It also proposes that *universities should set an example to the rest of society* and urges *cooperation* with all segments of society in the pursuit of practical and policy measures to achieve sustainable development.

Source: http://www.iisd.org/educate/declarat/swansea.htm

1993 Kyoto Declaration, Japan

The Kyoto Declaration on Sustainable Development was adopted in November 1993 during the Ninth Round Table of the International Association of Universities, attended by leading figures from 90 universities. The meeting was devoted to analysing *the role of universities in sustainable development* in the 21st century. Following the discussions, the participants approved the text of the declaration, which takes into account the content of the Halifax Declaration and the Swansea Declaration.

The declaration calls on universities to *establish and disseminate a clearer understanding of sustainable development*, using all the resources within their reach and recognizing the significant *interdependence and international dimensions of sustainable development*. The text also emphasizes *the ethical obligation of the present generation* to overcome those practices of resource utilization which lie at the root of environmental unsustainability. It aims to *enhance the capacity of the university to teach and undertake research and action* in society in sustainable development principles. In addition, it signals the *need to cooperate with one another and with all segments of society* in the pursuit of practical and policy measures. Finally, it encourages universities to *review their own operations and implement the ways and means* to give life to the Declaration.

Source: http://www.unesco.org/iau/sd/sd_dkyoto.html

1993 Copernicus Charter

This project was developed by Copernicus, an inter-university environmental cooperation network set up by the former Association of European Universities. The Charter aims to raise consciousness within European universities of the necessity to work together to preserve the future and was presented in Barcelona in 1993, two years after it had been approved and signed by the rectors of 213 universities.

The Charter expresses the *collective commitment* of a large number of universities to *introduce the concept and objectives of sustainable development* into all areas of their activity, above all in institutional commitment, the teaching of environmental ethics, the training of university employees, the development of programmes in environmental action, interdisciplinary and collaborative education, the dissemination of knowledge, the creation of higher education networks and international partnerships with other sectors, the development of life-long learning programmes, and technology transfer.

Source: http://www.copernicus-campus.org/sites/charter_index1.html

1994 Barbados Declaration

This Declaration was made as part of the Global Conference on the Sustainable Development of Small Island Developing States promoted by the UN and held in Bridgetown, Barbados, in 1994. The conference was attended by delegates from the governments of small island developing states and from non-governmental organizations, who drafted and presented the final declaration. The document declares the need to *improve the quality of education, training and human resource development* to meet the challenges of sustainable development in small islands.

Source: http://www.sidsnet.org/docshare/other/BPOA.pdf

1996 *Learning: The Treasure Within*, a report presented to UNESCO by the International Commission on Education for the Twenty-first Century

This document is the report presented to UNESCO by the International Commission on Education for the Twenty-first Century, chaired by Jacques Delors and made up of 14 leading figures from various cultural and professional backgrounds. Although this is not a declaration, the text proposes valuable ideas on the foundations of education. It highlights the importance of *considering education as a whole*, which helps to provide the inspiration and guidance for educational reforms, both in the creation of programmes of study and in the definition of new teaching policies. The document is also a reference for future texts as its describes the *four pillars of education*:

Learning to know, combining a sufficiently broad general education with the possibility of in-depth work on a selected number of subjects ...

Learning to do, which, in addition to learning to do a job of work, should, more generally, entail the acquisition of a competence that enables people to deal with a variety of situations, often unforeseeable, and to work in teams ...

Learning to live together, by developing an understanding of others and their history, traditions and spiritual values and, on this basis, creating a new spirit which, guided by recognition of our growing interdependence and a common analysis of the risks and challenges of the future, would induce people to implement common projects or to manage the inevitable conflicts in an intelligent and peaceful way.

Learning to be, to ensure that none of the talents which are hidden like buried treasure in every person remain untapped and to create the conditions in which people can act with greater freedom, reasoning and personal responsibility ...

Source: http://unesdoc.unesco.org/images/0010/001095/109590eo.pdf

1997 Thessaloniki Declaration, Greece

This Declaration was presented in 1997 at the close of the Thessaloniki International Conference on Environment and Society: Education and Public Awareness for Sustainability, organized by UNESCO and the government of Greece. The text was signed by representatives of governmental, inter-governmental, and non-governmental organizations and the civil society at large from 85 countries.

The text reaffirms that *education and training* should be recognized as one of the *pillars of sustainability*. It also stresses that education is an indispensable means to give to all women and men in the world the *capacity to own their own lives*.

The declaration calls on governments, public administration, the scientific community, universities, non-governmental organizations and international networks to *consider education a priority area of action* and to work towards the *reorientation of education as a whole towards sustainability*.

Source: http://www.mio-ecsde.org/old/Thess/declar_en.htm

1998 World Declaration on Higher Education in the Twenty-first Century: Vision and Action

Participants in the 1998 World Conference on Higher Education (WCHE) adopted the World Declaration on Higher Education for the Twenty-First Century: Vision and Action and the Framework for Priority Action for Change and Development of Higher Education.

In 2003 UNESCO met with 400 higher education partners from 120 countries as a follow-up to the implementation of the World Declaration on Higher Education presented at the WCHE in 1998, and affirmed that:

The core missions of higher education systems (to educate, to train, to undertake research and, *in particular, to contribute to the sustainable development and improvement of society as a whole*) should be preserved, reinforced and further expanded, namely to educate *highly qualified graduates and responsible citizens* and to provide opportunities for higher learning and for learning throughout life. Moreover, *higher education has acquired an unprecedented role in present-day society*, as a vital component of *cultural, social, economic and political development* and as *a pillar of endogenous capacity-building*, the consolidation of *human rights, sustainable development, democracy and peace*, in a context of justice.

Source: http://portal.unesco.org/education/es/ev.php-URL_ID=19189&URL_DO=DO_TOPIC&URL_SECTION=201.html

2000 The Earth Charter

The Earth Charter was presented in 2000 and is a synthesis of values, principles and aspirations shared by a growing number of men and women across all the regions of the world. The principles of the Earth Charter reflect extensive international discussions conducted over a period of several years. By October 2007 the document had been endorsed by 17,908 groups, individuals and organizations.

The definitive text declares the need to:

Empower every human being with the education and resources to secure a sustainable livelihood, and provide social security and safety nets for those who are unable to support themselves.

Affirm gender equality and equity as prerequisites to sustainable development and *ensure universal access to education*, health care, and economic opportunity.

Integrate into formal education and life-long learning *the knowledge, values, and skills needed for* a sustainable way of life.

Promote the contribution of the arts and humanities as well as the sciences *in sustainability education*.

Recognize the *importance of moral and spiritual education for sustainable living*.

Source: http://www.earthcharter.org/

2000 Millennium Declaration

The Millennium Declaration was approved at the General Assembly of the United Nations by 189 nations and signed by 147 heads of state and government at the United Nations Millennium Summit held in September 2000. *The declaration establishes the Millennium Development Goals (MDGs)* that participating countries will endeavour to meet by 2015. Although the text does not make specific reference to higher education, one of its goals is to provide universal primary education.

Source: http://www.un.org/millennium/declaration/ares552e.pdf

2001 Lüneburg Declaration, Germany

The Lüneburg Declaration on Higher Education for Sustainable Development was adopted in October 2001 in Lüneburg, Germany, during the International Copernicus Conference, Higher Education for Sustainability – Towards the World Summit on Sustainable Development 2002.

The text calls on higher education institutions, non-governmental organizations, stakeholders, governments, the United Nations and UNESCO to *unite efforts* with the aim of *meeting the challenges posed by sustainable development*, through education in general and higher education in particular.

Source: http://www.lueneburg-declaration.de/downloads/declaration.htm

2002 UBUNTU Declaration on Education, Science and Technology for Sustainable Development

This Declaration was presented at the World Summit on Sustainable Development held in Johannesburg, South Africa in 2002. The text was created by 11 international organizations dedicated to education and science, including UNESCO, the United Nations University, the African Academy of Sciences, the International Council for Science, the International Association of Universities, Copernicus-Campus, the Global Higher Education for Sustainability Partnership, the Science Council of Asia, the Third World Academy of Sciences, University Leaders for a Sustainable Future and the World Federation of Engineering Organizations.

The UBUNTU Declaration is a *major effort to make integrated solutions work* for sustainable development and to *mobilize the education sector* to contribute to sustainable development. It stresses that *education is critical in galvanizing the approach to the challenges of sustainable development* and emphasizes the need to *create a global alliance* and work to review the programmes and curricula of colleges and universities, in order to better address the challenges and opportunities of sustainable development.

Source: http://www.ias.unu.edu/research/ubuntu.cfm

2005 United Nations Decade of Education for Sustainable Development (2005–2014)

In December 2002, the General Assembly of the United Nations proclaimed the ten-year period beginning on 1 January 2005 the United Nations Decade of Education for Sustainable Development (Resolution 57/254). The General Assembly designated UNESCO as the lead agency in the promotion of the initiative. The international implementation framework was approved during the 57th UN General Assembly in 2004 and was presented to the community on 1 March 2005.

The initiative aims to encourage *changes in behaviour that will create a more sustainable future in terms of environmental integrity, economic viability, and a just society for present and future generations*. The general goal is to *integrate the principles, values, and practices of sustainable development into all aspects of education and learning*, which will be achieved through the following specific objectives:

- Facilitate *networking, linkages, exchange and interaction* among stakeholders in education for sustainable development
- Foster an *increased quality of teaching and learning* in education for sustainable development
- *Help countries make progress towards and attain the millennium development goals* through education for sustainable development efforts
- Provide countries with *new opportunities* to incorporate education for sustainable development into education reform efforts.

Source: http://portal.unesco.org/education/en/ev.php-URL_ID=27234&URL_DO=DO_TOPIC&URL_SECTION=201.html

2005 Alliance of Civilizations

Presented in 2005 by the Secretary-General of the United Nations 2005 with the joint support of the *President of the Government of Spain, José Luis Rodríguez Zapatero, and the Prime Minister of Turkey, Recep Tayyip Erdoğan*, the *Alliance of Civilizations* is confirmation of a broad consensus between nations, cultures and religions that all societies are intimately linked and interdependent in their search for stability, prosperity and peaceful coexistence.

The Alliance aims to address the widening gulfs between societies by instating a model of *mutual respect between nations with different cultural and religious traditions* and contributing to the promotion of multilateral action. To guide this initiative, the UN Secretary-General created a *High-Level Group* made up of a number of leading international figures. The group presented its first *Report in 2006*, in which it *recommends a viable action plan* for nation-states (at the regional, national and international level), international organizations and civil society in the hope that it will foster harmony between the nations and cultures of the world.

The report recognizes *education as one of the principal areas of action* for achieving the objectives proposed by the Alliance. The recommendations in this field focus on the adaptation and expansion of existing initiatives and establishes the following general guideline:

Governments, multilateral institutions, *universities*, education scholars and policy-makers should *work separately and together to expand global, cross-cultural, and human rights education*.

Source: http://www.unaoc.org/repository/HLG_Report.pdf

2007 Communiqué of the 34th session of the UNESCO General Conference, Ministerial Round Table on Education and Economic Development

The Ministers of Education of 96 countries, meeting in Paris, discussed the relationship between education and economic development. The Round Table addressed the following themes:

- The rights to education and development
- The contributions of education to economic growth
- Education and sustainable development
- Partnerships for education and economic development.

They set the discussion in the context of realizing the Millennium Development Goals and those of Education for All and ensuring that *education contributes to peace, broader social development, active citizenship and the promotion of human values*. In an era of unprecedented change, they recognized that *education systems must respond with innovative and different approaches*.

Source: http://unesdoc.unesco.org/images/0015/001542/154229e.pdf

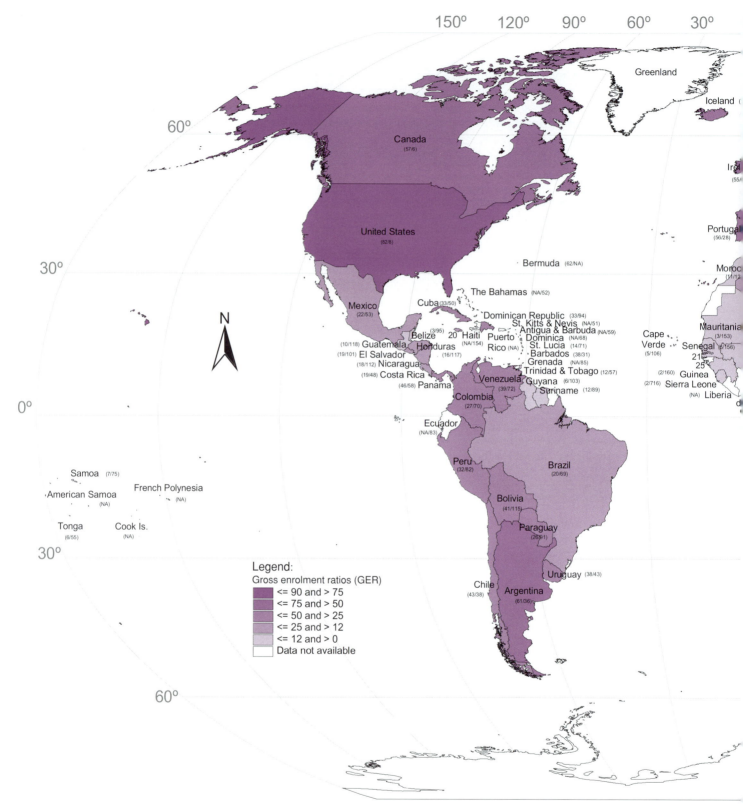

Legend:
Gross enrolment ratios (GER)

	<= 90 and > 75
	<= 75 and > 50
	<= 50 and > 25
	<= 25 and > 12
	<= 12 and > 0
	Data not available

Notes

This map shows a correlation: in general, countries with high GER have a better place in the ranking of HDI.
The first number is GER and the second is HDI rank.

Sources: UNESCO Institute for Statistics.
United Nations Development Programme, *Human Development Report 2006*, Statistical Table 1.

MAP 2 Higher education gross enrolment ratios (GER) by country and human development index (HDI), 2006

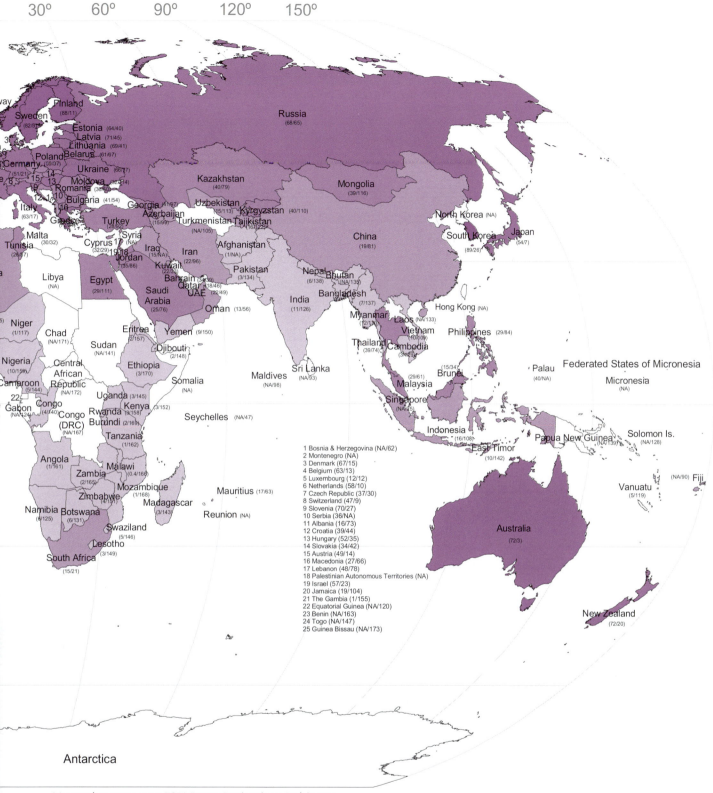

Vector layer source: ESRI Data; Projection: Robinson

MAP 2   liii

PART I
GLOBAL ISSUES ON THE ROLE OF HIGHER EDUCATION FOR HUMAN AND SOCIAL DEVELOPMENT

A

Present and future challenges for higher education's role in the context of globalization

Abstract

Universities worldwide are being called on to fulfil more and more roles, often with fewer resources. As a result, academic missions may become dispersed and the quality of the work may decrease. In this era, the function of universities as institutions devoted essentially to teaching and research may be weakened by the struggle to be entrepreneurial and market-relevant (Ben-David, 1977; Clark, 2004; Geiger, 2004). The academic drift of the 21st century raises concerns about the core functions of universities and how contemporary changes have affected academic missions. This paper mainly discusses research universities, which, as the leading and most influential academic institutions, have been most affected by this expansion of roles (Neave, 2000; Altbach and Balán, 2007). The goal of this paper is to examine the changing missions of universities and the impact on academe worldwide.

I.1
THE COMPLEX ROLES OF UNIVERSITIES IN THE PERIOD OF GLOBALIZATION

Philip G. Altbach

THE CORE MISSIONS

Since their establishment in Europe in the 12th century, universities have frequently been asked to undertake essential roles. Only when they were considered irrelevant were they isolated, as when the Enlightenment largely bypassed the European universities still mired in disputes between Catholics and Protestants from an earlier period (Perkin, 2006, pp. 172–3). Academic institutions have often been in conflict with their societies over missions and roles, and sometimes over ideology and politics. This tension has contributed to the creativity of universities over time, but has at times placed overwhelming burdens on them.

In the contemporary period, the teaching mission of the university is a central responsibility. The goal is to educate people to work effectively in an increasingly technological world – that is, to provide the technical skills needed for a growing number of jobs and professions that require sophisticated knowledge and an education that instils the ability to think critically. In many countries, general education is also considered a key university goal. Teaching has been the core role since the beginning.

However, this function has become more complex and variegated, ranging from general education for undergraduates to advanced doctoral instruction and supervision in the most specialized fields.

Research is the other core function of universities, dating back to the establishment of the University of Berlin by Wilhelm von Humboldt in the early 19th century (Ben-David and Zloczower, 1962). It has come to be the central value of top-tier universities in all countries, and academic rewards and institutional prestige for individual faculty members are bestowed largely on the basis of research productivity. Research is defined in different ways by various disciplines and can take many forms. Pure research – the discovery of new knowledge – is generally considered the gold standard in terms of recognition and prestige. Nobel prizes are won for pure research. Applied research – increasingly emphasized as universities seek to generate income from research output – applies scientific discoveries to problems, commercial products or related practical goals. Research in the humanities may deal with interpreting texts or gaining insights on literature. Historical research may work from original data or may reanalyse existing research. Research in many scientific fields requires significant funding for laboratories and equipment. In other disciplines, research may need only basic library or internet resources. Research can thus take many forms and have different purposes. The focus on discovery, interpretation and originality links the vast array of research themes, methodologies and orientations.

UNIVERSITIES AS NATIONAL INSTITUTIONS

Universities have from time to time functioned as the central institutions for national development. Nationalist ideologies, for example, were nurtured in European universities in the 19th century. Universities were seedbeds of nationalism in many colonized nations in the 19th and 20th centuries. In these cases, the ideas that led to the establishment of modern nations were, in part, developed by the academic community. Nations also used universities in their efforts to modernize. Humboldt's reformed University of Berlin was intended to contribute to Germany's national resurgence, as were the imperial universities established in Japan following the Meiji Restoration in 1868. Similarly, the American 'land grant' public universities were designed to contribute in terms of teaching, research and service to the development of the USA following the end of the Civil War in 1865. In these cases, universities were integral contributors to national development.

Universities have also played a central role in the growth of developing countries. In Latin America, the emergence of national universities following independence from Spain contributed to nation-building throughout the continent. These universities not only educated the nation but also provided ideas on national development (Ordorika and Pusser, 2007). In other parts of the developing world, universities have played a similar historical role – as incubators of nationalistic ideas, educators of the emerging governing class and providers of the technical expertise needed for nation-building (Ashby, 1966).

National universities in many parts of the developing world continue to serve as central institutions for nation-building, research and training. In Mexico, for example, the National Autonomous University of Mexico (UNAM), the main national university, produces most of the nation's published research and has traditionally educated the nation's political and intellectual leaders (Ordorika and Pusser, 2007). These state-sponsored universities are still central to national development, despite the emergence of diversified academic systems in many developing countries.

CENTRAL ACADEMIC ROLES

From the outset, universities have provided vocational education and training for the top professions, thus developing a direct long-term link to the economy and to the practical needs of society. Due to the ever-increasing sophistication of the economy, academic institutions have been obliged to provide training for a growing number of professions. The first universities formed centres of learning for the core professions of the time: law, the priesthood, medicine and the academic profession itself. Today's universities are largely responsible for educating business executives, engineers, architects, social workers, veterinarians and many other professionals. Specialized academic institutions provide training for certain professionals, such as school teachers in a number of countries and military officers in many; these institutions

may have university status. The vocational role of higher education has become universal and more complex. In most cases, this function combines applied training with education in relevant basic academic disciplines.

THE PRESERVATION AND DISSEMINATION OF KNOWLEDGE

Even in the age of the internet, universities are repositories and organizers of knowledge. Academic libraries have traditionally been centres for preserving and organizing the cultural and intellectual heritage of a society. Libraries not only collect books and journals (the essential elements of knowledge), they also organize scholarly and scientific material of all kinds for effective use and preserve it for future generations. Even in the age of digital storage, libraries remain essential parts of universities and of the organization and preservation of knowledge (Baker, 2001). Universities help to organize knowledge, without cost to either the academic community or the general public. Thus, universities constitute an alternative to the growing commercialization of knowledge by for-profit service providers. The Massachusetts Institute of Technology's 'open courseware' project, which provides much of the content of most MIT courses on the internet, is an impressive example of how free access to knowledge can be provided by harnessing the intellectual work of the faculty and by organizing and disseminating material.

Universities preserve other cultural and scientific artefacts, ranging from works of art to collections of insects. Universities often sponsor museums and provide access to a wide audience. These museums are repositories that are often linked to the institution's academic programmes. In many countries with limited resources and little expertise in preserving cultural and historical treasures, universities are the only institutions capable of collecting, cataloguing and preserving such items. For example, Mexico's UNAM serves as the nation's national library and sponsors several respected museums.

UNIVERSITIES AS INTELLECTUAL CENTRES

Universities almost everywhere have become key creative institutions. Many professors, in addition to their teaching and research, involve themselves in the intellectual life of society as commentators, experts or analysts. Some are public intellectuals. The work of many academics can be seen on the opinion pages of major newspapers or on serious television talk shows. Academic life provides time, intellectual stimulation, debate and, in most countries, the protection of academic freedom, which encourages participation in societal debate and analysis (Altbach, 2007).

Academics also serve as experts on a wide variety of topics. Professors are asked to provide analysis for the government, the media and the public on topics ranging from space exploration to Egyptian mummies. Scientists provide expert analysis of environmental issues. Sociologists analyse social conflict. University professors are the largest community of experts in any society, and many play key roles in interpreting science and scholarship for a wide audience. Professors sometimes bring their expertise directly to the government by serving as ministers or taking other posts. They occasionally run for public office. They often engage in oppositional politics by providing ideas or analysis and sometimes by participating directly in political activism.

Academics have from time to time been involved in social and political movements. They were engaged in the rise of nationalism in Europe and in many developing countries. They were key participants in the European revolutions of 1848 and in the Latin American reform movements of the early 20th century that led to the Cordoba Reforms of higher education and to significant democratic change.

Students also participate in intellectual, social and political life beyond the campus. Student activist movements frequently stimulate political conflict and sometimes reform or even revolution – for example, in the European nationalist movements of the 19th century, the independence struggles in developing countries, and the activist movements of the 1960s and 1970s worldwide. Universities provide an atmosphere of ideas, freedom and debate that stimulates student activism and social involvement.

Academic institutions frequently sponsor journals and other publications that contribute to intellectual life. Some even own or manage television and radio stations. These enterprises help to educate people and add to the wealth of ideas in society. Universities, as non-profit organizations with guarantees of academic freedom, are uniquely suited to provide the autonomy for both individuals and groups to engage in intellectual creativity, dialogue and analysis.

UNIVERSITIES AS INTERNATIONAL INSTITUTIONS

Academic institutions operate in a global environment and bring science and scholarship from around the world to a local community. Universities are the central links with the international scientific community. They have the necessary intellectual and scientific infrastructure, through information and communication technologies (ICTs) and informal networks. Professors are involved with international research in their disciplines and fields. Academic institutions are engaged in exchange programmes, the hosting of international staff and students,

collaborative international research projects, and other activities. More than any other segment of society, universities are engaged constantly in the international exchange of ideas, data and knowledge.

In developing countries, universities are the central link to world science, scholarship and intellectual life. In much of Africa, where internet infrastructure remains inadequate, universities are the best-connected institutions. Academic communities use the main international languages of science, and many in the academic community have studied abroad.

ACCESS AND EQUITY

Universities provide the education needed for most skilled occupations and professions in society. For almost a century, universities have also been seen as instruments for social mobility – a way for individuals to obtain the skills they need to improve their incomes and status. Massification has, of course, brought access to a wider section of the population. Many countries and academic institutions have also developed strategies to enhance access for underserved populations – racial, religious and ethnic minorities, women and low-income groups. Scholarship, bursary and loan programmes, as well as a variety of affirmative-action efforts, have been put into place. Access to higher education is recognized as an important societal goal. Almost everywhere, even in countries where a large proportion of the relevant age cohort has access to post-secondary education, problems of equity remain. Typically, higher status socioeconomic groups have greater access than others. In developing countries, the goals of both access and equity remain to be achieved. In the North, while access is widespread, equity is still problematic.

ENGINES OF ECONOMIC DEVELOPMENT

From their origins, universities have stimulated local economies. Any university generates economic benefits for its community through local purchases, property investment and expenditures by students and faculty. Starting with the Humboldtian reforms in Germany, the rise of the 'land grant' universities in the USA, and the establishment of the Japanese imperial universities in the 19th century, universities have been designed to contribute directly to economic development. Universities support knowledge- and technology-based industries that make use of the knowledge produced by the institutions – including skills of graduates and scientific innovations. Universities have contributed to this development by establishing science parks and even by investing in companies that use university-based knowledge. Universities are often included in government economic plans. Societies increasingly count on universities to contribute both directly and indirectly to economic and technological development. China is an excellent example of a country where academic institutions have been recognized as central to development; several key Chinese universities have built science parks and established companies to take advantage of academic research (Ma, 2007).

GENERAL EDUCATION

In a few countries, such as the USA, universities have from their origins provided first-degree students with a broad general education in the liberal arts and sciences. The idea of general education, as it has evolved, is to provide students with a broad grounding in the basic knowledge they need in contemporary society and also with skills in logic, critical thinking and writing. The curriculum in much of the world has traditionally been based on specialized knowledge in specific disciplines and has not included general education. There is now more discussion of the role of general education, and some countries have added this to the university curriculum.

HISTORICAL PERSPECTIVES

Medieval universities were established to educate men for the legal, medical and religious professions. They also preserved knowledge through their libraries and undertook the specific work of translating scientific and other literature from Arabic to Latin and disseminating it in Europe. Universities have been subject to different forms of external authority. In the 13th century, the Roman Catholic Church and the French monarchy founded the University of Paris, one of the first and most significant universities. In Italy, students were instrumental in establishing universities in Salerno, Padua, Bologna and elsewhere, and had a dominant role in governing them. Medieval universities were mainly focused on professional education, but they also had other functions. They engaged in intellectual, religious and, occasionally, political life. For example, the University of Paris helped to settle a schism in the Catholic Church in 1409 (Perkin, 2006, p. 168). In the 16th century, the ideas that led to the Protestant Reformation came from the universities in Germany. Universities thrived when they were engaged in professional education and the intellectual life of society.

When universities cease to be engaged with society and with the emerging scientific and political developments of an era, they tend to be moribund. Beginning in the 17th century, most European universities turned inward. They played almost no role in the Enlightenment and were in the doldrums. Their role was limited to training priests and a few civil servants (Perkin, 2006, p. 173).

The tremendous creativity of the Enlightenment and the technological innovations of the Industrial Revolution largely took place outside of the universities. The idea that universities were truly 'ivory towers' designed to be separate from society, unwilling to open their doors to the emerging middle classes, meant that universities were largely uninvolved in the dynamic scientific and political developments of the era. With only a few exceptions, universities received little public financial support because they were not perceived as contributing significantly to society. Napoleon, for example, was so unimpressed with the French universities of the *ancien régime* that he abolished all of them – and replaced them with the vocationally oriented *grandes écoles*.

When Wilhelm von Humboldt reformed the University of Berlin in 1810, the modern research university was established. First in Germany and then elsewhere, academe began to recover. Research universities were not only committed to bringing research to the centre of the academic enterprise but also to linking research to applied science and national development. Towards the end of the 19th century, American land grants expanded the research university concept to include the role of direct service to society and the key function of engagement with agriculture and industry. These developments, pioneered in Germany and the USA, spread elsewhere and brought universities back to the centre of society. Since the early 20th century, universities or university-related laboratories have been involved in key scientific and intellectual developments in most countries. The development of radar, atomic energy and many pharmaceuticals illustrates this point.

Historically, scientific research has not always been conducted mainly in universities. The 'academy of science' model – used in the former Soviet Union and to some extent still in practice in Russia, China and differently in the National Centre for Scientific Research system in France – concentrated research in scientific institutes that were separate from universities (Vucinich, 1984). Universities were mainly focused on teaching and did not have significant funding for research. It is generally agreed that separating research entirely from teaching is not the best way of organizing either, and there is a worldwide trend towards combining the two functions in universities.

Clark Kerr coined the term 'multiversity' to capture the historical evolution of the modern university (Kerr, 2001). He pointed out that the American research university, considered by many the most influential contemporary academic model, combines the English collegiate tradition, the German research idea and the American value of service to society. The American variant of the

German research university has, over time, taken on many new roles and is without question a key pillar of the knowledge economy.

THE IMPLICATIONS OF MASSIFICATION

Since the Second World War and especially after the 1960s, enrolment in higher education increased dramatically worldwide, doubling from 40 million in 1975 to 80 million in 1995 and perhaps reaching 150 million in 2007. While much of the growth between the 1960s and 1990s occurred in developed countries, current growth is mainly in developing countries. The proportion of the age group participating in higher education has increased from 10% or less in most developed countries to over 50% today, although some of the poorest countries still enrol just a few per cent of the relevant age group; worldwide, the proportion is about one quarter (*Higher Education in the World 2007*, p. 384). In developing and middle-income countries, where participation rates remain modest – 20% in China, somewhat less than 10% in India and just a few per cent in much of sub-Saharan Africa – expansion is gearing up. Only the USA and to some extent Canada had mass higher education systems prior to the 1960s (Trow, 2006). Most of the growth of the coming half-century will happen in developing and middle-income countries (Task Force on Higher Education and Society, 2000).

Massification was, without question, the dominant force in higher education in the latter half of the 20th century and will continue to have an impact in the 21st century. The emergence of mass higher education systems with different kinds of post-secondary institutions serving diverse segments of students has been a revolutionary change. Nevertheless, this shift occurred in most countries without much planning. For centuries, higher education was considered the preserve of a small elite, and academic institutions tended to be small and fairly uniform. Mass higher education meant not only an expansion in the number of students but also a dramatic increase in the number and kinds of academic institutions. Massification necessitated the emergence of a differentiated academic system with institutions serving separate purposes.

The emergence of post-secondary institutions with different purposes, goals, students, facilities and academic staff has altered the landscape of higher education worldwide. New kinds of institutions with different missions have extended the role of higher education in unprecedented ways. Vocationally oriented academic institutions have absorbed much of the mass demand in many countries. In the USA, community colleges, which are mainly vocational and typically require only a high school diploma for entry, prepare students for many kinds of jobs that call for technical training. Community colleges also provide general education courses that can lead to transfer to a four-year baccalaureate college or university. One of the most effective elements of the US higher education system is the coordination between the various kinds of institutions, which allows students to transfer from one kind of institution to another and take their academic credits with them (Altbach, 2001). Not only do community colleges allow almost universal access, they provide vocational training in a wide range of fields and, for a minority of students, upward transfer options within the system. There is a wide array of entry-level post-secondary institutions around the world, such as the *Fachhochschulen* in Germany, the *instituts universitaires de technologie* in France and many others. While these institutions do not generally provide the relatively easy mobility of the American community college, they do satisfy important access and vocational needs in society. Many countries, including China, are examining the community college model.

There has also been an expansion of a relatively broad range of baccalaureate and master's-degree-equivalent universities, which provide access and meet new academic needs. These universities represent both the public sector and the rapidly expanding private sector. At times their curricula are specialized. In general, these universities have modest entry requirements so as to provide fairly wide access to students. They focus mainly on teaching but often have some interest in research, and are frequently involved in a range of social service activities.

Research universities form the pinnacle of the academic system, typically serving only the most able students and constituting only a modest number of institutions (Clark, 1995; Altbach and Balán, 2007). As the most complex institution in the system, the research university combines both basic and applied research with teaching at a range of levels, from baccalaureate to doctoral. Research universities generally offer specializations in the mainstream academic disciplines, and many also have professional schools in fields such as law, management, medicine, engineering and education. Interdisciplinary research programmes and institutes in emerging fields such as biotechnology, as well as science parks and other links with industry and commerce, add to the complexity of research universities. In most countries, these universities obtain the largest proportion of research funds – often 80% or 90% of all R&D money available to higher education.

In increasingly complex academic systems, specialized academic institutions have emerged, three of the most famous being the prestigious Indian Institutes of Technology, which focus on engineering and related disciplines; INSEAD, a prestigious school of management in France; and the University of California at San Francisco, which focuses on medicine and the biomedical sciences. Specialized schools in law, veterinary science, pedagogy and many other disciplines also exist in academic systems. Whether created by the government or having emerged over time to meet perceived market needs, academic systems are by now highly differentiated in most countries. They are the result of both massification and the educational and research needs of modern society.

Mass higher education has brought with it greater inequality in academic systems – disparities between the high-quality universities at the top and the many modest or low-quality mass-access institutions at the bottom. It is likely that the top institutions have improved in industrialized countries, while worldwide the bottom sector has declined in quality. Massification inevitably creates more variations and diversity in academic systems. It creates opportunities for access that are unprecedented in world history, but at the same time it creates systems that are less equal and more difficult to support financially.

THE PROBLEM OF THE PUBLIC GOOD

One of the serious debates about higher education in the past several decades relates to whether it is a *public* good – one which adds value to society by educating its people, who will then be productive citizens – or a *private* good – one which mainly benefits individuals, who earn more money and enjoy other advantages as a result of their education (Bloom et al., 2006). The logic of the debate is, of course, that if higher education is a private good, then those who benefit from it – the students – should pay. If higher education is mainly a public good, then society has a responsibility to provide support. The argument is as much one of philosophy, ideology and politics as it is of economics. Those advocating the private-good stance are motivated both by their interpretation of economic realities and by a belief that the state cannot afford to pay most of the cost of mass higher education. In recent years, private-good advocates have prevailed to a significant degree. As a result, higher education budgets in many countries have stagnated or been reduced. Public academic institutions have been asked to fund an increasing portion of their costs by increasing tuition fees, becoming more commercialized and selling their services to the market (Kirp, 2003; Geiger, 2004).

The cost of providing higher education has increased greatly in recent decades. The demands of mass access combined with the increased costs of research universities have placed greater pressure on the state to provide funding. Due in part to the private-good ideology, public authorities in many countries have shifted the financial responsibility for higher education to the 'users', that is, students and their families. In some cases, loans and other funding programmes have been introduced to lessen the financial burden (Johnstone, 2006). Whether it is in fact beyond the financial ability of the state to support expanded access to higher education is arguable. In any event, most countries have in fact chosen to shift a significant part of the financial obligation to students.

One problem with the contemporary emphasis on the private good is the fact that research universities are public-good institutions. While their graduates benefit from their academic preparation and degrees, much of the work of research universities emphasizes the public good. Basic research, for example, may in the long run result in commercially valuable products, but the research itself generally yields little direct profit. Basic research is a public good and therefore requires support. Research universities require basic research infrastructure, including talented (and often highly paid) professors, up-to-date laboratories and other facilities, and graduate and often postdoctoral programmes. They must have an academic culture that fosters a research-oriented environment (Ben-David, 1991). Furthermore, many of the services performed by research universities are non-commercial. Research universities have been asked to commercialize their research and other activities. This may distort their most important missions and in the long run weaken them (Washburn, 2005; Sörlin and Vessuri, 2007). Research universities also sponsor a wide array of service and outreach activities, including concerts, performances, art exhibitions and occasionally museums. These activities have little commercial potential.

Mass higher education is intended to provide access to students from all social classes. While it is possible for students from wealthier segments of the population to pay tuition fees for higher education, students from poorer backgrounds may find the costs unaffordable and may be reluctant to take out student loans. Without arrangements for scholarships and grants, a private-good approach may in some ways limit access to higher education for a significant part of the population.

The idea of the public good as a key factor in supporting higher education relates directly to the roles that academic institutions can play in society. Many of the complex activities of post-secondary institutions – from cultural and outreach activities to the most advanced basic research – are directly linked to the public good.

CONTEMPORARY CHALLENGES

In playing the complex and highly important roles that have been discussed in this paper, universities face significant challenges. The public-good ideal has been called into question and a variety of related problems have emerged.

Private higher education is rapidly expanding in many parts of the world and now enrols more than half of all post-secondary students in much of Latin America, the Pacific Rim and other areas (Altbach and Levy, 2005). With the exception of some institutions in the USA and Japan and a handful of other examples, private academic institutions are seldom high-prestige universities, have limited purposes and programmes, and depend exclusively on tuition income for survival. Many are either formally or informally for-profit schools. The private sector in higher education is, almost by definition, a private good, that is, students are charged for a specific higher education programme that they hope will contribute to their career and advancement. With few exceptions, private institutions have neither the commitment nor the ability to participate in research or service roles. They can seldom build the facilities needed for advanced research, they rarely offer advanced degrees in the sciences or other fields that require expensive facilities, and they are largely uninterested in the cultural and social roles of higher education.

The privatization of public higher education has also contributed to narrowing the roles of universities. In many countries, public universities now receive a smaller proportion of their budgets from government sources. As a result, they must generate their own income from tuition fees, research, consulting, commercial enterprise and other sources. This privatization has meant that the broad traditional purposes of the university – most of which do not readily produce income – have to some extent been de-emphasized while potentially income-generating activities have become more central.

The marketization of higher education is closely related to privatization. The functions of the university are increasingly subjected to market forces. Knowledge that can earn income is valued and supported. Fields that produce little income are de-emphasized or even discarded. Tuition fees are an example of market forces at work. More academic institutions charge tuition fees, which in many instances are increasing. Students are sometimes charged differential fees. In countries ranging from Uganda to China, some students pay low government-subsidized fees, while others are charged much higher amounts. Entrance standards are sometimes adjusted for high-fee-paying students as well. Research facilities and faculty time are 'sold' to companies and other organizations as a way of earning income – at the expense of basic research that does not earn quick profits. Competition has increased among academic institutions in an effort to lure students, attract profitable research projects and generate prestige. The current emphasis on league tables and rankings is very much part of the marketization of higher education (Sadlak and Liu, 2007).

All of these challenges are related to the demands made on universities to be more financially self-sufficient and market driven. This trend creates an immense contradiction between these new emphases and the role that universities have played over the past century in providing access to ever larger numbers of students. Marketization trends are often in conflict with higher education's goal of providing equity and the chance to obtain skills and better employment to underserved populations. Access and equity require that, through scholarships or other programmes, higher education be made affordable for segments of the population that have traditionally been unable to afford expensive higher education.

Increasingly complex goals require larger and more sophisticated academic institutions. Clark Kerr (2001) pointed out in 1963 that universities require larger and more complex administrative and governance structures to fulfil all their new roles. Added to this need is the requirement of increased accountability – not only for the expenditure of funds but also for the performance of many aspects of the academic enterprise, including student achievement and faculty productivity. Traditional academic governance, which typically left major decisions in the hands of senior professors and included few administrative resources, does not work well in the large, complex institutions of the 21st century. Universities need administrative structures that can coordinate the various elements of the institution and carefully allocate and measure resources. Professionals are required in the areas of financial management, student services and many others. To handle their more diverse functions, universities have added offices to deal with legal matters, intellectual property, relations with business and industry, psychological counselling for students and other areas. Faculty members can no longer administer and manage these universities.

Traditional academic decision-making patterns no longer function well. New governance arrangements such as senates to managing committees have been established. These bodies include both managers and academics, and in some cases students and stakeholders from outside the university. Academic institutions and systems are experimenting with management patterns that take into account the new realities of higher education.

Accountability is an additional reality, created by the

size and complexity of academic institutions and systems. Funders of higher education – usually government authorities – demand information about the management and performance of academe. This requires an additional layer of management as well as the unprecedented collection of data on all aspects of university affairs. Internal data are needed to ensure efficient management. Performance indicators and other reports must be generated for funders and other groups. Universities have become complex organizations that require sophisticated management systems and new ways of governing the academic enterprise. They are, at the same time, bureaucracies and communities of scholars. The challenge of management and governance is to reconcile these different and sometimes contradictory realities.

THE SPECIAL CHALLENGES OF DEVELOPING COUNTRIES

The issues discussed in this paper are relevant to all countries and circumstances. Developing countries, however, face additional challenges that make building an effective university system more difficult. The heritage of colonialism in many parts of the developing world and the fact that contemporary universities are Western institutions with few links to indigenous intellectual traditions make it more difficult to build successful universities (Altbach, 1998; Shils and Roberts, 2004). Colonial authorities were reluctant to permit much expansion of higher education and generally kept higher education institutions small and limited in size and scope. The institutions were mainly intended to train members of the colonial administration, so at the time of independence most higher education systems were small, weak and limited in scope.

Massification occurred later and more intensively in developing countries than in industrialized nations. The existing academic systems, enrolling a tiny fraction of the relevant age groups, often under 1%, have found it difficult to cope with expansion. In the coming decades, most worldwide expansion of higher education will take place in developing countries, which are less able to afford rapid expansion. The institutions have felt immense pressure to provide qualified academic staff and campus facilities (for example libraries, classrooms and laboratories). One key issue is how to finance expansion so as to provide more access; governments have often found this task impossible (Task Force on Higher Education and Society, 2000).

The failure to meet the demand for access has led to a series of problems that have plagued developing countries. It has proved impossible to severely limit enrolments, so academic institutions have become increasingly overcrowded. The facilities cannot accommodate all the students admitted to study, and as a result students cannot gain access to classrooms or libraries. In part as a means of limiting enrolment without denying access, many universities have implemented draconian procedures to eliminate students who cannot keep up with the work. The overall quality of higher education has declined in much of the developing world as a result of overcrowding and inadequate resources.

As discussed above, the financial crisis has contributed to the rise of private higher education. The fastest-growing private higher education sectors are in developing and middle-income countries. With some notable exceptions, the new private sector is intended to absorb demand for access at the bottom of the higher education system. Many private institutions are for-profit, with narrow aims and limited curricula (Altbach and Levy, 2005).

In many countries, while access has been significantly expanded, equity has not been achieved. Students who gain access to less-well-established academic institutions receive a questionable education, and many are unable to complete their degrees. In some places, failure to coordinate academic degrees with the job market has resulted in educated unemployment. The causal factors include the inadequate quality of the graduates of many universities and the economy's inability to keep up with the production of degree holders. The Indian prime minister, for example, recently complained about the low quality of many undergraduate colleges, which put graduates at a disadvantage in the job market.

These problems weaken the ability of universities in developing countries to fulfil all their missions, especially those related to the public interest. Even flagship research-oriented universities are often unable to fully engage with the international scientific community, sponsor top-level scientific research, maintain good libraries and information technology infrastructure, and so on. Even at these universities, the pressure of numbers is great and funds are inadequate. Indeed, in some cases, such as at Makerere University in Uganda, high-fee-paying students are admitted for evening classes in order to earn extra funds. The extra teaching and other money-earning activities leave professors with little time for research. Research universities in developing countries need both funding and autonomy in order to take their place in the international research-university network. As part of this world network, these institutions must keep up with their peer universities in industrialized nations.

Nevertheless, in many ways, universities in developing countries are falling further behind.

The challenges are very great indeed: funding; balancing the consequences of massification with the maintenance of quality; supporting world-class professors; forming an academic culture dedicated to academic freedom, intellectual competition and meritocracy; and providing a quality education to undergraduate students. Developing countries, like the rest of the world, require a differentiated academic system, with mass access at the bottom and a small research-focused sector at the top. Mission differentiation is difficult to build where it has not existed previously, but it is central to a successful academic system.

CONCLUSION

Universities are multifaceted institutions in all societies. They are especially important to the knowledge economies of the 21st century, but their roles extend far beyond this. Universities are quintessential public-good institutions; they are an essential underpinning of intellectual life in all societies, and especially in developing countries. They are key international links for science, scholarship, culture and ideas. Understanding the complex roles of universities is a first step towards providing the needed support – not only appropriate public funding but also academic freedom and autonomy. Too often, the government and the public see universities merely as economic engines and training grounds for key personnel. As argued herein, they are much more than this. Universities play an important role in economic development, but this is only part of their broader mission.

Due to the tremendous pressure placed on higher education institutions to cope with increased numbers of students and societal demands in a context of inadequate resources, universities have become mainly reactive institutions that deal with new responsibilities as best they can. They can be creative only in ways that permit them to respond to external pressures. There seems to be neither the time nor the resources to consider new approaches to educating students or serving society. In much of the world, higher education institutions are part of increasingly competitive societies. As a result, society asks them to react to the pressures of competition.

Are these trends a good thing for higher education and, in the long run, for society? Universities have been forced to give up part of their essential role as centres for intellectual and cultural life and as social analysts and critics. They have less 'space' for creative and independent work. There is less autonomy for decision-making and for thought.

At the same time, universities are linked as never before to the practical needs of society as dictated by governments (for public institutions) and by the market (for both public and private institutions). At the beginning of the 21st century, the pendulum has swung way too far towards the government and the market, at the expense of the traditional autonomy of academe. Society would be better served by a more balanced academic environment in which universities could be more attuned to the broader public interest and to the traditional values of academic autonomy and independence.

This paper has mainly discussed the top tier of the academic system: the research universities that provide the most advanced education, a home for public intellectuals and the greatest number of international linkages. These institutions need special understanding, care and support. In most countries, the main exception being the USA, they are public institutions. Research universities do not represent the entire academic system. Most students attend universities that focus mainly on teaching, and most academic staff teach at such universities. These institutions also deserve support because they provide most education and training.

Universities serve many purposes in contemporary society and they deserve support, not only for their direct economic role. Societies that ignore the manifold purposes and roles of universities will be much weaker. Universities are engines of the knowledge economy, but they serve the humanistic and cultural goals of society and of individuals.

REFERENCES

Altbach, Philip G. (1998) Twisted roots: the Western impact on Asian higher education. In: Altbach, P.G. *Comparative Higher Education: Knowledge, the University, and Development*. Chestnut Hill, MA: Boston College Center for International Higher Education, pp. 55–80.

Altbach, Philip G. (2001) The American academic model in comparative perspective. In: Altbach, P.G., Gumport, P.J. and Johnstone, D.B. (eds) *In Defense of American Higher Education*. Baltimore, MD: Johns Hopkins University Press, pp. 11–37.

Altbach, Philip G. (2007) Academic freedom: international realities and challenges. In: Altbach, P.G. *Tradition and Transition: The International Imperative in Higher Education*. Rotterdam, Netherlands: Sense Publishers, pp. 49–66.

Altbach, Philip G. and Balán, Jorge (eds) (2007) *World Class Worldwide: Transforming Research Universities in Asia and Latin America*. Baltimore, MD: Johns Hopkins University Press.

Altbach, Philip G. and Levy, Daniel C. (2005) *Private Higher*

Education: A Global Revolution. Rotterdam, Netherlands: Sense Publishers.

Ashby, Eric. (1966) Universities: British, Indian, African. Cambridge, MA: Harvard University Press.

Baker, Nicholson (2001) Double Fold: Libraries and the Assault on Paper. New York: Random House.

Ben-David, Joseph (1991) Scientific Growth: Essays on the Social Organization and Ethos of Science. Berkeley, CA: University of California Press.

Ben-David, Joseph (1977) Centers of Learning: Britain, France, Germany, United States. New York: McGraw-Hill.

Ben-David, Joseph and Awraham Zloczower (1962) Universities and academic systems in modern societies. European Journal of Sociology 3(1), pp. 45–84.

Bloom, David E., Hartley, Matthew and Rosovsky, Henry (2006) Beyond private gain: the public benefits of higher education. In: Forest, James and P. Altbach (eds), International Handbook of Higher Education. Dordrecht, Netherlands: Springer, pp. 293–308.

Clark, Burton R. (ed.) (1995) Places of Inquiry: Research and Advanced Education in Modern Universities. Berkeley, CA: University of California Press.

Clark, Burton R. (2004) Sustaining Change in Universities: Continuities in Case Studies and Concepts. Maidenhead, UK: Open University Press.

Geiger, Roger L. (2004) Knowledge and Money: Research Universities and the Paradox of the Marketplace. Stanford, CA: Stanford University Press.

GUNI (2006) Higher Education in the World 2007: Accreditation for Quality Assurance: What is at Stake? Basingstoke, UK: Palgrave Macmillan.

Johnstone, D. Bruce (2006) Financing Higher Education: Cost-Sharing in International Perspective. Rotterdam, Netherlands: Sense Publishers.

Kerr, Clark (2001) The Uses of the University. Cambridge, MA: Harvard University Press.

Kirp, David L. (2003) Shakespeare, Einstein, and the Bottom Line: The Marketing of Higher Education. Cambridge, MA: Harvard University Press.

Ma, Wenhua (2007) The flagship university and China's economic reform. In: Altbach, P. and Balán, J. (eds) World Class Worldwide: Transforming Research Universities in Asia and Latin America. Baltimore, MD: Johns Hopkins University Press, pp. 31–53.

Neave, Guy (ed.) (2000) The Universities' Responsibilities to Society: International Perspectives. Amsterdam: Elsevier Science.

Ordorika, Imanol and Pusser, Brian (2007) La máxima casa de estudios: Universidad Nacional Autónoma de México as a state-building university. In: Altbach, P. and Balán, J. (eds) World Class Worldwide: Transforming Research Universities in Asia and Latin America. Baltimore, MD: Johns Hopkins University Press, pp. 189–215.

Perkin, Harold (2006) History of universities. In: Forest, James and Altbach, P. (eds) International Handbook of Higher Education. Dordrecht, Netherlands: Springer, pp. 159–206.

Sadlak, Jan and Liu, Nian Cai (eds) (2007) The World-Class University and Ranking: Aiming Beyond Status. Bucharest, Romania: UNESCO-CEPES.

Shils, Edward and Roberts, John (2004) The diffusion of European models outside Europe. In: Rüegg, W. (ed.) A History of the University in Europe, Volume III. Cambridge, UK: Cambridge University Press, pp. 163–230.

Sörlin, Sverker and Vessuri, Hebe (eds) (2007) Knowledge Society vs. Knowledge Economy: Knowledge, Power and Politics. New York: Palgrave Macmillan.

Task Force on Higher Education and Society (2000) Higher Education in Developing Countries: Peril and Promise. Washington, DC: World Bank.

Trow, Martin (2006) Reflections on the transition from elite to mass to universal higher education access: forms and phases of higher education in modern societies since World War II. In: Forest, James and Altbach, P. (eds), International Handbook of Higher Education. Dordrecht, Netherlands: Springer, pp. 243–80.

Vucinich, Alexander (1984) Empire of Knowledge: The Academy of Sciences of the USSR (1917–1970). Berkeley, CA: University of California Press.

Washburn, Jennifer (2005) University, Inc.: The Corporate Corruption of Higher Education. New York: Basic Books.

SPECIAL CONTRIBUTION I.1
Contemporary challenges for public research universities[1]

Imanol Ordorika

Globalization has substantially modified the nature of contemporary nation-states as the principal organizers of capital accumulation and as bearers and creators of national identities (Evans et al., 1985; Castells, 1996). The nation-state's progressive withdrawal from higher education, made evident by the reduction in public resources (Altbach and Johnstone, 1993; Johnstone, 1998), has led to an increase in competition for individual and/or institutional resources from the state and vis-à-vis the market (Marginson, 1997; Marginson and Considine, 2000; Pusser, 2005). Consequently, the traditional autonomy of academic institutions and their professionals from nation-states and markets has been significantly reduced (Slaughter and Leslie, 1997; Rhoades, 1998).

GLOBALIZATION AND HIGHER EDUCATION: THE ECONOMIZATION OF THE UNIVERSITY

Due to globalization and internationalization processes, as well as changes in the nature of nation-states, initiatives for accountability have been promoted in almost every area of societal life. The public sphere has been called into question and the weight of market relations in every type of social interaction has increased. Globalization has been a product of this and has in turn promoted a growing economization of society and the erosion of all that is considered 'public' (Wolin, 1981), as well as changes in the nature and capacity of nation-states (Evans et al., 1985) and the continuous expansion of markets, particularly within the realm of education and the production of knowledge (Readings, 1996; Marginson, 1997; Slaughter and Leslie, 1997; Marginson and Considine, 2000). All these factors go some way towards explaining society's loss of trust in universities as institutions that rely heavily on public resources.

The crisis of 'publicness' and eroded societal trust in the realm of education has been expressed in constant challenges to the efficiency, productivity, equity and quality of large educational systems (Díaz Barriga, 1998). Criticism of the state of education and demands for accountability have put assessment, evaluation and certification policies at the core of public educational guidelines worldwide. The diversification and dissemination of academic institutional assessment and evaluation is a consequence of international dynamics generated by international organizations – such as the OECD or the World Bank – as much as a response to the adoption of the discourse and practice of evaluation and accountability by nation-states and educational administrators at the local level (Coraggio and Torres, 1997; Díaz Barriga, 1998; Ordorika, 2004; Bensimon and Ordorika, 2005).

Higher education institutions, and the nature of the academic work that is performed within them, have suffered changes that have no precedent in the history of post-secondary instruction (Lyotard, 1990; Readings, 1996; Slaughter and Leslie, 1997; Barnett, 2000). Until the 1970s, higher education had expanded continuously in terms of student enrolments, the number of teaching staff and the availability of financial resources. According to the World Bank (2000) student enrolment ratios through-

out the world grew from 9% to 14% between 1965 and 1975, with low- and middle-income countries moving from 4% to 7% and high-income countries from 20% to 33%. Since the 1980s, however, public resources for higher education have been reduced significantly in almost every country (Altbach and Johnstone, 1993; World Bank, 1994, 2000; Johnstone, 1998). Tertiary education expenditure per student as a percentage of GNP per capita diminished from 163% to 77% overall between 1980 and 1995; low- and middle-income countries dropped from 259% to 91%, and high-income countries from 39% to 26% (World Bank, 2000).

The fiscal crisis of universities has been accompanied, both as a cause and as a consequence, by a redefinition of the meanings, goals and practices of higher education. Ideas of universities as broad cultural societal projects or as institutions that focus on the production of public goods have moved into a marginal or solely discursive realm (Readings, 1996; Marginson, 1997). These notions have been substituted by a renewed emphasis on the links between higher education and markets (Marginson, 1997; Slaughter and Leslie, 1997; Marginson and Considine, 2000; Pusser, 2005), by a schema of 'entrepreneurial universities' (Clark, 1998), by notions of excellence (Readings, 1996), by the centrality of managerial concepts and goals, such as 'productivity' or 'efficiency', and by the increasing privatization of educational supply and financing (Slaughter and Leslie, 1997).

Globalization in higher education also occurs to a large extent through the emergence of new markets and market relations for higher education institutions and their 'products'. The adoption of market practices or of routines that try to imitate these practices (markets, pseudo-markets or fictitious markets) has become one of the most outstanding characteristics of contemporary higher education (Slaughter and Leslie, 1997; Ordorika, 2002, 2004).

PRODUCTIVITY AND THE HIERARCHICAL FIELD OF HIGHER EDUCATION

Higher education at the global level constitutes a worldwide field of influence. Within this field, elite research universities interact directly with each other within common global networks, assume leading roles within national higher education systems and, in most nations, are closely involved in government policy. They also respond to more localized constituencies (Marginson and Ordorika, forthcoming).

The international field of higher education is uneven, hierarchical and permanently contested (Bourdieu and Johnson, 1993). Universities are positioned within this field on the basis of their historical circumstances, university traditions and local settings, particularly the possession of financial and cultural capital (Naidoo, 2004), as well as through position-taking strategies that are also historically conditioned. To a large degree, international positioning is based on adherence to international standards of research productivity (Marginson and Ordorika, forthcoming).

Research productivity is fundamental in establishing a university as a prominent institution at international and local levels. The networking and global interacting potential of institutions is strengthened if they adhere to the dominant productivity model. They therefore constantly reproduce it, purposefully or not. Their national prominence and influence on public policy have also become increasingly dependent on their research productivity. This often hampers the institution's ability to commit to local problems and constituencies.

With globalization, international competition and the stratification of higher education have become more salient, and competition for social and academic prestige more central to the aims of institutions. Cross-border institutional activities and academic mobility have increased. Global communications and mobility have created the conditions for the emergence of a global market in higher education. Consequently, competition among elite universities is now worldwide and has moved closer to capitalist economic forms.

Positions within this global market are mediated by comparative rankings of research performance or university status (for example the Shanghai Jiao Tong *Academic Ranking of World Universities* and *The Times Higher Education Supplement* world university rankings). Worldwide attention to university rankings is a sign of the new global market. Comparisons reflect and reinforce the structure of these markets as a system of power. For example, the leading national research universities outside the Anglo-American world are now increasingly overshadowed by universities like Harvard, Stanford and Oxford. This affects not only the global standing of national research universities, but also their position at home.

In this context, the perception of institutional and individual competition within an international market for higher education reinforces the presence of businesslike practices and concerns. The focus on research productivity and (in a significantly minor proportion) teaching productivity becomes central to the notion of institutional self-positioning in the worldwide field of higher education. The concern of public officials and university administrators is how to reach higher levels of research performance with the most efficient levels of investment in material and human resources, that is, how to increase academic productivity.

HEGEMONY AND THE NARROWED ROLE OF THE UNIVERSITY

University rankings show a highly unequal distribution of resources and status. The top research universities are in the USA and a few are in the UK.[2] Ranking measures themselves reproduce and strengthen this pattern of domination. They give the advantage to wealthy nations that invest in science-based research and benefit English-speaking nations because English is now the only global research language (Marginson and Ordorika, forthcoming).

More significantly, the nation- and state-building commitments of national and local universities are outside the scope of international performance and productivity standards for higher education. Universities' orientation towards local constituencies and their impact on local, regional and national development is difficult to measure and goes beyond traditional criteria of academic performance and research productivity. International trends drive universities away from local commitments and diminish their role as state-building institutions (Ordorika and Pusser, 2007).

The outcome of this hegemonic pattern is that higher education is subject to a high degree of US domination. US hegemony is made clear in the normative character of an idealized model of the American research university and of the stratified and competitive American public/private higher education system, which combines a high level of overall participation with the extreme concentration of wealth, academic authority, academic resources and social status in the leading universities. This model is very different from that which has developed in most nations, especially in Latin America which has historically emphasized the contribution of the university to national democracy and placed the research university at the centre of national politics and culture. It also differs from the more homogeneous systems of Western Europe, sustained by state investment, in which all research universities enjoy similar status and access to resources.

The norm of the idealized American research university is propagated by international organizations, such as the OECD, UNESCO and the World Bank, in their advice to policymakers in peripheral countries and in the conditions attached to World Bank loans. These narrow performance- and productivity-oriented higher education guidelines and policies have become essential components of dominant neo-liberal policy ideologies in most other nations. They constitute the basic premises of mainstream research literature in higher education studies and appear as the only common-sense alternatives in mainstream public debate. In this way the idealized model of research performance and productivity has been translated into simplistic formulas that are reproduced without sufficient analysis in many countries and universities (Ordorika and Pusser, 2007).

DIVERSITY AND DIFFERENCE IN HIGHER EDUCATION

In spite of great similarities between systems and institutions in the world, there is no single, unifying idea of the university (Bonvecchio, 1991; Wittrock, 1993). On the contrary, diverse and distinct major university traditions operate at the national, meta-national or regional levels. Some models or traditions[3] are defined by national borders, or are post-colonial; others are tied to cultural or geographical proximities. Even though some of these models have had more international influence than others, they all represent robust university traditions in their own domains.

In this global era in which models, ideas and policies are freely communicated across national boundaries, one would expect these different traditions to contribute collectively to the development of international higher education. This is not the case, however, for the hegemony of the North American model and its 'idea of a university' exercises a powerful and often disruptive influence. Trends towards global standardization partly reflect the emergence of common guidelines and systems in higher education but they also reveal cultural and material differences and inequities.

Moreover, a narrowly defined idealization of the North American elite research model of higher education – which corresponds to a virtually unique relationship between university and industry, existing only in the USA – becomes harmful and dangerous when it is romanticized and transposed to the rest of the world. Business inclinations as well as market orientations and market-like behaviour are characteristic of the top tier of US higher education institutions, which have increasingly narrowed their role to knowledge production with significant capital-accumulation purposes. Adherence to this paradigm in other prominent countries whose accumulation processes are different can be harmful. Public research universities in peripheral countries are historically more diverse in the range and nature of their tasks and social responsibilities; therefore, harnessing them to research productivity and performance goals put forward in the form of international standards by dominant systems and institutions can easily erode their commitment to society at large.

DIVERSITY AND COMMITMENT TO SOCIETY: UNIVERSITIES ON THE PERIPHERY

Institutions, policymakers, and even teaching staff and students worldwide have a difficult time avoiding these hegemonic trends. While there have been important instances of resistance, alternatives to the dominant model are virtually non-existent. In order to build alternatives and expand the notion of the contributions of higher education to society, there is a need to be aware of the homogenizing effects of productivity-driven policies, their impact on the narrowing of university goals and their detrimental consequences on the social responsibilities of universities. For this purpose it is increasingly important to understand the loaded nature of concepts and notions of research performance and productivity that are so closely linked to market-oriented institutions of higher education.

Through a process that we can label *marketization* or *commodification*, higher education has been aligned to the requirements and practices of diverse markets both at national and international levels. In this global context, research universities have been integrated, willingly or not, into a global market with a centrally established system of assessment through international rankings. These international rankings promote, reproduce and reify research performance and productivity indicators as the only sources of value on which to base societal appreciation for higher education institutions and academic work.

Standardized measures of academic output become an international homogenizing force that throws universities with diverse origins, traditions and roles into a common process of competition in uneven conditions and with unequal possibilities for success. In this way, the global higher education market works as a powerful mechanism for reproducing inequities between different types of universities that come from diverse regions or countries and have extremely differentiated access to intellectual and material resources.

The reproduction of the global higher education market is based on two distinct but closely interconnected processes: alignment and hierarchical stratification. Alignment arises from the normative character of the productivity-oriented model discussed above and its homogenizing effect on the diversity of projects and university traditions. Hierarchical stratification occurs through the establishment of a 'pecking order' of institutions based on international status and power, as measured by the international productivity standards fashioned by those institutions that shape the hegemonic model.

Many universities on the periphery of the hegemonic model, certainly those in peripheral countries (in Latin America for example), have maintained differentiated traditions and have played central roles in the development of nation-states. Most of these, willingly or under coercion, have entered a conflictive process of homogenization and conformity leading towards the global hegemonic model. Entering a transition process that involves subordination to the extraneous North American model for research universities and unequal competition with top North American institutions is enormously risky for peripheral universities and the countries in which these are based. The legitimacy and foundations of national institutions are gradually eroded by unfair and unjustified comparisons with the bearers of the productivity models. The distinctive character of national systems and universities is lost, giving way to uprooted institutions that qualify badly in international rankings and also have a diminished impact on the national and local realities to which they should respond.

The emergence of an international higher education market constitutes a significant challenge for national research universities: how to participate in the global realm of colleges and universities on the basis of their own nature and distinctive character and to avoid diluting these in the face of hegemonic models and dominant international guidelines. Alignment and homogenization must be confronted by reestablishing different traditions and university models.

The diversity of regional and national contexts and of university traditions makes it impossible to propose one single alternative to the restrictive market-driven hegemonic model. However, a common theme is the reconstruction of societal appreciation of higher education, based on ascribing greater value to the contributions of higher education to society beyond market interactions and the fulfilment of administrative practices. One possibility is to think about re-creating the university along the lines of the following broad set of social commitments and responsibilities:

1. To provide a privileged space for relating global trends to national identities, building up local social understanding and promoting interaction between diverse cultures and beliefs, ethnic groups, migrant and resident nationalities, genders, social classes and other societal groups.
2. To act as the only public institution that promotes reflective understanding and grounded critique of contemporary society and its relations with the environment (Pusser, 2006).
3. To bridge the gap between specialized knowledge and society as a whole, in

the context of the knowledge society and the information economy, as it is the only existing institution in contemporary society capable of doing so (Fuller, 2001).

4. To act as the main institution in re-creating and constructing contemporary shared values and societal understanding, and serve as an essential space for shaping diverse constituencies for a broad set of interactions within society and with the environment (these include training for work and employment but go beyond these objectives).

5. To act as a fundamental establishment for the production of knowledge, addressing a broad range of societal concerns, demands, and problems in diverse areas, including, but moving beyond, the narrow reach of production requirements and market demands.

In the face of a hierarchical field of domination and a hegemonic understanding of what constitutes a successful university in contemporary society, the challenge for peripheral universities is how to preserve their diversity of traditions and responsibilities through a broad commitment to society. It is along these lines that a wide variety of alternatives should be developed, re-creating multiple concepts of the university rooted in distinct traditions and historical conditions.

REFERENCES

Altbach, P.G. and Johnstone, D.B. (1993) *The Funding of Higher Education: International Perspectives*. New York: Garland Publishing.

Barnett, R. (2000) *Realizing the University in an Age of Supercomplexity*. Buckingham, UK/Philadelphia, PA: Society for Research into Higher Education and Open University Press.

Bensimon, E. and Ordorika, I. (2005). Mexico's Estímulos: faculty compensation based on piece-work. In: R. Rhoads and C.A. Torres (eds), *The University, State, and Market: The Political Economy of Globalization in the Americas*. Stanford, CA: Stanford University Press, p. 400.

Bonvecchio, C. (1991) *El Mito de la Universidad*. Mexico City: Siglo XXI Editores.

Bourdieu, P. and Johnson, R. (1993) *The Field of Cultural Production: Essays on Art and Literature*. New York: Columbia University Press.

Castells, M. (1996) *The Rise of the Network Society*. Cambridge, MA: Blackwell Publishers.

Clark, B.R. (1998) *Creating Entrepreneurial Universities: Organizational Pathways of Transformation* (1st edn). Oxford; New York: Published for the IAU Press by Pergamon Press.

Coraggio, J.L. and Torres, R.M. (1997) *La Educación Según el BancoMundial: Un Análisis de sus Propuestas y Métodos* (1st edn). Buenos Aires: Centro de Estudios Multidisciplinarios. Miño y Dávila Editores.

Díaz Barriga, A. (1998) Organismos internacionales y política educativa. In: C.A. Torres, A. Alcántara Santuario and R. Pozas Horcasitas (eds), *Educación, Democracia y Desarrollo en el Fin de Siglo* (1st edn). Mexico City: Siglo XXI Editores, p. 288.

Evans, P.B., Rueschemeyer, D. and Skocpol, T. (eds) (1985) *Bringing the State Back In*. Cambridge, UK: Cambridge University Press.

Flexner, A. (1994) *Universities: American, English, German*. New Brunswick, NJ: Transaction Publishers.

Fuller, S. (2001) *Universities as vehicles for the governance of knowledge from the standpoint of social epistemology*. Paper presented at the UNESCO Forum on Higher Education, Research and Knowledge Colloquium on Research and Higher Education Policy: 'Knowledge, Access and Governance: Strategies for Change'.

Geiger, R.L. (2004) *Knowledge and Money: Research Universities and the Paradox of the Marketplace*. Stanford, CA: Stanford University Press.

Johnstone, D.B. (1998) *The Financing and Management of Higher Education: A Status Report on Worldwide Reforms*. Washington, DC: World Bank.

Kerr, C. (2001) *The Uses of the University* (5th edn). Cambridge, MA: Harvard University Press.

Lyotard, J.F. (1990) *La Condición Postmoderna: Informe Sobre el Saber*. Mexico: REI.

Marginson, S. (1997) *Markets in Education*. St. Leonards, NSW: Allen & Unwin.

Marginson, S. and Considine, M. (2000) *The Enterprise University: Power, Governance, and Reinvention in Australia*. Cambridge, UK/New York: Cambridge University Press.

Marginson, S. and Ordorika, I. (forthcoming). El central volumen de la fuerza (The hegemonic global pattern in the reorganization of elite higher education and research). In: C.J. Calhoun and D. Rhoten (eds), *The Transformation of 'Public' Research Universities: Shaping an International and Interdisciplinary Research Agenda for the Social Sciences*. New York: Social Science Research Council Press.

Naidoo, R. (2004) Fields and institutional strategy: Bourdieu on the relationship between higher education, inequality and society. *British Journal of Sociology of Education*, **25**(4), pp. 446–72.

Ordorika, I. (2002) Mercados y educación superior. *Perfiles Educativos*, **XXIV**(95), pp. 98–103.

Ordorika, I. (2004) El mercado en la academia. In: I. Ordorika (ed.), *La Academia en Jaque: Perspectivas Políticas Sobre la Evaluación de la Educación Superior en México*. Mexico City: CRIM-UNAM/Grupo Editorial Miguel Angel Porrua, pp. 35–74.

Ordorika, I. and Pusser, B. (2007) La máxima casa de estudios: The Universidad Nacional Autónoma de México as a state-building university, in P.G. Altbach and J. Balán (eds), *The Struggle to Compete: Building World-class Universities in Asia and Latin America*. Baltimore, MD: Johns Hopkins University Press.

Pusser, B. (2005) *Educación Superior, el*

Mercado Emergente y el Bien Público. Mexico City: Grupo Editorial Miguel Angel Porrua.

Pusser, B. (2006) Reconsidering higher education and the public good: the role of public spheres. In: W.G. Tierney (ed.), *Governance and the Public Good*. Albany, NY: State University of New York Press.

Readings, B. (1996) *The University in Ruins*. Cambridge, MA: Harvard University Press.

Rhoades, G. (1998) *Managed Professionals: Unionized Faculty and Restructuring Academic Labor*. Albany, NY: State University of New York Press.

Slaughter, S. and Leslie, L.L. (1997) *Academic Capitalism: Politics, Policies, and the Entrepreneurial University*. Baltimore, MD: Johns Hopkins University Press.

Wittrock, B. (1993) The modern university: the three transformations. In: S. Rothblatt and B. Wittrock (eds), *The European and American University Since 1800: Historical and Sociological Essays*. Cambridge, UK/New York: Cambridge University Press.

Wolin, S.S. (1981) The new public philosophy. *Democracy: a journal of political renewal and radical change*, **1**(October), pp. 23–36.

World Bank (1994) *Higher Education: The Lessons of Experience*. Washington, DC: World Bank.

World Bank (2000) *Higher Education in Developing Countries: Peril and Promise*. Washington, DC: World Bank.

NOTES

1 This paper is one of the outcomes of a broader research project on globalization and higher education that I share with Dr. Simon Marginson (University of Melbourne, Australia). I am deeply indebted to my colleagues Simon Marginson, Brian Pusser (University of Virginia, USA), and Humberto Muñoz (Universidad Nacional Autónoma de México) for the intellectual contributions and thoughtful criticism they provided during the preparation of this work.

2 The top 100 universities in the Jiao Tong world ranking (2005) include 52 from the USA and 17 from other English-speaking countries, with the remainder from Western Europe and Japan.

3 I am referring here to models such as the US *elite research university* (Kerr, 2001; Geiger, 2004), the *state-building university* in Latin America and peripheral countries (Ordorika and Pusser, 2007), and the *Napoleonic and Humboldtian* traditions in continental Europe (Wittrock, 1993; Flexner, 1994).

I.2

THE UNIVERSITY OF THE 21ST CENTURY: POLITICAL AND SOCIAL TRENDS OF GLOBALIZATION – CHALLENGES FOR HIGHER EDUCATION

Federico Mayor-Zaragoza

Abstract

Globalization is intensifying economic differences and social and cultural divisions. Democratic principles, rather than the laws of the market, need to be used to guide human behaviour and economic policies. 'It is foolish to confuse value with price', wrote the great poet Antonio Machado. Those in power have been foolish and have irresponsibly abandoned the ideologies and ideals that the university community has striven so hard to preserve through the years.

The world is in a deplorable state: the democracy embodied in the United Nations, designed by Roosevelt, has been replaced by a plutocracy (G7/G8) and a hegemonic power. Furthermore, states have been weakened by the transfer of much of their power to big multinational companies that do as they please, with total impunity, at a supranational level. They are involved in all kinds of trafficking (arms, capital, patents, drugs and even people) and make use of tax havens. They invest more than US$3 billion per day in arms (not counting the missile defence shield that the US government wants to implement in contravention of the 1988 treaties), while more than 60,000 people die of hunger.

Universities can remain silent no longer. The functions of
- training
- assessment
- production

are now more important than ever. Daring to know, and knowing how to dare. Universities – with European leadership – must be a beacon and watchtower in the 21st century.

> I hold with what has been said:
> Justice must be done,
> despite law and customs,
> despite money and alms.
> (Pedro Casaldáliga, 2006)

CONTEXT

The process of 'globalization' has replaced universal ethical principles with market laws. This has led to a situation that is truly worrying and requires firm and urgent solutions that can only be implemented – as brilliantly intuited by those who drafted the Charter of the United Nations in 1945, at the end of a horrific world war – by the 'peoples', for the people, and not by the powerful, short-sighted and limited individuals who respond to immediate-term interests. 'It is foolish to confuse value with price', warned Antonio Machado in one of his proverbs, drawn from his Castilian background, that I like to quote. Those in power have been foolish. They have exchanged the values of justice, liberty, equality and solidarity – on which the construction of a peaceful and creative world should be based – for the norms that govern commercial transactions. 'The peoples' have been replaced by the states, which are being increasingly weakened, to the benefit of big transnational corporations. In addition, the United Nations that, in Roosevelt's design, constituted a 'democratic' system on a planetary scale, has been sidelined in favour of the group of the richest countries on earth (G-7/G-8).

THE WIDENING GAP BETWEEN RICH AND POOR

The divide separating rich and poor has been widened instead of being narrowed, and the rents in the social fabric have not been mended. The attempt to staunch wounds caused by rancour and animosity has been made using thorns and bullets instead of generous aid, dialogue and understanding. Whether or not we wish to acknowledge it, in 2007 we are heading, with more or less reluctance, towards a war economy that is gradually concentrating economic power in very few hands and that will use any pretext to reach colossal proportions. The Iraq war, based on false premises, gave the war industry a huge boost. Now, unable to extend the number of 'enemies' – due to another resounding failure of war – the current US administration has managed to extend the tentacles of its military power, in the face of the deafening silence of the European Union. Added to the anti-missile shield – which breaks the agreements reached with such difficulty between the two superpowers in Reykjavik at the end of the cold war – is the massive rearmament not only of Israel but also of all the countries in the Gulf region.

It has been calculated that US$3 billion are invested in arms each day. This amount will undoubtedly increase in the coming months and years. We invest 365 times less than this on food. Indeed, the World Food Programme only has an *annual* budget of US$3 million. As a result, approximately 60,000 people die of hunger every day. Are the US military really looking for weapons of mass destruction? The name of such weapons is *hunger*. Poverty and misery are spreading everywhere and are breeding grounds of frustration at so many broken promises. From these breeding grounds emerge radicalization and feelings of revenge, foci of violence, desperate people who – often at the risk of their own lives – try to reach the shores of plenty or immolate themselves in protest, defeat or ignorance. The use of violence, regardless of its origins, is absolutely unjustifiable. But we must make an effort to identify its roots, to explain what causes it.

Contrary to what was expected, globalization does not heed working conditions, power mechanisms or respect for human rights. The only thing that is important is the deal. From the most atrocious dictatorships, to countries that are trying to rise or re-emerge from secular colonialism and subjection, from China to Ecuador and Gabon, what is important is buying and selling, exploiting natural resources, and privatizing goods that were previously considered to belong to the public. Thus, through takeovers and major mergers, the world panorama has become more rarefied with increased disparities. Worse still, the responsibilities of those who carried out the functions of government in the name of their citizens have disappeared. Economic, social and environmental impacts; cultural standardization; the lack of moral references and so on have been largely brought about by the 'faceless power' of the big multinationals, which act as they please with total impunity.

Everything seems to be affected: the main beneficiaries of the war economy can see how the poverty rate is increasing in their own country. While they are able to reach the moon and develop the greatest technological prowess, they are completely unprepared when hit by natural disasters, such as hurricane Katrina. A bridge recently collapsed in Minneapolis in the state of Minnesota, even though technical studies had detected faults more than six months previously. There are hundreds of other similar cases in the USA. The presidents of the USA and the other most powerful countries on Earth should thoroughly read and understand the 1918–1919 reflections and projects of President Woodrow Wilson (the Covenant of the League of Nations promoting 'lasting peace'), and of Franklin Delano Roosevelt in 1944–1945 (the International Bank for Reconstruction and Development and the International Monetary Fund; United Nations Organization). Both presidents believed that the solution to the world's problems could only be reached by the people themselves. They considered that different peoples needed to come together, united by a common destiny, in organizations in which cooperation, dialogue and comprehension would be facilitated.

The aim was to prevent and anticipate future events, and to be totally committed to the welfare of future generations. The preamble to the UN Charter, which I like to quote, says: 'We the peoples of the United Nations are determined to save succeeding generations from the scourge of war' Who? 'We the peoples.' 'Save', that is, we build peace daily through our behaviour. To achieve what? To ensure that our descendants do not have to experience the scourges of confrontation, humiliation, exclusion, discrimination and violence. The solution, therefore, is to unite the peoples in one international organization, guided by universally accepted principles. The Universal Declaration of Human Rights, promoted by the General Assembly of the United Nations on 10 December 1948, constitutes a compendium of the ethics on which to base personal and collective action to provide humankind with 'freedom from fear and want', as stated in the preamble to the Declaration.

To achieve this, we must keep the future in mind, know that the past can be described and has to be reliably described, but also be aware that it has already been written. What future generations must be able to write with total freedom is the future – their present. To attain this, it is essential to encourage the ability to anticipate, to foresee and to act in time. It is not enough to know the right treatment; it must also be applied at the right time. Based on my experience in the diagnosis of postnatal disorders that can develop irreversibly with severe mental deterioration, I published *Tomorrow Will be Too Late* (Mayor, 1984) to highlight the government actions that must be given priority so that they do not reach the point of no return. The aforementioned diseases have to be *treated in time* to stop them from becoming irreversible pathological disorders.

We need to act in time, draw on the lessons learnt in the past and always keep the future in mind (Mayor, 1996). Only then is it possible to walk with hope and self-esteem, in new directions towards the world of equal human dignity we yearn for. Equal dignity! If we all really believed in equal dignity for every individual human being, regardless of the colour of their skin, their ethnic background, their ideology, their beliefs and so on, most of the challenges we face could be resolved. However, in order to look forwards, knowing where we came from and what we have left behind, it is essential to eradicate the impediments and baggage that prevent us from walking free. We should press on and know how to distinguish what is important from what is urgent. The right institutions need to tackle the major economic, social, cultural, environmental, energy and moral challenges of our times. We should not be resigned, submissive citizens – receivers but not emitters – who observe what is happening around us passively and even with indifference.

THE 'SCOURGE OF WAR'

The United Nations Organization is an attempt at creating international order through an institution that provides guidelines for political action in international relations. It includes a number of organizations capable of establishing guidelines on health, employment, nutrition, education, science, culture, development, childhood and so on. The aim is to make international agreements work and to *get nations to work together* to 'spare us from the scourge of war'. The diversity and pluralism that constitute the wealth of humankind, and that are so feared by those who want to ensure their power of command over uniform and uniformed beings, must be inspired – as befits their common destiny – by the universally accepted ideals that the UNESCO constitution establishes in the name of 'democratic principles'. These are: justice, liberty, equality and solidarity. The constitution adds 'intellectual and moral solidarity', as only an attitude of solidarity will make it possible to achieve the supreme objective of equal dignity for all human beings and, as stated in Article 1 of the Universal Declaration, allow them to 'act towards one another in a spirit of brotherhood'.

Yet, as happened in the opening months of 1919 with the peace proposals of President Wilson, the interests of the immense war machine soon ruined this great project, which is so urgently needed and the absence of which is so conspicuous. As a result, we must continually remind ourselves of the reasons, given at the end of the two great 20th century wars, why brawn can prevail over the mind, and force over words.

In a masculine society (95% of decisions at world level continue to be taken exclusively by men), the perverse adage 'if you want peace, prepare for war' has been irrevocably implemented. It is always based on two equally perverse suppositions. The first is that humans have a tendency towards violence. The second, that subjects can be called on at any time to give their lives, if necessary, without argument and with blind obedience, for the causes that the omnipresent and indisputable powers

decide. Thus, the requirements for war are served: weapons and soldiers. Weapons are provided by manufacturers, who are gradually becoming the most important businesspeople on Earth. Soldiers are acquired by means of propaganda, biased information and fear; education that subjects rather than freeing, that emphasizes divisions instead of uniting; and training that makes automata of humans whose defining faculty is the ability to think, reflect and invent. Those who obey, often at the cost of their own lives, become heroes. 'Unknown' soldiers, but heroes. Those who dissent, retreat or desert are traitors. And we all know the fate reserved for traitors. All this explains why, against all the evidence, we are preparing for war instead of peace; why we tolerate the fact that 80% of humankind live precariously on 20% of all resources, while in the wealthy neighbourhoods of the global village less than 20% of humankind enjoys more than 80% of all resources, including – in the first place – knowledge. This also clarifies why the powerful are unwilling to accept the diversity that, to the extent of uniqueness, characterizes the human species. It explains why they are afraid of freedom of expression and unrestricted freedom of information. It also reveals why the powerful prefer democracy to consist of getting citizens to express their preferences every four or five years in a truly oppressive atmosphere of media interference, instead of really taking them into consideration, facilitating their participation and encouraging a culture of listening – the essence of democracy.

In the 1950s, hopes faded for a system that claimed to represent the 'peoples', but in fact consisted entirely of states – five of them (the victors in the war) with the power of veto. Instead of 'sparing' us from the 'scourge of war' and building peace, these states were preparing for war. It has taken many years of confrontation, bloody conflicts, revolutions and suffering of all kinds for humankind to realize, against the tide and against the practices that even today continue to muddy the dark horizon, that 'if you want peace, help to build it with your day-to-day behaviour', with your everyday attitude, with your hands stretched out but never raised.

DISTRIBUTION OF RESOURCES

The time of 'the peoples' has now arrived. The time of people has come. The 21st century really can become the century of people. Thanks to distance participation, in a few years, we will have real democracies, which will confound the manoeuvres that have characterized the different power scenarios throughout history. In a few years, women will finally be relevant in the decision-making. In a few years, the voice of the people will finally be heard in the government of nations.

At the UNESCO General Conference held in New Delhi in 1956, Pandit Nehru stated that the high function of the intellectual organization of the United Nations was to act as the 'conscience of mankind'. This is the mission of educators, creators, artists and scientists: in the midst of all the shouting and mêlée, remember the points of reference, the beacons that should guide our course.

'Acting towards one another in a spirit of brotherhood' required a better *distribution* of resources. This was the beginning of the 'new international order' that the United Nations attempted to put into effect, which was thwarted once more. Development for what? For whom? To provide citizens with the skills that would allow them to use their own resources, or at least contribute to the use of these resources, so that their living conditions could reach a minimum level that would prevent migration and brewing resentment; to ensure equal opportunities and the absence of discrimination due to place of birth, ethnic origins and so on; to make possible the supreme principle of equal dignity for all human beings. What kind of development needed to be promoted to reach these goals? The General Assembly argued for decades about the factors that should make up the perfect development model. Meanwhile, the resources that prosperous countries contributed to this development decreased.

In the 1960s, it became clear that development needed to be social, educational, cultural and scientific, as well as economic. It needed to be comprehensive. However, it took 50 years for the first world summit on social development to be held in Copenhagen. Let us no longer be fooled by those who insist that good economic development is needed to be able to distribute wealth adequately and equitably. That moment never arrives. Thus, on the eve of the 50th anniversary of its founding, the United Nations decided to focus the commemoration on three fundamental axes: social development, the fundamental role of women, and tolerance. However, in 1995 the commitments made in Copenhagen on social development fell into the vacuum created by the height of the market economy. The 'globalizers' were satisfied, and spent much time looking into the mirrors of their fortresses instead of opening doors and windows and looking at what was really going on in the world. So much so, that on 11 May 1996 the US president stated that results were so encouraging that it would be worth extending the economic criteria to a 'market society' and 'market democracy'.

In the 1970s, a distinction was rightly made between *immediate* aid (rescue aid) for getting out of dramatic situations, and *rehabilitation aid* for 'normalizing' situations of underdevelopment by fostering endogenous skills,

training, and knowledge and technology transfer so that countries could acquire skills. In 1974, the General Assembly agreed that the wealthier countries would facilitate the development of the more needy by means of aid that totalled 0.7% of their GDP. This is obviously a very reasonable percentage, as most rich countries retain 99.3% of their GDP. Sadly, we all know what happened. Soon, most countries, with the exception of the Scandinavian nations, reduced their contributions to laughable percentages. Aid was replaced with loans granted under intolerable conditions by the World Bank, *their* bank, the bank of the most developed countries, which, by the way, had omitted its 'surname': 'Reconstruction and Development'.

The borrowers were required to privatize, reduce their administrative force, and carry out infrastructure work in order to secure these loans. Such work would be undertaken by the lenders, since they had the qualified personnel and the machinery. How shameful that aid was replaced by loans, that poor countries became even poorer and ended up in debt and underselling the exploitation of their natural resources to major multinational concerns. Thus, financial flows were reversed: instead of moving from North to South, they began – to the disgust of a perplexed yet resigned humankind – to move from South to North. Today, there is a demand for the International Monetary Fund, the World Bank, and the World Trade Organization to radically change their methods. If they do not, popular resistance will achieve the transformations that commonsense imposes in a very short space of time.

SUSTAINABLE DEVELOPMENT

In her capacity as chairwoman of the World Commission on Environment and Development in 1983, Gro Harlem Brundtland, the Norwegian prime minister, came up with the notion of 'sustainable development'. This is development that allows for the renewal of natural resources that are consumed. Thus, we can stop the ecological deterioration caused by the process of industrialization and production and by a lifestyle that leads to the consumption of vast quantities of fuel and energy, all of which is in the hands of a privileged few. Development must respect the natural environment. A few years later, in 1992, the Rio de Janeiro Summit, called the Earth Summit, established global measures in Agenda 21. These measures aim for future generations to receive the legacy of a natural environment that does not restrict the quality of life of the inhabitants of the planet.

Like the Copenhagen commitments, the Rio agreements were not upheld by the richest and most powerful countries. The Kyoto Protocol for the reduction of greenhouse gas emissions, and carbon dioxide in particular, contains 'diluted' measures in terms of both the release of these gases and their re-uptake. However, even these were completely ignored by the Bush administration, because the measures were 'contrary to the interests of American industry'. The scientific community remained silent. Scientists and specialized institutions around the world did not raise their voices in disagreement, as they should have done, with yet another arbitrary decision of the American president. In August 2007, President Bush called a meeting in Washington, DC on climate change, thus confusing the issue. I have repeated endlessly that the best diagnosis is the one that allows you to effect treatment in time. New meetings, like the one called by the president of the USA, serve no other purpose than to delay the changes in direction that scientific rigour is urgently recommending.

It is time for action. If we want guidelines for general education on environmental matters, from the security of peace and never again from the peace of silence and mistrust and suspicion; if we want to create attitudes that promote environmental conservation, the construction of peace and the strengthening of democracy, we can use existing documents such as the Earth Charter. Since 2000, the Earth Charter has been a wonderful inspiration for action on many levels. It has led to participation in and contributions to the works of reflection of many panels and commissions. However, more than new diagnostic reports, recommendations and resolutions, what is needed is action. Major changes are required rapidly to reduce military spending and increase funds. This will meet the immediate demand of the world conscience: stop the death of thousands of people every day from starvation and from a lack of access to the right treatment for their health and quality of life.

Having analysed comprehensive, endogenous and sustainable development, the assistant administrator of UNICEF, Richard Jolly, wrote *Development with a Human Face* (Mehrotra and Jolly, 1987). This book was needed to make us realize that we had looked at many aspects and dimensions of the development process but had forgotten who its protagonists and beneficiaries should be. The beneficiaries were not those in urgent need but those who have turned the process of development into another source of income – one of the biggest – while most of humankind lives in ethically unacceptable conditions.

CITIZEN PARTICIPATION

Despite being marginalized, and despite the fact that international power is gradually being transferred from the 'democracy' of the United Nations to the 'plutocracy' of the G-7/G-8, the UN has not ceased to work to fulfil its mission by establishing guidelines and measures that, when put into practice, can rectify so many of the mistaken current trends. Thus, in addition to the summits and the aforementioned documents, the General Assembly of the United Nations passed a resolution in 1998 on the dialogue between civilizations; devised the Declaration and Programme of Action on a Culture of Peace (United Nations, 1999); and the Millennium Development Goals (United Nations, 2000). To facilitate the transition from a culture of force, brawn, imposition, violence and war to a culture of dialogue, understanding, conciliation and peace, we must encourage the participation of all citizens. All citizens must realize that they have to contribute, even if it is only by a small amount – a small seed – to the construction of the new world that we wish to pass on to our descendants. To achieve this, it is necessary to foster education in human rights and democracy, tolerance and mutual national and international understanding; to fight against all forms of discrimination; to promote democratic principles and practices in all areas of society; to combat poverty and achieve endogenous and sustainable development that benefits all and provides each person with a dignified way of life. More than 110 million signatures were obtained at the beginning of the century and of the millennium in favour of the Manifesto 2000 for a Culture of Peace and Non-violence. This manifesto committed signatories 'in my everyday life, in my family, in my work, my community, my country and my region to respect all life, reject violence, share with others, listen to understand, preserve the planet and rediscover solidarity'. The Declaration and Programme of Action (United Nations, 1999) contains a considerable number of measures that require urgent implementation. These include fostering freedom of expression and information, and the ability and role of women in decision-making.

MILLENNIUM GOALS

In 2000, 189 heads of government and state met at the headquarters of the United Nations to commit to meeting the eight goals that make up the Millennium Declaration before 2015. The first goal consists of eradicating extreme poverty and hunger. It has been calculated that 1.2 billion people (one in five) currently subsist on less than a dollar a day. 1.8 billion people (almost a third of the world population) live in a state of 'poverty'. Eight hundred million people suffer from malnutrition. Poverty is not exclusive to developing countries: it is calculated that, in many advanced countries, one fifth of the population lives below the poverty threshold.

The second goal is to achieve universal primary education. The third goal involves promoting equality between the sexes and the autonomy of women. The fourth consists of reducing infant mortality. The fifth aims to improve maternal health. The sixth is to fight AIDS, malaria and other diseases. The seventh involves ensuring environmental sustainability and the eighth consists of encouraging a global society for development.

The measures for achieving these goals are the result of the work of many specialists worldwide, and of first-class reports that, generally, do not require any amendments. We must now *quickly* convince ourselves of this, and *demand that those in power* stop postponing possible and feasible action, so that the few may become many, peacefully, without turmoil, 'in a spirit of brotherhood'. I frequently insist that the price of rejecting evolution is revolution. Revolutions do not tend to be good for anybody. We must understand that the difference between one and the other is the letter *R* for *responsibility*, and assuming this responsibility. In *The World Ahead* (Mayor, 1999), I examined, with the help of Jeröme Bindé, the state of the world at the end of the last century. A wealth of data and sources of information to analyse what needed to be done to meet the great demographic, healthcare, educational, energy, environmental, cultural and ethical challenges, was used. I proposed four 'new contracts': a new social contract, a new natural contract, a new cultural contract and a new moral contract. If based on sound principles, all these contracts flow like tributaries into the main river, which is a global endogenous development contract, *The Global Contract* (Fundación Cultura de Paz, 2001) that would enable the building of the other possible world that the vast majority of humankind is dreaming of.

Despite the chilling figures shown above, despite the images that move us from time to time, those who rule the world continue – with some exceptions – to be immersed in a culture of war and force. The tragic terrorist attacks of 11 September 2001 were a terrible cry for attention from the whole of humanity (many of whom were watching live). With the exception of some callous people (who are capable of inducing the blind single-mindedness that leads to terrorists destroying themselves), the whole world has come out on the side of life, on the side of the victims. By coincidence, only a few hours before the attack, the Food and Agriculture Organization of the United Nations (FAO) had announced from its Rome headquarters that over 35,000 children die every day, forgotten and unloved. However, out of sight, out of mind. We must always be aware of the things we do not see, so that they can also become motives for emotion, reflection and action.

Following the reprisals in Afghanistan, everyone indulgently looked the other way and tried to take on board the logic of the wounded giant's reaction. But then, inexplicably and inadmissibly, there was a terrible war based on lies, on false premises and on potential threats with no basis. In September 2004, President Lula proposed passing measures for eradicating poverty. Through justice, not through charity. It is time to honour the many broken promises. It is not a time for handouts, but for solidarity based on justice, on the equal dignity of all.

One recent image, which has had a great impact, showed the interlaced hands of the UN's Secretary-General Kofi Annan, presidents Lula, Lagos and Chirac, and the Spanish prime minister, José Luis Rodríguez Zapatero, who furthermore proposed, to the surprise of many, promoting the 'Alliance of Civilizations', the building of bridges between cultures and interaction between beliefs. At the Millennium Goals Summit + 5 (United Nations, 2005), held in September 2005, the heads of state and government gave the warmest welcome to the Alliance of Civilizations initiative by firmly reaffirming their good intentions and unanimously recommending the transition towards a culture of peace and dialogue throughout the world.

By mid-2007, few actions had been undertaken in favour of this great transition. However, many activities continue to fuel current trends, with the turbulent panorama that I mentioned at the beginning of this paper. Yet each day (and this is what must be highlighted), there are more reasons for hope; for the participation of people; the consolidation of democracy; and the profound reform of the United Nations (Ubuntu, 2006); for words to finally replace force, imposition and violence; for citizens no longer to be subjects, but to be members of the human family, able to develop their distinctive creative ability to the full; citizens who are no longer silent because they are aware of the voice they owe to future generations. The voice of life.

EUROPEAN HIGHER EDUCATION'S FUTURE ROLE

What are the main functions of higher education in contributing to all aspects of this potential world? How can we mobilize political will to provide solutions to the major challenges facing the world?

FUNCTIONS OF HIGHER EDUCATION
The main functions of higher education at national and

international level (particularly at the European Union level) are:

- *Training:* to transmit and disseminate up-to-date knowledge; to generate new knowledge and ensure the progress of knowledge; to promote excellent qualifications for professionals; and to strengthen democracy.
- *Consultation:* to improve the social dimension of higher education by facilitating its active participation in society. Such participation could involve advisory services for governments and parliaments on matters of profound public impact (current examples include climate change, avian flu, energy sources, neurological diseases and so on) and in setting national priorities. Europe should be, above all, a world reference for democratic behaviour. Higher education must produce highly qualified graduates and responsible citizens (UNESCO, 1998).
- *Prevention:* the duty of global forecasting, which will allow higher education to play an active role in society, especially in meeting new social and environmental needs. It will help society to plan for the future and be in charge of its own destiny (Tanguiane and Mayor, 2000). Universities must be a global watch tower (EC, 2006).

UNIVERSITIES IN SOCIETY AND FOR SOCIETY

- *The cultural and ethical mission:* today, higher education and research are essential for the sustainable cultural, socioeconomic and ecological development of people, communities and nations (UNESCO, 1998).
- *Autonomy, social responsibility and academic freedom.*
- *Education, higher education, economy and profitability:* education is not a branch of the economy. Nor is the educational process, its aims or results comparable to those of the economy.

Education is a vital function and an essential sector of society in and of itself – a condition of society's existence. Without it, there can be no 'full' society, because it brings together cultural, social, economic, civic and ethical functions. It ensures the continuity of society, and transmits the knowledge, skills and experience accumulated by humankind throughout history. It provides the skills that will allow society to programme, innovate and change, *even* in the area of the economy (Tanguiane and Mayor, 2000).

Higher education is essential for social progress, production, academic growth, affirming cultural identity, maintaining social cohesion, fighting against poverty and promoting a culture of peace (UNESCO, 1996).

One of the main missions of universities is to serve society and to contribute to resolving the major problems it faces (UNESCO, 1998).

Furthermore, universities must foster closer cooperation with the private sector. Industry must understand that there will be no future progress if the rate of innovation is not increased (EC, 2006). Incentives, particularly through tax laws, may increase the involvement of businesses, which is currently low.

We can only transform reality if we have complete, in-depth knowledge of it. It is important to use a transdisciplinary and multidisciplinary approach to contribute to this knowledge.

INTEGRATING EDUCATIONAL EFFORTS AND POLICIES

Educational efforts and policies should be integrated in:

- Autonomous communities
- States
- Europe.

It is essential to ensure proper coordination between the universities of autonomous communities and those of states.

Focusing on Europe, the basic objective is to maximize the potential of universities and to increase their ability to provide the EU with the skills and the application of knowledge required for 'European quality' and competitiveness. However, we should bear in mind that what is important in the long term is the crucial contribution of higher education to a European Union with consolidated participatory, inclusive and anticipatory democracies (EC, 2006).

With 4,000 institutions, more than 17 million students and 1.5 million employees (of which 435,000 are researchers), European universities have tremendous potential (EC, 2006). Universities can contribute to implementing the Community Lisbon Programme (Commission of the European Communities, 2005) through political dialogue and mutual learning, especially within the Education and Training 2010 Work Programme.

MOBILITY OF TALENT

- *Lisbon Summit 2000:* Europe should be the leader of the knowledge-based economy by 2010. It is essential to hold onto the best talent (in terms of lecturers, researchers and students) by offering them the opportunity to train in centres of excellence abroad, but with opportunities to come back to European universities and centres.
- *ERC (The European Research Council):* the ERC and its EU resource fund was launched on 1 January 2007.

It aims to promote basic research in all disciplines. Likewise, a major European university fund should be established that answers to a European university council. Such a council should include existing higher education organizations. It should cooperate closely with the Bologna Process, the ERC and related organizations. It is also essential to increase community programmes such as Socrates, Leonardo, Erasmus, Tempus, Marie Curie and so on, and the loans provided by the European Investment Bank Group and the structural funds. The financing mechanisms must be flexible and free from the slow bureaucratic requirements of the European Union (EC, 2006).

- *ISE (Initiative for Science in Europe):* this institution maintains the impetus achieved by the ERC, with the *entire* scientific community united as a partner at the national (COSCE) and European (ISE) level (ISE, 2007).

MAIN PERSISTING PROBLEMS

- *Student access* (by *merit*, established in article 26.2 of the Universal Declaration on Human Rights). Improved use of existing EU programmes for mobilizing students. The promotion of financial instruments, in basic and cooperative projects (EC, 2006).
- *Access of teaching staff, quality assurance*. Some 'universities' discredit the higher education system. *Quality alone* should guide university life. Improve the access of university teaching staff to research posts. Avoid premature lifetime appointments: the system of five-year contracts should be used. Once an employee's ability has been accredited, tenure (as used in the USA) is a good option.
- *Application of science, patents* (van Ginkel, 1995; Salaburu, 2007). 'There is no applied science if there is no science to apply' (Houssay, 1965). The contribution of universities to research must therefore improve. Furthermore, there is no applied science if there is a lack of ability to transfer knowledge to patents and licences. *Both* are essential for leadership in 'the knowledge-based economy' (EC, 2006). Giving universities the flexibility to generate alternative sources of income is essential to guaranteeing their financial strength (La Caixa, 2007). In summary, they require an organized structure that is able to compete and to take risks (Gabilondo, 2006).

BIBLIOGRAPHY

Casaldáliga, Pedro (2006) *Antología personal.* Trotta.

Commission of the European Communities (2005) Common Actions for Growth and Employment: The Community Lisbon Programme.

EC (2006) Communiqué of the European Commission to the European Parliament and Council: *Carrying out the reforms necessary for modernizing the higher education sector: education, research and innovation,* M. Figel and M. Potocnik. Contribution of F. Mayor in monitoring the informal meeting of heads of state and government at Hampton Court.

Fundación Cultura de Paz (2001) *El contrato global.* Madrid.

Gabilondo, Ángel (2006) 2010: odisea en el espacio de educación superior, *El País.*

Ginkel, Hans, J.A. van (1995) University 2050. The organization of creativity and innovation, *Higher Education Policy,* **8**(4), December.

Houssay, Bernardo (1965) Nobel laureate in Physiology and Medicine.

ISE Green Paper (2007) European Commission: *Inventing our Future Together,* ERA, *New Perspectives,* 4 April.

La Caixa (2007) *Universidades americanas y europeas, cuestión de Estado.* Servicio de Estudios de la Caixa, April.

Mayor, F. (1984) *Mañana siempre es tarde.* Espasa-Calpe. (English version 1987).

Mayor, F. (1996) *Memoria del futuro.* UNESCO.

Mayor, F. (1999) *Un mundo nuevo (Un monde noveau, The World Ahead).* Paris: Odile Jacob.

Mehrotra, S. and Jolly, R. (1987) *Development with a Human Face.* Oxford: OUP.

Salaburu, Pello (2007) *La universidad en la encrucijada. Europa y EE. UU.* Spain: European Academy of Science and Arts.

Tanguiane, S. and Mayor F. (2000) *L'enseignement supérieur au XXI^{éme} siècle,* Paris: Herm Sc. Pub.

Ubuntu (World Forum of Civil Society Networks) (2006) *Reforma en profundidad de las organizaciones internacionales.* Geneva, November.

UNESCO (1996) Declaration on Higher Education, Latin America and Cuba. Havana, Cuba.

UNESCO (1998) Declaration at the World Conference on Higher Education, Paris.

United Nations General Assembly (1999) Declaration and Programme of Action on a Culture of Peace. Resolution of 13 September.

United Nations (2000) Resolution on the Millennium Goals, September.

United Nations General Assembly (2005) Summit on Millennium Goals + 5, September.

The university and cosmopolitan citizenship

Gerard Delanty

Universities are undergoing major change today and we need to rethink quite fundamentally the very idea of the university in a world that is entirely different from earlier periods when the university as an institution emerged. The emergence of global public culture is a new context in which to understand the contemporary significance of the university, which is an institution that can play a key role in shaping social and human development in a global age. The thesis of this paper is that the university is an agent of cosmopolitanism insofar as it makes possible the broadening of the socio-cognitive horizons of societies. In this sense, the university is one of the few institutions in society that is specifically related to the development of collective learning processes. Although universities no longer dominate the field of knowledge production, they have a central role to play in linking knowledge and citizenship. This means more than simply being knowledge producers; it is also a question of social and human development and challenges that are as much socio-cognitive as technical. Universities have the potential to play a leading role in shaping the social and cultural horizons of the knowledge society.

DEFINING THE UNIVERSITY AS AN INSTITUTION

It is helpful to place the current situation in a historical context, which for the sake of simplicity can be characterized as one of globalization. The word 'university' itself is Latin in origin: *universitas*, a term suggestive of community, simply designated a defined group of people pursuing a collective goal. The term was not exclusively applied to universities and indeed many of the ancient universities – Plato's Academy and Aristotle's Lyceum, for example – did not use it to refer to themselves. Universities emerged around the idea of governance and the many forms of the university from the early Middle Ages onwards reflected the diver-

sity of forms of governance, which ranged from craft guilds and municipal corporations to state schools. Therefore, despite its ancient origins, the university is actually an institution of modernity. Virtually all the major universities were created in the modern age and the medieval universities were reconstituted in this period. Today, with the spread of universities beyond the West, a new age of the university is beginning.

In terms of cultural definitions, it is possible to refer to a tension between a reproductive and a transformative conception of knowledge that underlies the university. The former was embodied in Newman's famous notion of the transmission of the received wisdom of the past, which was essentially what liberal education was all about. The latter was contained in von Humboldt's vision of a more transformative conception of knowledge. Central to this was the idea that the combination of teaching and research creates a more enlightened kind of knowledge, which leads to a spiritual transformation in the student. The cultural model of knowledge was the idea that there was an essential unity to knowledge: a unity of teaching and research, and an underlying unity of culture. This classical vision of the university was clearly connected with a notion of human development, although it was not a vision that was centrally concerned with social development. This difference sets the classical university apart from the contemporary university, which has become inextricably bound up with all aspects of social development. Moreover, today we cannot make assumptions about the fundamental unity of knowledge.

Universities played a major socio-cognitive role in shaping the culture of the nation-state and were agents of secularization. They played an important role in the Industrial Revolution, especially in Germany. The rise of the professional classes was connected to civic universities in Britain, whilst in the USA state universities,

created by the Land Grant Act, had a similar function. Professional and vocational training was one of the functions the university played in the process of modernization, for modern society required the accreditation of expertise. Of course, the university was the key to the advancement of scientific research and became a key player in the R&D policies of most states in the period following the Second World War. It is important to see that, since the 19th century, the university has been far from being an ivory tower that is isolated from the wider society. The university has always been a key agent in the formation of modernity in terms of culture and economic and social development. Universities throughout Europe and North America were very different, depending on their relation with the state, professional bodies and the market.

Universities are regulated by three principles: the state, the market and the self-regulating professions. It is possible to see a movement from the university as based exclusively on an autonomous professional organization to being regulated by the state and by the market. Medieval universities in Europe were almost exclusively based on self-governing corporations in which professors determined the form of the university. With the rise of modernity, the state became more important, and with industrial and professional society the market played an increasingly predominant role. Today, the market, which is now a global one, is clearly more important in shaping the fortunes of the university than in the past. Although much diminished, the self-regulating capacity of the university still remains.

THE KNOWLEDGE SOCIETY

One of the features of the present day is the knowledge society. It is commonly held that the university cannot have an enlightening role for it no longer controls the field of knowledge. The classical modern university could at least claim to be the privileged site of knowledge production, for the elites largely produced and consumed knowledge. However, today with mass society becoming an increasingly knowledge-based one, knowledge ceases to be the privilege of the university. The various functions of the university – teaching, research, vocational training, intellectual and cultural transmission – are becoming unbundled. Yet despite signs of the fragmentation of the university, the identity of the university as an institution consists of the unity of these functions, which in different ways are connected with the various dimensions of human and social development.

The more the university becomes implicated in social issues, the more it loses its autonomy. While some critics stress an increase in managerial power, others stress market values and information technology, especially in the area of the online provision of higher education. This leads to the charge of the 'post-university' embracing consumerism and losing its moral purpose. According to various authors, the university is fully integrated into capitalism, in particular techno-science, and, as a new managerialism takes over what was once academic self-government, there is a resulting loss of academic freedom.

These developments have led to a great deal of speculation about the emergence of global mega-universities, corporate universities, and even virtual universities. Building on industry–university links established over the past two decades, it has frequently been noted that universities are also moving closer to digital degrees. The growth of vocational training, distance learning and the move to make course curricula the property of the university are examples of how universities are reducing labour costs while expanding enrolment.

To what extent is the university in a crisis as a result of the knowledge society and the context of globalization? There is much to suggest that the old idea of the university has been undermined by recent developments. There is a clear need for a historical contextualization of the univer-

sity. The recent debates on the demise of the university tend to be based on a historically inaccurate view of earlier models of the university as a golden age. While the augmented instrumentalization of the university by market values is an undeniable and probably irreversible development, it is by no means specific to the contemporary university. Universities have been deeply involved in industry since the late 19th century. Globalization is not bringing about a homogenization of universities. Indeed, if anything, the contrary is occurring. Globalization can be seen as opening up different routes for the university. Globalization is not merely a matter of the homogenization of the world by markets and communication. This is also reflected in the diversity of universities and institutions of higher education.

There is no doubt that it is in the developing and non-Western world that the major developments are occurring, with China and India in the lead as far as change is concerned. Until now, the question of the university was mostly discussed with regard to European and American examples. As a result, much of the recent debate has been whether something like an Americanization of the university is occurring. The reality is far different. A global perspective reveals that universities and institutions of higher education are emerging at a rapid rate in many parts of the world, especially in Asia, and that there is no one dominant model.

A global perspective on universities suggests that there has been a tremendous expansion in universities worldwide and that there is no one particular model emerging. Universities are not disappearing, nor are they simply becoming dominated by the market. What we find is a complicated interaction of the state and market, with professional associational factors playing a major role in research-led institutions. Globalization is not a single process. It is a term to describe an interconnected world, not a single world. For some, processes of globalization open up new emancipatory possibilities while for others globalization leads to the loss of

autonomy and the fragmentation of the social world. We cannot neglect the multifaceted nature of globalization, which is best seen as a relational dynamic rather than a new kind of reality. Globalization – which is highly heterogeneous – can be understood as a tension between various interacting processes, one of which is global public culture.

Until now, universities have not been part of this, but it is possible to see them becoming more important players. As they do so, they may assist in resisting global corporate globalization by providing an alternative kind of culture that is more allied to global public culture. Furthermore, it is difficult to speak of a single new idea of the university, for the same reason as in the past. This is simply because there are too many different kinds of universities for this to be meaningful. However, this does not mean it is meaningless to speak of the university as an institution and to see corporate globalization everywhere.

THE UNIVERSITY AND COSMOPOLITANISM

The university can be a cosmopolitan institution that contributes to global public culture by cultivating a cosmopolitan citizenship. As an institution of knowledge production, the university's contribution to society is to develop and enhance global public culture by connecting citizenship and knowledge. In this way, it may be possible for the university to influence the knowledge society in ways that are not entirely based on market forces. One way it can do this is by incorporating more and different kinds of knowledge into the academy.

The term 'knowledge society' should be used in a broad sense to include not merely the application of science and technology in the economy, or as another term for the 'information society'. Knowledge is increasingly inseparable from citizenship and from democracy. Knowledge is also about the interpretation of knowledge and in addition to this reflexive aspect, it also has a cosmopolitan dimension in that it is unbounded and open.

Cosmopolitanism is a site of interaction and of cultural encounters as well as socio-cognitive development. Cosmopolitanism is connected with transcendence, that is, the way societies evolve through going beyond their present condition; it concerns the opening of horizons and new ways of seeing the world. Cosmopolitanism gives expression to the utopian aspiration to transcend the immediate context of existence without necessarily rejecting it in the name of an unattainable alternative. A key dynamic is the local–global relation, for cosmopolitanism arises when the local contexts of interpretation are transformed in light of the encounter with the global. Universities are located in a space that is neither global nor national, but the interaction of both. For this reason, they can be seen as having a particularly significant role to play as cosmopolitan agents of social change. In distinguishing between globalization and cosmopolitanism, the latter can be regarded as expressing a certain resistance to global market forces and thus as having a closer connection with social development.

In this respect, central to the university is cosmopolitan citizenship, that is, new kinds of citizenship that embody a non-instrumentalized rationality. The following three arguments can be made.

First, the argument that the turn from the state to the market fundamentally alters the historical purpose of the university can be challenged on the grounds that it exaggerates current developments in the area of the market. The university is still a major vehicle of cultural citizenship, especially in countries where civil society is weak – China and Iran, to name but two of numerous other examples. In eastern Europe, universities now have a major role to play in reshaping societies. Latin American universities were important for opening up opportunities for women. Universities throughout the world have been tremendously important in cultivating democratic values and in

extending cultural citizenship. They have, for example, brought about a critical and reflexive awareness of issues relating to minorities, multiculturalism, human rights, feminism and cultural heritage. While in the past much of the critical capacity of the university was subordinated to defining the cognitive structures of the nation-state, today the cultural mission of the university has extended into the broader domain of cosmopolitanism in the cultivation of post-national kinds of citizenship. The capacity of the university to define cognitive structures for society is one of the major themes in the sociology of the university discussed earlier. There is much in this that is still relevant to the current situation as far as social and human development are concerned.

Universities can be major sites of cosmopolitan knowledge, that is, locations of the meeting of cultures. In this respect, they can be agents of democracy and give expression to excluded forms of knowledge. If we need a new idea of the university for the 21st century, maybe this could be one of the tasks – to give expression to an alternative to global corporate culture. This is one of the most important social and cultural challenges, and universities represent an alternative to market rationality. Furthermore, they are not exclusively agents of states.

Second, in many countries higher education is central to social citizenship, which is an important dimension of social development. In the UK, for instance, the question of widening participation in higher education is one of the main aims of government policy in the area of social citizenship. In the view of many critics, this has the disadvantage of a trade-off between the social question of widening participation and the cultural question of an overriding commitment to science. The defenders of liberal education make much of this, seeing only a loss in the cultural dimension. For good or for bad, higher education is increasingly being forced to be an agent of social change. There is no sign of this abating and, in fact, the separation of

mass education from research-based activities has long been a feature of the American university. One of the best examples of the role of the university in extending social and cultural citizenship is the Open Society Foundation, funded by George Soros. Aside from being an interesting example of how globalization is not undermining higher education but supporting it, the Open Society testifies to the critical role higher education is playing in reconstituting civil society in post-communist societies. However, it is also possible to find examples in Latin America of universities that are playing a major role in economic and social development. Universities have been central in increasing social mobility and in generating wealth for developing societies.

Third, along with cultural and social citizenship, technological citizenship has become a new form of citizenship, which goes beyond social citizenship and, indeed, cultural citizenship and pertains to challenges to society that new technologies are creating. In the context of the knowledge society, the question of technological citizenship is especially important for the university to define a new identity for itself. Technology, especially techno-science, is shaping the world according to the dictates of global market forces and is one of the major societal discourses today in which rights and democracy are framed. As science is no longer exclusively based in the university, it is not far-fetched to propose that universities have an important role to play in linking technology to citizenship and in bringing about a democratization of science and technology. Universities are heavily implicated in the new techno-science, as a result of partnerships with businesses. However, in a situation in which universities do not entirely control the production of science and technology, their significance lies instead in their ability to produce democratic discourse and enhance citizen participation in the field of knowledge production.

There are undoubtedly tensions between these dimensions of citizenship.

For instance, widening participation – the dimension of social citizenship – can undermine the cultural role of the university, but it can also enhance it. Perhaps it can be suggested that the term 'university' today means the interconnection of different societal discourses: cultural, social and technological. Whilst these are fragmented in the wider society, they are connected in the university. The university no longer has a monopoly over knowledge in the broad sense of education, nor does it exclusively define science. Yet it is a vital institution in the public sphere that contributes to civil society and citizenship by connecting societal discourses. The public sphere today is part of the knowledge society in which knowledge is not only more widely available but is also more and more contested as increasing numbers of social actors are drawn into it. It is possible to see universities in the knowledge societies of the 21st century as having the role of public spheres, that is, discursive sites in society where social interests engage with the specialized worlds of science and where national and global forces meet. This suggests a notion of cosmopolitan citizenship.

CONCLUSION

To conclude, we need a new idea of the university today. There is no going back to the golden age of the medieval university and much of the humanistic vision of the modern university was elitist and does not adequately reflect what the university has been in the past. Globalization is not bringing about the end of the university, nor is it bringing about a single commercial kind of university order. A sober assessment of the current situation shows that there is a huge diversity of universities and that the sector as a whole is a significant part of what can be called global public culture. As a knowledge-producing institution, the university today should become the cosmopolitan site of global public culture that brings together different kinds of knowledge and cultures. Since the university can no longer define what counts as knowledge in the way that it once could, and since knowledge is no longer produced exclusively by and consumed within the university, the task of the university should instead be to connect different kinds of knowledge. In this way, it can be an actor in the public sphere and one of the major sites of global public culture. If truth means anything, it must be a post-universalistic conception of truth, as the essential contestability of knowledge claims, and the challenge of living without certainty. Thus, one of the challenges of the university today is for it to become a cosmopolitan actor in the global knowledge society by forging new links between knowledge and citizenship.

SPECIAL CONTRIBUTION I.3

Aziza Bennani

The contribution of higher education to multicultural existence: present and future challenges

The process of globalization and the interdependence of societies – largely the result of the circulation of ideas and people – show that multicultural coexistence is essential to guaranteeing world peace and security, particularly in the context of the permanent transformation of multicultural and mixed-race societies.

As this matter is primarily strategic, education in general – and higher education in particular – plays the fundamental role of an element for transforming society. Yet when we approach the matter in relation to the Arab world, we must bear in mind that any generalization inevitably masks the idiosyncrasies, especially in the case of a world that is both unique and plural, and characterized by multiple educational systems that are sometimes very different.

Indeed, though levels of education are generally low,[1] they differ depending on the various national and political regimes and their resulting options; the different levels of development (in terms of economy, health, standard of living and so on); the human resources (the lack, in some cases, of teaching and high-level research personnel, brain drain and so on); and the financial resources available to absorb the potential number of students (countries with larger populations have fewer financial and energy resources and vice versa). Therefore, providing quality education becomes a matter of merit rather than elite status.[2] Thus, when discussing higher education in Arab countries, we should not forget the differences in a diverse world with different levels of education.

Today, in parallel with an urgently required improvement in educational levels, the educational systems of Arab countries are facing the new global challenges of the modern world. These include the rapid development of science and technology, the demands of the creation of knowledge societies, and the growing competition between increasingly multicultural and interdependent societies dominated by market forces. Such challenges require all the world's educational systems to adopt new roles and readjust their traditional missions.

In addition, our world is becoming ever more insecure and dangerous, due to the intensification of fanatical ideologies, nationalism and cultural and religious fundamentalism that increase the number of conflicts. These are multifaceted phenomena. Unfortunately, however, they are markedly polarized in terms of the West's relationship with the Arab world, which is united by Islam as a majority religion (though it coexists with minorities belonging to the other two monotheistic religions) and by Arab-Islamic culture.

In this context, and in the face of the fear inspired by the 'clash of civilizations' thesis of messianic Hegelian affinity, various figures, government institutions and

NGOs that defend values of multicultural coexistence and respect for difference, harmony and peace have mobilized in recent years in favour of intercultural dialogue. This highly topical desire for reflection and action has been reinforced by the Alliance of Civilizations[3] – a strategically important initiative that sees the current situation as a global phenomenon requiring both a global solution and the mobilization of all citizens. In addition, this global movement places special emphasis on the fundamental role of education.

The Alliance of Civilizations provides an excellent opportunity for higher education in general, and in the Arab world in particular, to join its initiative. This will enable higher education to highlight its prominent role in this area. It is important to underscore the perspectives provided by the *Universal Declaration on Cultural Diversity* and the Convention on the Protection and Promotion of the Diversity of Cultural Expressions adopted by UNESCO in 2001 and 2005, respectively.

Universities are, by definition, sites with multiple users; they are, in essence, areas for dialogue and for the exchange of ideas that are open to alterity, or 'otherness', and all that is universal. The Arab world knows this from experience, as in the past it created famous universities such as Al-Qarawiyin in Fez, Zitouna in Tunis and Al-Azahar in Cairo in the 8th, 9th and 10th centuries, respectively. This contributed to creating an international – or at least interregional – space devoted to developing knowledge, fostering intellectual curiosity, assessing ideas on the basis of their scientific merits, promoting ethical conduct, learning to respect diversity, understanding alterity, appreciating exchange and so on. Unfortunately, although the Arab world still has outstanding academic skills (sometimes developed outside its respective national borders), few Arab academic centres have managed to achieve the same level of excellence and fame in modern times.

In 1972, Arab education ministers agreed on the need to reform their educational systems. They decided to draw up an education strategy, known as the Development Strategy for Education in the Arab World, to achieve specific 'national and human goals'. To this end, they adopted 'Arab and Islamic culture, theories of education for training people and for preparing the society of the future'.[4] The challenges of globalization and the objectives of the UNESCO World Report produced by Jacques Delors (*Learning: The Treasure Within*)[5] were also taken into consideration in the Strategy.

The director general of the Arab League Educational, Cultural and Scientific Organization (ALECSO) explained that the Strategy formed part of the efforts of the Arab nation to 'form a new man … promote dialogue, mutual understanding and cooperation with a view to building Arab-Islamic civilization'; construct the society of the future; and promote prosperity, peace and justice for all.

The Strategy was also inspired by the principle in the Delors report of 'education for learning to live together', for 'developing an understanding of others, appreciating interdependence, carrying out joint projects, learning to manage conflicts, showing a spirit of respect for multiple values, mutual understanding and peace'.[6]

The Strategy took six years to draw up and the result was made public at the Khartoum conference in 1978, which became an important milestone for several countries in the region. It was updated between 2003 and 2004.

The Strategy consists of 12 fundamental principles: humanism, faith, patriotism, nationalism, development, education for democracy and human rights, education for science, education for work, education for life, education for strength and building, comprehensive education, and education for authenticity and innovation.[7]

The second principle concerns education for faith in God, in Islam and in other monotheistic religions. It prizes values such as virtue, love, mutual aid in defence of the truth and of good, and the brotherhood of all human beings.

The third and fourth principles are dealt with from a hierarchical perspective: firstly, individuals belong to their country; secondly, to the Arab nation; thirdly, to humankind as a whole. The sixth principle – education for democracy and human rights – is not stated explicitly and does not give rise to the desired development in this area.

The Strategy is of a highly general, not very pragmatic and non-urgent nature. It also seems introverted, oriented towards its own world and not much concerned with the need to reconcile the specific with the universal – 'plurality and shared citizenship', to use the phrase of Pérez de Cuéllar in the UNESCO World Report *Our Creative Diversity*.[8] Nevertheless, it reflects an undeniable desire for change – the real touchstone of the Strategy – and constitutes a general framework of reference for the various countries involved. Each country maintains complete freedom to implement the Strategy depending on political will, specific needs and the available human and financial resources.

Since 1981, in the framework of joint reflection on educational matters, a series of regional conferences has been organized on higher education and scientific research.[9] These focus on different topics: objectives, methods, syllabuses, specialities, internal and external assessment, implementation of the knowledge society, the quality of education, adaptation to market rules and so on. These topics have been approached from the perspective of renewal and adaptation to the new demands of the global context. However, approaches are always in accord with essential Arab values.

The regional conference held in Beirut in 1998 under the auspices of UNESCO was specific because it formed part of the international organization's wide-ranging activities aimed at defining basic principles for reforming higher education throughout the world. The topics discussed included contributions to major global issues, to the labour market, to economic development, to the requirements of the educational system, to scientific progress, to the quality of education, to regional and international cooperation and so on.

The Arab League Summit held in Riyadh in 2007 was an important event because it saw the approval of a document drawn up by ALECSO entitled the *Plan for Education, Higher Education and Scientific Research in the Arab World*. The fact that the Riyadh Declaration dedicates so much space to the topic is in itself unprecedented in the history of Arab summits. This illustrates the political leaders' great interest in redefining the function of Arab universities in the 21st century.

The document focuses on the new reality of the market – largely based on immaterial activities – that requires new multidisciplinary knowledge and new kinds of skills in order to achieve high-level productivity. Particular emphasis is placed on the need for reviewing courses, restructuring syllabuses, training teaching personnel appropriately and adapting better to the labour market. These matters were debated in the Fourth Arab Forum on Education in Amman, Jordan (24–25 April 2007).

The Strategy, as well as the declarations and recommendations of the different regional conferences on higher education and scientific research in the Arab world, show that the subject of the contribution of higher education and scientific research to multicultural coexistence is absent from the agendas of the institutional authorities. It is also absent from higher education sites in other parts of the world, as it is considered a political issue, rather than a strategic matter for academic debate and research.

Furthermore, the specialist literature includes only a few reports on action projects and declarations from meetings of experts on the matter.[10]

At the Council of Europe Ministerial Conference on intercultural education held in Athens in November 2003, the director general of ALECSO stated that 'the Arab world is also looking for ways that allow it to approach others ... to

replace the culture of hate and force with a culture of dialogue and reconciliation'.[11] He highlighted the desire to consolidate a conceptual framework through higher education and scientific research. In addition, he discussed exploring new tools for mutual knowledge and understanding that could help change perceptions and promote adaptation to the new demands of coexistence – 'living together' – in a multicultural world.

Nevertheless, there are only faint traces of some of these intentions in the programmes and actions. Apart from a few exceptions, not many mechanisms have been adopted to promote quality education; education in shared values; education for national and global citizenship; or education for dialogue (especially with those who have different convictions). Dialogue should be considered not as an end in itself but as a strategy for guaranteeing the required multicultural coexistence (both inside and beyond national borders and on an international scale). Such dialogue should not just be based on tolerance of others but also, above all, on enrichment through difference. Thus, education for dialogue is education for peace.

It is important to remember, for example, that only four universities in Arab countries (Jordan, Lebanon, Morocco and Palestine) are among the 62 universities from 42 countries that responded to the survey on education and intercultural dialogue in higher education, undertaken in 2004 by the International Association of Universities (IAU).

In this necessary and difficult task, the Arab world must fight simultaneously against stereotypes and disinformation regarding how they are perceived by others. The Arab world must regain control over its own image, without resorting to the often distorting lens of Orientalism (Edward Said, 1994).[12] This is an essential task that can only be carried out by means of endogenous scientific research.

Beyond the Arab world, the issue of multicultural coexistence must be central to any educational policy. Multicultural

coexistence is a major challenge for all educational systems in today's globalized world. Therefore, common policies and strategies need to be designed that are aimed at promoting and disseminating shared values among the members of the new multicultural community. The multiplier effect of higher education in this regard is considerable.

Salah Stétié, a Lebanese poet and diplomat, holds that 'Arabs, especially today, must integrate their Mediterranean (and, I would say, universal) dimension into their profound historical and religious background'.[13] They would thus be able to incorporate their regional concerns into a wider dimension, in accordance with the needs of today's globalized world.

In order to contribute to promoting multicultural coexistence, higher education in general must encourage a new kind of cooperation through inter-university networks, UNESCO chairs, national commissions for UNESCO, international and interregional associations, and intercultural and inter-institutional interlocutors at the interregional and international levels (ALECSO, the Islamic, Educational, Scientific and Cultural Organization (ISESCO), UNESCO, UNDP, Council of Europe, Euro-Mediterranean and Euro-Arab institutions and so on). The creation of an award for higher education institutions that excel in promoting multicultural coexistence could be a useful incentive.

Joint research is necessary to consolidate a conceptual framework, explore new analytical methods and seek new forms of knowledge, thought and action. It is also required to adapt to values themselves. It would also be helpful to create tools for understanding multiculturality and the numerous shared values that make it possible to benefit from enriching diversity and to promote coexistence and peace.

Furthermore, it is essential to thoroughly examine teaching materials, in order to remove all references contrary to these values.[14] Historical and religious subjects (not related to any dogma) must be approached from a more balanced perspective. The teaching of philosophy – a subject that is essential for fostering free thought, discovering alterity and deciphering the complexity of the world around us – should be made general in all countries. In Morocco, for example, the process of democratization was accompanied by the reinstatement of this subject.

Of course, in order to ensure the application of appropriate policies, strategies and mechanisms for promoting multicultural coexistence through higher education, it is necessary to raise the awareness of educators, researchers, high-level political leaders and institution directors so that they incorporate these matters into their respective agendas.

The failure of the various 'models' for integrating immigrant populations – basically from Arab-Islamic culture – into European countries has given rise to intense debate. The main concern consists of promoting harmonious multicultural coexistence by means of specific solutions aimed at remedying the negative consequences of multiculturalism in the different societies, and at making diversity a source of enrichment rather than conflict.

The Council of Europe (mainly through its Steering Committee for Higher Education and Research (CDESR)) considers that higher education can play an essential role in this matter – not only in the European Union countries but also in the whole of the Euro-Mediterranean region. The project launched in this area is based on a novel vision oriented towards action and the development of specific teaching tools. It also places great importance on regional cooperation, especially with the Arab world.

Taking as a reference the fundamental values of human rights and democracy and the principles stated in the Convention on the Protection and Promotion of the Diversity of Cultural Expressions (2005), and with a nod to the United Nations Alliance of Civilizations initiative, in 2005, the Council of Europe approved a plan of action and a statement on a strategy for developing intercultural dialogue.[15] Within this framework, it launched a pilot project, 'Universities as Sites of Citizenship', and declared 2008 the European Year of Intercultural Dialogue.

Thus, we consider that developing similar programmes and actions within the European Union and in cooperation with other regions, with special emphasis on the Arab world, could contribute to counteracting the idea of the clash of civilizations and help to bring about a world of harmony, stability and peace.

The problem of multicultural coexistence therefore provides interesting perspectives in favour of fruitful international cooperation for universities and research centres.[16] This will enable the entire academic world to contribute effectively to the creation of a world in which there is greater understanding, harmony and peace, to the benefit of the human family, which, after all, shares one destiny. This world will only be possible if we turn towards the mixing of cultures, multicultural coexistence and the universal.

NOTES

1   cf. ALECSO (2006) *Stratégie de développement de l'éducation dans le monde arabe* (updated). Tunis, p. 37; and the UNDP (2006) Report on the Arab World.
2   Federico Mayor Zaragoza (1998), Regional Arab Conference on Higher Education, Beirut.
3   cf. Kristina Kausch and Isaías Barreñada (2005) (eds) *Alianza de civilizaciones, seguridad internacional y democracia cosmopolita.* Madrid: Complutense, Colección Estudios Internacionales.
4   Stratégie de développement de l'éducation dans le monde arabe, op. cit., p. 8.
5   World Report produced by Jacques Delors (1996) *Learning: The Treasure Within: Report to UNESCO of the International Commission on Education for the Twenty-first Century: Highlights.* Paris: UNESCO, 11 April.
6   *Stratégie de développement de l'éducation dans le monde arabe*, op. cit., p. 16.
7   Ibid., pp. 76–84.
8   cf. World Report produced by Pérez de Cuéllar (1996) *Our Creative Diversity.* Paris: UNESCO, p. 78.
9   The following is a list of the regional conferences on higher education held in the Arab world to date: Algiers 1981, Tunis 1983, Baghdad 1985, Damascus 1989, Benghazi 1991, Algiers 1999, Riyadh 1999, Beirut 2000, Cairo 2001, Damascus 2003, Sanaa 2005. The next conference is scheduled for late 2007 in Beirut.
10 cf. the Council of Europe Ministerial Conference on intercultural education, held in Athens, November 2003; *L'édu-cation et le dialogue interculturel dans l'enseignement supérieur*, seminar by experts from the IAU, Budapest, November 2004; *Statement on the Contribution of Higher Education to Intercultural Dialogue*, Council of Europe. (2006) http://www.coe.int/t/dg4/highereducation/News/Intercultural%20dialogue_EN.pdf.
11 cf. the interview with Director General Mongi Bousnina, at www.coe.int, Council of Europe.
12 Said, Edward (1994) *The Politics of Dispossession.* New York: Random House.
13 cf. 'Regards croisés Europe-monde arabe: l'indispensable dialogue'. In: *Dialogue interculturel: fondement du partenariat euroméditerranéen.* Lisbon: Multitema, 1999, p. 15.
14 For example: the meeting organized in Lyon in 2005 by UNESCO, the Council of Europe and ALECSO, with the participation of several Arab and European countries; the cycle of comparative studies of school manuals carried out within the framework of Euro-Arab dialogue by the French and Moroccan commissions for UNESCO in 2005 and 2006; the conference on school manuals '*Penser et construire la paix à travers une conception innovatrice du manuel scolaire*', UNESCO, 23–24 June 2007, with the participation of several Arab and European countries, as well as ALECSO.
15 cf. the 3rd Summit of Heads of State and Government, Warsaw, 16–17 May 2005 and the Council of Europe Ministerial Conference, Faro, 27–28 October 2005.
16 cf. '*L'éducation, une passerelle pour le dialogue euro-arabe?*', in *Prospects. A quarterly review of comparative education.* 33(128) December 2003. UNESCO-IBE

Higher education and its institutions and the civilizational paradigm crisis: Reflections, analysis and proposals from the perspective of a forum of international civil society organizations

Josep Xercavins i Valls

PERSONAL CONTEXT

Some years ago, as a university lecturer, I had the opportunity to reflect on the various topics relating to higher education (HE) and higher education institutions (HEIs) that are the subject of this report at events such as the 1998 UNESCO Conference (Xercavins, 1999). Notwithstanding this, I have decided to write this paper without reverting to that context and those reflections and to resort instead to more recent experiences. Since 2000, I have worked at the World Forum for Civil Society Networks (www.ubuntu.upc.edu), which basically comprises international NGOs; it is in this context that I have developed my thoughts on the aforementioned matters. The Forum's slogan is 'To make another world possible, let us reform our international institutions' (www.reformcampaign.net). I would like my paper to reflect as closely as possible the thoughts that the aims and topics of this report inspire in me. Thus, I shall go beyond the everyday to consider deep-seated concerns.

CIVILIZATIONAL CRISIS, ABSENCE OF A PARADIGM AND THE MULTIFACETED NATURE OF THE PROBLEM

What worldview shapes my thoughts and, as a result, my deliberations and proposals?

Some of the characteristics by which we may identify this new civilizational paradigm crisis are the magnitude (which is both quantitative and qualitative) and, in particular, the speed, acceleration and interrelation of the changes occurring as a result of new scientific knowledge (stemming from the fields of physics and biology in the 20th century, but which has not yet been fully assimilated in philosophical terms). These characteristics lead us to make tentative attempts to deal with and interpret this new model, for which, at the moment, we lack the necessary depth and *enlightenment* as regards complexity and uncertainty.

Another characteristic of this moment in history is the multifaceted nature of the crisis and the absence of role models. I am sure that this report will enlighten us as to other dimensions of the crisis (development, economics, governance, society, higher education and ideology, for example) that require a new paradigm of interpretation, analysis and proposition.

IN THIS CONTEXT, WHAT SHOULD HEIs BE AIMING FOR?

From my political and ideological standpoint, the ultimate, all-encompassing aim of HEIs is to be centres for the generation and transmission of knowledge that function in the service of society. They should be able to throw off the shackles of established (and, as far as our hypothesis is concerned, obsolete) models and invest their energies and assets in developing new guidelines for interpretation, new methodologies for analysis and proposition and new *settings* in which new paradigms may be born. These new paradigms will enable us to understand and help us to shape (this point is explained in more detail in the next section) and *shed light* on the new, emerging civilizational reality.

In this context, the practical autonomy of HEIs to define their mission, vision and strategy beyond short-term, sectorial or specific interests, such as those that are strictly economistic (this point is also developed further in the next section), must be recovered if the proposed aim is to be achieved.

I would like to make a final point, a fine one but one which may well be revealing: let us rechannel the energy that young lecturers and researchers invest in competing against each another in their academic careers (which in fact works *against* them) so that, being less conditioned by outdated models, they can spend their most vital years in *bringing to light* the best they have to offer.

Box 1 A new world crisis without precedent

I share the view held by analysts (Burcet, 1997) who claim that the quantitative and qualitative levels of discontinuous changes in scale (which are in general related to exponential growth at the stage at which the curve is steepest) with regard to a multitude of phenomena and phenomenologies (world population, world economy, environmental imbalances, social imbalances, knowledge and skills in science and technology, physical and virtual communication skills and so on) are comparable, as a kind of macro-state, with the great revolutions in ways of living that have taken place on Earth, such as the agricultural and industrial revolutions from which new civilizational realities (in the most common and historicist meaning of the expression) have arisen.

All these revolutions, in the most Kuhnian (Kuhn, 1975) sense of the word – including, if the hypothesis is true, the one that we are at present undergoing – constitute a civilizational paradigm shift away from *what came before* those revolutions or paradigm crises, and give way to a highly significant period in which there is no basic explanatory archetype for the new, emerging civilizational macro-state and reality.

This period is characterized by society's and particularly HEIs' efforts to *shatter the corpus built upon the old ideas*, in a vain attempt to continue analysing and explaining reality from a *pre-crisis standpoint*.

The present revolution, like those before it, is undergoing a period of confusion and suffering from an obvious and real inability to respond to the great challenges posed, with the added problem that the feeling of frustration and even of decline is – although logical and natural – a handicap that must also be overcome.

CONCERNING OTHER POSSIBLE WORLDS: FUTURE PERSPECTIVES AND ACTION

One of the most popular movements initiated at the start of this century in 2001 is the World Social Forum (Porto Alegre, Mumbai, Nairobi and so on) and the well-known slogan 'Another world is possible', which offers an alternative vision to the status quo.

In the framework of ideas put forward in the preceding section, this slogan reflects the idea of 'a crisis in terms of what went before' but positions itself, in political and ideological terms, as 'a crisis in terms of the situation as it stands', in terms of the current world which we wish was different, particularly since the emergence of neo-liberal economic globalization. *It is a slogan denoting crisis* and a positive affirmation of the will to find a satisfactory way out of this crisis (although the way has only been vaguely sketched out in terms that are negative or contrary to the current situation, which is characterized by multiple or multidimensional situations, generally related to the aforementioned type of globalization). However, it is not *a phrase denoting a paradigm shift* as such, but simply a phrase revealing a desire for change and expressing the political and ideological will to achieve it.

It is certainly true to say that another world is possible, particularly in political and ideological terms. There is no determinist theory obliging us to think that the world in which we live must be as it is, at the very least in ideological terms.

However, the issue is more complex than that. In my opinion, and in keeping with the discussion in the preceding section, the heart of the matter lies in the fact that at present the civilizational paradigm crisis we are undergoing is a (Kuhnian) revolutionary crisis, which as such, if the hypothesis is correct, sheds light on *a different world*, or, in other words, on *another possible world*, and will continue to do so. From this perspective, we should point out, therefore, that it is not so much that another world is

possible – except in the aforementioned political–ideological sense – but rather that this other world is already coming to light. The problem is that, in the absence of clear determinist indicators, we do not know what this other world will be like, or, most importantly, whether it will be what we were hoping for or altogether undesirable.

Clearly, this change is not independent of or alien to the actions of humankind now and in the future. Therefore, it would be wise to bear in mind that (a) another world is coming into being, and we are beginning to see it, (b) *this other world may take a number of different forms* and (c) *the world that we end up with* will be the result of the uncertain evolution of a complex system, of which humankind is a subsystem (hereinafter I shall be referring to the *human subsystem*) that drives and shapes this evolution. As such, it is one of the most important and decisive of these subsystems.

It is on this last point that the two levels of analysis described – that which foresees a shift in the world's civilizational paradigm and that which, in political and ideological terms, prescribes and formulates this shift in terms of making what is desirable possible – come together, converge and establish dialectical contact.

This last statement leads me to consider another point that is also fundamental. Hypothetically perceiving a civilizational paradigm shift allows and obliges us to carry out prospective work. As mentioned, if a revolutionary civilizational paradigm crisis casts light on a different world that may take on a number of guises, then it is essential to analyse what these possible scenarios, these possible other worlds, might be, particularly from the perspective of the role that the human subsystem's actions would have played and will play in *making these other worlds possible*. This is especially important if, from the perspective of the human subsystem's political and ideological will and action, we wish the result of the change to be (a) the building and

implementing of a framework of prospectivist action that contributes to *shaping, guiding and governing* this other world, and (b) the other possible world that we wish for and have explicitly been working towards.

Let us not forget that a lack of foresight and action, which in prospectivist terms is known as a business-as-usual scenario, would make the revolutionary civilizational change much more *open-ended*. As much as I hold the phrase 'Another world is possible' to be true, I repeat, there is not just one other possible world but many. The positions and initiatives taken by society in favour of or against this or that other world will shape the results of this change and will be essential to *ascertaining which of the various possible worlds will come into being*. As I write, in a spirit of enlightened pessimism, I can see similarities between many of the changes that have been made possible by science and technology, which are undesirable from an ideological perspective, and Aldous Huxley's vision in *A Brave New World*.

IN THIS CONTEXT, WHAT SHOULD HEIs BE AIMING FOR?

It is very important for HEIs to become, consciously and intentionally, analysts of the big changes that are happening and of possible initiatives in shaping, anticipating, intervening in and guiding these changes towards another possible world. What other world? For me, the only desirable world is one that is more human, fairer, more equitable, more peaceful, more diverse, more compassionate and more sustainable, although its ultimate definition and ideological conception is beyond the scope of this report, as I understand it.

This prospectivist, scientific endeavour is, I feel, a duty inherent to the history and future of HEIs. (See the Hawaii Research Center for Future Studies at http://www.futures.hawaii.edu/index.php.) Furthermore, this endeavour should be as clear as possible, in social terms, so that it sparks debate, raises awareness and leads the human subsystem to position itself and take political and ideological action in the face of the existing problems.

This is the role that a political activist, in a globally organized civil society, would expect of HEIs serving the interests of humankind, which is now facing the greatest challenges since the beginnings of life on Earth.

THE ECONOMIC GROWTH PARADIGM CRISIS AND HIGHER EDUCATION AND ITS INSTITUTIONS

As is well known, but also often forgotten, the ultimate aim of the economy is to distribute and allocate resources to satisfy human needs, which is something we cannot – and of course should not – dismiss. In this text I shall refer to this aim, as the basic economic fact.

Which, how many and whose human needs are to be met has much to do with the human development model that we take to be socially desirable. The options for this model are closely related to each other, as well as being incompatible with the economic model followed by the basic economic fact, particularly when it comes to allocating resources.

In any case, in the context of this basic economic fact resources are always scarce. Most of those extracted from the Earth are progressively running out, and certainly in the medium term they are unlikely to be supplemented by the conquest of other parts of the solar system. Human needs are always unlimited, especially for some, who are now paying to travel in space, perhaps to experience the nocturnal darkness cloaking poverty on Earth.

If this were not enough, we also know and can be ever more sure of the fact that the economic growth model is based on unsustainable trends of production and consumption that are exhausting the world's resources and that, because of the waste that is inevitably generated (according to the second law of thermodynamics), this is having a high impact on our habitat and, above all, on the life of the numerous species, including ours, that are alive on planet Earth.

IN THIS CONTEXT, WHAT SHOULD HE AND HEIs BE AIMING FOR?

If I had to give priority to a single one of the challenges facing HE and HEIs, it would be the construction of a paradigm other than an economistic one or one of economic growth. The theoretical and practical efforts and the changes in values at many levels that this would require, the new concept of human development which would have to free itself from its economistic ties – in short, all the changes that the construction of a new paradigm would entail – are so paradigmatic (in the Kuhnian sense given to the term here) that they would involve moving from the industrial age or the age of *economics* to an era of intangible, immaterial *knowledge* and of equity and *solidarity* in the use and distribution of resources – two aims which are inextricably linked.

This change in paradigm that HE and HEIs must face is so important that it includes changes in other paradigms such as (in order of importance) the sustainability paradigm (see Box 3) and the neo-liberal paradigm (on which I will not elaborate further, given that I am sure there will be more in-depth analyses of this in this report).

GLOBALIZATION, THE CRISES OF INTERNATIONAL MULTILATERAL ORGANIZATIONS AND STATE SOVEREIGNTY, WORLD DEMOCRATIC GOVERNANCE AND HE AND HEIs

If, despite the *uncertainty* and *difficulties* inherent in analysis in the current age, we were to use a single word and concept to

Box 2 The basic economic fact – is it being met?

In any event, the economic growth paradigm is only one of many models or systems for allocating and distributing resources that can drive the basic economic fact discussed here. However, at this crucial point, we must once and for all realize that there is no *natural law or constitution drawn up by man* that obliges us to function according to this paradigm or model of economic growth.

The capitalist model (I would like to stress the fact that real communism followed the same model, except in the case of the ownership of the means of production, and that I am therefore not alluding to other ideological debates that would be outside the scope of this paper) needs economic growth entailing the accumulation of wealth by a few who apply a merely economistic activity regardless of their direct social interest. Essentially, through the creation of paid human employment, these few theoretically end up redistributing wealth and therefore make it possible for certain human needs to be met, in our globalized world, for humanity as a whole.

However, because economic growth increasingly relies on, first, high levels of consumption by an increasingly small minority whose income levels continue to rise (the world's wealthiest) and, second, greater productivity (per product unit and per producer unit), directly related to neo-liberal economic globalization (again, something which is outside the scope of this paper), it is leading to an ever more deficient redistribution of the wealth produced during, and as a result of, this growth.

Indeed, the current levels resulting from the creation of paid employment, in relation to the working population and particularly the economic growth achieved, places this economic growth paradigm in dispute purely because of socioeconomic factors that are internal to the model. According to the International Labour Organization (ILO, 2007), the global unemployment rate was 5.6% of the active population in 1993 and 6.3% in 2006. In conjunction with the sustained growth of the world's GDP in the past decade, at around 4.1%, the corresponding ratio of employment to the working population has decreased by more than one percentage point.

Thus it goes without saying that the growing abyss between the richest (who are fewer and fewer in number) and the poorest (who are ever more numerous), in addition to the world poverty rates that we know so well, are pressing us to acknowledge the fact that, with the current model, the main aim of the basic economic fact – that is, to meet the needs of humanity as a whole – is not being achieved.

The sustainability paradigm is a revealing example of thought on paradigmatic topics (previous paradigm, paradigm in crisis, new paradigm and so on) and particularly of the problems that, in the process of change, these topics can entail.

Without doubt, the *sustainability* paradigm is one of the first *clear, recognizable* components of the new *corpus constructo* of the civilizational change in which we are immersed. It is also an interesting *part of the new paradigm* that has been, up until now, engulfed by outdated paradigms that mask it, render it useless and prevent it from gaining a foothold and advancing.

I have on other occasions said that it is an insult to the planet Earth and its species to talk of sustainable growth and not sustainable development (Xercavins, 2001). However, this reality (which Europe in its entirety *claims* to be moving towards) in essence entails the capture or radical absorption of the *dangerous* emerging paradigm by the outdated, but nevertheless still dominant, paradigm of economic growth. This is why, I insist, the priority objective of HE and HEIs that I have discussed above is so important. Although there are of course many more things that need doing, only by placing the economic growth paradigm in a state of crisis will we finally allow the sustainability paradigm to emerge.

---

characterize the great revolution in which we are immersed, the human ways of life on Earth and the new civilizational reality that is emerging, that word would undoubtedly be 'globalization' and the concept would in principle be that of a 'global world', although these terms are also shrouded in uncertainty.

It is precisely this point that I will be exploring in the final section of this paper. The aforementioned changes in scale in almost all spheres of life and, as part of this, the *incommensurable leap* from the local to the global (and vice versa, which has far-reaching implications), include an added dimension of the civilizational paradigm crisis considered here, a dimension which is fundamental and has an identity of its own: that of politics and present-day political systems and institutions.

Throughout history, politics has always lagged behind dynamic change, and continues to do so, regulating and acting retrospectively. Clearly, we find ourselves in a situation in which politics is *lagging behind* globalization. This is particularly so at the global scale. Current politics is designed for, and was effective at, the scale of the nation-state, and of course within it. The world's division into nation-states was completed with decolonization after the Second World War (although many of these states do not in any way match the national model that emerged as a result of the French Revolution), and the relations between states have shaped international politics (between countries) since then. International multilateral organizations (organizations of states and not institutions with their own political power beyond those states) made up (and still do?) the playing field of international politics.

However, if the basic premises of this article are correct, the reality of globalization far surpasses this system of international organizations and international politics, places it in a state of crisis and radically decreases its effectiveness.

Large international corporations (and their perpetual delocalization and physical movement, in addition to virtual financial operations on a global scale) and the grand new themes and challenges facing humankind at this moment (the environment, information and communication, among others) operate beyond borders and therefore cannot be governed (in the sense of politics governing the economic and social spheres of life and human relations) by the actors (countries) and their organizations (present-day international organizations) that have been conceived and created within the old but still prevalent political paradigm.

On more than one occasion (see http://www.ubuntu.upc.edu/index.php?lg=eng&pg=2&ncom=22), I have used the following fact as an example of this: the USA is fully entitled, by international law, not to comply with the Kyoto protocol. It is precisely when what is illegitimate and extraordinarily dangerous to humanity is, under present-day conditions, legal that legislation must change. Clearly, the current model of international politics is in a profound state of crisis and in need of in-depth reform, although much of this reform cannot take place within the current paradigmatic framework. The reform should contain and above all facilitate, in a dynamic way, changes in paradigm that would allow governance in the future.

In this context, to cite just one example, state sovereignty, a basic principle and fundamental paradigm of the United Nations as it emerged after the Second World War, should give way to new (and/or reformed) international institutions dealing with world democracy and governability. At least in certain spheres (those of global public assets such as the environment and cultural diversity and global public evils such as international crime) this sovereignty should move to a global political scale on which it is possible to legislate (democratically, of course) with universally enforceable effects.

IN THIS CONTEXT, WHAT SHOULD HEIs BE AIMING FOR?

Despite their internal logic and common sense, the above statements are extremely distasteful to the political status quo. Therefore, only constructive and analytical agents who are revolutionary (in the sense employed here) in their propositions can and should oppose it.

I do not believe there is a more ideal space-time than now for HEIs and their networks, if they are required to and, above all, if they allocate time to it, to take this road, which may be perilous but is the only way forward.

Fortunately, for once there is no need to start from scratch, because various thinkers were ahead of their time and traced this path clearly. Kant, Russell and others saw humanity as a whole that considers and governs itself, because as a whole it interacts in a complex way with its parts, with our planet and with the future of both. This so-called globalized world has a magical connection to the other globalized world that many of us are currently walking towards, in order to make the other world we wish for possible.

REFERENCES

Burcet , Josep (1997) *Ingeniería de Intangibles*. Valencia, Spain: Germania.

ILO (2007) *Global Employment Trends*. Short report . Geneva: ILO, January.

Kuhn, Thomas S. (1975) *The structure of scientific revolutions*. Mexico: Fondo de Cultura Económica.

Xercavins, Josep (1999) Mobilitzant els poders dels 'sabers' and Los retos de la Educación Superior en el siglo XXI, la globalización y los nuevos objetivos-misión formativos e investigadores de las universidades. *Sostenible?* Barcelona, Spain: the UNESCO Chair at UPC in Technology, Sustainable Development, Imbalance and Global Change, March.

Xercavins, Josep (2001) ¿De qué hablamos cuando hablamos de desarrollo sostenible? *La Vanguardia*, 25 November.

I.3

GLOBALIZATION AND MARKETS: CHALLENGES FOR HIGHER EDUCATION

Deepak Nayyar

Abstract

The object of this paper is to reflect upon the intersection of, and explore the interconnections between, globalization and higher education. It outlines the essential characteristics of globalization, with an analysis of its dimensions and implications (in particular, exclusion). It shows that, over the past three decades, globalization has been associated with uneven development and asymmetrical consequences for both countries and people. This sets the stage in the wider context of development. The paper then develops an analytical framework to consider how globalization relates to and influences the world of higher education. It argues that the retreat of the state and the advance of the market have changed the national context, and that the spread of markets is beginning to exercise a significant influence on higher education. There are inherent dangers to such commercialization, but there are also some opportunities to learn from markets. This paper also shows that the gathering momentum of globalization, which has changed the international context, is beginning to reshape higher education. The associated globalization of education has major positive and negative implications for development. Markets and globalization together could transform the world of higher education. However, education as business, particularly in universities, is not conducive to economic development and social progress. Therefore, countries should formulate policies for higher education in the pursuit of development, so as to minimize the dangers and capture the opportunities created by markets and globalization.

INTRODUCTION

The spread of education in society is at the foundations of success in countries that are latecomers to development. The most striking examples in recent history are the success stories in East Asia that are now perceived as role models. Education is both a means and an end. It is a means of raising levels of productivity and mobilizing the most abundant resource in economies – labour – for the purpose of development. It is an end in so far as it makes a basic contribution to improving the quality of life for people as individuals and for society at large. The essence of development, after all, is the well-being of humankind. Development must therefore provide ordinary people with the rights, opportunities and capabilities they need to exercise their own choices for a decent life. Education is critical in every dimension. The relative importance of its components may change over time: from primary education and adult literacy to vocational education, higher education, technical education or professional education. Nevertheless, investing in human beings is always important, at every stage of development. The returns to society may accrue after a time lag but are always high. In the quest for development, primary education is absolutely essential because it creates the base. Higher education is just as important, however, for it provides the cutting edge. And universities are the lifeblood of higher education. Islands of excellence in professional education or scientific research are valuable complements but cannot replace universities, which provide educational opportunities for people at large. Such broad-based higher education alone creates capabilities at a micro level that provide the foundations of development at the macro level. This is, perhaps, among the most important lessons to emerge from the experience of latecomers to industrialization during the 20th century.[1]

In reflecting on the future at this conjuncture, it is imperative to recognize that globalization and markets are not only shaping the process of development everywhere, but are also transforming the world of higher education at a pace that would have been difficult to imagine just two decades ago. The retreat of the state and the advance of the market have changed the national context, while the spread of markets is beginning to exercise a significant influence on higher education. At the same time, the gathering momentum of globalization, which has changed the international context, is beginning to reshape higher education. Markets and globalization together have the potential to bring about profound changes in higher education, which could be negative or positive, but education as a business concern cannot be conducive to development. The object of this paper is to reflect upon the intersection of, and explore the interconnections between, globalization and higher education in prospect, rather than retrospect, situated in the wider context of development.

The structure of this paper is as follows. The first section outlines the essential characteristics of globalization, with an analysis of its dimensions and implications (in particular, exclusion) to set the stage. The second section considers the development experience of the world economy during the last quarter of the 20th century to show that globalization is associated with uneven development and asymmetrical consequences for both countries and people. The third section develops an analytical framework to consider how globalization relates to, or influences, the world of higher education. The fourth section examines what globalization means for higher education in different spheres, with some reference to the implications of markets and commercialization for universities. The fifth section focuses on the globalization of higher education and discusses its consequences for both people and education in the development process. In conclusion, the final section addresses a question that is simple enough to pose but difficult to answer: what is to be done?

GLOBALIZATION: DIMENSIONS AND IMPLICATIONS

Globalization means different things to different people. What is more, the word globalization is used in two ways, which is a source of some confusion. It is used in a *positive* sense to *describe* a process of integration into the world economy, and in a *normative* sense to *prescribe* a strategy of development based on a rapid integration with the world economy.

Even its characterization, however, is by no means uniform. It can be described, simply, as an expansion of economic activities across national boundaries. There are three economic manifestations of this phenomenon – international trade, international investment and international finance – which also constitute its cutting edge. But there is much more to globalization. It is about the expansion of economic transactions and the organization of economic activities across the political boundaries of nation-states. More precisely, it can be defined as a process associated with increasing economic openness, growing economic interdependence and deepening economic integration in the world economy.

Economic *openness* is not simply confined to trade flows, investment flows and financial flows. It also extends to flows of services, technology, information and ideas across national boundaries. But the cross-border movement of people is closely regulated and highly restricted. Economic *interdependence* is asymmetrical. There is a high degree of interdependence among countries in the industrialized world. There is considerable dependence of developing countries on industrialized countries. There is much less interdependence among countries in the developing world. Economic *integration* straddles national boundaries as liberalization has diluted the significance of borders in economic transactions. It is, in part, an integration of markets (for goods, services, technology, financial assets and even money) on the demand side, and, in part, an integration of production (horizontal and vertical) on the supply side.

The gathering momentum of globalization has brought about profound changes in the world economy, which are clearly reflected in its three important dimensions: trade, investment and finance.[2] The second half of the 20th century witnessed a phenomenal expansion in international trade flows. Consequently, an increasing proportion of world output entered into world trade. The share of world exports in world gross domestic product (GDP) rose from 6% in 1950 to 14.3% in 1975 and 20.2% in 2000. For the industrialized countries, this proportion increased from 13.6% in 1975 to 16.7% in 2000. For the developing countries, this proportion increased from 17.5% in 1975 to 31.2% in 2000. The story is almost the same for international investment flows. The stock of foreign direct investment in the world, as a proportion of world output, increased from 4.4% in 1960 to 6.1% in 1980 and 20% in 2000. Over the same period, world foreign direct investment flows as a proportion of world gross fixed capital formation rose from 1.1% in 1960 to 2.3% in 1980 and 22% in 2000. The growth in international finance has been explosive – so much so that, in terms of magnitudes, trade and investment are now dwarfed by finance. The expansion of international banking is phenomenal. The international market for financial assets has experienced similar growth. There is a growing international market for government bonds. The size of international foreign exchange markets is staggering. Global foreign exchange transactions have soared – from US$60 billion per day in 1983 to US$1.49 trillion per day in 1998. By comparison, in 1997, world GDP was US$82 billion per day and world exports were US$15 billion per day, while the foreign exchange reserves of all central banks put together were US$1.55 trillion.

Such aggregates do not reveal that the spread of globalization is uneven. The exclusion of people and countries from the process is a fact of life. Consider some figures, for 2000, on international trade, international investment and international finance, which constitute the cutting edge of globalization.[3] Industrialized countries accounted for 64% of world exports, while developing countries accounted for 32% and transitional economies for the remaining 4%. Industrialized countries accounted for 82% of foreign direct investment inflows in the world economy, whereas developing countries accounted for 16% and transitional economies for the remaining 2%. Industrialized countries accounted for 95% of cross-border mergers and acquisitions in terms of purchases, whereas developing countries accounted for just 4% and transitional economies for a mere 1%.

This sharp divide between rich and poor countries is no surprise, but the spread of globalization is just as uneven within the developing world. No more than a dozen developing countries are an integral part of the globalization process: Argentina, Brazil and Mexico in Latin America; and China, Hong Kong, India, Indonesia, South Korea, Malaysia, Singapore, Taiwan and Thailand in Asia. During the 1990s, these countries accounted for 70% of total exports from the developing world and 75% of manufactured exports from the developing world, absorbed almost 72% of foreign direct investment flows to the developing world and received about 90% of foreign portfolio investment flows to the developing world.[4] Countries in sub-Saharan Africa and West Asia are simply not in the picture, and many countries in Latin America, South Asia and the Asia-Pacific region are left out altogether. The exclusion of the least developed countries, everywhere in the world, is almost complete.

The exclusion of poor countries and people extends beyond trade, investment and finance, in so far as their access to globalization is exceedingly limited in terms of communication and technology. Indeed, the excluded are barely connected with the globalized world. For example, in 2000, the distribution of internet access was most unequal: of the world's internet users, 75.8% were in the industrialized countries, 18.4% were in Asia, just 4.6% were in Latin America and the Caribbean, and a mere 1.2% were in Africa.[5] Similarly, in 1999, the access to telecommunications systems was most unequal: there were 100–125 telephone lines per 100 inhabitants in the countries of the Organisation for Economic Cooperation and Development (OECD) compared with 25 telephone lines per 100 inhabitants in the rest of the world. The difference was much greater in other modes. In the OECD countries, for every 100 people, the number of personal computers ranged from 25 to 30 while the number of mobile phones ranged from 20 to 40. In the rest of the world, the number of personal computers and mobile phones per 100 people was less than 5.[6] These are averages for the non-OECD world. Obviously, such access

was probably far less in most developing countries and minimal in the least developed countries.

Globalization has, indeed, created opportunities for some people and countries that were not even dreamed of three decades ago. But it has also introduced new risks, if not threats, for many others. It has been associated with the deepening of poverty and the accentuation of inequalities. The distribution of benefits and costs is unequal. There are some winners: more in rich countries than in poor countries. There are many losers: numerous both in rich countries and poor countries.[7] It is perhaps necessary to identify, in broad categories, the winners and the losers. The asset-owners, profit-earners, rentiers, the educated, the mobile and people with professional, managerial or technical skills are the winners, whereas the asset-less, the wage-earners, the debtors, the uneducated, the immobile, the semi-skilled and the unskilled are the losers.[8]

At the same time, globalization has introduced a new dimension to the exclusion of people from development. Exclusion is no longer simply about the inability to satisfy basic human needs in terms of food, clothing, shelter, healthcare and education for large numbers of people. It is much more complicated. The consumption patterns and lifestyles of the rich associated with globalization have powerful demonstration effects. People everywhere, even the poor and the excluded, are exposed to these consumption possibility frontiers because electronic media have spread the consumer message far and wide. This creates both expectations and aspirations. But the simple fact of life is that those who do not have the incomes cannot buy goods and services in the market. Thus, when the paradise of consumerism is unattainable – which is the case for common people – it only creates frustration or alienation. The reaction of people who experience such exclusion differs. Some seek short cuts to the consumerist paradise through drugs, crime or violence. Some seek refuge in ethnic identities, cultural chauvinism or religious fundamentalism. Such traditional or indigenous values are often the only thing that poor people can assert to bring identity and meaning to their lives. Outcomes do not always take these extreme forms, but globalization inevitably tends to erode social stability.[9] Thus, economic integration with the outside world may accentuate social tensions or provoke social fragmentation within countries.

In this context, it is essential to recognize that economics provides a critical but limited perspective on globalization, which is a multidimensional phenomenon. It extends far beyond the economy to polity and society. It would be no exaggeration to say that the whole is different from, and possibly greater than, the sum total of its parts. The multiple dimensions – political, social and cultural – deserve mention, even if briefly.

In the political dimension, the momentum of globalization is such that the power of national governments is being reduced through incursions into hitherto sovereign economic or political space, without a corresponding increase in effective international cooperation or supranational government to regulate or govern this market-driven process.[10] Simply put, there is a mismatch between economies that are global and polities that are national or local.[11]

In the social dimension, a market economy may be seen as a necessary and indeed desirable attribute of globalization, but the creation of a market society may not be a desirable outcome. If the pursuit of material well-being becomes a dominant and, for some, exclusive objective, then the culture of materialism or simply the quest for money might spread into all spheres of life. A reasonable utilitarianism could then be transformed into Narcissist hedonism. The norms and values that are the foundations of civil society, in which individuals have an obligation to society, could be eroded. Social norms and social institutions, so essential for the market economy itself, could be weakened.

In the cultural dimension, the global spread of cultural impulses is at least as important as that of economic impulses. Youth culture in cities everywhere, across the world, is globalized, as manifested in jeans, T-shirts, sneakers, jogging, fast food, pop music, Hollywood movies, satellite television, 24/7 news channels, the internet and so on. Consumerism is indeed global. Even corruption and crime have become similar everywhere. The communications revolution and the electronic media have played a key role in all this. But modernity and tradition do not always mesh together, and this could plant seeds of conflict in societies. What is more, the homogenization of culture associated with globalization is not desirable, for cultural diversity is as important as biodiversity.

GLOBALIZATION: CONSEQUENCES FOR DEVELOPMENT

The globalization process, which gathered momentum during the last quarter of the 20th century, has brought about profound changes in the international context. It could have far-reaching implications for development. The reality that has unfolded so far, however, belies the expectations of ideologues. The development experience of the world economy from the early 1970s to the early 2000s, which could be termed the age of *globalization*, provides cause for concern, particularly when compared with the period from the late 1940s to the early 1970s, which has been described as the *golden age of capital-*

ism. Any such periodization is obviously arbitrary, but it serves an analytical purpose.[12]

Growth did not accelerate. It slowed down. During the 1960s, the average growth rate of world GDP per capita was 3.5% per annum. Deceleration set in thereafter. The average growth rate of world GDP per capita was 2.1% per annum during the 1970s, 1.3% per annum during the 1980s and 1% per annum during the 1990s.[13] This growth was more volatile than in the past, particularly in the developing world.[14] It was also unevenly distributed across countries. Between 1985 and 2000, the growth in GDP per capita was negative in 23 developing countries, 0.2% per annum in 14 developing countries, 1.2% per annum in 20 developing countries, 2.2% per annum in 12 developing countries, and more than 5% per annum in just 16 developing countries. Over the same period, growth in GDP per capita was negative in 17 transition countries and 1.8% per annum in 22 industrialized countries.

Available figures suggest divergence, rather than convergence, in income levels between countries and between people. Economic inequalities increased in the late 20th century as the income gap widened between rich and poor countries, between the rich and the poor in the world's population, and also between rich and poor people within countries. The ratio of GDP per capita in the 20 richest countries to GDP per capita in the poorest 20 countries of the world rose from 54:1 during the period 1960–1962 to 121:1 during the period 2000–2002.[15] The income gap between people has also widened over time. The ratio of the average GNP per capita in the richest quintile of the world's population to that of the poorest quintile of the world's population rose from 31:1 in 1965 to 60:1 in 1990 and 74:1 in 1997.[16] Income distribution within countries also worsened. This is borne out by a study on trends in income distribution from the 1960s to the 1990s for 73 countries comprising developed, developing and transitional economies. It shows that income inequality increased in 48 countries, which account for 59% of the population and 78% of the PPP-GDP in the sample of 73 countries. Income inequality remained the same in 16 countries, which account for 36% of the population and 13% of the PPP-GDP in the sample of 73 countries. Income inequality decreased in just 9 countries, which account for 5% of the population and 9% of the PPP-GDP in the sample of 73 countries.[17] The increase in income inequality was striking in some industrialized countries. Between 1975 and 2000, the share of the richest 1% in gross income rose from 8% to 17% in the USA, from 8.8% to 13.3% in Canada and from 6.1% to 13% in the UK.[18]

The incidence of poverty increased in most countries

of Latin America, the Caribbean and sub-Saharan Africa during the 1980s and 1990s. Much of Eastern Europe and Central Asia experienced a sharp rise in poverty during the 1990s. However, East Asia, Southeast Asia and South Asia experienced a steady decline in the incidence of poverty during this period. Most of this improvement, however, is attributed to changes in just two countries with large populations (China and India).[19]

The employment situation during the last quarter of the 20th century provides a sharp contrast with the preceding quarter century, during which full employment was almost the norm in industrialized countries. Unemployment in industrialized countries has increased substantially since the early 1970s and has remained at high levels since then. During the 1980s and 1990s, the unemployment rate was in the range of 10% in the European Union and about 7% in the OECD countries. The exception is the United States, where the unemployment rate remains around 5%. In contrast, Japan has witnessed a sharp increase in the unemployment rate from near zero to more than 5%.[20] In developing countries, employment creation in the organized sector continues to lag behind growth in the labour force, so that an increasing proportion of workers are dependent upon low-productivity and casual employment in the informal sector. Inequality in terms of wages and incomes has registered an increase almost everywhere in the world. This has been associated with an increasing casualization of the workforce: employment opportunities in the organized sector have stagnated, so labour absorption is possible largely in the informal sector of economies.

It would seem that globalization is characterized by uneven development. For a few rich countries and rich people, it has led to prosperity. For many poor countries and poor people, it has led to marginalization if not exclusion. The benefits have accrued essentially to the industrialized world and a small number of developing countries. For many developing countries and their people, the process of integration with the world economy has not yielded benefits in terms of economic growth or poverty reduction, either because they did not create the necessary preconditions or because the process of integration was too rapid. The least developed countries and their people have simply been marginalized and almost excluded from the process.

In retrospect, it is apparent that globalization has been associated with simultaneous, yet asymmetrical, consequences for countries and people. There is inclusion for some and exclusion or marginalization for many. There is affluence for some and poverty for many. There are some winners and many losers. The celebrated economist Joan Robinson once said: 'There is only one thing that is worse than being exploited by capitalists. And that is not being exploited by capitalists.' Much the same can be said about markets and globalization, which may not ensure prosperity for everyone but may, in fact, exclude a significant proportion of people.[21]

It would seem that globalization has created two worlds that co-exist in space even if they are far apart in well-being. For some, in a world more interconnected than ever before, globalization has opened the door to many benefits. Open economies and societies are conducive to innovation, entrepreneurship and wealth creation. Better communications, it is said, have enhanced awareness of rights and identities, just as they have enabled social movements to mobilize opinion. For many, the fundamental problems of poverty, unemployment and inequality persist. Of course, these problems existed before, but globalization may have accentuated exclusion and deprivation, for it has dislocated traditional livelihoods and local communities. It also threatens environmental sustainability and cultural diversity. Better communications, it is said, have enhanced awareness of widening disparities. Everybody sees the world from the viewpoint of their own lives. Therefore, perceptions about globalization depend on who you are, what you do and where you live. Some focus on the benefits and the opportunities. Others focus on the costs and the dangers. Both are right in terms of what they see. But both are wrong in terms of what they do not see.

On balance, it is clear that both countries and people suffer from exclusion.[22] Too many people in poor countries, particularly in rural areas and the informal sector, are marginalized if not excluded. Too few share in the benefits. Too many have no voice in its design or influence on its course. There is a growing polarization between the winners and the losers. The gap has widened between rich and poor countries, between rich and poor in the world's population, and also between rich and poor people within countries. These mounting imbalances in the world are ethically unacceptable and politically unsustainable.[23]

TOWARDS AN ANALYTICAL FRAMEWORK

An obvious question arises. How can this globalization process relate to, let alone influence, the world of higher education? The simple answer lies in two factors underlying the process of globalization. For one, globalization is driven by market forces – whether the threat of competition or the lure of profits. For another, globalization is driven by the technological revolution in transport and communications, which has set aside geographical barriers so that distance and time matter little. Economic analysis also enables us to provide a more complete and analytical answer.

In any economy, education is an integral part of the social infrastructure and an essential component of social consumption. Until not so long ago, most education was produced and consumed within national boundaries. It was what economists describe as 'non-traded'. In this attribute, education in general and higher education in particular were not significantly different from services as distinct from goods. Services possess two unique characteristics. First, the production of a service and its consumption are, as a rule, simultaneous, because services cannot be stored. Second, the producer and the consumer of a service must interact with each other, because the delivery of a service requires physical proximity.

In principle, it is possible to make a distinction between traded services, non-traded services and tradable services. In the world we knew just a quarter of a century ago, education was essentially non-traded across borders. But globalization has changed the world since then. The distinction between traded, non-traded and tradable services, which was always far from clear, has become more blurred on account of rapid technical progress and the changes in organization and production that the world economy witnessed during the late 20th century.

Trade in services may be defined as international transactions in services between the residents of one country and the residents of another country, irrespective of where the transaction takes place. International trade in services so defined can be divided into four categories:

1. those in which the producer moves to the consumer;
2. those in which the consumer moves to the producer;
3. those in which either the producer or the consumer moves to the other; and
4. those in which neither the consumer nor the producer moves to each other.[24]

In the first three categories, physical proximity of the producer and the consumer is essential for the international service transaction to take place. This is in conformity with the characteristics of services. In the fourth category, however, such physical proximity is not necessary and international trade in services is similar to international trade in goods.

Conventional examples of international trade in services fit into each of these categories. Guest workers, body shopping,[25] hotel chains and department stores are examples of situations in which the producer of a service moves to its consumers. Tourism provides the most obvious example of situations in which the consumer of a service moves to the producer. Higher education is the other traditional example, as students from all over the world move to study at Harvard or MIT in the US and at Oxford or Cambridge in the UK. Entertainers, performing artists and professional athletes provide examples of situations in which either the producer moves to the consumer or the consumer moves to the producer. Traditional banking, shipping and insurance services provide examples of situations in which neither the consumer nor the producer moves to the other, as these services can be disembodied from the producer and transported to the consumer.

Over the past two decades, there has been a discernible increase in the possibilities for international trade in services, without any perceptible decrease in the degree of restrictions on such trade, which is attributable to technological change on the one hand and a near-revolution in transport on the other.[26] Taken together, these developments have had the following consequences: first, non-traded services have become tradable; second, some altogether new services have entered the realm of international transactions; and third, the possibilities for trade in erstwhile traded services have become much larger. The technological revolution in transport and communications has made hitherto non-traded services tradable, either by a dramatic reduction in the cost of transport, which increases the mobility of the producer and the consumer of a service, or by developing means of communication, such as satellite links or video transmissions, which eliminate the need for proximity between the producer and the consumer of a service. At the same time, the revolution in telecommunications and information technologies has created an altogether new species of traded services.

These developments have transformed not only the possibilities but also the realities of higher education transactions across national boundaries. For a long time, as a service, higher education was tradable in one category alone – where the consumer of a service moved to the producer – as students from different parts of the world went to study in premier universities, mostly in industrial societies. Of course, there is a rapid expansion and diversification of this process in terms of student numbers and geographical spread. But that is not all. Cross-border higher education transactions have entered each of the other three categories:

1. those in which the producer moves to the consumer, as universities, particularly those in English-speaking industrial societies, have established campuses in different parts of the world;
2. those in which either the producer or the consumer moves to each other, as universities run short courses or summer schools either on their own campuses or in facilities leased in students' home countries; and
3. those in which neither the producer nor the consumer

moves to each other, as distance education, satellite television and open courseware dispense with the need for physical proximity between the teacher and the taught.

IMPACT OF GLOBALIZATION ON HIGHER EDUCATION

The spread of markets and the momentum of globalization during the past two decades have transformed the world of higher education almost beyond recognition. Market forces, driven by the threat of competition or the lure of profit, have led to the emergence of higher education as business. The technological revolution has led to a dramatic transformation in distance education as a mode of delivery. This is discernible not simply in the national context, but also in the international context, with a rapid expansion of cross-border transactions in higher education. It is clear that markets and globalization are transforming the world of higher education. The ways and means of providing higher education are changing. But the process does not stop there. Markets and globalization are shaping the content of higher education and influencing the nature of institutions that provide higher education.

In reflecting on the content, it is appropriate to make a distinction between higher education, professional education and distance education. These are neither mutually exclusive nor exhaustive, but the distinction is useful for analytical purposes.

In the world of higher education, markets and globalization are beginning to influence universities and shape education, not only in terms of what is taught but also of what is researched. In the sphere of teaching, there is a discernible departure from the liberal intellectual tradition in which education was about learning across the entire spectrum of disciplines. Students' choices were shaped by their interests. There was never perfect symmetry. Even so, universities endeavoured to strike a balance across disciplines, whether literature, philosophy, languages, economics, mathematics, physics or life sciences. But this is changing, as students and parents display a strong preference for higher education that makes young people employable. The popularity and availability of courses are thus being shaped by markets. Student employability is not simply a force that is pushing to create more places for vocational courses in higher education. It is also inducing universities to introduce new courses for which there is a demand in the market, because these translate into lucrative fees as a major source of income. Similarly, markets are beginning to

exercise an influence on the research agenda of universities: resources for research in life sciences, medicine, engineering and economics are abundant, while resources for research in philosophy, linguistics, history and literature are scarce. There is a premium on applied research and a discount on theoretical research.

The world of professional education is also being influenced by markets and globalization. The obvious examples are engineering, management, medicine and law. Markets exercise some (albeit limited) influence on curricula. Furthermore, globalization is encouraging the harmonization of academic programmes. The reason is simple. These professions are becoming increasingly internationalized. Therefore, the context is more global and less national, let alone local.

The world of distance education is somewhat different and could provide a silver lining to the cloud. Market forces and technical progress have opened up a new world of opportunities in higher education for those who missed the opportunity when they finished school or did not have access earlier. Of course, these opportunities come at a price that may not be affordable for some, particularly in developing countries or transition economies.

All this suggests that globalization is changing the form and shaping the content of higher education. At the same time, markets are beginning to influence the nature and culture of universities, which are the most important institutions in higher education.

There is a discernible commercialization of universities, although it is at its early stages and has not yet spread everywhere. Even so, it is important to analyse the underlying factors.[27] The process began with the resource crunch in governments that led to a financial squeeze on universities. It coaxed universities into searching for alternative sources of income. Entrepreneurial talents, which were rewarded by the market and admired by some in society, legitimized such initiatives in universities. The importance of traditional academic values diminished as competition among universities for scarce resources intensified. This sequence of developments came to be juxtaposed with the emergence of a wide range of opportunities for universities to earn money in the marketplace, based on their comparative advantage in knowledge with enormous potential for applications in management and technology.

Such commercialization has been reinforced by the forces of supply and demand. On the demand side, there is a burgeoning desire for higher education that is driven by a combination of individual aspirations and corporate needs in a changed national and international context. On the supply side, higher education almost everywhere is dominated by large public universities, which are somewhat inefficient and resistant to change. The safeguards implicit in academic freedom and the security guaranteed by tenure appointments, taken together, often create situations in which professors and administrators are not quite accountable to students, let alone to society. In developing countries, the problem is compounded because the opportunities for higher education in public institutions are simply not enough.

If we read between the lines, the situation in higher education is not very different from that of the healthcare sector before the advent of private enterprise. Unless corrections are introduced, the world of higher education might be caught in a pincer movement. At one end, the commercialization of universities means business in education. At the other end, the entry of private players into higher education means education as business. There are inherent dangers to such commercialization, but there are also opportunities to learn from markets.[28] It is clear that dangers and opportunities are closely intertwined in this process of change. These emerging realities cannot be ignored because the world of higher education is at some risk. The culture of markets and the advent of commercialization could erode both values and morality, which are the lifeblood of higher education.

GLOBALIZATION OF HIGHER EDUCATION

There can be little doubt that the globalization process is exercising a significant influence on the world of higher education. But that is not all. At the same time, there is a globalization of higher education, which, in turn, has significant implications. It has implications for people and countries, as well as for higher education and development. Let us consider each in turn.

In considering what the spread of globalization into higher education could mean for people and countries, there are three important manifestations worth noting.[29]

First, the *globalization of education* has gathered momentum. This has two dimensions. The proportion of foreign students studying for professional degrees or doctorates in the university system of the major industrialized countries – in particular the USA – is large, and more than two-thirds of these students simply stay on. The situation is similar in Europe, albeit on a smaller scale. At the same time, centres of excellence in higher education in labour-exporting developing countries are increasingly adopting curricula that conform to international patterns and standards. Given the facility of language, such people are employable almost anywhere.

Second, the *mobility of professionals* has registered a phenomenal increase in the age of globalization. It began with the brain drain. It was facilitated by immigration laws in the USA, Canada and Australia that encouraged the entry of people with high skills or professional qualifications. This process has intensified and diversified. It is, of course, still possible for scientists, doctors, engineers and academics to emigrate. But more and more professionals – such as lawyers, architects, accountants, managers, bankers and those specializing in computer software and information technology – can emigrate permanently, live abroad temporarily, or stay at home and travel frequently for business. These people are almost as mobile across borders as capital.

Third, the reach and spread of *transnational corporations* is worldwide. In the past, they moved goods, services, technology, capital and finance across national boundaries. Increasingly, however, they have also become transnational employers of people. They place expatriate managers in industrialized and developing host countries. They recruit professionals from both industrialized countries and developing countries for placement in corporate headquarters or affiliates elsewhere. In developing countries, they engage local staff who acquire skills and experience that make them employable abroad after a time. They move immigrant professionals of foreign origin, permanently settled in the industrialized world, to run subsidiaries or affiliates in their countries of origin. They engage professionals from low-income countries, particularly in software but also in engineering and healthcare, to work on a contract basis on special non-immigrant status visas, a practice that has come to be known as 'body shopping'. This intra-firm mobility across borders easily spills over into other forms of international labour mobility.

The professionals at the top of the skills ladder are almost as mobile as capital. Indeed, we can think of them as globalized people who are employable almost anywhere in the world – and the world, so to speak, is their oyster. In a sense, it is a part of the secession of the successful. The story is similar but not the same for contract workers or those involved in body shopping, for they are somewhere in the middle of the skills ladder. In both cases, however, the globalization of higher education has made this possible. Nevertheless, there is a crucial asymmetry. The investment is made by the home countries. The returns accrue to the host countries. This process is associated with the privatization of benefits and the socialization of costs. For the home countries of these people, there is an externalization of benefits and an internalization of costs.

The World Trade Organization (WTO) regime and the General Agreement on Trade in Services have major implications for higher education that need careful consideration. This multilateral framework embodies the most-favoured-nation clause and the national treatment provision. The right of establishment, or commercial presence, for service providers is also integrated into the agreement. This is not yet universalized, but allows for sector-by-sector negotiations. Higher education is on the agenda. A multilateral regime of discipline for international trade in higher education services is therefore on the anvil. A discussion of higher education in the context of the WTO would be too much of a digression, but I would like to highlight two possible implications and consequences for higher education in the wider context of development that relate to the quality and nature of education.

In developing countries, the globalization of higher education is influencing the quality of education in two ways. There is a striking proliferation of sub-standard institutions charging high fees and providing poor education. There is little if any accountability to students because, in most developing countries, there are no consumer protection laws or regulators for this market. Such an adverse selection of service providers in higher education is a real problem. Of course, there are some good institutions entering the domain of providing higher education across borders, but these are few and far between. Unfortunately, even these institutions are susceptible to the practice of double standards: the global and the local. It might be unfair to cite examples, but it would be instructive to compare the academic content and standards of the programmes run by such reputable institutions through campuses at home, through distance education and on campuses abroad. Clearly, unfettered markets without established regulators in higher education are bound to have an adverse effect on the quality of education.

The globalization of higher education is also changing the nature of higher education in the developing world. Its links with and relevance to the society in which the higher education is provided are somewhat tenuous, because its content and scope are determined in industrial societies. What is more, there is a clear and present danger that an internationalized higher education system may stifle rather than develop domestic capabilities in the higher education systems of the developing world, particularly in the least developed countries.

CONCLUSION

In a world of unequal economic and social opportunities, higher education provides the only means of faring better, whether we think of people or of countries. Theory and evidence both suggest that the development of a physical and social infrastructure, particularly in education, creates the necessary *initial conditions* for a country to maximize the benefits and minimize the costs of integrating with the world economy in the process of globalization. Thus, for countries that are latecomers to industrialization and development, a premature, passive, market-driven insertion into the world economy, without creating the *initial conditions*, is fraught with risk. It is not just about an unequal distribution of costs and benefits between people and between countries. The spread of education in society is critical. So is the creation of capabilities among people. In this, higher education provides the cutting edge. It is at the foundations of development in countries that are latecomers to industrialization. This is the essential lesson that emerges from the success stories of Asia in the second half of the 20th century.

At the beginning of the 21st century, it is clear that the wealth of nations and the well-being of humankind will depend, to a significant extent, on ideas and knowledge. In the past, land, natural resources, labour skills, capital accumulation and technical progress were the sources of economic growth and economic prosperity. In the future, knowledge is bound to be critical in the process of economic growth and social progress. Without corrections, the widening gap between the haves and the have-nots could then be transformed into a widening gap between the 'knows' and the 'know-nots'.

The most appropriate conclusion is provided by an old Buddhist proverb: 'The key to the gate of heaven is also the key that could open the gate to hell.' Markets and globalization provide a mix of opportunities and dangers for higher education. I have not provided an answer to the question I posed at the outset: what is to be done? However, a simple prescription would be appropriate. We should not allow markets and globalization to shape higher education. Instead, we should shape our agenda for higher education so that we can capture the opportunities and avoid the dangers unleashed by markets and globalization.

NOTES

1   See, for example, Amsden (1989) and Wade (1990).
2   For a more detailed discussion, as also for sources of the figures cited in this paragraph, see Nayyar (2006).
3   For figures on the share of country groups in world exports, see UNCTAD, *Trade and Development Report 2003*. For figures on the share of country groups in foreign direct investment inflows, as well as cross-border mergers and acquisitions, see UNCTAD, *World Investment Report 2002*.
4   The share of these 12 countries in total exports and manufactured exports from developing countries is calculated from data in UNCTAD *Handbook of Statistics 2002*. Their share in foreign direct investment inflows to the developing world is calculated from data in the UNCTAD *World Investment Report 2002*. The figures on the share of these 12

countries in portfolio investment flows to the developing world refer to the period 1992–1997 and are drawn from UNCTAD, *World Investment Report 1998*, p. 15.

5 The International Telecommunication Union (ITU) reports that, in 2000, the number of internet users in the world was distributed as follows: 137 million in North America, 110.8 million in Europe, 38 million in Japan, 8.2 million in Australia/New Zealand, 71.3 million in Asia, 17.7 million in Latin America and the Caribbean, and 4.6 million in Africa.

6 See Observatoire de la Finance and UNITAR, *Economic and Financial Globalization: What the Numbers Say*, New York and Geneva, 2003, p. 23.

7 For a critical perspective on the implications of globalization for development, see Stiglitz (2002), Nayyar (2003) and Kaplinsky (2005). See also World Commission on the Social Dimension of Globalization (2004).

8 For a more detailed discussion, see Nayyar (2003).

9 This argument about reactions in the form of chauvinism or fundamentalism is set out by Streeten (1996), who also cites Benjamin Barber, *Jihad vs. McWorld*, Random House, New York, 1995, on this issue. The hypothesis that there are actual or potential sources of tension between global markets and social stability is developed, at some length, by Rodrik (1997).

10 For a discussion on the intersection between the economic and the political in the context of global governance, see Nayyar (2002a).

11 Cf. World Commission on the Social Dimension of Globalization (2004).

12 The quarter century that followed the Second World War was a period of unprecedented prosperity for the world economy. It has, therefore, been described as the *golden age of capitalism*. See, for example, Marglin and Schor (1990) and Maddison (1982). The *age of globalization*, however, is not a phrase that has been used in the literature to describe the world economy during the last quarter of the 20th century. It was suggested in an earlier paper by the author (Nayyar, 2003), as this periodization facilitates comparison.

13 For the figures on growth rates in GDP per capita cited in this paragraph, see Nayyar (2006).

14 For figures on the volatility of growth in the world economy during the period 1975–2000, see World Bank, *World Development Indicators 2003*. For figures on the volatility of growth in developing countries during the period 1980–2000, as compared with the period 1960–1980, see UNCTAD, *Trade and Development Report 2003*, p. 59.

15 From 1960–1962 to 2000–2002, in constant 1995 US dollars, GDP per capita in the 20 richest countries rose from 11,417 to 32,339, while GDP per capita in the poorest 20 countries barely increased from 212 to 267 (World Bank, *World Development Indicators 2003*).

16 For 1965 and 1990, these ratios are obtained from UNCTAD, *Trade and Development Report 1997*, p. 81. For 1997, the ratio is obtained from UNDP, *Human Development Report 1999*, p. 3.

17 See Cornia and Kiiski (2001).

18 See Atkinson (2003).

19 For supporting evidence, see World Bank, *World Development Report* and *Global Economic Prospects*, various issues.

20 Cf. International Labour Organization (ILO), *Global Employment Trends* and OECD, *Employment Outlook*, various issues.

21 For a more detailed discussion, see Nayyar (2007).

22 For a detailed discussion and figures, see Nayyar (2003) and Nayyar (2006).

23 This proposition is set out, as also explained, in the Report of the World Commission on the Social Dimension of Globalization (2004).

24 For an economic analysis of international trade in services, see Nayyar (1988).

25 For example, the practice of engaging professionals from low-income countries, particularly in software but also in engineering and healthcare, to work on a contract basis on special non-immigrant status visas.

26 See Nayyar (1988).

27 For a perceptive analysis and lucid discussion, see Bok (2003).

28 For a more detailed discussion of dangers and opportunities, see Bok (2003) and Nayyar (2008).

29 For an analysis of cross-border movements of people in a globalizing world, see Nayyar (2002b).

BIBLIOGRAPHY

Amsden, Alice (1989) *Asia's Next Giant: South Korea and Late Industrialization*. New York: Oxford University Press.

Atkinson, Anthony (2003), Income inequality in OECD countries: data and explanations, *mimeo*, Oxford.

Bok, Derek (2003) *Universities in the Market Place: The Commercialization of Higher Education*. Princeton, NJ: Princeton University Press.

Cornia, G. Andrea and Kiiski, Sampsa (2001) Trends in Income Distribution in the Post World War II Period: Evidence and Interpretation. WIDER Discussion Paper No. 89, Helsinki: UNU-WIDER.

Kaplinsky, Raphael (2005) *Globalization, Poverty and Inequality*. Cambridge: Polity Press.

Maddison, Angus (1982) *Phases of Capitalist Development*. Oxford: Oxford University Press.

Marglin, Stephen and Schor, Juliet (eds) (1990) *The Golden Age of Capitalism*. Oxford: Clarendon Press.

Nayyar, Deepak (1988) The political economy of international trade in services, *Cambridge Journal of Economics*, **12**(2), pp. 279–98.

Nayyar, Deepak (2002a) Towards Global Governance. In: Deepak Nayyar (ed.) *Governing Globalization: Issues and Institutions*. Oxford: Oxford University Press.

Nayyar, Deepak (2002b) Cross-Border Movements of People. In: Deepak Nayyar (ed.) *Governing Globalization: Issues and Institutions*. Oxford: Oxford University Press.

Nayyar, Deepak (2003) Globalization and Development Strategies. In: John Toye (ed.) *Trade and Development*. Cheltenham: Edward Elgar.

Nayyar, Deepak (2006) Globalization, history and development: a tale of two centuries, *Cambridge Journal of Economics*, **30**(1), pp. 137–59.

Nayyar, Deepak (2007) Development Through Globalization? In: George Mavrotas and Anthony Shorrocks (eds) *Advancing Development: Core Themes in Global Economics*. London: Palgrave.

Nayyar, Deepak (2008) Globalization: What Does It Mean For Higher Education? In: Luc Weber and James Duderstadt (eds) *Globalization in Higher Education*. Paris: Economica, forthcoming.

Rodrik, Dani (1997) *Has Globalization Gone Too Far?* Washington, DC: Institute for International Economics.

Streeten, Paul (1996) Governance of the Global Economy. Paper presented to a Conference on Globalization and Citizenship, UNRISD, Geneva.

Stiglitz, Joseph E. (2002) *Globalization and its Discontents*. London: Penguin/Allen Lane.

Wade, Robert (1990) *Governing the Market: Economic Theory*

and the Role of Government in East Asian Industrialization. Princeton, NJ: Princeton University Press.

World Commission on the Social Dimension of Globalization (2004) *A Fair Globalization: Creating Opportunities for All*. Geneva: International Labour Organization (ILO).

Box I.1   Rethinking human and social development: the perspective of Gross National Happiness[1]

Introduction: Early concepts of human and social development

The 4th century, BC Indian statesman and philosopher Kautilya asserted: 'In the happiness of the people lies the legitimacy and the happiness of the ruler' (Kashyap, 2003).

Almost 21 centuries later, during the French Revolution, Jeremy Bentham (1907), the brilliant English economist, was arguing that the proper objective of a government is to provide 'the greatest happiness of the greatest number [of its citizens]'.

Under classical liberal economic theory, happiness was already an economic measurement used interchangeably with utility as well as the general welfare. Classical liberal economists attempt to quantify happiness through measurements of consumption and profits. Since higher income could allow higher consumption leading to more happiness, so income per capita was used as the standard measure for well-being and development. At the national level, gross domestic product (GDP) or its variant, gross national product (GNP), was considered to be a measure for development. It was soon found that this measure was faulty for ignoring:

- differences in domestic price levels
- inequalities in the distribution of income between different groups of people leading to group 'unhappiness'
- allowance for military expenditure, pollution, social ills like crime, and the value of leisure and consumer durables.

Gradually, it was perceived that income and economic growth cannot adequately capture the complexity of human and social development. As early as 1962 Simon Kuznets wrote in *The New Republic* 'The welfare of a nation can scarcely be inferred from a measurement of national income' (Kuznets, 1962). The faster the economy grows the more rapidly natural resources are depleted, leading to scarcity, and more fossil fuels are burnt, polluting the environment. Indicators covering health, education, employment, housing, environment and basic human rights are too important to be ignored.

The ideas stemming from Richard Easterlin's work suggest that as economies get richer, people can afford to question the need for further riches (Easterlin, 1974) and, according to Sen's capability approach, people also needed

expanding capabilities or freedom to improve their lot through better 'doings' and 'beings' (Sen, 1992).

Adjusted income as a measure of social and human development

GNP was adjusted for factors like leisure, underground economy and environmental damage and a 'measure of economic welfare' (MEW) was adopted as being more realistic. Although these adjustments were sensible, putting them into numbers created serious problems.

The United Nations Development Programme developed another more acceptable indicator, the Human Development Index (HDI) which combines income, life expectancy, adult literacy and school enrolment supplemented by measures such as gender empowerment (Gender-related Development Index (GDI) and the Human Poverty Index (HPI). HDI scores are now available for more than 170 countries. This has also been criticized for failing to capture important elements of the complexity of human well-being (United Nations University, 2007).

The Genuine Progress Indicator (GPI) has been developed providing 'explicit value to [some of these complexities such as] environmental quality, population health, livelihood security, equity, free time and educational attainment. It values unpaid voluntary and household work as well as paid work'. It counts sickness, crime, and pollution as costs not gains' (webmaster@gpiatlantic.org). GPI incorporates 26 social, economic and environmental variables. This indicator has been endorsed by 400 eminent stakeholders, including Nobel Laureates, as an important step 'in moving towards the society we want to create' (webmaster@gpiatlantic.org).

A new paradigm for social and human development: the concept of subjective well-being (SWB) and gross national happiness

In recent years a paradigm shift has occurred in the concept of development. All the indicators mentioned above deal with objective measures of quantifiable characteristics. If achievement of happiness is the goal, subjective assessment is necessary for measuring social and human development, argue some development specialists of today.

The concept of social and human development was moved forward from a subjective

point of view through the articulation of gross national happiness (GNH) by the king of the small Himalayan Kingdom of Bhutan in 1972. That signalled the king's commitment on building the economy that would serve his country's unique culture based on Buddhist spiritual values. The concept of GNH claims to be based on the premise that true development of human society takes place when material and spiritual development occur side by side to complement and reinforce each other. The four pillars of GNH are the promotion of equitable and sustainable socio-economic development, preservation and promotion of cultural values, conservation of the natural environment and establishment of good governance. During the past two decades Bhutan's development plan has been guided by the principles of GNH.

More recently, the economic and planning ministers of the South Asian Association for Regional Cooperation (SAARC) adopted the concept of GNH and its four pillars among the principles and strategies for the eradication of poverty in South Asia (Acharya, 2004).

From a methodological point of view, it should be noted that non-material components of happiness cannot be measured objectively. It is something in the minds of people and consequently can be measured only by asking questions in various contexts: clinical interviews, life-review questionnaires and survey interviews. Questions can be posed in different ways: directly or indirectly with single or multiple items.

Finally, the United Nations University has recently published five volumes on human well-being, which claim to correct many of the pitfalls of the Human Development Index. According to the authors, 'well-being' is a multi-dimensional concept embracing all aspects of human life: economic, freedom to achieve valuable 'doings' and 'beings', health, education, employment, housing, good environment, human security and basic human rights. The research behind the volumes makes a case for using information about people's perceptions or satisfactions to make policy choices, and considers future directions for participatory processes in well-being research. The research also reconfirms that 'happiness is not always closely associated with income or health: wealthier people are not necessarily happier' (United Nations University, 2007).

We have observed from the above analysis that simple objective quantitative methods cannot measure well-being, the essence of social and human development, correctly. However, any measure of happiness should be disaggregated to regional and local levels; should reflect well-being according to different aspects of life; should combine both economic and non-economic aspects of life and use a combination of qualitative and quantitative, subjective and objective indicators.

We have also noted that the strategies for social and human development will now have to be designed by specialists with an interdisciplinary expertise depending on the context and on the aspect of life under consideration.

NOTE

1   We would like to thank Bikas C. Sanyal for his work as principal writer of this text.

REFERENCES

Acharya, Gopilal (2004) *Operationalizing Gross National Happiness*, Kuensel on line, 22 February 2004 (accessed 13 October 2007).

Bentham, J. (1907 [1789]) *An Introduction to the Principles of Morals and Legislation*. Oxford: Clarendon Press.

Easterlin, R. (1974) Does Economic Growth Improve the Human Lot? Some Empirical Evidence. In: David, P.A. and Reder, M. (eds) *Nations and Households in Economic Growth: Essays in Honour of Moses Abramovitz*. New York and London: Academic Press.

Kashyap, S. (2003) *Concept of Good Governance in Kautilya's Arthashastra (meaning Economics)*. New Delhi: Indian Council for Social Science Research (ICSSR).

Kuznets (1962) How to judge quality, *New Republic*, 20 October.

Sen, A. (1992) Capability and wellbeing. In: Sen, A. and Nussbaum, M. (eds) *The Quality of Life*. Oxford: Clarendon Press.

United Nations University (2007) *Policy Brief Number 3*, Finland: UNU-WIDER.

SPECIAL CONTRIBUTION I.5
The new role of globalized education in a globalized world

Deane Neubauer and Víctor Ordoñez

As we search for new roles for higher education amidst the social, economic and political changes wrought by globalization, it is useful to reflect on the historic functions performed by universities. Essentially, these functions have been knowledge creation, knowledge transmission and knowledge conservation. Over the years, other important social activities have been included, in different societies and cultures, and at different times, in the functions that universities carry out. These include the production and reproduction of elites and professional classes, the expansion of higher education to other social strata through its democratization and massification, the creation, distillation and dissemination of scientific knowledge, and the codification and conservation of linguistic and cultural practices. History has shown that higher education institutions have the ability to adapt, however slowly and conservatively, to wide-reaching social change. Opportunities for new kinds of inquiry have been created, disciplines have been newly fashioned that are appropriate for the detailed study and transmission of these lines, and social values of open inquiry and opportunity have been championed, albeit unevenly.

The challenge that rapid globalization presents to universities is whether they can continue to adapt, no longer slowly or organically but in the quantum leaps required by new realities. Knowledge is not what it used to be, or more accurately, knowledge is now created, transmitted and conserved through modalities, institutions and configurations that were previously unknown, and at speeds once unimaginable. Universities no longer enjoy an exclusive or even a priority role in the new environment of internet access, media overload, and corporate- and lifestyle-customized products. They remain essential, but they also need to accept that they must change. In a context in which there are competing knowledge providers, they must recognize these competitors and form networks and partnerships with them in a way that strengthens all the parties involved.

There have always been connections between universities and the sectors of society that they serve and for which they provide the human resource base. However, with the pressures brought about by globalization and an accelerated pace of development, these connections take on new urgency and primacy. The world of employment has changed around the world, and universities must prepare their graduates for careers and jobs for which academic programmes do not as yet exist. For this to happen, more intense collaboration is vital. Globalization has promoted progress in the area of rapid and flexible competitiveness, but has done so in a largely uneven and inequitable way. Especially in developing countries, universities are looked upon as having the potential to correct the widening equity divide by preventing the human resource base from being left too far behind their counterparts in other countries. Universities can respond to this call only if they are closely allied to the country's productive and economic sectors. A look at the contributions that universities will be making in this revised context reveals academic programmes for which students alternate years on campus with years working in industry, government or the social sector; academic research councils in which individuals from industry and other sectors participate fully in the formulation of research agendas and study programmes; and teaching posts provided to people outside academic circles who can contribute to the development of the flexible, updated human resource base needed in a globalized, rapid, competitive world. Another development with a slightly different twist and an unpredictable outcome is a startling increase in the privatization of intellectual property, as teaching staff seek to own and commercialize their intellectual contributions to the overall knowledge process.

The pressures of globalization on developing countries produce some of these dynamics, but create whole new sets of problems as well. Universities in developing countries no longer have the luxury of developing at their own pace, because of the risk of being left behind in the global race. However, unlike their more well-endowed counterparts in developed countries, they do not have even a fraction of the financial resources needed to keep up. Yet if their countries are not to be left behind, they have no choice but to strive to provide internationally comparable and competitive programmes. This tension has brought the private sector into higher education in ways that differ remarkably from the historical role of private higher education in developed countries. This is especially true of the USA, where a tradition of higher education for the public good has resulted in a historical convergence of purpose between private and public institutions. This convergence is less clear in the developing world, especially in the very rapidly growing economies of China and India, where the temptation to skim the market for well-paying students leads all too often to the provision of inferior and highly specialized courses that pay little attention to issues affecting either the broader public good or a significant qualitative increase in knowledge. In the worst-case scenario, this sub-sector threatens to become a net 'taker' from the knowledge quota, rather than a net contributor.

In spite of these tensions one finds that developing countries are well aware that they cannot, and indeed should not,

merely replicate Western higher education models. Hence their search for relevant and yet indigenous forms of higher education, in terms of delivery modes, programme content, and even areas of research. This is especially true in the realm of knowledge conservation, and particularly in the field of the preservation and enhancement of cultural and national identities and heritages. In a world in which globalization has established English as the default language, the work of universities in preserving languages and the cultures they embody and represent is critical, and is unlikely to be performed by any other set of social institutions. The consequences of globalization-induced homogenization (or of the opposite reaction: the polarization of cultures), especially in the cultural forms promoted by the mass media, make this task of cultural and language preservation by universities vital for the promotion of a healthy and harmonious society. While repositioning themselves as effective agents in the global knowledge economy, universities must also preserve the character of their specific national higher education systems and transmit key elements of national cultural identities and traditions. Ironically, this vital role contributes to the resource problems experienced by universities as they continue to suffer a gradual withdrawal of governmental funding.

The emergence of these new roles and responsibilities is changing the way universities see themselves, seek resources, and respond to social signals to align their actions with perceived social needs. These forces and tensions are doing much to redefine historic notions of the responsibilities of public higher education towards the public good. This may well be the initial conceptual framework within which universities in a globalized, knowledge-saturated world can define their distinctive arena or unique niche in society. The new vectors include the role of universities in providing services to society (far above the conventional third-place status, under teaching and research, that has traditionally been assigned to this role); the

inherent tensions between acting as the handmaidens of government and as social critics; the responsibilities of their role as a collective and heterogeneous set of social consciences; and their role as predictors and precipitators of social and scientific change.

One likely new pathway will be the development of new foci of inquiry and, through them, of new disciplines. This has begun to happen with the study of globalization itself, which has produced both research and instructional programmes (and in a few isolated instances even service programmes, albeit to this point successfully disguised as occupation-related leadership courses). One can reasonably argue that the pace of change under the impress of globalization has been so rapid and extensive that much of the knowledge that is imparted in basic and higher education institutions and in schools refers to a world that no longer exists. The tensions between the conservation of history and irrelevance have been painfully sharpened by globalization's irreverent drive towards change and its insensitivity to what is displaced by such changes. New research and instructional programmes have an urgent responsibility to describe and analyse this emergent world. Put another way, the world that globalization has created produces consequences – problems *and* predicaments – that are not successfully accommodated within existing disciplinary boundaries. New knowledge constellations and modes of inquiry are required and are already taking shape.

Some of these new disciplines are likely to be formed around public policy and its many controversies. One example is global warming and climate change – problems that extend far beyond conventional disciplines and their limitations of expertise. Another example, related to the former, but with significantly different implications is sustainability, with its potential sub-fields of social and cultural sustainability and agricultural and rural sustainability (in what has become, since the year 2000, an urbanized world). The knowledge explosion itself is likely to produce new hybrid disciplines much in the same way as they have developed over the past 60 years with the creation of telecommunications, information and computer science, and marketing. One would expect the dramatic changes in digital technologies and the virtual elimination of the practical costs of digital information storage to engender new ways of studying cultural change, consumption and style in conjunction with communication. Just as the increased pace of social change due to the rapid introduction of digital innovation affects society, so will higher education be pressured to study such phenomena with rigour, and to invent knowledge frameworks that extend society's understanding of them as well as assisting with policy responses to them. The cultural wars partially engendered and partially stirred up by globalization suggest the possibility of an entirely new platform on which to erect peace studies and the serious pursuit of new inquiries into the nature and resolution of human conflicts.

The development of these new foci of inquiry and emergent disciplines has in turn led to the evolution of new ways of addressing them. In an ever more complex and interconnected society, universities now conduct their work in new ways, such as in increasingly close cooperation with other sectors of society and with partners across national and regional boundaries. The ease and speed with which information is shared and transmitted has enabled a redefinition of communities of research and inquiry. While they may still have higher education institutions as hubs, they now routinely include the corporate sector, government agencies or sponsoring bodies, groups of international academic colleagues and civil society. Perhaps the growth industry of global higher education lies at the intersection between conventional cross-border education represented by the exchange of students and teaching staff, and the new networks, partnerships, consortia and forms of association currently being invented and defined. The result is a *global education community* that is tak-

ing shape and beginning to assess its strengths and possibilities. Like many other globalization phenomena, these events mix traditional frames of reference in a radical way, simultaneously promoting homogenization and difference by reaching for what is global, while at the same time intensifying what is local.

Fundamentally, the academic marketplace is no longer confined to national settings. More than ever, knowledge is becoming universal and crossing borders of all kinds with unpredictable consequences. Its pursuit and advancement are based on the free exchange and circulation of ideas across scientific fields, geographic boundaries, political systems, and academic disciplines. Predictions that the number of students travelling abroad will double within the next five years are accompanied by the unparalleled growth of cross-border education. Both imports and exports abound in this new global market. As societies grapple with a quantum leap in demand for higher education and the inability of both their public and private sectors to meet this demand, governments, at first reluctantly and then willingly, admit the access possibilities of branches of overseas universities and the manpower development potential of their programmes. In many countries, policy frameworks governing the operation and regulation of such cross-border institutions are only now being deliberated and defined. In such places as China, Korea and Southeast Asia, for example, governments struggle to maintain their sense of control over the proliferation of offshore campuses, while admitting the need to obtain greater access to them under appropriate institutional arrangements.

It is clear to us that distance education, both cross-border and national, is in the early, albeit dramatic, stages of development. Open universities are at the centre of this phenomenon. Each of the major open universities in Bangkok, Shanghai, Delhi, London, Arizona and other cities serves literally hundreds of thousands of students. Contemporary instructional technology and quality con-

trol mechanisms have made it possible to expand higher education access to enormous numbers of students in a way that would have been impossible under the old distance education systems. And while initial course development and the setting up of infrastructure needed for delivery makes this model more expensive in the beginning, successive iterations over time dramatically reduce unit costs. At the aggregate social level, as the numbers benefiting from distance education continue to grow and effective per-student costs decline, the resulting capacity will address the problems of access resulting from the massification of global higher education. The ultimate test will be the issue of quality. The advocates and proponents of distance education are working steadfastly to maintain and demonstrate quality; this includes a quiet but considerable increase in investments by corporations in their own versions of higher education to meet constant workforce demands. The *worst* possible outcome of this would be for these massive distance education endeavours to end up as second- or third-rate enterprises specializing in providing low-unit-cost education to those unable to obtain it elsewhere in the market. The *best* possible outcome would be for distance education, spurred along by innovative technologies, to lead more traditional educational institutions and their delivery modalities towards new ways of functioning, and to successfully challenge emergent student populations characterized by preferences for new learning solutions.

Inevitably, the globalized world involves the rapid forming, reforming and un-forming of knowledge societies. With knowledge as the dominant currency of future growth and development, universities have little choice but to recognize their ever-changing roles as creators, transmitters and preservers of knowledge at the service of society as a whole. And, in ways that we are just beginning to appreciate, they must not only perform these roles for young adults preparing for their first jobs, because the technical requirements of specific professions have become so complex and are evolving so rapidly that even the best pre-service education becomes outdated a few years after it is acquired. A recent study indicates that engineers, for example, need fundamental retraining to update their knowledge five years after graduation. In light of this, the university must be aware that it has a role to play, not only in producing new engineers, but also in servicing the current engineering workforce with programmes that keep them updated, relevant and effective. Addressing the problem of the short lives of professions and set bodies of knowledge will become a constant task in universities.

The knowledge society is a society based entirely on lifelong learning. Until recently, lifelong learning stood for the kinds of highly optional education provided for casual learners of advancing age. Slowly the term expanded to include the retraining of individuals in the workforce whose jobs were being restructured. It is now seen as an *inherent requirement* that must be met if one is to be professionally responsible to one's knowledge obligations. This awareness of the changed nature of lifelong learning will, we predict, continue to radically transform higher education demand and access figures. What is now optional will become compulsory.

We already see some implications of these outcomes in the economics of what was formerly called 'university extension' in many of the public and private educational institutions of the USA. What were once convenient or service-oriented adjuncts to the 'real' educational enterprise (and thus somewhat 'quaint' when all was said and done) have become sources of fresh revenue for cash-strapped universities, often serving many more students than the other branches of the institution. A further implication is the impact of all this, both for good and ill, on teaching staff, resulting in a vast expansion in the employment of part-time, contract staff and a parallel decline in traditional, permanent career positions. This shift threatens to create an invidious two-tier class system within the teaching staff, but it also promises to revolutionize current patterns of retirement and the utilization of 'older' minds in the overall knowledge enterprise. Universities are currently operating a staffing structure that owes everything to the work demands and structures of traditional industrial enterprise; much of contemporary higher education is modelled on the Industrial Revolution and its successive developments. People are hired and retired in relation to a once extant, but now obsolete, combination of biological ageing and the need to create new job opportunities within higher education. To deliberately oversimplify an important point, the form of higher education that is aligned with the requirements of lifelong learning in a knowledge society will be based on minds and what resides within them, rather than obsolete age-related notions about the bodies that carry these minds about. Once again, demand will redefine capacity.

Far beyond the limits of their (essential) function of catering to market-driven demands for professional updating, universities must serve knowledge societies in a more fundamental sense. Their ultimate responsibility is to contribute meaningfully to the total development of their societies. They must reach out to and serve those who shape this development: the political, economic and social leaders of society. This includes those responsible for the education of society at levels below higher education, who ensure that there is an adequate number of well-qualified teachers in school systems. Higher education must ensure that society continues to be equipped to address its most pressing societal problems, to expand its innovation and research capacities, and to foster the values needed for a productive, cohesive, harmonious and ethical society, in terms of good governance and participatory democracy. The overall welfare of countries will depend a great deal on the extent to which universities can fulfil their role as supporters of these broader goals.

CONCLUSION

There are three conundrums in what is generally called the 'politics and economics' of higher education in the emergent knowledge society. These strike us as issues of such prominence that they must be addressed immediately in policy processes if they are to have any hope of a successful resolution.

The first is the transmutation of the 'digital divide' problem. Initially, it referred to the gap between those with computing capability and those without. Various organizations throughout the world have worked hard to take capacity and capability to places where it was formerly lacking. Now, however, we are faced with the boundary-destroying nature of digital proliferation. As indicated above, universities themselves are in danger of being hierarchically divided by their abilities to keep abreast of these developments, which represent a quantum leap in the demands and requirements of addressing the digital divide.

The second is the issue of value within information. The changing economic dynamics of information and knowledge companies and the extraordinary growth of their products have created an 'informational field' of an extent and density never seen before. In the midst of this explosive blizzard of information lie the coherence-generating devices and processes we label 'search'. Determining the pathways and value-ways through this information blizzard towards knowledge coherence constitutes a problem of unprecedented proportions for higher education (conceived of as collections of knowledge organizations). The quantity of new resources required by such institutions to successfully navigate these transformations will be of great magnitude. Public policy must be fully implicated in providing the capacity to deal with these changes. If not, public institutions, at the very least, will fail to breast this challenge.

Finally, there is the complex issue of which knowledge to conserve in a world that is being rapidly globalized, and the same can be asked of the two historic functions of universities – teaching and research. What to teach is an increasingly pressing dilemma, and one which universities are particularly ill-equipped to resolve, given their historically conservative decision-making processes. Meanwhile, with research issues, universities face the prospect of extending C.P. Snow's famous 'two cultures' problem[1] to the whole of global education. The instrumental value of science and technology, and its imperative alignment with economic development, threaten to displace the study of humanities (and to some extent the social sciences) within university priorities.

These are only three of the policy issues that globalization is challenging higher education to solve. Those responsible for higher education must grapple with these and other issues still to emerge, and they must grapple with them with a sense of perspective, an instinct for the future, and a vision of the role of the university within that future. If they do so, no matter what forms, modalities and connections higher education adopts, it will continue to be a guiding light and a driving force for development in the societies it serves, as it has been throughout history.

NOTE

1   C.P. Snow (1959) The Two Cultures, Rede Lecture delivered 7 May, Senate House, Cambridge, UK. Subsequently published (1959) as The Two Cultures and the Scientific Revolution, Cambridge, UK: The Cambridge University Press.

SPECIAL CONTRIBUTION I.6
The social relevance of higher education

Jean-Marie De Ketele

There is a wealth of texts on the quality of higher education: many concepts appear or reappear, such as quality assurance, quality management, quality assessment and accreditation (GUNI, 2007). However, the concept of quality is difficult to define, due to its multidimensional and relative nature. Effectiveness (the relationship between the observed and expected effects) and efficiency (the relationship between the observed effects and the investment made) are two essential aspects of quality. However, higher education can be effective and efficient without being socially relevant, if the desired and observed effects do not serve society. Some believe that if we add a third concept, that of equality, the requirements of society will be taken into consideration. Indeed, an educational system (and therefore a higher education institution) would be much more equitable if the benefits it provided were less concerned with the characteristics of the students (sex; social, cultural, ethnic, economic and geographic background; and so on). Clearly, this would represent a new and important step forward. However, it is not sufficient. This paper's thesis can be summed up in a few words: the first and last criteria for assessing higher education should be social relevance. Nevertheless, the limits of social relevance must be clearly established. The concept should not be focused exclusively on economic development, as some arguments propose.

RELEVANCE INVOLVES CONTRIBUTING TO THE DEVELOPMENT OF A PROJECT FOR A MORE JUST SOCIETY

To be relevant, higher education institutions have to incorporate their goals into a project for society. A first concept might be that higher education produces and disseminates knowledge in order to allow society to develop, as the development of science and technology creates a 'cognitive society'. This is the belief of many countries, including those of the European Union (EU) and North America. They have given this concept official status in several international meetings. The work of various European conferences (starting with the Lisbon conference), the OECD conference and, to a lesser extent, that of the World Trade Organization (WTO) has been along these lines: the economic development of regions depends on the effort invested by the institutions that produce and disseminate new scientific and technological knowledge. As a result, institutions must open up to the world of business. The more companies can exploit this new knowledge, the more wealth they can produce. This idea is based on the premise that higher education contributes to economic development, which, in turn, contributes to the development of society.

An increasing number of people are speaking out against this excessively simplistic concept, which has been contradicted by many factors. These can be summed up as follows:

- The wealth produced by the corporate world as a result of scientific and technical knowledge transfer exclusively serves the interests of the most wealthy and powerful, to the detriment of the interests of the weakest, and even to the future of humanity

- An increasingly large segment of the world's population lacks the most basic requirements of society (access to water, food, health, security, conservation of the environment and so on), despite the extraordinary developments of science and technology in recent decades

- In addition to the growing divide between the richest and the poorest regions, which some attribute to the absence or poor quality of higher education in the least developed countries, a similar divide is being created in the so-called developed countries, including those with the best-rated universities in the world.

Thus, in Great Britain, whose universities are the highest rated in international classifications, more than 20% of families live below the poverty line.

These observations have led some institutions, such as the Observatory of the European University, to add a social dimension to the economy-oriented conception of social relevance (Schoen et al., 2007). In that paper, the authors proposed that higher education should be assessed using eight sub-dimensions or assessment scales. The first four sub-dimensions refer to the economic dimension: human resources, intellectual property (scientific production, ownership), spin-offs and industry contracts. The last four sub-dimensions deal with contracts with public bodies, participation in political decision-making, involvement in social and cultural life, and public understanding of science. This concept is indeed more advanced than the first one. However, two aspects of it should attract our attention. The first is the parallelism and juxtaposition established between the two orientations, that is, the economic dimension is not seen as an integral part of the social dimension. The second aspect is the list of indicators identified by the work of the Observatory of the European University: of the 43 listed indicators, 36 belong to the economic dimension and its four sub-dimensions, whereas only seven indicators belong to the social dimension and its four sub-dimensions. This analysis reveals much about the weight given to the first dimension.

A third concept was developed during preparatory work for the World Conference on Higher Education (UNESCO, 1995, 1998) and in the conclusions of the meeting held in Paris in October 1998. In the 1995 document, UNESCO specified the approach that should be applied to the social relevance of higher education:

Relevance refers to the role of higher education as a system and the role played by each institution in society, and to what society expects from higher education. It must

include topics such as: democratizing access; increasing the opportunities for taking part in higher education at different stages in life; links with the world of employment; and the responsibility of higher education towards the entire educational system. It is also important for the community to participate in higher education in the search for solutions to the most urgent problems facing humanity, such as overpopulation, the environment, peace, international understanding, democracy and human rights. The importance of higher education is perhaps best expressed through the variety of 'academic services' it offers society.

In the orientation documentation distributed to the 5,000 participants at the world conference, the chapter on relevance included the following:

To be relevant is to seek …
… policies
… the world of employment
… other levels of the educational system
… the culture and cultures
… of everyone
… in all places and at all times
… students
… teachers
    Encounters for moving toward sustainable, harmonious development and correcting imbalances:
… both more internationalization and more contextualization
… more fundamental research and more applied research
… sustainable human development and peace culture

The participants at the World Conference lent such orientations legitimacy by organizing them into three related concepts:

- relevance
- quality
- internationalization.

This idea of relevance takes into consideration the needs of people and society. The economic aspect and opening up to the world of employment are included in

only one of the many dimensions to be taken into account. Therefore, economic considerations do not have the exclusive weight they are given in the first conception or the priority granted to them in the second. In this third conception, the three traditional missions of higher education (teaching, research and service) must, above all, contribute to attaining goals as important and urgent as the eight Millennium Development Goals:

- Eradicate extreme poverty and hunger
- Achieve universal primary education
- Promote gender equality and empower women
- Reduce child mortality
- Improve maternal health
- Combat HIV/AIDS, malaria and other diseases
- Ensure environmental sustainability
- Develop a global partnership for development.

David E. Bloom (2003) shows his surprise, and rightly so, that at the World Summit on Sustainable Development held in Johannesburg:

higher education was not mentioned as an instrument for achieving even one of the United Nation's Millennium Development Goals. Yet, attainment of every single one of them will be much easier if a country has a strong and productive higher education system. (p. 14)

RELEVANCE IS A SOCIAL CONSTRUCT THAT IS CONSTANTLY BUILT AND REBUILT

In a paper delivered in Barcelona in 2005, Marco Antonio Rodrigues Dias noted that between 1994 and 1995, the World Bank (*Higher Education: the Lesson of Experience*) and UNESCO (*Policy for Change and Development in Higher Education*) made the same diagnosis of the relationship between higher education and society. However, their conclusions were radically different:

The UNESCO document held that higher education is a public asset that must become internationalized on the basis of solidarity and cooperation. Its proposals can generally be grouped into three major areas (relevance, quality and internationality). In contrast, the priorities for reform in the World Bank document included the following: increasing integration with the private sector and with companies, which should be members of university governing bodies; implementing market-oriented policies, specifically policies for managing higher education institutions; and boosting institutional diversification, with privatization as a priority.

In light of the different impacts these two documents have had on higher education reforms in a certain number of countries, Dias states that a conceptual, political and organizational effort is needed. He mentions various concepts that require continued work, including 'justice', a 'just society', 'public good', 'public service' and 'public commitment', among others. In addition to these, there are other, more action-oriented concepts, such as accreditation, that need to be explored further in light of the basic concepts.

THE CONTRIBUTION OF THEORIES OF JUSTICE

There can be no doubt that the works of Rawls (1971) on justice have had, and continue to have, a considerable impact. His theory of justice rests on three principles. The first is the *principle of equal liberties:* each person must have the greatest fundamental liberties that are compatible with all people enjoying the same liberties. The fundamental liberties are freedom of thought, religion, expression, assembly and choice of profession; the right to a fair trial; the right to hold personal possessions; and the right to vote and stand for office. The second principle is *the principle of fair equality of opportunity:* all members of society must have equal access to all social positions on the basis of merit. Inequalities in probability, due to inequalities in preferences, tastes and ambitions are not unjust from the point of view of this principle. However, it is important to neutralize as far as possible

the impact of social background on peoples' careers. The third principle is the *principle of difference:* society is a system of diverse social positions with different corresponding expectations in terms of income, wealth, power and leisure. However, these inequalities in socioeconomic advantages are not unjust if they contribute to improving the prospects of those occupying more disadvantaged social positions. We cannot aim for equal results but we can aim for equal opportunities.

This theory has inspired numerous works, including those of Amartya Sen, who has influenced the indices prepared by the United Nations Development Programme (UNDP). The main criticism that Sen (1999) levels at Rawls is that the theory of justice is based on 'primary social goods', which include fundamental liberties, opportunities to access different social positions, and socioeconomic advantages. For Sen, a better approach to social justice should be based on people's 'abilities'. For him, injustice arises from the failure of certain members of society to achieve 'basic abilities', that is: the ability to feed oneself, to dress oneself, to provide shelter for oneself, to move, to educate oneself, to take care of oneself and so on. The role of society – and, therefore, of higher education as a component of society – is to allow more people to obtain these basic abilities. When everyone has all attained these abilities, it will no longer be possible to compare the different social strata.

At a conference held during the French Social Weeks (Paris, 24 November 2006), Philippe van Parijs used the works of Rawls and Sen to establish 'four conditions for any plausible conception of justice today'. *The first condition* states that any plausible theory of justice today must try to achieve equal respect for all of the conceptions of a good life that exist in our pluralist societies. *The second condition* involves equal concern for the interests of everyone. *The third condition* postulates that any plausible conception of justice today rests on the obligation of personal responsibility, not in terms of results or lev-

els of well-being, but in terms of making the most of opportunities, possibilities and real liberties and, therefore, exercising one's abilities. *The fourth condition* formulates the idea that an inequality is justified if and only if the victims of the inequality obtain some benefit.

The university studies of the aforementioned authors show that the concept of justice is a 'social construct' that must constantly be rebuilt as society evolves. The relevance of higher education – in terms of its contribution to the development of a more just society by producing new knowledge, training people and undertaking civil service – is also, therefore, a social construct. Dias (2005) also states that 'in fact, in the social sphere, neutrality does not exist'. Petrella (2003) shares this idea and complains that certain scientists equate rigour with neutrality. Producing relevant knowledge to respond to the requirements of a more just society means making value choices (no neutrality) whilst maintaining tremendous scientific rigour:

> Rigour is urgently required, particularly in three areas ... Firstly ... the different scientific disciplines should guarantee scientific rigour above all, even if this means ensuring real and effective transdisciplinary work and the increased responsibility of scientists to the community and to future generations (through the application of the principle of caution, among others). Secondly, the subject of globalization comes to mind. The predominant theories today in this field are based on theses that are not beholden to any criteria of scientific validity, such as the thesis of historic 'naturalness' and therefore the 'inevitability' of the current forms and contents of the economic and financial globalization of western economies. Thirdly, and lastly, is a vast domain that covers the concepts and realities relating to humanity, the world community, common global goods and international law and, through them, the notions and phenomena of sovereignty (what sovereignty? whose? how?), security (whose? what? by whom?), political representation at the world level, world gov-

ernment (and I do not mean that great scientific and political fraud that hides behind the term 'government'), world public services, a tax system with the objective of redistribution and local/global relations. In this field, scientists are at the beginning of a great adventure of knowledge. But we cannot postpone it. Slogans … cannot replace the theses that are based on a solid labour of theoretical and empirical validation. (pp. 142–4)

These hard-hitting proposals show that the concept of social relevance still remains to be (re)constructed and that scientists and higher education institutions can no longer avoid it.

THE CONCEPTS OF PUBLIC GOODS, SERVICES AND COMMITMENTS

Higher education institutions are under tremendous pressure: private financing of research (and therefore the control that goes with it) is increasing considerably; the demands of educating and training a varied and numerous public (laudable in itself) have taught certain institutions the usefulness of selling their services for profit and setting up forms of government similar to those of private companies; enterprise universities are multiplying in certain countries, such as Australia and the United States. Due to the training offered in foreign countries – mainly through new technologies – this type of university is turning education into a lucrative market that attracts ever larger sums of money. Thus, an increasing number of universities seek resources that supplement public funding, but that become increasingly difficult to control (Currie, 2003; Knight, 2003; Dias, 2005). The commercialization of education, advocated by the World Trade Organization, tends to make the criterion of social relevance invisible, despite all the spoken and written efforts (or 'doublespeak', according to Dias, 2005) made to justify actions in terms of contributions to society. The idea of justice (an essential component of social relevance) must be associated with the concepts of 'public goods', 'public services' and 'public commitments'.

The noun form of *good* means something that is useful for a specific purpose. When this purpose is not strictly individual or is not available to certain people using their own resources, but does serve a public purpose (responding to the needs of society, its conservation and its development), it becomes a public service. This is the case with education: it is a *public service* based on solidarity and contribution to the development of society. Elie Jouen, Secretary General of the NGO Internationale de l'Éducation (quoted in Dias, 2005) expresses this idea of public service very well:

> The state is responsible for coordination (of its public system) and contributes financially, either partially or fully, to its correct functioning. When organizing public services, the state implements policies that redistribute wealth in favour of those who are favoured [sic Translator's note]. Everyone receives according to their needs. The privatization of public services is based on the concept of a service transformed into a good that must be purchased. Then, everyone receives according to their resources rather than their needs. The state does not fulfil the function of redistributing wealth. This is the basic difference between public and privatized services and is the foundation for completely different societies.

Of course, the label *public* is not always a guarantee of a genuine public service. Similarly, the label *private* may involve different situations, from institutions with commercial goals (private in the strict sense) to institutions that are not directly under state control but offer a genuine, not-for-profit public service within the framework of a specific project (this is the case of many private institutions governed by state subsidy agreements). While the criterion is the public service provided, it is also true that the state cannot abdicate its mission to ensure that everyone is provided with a quality public service according to their needs (access and the chance of updating their 'abilities' in the sense used by Sen). Such a service should also take into

account the development requirements of society. As Dias (2005) points out, the commitment of the state and the international organizations involved in guaranteeing public services rests on three principles: equality, permanence and adaptability. *Equality* means that everyone, according to their needs and without discrimination, has the right to public services. This is also true of higher education, as indicated in the Universal Declaration of Human Rights (1948) and the World Declaration on Higher Education for the Twenty-First Century (1998). The principle of *permanence* means that public services must be guaranteed permanently and without interruption. The principle of *adaptability* means that public commitment ensures that public services adapt to the evolution of society (its changes and requirements, and the new knowledge and technology that make it possible to respond to them). Not only are higher education institutions public services, but they also have to make a public commitment to studying public services. The knowledge produced and academic critical judgment skills ensure that these functions are fulfilled.

THE CONCEPTS OF QUALITY, QUALITY ASSURANCE, ACCREDITATION AND INTERNATIONALIZATION

The public services offered by higher education institutions are essential components of their mission and therefore of their strategic plans. They are essential indicators of social relevance. Furthermore, these services (teaching, research and responding to the needs of society) must be of a high quality. The first priority is the criterion of relevance: relevant goals must be set. The criterion of quality (and therefore the quality-assurance and accreditation mechanisms involved) is subordinate to relevance: quality actions may be undertaken that are not relevant or are not the most relevant in terms of the needs of society. If relevance is a social construct that must constantly be (re)built, then so is quality, as it is absurd to consider a model that has unique standards. While the formulation of some quality criteria has a certain universality, the indicators must be put into context in space and time and continually adapted. There is a natural tendency to favour only quantitative indicators, due to the ease with which they can be measured. We should be wary of this tendency. Although he inspired the Human Development Index (HDI), Sen (1999) points out the risk of skewed interpretations, not just because the HDI has statistical shortcomings that are hard to avoid, but also because it only takes into account three of the easier-to-measure dimensions (education, longevity and standard of living). This tool does not take into consideration such essential 'abilities' as political freedoms, participation in social life and security (see the analysis by Farvaque, 2003).

The work of the UNDP on the HDI, and of GUNI (2007) on factors to take into account in accreditation, represent very important advances. However, work in these areas needs to continue since, as with all scientific research (particularly that with a strong social component), there is always progress to be made. As Sen pointed out in connection with the HDI, a critical examination must take into account what is missing as well as what is present. Such an analysis of the results of GUNI research undertaken using the Delphi method reveals some interesting facts. In the table that uses large regions (Africa, Latin America, the Caribbean, Asia Pacific, the Arab States, Europe and North America) to present the most important factors in an accreditation system and on which the participants are in most agreement, the most common factors are:

- good governance, transparency and accountability (six regions out of six)
- qualifications and quality of teachers and researchers (six regions out of six)
- quality of the academic courses (four regions out of six)
- optimization and good management of resources (three regions out of six);
- relevance of the courses and syllabus (three regions out of six).

The concept of relevance appears at least three times, though it refers mainly to courses and syllabuses. This could essentially mean that it is related to adaptation to the labour market, which is desirable, but insufficient with respect to the idea of social relevance that we have described. This table contains no mention of the factors that affect such urgent needs as those stated in the Millennium Goals, for example. When these factors are opened up to society, they tend to be restricted to the labour market or to the development of the country (four of the eight factors cited by the Arab States and one of the six cited by Europe). The favoured factors are classic examples that also reveal the main effects of the pressures brought to bear by organizations such as the World Bank, the OECD and the EU. Factors such as solidarity, international cooperation with the universities of developing countries, and contribution to the urgent needs of humanity are some on which consensus has not yet been reached. They are, however, key aspects of the social relevance of higher education institutions, as highlighted by the World Declaration on Higher Education for the Twenty-First Century. In a practical way, the concept of social relevance still has to be constructed.

REFERENCES

Bloom, D.E. (2003) Des idées à l'action pour une réforme de l'enseignement supérieur. In: Breton, G. and Lambert, M. (eds) *Globalisation et universités. Nouvel espace, nouveaux acteurs.* Québec: Presses de l'Université Laval and UNESCO, pp. 151–66.

Currie, J. (2003) Universités entrepreneuriales: de nouveaux acteurs sur la scène mondiale (le cas australien). In: Breton, G. and Lambert, M. (eds) *Globalisation et universités. Nouvel espace, nouveaux acteurs.* Québec: Presses de l'Université Laval and UNESCO, pp. 197–214.

Dias, M-A. (2005) *Social Commitment of the Universities Against the Commercialization Attempts.* Barcelona (Technical University of Catalonia):

document written for the meeting of Nobel Prize winners on the social commitment of universities.

Didriksson, A. and Herrera, A.X. (2007) Universities' new relevance and social responsibility. In: GUNI (2007) *Higher Education in the World 2007. Accreditation for Quality Assurance: What is at Stake?* New York: Palgrave Macmillan, pp. xli–xlv.

Farvaque, N. (2003) *Conventions et institutions d'évaluation dans l'approche par les capacités de Sen: des repères pour l'action publique?* Paris: Communication to the Symposium 'Conventions et institutions. Approfondissements théoriques et contribution au débat politique', 12–13 December 2003, Grande Arche de la Défense, Paris.

GUNI (2007) *Higher Education in the World 2007. Accreditation for Quality Assurance: What is at Stake?* New York: Palgrave Macmillan, GUNI series on The Social Commitment of Universities 2.

Knight, J. (2003) Les accords commerciaux (AGCS): implications pour l'enseignement supérieur. In: Breton, G. and Lambert, M. (eds) *Globalisation et universités. Nouvel espace, nouveaux acteurs*. Québec: Presses de l'Université Laval and UNESCO, pp. 87–116.

Petrella, R. (2003) Le mur mondial de la connaissance. In: Breton, G. and Lambert, M. (eds), *Globalisation et universités. Nouvel espace, nouveaux acteurs*. Québec: Presses de l'Université Laval and UNESCO, pp. 139–48.

Rawls, John (1971) *A Theory of Justice*. Cambridge, MA: Belknap Press of Harvard University Press.

Schoen, A., Laredo, P., Bellon, B. and Sanchez, P. (2007) Observatory of the European University. *Prime Position Paper*. Brussels: CE (March 2007 version).

Sen, Amartya (1999) *Development as Freedom*. New York: Random House.

Van Parijs, P. (2006) *Qu'est-ce qu'une société juste? La pensée philosophique contemporaine*. Paris (La Défense): Lecture at the French Social Weeks, 24 November 2006.

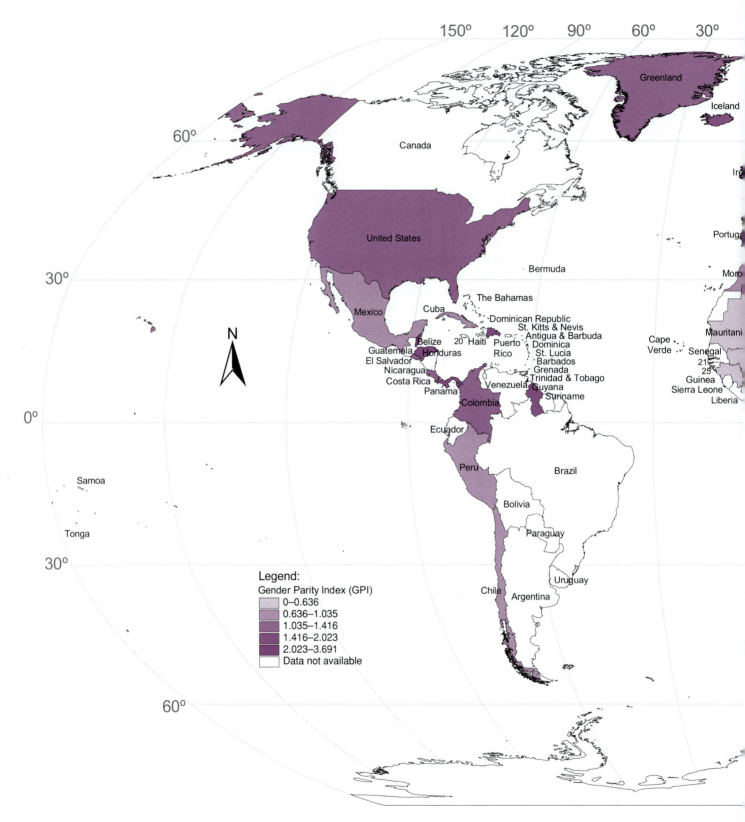

Legend:
Gender Parity Index (GPI)
0–0.636
0.636–1.035
1.035–1.416
1.416–2.023
2.023–3.691
Data not available

Source: UNESCO Institute for Statistics.

Notes
This map shows the ratio of the female-to-male in tertiary education.
A gender parity index of 1 indicates parity between sexes.
Classification method: natural breaks (Jenks optimization)

MAP 3 Gender parity index in tertiary education

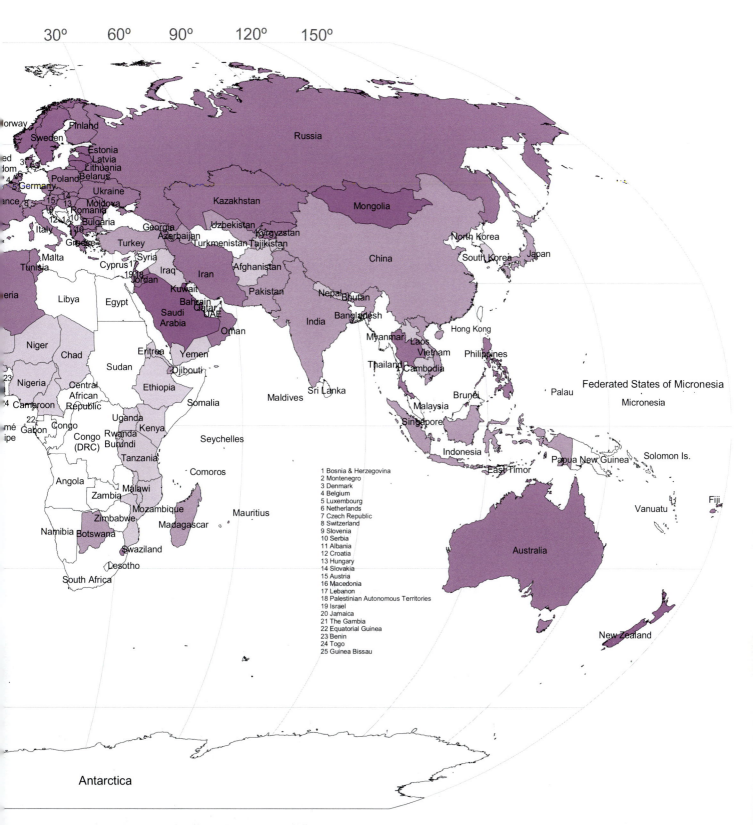

1 Bosnia & Herzegovina
2 Montenegro
3 Denmark
4 Belgium
5 Luxembourg
6 Netherlands
7 Czech Republic
8 Switzerland
9 Slovenia
10 Serbia
11 Albania
12 Croatia
13 Hungary
14 Slovakia
15 Austria
16 Macedonia
17 Lebanon
18 Palestinian Autonomous Territories
19 Israel
20 Jamaica
21 The Gambia
22 Equatorial Guinea
23 Benin
24 Togo
25 Guinea Bissau

Vector layer source: ESRI Data; Projection: Robinson

B

The emerging roles of higher education: Implications for education, research, civil engagement and institutional development

Abstract

Globalization presents a particularly challenging context for re-examining the educative purpose of higher education for human, community and social development. In the very first place, development itself is rarely explicitly claimed as a deliberate focus of most institutions of higher education. Given that the fundamental purpose of higher education is intellectual and moral development, this is not only a very strange stance but also one that is increasingly problematic and indeed ethically indefensible. In the face of the complexities of this late modern age, where 'bads' as well as 'goods' are circulating the globe with ever-increasing frequency and causing ever-more destructive impacts on nature and society alike, it is becoming glaringly obvious that new ways of 'seeing' the world and 'dealing' with issues in it are urgently needed if sustainable futures for societies are to be achieved across the globe.

If, as the substantive argument in this chapter holds, we humans have become victims of our own paradigmatic inadequacies in a manner that now threatens the very sustainability of life on earth, then higher education is duty-bound to do all it can to transform prevailing epistemic assumptions and to liberate human and social development in the further pursuit of the considered and inclusively responsible life.

INTRODUCTION

There is a strange and inexplicable reluctance by institutions of higher education across the entire globe to overtly promote the fact that they are, first and foremost, agencies of human and social development. The word *development* for instance, rarely appears in the mission statements of universities or technical colleges, nor is it even included within the list of roles or purposes or functions that the academy at large explicitly does claim for itself. Moreover, the roles that are promoted by academic institutions, including the classical trinity of teaching, research and outreach or service, are just that: roles. They are means not ends; processes that lack reference to any nominated purposes or aims or, importantly, contexts. Yet when they

are explored in any detail, teaching, research and outreach are all means that are related to such vital human and social developmental ends as the bringing forth of latent capabilities, the advancement of knowledge, and indeed to 'betterment' in a wide variety of social, cultural and material contexts. The educative purpose of higher education is perforce contextual, although, yet again, the academy seems to show little overt appreciation of that by the manner of its essentially uncritical commitment to what it continues to regard as the tried and true practices of education.

Significantly, the meaning of *educere*, one of the two Latin roots of education, also means unfolding and bringing forth, and thus education and development are essentially synonyms. Yet academics are notoriously uncomfortable with the idea of being agents of development and change. At their best, of course, even though they might not appreciate the fact, they are clearly facilitators of improvements in the human condition through the intellectual, moral, aesthetic and even spiritual development that they nurture in those with whom they critically engage – students and all other 'stakeholders' alike. Simply put, higher education fundamentally ought to be explicitly about such epistemic development. It should be conducted in such a way that all aspects of human knowing are integrated into cognitive systems that, in their own inherent systemic complexity, are most appropriate for dealing with the complex issues that characterize the late modern times in which we live: for there is strong evidence to suggest that these cognitive systems – the 'knowledge structures and the processes through which information is organized and made usable' – can, under appropriate circumstances, develop 'from a state of simple, absolute certainty into a complex, evaluative system' (West, 2004).

EDUCATIVE PURPOSE AND DEVELOPMENT

The purpose of higher education, to borrow from Socrates, should be the development of

---

Richard Bawden

competencies for knowing how to live the 'considered life' within the context of the times: to promote living a life 'which is well informed, has worthwhile goals and is lived discerningly so that one can respond to others well, and live flourishingly for oneself' Grayling (2004, p. 36). As I shall take pains to emphasize below, this 'discerning response to others' must be inclusive of all of the living world and not just our fellow human beings. This more global, holistic perspective on the educative purpose is the central contextual challenge of today if we humans and all the other communities of nature with which we are inexorably interconnected, and oft-times embedded, are to enjoy a sustainable tomorrow together.

There is a moral imperative here that also demands our intellectual and aesthetic attention, for as Leopold (1949, p. 224) has submitted, '[a] thing is right when it tends to conserve the integrity, stability and beauty of biotic communities. It is wrong when it tends otherwise': and 'tending otherwise' is certainly an all-too-frequent trajectory in this globalizing era. Higher education should be preparing humanity to deal with contemporary issues that, in their complexity, represent clear threats to sustainable ways of being. Their complexity lies not just with the fact that they comprise many different components that interact, often on a truly global scale, but also because they require collective human judgments for actions that must embrace moral, aesthetic and even spiritual dimensions in equal part to their intellectual aspects. To commit to such an educative purpose is no easy matter, as people all across the globe struggle to deal with the complexity and vagaries of a 'risk society' that, in part at least, has been induced by the very manner in which we continue to treat the world about us (Beck, 1992). Under our current circumstances, as Dietz et al. (2003) submit: '[d]evising ways to sustain the earth's ability to support diverse life, including a reasonable quality of life for humans, involves making tough decisions under uncertainty, complexity, and substantial biophysical constraints as well as conflicting human values and interests'.

The core of the argument to be presented here is that whatever higher education institutions have done in the past – whatever roles they have adopted, functions they have served, purposes they have pursued, worldviews they have assumed, and paradigms they have generated, expressed and nurtured – needs to be critically reappraised for its adequacy in light of the challenges arising from the complex circumstances in which we humans currently find ourselves, wherever we are in the world. This is especially challenging in light of the realization that local actions can have global consequences that could render them unsustainable in the future thereby making them irresponsible and morally indefensible acts in the present. Meanwhile, the ever-increasing tendency for the flow of goods and services, capital and labour, technologies and institutions, and indeed ideas themselves across the entire globe, while indisputably beneficial in many regards, also presents threats and risks to the sustainability of both human and entire biotic communities through their consequences – intended or otherwise. Each of these global flows can be regarded as constituents of the phenomenon that is being termed 'globalization', even though that term is most often associated only with the idea of a market-led, integrated world economy achieved through free trade across the world, and that has technological innovation and policy reform as the two essential 'drivers' of its continuing development (Wolf, 2004).

In this current age of the 'globalizing civilization' that has come to characterize late modernity – or as Delanty (2001) prefers, organized modernity where the technological and technocratic experts 'rule' – it is an irresponsible perversity for higher education institutions to fail to appreciate the vital importance of a focus on contextual human and social development, and to not accept it as their primary educative purpose. Modern universities, with their particular emphasis on the generation and transmission of technical knowledge, have, after all, been a primary source of the emergence of organized modernity. Ironically, they are now increasingly a victim of it while, somewhat paradoxically, they are also becoming increasingly aware of this situation and conscious of its implications with regard to their traditional responsibilities and role as prime developers of paradigms of development that are appropriate to the contexts of the times. There are even signs that some at least within academia are beginning to respond to a call for the reappraisal of the purpose, functions and practices of institutions of higher education that are responsive to the contextual needs of contemporary society through their critical engagement in dialogue and discourse with the citizenry in their dealings with the problematic issues of the day (Fear et al., 2006).

In reassuming those dialogic responsibilities with respect to human and social development, institutions of higher education will have to pay specific and critical attention to their own development – in intellectual, moral, material and even spiritual terms. Any shift by universities to what might be termed a 'development focus' (Bawden, Busch and Gagni, 1991) must therefore be achieved from a critical stance towards the nature, the momentum and the increasingly obvious inadequacies of the march of modernity, and to the logic and relevance of the intellectual and moral foundations of the development paradigm that supports it. Accordingly, the 'late modern condition' is an expression of a crisis of paradigms as much as anything – of an inadequacy of the prevailing way that we have come to view, value and treat the world about us, and to understand the implications of our actions in it.

MODERNITY AND THE MODERNIZATION PROJECT

The fundamental theme of modernity, all along, has been the promotion and active promulgation of the ideology of development as material improvement. Higher education in its broadest sense has played a very important role in guiding the 'unfolding' of an improved future in this context, as it has become the present. Indeed it could be argued that over the past half millennium or so, universities have been the most important and certainly the most sustainable institutions of all in defining the essential technocentric characteristics of the modern age as it has developed from the early (liberal modernity, as Delanty (2001) has it) to the present late stage (organized modernity). The whole essence of modernity and of the modernization project has been 'developmental progress' through the application of rational thought for decision-making in a deliberate and inexorable movement away from the mysticism and feudalism of medieval times. The promise became 'control over nature through science, material abundance through superior technology, and effective government through rational social organization' (Norgaard, 1994, p. 1), and central to this promise has been the development of particular ways of thinking, of modes of rationality and, indeed, of the very manner of thought itself. Now, however, these are proving grossly inadequate to the challenge of living the considered life within the emerging context.

The crux of the argument here is that progressive acts of development in the social and material worlds are functions of the intellectual and moral development of the actors who need (or ought) to be involved in those acts – either because they themselves are able to effect developmental change or because they are potentially affected by any changes that might be engineered by others. It follows then that the central educative purpose of institutions of higher education ought to be the explicit facilitation of epistemic development: of progressive, reflexive, critical, transformative learning that leads to much improved understanding of the need for, and expression of, responsible paradigms for living and for 'being' and for 'becoming', both as individuals alone and collectively as communities.

As responsible citizens of one world, we have in large part failed to live up to this critical ideal, and indeed have quintessentially rejected its implications. The extent and pervasiveness of social inequities and injustices, as well as overt conflicts and cultural abuses that continue to be pervasive across the entire globe, bear testament to just that. Furthermore, the quest for material abundance, which has come to characterize the aim and trajectory of modernity, has come at the price of significant resource depletions, environmental degradations, social injustices, inequities and conflicts. Such a material approach to development now poses threats to the very sustainability of life on earth itself, on a scale that we have never before confronted in the history of human interactions with the rest of nature. Although the globalization of trade in goods and services has become the most recent hallmark and inevitable dimension of the modernization project, it has been accompanied by the increasingly global spread of highly infectious diseases (often of animal origin), polluting chemicals and potentially hazardous radiations, criminal activities and stateless terrorism, the latter often motivated by religious fanatics who essentially 'yearn for martyrdom' in the face of their self-perceived isolation from their own societies as they turn increasingly to embrace modernity (Sageman, 2004).

Such is the nature, scope and risk potential of these destructive consequences of modernization that they are seen by some as representing nothing less than 'irreversible threats to the life of plants, animals and human beings' (Beck, 1992, p. 13). Under these circumstances it is impossible to disagree with Beck's claim that many of the problematic issues that we currently face in the world 'result from techno-economic development itself'. Thus while modernization has come to mean progress and development, the paradox is that it has proved to have an inherently destructive as well as creative side with the production and transmission of what have been referred to as 'bads' emerging as unintended consequences of the production and transmission of 'goods' (Beck, 1992). As Beck contends, while modernization has certainly resulted in significant control of nature to ends that suit human needs and wants, it has also resulted in a host of associated risks and hazards to both biophysical and sociocultural environments. And all of this is indeed happening on a truly global scale where the 'transformation of the unseen side effects of industrial production into global trouble spots is therefore not at all a problem of the world surrounding us – not the so-called "environmental problem" – but a far reaching institutional crisis of industrial society itself' (Beck, 1996, p. 32).

There are vital echoes here of Einstein's famous dictum that 'the world we have made, as a result of the level of thinking we have done so far, creates problems that we cannot solve at the same level of thinking at which we created them' (quoted in MacHale, 2002). The profound cognitive challenge that this represents deserves far more attention than it currently seems to attract.

Witness the impact that the carbon emissions from the burning of the hydrocarbon fuels that provide the essential energy for industrialization are unquestionably having on the climate across the entire globe. A global issue like this demands attention on a truly global scale in a manner that reflects a similarly global commitment to 'different levels of thinking'. At the very moment of writing (September 2007), not one but two international meetings are being held in the USA to address the issue of climate change (one convened by the United Nations for national leaders to find a suitable replacement for the Kyoto Protocol and to commit their governments to it, and one convened by the President of the USA for leaders of the 25 'big emitters' to explore an agenda for reducing emissions). However, there is no apparent reference whatsoever, in either of these meetings, to the epistemic changes that are essential for dealing with the systemic complexity of the matter at hand. There are not even any signs that the need for epistemic transformation is appreciated, let alone being addressed. And of course this epistemic deficiency is greatly amplified when other confluent aspects of 'development' are factored in, including the accelerating demands for energy made by rapidly industrializing nations such as China, India and Brazil that are occurring at a time when oil production is seemingly already at its peak (Mick Winter, 2007).

At the heart of this immanent crisis, and as a central feature of the problematic aspect of the entire emergent phenomenon that is globalization, is the matter of the way things are known in the name of science, valued in the name of economics, done in the manner of technology, and assured in the name of public policy and mechanisms of governance. Particularly evident from the prevailing perspective on late modern development is the exclusion of both the normative and the emotive from formal educational paradigms and pedagogies. Just as the citizens of civil society have been overwhelmed by the technical knowledge of the experts, so too have they abdicated their responsibilities for moral reasoning to institutions such as the church, the state, science, or the market (Busch, 2000). The result is the loss of competencies in moral and aesthetic judgment and a consequential impoverishment of what have been called our appreciative systems (Vickers, 1983). It is these systems that determine the way that we each 'see' (reality judgment) and 'value' (value judgment) various situations in the world about us, which, in turn, condition the manner by which we make 'instrumental judgments' (what is to be done) and take executive actions: in sum, how we each contribute to the social world (Jackson, 2000), or more specifically, to the communities to which we belong.

THE NATURE AND SIGNIFICANCE OF DEVELOPMENT PARADIGMS

The distinction between societies and communities is of great significance to the arguments being presented here for the transformation of the educative purpose of higher education and of the institutions that provide it. The contemporary emphasis on the 'it' of societies rather than the 'thou' or 'you' of communities illustrates very clearly the central thrust of the modernist agenda, while also providing a focal point for its reform. The distinction is of course far from new, with Ferdinand Tönnies in the late 1880s distinguishing between a *Gemeinschaft* (community) characterized by mutual relations of trust and caring that is supposedly eclipsed by a focus on a much less personally interactive *Gesellschaft* (society) as a function of the onrush of modern urban civilization that he claimed for those times (Mendes-Flohr, 1989).

As civilization has continued to 'rush on', this emphasis on the 'it' of society has become ever more pronounced and along with it, a loss of emphasis on the 'thou' of community. The citizenry, the individuals and communities of the lay public, have been increasingly objectified as consumers and as members of abstract social sectors that can be regulated and governed, rather than trustingly embraced and discursively engaged. Higher education has closely reflected these changes, as the age of organized modernity – with its emphasis on science, technology and liberal economics – has continued its march from its emergence in the early part of the 20th century. Far from the ideal encouraged by von Humboldt and other German idealists – that is, of the beginning, in the 19th century, of the university as an active and autonomous agent in the cultural transformation of the nation-state (Readings, 1996) – institutions of higher education have progressively lost their autonomy, as well as their character as institutions nurturing *Gemeinschaft*. In contrast to retaining their autonomy from other state (social) institutions, they have instead been virtually colonized by other institutions of the state resulting in the creation of what Etzkowitz and Leydesdorff (1997) refer to as 'a triple helix' of interdependence that involves 'the three great monoliths of industry, governance, and the academy'. These are co-evolving, it is argued, in such a manner that each has come to uncritically serve the needs of the other, while also increasingly assuming organizational, structural, cultural and dispositional characteristics in common with each other (Kerr, 1982). Most significantly, they have also come to both share and mutually defend a paradigm for development in spite of the fact that it is proving to be increasingly inadequate to the task of dealing with the complexity, contingency, contestability and confluency that is characteristic of the contemporary *problématique*.

As Guba and Lincoln (1994) have emphasized, paradigms are differentiated through three different sets of assumptions: beliefs about the nature of nature (ontologies), beliefs about the nature of knowledge about that nature (epistemologies), and beliefs about the nature of human nature particularly with respect to the nature and role of values (axiologies). Paradigms therefore also differ in the practical expressions of these beliefs (methodologies). The prevailing paradigm of development in late modernity is well exemplified in the endeavours of so-called 'international development' based as it is on theories of 'modernization', 'industrialization', and 'dependency' (Escobar, 2000). Norgaard (1994) nominates five particular epistemological and meta-physical beliefs – atomism, mechanism, universalism, objectivism and monism – that he believes have become so central to the way we have come to see the world, and thus so embedded in our public discourse, that they exclude other beliefs which, he argues, 'are more appropriate for understanding the complexities of environmental systems and which are more supportive of cultural pluralism' (Norgaard, 1994, p. 62). The dominant paradigm of modernization, to which the higher education sector has lent strong paradigmatic support, has become an expression of an instrumental logic of 'productionism' with unashamed epistemological foundations in 'technical rationality' and 'mechanistic reductionism'.

The methodologies for development that continue to dominate emphasize technical infrastructure enhancement and enhanced social control that is achieved through 'institutional bureaucratization' and regulatory governance. Higher education continues to play a seminal role here both in the further development of this approach and in its promulgation as the essential source of 'training' for scientific and technical 'expert counterparts'.

The fundamental parameters of the modernist mantra for international development are material growth and efficiency of production with an unapologetic emphasis on 'perpetual economic growth in industrialized countries and convergence toward the rich country model in poorer countries' (Raskin, 2000). The key drivers, as stated earlier in the context of the globalization of trade, are technological innovation and policy 'reformation' (Wolf, 2004). Far from embracing the notion of the considered life including respect for the integrity, stability and beauty of nature, the methods and practices of the modernist paradigm present a worldview of the benefits of exploitation and manipulation of a nature that is construed as a 'pool' or source of natural resources.

With all its conceptual and practical limitations, it is difficult to both understand and accept the centrality of economic institutions and what Harmon (1984) referred to as 'the paramountcy of economic rationality' in the orthodox development paradigm. Yet in spite of the obvious inadequacies of the 'econo-centricity' of development orthodoxy in practice, in spite of the epistemic limitations that neo-liberalism presents to the development paradigms, and in spite of the view espoused by some that 'it has led to, and contributed to, the great global problems of our day', the basic assumptions of the modernist paradigm have, for the most part, seemed 'right headed and inescapable and generally uncritically accepted' (Harmon, 1984, p. 16).

Again it must be emphasized that the academy has played a central role in uncritically promoting – and indeed emulating – these principles. As Yankelovich (1991, p. 8) has put it, the 'pervasive march' of the 'culture of technical control' and its empiricist/instrumentalist epistemological foundations achieved 'through the application of expert thinking in science, technology, economic enterprises, government, the policy sciences, and large organizational structures' has all occurred with the willing acquiescence, and indeed scholarly support, of the academy. Little thought has been given, he argues, 'to strategies for preserving the benefits of the Culture of Technical Control while at the same time curbing its excesses' (Yankelovich, 1991, p. 9).

No longer a source of critique and sceptical reflexivity of cultural and societal change, institutions of higher education have all too commonly been captured by, and now merely aid and abet, the prevailing modernist corporate paradigm of instrumentalism and materialism, to the extent that they themselves have become archetypes of it. They have even uncritically accepted the language and metaphors of the modernist discourse for their own organizational principles and structures with its roots in the Taylorist logic of the arrangement of people in mechanical relationships 'so as "to fit" the strategies and needs of business, to "take instructions", to "implement orders" and to act unthinkingly, robot-like in pursuit of "rational" objectives set top-down by others' (Franklin, Hodgkinson and Stewart, 1998).

Readings (1996) has even suggested that, in this age of globalization, universities have essentially *become* transnational global corporations, while opining that 'it is no longer clear what the role of universities is within a society, nor what the exact nature of that society is'. And this is particularly so as national societies and cultures themselves are increasingly unsure of their own identities, character, and responsibilities in the face of the seismic 'forces' of globalization.

The lack of criticality has also allowed the instrumental-rationalist pattern of thinking to dominate education itself to the virtual exclusion of all other forms of knowing and understanding. This has led, in turn, to the elevation of university scientists/teachers to positions of social dominance by virtue of their status as experts, reflecting what Gadamer (1975) has referred to as 'the idolatry of the scientific method and of the anonymous authority of the sciences'. And a very unfortunate consequence of this 'peculiar falsehood of modern consciousness' (Gadamer, 1975) has been the emergence of a climate of cognitive authoritarianism where 'rationality of thinking for oneself diminishes as society's knowledge gathering activities expand to the point of requiring a division of cognitive labour into autonomous expertises' (Fuller, 1988).

Such has been the cultural retreat from criticality that the relationship between universities, as the source of 'expert knowledge', and the general citizenry has become increasingly adversarial rather than mutually supportive, with the result that there is a continuing decline in the quality of public participation in their own affairs accompanied by the erosion of self-governance (Yankelovich, 1991). This inertia threatens the very foundations of democracy, grounded as they are in participation and collective judgment, and employing as they do a plurality of ways of knowing and valuing and coming to judgment (Yankelovich, 1991). At the same time, the rhetoric of development emphasizes the honourable goal of 'spreading democracy' across the globe – even if it takes military force and foreign occupation to achieve just that.

None of this could be happening at a worse time in history, given the immensely complex challenges associated with the dynamics of globalization, with all that that implies in relation to inter- or transnational governance, to cultural and societal transformations, and to the responsible treatment of the environment; all on a truly global scale.

Was there ever a more critical moment to heed the call for universities to become much more engaged 'in the resolution of the most pressing social, civic, economic and moral problems' of the day (Boyer, 1996)?

THE WINDS OF CHANGE

Most fortunately (and fortuitously), there is increasing evidence, as intimated earlier, that there are those within the academy who are indeed heeding that call (Fear et al., 2006). This growing appreciation is coinciding with an ever-growing recognition within societies and bureaucracies alike that current approaches to material and social development are indeed not only failing to fulfil their promises but are contributing to the *problématique*. The

coincidence of social awareness of the need for changes in the prevailing approach along with critiques both within the academy and beyond it that question the very rationality and governance of development (Escobar, 2000) – as well as the very aims and purposes of modernization itself (Beck, 1992) – is spawning significant changes of thinking and of practice alike.

Norgaard, as one who is prominent among these critics, calls for a fundamental reconstruction of the character of development such that it embraces a paradigm of co-evolution 'of social and environmental systems' and a 'co-evolutionary cosmology that stresses the communal nature of knowing' (Norgaard, 1994, p. 99). While criticizing the pre-eminent role that has been given to atomistic science and technology in the development process, his argument is not for their rejection, but for their reorientation into a process that 'admits, helps us see, lends legitimacy to and identifies the advantages of a diversity of ways of knowing, valuing, organizing and doing things'. Uphoff (1992, p. 289) adopts a similar line in arguing for a reorientation of mechanistic scientific thinking in development, observing that 'if we cannot eliminate straightaway all material and mental obstacles to human fulfilment, we can begin by revising our scientific and day-to-day thinking along the lines that various disciplines are charting'. Not all of our present thinking and ways of doing things need to be abandoned, but we ought to 'dethrone those methodologies that restrict positive-sum outcomes in the name of rigor, by equating the closed systems we create analytically through our minds with the multiple open and overlapping systems that exist all around us'.

Innovative intellectual constructs and theories are emerging that provide novel paradigmatic perspectives on the development process (for example Sen, 1999), and on the moral dimensions of development (for example Crocker, 1991). These initiatives are finding expression through emerging paradigms that are 'people centered' (Korten and Klaus, 1984), 'rights-based' (Pettit and Wheeler, 2005), and 'participatory' (Crocker, 2003) and which are, in turn, all embraced by the powerful worldview of 'development as freedom' that Sen (1999) promotes. The case for a perspective of development as freedom, and for the associated formulations as *rights*, rests on the three propositions that (a) they have intrinsic importance, (b) they have a consequential role in providing political incentives for economic security, and (c) they play an important role in the genesis of values and priorities (Sen, 1999, p. 246). These assertions further highlight the significance of the moral dimensions of the emerging paradigmatic shift, while also emphasizing the concomitant need for the development of moral consciousness and ethical competencies as key factors, along with intellectual development, in the transformative development of 'development for transformation'!

Cognitive psychology provides some very important insights here in terms of guiding response frameworks from the academy to these epistemic challenges, and at base is the need to address the very processes of knowing and understanding. As Bernstein (1983, p. 113) observes: 'if we are to understand what it is to be human beings, we must seek to understand understanding itself, in its rich, full, and complex dimensions'.

A number of very significant theories have been developed regarding intellectual and moral development, both in childhood (Kohlberg, 1963; Piaget, 1969; Hoffman, 1970) and beyond (Perry, 1968; Gibbs, 2003). While the schema presented by the different works differ in their details (West, 2004), their central theses about epistemological, ontological and axiological development through childhood, adolescence, early adulthood and indeed throughout life, are in strong overall agreement. It would seem that such epistemic developments have elements that are, on the one hand invariant and universal, while on the other they rely in part 'upon the self's particular and somewhat unique experience' (Kohlberg and Ryncarz, 1990). In either case, epistemic changes of significant proportions can be achieved essentially through a combination of both cognitive challenge (Salner, 1986) and changed existential circumstances (Gibbs, 2003).

Kitchener (1983) describes a three-level model of cognitive processing that provides a very important conceptual framework for the redesign of the academy's educative functions in response to the challenges that late modernity presents. She argues that cognitive developments can occur in cognition (dealing with the matter to hand), in meta-cognition (dealing with how we deal with the matter to hand), and in epistemic cognition (dealing with the limits of knowledge and epistemological assumptions). From this perspective, shifts in paradigms actually represent 'epistemic developments' that are expressed as 'more advanced' states of intellectual and moral understandings as they are reflected in action. Most importantly, complex cognitive frameworks and processes appropriate to the task of dealing with complex issues in the world can be developed by individuals and communities alike in which intellectual and moral 'ways of knowing' are integrated into critically appreciative learning systems (Bawden, 2000).

So even as it responds tentatively to the imperative to turn its attention to human and social development as its educative purpose, it is vital that the academy embraces the need to critically explore the nature of development itself. Such critical reflexivity must focus on both the nature and the challenges of intellectual, moral and spiritual development, as well as on the characteristics of the expression of these in terms of appropriate paradigms for, and responsible developments of, the material, social and cultural worlds. And all this must be set within the context of a critical review of the age of organized modernity that is increasingly characterized by the globalizing tendency that clearly demands intellectual, moral and spiritual refinement, if not outright systemic transformation.

SUMMARY AND CONCLUSIONS

The context of globalization that increasingly characterizes this age of late, organized modernity, presents significant challenges to the educative purposes and functions of institutions of higher education, wherever they are located in the world. It particularly demands a critical appreciation of complexity from a number of different aspects. These include the inherently grand scale of global phenomena as well as the intricacies of a multitude of interacting elements including people across that scale. It also includes the interactive components of the cognitive systems of those who need to be collectively involved in public judgments about what needs to be done in the name of 'considered and sustainable collective lives', which embraces an ethos of care for other communities – human and the rest of the biota of nature alike. Complex too are the conceptual foundations of sustainability and the everyday practicalities of its expression as sustainable development in the face of features like contestability, contingency and contextuality, which are all far removed from the certainties and objectivities of the technocentric paradigm of development that continues to prevail.

As Redclift (1987) has pointed out, the problem with achieving sustainable development, even if adequate intellectual foundations could be established, is related to the overriding structures of the international economic development system, 'which arose out of the exploitation of environmental resources' in the first place, and which frequently operate 'as constraints on the achievement of long-term sustainable practices'. Sustainable development, he concludes, presents a perspective that recognizes 'that the limits of sustainability have structural as well as natural origins.' While sustainability and sustainable development remain contestable constructs (Davison, 2001), they are central aspects of emerging approaches to what we might now refer to as 'post-industrial' paradigms of development which demand, above all else, the development of human cognitive systems for individuals and communities alike.

Essentially, to paraphrase Milbraith (1989), our institutions of higher learning need to commit themselves to helping the citizenry at large to 'learning our way out' of the modernist dilemma by critically engaging in the transformative and participatory processes of what he referred to as 'social learning' – people learning with, from, and through others as they engage together as learning communities, seeking inclusive improvements to the circumstances in which they collectively find themselves or anticipate finding themselves in the future as it continues to unfold.

While such learning will need to focus on all three levels of cognitive processing, special emphasis must be placed on the epistemic dimensions of cognition that contribute so much to the character of our paradigms. If indeed, as has been argued throughout this piece, we have become victims of our own paradigmatic inadequacies in a manner that now threatens the very sustainability of life on earth, then higher education is duty-bound to do all it can to transform prevailing epistemic assumptions and to liberate human and social development in its further pursuit of the considered life.

REFERENCES

Bawden, R.J. (2000) Valuing the epistemic in the search for betterment. *Cybernetics and Human Knowing, 7*, pp. 5–25.

Bawden, R.J., Busch. L. and Gagni, A. (1991) The agricultural university for the twenty-first century. *Impact of Science on Society*, **164**, pp. 353–66. (Adapted from keynote paper for Workshop on Agricultural Universities for the Twenty First Century. Reston, Virginia, October 1988.)

Beck, U. (1992) *Risk Society: Towards a New Society*. London: Sage.

Beck, U. (1996) Risk, society and the provident state. In: U. Beck, B. Szerszynski and B. Wynne (eds) *Risk, Environment and Society: Towards a New Ecology*. London: Sage.

Bernstein, R.J. (1983) *Beyond Objectivism and relativism: Science, Hermeneutics and Praxis*. Philadelphia: University of Pennsylvania Press.

Boyer, E.L. (1996) The scholarship of engagement. *Journal of Public Service and Outreach*, **1**, pp. 11–20.

Busch, L. (2000) *The Eclipse of Morality*. New York: Aldine de Gruyter.

Crocker, D. (1991) Towards development ethics. *Word Development, 19*, pp. 457–83.

Crocker, D. (2003) *Participatory Development: The Capabilities Approach and Deliberative Democracy*. Working Paper. Institute of Philosophy and Public Policy, Institute of Public Affairs. University of Maryland.

Davison, A. (2001) *Technology and the Contested Meanings of Sustainability*. New York: State University of New York Press.

Delanty, G. (2001) *Challenging Knowledge: The university in the knowledge society*. Buckingham: The Open University Press.

Dietz, T., Ostrom, E. and Stern, P.C. (2003) The struggle to govern the Commons. *Science*, **302**, pp. 1907–12.

Escobar, A. (2000) Beyond the search for a paradigm? Post-development and beyond. *Development*, **43**, pp. 11–14.

Etzkowitz, H. and Leydesdorff, L. (1997) *Universities in the Global Economy: A triple helix of university, industry and government relations*. London: Cassell Academic.

Fear, F.A., Rosaen, C.L., Bawden, R.J. and Foster-Fishman, P.G. (2006) *Coming to Critical Engagement: An autoethnographic exploration*. Lanham, Maryland: University Press of America.

Franklin, P., Hodgkinson, M. and Stewart, J. (1998) Towards universities as learning organisations. *The Learning Organization*, **5**(5), pp. 228–38.

Fuller S. (1988) *Social Epistemology*. Bloomington, IN: Indiana University Press.

Gadamer, H-G. (1975) Hermeneutics and social science. *Cultural Hermeneutics*, **2**, pp. 307–16.

Gibbs, J.C. (2003) *Moral Development and Reality: Beyond the theories of Kohlberg and Hoffman*. London: Sage Publications.

Grayling, A.C. (2004) What is the Good Life? *Journal of the Royal Society for the Arts*. July, pp. 36–7.

Guba, E.G. and Lincoln, Y. S. (1994) Competing paradigms in qualitative research. In: N.K. Denzin and Y.S. Lincoln (eds) *Handbook of Qualitative Research*. Thousand Oaks, CA: Sage Publications.

Harmon, W.H. (1984) Key choices. In: D.C. Korten and R. Klaus (eds) *Contributions Toward Theory and Planning Frameworks*. West Hartford, CT: Kumarian Press.

Hoffman, M.L. (1970) Moral development. In: P.H. Mussen (ed.) *Carmichael's Manual of Child Psychology* (Vol. 2, 3rd edn). New York: John Wiley.

Jackson, M.C. (2000) *Systems Approaches to Management*. New York: Kluwer Academic/ Plenum Publishers.

Kerr, C. (1982) *The Uses of the University* (3rd edn). Cambridge, MA: Harvard University Press.

Kitchener, K.S. (1983) Cognition, metacognition, and epistemic cognition: A three level model of cognitive processing. *Human Development*, **26**, pp. 222–32.

Kohlberg, L. (1963) The Development of Children's Orientation Towards a Moral Order. 1. Sequence in the development of moral thought. *Vita Humana*, **6**, pp. 11–33.

Kohlberg, L. and Ryncarz, R.A. (1990) Beyond Justice Reasoning: Moral development and consideration of a seventh stage. In: C.N. Alexander and E.J. Langer (eds) *Higher Stages of Human Development: Perspectives on Adult Growth*. New York: Oxford University Press.

Korten, D.C. and Klaus, R. (1984) Introduction. In: D.C. Korten and R. Klaus (eds) *Contributions Toward Theory and Planning Frameworks*. West Hartford, CT: Kumarian Press.

Leopold, A. (1949) *A Sand County Almanac*. New York: Oxford University Press.

MacHale, D. (2002) *Wisdom*. London: Mercier Press.

Mendes-Flohr, P. (1989) *From Mysticism to Dialogue: Martin Buber's Transformation of German Social Thought*. Detroit: Wayne State University Press.

Milbraith, L.W. (1989) *Envisioning a Sustainable Society: Learning our way out*. New York: State University of New York Press.

Norgaard, R.B. (1994) *Development Betrayed: The End of Progress and a Co-evolutionary Revisioning of the Future*. London: Routledge.

Pettitt, J. and Wheeler, J. (2005) Developing rights? Relating discourse to context and practice. *IDS Bulletin*, **36**, pp 1–8.

Piaget, J. (1969) *Judgment and Reasoning in the Child* (M. Warden, Trans.). Torowa, NJ: Littlefield Adams. (Original work published in 1928.)

Perry, W.G. (1968) *Forms of Intellectual and Ethical Develop-*

ment in the College Years. New York: Holt, Rinehart and Winston.

Raskin, P.D. (2000) Bending the curve: toward global sustainability. *Development*, **43**, pp. 67–74.

Redclift, M. (1987) *Sustainable Development: Exploring the Contradictions*. London: Methuen.

Readings, B. (1996) *The University in Ruins*. Cambridge, MA: Harvard University Press.

Sageman, M. (2004) *Understanding Terror Networks*. Philadelphia: University of Pennsylvania Press.

Salner, M. (1986) Adult cognitive and epistemological development in systems education. *Systems Research*, **3**, pp. 225–32.

Sen, A. (1999) *Development as Freedom*. New York: Anchor Books.

Uphoff, N. (1992) *Learning from Gal Oya: Possibilities for Participatory Development and Post-Newtonian Social Science*. Ithaca, NY: Cornell University Press.

Vickers, G. (1983) *Human Systems are Different*. London: Harper and Row.

West E.J. (2004) Perry's Legacy: Models of epistemological development. *Journal of Adult Development*, **11**, pp. 61–70.

Winter, M. (2007) *Peak Oil Preparedness. Preparing for peak oil, climate change, and economic collapse*. San Francisco: Westsong Publishing.

Wolf, M. (2004) *Why Globalization Works*. New Haven and London: Yale University Press.

Yankelovich, D. (1991) *Coming to Public Judgment: Making democracy work in a complex world*. Syracuse, New York: Syracuse University Press.

The purpose of higher education: A discussion based on Edgar Morin's thinking

GUNI Secretariat[1]

INTRODUCTION

This contribution addresses various fundamental questions that allow for a debate about higher education based on the thought of the philosopher Edgar Morin. This debate will take place particularly around his book *Seven Complex Lessons in Education for the Future*. It is worthwhile to point out that embracing or synthesizing the complete philosophical thought of Edgar Morin is far from the aim of this contribution.

More than ever before, the current state of global crisis and the complexity and uncertainty inherent in today's events reinforce the need to transform our way of thinking. In this regard, Morin defends education as a powerful and fundamental instrument in this transformation. With the *Seven Complex Lessons in Education for the Future*, he opens new horizons for the transformation in thinking, and gives a key role to education. Morin promulgates seven fundamental lessons for the future of education, which any culture should embrace, without exception.

Edgar Morin's thought proposes a transformation of higher education based on an authentic union between scientific disciplines, integrating also a deep capacity for self-criticism and reflectiveness on knowledge. This takes place by means of a holistic approach to knowledge, showing interdependency between all spheres of knowledge and the fundamental questions about man and life.

THE STATE OF THE WORLD AND THE NEED FOR A REFORM IN THINKING BY MEANS OF EDUCATION

Today's model of development has created more problems than solutions and has brought humanity to a profound crisis. Various antagonisms feed each other in this situation: antagonisms between nations, religions, the secular and the religious, modernity and tradition, democracy and dictatorship, rich and poor, East and West, and between North and South. It is in this context that the antagonist economic and strategic interests for profit making of superpowers and multinationals come together. This situation has brought significant imbalances: while some enjoy economic progress, a large part of humanity suffers poverty and misery. In addition, the 'survival' of the planet is at risk due to the environmental impact caused by the current model of development.

If we want Earth to provide for the needs of its inhabitants, societies must undergo a transformation. The world of tomorrow must be different from the world we know today. Democracy, equity, social justice, peace and harmony with our natural environment should be the key aspects to be considered in this transformation. Education is one of the most powerful elements to undertake and realize this transformation.

Today, this consideration has been pointed out by numerous authors, and similarly it was already mentioned in the 1996 report *Learning: The Treasure Within*, prepared for UNESCO by the International Commission on Education for the Twenty-first century. In this text, education is shown to be an essential instrument for humanity to reach the ideals of peace, freedom and social justice. The role of higher education is identically conceived in UNESCO's (1998) *World Declaration on Higher Education for the Twenty-first Century: Vision and Action*.

One of the main challenges today is to transform our way of thinking, with the purpose of integrating the complexity, the rapid changes and the unpredictability that characterizes the world today and reality itself. To achieve this, it is necessary to conceive a way of uniting and organizing the different types of knowledge, which are, at the moment, separated. This need for transformation demands a reform in thinking, necessary to conceive together the context, the global, and the multidimensional aspects of knowledge. In this regard, Morin invites us to reformulate our policies and educational programmes, with a long-term perspective and aiming to serve future generations.

HIGHER EDUCATION AND THE SEVEN COMPLEX LESSONS FOR THE FUTURE

In modernity, and with special intensity during the past decades, an overspecialization and compartmentalization of knowledge has taken place in higher education. This separation of different types of knowledge has been one of the aspects that have made it difficult to deepen our understanding of the fundamental aspects of human beings, life, and their interrelation with knowledge.

For higher education to contribute effectively to the understanding of the world, Morin proposes the integration of science and philosophy, as well as the integration of a number of fundamental elements for human understanding: the emotional, artistic, spiritual, and the psychological aspects. Thus, on the basis of a reform in thinking, the study and examination of human complexity and the human condition ought to be incorporated into higher education from a holistic approach.

This perspective broadens the outlook and purpose of higher education as we know it today. With the *Seven Complex Lessons in Education for the Future*, Morin proposes a model of higher education able to empower people, so that they discover and strengthen their human potential. This change would happen from self-understanding, the understanding of others, and the understanding of the world the person inhabits. This means a new vision and a broader role for higher education, which is still seen today as mainly providing professional capacity.

Within this framework for change, the book *Seven Complex Lessons in Education for the Future* provides seven key principles that the author believes should be incorporated into higher education.

EDUCATING IN THE BLINDNESS OF KNOWLEDGE: THE ERROR AND THE ILLUSION

Education, which principally generates and transmits knowledge, ignores human knowledge with its realities, imperfections and difficulties, and its tendency to create error and illusion.

Knowledge cannot be handled like a ready-made tool that can be used without studying its nature. Knowing about knowledge should figure as a primary requirement to prepare the mind to confront the constant threat of error and illusion that act as parasites on the human mind. It is a question of arming minds in the vital combat for lucidity.

It is necessary to introduce and develop the study of the cultural, intellectual, and cerebral properties of human knowledge, its processes and modalities, and the psychological and cultural dispositions that make us vulnerable to error and illusion.

EDUCATING ON THE PRINCIPLES OF PERTINENT KNOWLEDGE

There is a major problem that is still unsolved: how can we encourage a way of learning that is able to grasp general, fundamental problems and insert partial, circumscribed knowledge within them.

The predominance of fragmented learning divided up into disciplines often makes people unable to connect parts and wholes; it should be replaced by learning that can seize objects within their context, their complexity, and their totality.

It is necessary to develop the natural aptitude of the human mind to place all information within a context and an entity. We should teach methods of understanding mutual relations and reciprocal influences between parts and the whole in a complex world.

EDUCATING ON HUMAN CONDITION

Humans are physical, biological, psychological, cultural, social and historical beings. This complex unity of human nature has been so thoroughly disintegrated by education, divided into disciplines, that we can no longer learn what 'human being' means. This awareness should be restored so that every person, wherever he might be, can become aware of both his complex identity and his shared identity with all other human beings.

Thus, the human condition should be an essential subject of higher education. Starting from current disciplines, it is possible to recognize human unity and complexity by assembling and organizing knowledge dispersed in natural and social sciences, literature and philosophy, so as to demonstrate the indissoluble connection between the unity and the diversity of all humans.

EDUCATING ON EARTH IDENTITY

Knowledge of current planetary developments that will undoubtedly accelerate in the 21st century, and recognition of our Earth citizenship, will be indispensable for all of us. This should be one of the major objectives of education.

The history of the planetary era should be taught from its beginnings in the 16th century, when communication was established between all five continents. Without obscuring the ravages of oppression and domination in the past and present, we should show how all parts of the world have become interdependent.

The complex configuration of planetary crisis in the 20th century should be elucidated to show how all human beings now face the same life and death problems and share the same fate.

EDUCATING ON THE CONFRONTATION OF UNCERTAINTIES

We have acquired many certainties through science, but science has also revealed many areas of uncertainty. Higher education should understand the study of uncertainties that have emerged in the physical sciences (microphysics, thermodynamics and cosmology), the sciences of biological evolution, and the historical sciences.

We should teach strategic principles for dealing with chance, the unexpected and uncertain, and ways to modify these strategies in response to continuing acquisition of new information. We should learn to navigate on a sea of uncertainties, sailing in and around islands of certainty.

The abandonment of determinist conceptions of human history that claimed to predict our future, the study of major events and accidents of our century, which were all unexpected, and the unpredictable course of the human adventure should incite us to prepare our minds to expect the unexpected and confront it

EDUCATING ON UNDERSTANDING EACH OTHER

The understanding of each other needs awareness of its complexity. Understanding the human means understanding its unity within its diversity, and its diversity in its unity. Self-understanding and self-criticism are needed to capture the mechanisms of understanding. Empathy, identification with the other, projection, compassion and fraternity are needed in this process.

Understanding is both a means and an end of human communication. And yet we do not teach understanding. Our planet calls for mutual understanding in all directions. Given the importance of teaching understanding on all educational levels at all ages, the development of this quality requires a reform of mentalities. The mutual understanding between human beings, whether familiar or unknown to us, is vital to develop human relations outside the barbarous state of misunderstanding.

In this sense, misunderstanding must be studied from its sources, modalities, and effects. This is all the more necessary in that this study would focus not only on the symptoms, but also on the causes of racism, xenophobia and discrimination. Improved understanding would form a solid base for the education for peace, which we are attached to by essence and vocation.

EDUCATING ON HUMAN GENRE

Ethics cannot be taught by moral lessons. It must take shape in people's minds through awareness that a human being is at one and the same time an individual, a member of a society and part of a species. Every individual carries this triple reality within himself, and ethics should consider this reality. All truly human development must include joint development of individual autonomy, community participation, and awareness of belonging to the human species.

From there, the two great ethical–political finalities of the new millennium take shape: establishment of a relationship of mutual control between society and individuals by way of democracy, and the fulfilment of Humanity as a planetary community. Education should not only contribute to an awareness of our Earth-Homeland, it should help this awareness find expression in the will to realize our Earth citizenship.

FIRST STEPS IN THE DEVELOPMENT OF HIGHER EDUCATION FOR A REFORM IN THINKING

There are currently some projects that incorporate the first advancements in the development of higher education incorporating the reform of thinking. On one hand, we have the creation of multi-universities, such as the Real World Multiversity in Mexico. And on the other, there is the development of transdisciplinary postgraduate programmes, created with a prominent humanist outlook; in this sense, the University of Xalapa (Mexico) has developed a type of doctorate carrying this perspective.

As a result of the creation of the multi-university, Morin has proposed the creation of *Institutes of fundamental culture*, which can be developed in-house at a university or as independent institutions. They would offer education for a diversity of groups (students, citizens, professionals, business entrepreneurs, and so on) and in different moments (pre-university, during university studies and at post-university stage). These institutions would aim at educating to face life based on Morin's proposal. This is the fundamental education that would contribute to the reform of spirit, thought, knowledge and life.

Higher education as a whole, and with the participation of all the actors involved, is called to be the key actor in the development of this type of initiative, as well as in the active research of its results in the context of human development.

From the perspective shown in this contribution, human understanding, the understanding of the very same knowledge and complexity, sets the agenda for a reform in thinking, which is needed to live closer to human plenitude and to create harmony between individuals and cultures in the planetary era.

NOTE

1   GUNI Secretariat thanks Manuel Fernández for his work as principal writer of this contribution.

SPECIAL CONTRIBUTION I.8

Ethics and values in learning and teaching: Challenges for the role of human and social development in higher education

Swami Atmapriyananda

ABSTRACT

Globalization and staggering advances in science and technology have posed unprecedented, serious challenges to higher education. One of these is the enormous challenge to the ancient question of ethics and values. *Dharma*, the Sanskrit word for ethics and moral values, means holding together. With the decline of *dharma*, 'things fall apart; the centre cannot hold; there's anarchy everywhere'. Dark clouds of disintegration and anarchy loom large on the horizon of 'modern development' and are agitating the world's conscience. Humanity is faced by fundamental questions such as: 'What is education?' 'What is true development?' The developmental role of higher education is being subjected to scrutiny, and is in urgent need of being revised and revalued. This paper discusses some of these issues and reassesses the goals and the role of higher education in the light of the concept of human personality and the paradigm of human development that has been formed over thousands of years by Indian sages and seers, philosophers and thinkers. These ancient thoughts are then put into the context of the present. We end by describing a roadmap that would lead to a realm beyond ethics. Higher education faces many human and social development challenges in a globalized and technologically highly developed world, which is nevertheless desperate for peace and harmony. We suggest that these challenges can only be met by developing 'cosmic consciousness' in higher education institutions. Einstein described this as the 'most profound and most sublime feeling'.

HUMAN ASPIRATION VIS-A-VIS HUMAN DEVELOPMENT: THE 'VALUE SYSTEM' OF AN INDIVIDUAL

The concept of human development hinges primarily on the concept the human being, namely, on our answers to philosophical questions such as why we are here and what we are. This statement might appear rather too philosophical to be socially relevant. However, most of the ills plaguing so-called modern, developed societies may be due to an unclear understanding of what constitutes a human being.

Human development is also conditioned by human aspirations. In Indian thought, what a human being seeks or aspires to is called *purushartha*. Thousands of years ago, Indian thinkers classified aspirations into four categories, called the four *purusharthas*. These could also be called the fundamental human values, as they are the things a human being val-

ues, seeks, aspires to, prizes and pursues. The four *purusharthas* are: (1) *Dharma* (2) *Artha* (3) *Kama* and (4) *Moksha*. The approximate English translations are: (1) righteousness, morality, ethical quality of life and adherence to certain higher human values; (2) wealth and economic prosperity; (3) enjoyment or fulfilment of desires; and (4) freedom, emancipation and liberation. An educated (meaning enlightened) person is one whose life is predominantly guided by *purusharthas* (1) and (4), that is, by *dharma* and *moksha*. Individual development, therefore, is conditioned by a person's aspirations and goal orientation, that is, his/her value system. A materially developed individual may consider a spiritually developed person who is unconcerned about his/her material development to be undeveloped or underdeveloped, and vice versa. Human aspiration and the aspect of the human personality that an individual seeks to develop are therefore crucial to the concept of human development. Thus, the nature of human personality itself is relevant. In the next section, we discuss this in the light of Indian philosophical thought and paradigms.

THE FIVE-LAYERED HUMAN PERSONALITY

For centuries, Indian philosophers and thinkers have accepted that the human personality is essentially five-layered. Each layer is an autonomous 'self' or *atman*. The five layers together constitute the human being or *jivatman*. The layers are often referred to and imagined as 'sheaths' or *koshas* that encase the central core of the personality called *Atman* or 'individual self', in much the same way that a scabbard covers a sword. Each of the *koshas* is an autonomous self, which is governed by its own laws. The outermost *kosha* is the 'physical self' called *annamaya-atman*. This is matter and is governed by laws of material, physical science. The next, subtler layer within the physical sheath is the 'vital self' called *pranamaya-atman*, which is full of life energy. This self is governed by the laws of biological or life science. The next, sub-

tler layer within the physical and vital selves is the 'mental self' called the *manomaya-atman*. It is the repository of ideas, thoughts, imagination and so on, and is governed by the laws of mental science or psychology. The fourth layer, which is subtler than the outer three, is the 'intelligence self' called *vijnanamaya-atman*. This self is the seat of what we call 'intuition', which transcends cogitation and reflection. It is the decision-making self and is referred to as *buddhi* or 'subtle *intelligence*', in contradistinction to the *intellect*, which cogitates, debates and reflects without being able to decide. Decision-making at the individual and collective level makes or mars human life. The full development of this 'intelligence self' or *vijnamaya-atman* helps people to make the right decisions, to have unwavering convictions and intuitive perceptions. This self has led to the discovery of nature's secrets by scientists, or spiritual truths by seers and sages. The fifth and subtlest layer is the 'blissful self' called *anandamaya-atman*, which is experienced in the state of deep, dreamless sleep. It holds, sustains and reveals the blissful or joyful aspects of life, without which human existence would be unbearable.

EDUCATION AS THE MANIFESTATION OF INNATE PERFECTION: ETHICS AND VALUES FLOW NATURALLY FROM THE ATTEMPT TO MANIFEST THIS PERFECTION

Swami Vivekananda, one of the greatest saint-philosophers of modern India, gave the following definition of education (*Complete Works*, Vol. IV, p. 358): 'Education is the manifestation of the perfection already in man.'

This statement is based on the idea that a human being has a perfect innermost core, or *purna*. This core is eternally pure, eternally awakened and eternally free: *nitya shuddha, nitya buddha, nitya mukta*. Its essence is knowledge as awareness and consciousness. It is of the very nature (*swarupa*) of pure Existence (*sat*), pure Awareness (*chit*) and pure Bliss (*ananda*). When we test this model against actual experiential data, it is easy to prove its veracity. First, daily experience shows that every human wants to *exist*, the urge to survive being the most predominant impulse. Second, everybody wants to *know*, the desire for knowledge being an equally powerful impulse. Third, everybody wants to be *joyful*, happiness or pleasure-seeking being perhaps the most powerful impulse. Natural urges reflect one's fundamental nature; so much so that the three fundamental urges (the urge to *exist*, the urge to *know* and the urge to *enjoy*) reveal that the true nature of a human is Existence, Knowledge and Joy. The real core of the human personality can therefore be summed up as Existence-Knowledge-Joy. Everybody experiences these three aspects in their daily life. However, the concept that this triad is our real nature remains only vague. This is where 'education' plays a crucial role. According to Swami Vivekananda, the whole process of education involves uncovering, or discovering, this innate Perfection, which is of the nature of Existence-Knowledge-Joy. An educational technique for refining the five layers that cover the 'Perfection Core' can help this discovery to take place. What we call development therefore involves making the five layers increasingly transparent, so that the inner Perfection Core can shine through them in all its glory. Transparency through which

luminosity shines is called *sattva* in Indian philosophical parlance. The refinement of the layers, which we define as development, comes through proper education. Education is therefore the process of making the layers *sattvic*. Through this process, the Perfection that is already within a person simply manifests itself. This new way of looking at the concept of development engenders a powerful value system that is conducive to human dignity and empowerment, which leads to freedom. The next section examines how this individual development is related to collective or social development.

INDIVIDUAL VS. COLLECTIVE, MICRO VS. MACRO DEVELOPMENT: THE CONCEPT OF DYNAMIC EQUILIBRIUM; HOLISTIC OR TOTAL DEVELOPMENT

It is well known in the field of physical science that the microcosm and macrocosm are built on the same plane and that the two are in dynamic equilibrium with each other. An analysis of the microcosm can reveal the mystery of the macrocosm and *vice versa*. The total development of the human personality, often called holistic development, is only possible if all the five layers discussed above are fully developed. The holistic development table below gives a picture of the individual (human) and collective (social) development at each level of the five-layered personality.

Overemphasizing engineering and technology, to the detriment of fundamental sciences and humanities, will make a person clever and skilful. However, it will leave him or her emotionally starved and spiritually impoverished. Albert Einstein's powerful ideas are worthy of consideration in this context:

> It is not enough to teach man a speciality. Through it he may become a kind of useful machine, but not a harmoniously developed personality. It is essential that the student acquires an understanding of and a lively feeling for values. He must acquire a vivid sense of the beautiful and of the morally good. Otherwise, he with his specialized knowledge more closely resembles a well-trained dog than a harmoniously developed person. (1988, p. 66)

Holistic and integrated human development, which Einstein called harmonious development, is possible only through a combination of the disciplines that simultaneously and harmoniously develop the head, heart and hand. The Sanskrit terms used for these three areas are *jnana* (knowledge), *bhakti* (devotion) and *karma* (action), respectively. The Indian paradigm speaks of each of these as yoga or paths to achieving human fulfilment. Swami Vivekananda emphasized that these yogas should be combined harmoniously to achieve total

TABLE 1
Individual and social development at each layer of the personality

Layer of the personality	Individual (microcosmic) development	Social (macrocosmic) development
Annamaya (Physical)	Fulfilment of physical wants and needs like food, shelter, clothing and so on (education for physical welfare)	Development of physical sciences, technology and so on, which leads to collective physical well-being
Pranamaya (Vital)	Healthy body: nutrition, medicine, vitamins and so on (education for psychophysical welfare)	Development of health and life sciences, which leads to collective psychophysical well-being
Manomaya (Mental)	Cultivation of knowledge about various sciences, humanities and so on (education for knowledge)	Development of educational institutions at various levels for study and research, which leads to collective mental and moral well-being
Vijnanamaya (Intuitional intellectual)	Moral, ethical and spiritual education, intuitive understanding, creativity, and so on (education for higher values)	Development of institutions to promote the cultivation of higher human values, like sensitivity to human suffering, democracy, justice, equality and so on, which leads to collective intellectual well-being
Anandamaya (Blissful)	Music, fine arts, dance, painting, photography, aesthetic sensitivity, nature mysticism, feeling of oneness with nature and other peoples (education for peace and harmony)	Development of spiritually sensitized groups, organizations and so on, which can inculcate empathy, a feeling of oneness with others, selflessness and so on, which leads to collective spiritual well-being

human development. The emblem that Swami Vivekananda conceived for Ramakrishna Mission, an organization that he established more than a century ago for holistic human and social development, conveys this remarkable message of harmoniously combining *jnana*, *bhakti* and *karma* (*Complete Works*, Vol. VII, p. 204).

How is human development related to social development? The relationship between man and society has been a major topic of discussion in the social sciences. The Indian philosophical paradigm, which is in remarkable agreement with modern science, is the 'dynamic equilibrium' between the *microcosm* and the *macrocosm*. The role of education should be to develop this awareness in the individual. Thus, he/she will not be an isolated entity, but an integral part of a total system in which the microcosm and macrocosm are in 'dynamic equilibrium' with each other. The ancient values of truth, beauty and goodness emphasized by Greek philosophers and highlighted as *satyam*, *sundaram* and *shivam* by ancient Indian thinkers have been translated in the modern age as integrity, purity and unselfishness. These values will be spontaneously inculcated if education imparts this feeling of cosmic awareness or cosmic consciousness. We are like waves or bubbles in the infinite ocean of unbroken cosmic consciousness, which is in fact our real identity. The wave arises from the ocean, plays around for some time and merges back into the ocean again. The 'dynamic equilibrium' between the wave and ocean remains continuous and constant, but the ocean's consciousness is the ultimate reality of the individual wave. Education, in its development role, ought to engender this 'cosmic consciousness', that is, that the 'other' is also 'me' in reality, as both of us are integral parts of an undivided ocean of consciousness. Selfless love is in fact a feeling of oneness or union.

PUTTING THE VALUE-SYSTEM DEVELOPED FROM THE ABOVE PARADIGM INTO THE CONTEXT OF PRESENT DAY HIGHER EDUCATION INSTITUTIONS

How are the philosophical perspectives described in the above sections to be put into the context of present day higher education institutions? Three issues are relevant: what the values are and what they should be in the context of higher education institutions; how values could be inculcated in practice in these institutions; what roadmap leads one beyond these issues. An analysis of these issues is detailed below.

1. Higher education institutions, by definition, are those that *cultivate knowledge*. The cultivation of knowledge involves two aspects: cultivation for one's own sake, one's own edification and fulfilment and for the pure joy that such cultivation engenders; cultivation to share knowledge and disseminate it to society at large. The first aspect involves inquiry, investigation and exploration. The second aspect addresses service through sharing and giving. Emancipation from ignorance through the cultivation of knowledge is the main objective of higher education institutions. Such institutions should therefore inculcate both individual emancipation (through inquiry) and collective emancipation (through sharing knowledge). Inquiry engenders depth (intensity), while dissemination gives rise to breadth (extensity). A harmonious blend of intensity and extensity is the highest value that higher education institutions should instil.

2. How are these values inculcated? Values are instilled by the example of teachers; the right environment; and peer groups that are focused on pursuing and sharing knowledge. Intellectual property rights and copyright laws have reduced knowledge to a commodity that is imparted to the highest bidder. In contrast, a feeling of the sense of the sacredness of knowledge automatically inculcates the higher values we have discussed. Education institutions are as sacred as places of worship and prayer. Teachers and students are engaged in the 'humble adoration of an illimitable intelligence' (Einstein). These 'worshippers' should therefore live in an austere, even ascetic, environment, which is devoted to the pursuit of higher knowledge. Thus, an environment should be created in which values are absorbed rather than taught. In the institutions run by Ramakrishna Mission, a charitable and philanthropic organization rooted in a profound spiritual ideology, each and every student, or *vidyarthi*, the Sanskrit word for seeker of knowledge, has to take certain 'vows', called *vrata*. These vows are made in a ceremony attended by all the teachers, monk-administrators and seniors. Students then embark on the sacred task of learning. All the students who are administered these vows by the teacher, or *acharya*, are then accepted ceremonially by their seniors as belonging to a happy community of knowledge seekers. This solemn ceremony makes a deep impression on the minds of the students. In a sense, this is a sublime antidote to the ragging that is used to initiate new students in other higher education institutions. As higher education institutions are sacred places of knowledge worship, they should remain absolutely immune to any kind of political activity.

3. Lastly, what is the roadmap for going beyond ethics and values? What lies beyond? Beyond is the cosmic awareness discussed in the above section. Ethics and values not only point to the realm beyond, but also lead to it. Realizing the cosmic dimension of one's personality is the culmination and pinnacle of the path from ethics and values. Einstein calls this realization – this awareness – the 'noblest mainspring of all scientific research'. There is perhaps no better way to end this paper than with Einstein's inspiring words:

The most profound and the most sublime experience that one can have is the sensation of the mystical. It is truly the sower of all science. A person who is a stranger to this emotion, who can no longer marvel and wonder in rapt awe, is as good as dead. To know that what is impenetrable really exists, manifesting itself as the highest wisdom and the most radiant beauty, that our dull faculties can comprehend only in the most primitive forms – it is this knowledge, this realization that constitutes true spirituality. This *cosmic mystical consciousness* is the noblest mainspring of all scientific research. (1988, p. 11)

Despite all our vaunted globalization, the world today is full of panic, strife, conflict and dissension. Therefore, it is time we listened to the Music of the Spheres that perpetually arises from the Cosmos, singing in lofty strains the joy and glory of realizing our true nature as the Infinite Cosmic Consciousness. This is the highest value that a human being can attain and that alone can ensure global peace and harmony.

REFERENCES

Einstein, Albert (1988) *Ideas and Opinions*, Rupa and Co., India.
Vivekananda, Swami (1978–79) *Complete Works* (9 volumes), Mayavati Memorial Edition, Advaita Ashrama, Kolkata, India.

The concept of global citizenship in higher education

Mary Stuart

INTRODUCTION – THE ISSUE

Globalization provides us with an opportunity to consider and develop a new conception of a university and its role in an increasingly interconnected world society. (Brown, 2007, p. 29)

Citizenship as a concept is hotly contested and there is no single definition, but many writers would promote the idea of active citizenship that is defined in terms of involvement in civic life, an idea of participation and voice, and civil rights and responsibilities to the community (Hall and Williamson, 1999; European Commission, 1998). As Preece (2006) points out, many definitions of active citizenship include education:

Strategies that are effective at local levels include participatory, democratic, awareness-raising initiatives that encourage self-help (often community self-help) and facilitate a mixture of formal, informal and non-formal education.

However, as societies are changed by migrations, some forced and others chosen, and as national communities become more fluid and interrelated, it is now difficult to talk about citizenship simply in the context of one form of nationalism, as there are many. Active citizenship can be a powerful mechanism for delivering:

- Civic engagement
- A real contribution to sustainable development through understanding and responding to the needs of the world and of local communities
- Increased employability
- Greater mutual understanding of difference
- Social inclusion and community regeneration.

Higher education institutions (HEIs) across the world are entering a new phase of development which involves changing relations with students in a more competitive market, changing relations with research fundraisers and increasing engagement with the workplace. In a global society, HEIs need to respond by creating new ways of working to meet these challenges.

At a time when there are significant global conflicts, issues of poverty and questions about sustainability and economic development, engaging higher education institutions to prepare their students to address world citizenship issues is vital. As with notions of active citizenship, there are many definitions of global citizenship. However, Oxfam has defined global citizens as people who are aware of the wider world and have a sense of their own role within it; who respect and value diversity and understand global economics and social and political issues; and who will challenge social injustice and participate in and contribute to communities at different levels from the local to the global (Oxfam, 2006). Global citizenship as an idea is also contested. How can there be global citizens in the age of globalization when there is no world democracy and markets determine everything? The principles of active citizenship in a global context are, I would argue, even more important because of these challenges.

In this chapter I suggest that, just as society has developed a much more integrated sense of global awareness, HEIs need to focus their activities much more on notions of global–civic responsibility rather than on national citizenship when educating their students, engaging in research, working with employers and establishing local and wider partnerships.

THE CURRENT SITUATION

Higher education institutions have always been concerned with educating their students as active citizens, although this mission has not always been successfully fulfilled (Harkavy, 2006). Meanwhile, as people's mobility increases, the homogeneity of the nation state is dissolving, as Scott (2006, p. 21) points out:

many nations [...] have become multi-cultural societies: they are no longer ethnically and culturally homogeneous, which has shaped their 'home' higher education systems …

This suggests that HEIs need to think differently about the social context of students, not only in terms of similar/different experiences of home/international students but also in terms of how societies are becoming more interconnected and interdependent. Recently, several social theorists (Beck, 2006a and b; Szerszynski and Urry 2002, 2006; Delanty, 2006) have argued that examining issues from the point of view of nation-states provides a false set of premises and have proposed a more 'cosmopolitan outlook'. Beck encapsulates this view when he points out that 'the founding duality of the national outlook – foreigner–native – no longer adequately reflects reality' (Beck, 2006b, p. 26). This is not to say that national imagining and the nation-state no longer exist, but that nations have been and are being transformed (Delanty, 2006). In other words, the idea of a 'cosmopolitan outlook' supersedes the national outlook rather than destroying it. This means that personal and group biographies are becoming increasingly 'liquid' and trans-spatial (Bauman, 2000).

Communications are faster than ever before and global capital is genuinely global.

As Albow says:

The point at which capitalism finally became global and outside the control of any one nation found the world's main banking centre in Tokyo, the world's main equity market in New York and its main foreign exchange centre in London.

… World society … is now of a shape where its history leaves it with uncertain and unclear organization. (1996, p.113)

Economic change has made the position of nation-states more precarious and produced a world where cooperation and collaboration between states is vital. This means that engagement with multinational organizations is an essential component of national governance in all parts of the world. Beck (2006a) says:

There is only one thing worse than being overrun by multinationals; that is *not* being overrun by multinationals. (p. 52)

To apply the idea of active citizenship that highlights civic responsibility and participation in the global arena, we can look at the principles of the Millennium Development Goals, agreed in 2000. These goals, which are discussed elsewhere in this collection, offer a reference point for HEIs to develop a programme for global citizenship in teaching, research and enterprise activities.

New technologies have reduced the distance between different peoples and have warped our sense of time. Frand (2000) describes how many of the students of today are digital natives. He identifies ten characteristics of the information-age mindset, particularly highlighting the compression of time and the ubiquitous nature of connectivity. In higher education, the opportunities for global interaction through technology have not yet been fully grasped.

Delors (1996) produced a report on education and training for the 21st century which also highlighted the need for engagement with a global society:

People need gradually to become world citizens without losing their roots and while continuing to play an active part in the life of their nation and their local community.

MAIN TRENDS FOR THE FUTURE OF HIGHER EDUCATION

The higher education sector is trying to respond to these economic, social, technological and political changes. Across the sector in different parts of the world the focus has moved away from the recruitment of international students, which was initially seen as the appropriate response to globalization, and is now far more concerned with developing more international outlooks and practices. This has included developments in the curriculum (Bourn et al., 2006). The Observatory on Borderless Higher Education conducted research in 12 countries, including Australia, Germany, Malaysia,

the United Arab Emirates and India. The resulting report found that 'internationalization' was high on the agenda of HEIs across these different contexts with a particular emphasis on economic competitiveness, but that 'global citizenship' was not really articulated, although many of the issues of global significance were seen to be important (Middlehurst and Woodfield, 2007). This indicates that there is still some way to go for universities to engage with global realities and realize the importance of their new civic responsibilities.

In the USA, the American Council on Education expressed concern about the lack of engagement of the higher education sector with civic issues in a global context (Ehrlich, 2000). A declaration of the role of universities in developing their own civic responsibility was agreed, and over 50 US University Presidents have now signed the declaration. At its heart is the recognition that global action and local action are intertwined. However, Harkavy argues that in the USA, universities have never really fulfilled their civic mission and one wonders if the declaration is simply another 'eloquent rhetorical pledge of support' (Harkavy, 2006, p. 17).

The UK prime minister's initiative 2 (British Council, 2006), while highlighting the importance of encouraging students from different parts of the world to study in the UK, also highlights global university partnerships to address issues of poverty and disease, and increase mutual understanding. However, here too the main focus remains on attracting high-fee-paying international students to bolster the funds available to universities. In other words, 'internationalization' does not fully address the moral responsibilities involved in a sense of 'civic' engagement and applied to a global environment.

An example of where the idea of global citizenship is explicit in the management and curriculum of education comes from India. The City Montessori School (CMS), which includes students across all the education sectors including higher education, has at its heart a belief in education for world peace. Students are encouraged to see themselves as 'world citizens' with responsibilities and rights to and for the world. The education programme is highly academic and includes student participation in international conferences from a very young age. Students meet with other students from different parts of the globe and with senior leaders at events such as the Chief Justices Conference that is held annually at CMS. Here, leading figures in the legal profession are held to account by the students and the participants discuss issues of global significance such as human rights, peace, mutual understanding and civic participation. Examples from the European region include the work that 'Engineers against Poverty' are carrying out with universities to develop a curriculum in engineering that explores solutions for the needs of developing nations rather than for those of the developed world. Equally, in the field of information technology, the Collegium for Development Studies and the IT Virtual Faculty at Uppsala University, in collaboration with Sida (Swedish International Development Cooperation Agency) and ideal/ICT4Africa, have been looking into global information technologies and their relationship to poverty reduction and to the development of global citizens. This project points out the challenges involved: while IT development is a vital component of enabling better understanding between people and an important tool for creating more global spaces to discuss world issues, it is sporadic and rooted in the interests of particular groups and organizations. It seems that universal access has not been secured and that access is determined differently in different contexts. Many of these examples, while indicating that there is a growing groundswell of concern about the role of higher education in global issues, reveal little systematic engagement with the issue of developing global citizens from student bodies, and universities need to work together to make this happen.

STRATEGIES AND ACTIONS

There are many possible responses, and many individual institutions are attempting to engage with these issues at a local level. In an attempt to be truly global and to understand what global citizenship means, a group of HEIs from across the globe have joined together to consider how they can respond to the much more fluid and interrelated global society that finds local expression in institutions and classrooms. The approach draws on cosmopolitan social theory (Beck, 2006a) and is attempting to transform institutions and make them responsive to global needs. This involves not simply thinking about growing international markets and responding to international student needs, but also responding to a more complex world that is economically and socially dependent. The rest of this paper describes this initiative and offers an example of institutional transformation that is being undertaken to respond to a cosmopolitan world.

The Centre for Global Citizenship is based at Kingston University, London, and has partners from institutions from across the globe. It acts as a catalyst for activity for members of the network and enables the sharing of good practices between the network members. It makes particular use of technologies to support communication between the partners and their different communities across the globe and organizes virtual seminars and discussions on ethical internationalization, global citizenship issues and sustainable development for institutions. As the Centre is international, virtual collaborative work plays a vital role. The aim of the Centre is to ensure that students and staff in partner institutions are more able to respond to a multidiverse global world.

Kingston University itself has focused part of its work for global engagement on issues of sustainability. This project, described in the report at the end of this paper, is part of a whole programme across the university to educate its students for an ethical sustainable future. The university has achieved fair-trade sta-

tus and has the goal of being carbon neutral by 2016. Another example of how this global citizenship approach works in practice can be found at one of the participating universities, the University of Bradford, in the north of England.

AN EXAMPLE OF GOOD PRACTICE

The Bradford Metropolitan District is the tenth largest in the UK and is situated in the West Yorkshire conurbation. The District formerly had an economy based on the textile industry and is home to several major textile organizations. It has a large immigrant community from Japan that was initially attracted by employment in the textile industry and has subsequently settled in the district, creating a society that is rich in its diversity but challenging for social cohesion.

The University of Bradford is located within the inner city. It traces its origins back to the provision of science and technology courses and received its Royal Charter as a University in 1966.

The past two decades have witnessed significant social and community tension, leading to riots in 1995 and 2001. The University's Corporate Strategy commits it to being 'at the heart of our communities'. In the context of Bradford, this is a particularly interesting challenge in that its communities are clearly to be found within West Yorkshire but also within Pakistan. Any approach made by the University to securing community engagement needs to take account of different cultural practices and lifestyles, and to adopt a local focus. An example of the nature of cosmopolitanism in Bradford can be found in the statistics of 'school absenteeism', as children are taken out of school for extended periods to spend time in Pakistan with relatives. It is quite common to work with people born and bred in Bradford who have spent a number of years at school in Pakistan, and this reflects the extended nature of this society. For many, these people are neither Pakistani nor British. That in itself causes a major rethink of what we mean by nationalism and the issue of 'place' in determining perceptions (Delanty, 2006).

What is very evident is that Bradford as a district is inextricably linked to Pakistan as a country.

Currently a large proportion of students within the University are from Pakistani families living either in Bradford or in other cities. This creates a campus culture that is different to many others and provides a high degree of challenge and opportunity.

It was considered to be vital that the University should work with all its communities in an inclusive and strategic way. The challenge of the developing global economy, the comparatively low skill levels in Bradford compared with the rest of the UK and the underdeveloped nature of the Pakistan economy were key factors. Rather than starting with the global community, Bradford decided to start with the 'local global' community.

The University was approached by a member of the local Pakistani communities to see if it would assist their young people educationally. The University established a project known as 'the Junior University' to pilot an early years outreach project. The scheme ran on a Saturday morning and was arranged to help students with homework, provide additional understanding in the areas of mathematics and science, and help with revision for public examinations. It was enormously popular. The first graduates of 'the Junior University' have now moved into higher education, graduated and found appropriate employment. The 'Junior University' project continues and is clearly linked to improved school attendance and exam results,

Moving on to the connected global community in Pakistan, the University has developed a strategic approach based on a number of fact-finding visits and discussions. It does not aim to develop campuses abroad but rather focuses on partnerships and the full involvement of local academics, communities and teachers.

There are many educational challenges in Pakistan and the role that the University can play is limited, but it is cru-

cial that it engages with its global communities. The strategy is therefore based on activities consistent with the University's mission and local needs. A variety of initiatives are under way including creating connections with the Shaukat Khanum Memorial Cancer Hospital and Research Centre in Lahore. This enables the University to engage in partnerships within a research and teaching area in which there is considerable strength in Bradford. The connection will include training radiographers and oncology nurses, research links with the Institute of Pharmaceutical Innovations, and other specialist work.

Bradford University also has a partnership with the University of Azad Jammu and Kashmir (AJKU) which has a campus in Mirpur, some of which was too badly damaged in the earthquake to be able to go on providing academic courses.

These are just a few of the examples of the approach the University is taking. It is designed to acknowledge the interconnectedness and interdependence of Bradford and Pakistan and to assist in a new notion of civic engagement for universities.

CONCLUSIONS AND FINAL COMMENTS – A LONG WAY TO GO IN RETHINKING OUR PROCESSES

The activities described above are part of a growing understanding of the interdependence of institutions and of our global world. The old response consisting of a simple call for national higher education is increasingly in decline, and new forms of international education provision are developing. Whether these are equal partnership arrangements where learning happens in different locations or other arrangements for learning in different environments, students in higher education increasingly want curricula and institutional environments that recognize the changed global economy and society. In this climate, thinking about students as interconnected is more appropriate and leads to a more mutually beneficial international higher education system. We are at the start of this engagement and it is difficult to predict or understand how the

new world will develop, but preparing all our students to be global citizens who are well versed in global issues can only be an advantage and will certainly foster better understanding between cultures within our different localities.

REFERENCES

Albow, M. (1996) *The Global Age*. Cambridge: Polity Press.

Bauman, Z. (2000) *Liquid Modernity*. Cambridge: Polity Press.

Beck, U. (2006a) *Power in the Global Age*. Cambridge: Polity Press.

Beck, U. (2006b) *The Cosmopolitan Vision*. Cambridge: Polity Press.

Bourn, D. McKenzie, A. and Shiel, C. (2006) *The Global University: The Role of the Curriculum*. London: Development Education Association.

British Council (2006) http://www.british council.org/learning-international-exp erience.htm (accessed 12 January 2007).

Brown, R. (2007) Internationalising Higher Education: a Financial or Moral Imperative? Summary of a consultation held at St Georges Hse, Windsor Castle, 25–26 January 2007. London: CIHE/SRHE.

Delanty, G. (2006) The Cosmopolitan Imagination: Critical Cosmopolitanism and Social Theory, *British Journal of Sociology*, **57**(1) pp. 25–47.

Delors, J. (1996) *Learning: The Treasure Within*. Paris: UNESCO http://www.uvm.dk/gammel/within.pdf

Ehrlich, T. (2000) (ed.) *Civic Responsibility and Higher Education*. Phoenix, AZ: Oryx Press.

European Commission (1998) *Education and Active Citizenship in the European Union*. Office for Official Publications of the European Communities: Luxembourg.

Frand, J. L. (2000) The Information-Age mindset: changes in students and implications for higher education, *Educause Review*, September/October, pp. 15–24.

Hall, T. and Williamson, H. (1999) *Citizenship and Community*. Leicester: National Youth Agency.

Harkavy, I. (2006) The role of universities in advancing citizenship and social justice in the 21st Century, *Education, Citizenship and Social Justice,* **1**(1) pp. 5–37.

Middlehurst R and Woodfield S (2007) Research project report 2005–2006: Responding to the Internationalization Agenda: Implications for Institutional Strategy. At http://www.heacademy.ac.uk/research/MiddleHurstWoodfield07.pdf (accessed 1 May 2007).

Oxfam (2006) *Education for Global Citizenship: A Guide for Schools.* Oxford: Oxfam.

Preece, J. (2006) Widening participation for social justice: poverty and access to education. In: Oduaran A and Bhola HS (eds) *Widening Access to Education as Social Justice.* UNESCO. Dordrecht: Springer.

Scott, P. (2006) Internationalising higher education – a global perspective. In: Kishun, R. (ed.) *The Internationaliza-tion of Higher Education in South Africa.* Durban: International Education Association of South Africa, pp.13–29.

Szerszynski, B. and Urry, J. (2006) Visuality, mobility and the cosmopolitan: inhabiting the world from afar, *British Journal of Sociology,* **57**(1) pp. 113–31.

SPECIAL CONTRIBUTION I.10
Higher education's contribution to sustainable development: the way forward

Leo Jansen[1]

SUSTAINABLE DEVELOPMENT AND THE OBLIGATIONS OF HIGHER EDUCATION

All men and women are a part of development in their place and level in society. The process of sustainable development (SD) requires that each of them attain the skills needed to handle the complex challenges of change and uncertainty, a large number of stakeholders, conflicting interests and rigid barriers of self-interest and short-term thinking on every level (Weaver et al., 2001). SD does not come about on its own; rather, it must be guided by long-term analyses and goals. This requires that higher education (HE) plays a double role: it must provide graduates with the attitude, knowledge and skills to lead this process, while also developing and delivering the knowledge to support research on SD.

Social learning (Wals, 2007) is a framework for developing the necessary skills, as SD is essentially a learning process on all levels. The characteristics of SD demand long-term integrated system changes. To gain broad support for these changes, all relevant parties must become involved. SD is a learning-by-doing process in which social challenges are met step by step by the social parties involved, supported by science and technology disciplines in a cooperative effort. The cumulative effect of such interaction is change in different domains and at dif-ferent levels (micro, meso and macro), which may lead to a societal transition to SD. Thus, by contributing to education and research, HE becomes a key player in social learning (Kibwika, 2006).

FROM ENVIRONMENTAL CARE TO THE TRANSITION TO SD

The process of SD did not appear overnight. Early warning signs were given in *Silent Spring* (Carson and Darling, 1962), followed by the Club of Rome's report *Limits to Growth* (Meadows et al., 1972). Around the same time, the OECD launched important principles such as 'normative forecasting' (Jantsch, 1969).

In its visionary report *Our Common Future*, the World Commission on Environment and Development (WCED) (Brundtland, 1987) connected the challenges of saving the environment and fighting against poverty. Nevertheless, the environment continues to deteriorate and the gap between the rich and the poor continues to grow. In terms of 'planet, people and prosperity', environmental protection covers 'planet', whereas SD integrates all three.

OBSTACLES TO CHANGE

In working towards a sustainable future, changes in culture and structure may affect the position and power of individuals and institutions. Resistance is expressed in bad attitudes, inabilities and defensive actions as a result of the stress between the need for (bureaucratic) certainties to keep society running and the need for flexibility towards change. This is manifested as opposition to long-term risks, insufficient innovative power and a rigid disciplinary organization of science.

The main remedy to these drawbacks is to shape conditions for developing broadly supported future views, as interest in long-term convergence is much stronger than interest in short-term rat races.

ATTITUDES

Even where resistance to change is not felt, urgency is lacking, especially in developed nations, where the direct deterioration of health and the environment has largely been overcome. In developing nations, however, environmental and economic problems are still matters of existential urgency. One fundamental barrier is the lack of willingness to accept a fair global distribution of environmental capabilities as a condition for common survival. SD requires cooperation, which goes beyond the search for individual certainties.

ABILITIES

Many groups, such as the Factor 10 Club (1997) and Robèrt et al. (2002), have developed visions of a sustainable future and a path thereto. However, responsible governments have proven incapable of developing long-term integrated visions of a sustainable future. The benefits of bureaucracy – providing certain expectations and responsibilities for civil stakeholders as a means of democratic control – conflict with the need to handle the uncertainties of fundamental change and cooperation in which the bureaucracy is just one partner. Nation-states operate in enlarging and changing circles under rules fashioned by history; this is reflected in the laborious implementation of international treaties like the Kyoto Protocol.

THE OPERATIONAL CHALLENGE OF SD
The main challenge of SD is to initiate evolutionary change in an unsustainable world. This evolution involves renewing integrated systems, making transitions and meeting the requirements of a growing population with growing prosperity. This will require SD education on all levels and in all modes of learning: formal, non-formal and informal (Dam-Mieras and Rikers, 2005). This education should focus on teaching skills, developing SD-oriented visions in civil society, integrating a future orientation in public policymaking and in public debate, transforming structures of society for SD, and breaking through barriers.

Systems renewal for SD is a complex social process that encompasses not only radical technological innovations but also changes in behaviour, organization, institutions, power relations and many other non-technical aspects. The latter may be even more decisive for implementation than the availability of 'technology'. Systems renewal requires a long-term future orientation on the part of a variety of stakeholders with conflicting interests in an environment in which the level of uncertainty is high.

The recognition of 'needs' as a starting point for innovation for sustainability, as set out in the Brundtland definition of sustainable development, deviates from the more traditional engineering- and business-related approach to innovation, which focuses on production and consumption in existing structures:

Humanity has the ability to make development sustainable – to ensure that it meets the *needs* of the present without compromising the ability of future generations to meet their own *needs*.

Meeting *essential needs* requires not only a new era of economic growth for nations in which the majority are poor, but an assurance that those poor get their fair share of the resources required to sustain that growth. (Brundtland, 1987)

As a societal transition process, SD comprises numerous innovation projects of varying origin, (scientific) environments, scopes and levels. These projects are often unrelated on the micro scale (niches), the meso scale (regimes) and the macro scale (landscapes), but are inspired by a general orientation. Transition is described as 'the result of developments in different domains, as a set of connected changes which reinforce each other but take place in several different areas, such as technology, the economy, institutions, behaviour, culture, ecology and belief systems' (Martens and Rotmans, 2002).

COOPERATION
The system's approach to transition requires transdisciplinary cooperation of clusters of societal parties, for example citizens, consumers and non-governmental organizations; corporations and other production organizations; and governmental institutions and organizations involved in science and education.

This was explored in a learning-by-doing setting by Dutch Sustainable Technology Development (STD) (Weaver et al., 2000), a long-term technological innovation programme for SD against the backdrop of a policy commitment by the Netherlands.

The players operate in different arenas, driven by different currencies and adopting different roles in the SD process. The Adaptive Integration of Research and Policy (AIRP) project (Hinterberger, 2003) developed a set of SD principles and delivered a methodology to set up and evaluate SD-oriented research and technology development programmes and projects.

DEMANDS ON HE IN THE SD PROCESS
A major condition for initiating system changes is the availability of competent players capable of developing SD options and initiating and managing change processes. The development of this capacity must, as far as possible, be congruent with sustainability principles (Weaver and Jansen, 2004). Thus, any SD programme depends on the extent of society's understanding of SD and awareness of its urgency. Both understanding and awareness, and elements of education and research, are necessary but are not sufficient conditions to initiate and execute SD-oriented programmes. In research, design is dependent on context

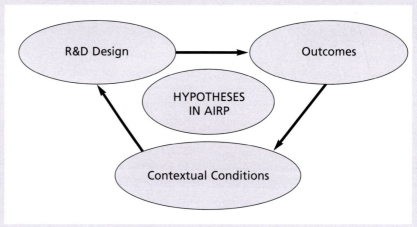

FIGURE 1 SD research in context

and outcomes are dependent on design. The outcomes in turn influence the context for further research (Figure I).

FUTURE HE

The SD learning process is a common and interactive undertaking. Institutions of HE are expected to take the lead as agents of change. Future HE, as a key player shaping the SD process together with other stakeholders, may meet society's SD demands by:

1. Educating graduates:
   * To be leaders, champions in the process of change, and/or
   * To keep 'everyday business' running, thus fostering the process of change.
2. Contributing to lifelong learning (for SD) in formal and informal learning and training activities and participating in processes of change.
3. Conducting participatory research:
   * Involving participants in social, spatial and technological planning, and
   * Encouraging students to acquire skills for transdisciplinary research.
4. Conducting institutional SD research on meeting societal challenges (industrial, regional and institutional):
   * Business-induced, comprehensive and transition- and system-oriented research
   * Product-oriented research in all phases – optimization, improvement and renewal of production and consumption systems
   * Process-oriented research on participatory decision-making, the relationship between representative and participatory democracy, new forms and bodies of international cooperation (new rules for new games), and so on.

In order to implement these options, HE institutions must develop visions and derive strategies. In these strategies, HE institutions must resolve the tension between accountability, which often results in short-term thinking, and flexibility, which is essential to the process of

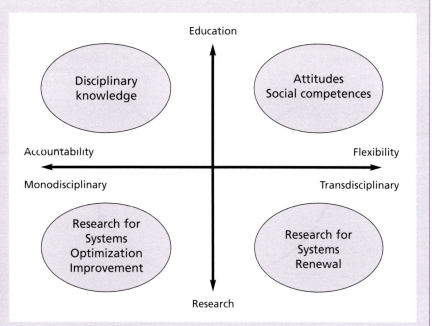

FIGURE 2 Areas of SD-related tension in HE

change. In HE, the need for some bureaucracy must be reconciled with the merits of a centre for creativity (Figure 2).

HE IN SD DEMANDS

The following are guidelines to finding a transitional path for HE in SD:

* Research and education are not separate worlds. Rather, they interact, complement one another and interact with society
* The core requirements for graduates are a sound education in their discipline, the ability to position their discipline in the context of SD, and the attitude and skills needed to cooperate with other disciplines and key 'non-scientific' players
* SD is not an isolated discipline. It must be integrated in all operations, activities and departments
* HE research must respond to society's problems.

DEMANDS ON EDUCATION

The options for future HE are reflected in:

DEMANDS ON GRADUATES

All graduates must be able to practise their profession under (future) conditions

of SD. They should be aware of possible implications outside their field of study. The more SD-determined students must be offered opportunities to acquire skills for inter- and transdisciplinary operations (Figure 3).

At TU Delft (Delft University of Technology), this was developed in a learning-by-doing process (Jansen et al., 2006).

DEMANDS ON LECTURERS

Demands on graduates obviously translate into similar demands on lecturers. However, many lecturers have not been trained to meet these demands. A minority have received education in this direction. Moreover, the career-development system and the disciplinary organization of science are hampering the development of scientific skills for SD. Personnel managers at higher education institutes (HEIs) should include these qualifications in the profiles for new appointments and career development and offer lecturers opportunities for them to gain SD qualifications.

At TU Delft, 'The Individual Interaction Method' (Peet et al., 2004) appeared to successfully connect courses to SD as a follow-up to disciplinary reviews conducted by the DHO, the Dutch network

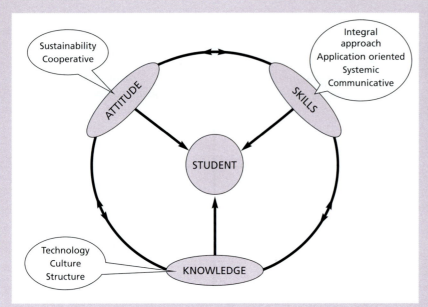

FIGURE 3 **Demands on graduates**

for sustainable development in HE (see e.g. Tellegen, 2006).

In Dutch universities providing professional/vocational education, lectureships (approximately 270 by 2006) involving knowledge circles of lecturers were established to enhance the quality of teaching, professionalize teaching staff, break through compartmentalization, strengthen capabilities for applied research and foster the circulation of knowledge (Daniels, 2006). Although some 20 lectureships are more or less directly related to SD, the skills acquired in these knowledge circles are also useful in education for SD in general.

DEMAND ON INSTITUTIONS

In order to integrate SD in HE, the entire education system, as well as its values and norms, must be rethought:

> It is critical to address the need, for example, to change mindsets, build a new vision of purpose, and inculcate new competences for training and research among the academic staff. (Kibwika, 2006)

Above all, the boards of HE institutions must recognize the necessity and urgency of SD, be convinced of the role of HE in SD and support initiatives to integrate SD in HE. In a framework of vision and strategy, curricula and graduation conditions should be adapted to new realities, and adequate educational forms, methods and resources should be developed. The facilities and resources (funding, time, personnel and so on) required to meet these demands should be provided by developing a structure and attitude of leadership and coordination.

This new attitude towards HE should be reflected in internal and external communication policies, in student recruitment and in innovative forms and methods of transferring knowledge to the public, for example distance education, participation in cultural events and so on. Links with business and public organizations can be strengthened without detriment to the principles of autonomy (Haddad, 2007).

Standards, such as Auditing Instrument for Sustainability in Higher Education (AISHE) certificates (Roorda, 2001, 2004), can measure the comparative progress of integration in HE institutions. The Engineering Education for Sustainable Development Observatory (AGS, 2006) identifies the top 16 universities that are already pursuing SD goals.

DEMANDS ON STAKEHOLDERS IN SOCIETY

Public and private stakeholders' recognition of the necessity and urgency of SD is an essential condition for the co-evolution of HE and society in SD. Although the reach of HE institutions is worldwide, most interactions with society take place at the regional level. Therefore, HE and society should interact in a regional framework of knowledge networks that promote cooperation among HE institutions. One such vehicle is the United Nations University (UNU) initiative to establish Regional Centres of Expertise (RCEs) for SD (Dam-Mieras and Rikers, 2005; Fadeeva, 2007), which function as regional connection points for SD knowledge exchange between social stakeholders (knowledge institutes, governmental institutes and bodies, community-based organizations and companies). In this area, HE may expect the following from its societal partners:

- A willingness to establish a vision of their role and position in the SD process
- An understanding of the essential skills required for SD
- Opportunities for on-the-job training explicitly to develop abilities and skills for (transdisciplinary) cooperation
- A willingness to reformulate and identify SD problems in a coherent, transdisciplinary manner
- A reflection of their demands in graduate profiles
- The inclusion of SD graduation conditions in HE accreditation (by law?).

DEMANDS ON RESEARCH

The most intriguing element of SD research is research on systems renewal, which comprises long-term transdisciplinary societal research. However, the economic system considers this type of research to be of public interest and expects the government to fund it. Corporations sometimes develop concepts but participate in funding only when it is in their economic interest.

Figures 4 and 5 show how SD-oriented activities fit into a coordinate system with two axes: interdisciplinary cooperation and social embedment.

In this context, HE research is expected to support the phases of systems research in which private corporations are not (financially) interested (right-hand quadrants in Figures 4 and 5) (Jansen et al., 2005). This requires HE to have a clear vision of the role of science in the SD process. Specifically, this involves a vision of the nature of research in general and of the short-, medium- and long-term orientations of research. Alternatively, SD could be strategically embedded in the mainstream research of all departments in order to fulfil external expectations (Mulder and Jansen, 2005).

REFERENCES

Alliance for Global Sustainability (AGS) (2006) *The Observatory: Status of Engineering Education for Sustainable Development in European Higher Education*. Barcelona: Technical University of Catalonia, p. 18.

Brundtland, Gro Harlem (1987) (chair) *Our Common Future*, World Commission on Environment and Development. Oxford/New York: Oxford University Press.

Carson, Rachel L. and Darling, L. (1962) *Silent Spring*. Cambridge, MA: Riverside Press.

Dam-Mieras, Rietje van and Rikers, Jos (2005) RCE-Europe: regional centres of expertise in the context of the UN decade for SD. In: *Proceedings 'Committing Universities to Sustainable Development'*. Austria: RNS TU Graz, pp. 202–3.

Daniels, Bianca (2006) Lectoren bij hogescholen. Rijswijk, The Netherlands: Quantes, www.scienceguide.nl.

Factor 10 Club (1997) *Statement to Government and Business Leaders*, Wuppertal Institute for Climate, Energy and Environment.

Fadeeva, Zinaida (2007) From centre of excellence to centre of expertise: Regional centres of expertise on education for SD. In: Arjen E.J. Wals *Social Learning Towards a Sustainable World: Principles, Perspectives, and Praxis*. The Netherlands: Wageningen Academic Publishers, pp. 245–64.

Haddad, Georges (2007) Quality of higher education: a complex approach, Special contribution B in GUNI, *Higher Education in the World 2007. Accreditation for Quality Assurance: What is at Stake?* Basingstoke: Palgrave Macmillan, p. xxxiv.

Hinterberger, F. (2003) *Adaptive Integration of Research and Policy for SD – Prospects for the European Research Area*, Project No. STPA – 2001-00007, final report.

Jansen, Leo, Holmberg, John, and Saverio Civili, Francesco (2005) *International Evaluation of UPC Environmental and Sustainability Research and Education*, UPC, November, http://www.upc.es/mediambient/ UPCSostenible2015.html.

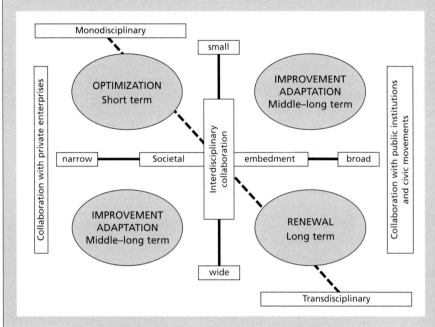

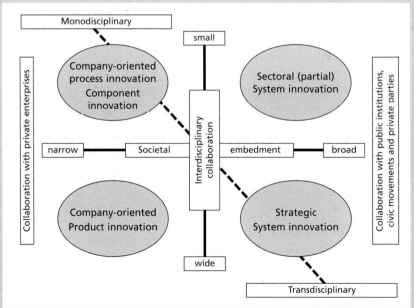

FIGURES 4 AND 5 **Modes of research in HE**

Jansen, Leo, Mulder, Karel and Pessers, Geerlinge (2006) Building capacity for SD: An evaluation of experiences at Delft University of Technology. In: Mulder, Karel F. *Sustainability Made in Delft*. Delft, The Netherlands: Eburon Academic Publishers, pp. 121–33.

Jantsch, E. (1969) Integrative Planning of Technology. In: Jantsch, E. *Perspectives of Planning*. Paris: OECD, pp. 179–85.

Kibwika, Paul (2006) *Learning to Make Change: Developing Innovation Competence for Recreating the African University of the 21st Century*. The Netherlands: Wageningen Academic Publishers, p. 207.

Martens, P. and Rotmans, J. (2002) *Transitions in a Globalising World*. Lisse, The Netherlands: Swets and Zeitlinger B.V.

Meadows, D.H., Meadows, D.L., Randers, J. and Behren, W.W. (1972), *The Limits to Growth*. A report for the Club of Rome's Project on the Predicament of Mankind. New York: Universe Books.

Mulder, Karel (2006) *Sustainable Development for Engineers: A Handbook and Resource Guide*. Sheffield, UK: Greenleaf Publishing.

Mulder, Karel and Jansen, Leo (2005) Evaluating the sustainability of research of a university of technology: towards a general methodology. In: Proceedings 'Committing Universities to SD'. Austria: RNS TU Graz, pp. 249–56.

Peet, D.J., Mulder, K.F. and Bijma, A. (2004) Integrating sustainable development into engineering courses at the Delft University of Technology: the individual interaction method, *International Journal of Sustainability in Higher Education*, **5**(3) pp. 278–88.

Robèrt, K.-H., Schmidt-Bleek, F., Aloisi de Larderel, J., Basile, G., Jansen, J.L., Kuehr, R., Price Thomas, P., Suzuki, M., Hawken, P. and Wackernagel, M. (2002) Strategic sustainable development – selection, design and synergies of applied tools, *Journal of Cleaner Production*, **10**(3) pp. 197–214.

Roorda, N., 2001, *AISHE – Auditing Instrument for Sustainability in Higher Education*. Duurzaam Hoger Onderwijs (DHO), Amsterdam, 2001, www.dho.nl/aishe.

Roorda, N. (2004) Policy development for sustainability in higher education – results of AISHE audits. In: Corcoran, P.B. and Wals, A.E.J. (eds) *Higher Education and the Challenge of Sustainability*. Dordrecht: Kluwer, pp. 305–18.

Tellegen, Egbert (2006) *Sociology and Sustainable Development*, Disciplinary Review Sustainable Development, Amsterdam: Dutch Network for Sustainable Higher Education, p. 75. www.dho.nl.

Wals, Arjen E.J. (2007) *Social Learning Towards a Sustainable World: Principles, Perspectives, and Praxis*. The Netherlands: Wageningen Academic Publishers, pp. 245–64.

Weaver, P., Jansen, L., Van Grootveld, G., Van Spiegel, E. and Vergragt, P. (2000), *Sustainable Technology Development*, Sheffield, UK: Greenleaf Publishing, p. 256.

Weaver, P.M. and Jansen, J.L. (2004) Defining and evaluating 'science for sustainability', International Conference on Sustainability Engineering and Science, Auckland. Conference Proceedings and Presentations, www.nzsses.org.nz.

NOTE

1   The author thanks Rietje van Dam-Mieras, Didac Ferrer, Karel Mulder, Nico Roorda and Paul Weaver for their stimulating cooperation and discussions, which contributed greatly to the insights in this paper.

Peter Taylor[1]

Abstract

This article examines issues relating to the development, delivery and evaluation of higher education curricula that aim to facilitate learning in the context of human development and social change. The paper begins by reviewing alternative conceptual and philosophical approaches that underpin higher education curricula, based on differing perspectives on knowledge and power, and the interplay between these in a time of globalization and growing complexity. It draws on evidence of existing relationships between curricula in higher education institutions and curricula at other levels of education systems, and the dominant pedagogical approaches that are determined by these relations. The paper identifies a range of key elements currently found in higher education curricula internationally – including citizenship, sustainable development and multiculturalism – which are consistent with the notion of human and social development. It then considers the range of potential learning needs in a globalizing world that may be addressed by higher education institutions. Taking into account issues of existing capacity, as well as needs for institutional strengthening, the paper finally suggests some key elements for the design, delivery and evaluation of interdisciplinary curricula that will help to meet learning needs in the future.

INTRODUCTION: CHALLENGES FOR HIGHER EDUCATION (HE) CURRICULA IN A GLOBALIZING WORLD

Higher education institutions (HEIs) have arrived at a critical moment in their long evolution as global and local producers and disseminators of knowledge. As noted in many of the papers in this report, due to the advent of globalization and the intensification of international competition, knowledge has come to be seen as an increasingly important determinant of the wealth of nations. Consequently, access to knowledge and the ability to disseminate it have become a major source of competitive advantage. In some quarters, knowledge itself is seen as the most powerful driver of social and economic progress in the world today (World Bank, 2002), and tertiary education is perceived as necessary 'for the effective creation, dissemination, and application of knowledge and for building technical and professional capacity' (ibid., p. xix). Universities, it is stated, should become more innovative and responsive 'to the needs of a globally competitive knowledge economy and to the changing labour market requirements for advanced human capital' (op. cit.). Knowledge itself becomes critical to the idea of development as the achievement of 'good change' (Chambers, 2005), not just in terms of availability, but also in terms of how we use knowledge to understand knowledge.

In the face of globalization, however, critics such as Olsen (2000) have claimed that the relationship between universities and society is deteriorating, and have identified HE as a service company, with society as its marketplace. Knowledge is increasingly seen as a commodity, with possession over the means of its production leading to the establishment of loci of power that support the far-reaching influence of relatively few over the majority. The potential for universities to support and nurture human and social development – especially in the South, where such an approach has been well understood in recent times and in some cases practised for centuries – is being eroded by constant shifts in policy and politics. Through the policy goals of efficiency, effectiveness, responsiveness and competition embodied in many HE reform programmes, 'national authorities transform their public higher education systems from national organizations with global social roles into global players mainly operating on the basis of economic considerations' (ibid. p. 374). These trends tend to result in raised tuition fees, reduced programmes and staff positions, increased teaching loads and greater numbers of part-time teaching staff. As a result, a more technocratic management style is adopted and alliances are formed with corporations and the private sector. This situation tends to reduce the autonomy of university teaching staff and subordinate the humanities and social sciences to the technosciences. As a consequence, HEIs may become increasingly alienated from poor and socially excluded communities and local concerns, even when they teach courses and undertake research in the name of 'development'.

Since education at all levels is playing an ever more critical role as a transmitter and reproducer of a complex fabric of knowledge and power relations, we now urgently need to question its purpose, as well as the distribution and use of the means that are put at its disposal to achieve this purpose. We need to explore ongoing transformations of the purposes and priorities of HE according to new global standards and the transfer of policies, curricula and assessment methods between countries. Curricula, in particular, offer us a glimpse of the challenges facing HE in a globalizing world, and the emerging roles of HEIs as key actors in human and social development.

Although there are many exciting curriculum innovations in HEIs around the world, the ways in which the curriculum is conceptualized and developed vary greatly. The pedagogical approaches associated with curricula appear in many different forms and are rooted, as this paper will argue, in the interrelationships between knowledge and power. As HEIs struggle to meet increasing demands in a world characterized by complexity and uncertainty, in a global context where the desire for economic growth seems to be in tension with the need to assure the basic human rights of all the world's peoples, curricula offer them the opportunity to reimagine and demonstrate their educational function and purpose. One source of opportunity may come through introducing new content, increasing interdisciplinarity and bridging the gap between advances in different disciplines. Going further, we could imagine changes throughout the curriculum experienced by all HE students, whereby traditional areas of study such as the humanities or the sciences are transformed through a transversal curriculum that is more problem-focused and linked to real-world challenges and issues. This is not an impossible dream; many institutions around the world already are attempting this.

There are many challenges to overcome, however. How should educators navigate the complex fabric of power relations both inside and outside their institutions that determines what is taught, by whom and how? What are the alternative conceptual and philosophical approaches that underpin HE curricula, based on differing perspectives on knowledge and power? How do HEIs make sense and use of the most appropriate and relevant curricular and pedagogical approaches as they struggle with the need to introduce and build new elements in their teaching programmes – including citizenship, conflict resolution and peace-building, sustainable development

and multiculturalism – that are consistent with the notion of human and social development? What are the institutional constraints and obstacles that must be overcome in order for curriculum innovation to truly take hold? This paper addresses these questions by looking forward to alternative visions of the educational purpose and curricula of HEIs in the age of globalization.

EXPLORING CURRICULA AND PEDAGOGY IN HE

Education is not the filling of a pail, but the lighting of a fire. (W.B. Yeats)

Curriculum development may be understood as 'all the learning which is planned and guided by a training or teaching organization, whether it is carried out in groups or individually, inside or outside a classroom, in an institutional setting or in a village or field' (Rogers and Taylor, 1998). For HEIs to contribute to human and social development through the education they provide, their curricula should be derived through a process of dialogue on the ideologies, philosophies and epistemologies of knowledge and learning. Thus, the purpose of education is to transform rather than transmit; to provide the opportunity to 'light the fire' rather than 'fill the pail', as Yeats reminded us; to inspire, provoke and motivate. A curriculum is grounded in the context in which learning takes place, and it is necessary to contextualize experiences that lead to wider generalizations. It is an embodiment of values: people are its foundation as living theory. A curriculum may be conceived as a 'space' in which all these varying elements may come together.

THE MAKING OF A CURRICULUM
Current trends in HE curriculum development suggest that this vision of education is not widely held, however. A more dominant view is that of education as a means of providing a well-equipped workforce for a globalizing economic world. Reuben (1996) tracked changes in the education programmes of eight American universities over a number of years and revealed the tensions emerging over curriculum and educational purpose. She concluded that the universities' belief that knowledge could lead to human and social improvement was so challenged that they lost their faith 'in the power of knowledge to elevate individuals and the world' (p. 265). Palmer (1998) noted the educational trend towards an objectivist study of reality, and criticized it on the grounds that it treats all things – and people – as objects. Imagining a different future – in which HEIs *subjectify* and even *co-create* knowledge as a means of building a new, transformative

purpose for education – could have significant implications for curriculum development.

The notion of a curriculum that is created and based, at least in part, on local knowledge generation (by either individuals or groups) is both provocative and challenging because learning in HE often focuses on an analytical understanding of the macro, the mass and the systemic. The personal and particular dimensions of knowledge – including the emotional, the artistic, the spiritual and the psychological (Heron, 1999; Heron and Reason, 2001) – are often neglected. Nevertheless, these aspects are critical to developing a sense of agency and power. They are vital ingredients that individuals and groups need in order to become effective agents of change, since they enable learners to become more conscious of the powerful, internalized and often hidden factors that constrain agency (Pettit, 2006). We need to inquire into the very nature of knowledge, using knowledge itself to understand this, and shape curricula on this basis. Unfortunately, it is rare to see genuine, open dialogue on curriculum process and product that draws on alternative perspectives of knowledge and power.

What prevents a shift towards a new vision of HE curricula and education? One key factor is the varying degree of autonomy of teachers and even institutions. In some universities, teachers and lecturers are able to make quite wide-ranging decisions on curriculum development, subject to the approval of the institution. In many HEIs, however, overall curriculum development often remains the responsibility of a few – an elite group located at the top of a hierarchy. Discussions about curriculum development tend to involve a small number of individuals in senior academic and, in some cases, government positions. These discussions usually focus on the content of teaching. Such small, privileged groups may assume that they are aware of the reality of the external environment, and that their own theoretical understanding and experience are sufficient to develop curricula that will bring about effective learning. They may also assume that learning will take place through the transmission of knowledge, and that the subject-related expertise of the teaching staff is sufficient to convey knowledge to the learners. Curricula developed using these approaches rarely provide guidance to teachers and learners on how to facilitate the learning process (Taylor, 1998). Even in universities where teachers have a greater degree of autonomy in the curriculum development process, there is rarely any mechanism or agreed-upon principle for increasing the involvement of other stakeholders. The lecturer is still considered the expert, and it is assumed that he or she will deliver the goods as a result of expertise garnered through professional activities such as academic study and research, or through personal linkages with the 'industry' in which graduates will be employed. Authority over what will be taught to the majority is vested in the minority.

Various authors have proposed curriculum development models that go far beyond listing the content to be dealt with in a specified time. Skilbeck's (1984) systematic model for curriculum development outlines five main steps: situation analysis, goal setting, planning, implementation and evaluation. This does not create a blueprint, since each step provides opportunities for a variety of decisions and actions. It places emphasis on the learner, since an important aspect of this approach is the development of learning outcomes, written in terms of what learners should be able to do at the end of a given period of study (although the value of highly specific objectives for all learning contexts is certainly debatable). It also requires an understanding of the external situation or the context of the training programme in question. It is still possible, however, for this approach to be applied by an unrepresentative minority. Situation analysis may well be invalid if it involves an individual or a small group of curriculum developers basing their work on their own narrow perception of external reality, or if it fails to consider issues of power. In such a case, there would be justifiable criticism that the predetermination of learning outcomes – and hence the selection of content, methods and materials – is inequitable. For this reason, interest is growing in more participatory approaches to curriculum development (Taylor, 2003) that seek to involve different stakeholders in meaningful ways throughout the various stages of the curriculum development process. Such approaches offer exciting possibilities for participation that are not just mechanistic or instrumental. Since power relations are often internalized by those who find themselves marginalized from decision-making processes, consciousness raising – which can lead to a new understanding of education's potential for transformation and positive change – is itself a critical part of any participatory curriculum development process.

Curriculum change is difficult, however, and resistance is often encountered. How can we support the development of curricula that are inclusive, just, democratic and based on transformative and more participatory processes? Different visions of change call for alternative ways of combating resistance: through structural means (Weiler, 1991; Olsen, 2000; Cloete, 2002); through an understanding of power relations (Bourdieu, 1990); or even through an integration of these visions for change (Freire, 1972; Giroux, 1993; Lynch, 1999). The philosophy and practice of curricula in HEIs are influenced strongly by what happens in the schools and colleges where future HE students first experience education (Apple, 1993; Bourner, 1998; Karmadonov, 2003).

RELATIONSHIPS WITHIN FORMAL EDUCATION SYSTEMS AND THEIR IMPACT ON HE CURRICULA

Bourner (1998) observes that students entering HEIs 'bring expectations about the nature of learning and education from their senior schools'. They expect HE to be like the education they have experienced previously (as do newly appointed ministers of education, as someone once remarked). But if this previous education has been top-down, based on the transmission of knowledge, students will expect nothing more from the university. Many students entering university are more vulnerable and therefore heavily defended, especially when they have recently passed through the process of adolescence and its associated biological and emotional changes (Bourner, 1998). Regardless of age, they may also be entering a new and strange environment, which for many is well beyond their comfort zone. Consequently, students look for 'sameness' wherever they can, even in the pedagogical realm. Aside from practical issues of teachers' professional capacity to offer pedagogical alternatives, this 'sameness' may also be viewed as symbolic of society's mechanisms for cultural and economic reproduction, of which the school is an agent (Karmadonov, 2003), and where the identities of students, and their positions in society, are consolidated.

A formal curriculum may be viewed as the explicit framing of ways in which cultural, economic and social relations are reproduced, whilst the 'hidden curriculum' – which underlies all educational experiences – reinforces and nourishes dominant ideologies and belief systems. It is extremely difficult for students at HEIs to move beyond understanding their education as a continuation of the system that has been legitimating, delivering and evaluating their knowledge throughout their formative years. This is hopelessly inadequate preparation for human and social development, since it avoids many, if not all, of the real challenges, problems and opportunities associated with individual learning and growth, and particularly with wider, positive social change and transformation. Learners need to pay more attention to the nature of real-world problems and take advantage of opportunities to learn a range of skills and capabilities that draw on different fields of experience and knowledge, and that enable them to address complex problems in various contexts.

How best to teach such an approach through formal education is a major challenge. The recent emphasis on lifelong learning has been criticized (Rogers, 2003) for failing to acknowledge the natural tendency of all human beings to continue learning throughout their lives, even without the assistance of international commissions and national policy statements. There are some positive signs of a shift in thinking on this matter. The need for a more holistic understanding of learning was explored in the insightful Delors Report, Learning: The Treasure Within (Delors, 1996). The International Baccalaureate (IB) Programme[2] – which emphasizes global citizenship, the complexity of a global worldview, multicultural awareness, foreign language acquisition and community service activities – is being offered more widely. The recent report of the Commission on the Skills of the American Workforce[3] emphasizes global citizenship, intercultural skills and foreign language acquisition, which seem essential if individuals are to become active members of a global society. However, these aspects could also be viewed as instrumental skills that contribute to the overall economic output of the individual and his/her national economy. So, how can we establish a vision of learning that explicitly takes into account aspects of power and politics in curricula at all levels of education?

Regardless of whether HE is seen as part of a continuous process of lifelong education to which all should have access or as a privileged place of learning accessible only to the elite few, there has been remarkably little change in the perception of the need for the qualifications that HE offers and the associated route to desirable employment. More than 30 years after the publication of Dore's (1976) seminal book *The Diploma Disease*, the problem of qualification escalation – and the almost unbreakable red thread that connects qualifications and employment – seems not to have changed, and has even been reinforced. King and Martin's (2002) return to Foster's 'vocational school fallacy' theory in Ghana is a pertinent reminder of HE's tendency to perpetuate the goal of individual acquisition over wider human and social development. Foster's argument that the educational aspirations of poor people in any community could not be changed, and that they most want the education that gives them the greatest possibility of social mobility, still seems to hold true.

Higher education remains the ultimate educational dream for many because, although non-formal and vocational education may be more practically relevant to their immediate situations, children and their parents prefer to have access to mainstream education and to the examinations and certifications that allow them to move further up the educational ladder. Even a slim hope of success in such a national system is preferred to the null chance of upward mobility provided through non-formal and vocational education. Stories abound of innovative ways in which local movements have emerged in response to the desire, often expressed by parents, for young people to enter HE. Two examples of such innovations are Columbia's 'bench schools' (Hall, 1986), spontaneously created by parents so that their children could have access to formal, national standard-based education and therefore a chance at certification and HE, and the Centre for Creative Education in Costa Rica. New institutions that attempt to provide a curriculum that is relevant and attractive to both learners and other stakeholders are beginning to emerge around the world (South Africa[4] and Uganda[5] provide two examples).

PEDAGOGICAL IMPLICATIONS

In an era of HE massification and internationalization, with everything this implies for curricula, there is a growing trend towards education as 'pail-filling' and the transmission of knowledge as a set of facts that meet pre-identified needs or requirements. This suggests a worrying return to the practice of 'banking' knowledge, to use Freire's (1972) terminology. In many ways, this trend runs counter to many of the theoretical developments in HE pedagogy over the past 40 years. Bourner (1998) observes a shift in emphasis on the big issues in the field of learning in HE and identifies a pedagogical emphasis on the transmission of knowledge and understanding in the 1960s and 1970s, on personal and transferable skills in the 1980s, and on critical reflection in the 1990s. Now, in the 2000s, as fascination with the power of distance and e-learning grows through the incredible development of ICTs, there has been a shift away from pedagogies that stress critical reflection on experience. Arnold et al. (1995) distinguish between three main educational approaches. Conservative approaches are characterized by banking of knowledge, are often expert-centred, and view learners as passive recipients. Liberal approaches are characterized by self-directed individuals seeking growth, view learners as 'learning how to learn', and are often neutral on power issues. Transformational approaches, however, are characterized by collective reflection and action, especially by those who are (or who feel) oppressed, and are concerned with changing power relations and transforming socioeconomic systems.

For an emerging role of HE to support human and social development, at least some aspects of all three approaches may be valuable at different times. Ultimately, however, we need a much stronger emphasis on more transformational approaches than we see at present. Much of the formal 'learning' on offer – for example in schools, colleges and universities – has proved to be didactic, rote and top-down (Bawden, 2004; Mott, 2005). Often, the content of these learning experiences is narrow and deals with skills, methods or theory. They rarely pay conscious attention to power issues (related to faith, race or gender, for example) that are embodied through experience and fail to enable learners to explore *who* they are (as opposed to simply *how* they are) in a deeply reflective way. In addition, the curriculum often is not grounded in a sound conceptual framework for either social change or learning (Taylor et al., 2007). Although the emergence of a 'knowledge society' may suggest a levelling of hierarchies and a shift towards more equitable power relations, we should not lose sight of the dynamics of power and the structural forces that determine them (Apple, 1993). We need to question the claim that education should be neutral, as we are reminded by many 'popular educators', by those who ascribe to 'critical pedagogy' (Lynch, 1999), and by recent initiatives such as the International Working Group on University Education for Community Change (Mott, 2005).

Have we then entered a period of enormous tension, in which the trend towards massification, efficiency and effectiveness in HE has resulted in pedagogies that are closer to the transmission model, yet appear alongside significant efforts to raise the profile of more transformative, reflexive pedagogies grounded in the co-creation of knowledge? Is curriculum partly a dialogue about the roles of and responsibilities for learning? How do beliefs and values influence the way in which curricula emerge and come to life through the learning process?

TRENDS AND EMERGING AREAS IN HE CURRICULA AND PEDAGOGIES

Even though HEIs are under severe pressure to craft their curricula and pedagogies to fit with the constantly evolving demands of a 'global' context, there are highly promising trends within the HE sector that indicate movements in the two directions mentioned at the beginning of this article: a bridging between existing disciplines, and a move towards transversal curricula that is a radical shift from what is commonly practised in most HEIs. A wide range of innovations have emerged, including sustainability studies; development as a dialogical process involving change and movement in both the North and the South; emphasis on student service activities and service-learning programmes that put university resources towards understanding and correcting social problems; inclusion of the study of poverty production factors in curricula;[6] integration of participatory action research within curricula and as a pedagogical approach; and the rising prominence in academic institutions of individuals who are recognized as both academics and practitioners. All these factors help HEIs respond to their emerging roles and face the challenges associated with human and social development.

PROFESSIONAL AND/OR GLOBAL CITIZEN EDUCATION? IMPLICATIONS FOR HE CURRICULA

Professional education (as competition) and global citizen education (as cooperation) are often seen as oppositional, but may be practised somewhat synthetically by HEIs. The most professional of training programmes, such as law and medicine, typically involve some international aspects or offer the possibility of an international focus. Most undergraduates in the USA, for example, are expected to participate in at least one professional internship during their college years and to travel abroad for a semester. Even so, the emphasis on 'internationalization' within universities and curricula, which emerged in the 1990s, has so far not achieved the promise of 'global citizenship education', as advocated by writers such as Ansley and Gaventa (1997), who wish to see a deepening practice of democracy in HE research and education. Most internationalization goals focus on either (1) increasing the number of overseas students who come to study at an institution, or (2) establishing satellite institutions in countries where there is a demand for the university's degree programmes, but where the high costs of travelling to and living in a relatively expensive country present an obstacle.

Interest is growing in the emergence of curricula that support the education of those who will work in a range of 'development' professions in various international contexts. In *Educating for Real*, Hamdi (1996) considers professional training for architects, engineers and urban planners who plan to work in developing countries and notes that their training would be far more effective if it were organized in context: 'We need field-based programmes of working and learning from communities, located at sites where students confront real constraints with conflicts of values, priorities, timetables, with changes of mind, with client members who appear and disappear, with no access to photocopying machines, drawing tables, inventing not only how to respond physically and intellectually but also how to communicate' (p. 13). Woolcock (2002), writing on what master's degree students should be taught, compares professional training programmes (in law, business, medicine, the arts and the sciences) with training programmes for public policymakers and development workers. Woolcock argues that the extreme variation in the work situations of development workers makes it very difficult to give them adequate training, except for some very broad and flexible skills. Indeed, training a 'citizen of the world' is a much harder task because of the broad, dynamic nature of this designation. As Woolcock points out, other professions have a high level of socialization in a professional culture, whereas development work does not. His argument may point to the future instability of all professional cultures in a globalized economy. Since job markets and their requisite skill sets will be changing more rapidly than ever before, lessons learned from teaching development professionals – citizens of the world – to be highly adaptive may in fact need to be incorporated into more rigid forms of professional training. These professions and their respective practices are likely to see significant changes over the coming decades that will require similar adaptivity to a smaller, more dynamic world.

There are various challenges to overcome:

- How can professional education programmes that follow a transversal approach help develop students' ability to 'learn' citizenship without overloading the curriculum and placing huge demands on both students and teachers?
- How can we coherently manage the 'professional' components and other elements that enable learners to understand and play their part in human and social development? What additional resources are needed to support this?
- What can be done to overcome resistance by professional bodies that do not wish to see significant changes in the curricula of education programmes that provide new entrants to their various professions?

COMPLEX VIEW OF THE WORLD: INTER- OR TRANSDISCIPLINARY EDUCATION

Higher education institutions and their educational programmes face enormous challenges: a world characterized by uncertainty and the interplay between a vast array of complex interactions that the human race, as self-appointed guardians of this planet, has hardly begun to comprehend. Disciplinary studies that fail to make connections to real-world and real-time challenges and problems are not likely to be in a position to support useful learning in the years to come. An emphasis on soft systems – fuelled by the influential writings of Peter Senge, including *The Fifth Discipline* (1990) – has arisen from the growing appreciation that most real-world problems are too complex for a simple 'problem-solution' framework. Woolcock (2002) points out that development workers, for example, are often faced with incomplete data when trying to analyse situations and make decisions. In such cases, workers must draw on a variety of skills and methods, as well as basic knowledge of many disciplines, in order to make inferences and conceptual connections that lead to changes in understanding and practice. Bawden (2004) describes 'the promise of the learning turn' (p. 19) for universities, in which a primary focus of learning will be on 'the features, dynamics and designs of innovative systems of learning, or inquiring systems that represent, at the very least, powerful and relevant conceptual frameworks' (op. cit.). A 'learning turn' is needed within the academy if it is to respond appropriately and innovatively to Boyer's call for it to be 'of greater service to the nation and the world' (Boyer, 1990) in an age of reflexive modernization and societal sustainability. According to Boyer, new, critically reflexive learning systems must be designed in order to meet the challenges of the new modernity, which will become the foundation for extending a scholarship of engagement into a critical systemic discourse of engagement (p. 19).

A holistic revision of global education, such as that imagined in the Delors Report (Delors, 1996), has been shared by many other institutions around the world. Such a vision generally includes a commitment to interdisciplinary research that manifests itself in teaching programmes. However, this often seems harder to achieve in practice, perhaps because of the expectations by both teachers and students of a more expert-centred mode of learning. Some education programmes have attempted to use interdisciplinarity, and even systems approaches (arising from various scientific roots in the biological sciences, engineering and cybernetics theory), as the very essence of their curricula. Bawden and Macadam (1990) have written extensively on the Hawkesbury Agricultural College in Australia, which attempted to build an entire education programme on the principles of systems thinking and practice. Agricultural and environmental education programmes have often been at the forefront of innovation in this regard, although the broad field of adult education, and newer fields such as human rights education, are showing promise (Marlin-Bennett, 2002). Sterling (2004) and Capra (1996) both argue for systems thinking as the means to environmental sustainability. However, holism and interdisciplinarity in curricula have been advocated well beyond the environmental education arena.

The World Bank (2002) has recently advocated a move towards 'transdisciplinary study' (p. 37), in which greater emphasis is placed on problem-based learning, thus blurring the distinction between basic and applied research and integrating disciplines. This has particular implications for pedagogy: greater emphasis is placed on problem-based learning, experiential learning, active student engagement, applying knowledge in real-life situations, collaborative activities, and learning as a process rather than simply rote memorization. Vedeld (2004) proposes several ways in which interdisciplinary teaching focuses on both theoretical and practical experience-based skills, thereby increasing and professionalizing the

use of problem-based learning. Students are called upon to take responsibility for their own learning; they develop skills by identifying, selecting, translating and integrating knowledge from various disciplines within a coherent framework. The recently formed MacArthur Commission on the Education Needs of Development Professionals also advocates a problem-oriented approach that encourages transversal learning by incorporating a wide range of technical and social dimensions within a more 'general' curriculum.

A number of key challenges are associated with such approaches, including the need:
- to support teachers' ability to develop a pedagogical approach based on uncertainty and problem orientation
- for employers to recognize and facilitate employees' application of more holistic forms of knowledge and practice, thereby granting greater legitimacy to this form of learning
- for schools at lower levels of the education system to prepare students for interdisciplinary forms of learning and study, in order to enable them to make a successful transition to HE.

CURRICULUM AND SUSTAINABILITY ISSUES

Jansen writes in greater detail on the issue of sustainability elsewhere in this report, and Steinemann (2003) suggests examples of curriculum development that aim to promote sustainability within a university environment and help students become more effective problem solvers and professionals. It is suggested that students in a Sustainable Urban Development course work on projects to make their campus and community more sustainable. In the process, students learn how to analyse sustainability, work with decision-makers and put classroom knowledge into practice. Further, through such a course's emphasis on problem-based learning, students acquire critical cognitive and professional skills as they tackle complex, interdisciplinary, real-world problems. Courses such as these can build important bridges between theory and application, and between education and professional practice.

The notion of sustainability education is sparking increased interest. Carlson (2006) recently provided a useful overview of the emerging field of 'sustainability studies', a highly interdisciplinary approach based on the premise that a real move towards sustainability will require a shift in thinking in all disciplines, or even a shift in consciousness (Sterling, 2004). Carlson considers curricula, hiring practices and campus design as parts of the wider institutional emphasis on sustainability. The following are other examples of innovative HE programmes that explicitly address sustainability in a more holistic way:

- The College of the Atlantic:[7] a small, environmentally focused college in Maine with only 300 students. It offers a self-designed degree programme based on a philosophy of human ecology.
- The University for Peace:[8] the United Nations college in Costa Rica. The curriculum focuses heavily on poverty reduction, conflict resolution and sustainable development. Most members of the teaching staff are UN officials with extensive professional experience within the UN system.
- The EARTH University:[9] also in Costa Rica, this school has an experiential agricultural focus and invites students from tropical countries who might be able to replicate the school's sustainable farming methods in their home countries.
- The Earth Institute at Columbia University,[10] which encourages interdisciplinary study of climate change and agricultural practices for developing countries. The Institute is also actively engaged in its own large-scale development projects, the Millennium Villages and Millennium Cities. It is linked to some 24 other degree programmes throughout the university.

Key challenges in addressing sustainability issues through curricula include the following:

- The need for policymakers and funders of HE to recognize the value of studies that emphasize sustainability as a vital complement to studies seen as contributing to economic growth.
- The need for reform within HEIs, not only to appreciate the importance of sustainable development but also to allocate needed resources and provide an enabling environment for innovation and change in sustainability practice.
- The need for HEIs to engage closely in wider societal debates on the major global challenges of our times (for example climate change, environmental degradation, poverty and human rights), even if this requires moving beyond their current, recognized areas of 'expertise'.

EDUCATION FOR MULTICULTURALISM, PEACE AND ADDRESSING CONFLICT

Multicultural understanding is a goal that many HEIs would aspire to, even though curriculum innovation rarely seems to address this explicitly. One interesting example of an educational approach is that of the United World Colleges,[11] comprising twelve schools in twelve countries on five continents, with intentionally diverse student bodies. These colleges, which are actually secondary schools, have long tried to promote multicultural understanding by bringing together young students from all over the world to study in close-knit, tightly structured social environments. The first school was created in Wales in 1962. Most recently, two new schools opened in 2006, one in Costa Rica and one in Bosnia. The early schools focused on bringing together students from countries that opposed each other in the World Wars. The new schools have a similar goal: bringing together both sides of regional conflicts. Although not yet at the HE level, such an approach seems to have strong potential for helping young people develop an understanding of themselves as global citizens, thus preparing them for a different experience of HE than would be afforded through more conventional schooling systems.

Many HEIs offer educational programmes in peace-building and studies of conflict and war. Some, such as the University of Peace in Costa Rica and the United World Colleges, are actually devoted entirely to this theme. There have been courageous attempts to develop curricula in conflict-affected societies, which by necessity address conflict and peace quite explicitly in a range of ways. In Northern Ireland, for example, the UNICORE programme at the University of Ulster[12] offers various courses and training programmes on conflict resolution and reconciliation. The curriculum has expanded around the academic study of the local conflict – the Troubles in Northern Ireland – and the resolution of the same. Efforts have also been made at an international level, as illustrated by the UNESCO Colloquium on Curriculum Change and Social Cohesion in Conflict-Affected Societies (UNESCO, 2003), which framed its approach in terms of a 'dialectical relationship between formal education and violent conflict'. The report notes: 'Formal education is an inherently ideological instrument that is related to political violence in both intended and unintended ways. On one hand, authoritarian education systems can incite conflict when explicitly used as a weapon of oppression – that is, as media of repression, apartheid, discrimination, intolerance and the perpetuation of inequalities. On the other, education can be a means through which oppressed people can resist ideological domination and contribute to liberation' (p. 6). Although the colloquium focused mainly on school curricula, a number of important ideas arose regarding the processes of curriculum renewal and policy change, which are also valuable for curriculum development in HEIs.

Key challenges associated with such approaches include the following:
- The difficulty of integrating new areas of knowledge and practice within existing curricula that enable students to act as global citizens, to recognize the rights of others, and to work towards improved conditions for others in their local contexts, as well as at the national, regional and global levels.

- The difficulties associated with building institutional linkages between HEIs and other societal actors in order to contribute to and promote dialogue that supports greater understanding and tolerance in society.
- The need for HEIs to engage in and commit their support to processes that contribute to peace-building and conflict reduction by generating and providing needed knowledge on these issues.

ETHICS, VALUES AND CURRICULA

Rethinking the nature and development process of curricula has implications for the ethics and values of teaching and learning. Bateson (1973) proposed 'levels of learning', which provide an opportunity to critically examine the paradigms within which learning takes place, and to more clearly see which paradigms are best suited to an emerging understanding of human and social development. According to Bateson, level 1 learning occurs within the dominant paradigm, while level 2 sees the limits of this paradigm and recognizes the existence of other paradigms. Level 3 is an almost transcendental state of recognizing many alternative paradigms at once – the context of contexts. Sterling (2003) argues that the infiltration of neo-liberal management practice into education has locked most HE systems into level 1 learning, and that all efforts are directed at efficiency and effectiveness – the art of 'doing things better'. At this level, there is little questioning of the validity of the paradigm, its underlying ethics and values, and its social and environmental impacts. In order to bring ethics and values to teaching and learning, there must be a sense of consequentialism that can be used to analyse one paradigm against another; this, in turn, requires level 2 learning, which looks at alternatives, at 'how to do better things' rather than just 'how to do things better'.

Of course, putting such ideas into practice is challenging. Nevertheless, there are interesting examples to learn from. The Shepherd Programme for Interdisciplinary Study of Poverty and Human Capability[13] at Washington and Lee University in Virginia in the United States, an undergraduate degree created in 1997, requires that students combine academic work with a rigorous eight-week summer internship. The academic component builds bridges between various areas of study, including English classes that focus on the theme of poverty in literature, economics classes that dissect wage inequality or the economics of race and class, and psychology courses that examine the effects of poverty on children. Another innovation is taking place within the Community Development Action Programme at Vanderbilt University in Tennessee,[14] also in the USA, which trains professionals seeking to foster developmental change in human communities. Through analysis, students investigate the concept of human potential as the freedom to choose among opportunities. At the Autonomous University of Mexico (UAM), the Master's in Rural Development has for nearly 30 years been following a 'modularized' approach in which students combine research and action learning at grassroots organizations in Chiapas with formal study at the university. Students, professors and community members collaborate closely to learn about and contribute to social change processes. The Master's in Participation, Power and Social Change at the Institute of Development Studies in the UK is grounded in a process of critical reflection on experience and combines residential intensive-study periods with a longer period of action research in a work-based placement. For many years, the PRIA network in India has promoted close ties between educational institutions and community-based organizations, in order that the knowledge and experience of both might support transformative development processes, to the benefit of all (see Tandon, in this report).

Key challenges associated with values and ethics in HE curricula include the following:

- Difficulties in establishing open processes and transparent institutional mechanisms that support dialogue on contentious or disputed areas of knowledge.
- Slow progress towards the recognition of academic 'outputs' that take into account and place value on contributions to human and social development, in addition to the traditional metrics of peer-reviewed publications and successful bids for research funding, which often govern promotion and career prospects in HEIs.
- The need to encourage teaching- and learning-based engagement between HEIs, students, teachers and wider society in a range of pressing real-world issues, following approaches that are democratic and participatory, and that affirm the rights of all.

LOOKING FORWARD: CURRICULAR POSSIBILITIES FOR HUMAN AND SOCIAL DEVELOPMENT

This paper has considered a wide range of imperatives that influence the way in which curricula are designed and has provided some examples of curriculum innovation. It has not sought to provide a survey of initiatives from all over the world, as many institutions are making small-scale – and often very exciting – efforts to bring about change in their education programmes. From the above discussion, we might identify two broad thrusts that determine the nature of HE curricula. The first thrust relates to the arguments in favour of effectiveness and efficiency, which concentrate mainly on how we can do things better – and more cost-effectively – in a globalizing world, so that our graduates may compete as part of a global workforce, secure better-paid paid employment, and thus continuously increase the demand for the education HEIs offer. The second thrust relates more to an understanding of human and social development, as discussed by many of the contributors to this report, under which scientific and academic inquiry need not be abjectly objective. Rather, such inquiry should also allow for vision and imagination; link to the spiritual, emotional and ecological; embrace uncertainty and the possibility of alternatives; and encompass a plurality of visions.

In this time of rapid growth of for-profit and corporate universities with rather narrow aims of professional training and human capital development, it seems important to ensure that all HEIs enable their students to gain a critical consciousness of the world they inhabit. This should help them to better anticipate, articulate and animate alternative processes that can lead to widespread human and social development as opposed to uneven, temporary surges in economic growth that benefit only the minority. This is not to negate the imperative of economic growth that still eludes many regions of the world, where poverty is still endemic and where the livelihoods of many are characterized by despair and deprivation. It is more of a plea for balance, and for growth coupled with wisdom, justice, tolerance and attention to the rights of all.

But the road forward is difficult. Although this paper highlights examples of innovation and changing practice, other contributions to this report have focused on the many obstacles to significant curriculum reform. In a recent international survey of innovative HE programmes, Mott (2005) remarks on how many of the programmes that are most engaged and active in human and social development find themselves marginalized within universities. These programmes are mainly supported by members of the teaching staff who believe in the merits of alternative educational forms. These individuals often invest additional effort into their work and receive no special compensation for their efforts. In some cases, they may even jeopardize their own career prospects by promoting an understanding of knowledge that is not shared by the wider institution (Stoecker, 2005). Mott found that these programmes tend to receive little university funding to cover extra expenses and therefore must often seek outside donors to maintain themselves. They are not considered as marketable as more 'mainstream' programmes. Because of funding uncertainties and a lack of support from senior management, they may become vulnerable regardless of their strength and effectiveness.

If, however, HEIs are going to support the development of curricula that promote learning that is valuable to human and social development, we need to more fully understand the learning needs of our future 'global citizens'. As Sen (1999) put it, we need to develop a sense of the capabilities that are required for development and human freedom. In addition to the ongoing need for technical skills in a host of areas, one key learning need is the ability to make connections between many types of knowledge in the face of increasingly diverse problems and challenges, and to do this in a way that places equal value on the nature and quality of our relationships with the world at large. In this latter area, more curricular emphasis should be placed on what are currently more 'marginal' areas of our education programmes: emotional intelligence; knowledge of and the opportunity to adapt to and function in unfamiliar contexts; and collaborative skills for group work, often with individuals of highly diverse backgrounds and perhaps even across former conflict lines.

Certain methodologies offer potential for the development of such attributes. One promising approach for HEIs is to focus much more intensively on social engagement and place real emphasis on learning about learning (Boothroyd and Fryer, 2004). Action research and action learning have, for some time, been seen as a means by which citizens can acquire agency and translate this more effectively into practice within a highly complex and challenging environment. To this end, methods of popular adult education, participatory action research (Freire, 1972; Fals Borda, 2001) and participatory learning and action (Pretty et al., 1995; Chambers, 1997) have been widely used in the contexts of community development and social movement organizing, often with promising results. Nevertheless, these approaches and their ability to address established knowledge and power relations have not always been applied internally within curricula by HEIs, even though this may be an area of considerable opportunity. Some practitioner-academics, such as Farmer (2003), see such 'local' possibilities of engagement in development activities as having the potential to lead to much larger changes in the global system by linking service-learning to 'the broader goals of equality and justice for the poor' (p. 227). Participatory action research allows for the development of many relational skills at once: emotional intelligence, dealing with the 'other', adaptation to and immersion in new contexts, conscious inversion of power roles and experiential/applied learning. It also encourages systemic forms of integrative reflection and analysis. As noted by Taylor, Pettit and Stackpool-Moore (2007), 'Participation and participatory approaches in education have emerged as a means of not only promoting inclusivity, but as a means of recognizing and shifting power structures, and ultimately contributing to social change and transformation. This includes the recognition that knowledge is a means of propagating power; hence, participation must involve discourse around both power and knowledge. This perspective has economic, ideological and organizational implications for institutions that provide and aim to facilitate adult education and learning programmes' (p. 4).

Attention must also be paid to teaching methodologies. Adult literacy pedagogies are an important source of guidance for HE pedagogical practice in general. Drawing on the ideas of writers such as Freire (1972) and Mezirow (1991, 2007), transformative pedagogies – sometimes termed 'emancipatory learning' or understood as experiential learning – give clear guidance on shifting power structures within the classroom that can lead to greater participation and social development of students. When linked to more participatory curriculum development approaches (Taylor, 2003), these approaches and methods may become a powerful force for positive change in how HEIs achieve their educational purpose. Although these methods are often associated with adult learners, typically in non-formal education contexts, participatory curriculum development is also practicable in HE and even in secondary schools, as A.S. Neill's radically democratic Summerhill School[15] has demonstrated. There are also interesting examples of learning networks of educators[16] who come together to share stories, experiences, concepts and methods in order to take participatory practices beyond the field and classroom and operationalize them in the restructuring of power roles within the HEI itself. The aim is to transform the university into a reflexive learning organization rather than a didactic student production line. Nor should we ignore the enormous potential of new technological innovations, particularly new forms of distance and web-based learning. Hellman (2003) provides a very useful overview of the 'promise, problems and applications' of ICTs for development. She highlights some key advantages, but also notes a range of limitations and drawbacks of distance education in industrialized countries, as well as some particular problems (the 'digital divide', the danger of disadvantaging the already disadvantaged, certification and cost-effectiveness issues, the inappropriateness of imported courses, and the corresponding risk of neglect of the classroom).

In order to bring about a sea change in curriculum design in HEIs whereby process and product become inextricably linked, more decentralized and participatory, increasingly open to a wider variety of local needs and influences, and grounded in pedagogies that are holistic and systemic for both personal and professional development, significant shifts in institutional arrangements are needed. More input and engagement will be required from students, with less emphasis on knowledge as a commodity to be bought. More involvement will be needed from teachers in designing the courses they teach and in linking them together coherently with other courses and activities within their institutions. HEI governing bodies will need to recognize that university outreach to local communities is a high priority and that the learning and knowledge generated through these programmes directly influence curriculum development. It will be important to support such knowledge generation processes, which are informed by local voices and knowledge, and rooted in society's real problems. The active engagement of administrators, teaching staff and students in systemic participatory curriculum development processes will be critical.

But to achieve all these goals, intensive work is needed on both the outcomes and the processes of specific institutional change within the HE sector. Students and teachers at HEIs, as well as external collaborators and partners, are increasingly viewed – at least as evidenced in policy and 'mission' statements – as co-learners who collectively construct knowledge through equitable dialogue. In practice, however, the act of 'designing' a curriculum still tends to be perceived as a rational, cognitive process. Teachers – and especially institutional managers – are aware that they need to rationalize 'learning' by creating a curriculum that is approvable and accreditable, often by external bodies. This view is reinforced by the many quality assurance schemes that have emerged in recent years, and propagated further by funding councils that often establish the metrics by which quality is judged and seek to promote ever-wider standardization nationally, regionally and even internationally (an issue explored in depth by the GUNI in 2006). On one level, the resulting 'institutional monocropping' (Evans, 2004) enhances international mobility, but it perhaps also reduces local relevance and adaptation to the real problems and issues of the local context and the potential for curriculum design based on 'popular deliberation'. The models selected for replication tend to be based on those seen by others as desirable due to their regular appearance at the top of international ranking systems, particularly in the USA and the UK. A relatively small group of schools at the top of these rankings has a remarkable influence on the curricula of many other institutions around the world. This may increase power asymmetry in many HEIs, as they are under immense pressure to stay aligned with the criteria evaluated in the rankings or risk losing prestige. Breaking with these standards almost invariably leads to a drop in rank in the international tables, which is perceived externally as a loss in educational quality regardless of internal motivations. Nevertheless, growing numbers of institutions are now refusing to cooperate in the surveys that lead to such ranking exercises.

Ultimately, we need to take a more strategic and collective view of the growth and evolution of innovative curriculum development processes by establishing realistic – yet challenging – planning and implementation cycles for institutional strengthening. We should seek out and commend proactive engagement by institutional leaders in policy dialogues on education, development and change processes at both local and global levels. We need to establish strategic dialogues and partnerships with policymakers and funding agencies to ensure that curriculum innovations are supported and maintained in the long term. Without such strategic moves, we run the risk of undermining the curriculum as the bedrock of the educational experience at HEIs, with potentially dire implications for the essential role of HE in human and social development.

NOTES

1 The author gratefully acknowledges the contribution of Felix Bivens for his invaluable help in preparing this article.
2 http://www.ibo.org/
3 http://www.skillscommission.org
4 Institute for Urban Ministry, South Africa: http://www.tlf.org.za/ium.htm
5 The African Rural University: http://www.urdt.net/aru.html
6 See, for example, www.cefe.net/forum/Poverty_production.pdf
7 www.coa.edu
8 www.upeace.org
9 www.earth.ac.cr
10 www.earth.columbia.edu
11 http://www.uwc.org/home
12 http://www.incore.ulst.ac.uk/
13 http://www.washingtonpost.com/wp-dyn/content/article/2006/08/01/AR2006080100825.html
14 http://peabody.vanderbilt.edu/x3684.xml
15 www.summerhillschool.co.uk
16 For example 'Learning and teaching for transformation'; http://www.pnet.ids.ac.uk/guides/ltt/index.htm

REFERENCES

Ansley, F. and J. Gaventa (1997) Researching for democracy and democratizing research, *Change*, January/February, **29**(1), pp. 46–53.
Apple, M. (1993) What postmodernists forget: cultural capital and official knowledge, *Curriculum Studies*, **1**, pp. 301–16.
Arnold, R., B. Burke, C. James, D. Martin and B. Thomas (1995) *Educating for a Change*. Ottawa: Doris Marshall Institute.
Bateson, G. (1973) *Steps to an Ecology of Mind*. Paladin.
Bawden, R. (2004) Engagement, reflexive scholarship and the learning turn within the academy. Paper presented at the 6th ALARPM World Conference, South Africa, 21–24 September 2003.
Bawden, R. and R.D. Macadam (1990) Towards a university for people-centred development: a case history of reform, *Australian Journal of Adult and Community Education*, **30**(3), pp. 138–53.
Boothroyd, P. and M. Fryer (2004) Mainstreaming social engagement in higher education: benefits, challenges and successes. Paper presented at the UNESCO Forum Colloquium on Research and Higher Education Policy, Paris, 1–3 December 2004.
Bourdieu, P. (1990) *In Other Words: Essays Towards a Reflexive Sociology*. Stanford, CA: Stanford University Press.
Bourner, T. (1998) Bridges and towers: action learning and personal development in HE. Inaugural lecture at the University of Brighton, UK, 24 November 1998.
Boyer, E.L. (1990) *Scholarship Reconsidered: Priorities of the Professoriate*. The Carnegie Foundation for the Advancement of Teaching. San Francisco: Jossey-Bass.
Capra, F. (1996) *The Web of Life: A New Scientific Understanding of Living Systems*. New York: Anchor.
Carlson, S. (2006) In search of the sustainable campus, *The Chronicle of Higher Education*, **53**(9).
Chambers, R. (2005) *Ideas for Development*. London: Earthscan.
Chambers, R. (1997) *Whose Reality Counts?* London: Intermediate Technology Publications.
Cloete, N. (2002) *Transformation in Higher Education: Global Pressures and Local Realities in South Africa*. Lansdowne: Juta and Company Ltd.
Delors, J. (1996) *Learning: The Treasure Within*. Report to UNESCO of the International Commission on Education for the Twenty-first Century. Paris: UNESCO.
Dore, R. (1976) *The Diploma Disease: Education, Qualification and Development*. Berkeley, CA: University of California Press.
Evans, P. (2004) Development as institutional change: the pitfalls of monocropping and the potentials of deliberation, *Studies in Comparative International Development (SCID)*, **38**(4), winter, pp. 30–52.
Fals Borda, O. (2001) Participatory (action) research in social theory: origins and challenges. In: Reason, P. and H. Bradbury (eds) *Handbook of Action Research: Participative Inquiry and Practice*. London: Sage.
Farmer, P. (2003) *Pathologies of Power: Health, Human Rights and the New War on the Poor*. Berkeley, CA: University of California Press.
Freire, P. (1972) *Pedagogy of the Oppressed*, London: Penguin.
Giroux, H. (1993) *Living Dangerously*, New York: Peter Lang.
Hall, A. (1986) Education, schooling and community participation. In: J. Midgley et al., *Community Participation, Social Development and the State*, London: Methuen
Hamdi, N. (ed.) (1996) *Educating for Real: The Training of Professionals for Development Practice*. London: Intermediate Technology Publishers.
Hellman, J.A. (2003) The riddle of distance education: promise, problems and applications for development. Technology, Business and Society Programme Paper no. 9. Geneva: UNRISD.
Heron, J. (1999) *The Complete Facilitator's Handbook*, London: Kogan Page.
Heron, J. and P. Reason (2001) The practice of co-operative inquiry: research with rather than on people. In: Reason, P. and H. Bradbury (eds) *Handbook of Action Research: Participative Inquiry and Practice*. London: Sage.
Karmadonov, O. (2003) The role of universities in the construc-

tion of new social realities. IPF OSI fellow 2002–2003, www.policy.hu/karmadonov.

King, K. and C. Martin (2002) The vocational school fallacy revisited: education, aspiration, and work in Ghana 1959–2000, *International Journal of Educational Development*, **22**, pp. 5–26.

Lynch, K. (1999) *Equality in Education*, Dublin: Gill and Macmillan Ltd.

Marlin-Bennett, R. (2002) Linking experiential and classroom education: lessons learned from the American University-Amnesty International USA Summer Institute on Human Rights, *International Studies Perspectives*, **3**, pp. 384–95.

Mezirow, J. (2007) Adult education and empowerment for individual and community empowerment. In: Connolly, B., T. Fleming, D. McCormack and A. Ryan (eds) *Radical Learning for Liberation 2*. Maynooth: MACE.

Mezirow, J. (1991) *Transformative Dimensions of Adult Learning*, San Francisco: Jossey-Bass.

Mott, A. (2005) University education for community change: a vital strategy for progress on poverty, race and community-building. Report. Washington: Community Learning Project.

Olsen, J. (2000) Organisering og styring av universiteter. En kommentar til Mjosutvalgets Reformforslag. Oslo: ARENA Working Paper WP 00/02. In: Cloete, N. (2002) *Transformation in Higher Education: Global Pressures and Local Realities in South Africa*. Lansdowne: Juta and Company Ltd.

Palmer, P. (1998) *The Courage to Teach*. San Francisco: Jossey-Bass.

Pettit, J. (2006) Power and pedagogy, learning for reflective development practice. *IDS Bulletin*, **37**(6), November 2006.

Pretty, J. I. Guijt, J. Thompson and I. Scoones (1995) *Participatory Learning and Action: A Trainer's Guide*. London: International Institute for Environment and Development (IIED).

Reason, P. and H. Bradbury (2001) Inquiry and participation in search of a world worthy of human aspiration. In: Reason, P. and H. Bradbury (eds) *Handbook of Action Research: Participative Inquiry and Practice*. London: Sage, pp. 1–14.

Reuben, J. (1996) *The Making of the Modern University: Intellectual Transformation and the Marginalization of Morality*. Chicago: University of Chicago Press.

Rogers, A. (2003) *What is the Difference? A New Critique of Adult Learning and Teaching*. Oxford: NIACE.

Rogers, A. and P. Taylor (1998) *Participatory Curriculum Development in Agricultural Education: A Training Guide*. Rome: Food and Agriculture Organization (FAO).

Sen, A. (1999) *Development as Freedom*. Oxford: Oxford University Press.

Senge, P. (1990) *The Fifth Discipline: The Art and Practice of the Learning Organization*. New York: Doubleday.

Skilbeck, M. (1984) *School-Based Curriculum Development*. London: Sage.

Steinemann, A. (2003) Implementing sustainable development through problem-based learning: pedagogy and practice, *J. Professional Issues in Engineering, Education and Practice*, **129**(4), pp. 216–24.

Sterling, S. (2004) Higher education, sustainability, and the role of systemic learning. In: Corcoran, P.B. and A.E.J. Walls *Higher Education and the Challenge of Sustainability: Problematics, Promise, and Practice*. Netherlands: Springer, pp. 49–70.

Sterling, S. (2003) Whole Systems Thinking as a Basis for Paradigm Change in Education: Explorations in the Context of Sustainability. University of Bath: unpublished PhD thesis.

Stoecker, R. (2005) *Research Methods for Community Change: A Project-Based Approach*. California: Sage.

Taylor, P. (1998) Participatory curriculum development: some experiences from Vietnam and South Africa. In: *Training for Agricultural Development*, 1996–98, Rome: FAO, pp. 4–14.

Taylor, P. (2003) *How to Design a Training Course: A Guide to Participatory Curriculum Development*. London: Continuum.

Taylor, P., J. Pettit and L. Stackpool-Moore (2007). Learning and teaching for transformation: Insights from a collaborative learning initiative. In: Guerstein, P. and N. Angeles (eds) *Learning Civil Societies: Shifting Contexts for Democratic Planning and Governance*. Toronto: Toronto University Press, pp. 173–95.

UNESCO (2003) *Curriculum Change and Social Cohesion in Conflict-Affected Societies*. Colloquium report. Geneva, 3–4 April 2003. Geneva: IBE UNESCO.

Vedeld, P. (2004) 'The challenges of designing and implementing an interdisciplinary educational programme'. Centre for International Environment and Development Studies (Noragric), Agricultural University of Norway.

Weiler, K. (1991) Freire and a feminist pedagogy of difference, *Harvard Educational Review*, **6**, pp. 449–74.

Woolcock, M. (2002) Higher education, policy schools, and development studies: what should masters degree students be taught? Working Paper 2002-11 Cambridge: Von Hügel Institute.

World Bank (2002) *Constructing Knowledge Societies: New Challenges for Tertiary Education*. Washington: World Bank.

SPECIAL CONTRIBUTION I.11

Training for the profession of sustainable development: educational requirements for practical imperatives[1]

John W. McArthur and Jeffrey D. Sachs

INTRODUCTION

The challenges of sustainable development – including extreme poverty, disease, and ecosystem vulnerability – can only be solved by connecting insights from a range of disciplines. Progress requires that the contributions of social, health, earth, and engineering sciences be integrated and translated into practical and well-managed policies and programmes. Unfortunately, multidisciplinary training and problem-solving remain rare, with very few practical connections across communities of expertise, particularly between natural sciences and social sciences. Individual disciplines tend to value inward-looking specialization rather than outward-looking problem-solving. This therefore makes it rare for individual organizations or professionals to have the background required to conduct cross-disciplinary policy management or problem-solving.

As one example, consider the challenge of combating chronic hunger in sub-Saharan Africa. A core knowledge of agriculture is required to understand the biophysical factors that are contributing to the stagnation of crop yields and the technical solutions that could quickly boost food output and nutritional intake in rural areas. A background in environmental science is required to manage the agricultural land environment and to understand its interactions with climate change. An understanding of health and disease control is required to promote nutrition and labour productivity among farmers and to fight the parasites that contribute to under-nourishment. Familiarity with economics is required to ensure that both farm- and macro-scale policy solutions are economically sustainable and supportive of long-term solutions to the poverty trap. Knowledge of political science is required to understand investment promoters and inhibitors in rural areas. An understanding of anthropology is required to ensure that priorities and innovations are relevant and manageable in local contexts. Crucially, none of these individual areas of knowledge is sufficient on its own to solve the challenge of hunger, but all are necessary. The same need for multidisciplinary problem-solving arises across a range of policy challenges in developing countries, such as disease control, water management, energy service delivery, and adaptation to and mitigation of climate change.

In recognition of this pressing need for a new form of training and the organization of problem-solving strategies for development, the Commission on Education for International Development Professionals was established in early 2007 to identify the core cross-disciplinary educational needs to support problem-solving in the realm of sustainable development. The Commission's work is anchored in an understanding that professionals working in the field of sustainable development – whether in developing country ministries, inter-governmental organizations, developed country aid agencies, non-governmental organizations, or academic institutions – are not sufficiently prepared to overcome the challenges they are facing. While Ph.D. graduates and other advanced specialists provide significant contributions within distinct fields of knowledge, these contributions too often remain circumscribed within the intellectual and institutional silos of their respec-

tive disciplines. As a result, opportunities are typically lost for integrated policy solutions that are scientifically, politically and contextually grounded.

It remains an unresolved paradox that the parameters for policymaking in all sectors – such as education, health, and the environment – are set by finance ministries and other powerful fiduciary institutions, where the individuals who set the policy parameters tend to have extremely limited knowledge of the sectors whose outcomes they define. Through little fault of their own, the finance officials are typically classroom-trained in the theories of economics, with no background for evaluating the absolute or relative merits of a plan to control a disease, manage an ecosystem, or deliver an energy service. Nor do they typically have much exposure to the ground-level practicalities of policy management and project implementation. Yet the consequences are of the highest order when decisions affect, and sometimes even cost, millions of lives at a time.

The Commission therefore recommends that new educational programmes are needed to forge links across disciplines, with particular emphasis on bridging the natural and social sciences. A new type of generalist practitioner is needed, one who understands the complex interactions between fields and is able to effectively coordinate and implement the insights offered by subject-specific specialists. Meanwhile, specialists like physicians and Ph.D. graduates require mechanisms to round out their knowledge base for the practice of sustainable development so that they can contribute as effectively as possible to cross-disciplinary policy teams. Moreover, the rapid pace of scientific advancement and the requirements for skill upgrading through lifelong learning underscore the need for a 'life cycle' continuing education approach to sustainable development.

To this end, this paper outlines the Commission's preliminary findings for a new approach to educating development professionals. The Commission proposes a new, rigorous approach to training, embedded in practical experiences that

will draw from a diversity of delivery methods in order to address needs throughout the professional life cycle. Specifically, the proposed reforms target graduate-level degree programmes, lifelong learning initiatives, and organization-based training programmes. In this context, the Commission places particular emphasis on the need for a new class of professional: the generalist development practitioner.

KEY SKILLS REQUIRED

The core competencies required for sustainable development problem-solving can be grouped under two headings: (1) substantive knowledge for problem-solving; and (2) management and leadership skills for implementation.

1. *Substantive knowledge for problem-solving*. Informed decisions hinge on the ability to *analyse* a particular situation with an appreciation of the cross-disciplinary nature of issues that typically interact. However, choosing a course of action requires a sound ability to *diagnose* the core drivers of a situation and the practical steps that can most directly affect outcomes. In this regard, development practice requires core substantive expertise that covers the following range of disciplines:

   - *Agriculture*. A majority of the world's poorest people depend on agriculture for their livelihoods, although biophysical environments vary tremendously by region. Both food production and rural economic transformation often hinge on crop yields, which in turn hinge on soil fertility, availability of inputs and land management. Practitioners require basic knowledge of these topics, along with fishery and livestock management.
   - *Civil engineering*. Public infrastructure is essential to poverty reduction and economic growth, and often requires balance with environmental priorities. Policymakers require a basic technical background in issues pertaining to urban planning, trans-

port, water management, and waste management.

- *Economics*. Microeconomics is essential for understanding the ground-level incentives and practicalities of policy design. Macroeconomics is crucial for understanding how programmes interact with large-scale government decision-making and budgets, and the movements of goods, resources and services across countries.
- *Environment and climate science*. Large numbers of poor people live in fragile ecosystems and many developing countries are experiencing severe ecosystem degradation as human settlement expands and natural resource bases are mined. Coastal populations depend heavily on fisheries and marine management. Evolving ecosystems typically define transmission patterns of diseases affecting human, animal and plant health. All these dynamics are affected by climate patterns, which are shown to be shifting due to anthropogenic climate change. Policy diagnosis and prescription is foolhardy without a sound understanding of basic environmental and climate science.
- *Health sciences*. As just one example, child mortality rates in the poorest countries are often 30 to 50 times higher than in industrialized countries. Most interventions to reduce this gap require the implementation of basic and proven technologies. Practical knowledge is essential on basic 'life-and-death' issues pertaining to child health, along with other core areas such as reproductive health, maternal health, nutrition, infectious disease control (such as HIV/AIDS, malaria, and tuberculosis), and non-communicable disease control.
- *Politics, anthropology and social studies*. By mapping out key scientific and technical dimensions that underpin sustainable development, the Commission does not suggest

an approach to development in which social dynamics are overlooked. Quite the contrary, development professionals require basic skills in analysing culture, power and social relations at various levels: within households, within communities, and across societal groups.
- *Statistics*. Development professionals require an ability to evaluate statistical evidence of programme and policy results. Multivariate regression analysis and other basic techniques should form an essential part of any practitioner's toolkit.

2. *Management and leadership skills for implementation*. Development practitioners must be able to manage policies, programmes and projects. The following skills are essential in this regard:

- *Communication and negotiating*. Practitioners must be able to interact with colleagues, partners, and stakeholders from diverse backgrounds and disciplines. Whether practitioners are working at the ground level or in the political arena, interventions will only be successful if they have been developed with a keen understanding of power relations and cultural interactions.
- *Human resource management*. As professionals advance in their careers, they must be able to lead, mentor, and inspire ever-larger numbers of subordinates to achieve successful outcomes.
- *Financial management*. Practitioners must be able to design and manage programme and project budgets with transparency and efficiency.
- *Monitoring and evaluation*. Practitioners must be able to collect, monitor, and evaluate relevant data to inform and update policy and project implementation.
- *Project design and management*. Practitioners need to be able to design and manage work streams that measure progress against clear benchmarks. They also often require strong proposal-writing skills.

While the above management skills can be described as 'core competencies,' leading practitioners must also have skills of social entrepreneurship such that they can pull together a variety of political, financial and institutional resources to imagine, build, market and deliver new ideas. This requires coordination, resource mobilization, campaigning and vision building. It further requires the agility to respond to constantly evolving contexts and to lead change processes within and across organizations. Similarly to strategic political figures, top practitioners are able to garner support for innovative projects or interventions.

CURRENT GAPS

Although today's professional education programmes might provide development professionals with small subsets of the skills listed above, there are no programmes that systematically develop skills across the range of competencies above. The Commission's review of university degree programmes, executive training programmes, and organizational training programmes highlight the following gaps:

- *Degree Programmes*. Most academic degrees relevant to sustainable development, whether based on the natural sciences or social sciences, tend towards within-discipline academic specialization. Many universities around the world offer graduate degree programmes that focus on 'development studies', typically with a focus on either social sciences or environmental sciences, but these offer few opportunities for systematic, cross-disciplinary education or management training. Across these programmes, there are no consistent standards for prerequisite training, core curriculum or programme length. Too few programmes employ delivery methods that teach functional and practical knowledge, and students' opportunities for course-related fieldwork or internships remain all too rare. Furthermore, students trained by professors with purely academic backgrounds could often benefit from more efficient means of acquiring the practical skills needed to work in policy- and project-focused settings.

- *Lifelong-learning initiatives.* Mirroring the lack of degree programmes focused on cross-disciplinary learning, development professionals have almost no opportunities for refreshing and upgrading relevant skills throughout their careers. Executive education programmes typically focus on management techniques rather than substantive training. Medical doctors and Ph.D. holders have no obvious vehicles for complementing their specialist skills with core knowledge from related fields. Moreover, there are no reference points for objectively evaluating competencies across disciplines. How does an economist know, for instance, whether a colleague's disease-related research meets basic epidemiological standards? Or how does a health specialist know when a colleague's environment-related policy recommendation meets the latter field's basic standards? There is no clear metric for judging.
- *Organization-based training.* In organizations working in sustainable development, training programmes generally do not provide staff and management with multidisciplinary knowledge. Moreover, experts from a specific field of study are often promoted to assume ever-greater substantive and managerial responsibilities but with no corresponding training. While many professionals have some of the required competencies of a development practitioner, these experts often lack a sufficient understanding of the other relevant disciplines required to analyse and diagnose problems. Furthermore, they may not have the management skills required to function effectively at their level.

To address the three categories of gaps outlined above, the Commission has made the following preliminary recommendations, with the aim of supporting future generations of professionals as well as those currently working in the sphere of sustainable development.

- *New graduate degree programmes.* The Commission recommends the setting up of new graduate programmes for generalist development professionals, tentatively named a 'Master's Degree in Development Practice' (MDP). The core curriculum should cover each of the skill sets described above, including both coursework and fieldwork for a combined programme length of probably two years. Courses should be taught using a combination of case methods, lectures, field seminars, clinical practices, apprenticeships and global exchanges. Each course should focus on the context of development, the analysis and diagnosis of problems, and interactions with other relevant disciplines.

  Teaching staff for the programme will need to systematically integrate active practitioners with programme and policy experience. These senior professionals should be able to serve as mentors and be able to provide students with opportunities to serve as apprentices in various projects. At least one semester should be dedicated to fieldwork, which should be specifically designed to foster students' management skills, communication skills, and practical understanding and application of the core subjects studied.

  It should also be highlighted that the new MDP can provide an invaluable service to other discipline-based graduate programmes. Students on discipline-based master's degrees and Ph.D. programmes may be invited to take a joint degree with an extra year of cross-disciplinary policy-based study in the MDP programme. Moreover, the MDP will have several stand-alone survey courses, which might be of considerable interest to graduate students from discipline-based programmes.
- *Professional education for lifelong learning.* The Commission recommends the creation of executive education programmes to support multidisciplinary and multifunctional professional learning at all stages of individuals' careers. This may include online or virtual learning programmes, web conferences, interactive workshops, and professional networks that help to update practitioners with recent advances in their field. Certification systems should be made available for those who wish to demonstrate their proficiency in substantive and functional areas of competence. For example, professionals with backgrounds in economics or environmental management should be able to obtain certificates that demonstrate a basic knowledge of vector-borne disease control. The same certification processes should also be subject to expiration and periodic upgrading as relevant scientific knowledge progresses.
- *Organization-based training programmes.* Sustainable development-focused organizations should implement systematic skill upgrading programmes, both to ensure adequate training for new staff and to ensure adequate preparation for normal promotion paths. For example, a ministry of planning might wish to ensure that individuals have core training across the range of sustainable development competencies before assuming the responsibilities of a permanent secretary or director of planning. Likewise, the World Bank or UN system might wish to invest in similar levels of generalist substantive and managerial competency before promoting an individual to be a national director or resident coordinator, respectively.

  Aggressive strategies for in-service training could also include exchanges across organizations, as well as between organizations and university-based professional schools. Such strategies would also nurture successful practitioners through the provision of intra-organizational training. Staff should engage in short 'rotations' across the other areas of expertise to ensure that they have the opportunity to test and apply basic knowledge for meeting the challenges in each field, plus the basic technical language employed by the different groups of experts. Junior staff should receive systematic feedback and evaluation from senior specialist staff across the range of substantive and managerial skills required.

CHALLENGES TO REFORM

The Commission recognizes that some of these recommendations call for major reform. For example, universities and training schools would need to develop strategies to recruit and retain active practitioners who meet high standards as teachers and mentors, while providing necessary support that would allow them to continue working as practitioners. In many if not most cases, teaching staff will initially need to be recruited from existing within-discipline university programmes. There are also significant financial implications. Programmes would need to be affordable and accessible, given that remuneration in the field of sustainable development is typically modest, particularly at junior levels. Moreover, professional and organizational cultures would need incentives for welcoming and systematically respecting the insights of disciplines that are historically under-represented. This implies revising status quo hierarchies and designing new professional reward systems to encourage multidisciplinary acumen. The proposed reforms must also be accompanied by the formation of a structure of clear ethical standards and accreditation bodies, which would most likely be established by a newly formed association of professionals and development practitioners.

Nonetheless, the implementation of these recommendations would dramatically increase the opportunities for improving policies and programmes for sustainable development. By creating educational training programmes that target students, professionals, and organizations, the Commission's recommendations should assist professionals in developing the competencies required to be a skilled practitioner.

TOWARDS A FUTURE GENERATION OF MULTIDISCIPLINARY PRACTITIONERS

Throughout the formulation and early stages of the Commission's work, we found that there was tremendous agreement among practitioners and educators around the world on the need for a coherent new approach to educating professionals with the multidisciplinary skills required to solve the day-to-day challenges of sustainable development. Institutions as diverse as Georgetown University, Makerere University, Sciences Po, Tsinghua University, the University of Central Asia, and the University of Sussex have expressed interest in launching educational programmes to meet this need. The Commission is working with these and other partners to identify the practical aspects of programme design while it is preparing its detailed recommendations for final presentation in early 2008. New degree programmes are likely to be launched as early as 2009. It is conceivable that, as early as a decade from now, new international norms will be consolidated for training multidisciplinary development practitioners across a broad range of scenarios. By 2025, a new generation of skilled practitioners could be in place to support and lead day-to-day development problem-solving around the world. The growing complexity and interconnectedness of our planet's sustainable development challenge will require such professionalism. These future professionals, in turn, require training today.

NOTE

1   This article is based on a June 2007 document, 'Initial Findings and Preliminary Recommendations', prepared by the Commission on Education for International Development Professionals, which is co-chaired by the authors and hosted by the Earth Institute at Columbia University in collaboration with the John D. and Catherine T. MacArthur Foundation. The authors gratefully acknowledge the contributions of all Commission members and the Project Manager, Katie Murphy, in the formulation of the ideas presented here.

GOOD PRACTICE I.1

Training professionals in socially responsible values, attitudes and behaviour patterns (University of Concepción, Chile)

GUNI Observatory[1]

CONTEXT

There is a growing need in today's society for professionals who are able to pre-empt change, think ahead to the future and work effectively. At the same time, they must continue to be aware of the impact of their actions on society. Universities train the professionals and academics who become leaders in society. Consequently, graduates must be capable of making a commitment to human and social development in their countries, which means they must be prepared to conduct themselves professionally in a technically and socially responsible manner.

Changes and new needs and demands in the labour market, and in society in general, cause certain difficulties in terms of adapting syllabuses to the setting in which universities operate. Furthermore, when practical and professional perspectives are included in higher education, the social relevance of professional practices – and social responsibility in general terms – is often overlooked. However, it is possible to identify certain aspects of the training of future professionals that need improving.

In Chilean universities, there has been

debate and reflection on the need to include the teaching of values and social responsibility in higher education. One example of this is the Universidad Construye País project. Eleven Chilean universities take part in this project, which is coordinated by the University of Concepción. It aims to establish university networks for sharing experiences and thoughts to tackle these issues.

AIMS
GENERAL AIM
To train professionals from universities associated with the project in the values, attitudes and behaviour patterns that foster social responsibility.

SPECIFIC AIMS
1. To achieve measurable changes in the values, attitudes and behaviour patterns necessary to exercise social responsibility in students studying degree courses covered by the project.
2. To create a team of academics who are suitably qualified to train lecturers and students in social responsibility.
3. To include social responsibility in all curricula as a core objective.
4. To set up permanent support units – linked to associated universities by means of a network – for disseminating, teaching, learning and exercising social responsibility.
5. To establish a common programme for the ongoing teaching of social responsibility in the associated universities.

DESCRIPTION
This project forms part of the Universidad Construye País initiative, which was launched in 2000. The initiative is led by the NGO Participa, which brought together eleven Chilean universities for the common purpose of reflecting on the role of higher education institutions in Chile.

The project commenced in 2003 with the participation of the Southern University of Chile, the Pontifical Catholic University of Valparaíso, the University of La Frontera, the University of Bio-Bio, the University of Valparaiso, and the University of Concepción. The University of Concepción is ultimately responsible for the project and its management.

The Ministry of Education mainly finances the project through a grant awarded from its Competitive Fund programme. The University of Concepción also contributes funds in its capacity as the coordinating institution. The budget amounts to approximately €694,086 for the three years of the project's duration (2003 to 2006).

The project is divided into five basic activities:

- Assessment tools
- A diagnosis of students' perceptions of socially responsible behaviour
- The creation of support units for teaching social responsibility
- Teacher training
- Curricular changes

PROCESS
The following activities have been undertaken:

1. The creation of instruments to assess socially responsible values, attitudes and behaviour patterns in university students.
2. The diagnostic assessment of 5500 students from the six participating universities to analyse their self-attributed socially responsible values, attitudes and behaviour patterns.
3. The setting up of support units for social responsibility teaching. These units are made up of the heads of department of all the degree courses covered by the project and the project's management team. The support units have their own premises in all the participating universities. The mission of the support centres is to offer pedagogical support to university lecturers who wish to include social responsibility in the subjects they teach.
4. The training of lecturers from all the participating degree courses in each university. A total of 165 lecturers from the six universities have taken a 280-hour course whose outcome is a diploma in social responsibility. Participants had to devise activities for transferring the knowledge acquired on the course to the other academics in their faculty.

The most appropriate aims, contents, methodology and assessment method for training university students in social responsibility were defined. Subsequently, lecturers were trained and the necessary curricular changes for the participating degree courses were agreed. The implementation of these changes is currently in progress.

In parallel, work is being done at an interdisciplinary level to initiate and encourage cooperation among universities in issues such as strategies, learning methods, teaching/learning modules, and student assessment systems that include social responsibility indicators.

RESULTS
The final results will be available after the assessment phase of the project. Assessment will be based on a comparative analysis of data from social responsibility questionnaires completed by students before and after implementing the project.

Up to 2006, the most noteworthy results were as follows:

1. Validated instruments for assessing the self-attribution of values, attitudes and behaviour patterns associated with social responsibility had been created. These instruments had been tested on 5500 students.
2. A total of 165 academics had been trained to teach social responsibility to professionals.
3. Support units for teaching social responsibility had been set up in each of the six participating universities.
4. Degree courses involved in the project now include subjects with a social responsibility component, whether in terms of aims, methodology or assessment.

RECOMMENDATIONS

A number of aspects should be taken into account when a project of this nature is implemented:

1. The decision by university academics and administrative staff to take training in social responsibility should be voluntary. An institution's commitment should be expressed through specific actions carried out by its rector and management.

2. A prior process of reflection and analysis is required in order to obtain the commitment of the institution's academic and administrative staff. This process will lead to a consensus on the meaning of social responsibility, and its role and impact on course syllabuses.

3. The training of academics to teach social responsibility should include teaching/learning methodologies and assessment strategies for the social responsibility programme.

4. It is important to determine the students' perceptions of social responsibility training before designing and implementing the curricular changes needed to teach it. This information will prove useful in redesigning the educational model, as both lecturers and students will have taken part in the process.

5. Social responsibility training offers graduates the opportunity to incorporate social responsibility into their everyday working lives. The model designed under the programme incorporates social responsibility skills into graduate profiles and includes the concept of social responsibility in the aims, teaching strategies and assessment methods for at least two subjects in each degree course. There is no plan to run specific social responsibility classes in parallel to traditional subjects.

In conclusion, therefore, it should be underlined that the training of socially responsible professionals should:

- Be an institutional decision
- Commence with a definition of common indicators of professional social responsibility
- Be achieved through training academics who voluntarily make the commitment to educate socially responsible professionals
- Involve joint decision-making on curricular modifications to syllabuses.

NOTE

1   Text written by the Universities and Social Commitment Observatory with information provided by Gracia Navarro, University of Concepción.

SPECIAL CONTRIBUTION I.12

Higher education challenges emerging from the interchange between science and ancestral knowledge in Central and South America

Manuel Ramiro Muñoz

INTRODUCTION

The aim of this article is to explain the dynamics of change in higher education that have arisen as a result of interaction with the indigenous peoples of Central and South America.[1] First, the problems of indigenous peoples are described. Second, some characteristics of the influx of indigenous peoples into higher education institutions are given. Third, the most common experiences of indigenous peoples in higher education are analysed. Fourth, the higher education challenges emerging from the dialogue between science and ancestral knowledge are discussed. Finally, several conclusions are drawn.

THE NEGATION OF INDIGENOUS PEOPLES RENDERS THEM INVISIBLE

The indigenous peoples of Central and South America have been excluded from all levels of society. Examples of the ways in which the system has negated their existence and rendered them invisible can be found in legal, socioeconomic, cultural and epistemological areas.

LEGALLY

In most countries in the region, national identities were formed by negating the diversity of the country's ethnic and cultural roots. Within the framework of the monocultural nation-state, a concept of citizen was established that only recognized people who were male, white, propertied and heterosexual (Castro, 2002). This exclusive definition marked the course of state policies. It created a discriminatory, exclusive political culture, which is now one of the main obstacles to generating processes for recognizing and integrating the identity, culture and knowledge of indigenous peoples.

SOCIALLY AND ECONOMICALLY

The extent to which the existence of indigenous peoples is denied, rendering them invisible, is clearly shown by their low human development indicators. This situation puts both the personal and collective survival of indigenous people at risk. World Bank and IDB studies[2] show that, like the human development indicators, the income level of indigenous people is lower than that of the rest of the population (Hall and Patrinos, 2005). This occurs in a context that is riddled with inequality. In most of the countries in the region, the richest 10% receive from 40% to 47% of the total income, while the poorest 20% only receive between 2% and 4% (Ferranti et al., 2003). Several studies demonstrate that efforts to reduce poverty and increase the income of indigenous peoples in the decade 1994–2004 had only limited results. In addition, these studies reveal major shortcomings in the special social protection policies that have been specifically designed for indigenous peoples (Hall and Patrinos, 2005). Today, being indigenous in this part of the continent means being the poorest of the poor.

CULTURALLY AND EDUCATIONALLY

Negating the existence of indigenous groups to the extent that they become invisible has serious negative effects on their social and cultural development. In recent decades, governments, cooperation agencies and networks have taken positive measures to ensure higher levels of inclusion. Their efforts have been worthwhile, but the results have not been as good as expected. The essence of this kind of negation lies in the monocultural approach. It can also be found in an attitude towards relations with indigenous peoples that is hierarchical and not open to discussion. They are treated as if they are under legal age and their activities are taken to be culturally, socially and economically irrelevant. The many positive measures are aimed at quantitative rather than qualitative inclusion, and do not consider questions such as: What type of education, for what kind of development, are indigenous people gaining access to (Gorostiaga, 2000).

EPISTEMOLOGICALLY

There is an epistemological barrier – a kind of cultural illiteracy – in many academic sectors. These sectors assume a monocultural stance when dealing with indigenous peoples, and treat them as if they are minors. This type of negation, which makes the indigenous peoples invisible, is the one that most influences responses to indigenous peoples' demands for a high quality, relevant higher education system. Above all, it prevents dialogue between science and ancestral knowledge. Alcibíades Escué, a Colombian indigenous leader, has made a direct comment on this matter:

In the first wave of globalization,[3] it was debated whether black people and Indians had a soul; in order to recognize us as humans and as individuals with rights. We lost this debate and consequently there were 'rational' arguments for colonizing and enslaving us. Today, in the second wave of globalization, the discussion is more subtle but equally harmful. It is debated whether we have culture or folklore, languages or dialects, thoughts or myths. It has even been stated that our illiteracy in Spanish and Western thought is yet more evidence of our inability to think. As in the past, we are losing this debate. We are treated like minors. Consequently, arguments exist for imposing models on us, colonizing us and exterminating us as a culture and a people.[4]

This epistemological barrier will be broken when groups on both sides are prepared to leave the security of their certainties and open themselves up to the marvellous and uncertain territory of dialogue and encounter.

THE INFLUX OF INDIGENOUS PEOPLES INTO HIGHER EDUCATION

In the 1990s, the indigenous peoples burst into regional politics[5] as agents of their own development. This occurred in almost all the countries of Central and South America. Indigenous peoples are at the crossroads of international geopolitics. Their territories are frequently in the areas of the world that have the highest levels of biodiversity (in terms of germplasm, seeds and species). In addition, their lands have valuable natural resources (water, natural forests and oxygen) and rich mineral and hydrocarbon resources of high strategic importance (gold, platinum, petrol, gas and coal).

Within this context, indigenous peoples are fighting for the creation of intercultural higher education areas. This involves taking positive action to combat discrimination. It also involves transcending current university policies that are focused on access (grants, enrolment targets, programmes and institutes) and progressing towards the transformation of higher education institutes (HEI) and higher education systems. A feasible university project should be created to recover the idea of universities as places for dialogue and meeting places for different kinds of knowledge, perspectives, interests, cultures and peoples.

This effort by indigenous peoples is not far removed from other ways of thinking that are promoting changes in the model of knowledge production. Such changes are linked to the different aspects of cultural, social and economic life. Traditional academic disciplines are no longer the only way of organizing knowledge, and new disciplines are proliferating. Opportunities for acquiring skills, abilities and competences are multiplying. The resulting pedagogical systems are increasingly transdisciplinary and interdisciplinary. Such systems constitute the only way to consider and devise solutions to the major problems in the environment (Didriksson, 2002). This situation has arisen in a context in which knowledge linked with development is one of the factors that produces most added value in the economy. It is also a key factor in the development of indigenous peoples.

University procedures in which specialized knowledge is used to address increasingly profound problems with complex, far-reaching consequences are generally unsuccessful and are becoming obsolete. Problems that used to be presented within clear disciplinary boundaries have now become urgent transdisciplinary and interdisciplinary tasks that break with closed, hegemonic and rationalist conceptions of truth, certainty and validity.

Likewise, academic and curricular structures that are formal, rigid, fragmented and far removed from specific social, economic, political and cultural contexts can no longer be sustained. The creation and appropriation of concepts need to be linked to action and experience in real situations. 'Ivory tower' subjects must make room for significant learning scenarios. Methods that naively champion neutral, aseptic knowledge have come up against processes of creating and transmitting ethically and politically responsible knowledge: science with awareness (Max Neef, 2002).

The dialogue between concepts, experience and awareness is summed up by an aphorism of the Nasa indigenous people of southeast Colombia, whom UNESCO has recognized as masters of wisdom: 'Words without action are empty, actions without words are blind, words and actions without the spirit of community are dead' (UNESCO – Caracas, 1998).

AREAS FOR DIALOGUE BETWEEN SCIENCE AND ANCESTRAL KNOWLEDGE

The constitutions of countries in the region are beginning to recognize the legal, political, territorial, cultural and educational autonomy of indigenous people, as well as their independence of thought. As a result, two main types of experiences have arisen, namely: projects that are promoted by indigenous peoples (*ab intra*) and projects that are promoted from outside the indigenous communities (*ab extra*) (see Figure 1).

There are two types of higher education among the *ab intra* projects.

INDIGENOUS HIGHER EDUCATION

This is rooted in the principle of cultural autonomy and independence of thought. It is based on the history, culture and ideas of each indigenous people and focuses on strengthening their identity, autonomy and life projects. It is characterized by being highly relevant and effective. Its quality varies according to the circumstances.[6] It is undertaken in precarious conditions (in terms of infrastructure, funding, and so on). It mostly takes the form of indigenous schools and autonomous universities. In this type of higher education, the following institutions are outstanding: indigenous schools in Ecuador, Colombia and Bolivia; the Kallawaya Medical School in Bolivia; the Kawsay Unik Project of the indigenous peoples of Andean countries.

BILINGUAL, INTERCULTURAL HIGHER EDUCATION PROJECTS PROMOTED BY INDIGENOUS PEOPLES

This type of education is based on dia-

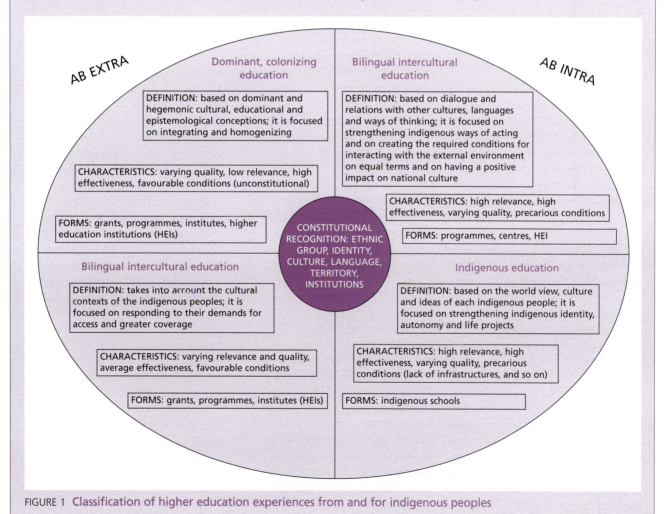

FIGURE 1 Classification of higher education experiences from and for indigenous peoples

logue and interchange with other cultures, languages and ways of thinking. It aims to strengthen indigenous people's own ways of acting; to create conditions for interacting with the external environment on equal terms; and to have a positive impact on national culture. This type of education is characterized by high levels of relevance and effectiveness. It varies according to circumstances as do the conditions under which it is carried out. The most common forms it takes are as follows: technical, vocational and professional training programmes, particularly for training teachers in higher education centres or higher education institutes. The following institutions are involved in this type of project: the University of the Autonomous Regions of the Nicaraguan Coast (URACAN); and the Intercultural Autonomous University of the Cauca Indigenous Regional Council (UAIN).

There are also two types of higher education in the second *ab extra* group of projects.

BILINGUAL AND INTERCULTURAL HIGHER EDUCATION PRACTICES PROMOTED BY THE HIGHER EDUCATION SYSTEMS

This type of education takes into account the cultural contexts of the indigenous people. It is focused on meeting indigenous peoples' demands for access, greater coverage and relevance. It generally has varying relevance and quality, and average effectiveness. This kind of education is usually carried out in more favourable conditions, as it is backed by the institutional weight of the higher education system and the HEIs. It often takes the form of enrolment targets, grants, programmes and institutions. HEIs have even been established with this type of education in mind.

Experiences in this category include the following: the Chilean government's grant programme for the Mapuche people; the undergraduate and postgraduate programmes for training teachers in ethnic education, run by public universities in Bolivia (the Universities of San Andrés and San Simón) and Guatemala (the University of San Marcos); master's

degrees at the Latin American Faculty of Social Sciences (FLACSO-Ecuador); the Mexican government's initiative to create ten autonomous, indigenous and intercultural universities (six of which have already been established); the master's course being developed at the Metropolitan Autonomous University, Xochimilco Unit; and in Guatemala, the diplomas and the EDUMAYA grants programme of the Rafael Landívar University. The Antioquia University and the National University of Colombia are also working in this area. In Ecuador, the Salesian Polytechnic University has a programme for training indigenous teachers.

DOMINANT, COLONIZING TYPE OF HIGHER EDUCATION

In contrast, here there is no place for dialogue between the sciences and ancestral knowledge. This type of education is based on dominant and hegemonic cultural, educational and epistemological concepts. Its effects are acculturation, integration of the indigenous peoples into the dominant culture, and cultural homogenization. In countries whose national constitutions include the concept of a multiethnic, multicultural and multilingual state, this kind of higher educational is unconstitutional. It usually takes the form of enrolment targets, grants and extension programmes. However, projects have also been created in this category under the 'indigenous universities' banner. The aim of these universities is to extend coverage; to qualify an indigenous labour force for the industries established in indigenous territories; and to make the processes of integration and colonization more effective.

HIGHER EDUCATION CHALLENGES IN THE REGION IN TERMS OF ANCESTRAL KNOWLEDGE

The first challenge is to change the strange monocultural way of evaluating peoples, cultures and knowledge. This approach is at odds with the plurality and diversity of the American continent, in which there is an enormous variety of languages and ways of being, acting,

feeling and thinking. South and Central America are part of a continent in which three major cultures meet. These are the Afro-American, American Indian and Latin cultures. Many different peoples, cultures and nations co-exist in this continent. The discourse of monocultural identity is a call to uniformity and sometimes even hinders real encounters. The possession of different characteristics or the ability to express oneself with passion is not part of this discourse.

The second challenge is to overcome the general tendency to imitate Europe and the USA, which exists on many levels. Such imitation has been widespread in Central and South America for several decades. This neocolonialism has been superimposed over the old, Eurocentric colonialism and has weakened the ability for autonomous thought. Imitation has continued despite the waning influence of the reference models, modernity and the North American lifestyle.

The third challenge involves the dialogue between science and ancestral knowledge. The major problems of the indigenous peoples – injustice, poverty, violence and the deterioration of the natural environment – are of such magnitude that it is impossible to tackle them using a scientific specialization in the hands of a fragmented human being. However, ancestral knowledge, which has been developed and applied in endogamic and ethnocentric contexts, does not provide solutions either. Problems are increasingly global and have ever more complex and worldwide consequences. The magnitude of such problems has created a need for urgent transdisciplinary and interdisciplinary tasks and led to real intercultural challenges. Any form of knowledge that is specific and closed in on itself has become obsolete in the face of these problems.

From both the new sciences and ancestral knowledge, searches have begun that encourage a move away from the concept of objectivity to one that includes the observer as part of knowledge; from knowledge that subjugates to knowledge that liberates; from absolute truths to approximate descriptions; from hierarchies to networks of interchange; from power as submission, to power as a collective construction; from 'to be or not to be' to being a developing person, who is present and participative; from nihilism, to re-enchantment with the world; from the battle of the sexes to reconciliation, from rigidity to flexibility, now seen as a strength; from structures to dynamic processes; from lineal time to plural conceptions of time; from natural selection to large-scale cooperation between the species; from fragmentation and the sum of the parts to the emerging plural, diverse order (*Agenda Mujer*, 1998).

The fourth challenge is to construct *universitas*, which are defined as places where meeting and dialogue can occur among sciences, knowledge, skills, cultures, peoples and nations. In these places, perspectives, approaches and interests should converge within a concept of universality that involves incessant, irreducible, rich dialectics between different, heterogeneous identities. Universality is not, therefore, taken to mean including the complete range of disciplines and professions. In such places, autonomy would be the affirmation of the creative nature of knowledge, of its reflective capacity to investigate and its power to innovate. This would create responsible, free-thinking environments that engender new ethical and political horizons to confront any new and old powers that try to impose their own reality. Here corporate awareness would be understood to mean that different social strata have joint responsibility and participate in a shared task from different positions and using different competences. Here, scientific activity would not be determined exclusively by how (methods) but also by why (objectives).

CONCLUSION: SOUTH AMERICA IS NOT ONLY LATIN

Indigenous peoples play a very important role in the region, due to their political prominence, their cultural importance and the new paradigms that they propose for relations between people and people, people and nature, and people and the environment in general. Their influx into the political, social, cultural and economic life of the region has helped people to realize that Latin America is not all that exists in the centre and south of the continent. There is also Indo-America, Afro-America and Caribbean America.

The situation emerging from the demands of the indigenous peoples is providing HEIs and national higher education systems with the challenging opportunity to bring together quality, relevance, coverage and effectiveness in university praxis. The indigenous peoples that have started out on the adventure of setting up higher education institutions have an opportunity to go beyond their own ethnic, educational, cultural and epistemological frontiers, using their own knowledge and methods to make a break with the past and undertake significant, wide-ranging innovation. Perhaps, the dialogue between the distinct ways of thinking of science and the ancestral knowledge of indigenous peoples will provide a wonderful opportunity to construct and devise solutions to the dramatic question posed by T.S. Eliot: Where is the wisdom we have lost in knowledge? Where is the knowledge we have lost in information? (Borrero, 2002).

REFERENCES AND BIBLIOGRAPHY

Agenda Mujer (1998) Grupo Vida-Mujer, Cali, Colombia.

Colombian Association of Universities (ASCUN) (2004) *Memorias Foro internacional sobre autonomía universitaria*. Bogotá, Colombia: ASCUN.

Borrero, Alfonso (2002) *Simposio permanente sobre la universidad*. Bogotá, Colombia: FES-ASCUN-ICFES.

Burton, R. Clark (1998) *Creating Entrepreneurial Universities*. London: Pergamon Press.

Castro Gómez, Santiago (2002) Ciencias sociales, violencia epistémica y el problema de la 'invención del otro'. In: *Colonialidad del saber: Eurocentrismo y Ciencias Sociales. Perspectivas Latinoamericanas*. Caracas, Venezuela: IESALC/UNESCO, Ediciones Faces/UCV, p. 149.

Didriksson, Axel (2002) *Universidad y pertinencia: El debate en la transición*. Lecture delivered at the University of San Buenaventura, Cali, Colombia. p. 10.

Dussel, Enrique (1999) *Taller sobre historia Indo-Americana*. Toribio, Colombia: Nasa Project.

Ferranti, D., Perry, G., Ferreira, F. and Walton, M. (2003) *Desigualdad en América Latina y el Caribe ¿ruptura con la historia?*, Mexico City: World Bank. URL <http://wbln0018.worldbank.org/lac/lacinfoclient.nsf/1daa46103229123885256831005ce0eb/718c516e8747517985256dc70076eeb5/$FILE/Inequality%20in%20LAC_presentation%20_spa.pdf>

Gorostiaga, Xabier S.J. (2000) En busca del eslabón perdido entre educación y desarrollo: Desafíos y retos para la universidad en América Latina y el Caribe. In: *La Educación en el horizonte del siglo XXI* (Coordinated by Carlos Tünnermann B. and Francisco López Segrera), Colección Respuestas no. 12, Caracas, Venezuela: IESALC/UNESCO

Hall, Gillette and Patrinos, Harry (2005) Pueblos indígenas, pobreza y desarrollo humano en América Latina: 1994–2004. Washington, DC: World Bank.

Hallak, J. (1999) *Globalization, Human rights and Education*. Paris: IIEP Contributions, no. 33.

López Segrera, F., Grosso, J.L. and Muñoz, M.R. (2002) *Educación permanente, calidad, evaluación y pertinencia*. Cali, Colombia: UNESCO/University of San Buenaventura. Colección Sapientia no. 8.

López Segrera, F., Grosso, J.L. and Muñoz, M.R. (2004) *América Latina y el Caribe en el siglo XX. Perspectiva y prospectiva de la globalización*. Mexico: Autonomous University of Zacatecas.

López Segrera, F., Grosso, J.L. and Muñoz, M.R. (2002) *Educación permanente, calidad, evaluación y perti-*

nencia. Cali, Colombia: University of San Buenaventura.

López Segrera, F., Maldonado, Alma and Muñoz, M. R. (2002) *Educación superior latinoamericana y organismos internacionales. Un análisis crítico.* Cali, Colombia: University of San Buenaventura.

Max Neef, Manfred (2002) *Desarrollo sin sentido.* Cali, Colombia: Diseñadores del futuro.

Mollis, Marcela (2003) *Las universidades en América Latina: ¿reformadas o alteradas? La cosmética del poder financiero.* Buenos Aires, Argentina: CLACSO.

Salmi, Jamil (2001) *La educación superior en un punto decisivo.* Bogotá, Colombia: University of the Andes.

Thulstrup, Eric W., Muñoz, M.R. and J.-J. Decoster (2006) *Building Research Capacity in Bolivian Universities.* Stockholm: Sida-SAREC.

UNESCO (2006) *Report on higher education in Latin America and the Caribbean 2000–2005. The metamorphosis of higher education.* Caracas, Venezuela.

UNESCO (1999) *III Encuentro de estudios prospectivos. Los escenarios de América Latina y del Caribe en el horizonte de 2020.* Río de Janeiro, Brazil: Ediciones IESALC/UNESCO.

UNESCO-World Bank (2000) *Higher Education in Developing Countries. Peril and Promise.* Santiago de Chile, Chile: Corporation for University Promotion.

UNESCO – Caracas (1997) *La educación superior en el siglo XXI. Visión de América Latina y el Caribe.* Colección Respuestas. Caracas, Venezuela: Ediciones CRESALC/UNESCO.

UNESCO – Caracas (1998) *Informe 1996–1997.* Caracas, Venezuela: Ediciones CRESALC/UNESCO.

World Bank (2003) *Constructing Knowledge Societies: New Challenges for Tertiary Education.* Washington, DC: World Bank.

NOTES

1   Studies and analyses of higher education and indigenous peoples have been carried out by UNESCO's International Institute for Higher Education in Latin America and the Caribbean (IESALC/UNESCO), the Inter-American Development Bank (IDB) and the *Fondo Indígena* (Fund for the Development of Indigenous Peoples in Latin America and the Caribbean).

2   There are two defects in the figures and studies on the poverty of indigenous peoples. First, there is limited access to data, as most information systems in these countries do not take into account the indigenous variable. Second, conventional indicators do not reflect indigenous perceptions of poverty.

3   According to indigenous peoples, the first globalization that affected them began in 1492.

4   Escué, Alcibíades (2005) Interview for the IESALC /UNESCO comparative study on higher education and indigenous peoples. Popayán, Colombia.

5   They participated in changing the constitutions of several countries. Legal, ethnic, cultural and linguistic pluralism has been included in these constitutions; the identity, autonomy and ancestral knowledge of indigenous peoples have been recognized, and their territories have been acknowledged. Supranational policies have played a key role in this process of constitutional recognition. Such policies include the International Labour Organization (ILO) Convention No. 169 Concerning Indigenous and Tribal Peoples in Independent Countries, which was ratified by 13 countries in the region. In addition, important new legislative instruments have been created. Examples are the United Nations Declaration on the Rights of Indigenous Peoples and the American Declaration on the Rights of Indigenous Peoples by the Organization of American States (OAS).

6   Quality factors and indicators are currently being discussed from the perspective of relevance.

GOOD PRACTICE I.2

Disciplinary integration to promote models of sustainability (Kingston University, United Kingdom)

GUNI Observatory[1]

CONTEXT

One of the functions of universities is to produce citizens who are highly professional and can take on social responsibilities that contribute to discussion, knowledge and solutions to current international challenges. These many challenges include the democratization of public institutions; the exhaustion of fossil fuels; and hunger and famines. Such responsibility and intervention on a worldwide scale is known as 'global citizenship'. It differs from the traditional concept of citizenship, which is linked to a nation (and, indeed, to a nation-state).

Universities should contribute to strengthening global citizenship. Kingston University (KU) aims to contribute to active citizenship from the following perspectives:

● Civic commitment.
● Making a real contribution to sustainable development that helps to under-

stand and respond to human development and local community needs.

- Increasing the employability of students.
- Contributing to the mutual recognition of differences. This is linked to university knowledge production and transfer and to cultural diversity.
- Promoting social inclusion and community regeneration by encouraging participation in higher education.

In this general framework, the KU aims to favour sustainable development, defined as a fundamental part of the cross-disciplinary competences that all students should currently acquire as part of their education.

Therefore, the KU has established a pilot project to include sustainability in syllabuses across all disciplines. The project is supported by the Higher Education Funding Council for England (HEFCE), which provides funding to promote curricular greening in higher education institutions.

DESCRIPTION

The Steering Group for Sustainability (SGS) was formed in 2002. It is a university group that helps to steer sustainability work within the institution. The group is representative of the University's diversity and includes members from six faculties, the university service sector and Kingston Student Union. Its activities focus on the environmental management of the campus and on the process of introducing sustainability criteria into teaching and research.

In 2003, a programme for introducing sustainability into the curriculum began. The aim was to reform the syllabuses in 2005, to coincide with the Decade of Education for Sustainable Development, promoted by UNESCO.

In 2005, the project obtained HEFCE funding, after taking part in a call for applications. The KU will receive an initial €204,394 followed by €510,986 annually for 5 years. Once the funding had been granted, the Centre for Sustainable Communities Achieved through Integ-

rated Professional Education (C-SCAIPE) was set up as a centre of excellence for teaching and learning. This centre is one of 74 centres of excellence for teaching and learning in UK universities. However, it is the only one that focuses on promoting sustainable development. Thus, it is a benchmark in sustainability for higher education institutions.

In 2007, the first stage of the programme was concluded, once preliminary studies had been undertaken and curricular reform had been approved. Reforms began in the 2006–2007 academic year.

For this pilot project, the KU considered that architecture and other related disciplines were the most suitable knowledge areas for introducing the concept of sustainability from a cross-disciplinary perspective. Fifty per cent of the UK's carbon dioxide emissions are produced by the construction industry, which thus has an important role to play in promoting sustainability. The current educational model for 'built-environment' professions encourages students to adopt a short-term mentality that focuses on the prospect of immediate financial rewards. However, professionals should develop some central concepts in order to obtain comprehensive knowledge about how human needs can be balanced with an environmental and social perspective.

OBJECTIVES

C-SCAIPE is a university body that aims to develop innovative teaching processes and links between active professionals and academics, using the resources of the university and other institutions.

It has the following objectives:

- Providing built-environment graduates with values and abilities that enable them to contribute to constructing a more sustainable society
- Developing initiatives for curricular integration and curricular greening in other university courses
- Increasing knowledge of the complex-

ity of the concept of sustainability in the university environment in general
- Working with other universities to implement similar processes, thus helping the KU to adopt a leading role in this field.

PROCESS

The main activities planned are to:

- Develop and design the curriculum
- Devise a teaching methodology
- Make education compatible with research
- Link the curriculum with professional practices and introduce the concept of sustainability.

C-SCAIPE operates in line with university policy at all times. It receives institutional support and encourages processes of change within the institution when required.

Although the plan is still in its initial stage, some activities have already been carried out, such as:

- The systematization of research into the embedding of sustainability into the curriculum.
- An audit of sustainability in the curriculum has been carried out. Sixty members of the University were involved in this audit, that is, 8% of permanent staff. These members represent six faculties and 49 disciplines (in particular, professionals and academics responsible for designing and implementing degree course curricula were interviewed).
- Curricular reform based on the audit results. This reform has already been approved and will be partially implemented in the 2006–2007 academic year.
- A new support system for promoting the inclusion of students. This system encourages student participation in redesigning the curriculum.

The results of the audit show that there is a high existing level of knowledge of and concern about sustainability in the Faculty of Art, Design and Architecture. On the basis of these results and with the input of lecturers from this centre, a new syllabus was drawn up, which aims to introduce the concept of sustainability into the curriculum across disciplines. This plan is promoted by the faculty with the support of C-SCAIPE.

RESULTS

An assessment was undertaken in 2006, twelve months after the plan had been implemented.

One of the main requirements for ensuring the success of the initiative is to attain self-funding in five years, when the HEFCE funding terminates.

To date, the main outcome of the project has been the drafting of a report on the results of the KU sustainability audit.

This report includes some very interesting data that could be used to help incorporate the sustainability curriculum into syllabuses. For example, 48% of the lecturers interviewed considered that it was necessary to incorporate into the syllabus at least one module that has sustainability as a core topic.

RECOMMENDATIONS

Practical initiatives that show the university's responsibility to education for sustainability should be developed. These could include the following:

- Adopting a system of university management or a system of environmental management that promotes a process of change in the institutional climate that, in turn, favours curricular change.
- Establishing processes for reflecting on and studying sustainability among teaching staff, students and other groups from the university community.

- Establishing networks and discussions with members to contextualize sustainable education across different degree programmes.

The specific steps that should be taken to set up a similar programme are as follows:

1. Sustainable education should be introduced as a key aspect of university syllabuses. The concept should be introduced into quality assurance, course review and lecturer assessment processes.
2. Institutional planning should be brought in line with sustainable education.
3. Education for sustainability should be extended into disciplinary and interdisciplinary areas.
4. A group coordinator should be established for embedding sustainability into all university activities.

NOTE

1   Text written by the Universities and Social Commitment Observatory with information provided by Sarah Sayce. Kingston University.

Andrei Marga
Translated by Rareş Moldovan, Roxana Gâz.

SPECIAL CONTRIBUTION I.13
Multiculturalism, interculturality and leadership[1]

In the context of globalization, the university is measured not merely in relation to its own mission, or to other universities in the country or the region; a university is inevitably measured in relation to the most competitive universities worldwide. This means that universities are required to produce and present 'cutting edge' scientific research on a par with that set by the top institutions; turn out graduates of the standard required by corporations for top-ranking positions; offer consultancy in the crucial areas of technology, economy, administration, health, the environment and policy; and produce significant interpretations and visions in the sphere of culture.

How should universities respond to this context of globalization? Universities act appropriately if they adopt self-programming, on a medium- and long-term basis, to mere adaptation to contexts; if they use their autonomy and academic freedom as an instrument for self-renewal and innovation, rather than as a basis for exempting themselves from outside appraisals; if they plead for the rationalization of an outmoded system, rather than moulding themselves to it; if they choose their profiles clearly (whether that profile be in research, teaching, services and so on), rather than mixing all these functions confusingly together; if they combine the open, accessible character of admissions with the selective and demanding character of graduation; if they balance, in their study programmes and curricula, the transmission of knowledge with discovery, information with training, data with application, and sciences with visions; if they adopt open and participative governance, and outcome-focused management; if they ensure an open, questioning and critical climate, capable of motivating both educators and students. 'The cultural turn' (see Marga, 2004, *Die Kulturelle Wende*) is occurring at the same time as the greatest market enlargement, *globalization*. Globalization confronts institutions and leaders with new situations, which are characterized by the meeting of multiple cultures, and by the need for *intercultural understanding*. As a consequence, among other factors, globalization obliges us to clarify multiculturalism, interculturality, and leadership, as well as the relationship between these concepts. I will examine these concepts in the following sections.

MULTICULTURALISM

Multiculturalism is the term frequently applied to what we are experiencing today. This phenomenon is not always precisely understood. A situation is considered multicultural 'when it results from a certain cultural diversity, from the pluralism characterizing any industrial society' (Riva, 2005). Diversity refers to lifestyles, technological acquisitions, concepts, value representations, behaviours and institutions, explanations, interpretations, value rankings and traditions.

To understand multiculturalism – and implicitly the fact that each of us comes into contact with diverse cultures – I propose to distinguish between three sources and three of its forms respectively. The first is *historical multiculturalism*, that is, the situation in which, in the same territory and as a consequence of history, cultures from different ethnic or religious communities co-exist. The second is *multiculturalism of migration*, which occurs when, in the same territory and as a consequence of immigration, different cultures with different origins meet. The third is *multiculturalism of restructurings* in which, in the area covered by an institution or a company, the different cultures related to different professions, generations, genders and so on, meet. Each of these three forms of multiculturalism is encountered in the context of globalization.

Because multiculturalism is increasingly an everyday experience for people, we cannot satisfy the immanent need for intercultural orientation without clarifying what *culture* means. This is not a simple task, as there are various possible definitions of the concept and multiple ramifications of culture in people's lives. Culture can be understood to mean the 'totality of that group's thoughts, experiences, and patterns of behaviour and its

concepts, values and assumptions about life that guide behaviour and how those evolve with contact with other cultures' (Jandt, 2007). I consider that a culture consists of values, practices, interpretations and, at the same time, awareness of one's identity.

INTERCULTURALITY

The reactions of people when meeting individuals from different cultures are highly varied; ranging from *culture shock* to *cultural integration* and *cultural conformity*. Each of these reactions brings into discussion 'cultural understanding'. If by *understanding* – as distinct from *description* or *explanation* – we mean the operation of acquiring the meaning or the sense of a phenomenon together with data about its genesis, then cultural understanding means more than describing or knowing a culture: it means the ability to place ourselves, even if only hypothetically, in the role of somebody who has embraced that culture (Dallmayr and McCarthy, 1997). Thus, current research into 'understanding culture' distinguishes between 'learning about a culture' and 'understanding a culture' (Varner et al., 2005).

Several steps are involved in the passage from 'contact' with another culture or between cultures, to 'understanding' it and then to effective 'intercultural understanding'. These steps lead one from the 'coexistence of cultures' to 'interculturality', which is based on communication. If by 'communication' one understands not merely a system of fast and unaltered transmission of information, but an operation whose purpose is to understand the other; if the other is considered not an object to manipulate, but a participant in the interaction; if participants see each other as partners in finding solutions to problems; if partners are ready to address and discuss the rules of their interaction (Marga, 1991) then we realize how complex intercultural communication and interculturality really are. Intercultural communication is not limited to the transmission of information from one culture to another, or to

simply living together in an informational universe (Ting-Toomey, 1999). It means, first and foremost, a motivating interaction in order to find solutions to common problems (Samovar and Poster, 2004). Communication is increasingly characterized as a 'complex process' with 'cultural dimensions' (Jandt, 2007).

Many aspects of intercultural communication have been discussed. In this paper I will mention only two: the identity of persons and groups; and religion and philosophy in intercultural communication.

Culture always brings *identity* into discussion, since:

> members of a culture share similar thoughts and experiences. One's culture is part of one's identity, and is taught to one's children. Culture also includes all the things that guide a group of people through life, such as myths, language and gestures, ways of communicating, economic systems, what kind of things they eat, and how they dress. People identify with being a member of a group. (Martin et al., 2002)

The long debate on personal and group identity can be summarized into three conclusions: identity is multiple (professional, ethnic, religious, national and so on), thus differentiated identities have to be taken into consideration any time the identity of a group or of an individual is discussed; identity is generated, not born; and globalization strengthens the process of constituting identity.

Many people are ready to enter intercultural communication as long as it is about technology, traditions for working the land, institutions, family life, food, literature and so on. However, they become more reticent when religion and philosophy are brought into discussion. These are considered to be explosive issues. Religion is considered too sensitive a subject (embodying as it does the most profound and private beliefs of people) to be accessible to intercultural communication. In such situations, the solution, in my view, is to promote a non-simplified concept of a religion, to continue the communication, and, from the outset, prevent people from feeling 'that this aspect of their cultural identity might be under interrogation' (Martin et al., 2002).

LEADERSHIP

In recent years, systematic knowledge about the role of a leader and successful leadership has been developed. Many assumptions of traditional political philosophy are being reconsidered. It is thus considered that leadership is a process by which a person helps others to accomplish objectives and directs an organization in a way that makes it more efficient and coherent, while leaders are people who carry out this process by applying procedures, personal decisions, values, knowledge and skills (Yukl, 1994).

But the meaning of 'leader' is still rather confusing. Our current language – especially when it is not connected to the development of specialized research – tends to mix bosses, managers and leaders as if they were the same thing. I propose that we should clearly distinguish between these three notions.

In current research on organizations, a 'leader' is considered to be different from a 'boss'. The boss is at the top of an organization, and the actions of his/her staff depend on his/her decisions and his/her power in the position. The leader also has authority, but authority granted by the ability to understand the organization within a context, to orient it according to new directions, and to make these convincing for everyone else. The manager, in his/her turn, is something else. Compared to the boss, the manager has the advantage of having enough knowledge on the functioning of the organization and on competences. Compared to the leader, the manager works in a given frame of strategic options. Only the leader can take the responsibility for changing major options.

Is there a need for leaders in organizations, companies or corporations? There is certainly no shortage of bosses. The fight to become a boss is a given, as soon as there is an opportunity. Managers are fewer, because the training of a real man-ager involves strenuous effort to learn and acquire the necessary abilities. With leaders, an organization is not only efficient, but also long-lasting; not just existent, but also competitive; not only conspicuous, but also relevant. Especially in the context of globalization, in which, as Robert Reich (1992) argued, success on the markets depends not on the 'high volume' of the product, but on its 'high value'. Therefore, the intelligence incorporated into the product and in its production requires qualified managers and valuable leaders (who lead not only physically, but are also effectively 'leaders in ideas, in actions').

The immediate question concerns how to *select leaders*. Bosses are the result of accessing a position (through election, appointment and so on), but neither a manager nor a leader is created because they have leading positions. Actually, many bosses are lousy managers, and will never become leaders. However, the passage from boss to manager or leader is not made through the simple effort of the person in question ('positions do not create leaders').

So how are leaders produced? Recent research indicates that three interconnected considerations are involved. The first refers to the fact that a leader is not self-proclaimed, but he/she is acknowledged. In addition, a leader is not simply a figurehead, but has a position that involves hard work. Cartwright and Zander's classic *Group Dynamics: Research and Theory* (1968) considered leadership as consisting of actions of:

> setting group goals, moving the group toward its goal, improving the quality of interactions among the members, building cohesiveness of the group, and making resources available to the group.

The second consideration is that a leader is made, not born. Miraculous endowments for leadership, a type of mysterious predestination, exist only for the naive. A leader is the product of a learning process in at least three dimensions: knowledge that can be used from the technical point of view, interaction abilities, and self-reflexivity. The third consideration is that we move in an environment of profound changes regarding the image of a leader. A leader 'is made' through 'continuous work and study', and he/she does not rely on success already obtained ('talent needs to be nurtured'). Both the traditional theory of the leader (chieftain, prince and so on), as a result of special traits(the trait theory), and the modern theory of the leader, as a product of exceptional circumstances (the great events theory), have lost their attractiveness when compared to the conception of a leader resulting from continuous learning (the transformational theory).

It must be observed that leadership is inseparable from *values*. Any decision or action of a leader has inevitable ethical consequences so that – in accordance with the Harvard Business School mission statement – the teaching of ethics has to be explicit, not implicit, and the community values of mutual respect, honesty and integrity, and personal accountability must support the learning environment. Recently, one of the most competent ethicists, Ottfried Höffe, pointed out that universities have to administer ethical values in five dimensions: capacity to assume self-responsibility; promotion of justice and tolerance; cultivation of reason, self-confidence and capacity for criticism; promotion of democracy; respect for universal human rights. Two implications are fundamental: universities can widely promote ethical values and their practice remains decisive; and their lecturers can preach ethics, but unless they practise it, ethical education remains purely formal (Marga, 2006).

GLOBAL AND INTERCULTURAL LEADERSHIP

The need for effective leaders in the institutions operating in our complex environment has been felt for several decades. Today, this problem should be solved by taking into account the context of globalization and that of its inherent multiculturalism. In some universities today, 'global leadership' and 'intercultural leadership' form part of the educational agenda. These topics should be included in university programmes. I would like to make four points on these two programmes, from the point of view of university education:

- First, the university as an institution needs to adapt to the situation of globalization and multiculturalism, taking into consideration the fact that new generations of graduates will be operating inside this situation, and that universities themselves are successful if they approach their own performance globally.

- Second, organizations should be run by competitive leaders. The metaphor of the organization as a 'machine' that can be projected, measured and directed – a modern metaphor that has been legitimated by cybernetics – is no longer appropriate. It needs to be replaced by the metaphor of *the organism*, which is more capable of acknowledging the fact that efficient organizations are now networks, communities, knowledge and learning systems. Leadership includes – as the *Blackwell Encyclopaedia of Management* (2007) shows – questions such as: What needs to be done? What can and should I do to make a difference? Are the performance and results good? What can and should I do to stimulate a diversity of approaches? How can I strengthen the role and the responsibility of followers? Am I the most proficient in my position? It is nowadays true that:

> change and global leadership are inextricably linked. The key challenges which face global leaders are linked to the changes that are occurring as organizations move from being bureaucratic machines to knowledge-based networks. Specifically, leaders must guide their organizations to produce results today, even as they push for transformation which will positively impact the future (Siehl, 2007).

- Third, *global leadership* today deals individually with cultural, ethnic and political representations that are larger than those present generations have been accustomed to. In addition, training for intercultural leadership has become part of university curricula. It is no longer sufficient to accept cultural differences, it is necessary to know and understand them. Thus, if we accept that universities train people in 'competences' – which means the knowledge, general and technical skills required for superior performance – then the formation of global competences and, at the same time, intercultural competences should become part of university programmes.

- Fourth, today we can access factual research on establishing *intercultural leadership competences*. Such research suggests what needs to be done in the university. According to this research, we should embrace the distinction between 'intrapersonal competences' (self-awareness, flexibility, curiosity, patience, imagination and so on), 'interpersonal competences' ('perspective taking', 'being non-judgemental') and 'intercultural competences' ('effective communication', 'appreciation of difference', 'local–global perspective', 'an understanding of how leadership is conceptualized in other cultures') (Sheridan, 2005). Anyone who acquires 'intercultural leadership competences' is able to perform specific tasks: to clarify his/her own notion of culture, which has to be well formed; to apply it; to understand his/her cultural background; to analyse and evaluate intercultural situations; to negotiate in these situations, to take decisions in a multicultural environment; to motivate participants in these situations; to form intercultural teams; and to exert intercultural leadership.

THE WISDOM SOCIETY

Recently, Paolo Blasi, a remarkable physicist reminded us that, due to several factors (competition in research, the pressure from society to transfer scientific knowledge, the search for funds, and the unstable work situation), new generations are engaging in more factual research, and looking for short-term solutions to problems without committing themselves to far-reaching projects. I would add that this situation is not only found in the field of scientific research, but is also connected to a more comprehensive orientation of culture towards immediate facts. At the same time, the predisposition to question what lies at the origin of the fact, of the immediate situation and of the custom is increasingly weak. This implies that there is less appetite for theory, system and project. In the 1980s, Habermas identified, as one of the consequences of this orientation, the apparent 'exhaustion of the utopian energies (*Erschöpfung der utopischer Energien*)' (Habermas, 1985). The dominant direction in today's culture is that of exploiting what is given, rather than asking what is possible. Moreover, a 'negative futurism' is developing – let's leave things the way they are, because they may become worse.

After analysing the application of the Bologna Declaration (1999), Blasi drew the conclusion that:

> the challenge of the European society today is to go beyond 'the knowledge society', and to evolve into what could be called a 'wisdom society'. Knowledge is conscious use of information; 'wisdom' means choosing one's behaviour on the basis of knowledge and shared values, in order to enhance the well-being of all, and the awareness that personal actions have social consequences. (Blasi, 2006)

Indeed, this is an important and pressing problem. Let us aspire to wisdom that is capable of enlightening people about their own responsibility. I believe that the author is too optimistic when he speaks about the quest for truth, the unity of knowledge, openness to the unknown and to other cultures, as simply 'restoration'. Our societies are now too complex for this to be the case. Still, he is right when he considers that today's universities are responsible for setting a larger and greater goal than producing and transmitting knowledge, in the projection of a 'developed and peaceful world'. Quite obviously, besides communication, teamwork, critical thinking and innovation, universities have to train the student to examine, test and – why not – articulate visions.

BIBLIOGRAPHY

Blasi, Paolo (2006) The European University – towards a wisdom-based society. In: *Higher Education in Europe*, **31**(4) December, p. 407.

Cartwright, D. and Zander, A. (1968) (eds) *Group Dynamics: Research and Theory* (3rd edn). New York: Harper & Row.

Dallmayr, Fred R. and McCarthy, Thomas A. (1977) (eds) *Understanding and Social Inquiry*. Notre Dame, IN: University of Notre Dame Press, p. 10.

Habermas, Jürgen, (1988) Die Krise des Wohlfahrtsstaates und die Erschöpfung utopischer Energien. In: Habermas, Jürgen (ed.) *Die neue Unübersichtlichkeit*. Frankfurt am Main: Suhrkamp Verlag.

Jandt, Fred E. (2007) *An Introduction to Intercultural Communication. Identities in a Global Community*. Thousand Oaks, CA: Sage Publications, p. 7.

Marga, Andrei (2004) *Die kulturelle Wende. Philosophische Konsequenzen der Transformation*. Cluj, Romania: Cluj University Press, pp. 195–226.

Marga, Andrei (1991) *Rationalitate, comunicare, argumentare*. Cluj, Romania: Dacia, pp. 251–75.

Marga, Andrei (2004) University reform in Europe: Some ethical considerations. In: *Higher Education in Europe*, **29**(4): 475–80. For a more comprehensive approach see also Andrei Marga (2006) *The Cultural Legitimacy of the European University*. In: *Higher Education in Europe*, **31**(4): 425–38.

Martin, Judith N., Nakayama, Thomas K. and Flores, Lisa A. (2002) *Readings in Intercultural Communication: Experiences and Contexts*. Boston, MA: McGraw Hill, pp. 21–31.

Reich, Robert B. (1992) *The Work of Nations: Preparing Ourselves for 21st Century Capitalism*. New York: Vintage Books, p. 82.

Riva, Kastoryano (2005) (ed.) *Quelle identité pour l'Europe? Le multiculturalisme á l'épreuve*. Paris: Presse de la Fondation Nationales des Sciences Politiques, p. 21.

Samovar, Larry A. R. and Poster, Richard E. (2004) *Communication Between Cultures*. Belmont, CA: Wadsworth, p. 15.

Sheridan, Eileen (2005) *International Leadership Competencies for U.S. Leaders in the Era of Globalization*. Dissertation. University of Phoenix.

Siehl, Caren (2007) Global leadership. In: Cooper, Cary L. (ed.) *The Blackwell Encyclopaedia of Management*, Malden, MA: Blackwell Publishing.

Ting-Toomey, Steela (1999) *Communicating Across Cultures*. New York: The Guilford Press.

Varner, Iris and Beamer, Linda (2005) *International Communication in the Global Workplace*. Boston, MA: McGraw-Hill/Irwin, pp. 2–12.

Yukl, G. (1994) *Leadership in Organizations* (3rd edn). Englewood Cliffs, NJ: Prentice-Hall.

NOTE

1   Based on the speech delivered at the conference Pathways Towards a Shared Future: Changing Roles of Higher Education in a Globalized World, UNU/UNESCO International Conference, Tokyo, 29–30 August 2007.

Abstract

Mankind is on the brink of a tragic era, in which the anarchic forces of the market and the incessant pressures upon natural resources on the verge of exhaustion will push sovereign states to increasingly dangerous rivalries. What will the role of research in higher education be, in response to the challenge of an active future contribution to human and social development? A good balance must be reached in the basic functions of research in order to avoid governance risks. While focusing only on the transformative function of research may pose dangers to the human dimension and development, unilateral concentration on responsible development aspects may generate reactive approaches and delay economic benefits. Disregarding the inclusiveness function may lead to slower development and even isolationism, and focusing on short-term issues is not good for long-term goals and future generations. We must reinforce research networks between 'Southern' and 'Northern', rich and poor, and developed and developing countries and institutions in order to bridge the gap between knowledge consumers and producers. This paper reviews aspects such as development, globalization and the inequality of nations; constraints and choices of the orthodox views of research; rethinking research and higher education to contribute to a better future; and knowledge integration for effective action.

INTRODUCTION

This is a time of renewed enthusiasm for higher education and research as the way forward to world development, with the establishment of millennium centres and science academies in Africa and other such initiatives in developing regions. Human and social development through higher education and research capabilities are appropriate themes in a report dedicated to the future role of higher education in an era of globalization. In this paper, however, I do not focus on the repeated promise that science, research and higher education are the surest routes to development. Instead, I argue that this can no longer be taken for granted and

concentrate on how international efforts in science and technology and higher education have missed the mark concerning unsolved issues and challenges in this domain, and on how research and higher education have grown in developing regions. I set out these ideas in this Introduction. In subsequent sections, I discuss and illustrate them and propose a rethinking of inherited perceptions with the aim of making science and technology relate more effectively and responsibly to society.

First, the intellectual rationale for science and research capacities being exclusively subordinated to the realization of practical ends as demanded by nation-states, and the universalistic approach that dismisses possible effects of national or other social and cultural dimensions upon the evolution of science, are both problematic, leading ultimately to undesirable if not tragic results. To a certain extent, this is a consequence of the prevailing ideology of scientists who, throughout the modern period, have resisted playing a political role in society. They refuse to see that, in practice, values other than the search for knowledge prevail. This corresponds to the form of education and professional training that excludes any link between the scientific endeavour and social concerns. This refusal by the scientific community to assume social responsibility can no longer be sustained because it has led to an out-of-control, conformist science without a conscience. Rethinking is overdue, given the current reality of the world and of certain countries in particular, if higher education and research are to bring about collective well-being and equity in society, (thereby improving the living conditions of most people, rather than just a small, better-off segment of the population), and salvage the Earth's environment.

Second, scientists have difficulty communicating across plural perspectives, conditioned as they are by a specialized and rather dogmatic scientific training. They generally feel uneasy about accepting and managing uncertainty, social variables and value commitments, and take comfort in reducing knowledge assessment to peer review of narrow technical issues. Basic science, however, is today recognized as being only a part of a much richer whole, where criteria and tasks of quality assurance explicitly involve additional values and interests (Funtowicz and Ravetz, 1992). New forms of governance are emerging at the crossroads between science and society as useful and relevant experiences in a changing world that affect both scientists and the beneficiaries of science. In the common space where scientists and different audiences begin to meet, we can hope to find out what elements experts provide to formulate and implement policy decisions and how these elements are actually used; only this common space can help the development of socially robust knowledge.

Third, we must rethink researchers' education. Arguments for reforms aimed at creating socially responsible scientists have grown in recent years, based on the need to democratize expert knowledge and provide pluralistic expert advice to democratic institutions and to the citizenry more broadly, thereby increasing the capacity to discuss and eventually meet citizens' expectations. Since knowledge is a major asset that allows involvement in framing issues for policy attention and in designing options, the 'whats' and 'hows' of knowledge and expertise become paramount. We know by now that the growth of a higher educated stratum in society does not necessarily ensure that individual countries in today's globalized world economy will reduce social and economic inequality; higher education may be necessary, but it certainly cannot bring about a more equitable and fair society on its own.

Fourth, in weaker countries with inadequate capacities and the wrong basic infrastructure – that is, with ineffective and unstable political and social institutions – higher education, science and technology have not reduced social and economic disparities but rather increased social and economic differentials between the knowledgeable and the ignorant. Something similar may occur with the growth of domestic research capacity. Higher education and research capacities have repeatedly been shown to work better for the rich. In the developing world, particular individuals with more assets (better education, more contacts and so on) may, and in effect do, succeed in science and technology research, but their success too often leaves their society untouched or increases inequality. It has been argued that doctoral students, under today's training conditions, may become skilled specialists in finding solutions rather than thinking about the problems of society and going beyond the mere technical terms of one specialty or another (Salomon, 2006). Research groups, institutions and even countries in the developing world are often presented as success stories not because they signal lasting positive structural change, but because donors, governments and experts need success stories.

All this, however, does not imply that poor countries would have been better off without higher education, science and technology – only that research capacity per se, without social guidance or oversight and isolated from other essential components of social and moral responsibility, cannot fulfil its potential for improving people's lives.

DEVELOPMENT, GLOBALIZATION AND THE INEQUALITY OF NATIONS

The idea of development, with its renewed approaches to economic and social growth, took root in the newly born United Nations of the 1940s and 50s. This continued during the 1960s and 70s, although by then two opposing trends in development thinking had become recognizable. One consisted of widening the scope of the development strategies pursued by explicitly including social considerations such as education, health, nutrition, employment, income distribution, basic needs, poverty reduction, the environment and so on (Seers, 1972; Sábato, 1975; Herrera, 1971; Stewart, 1985; Ukoli, 1985; Hountondji, 2006). The other was represented by a return to neoclassical thinking (largely through the influence of Friedman, 1962, and Solow, 1957).

The Humboldtian principles of the university and academic science, further elaborated by the sociological contributions of Weberians and Mertonians until well into the 20th century, had constituted a coherent normative system, which was challenged by attempts to deal with the massification of education in the post-Second World War period. Like development and growth approaches, mass education became an object of analysis in the 1970s, inspiring the notion of the knowledge economy, the human capital school of economic growth, the concept of manpower planning and, somewhat later, an agenda of academic capitalism and managerialism. In particular, Bell (1973) made the strong point, drawn from the growth theory of economics of the 1950s and 60s, that the human capital factor played an increasingly important role in explaining the sum total of economic growth (Sörlin and Vessuri, 2007). Post-industrial society, as described and envisaged by Bell, seemed to be the material underpinning for the mass growth of education in new generations.

In the late 1970s, there was a strong move towards open-market policies that emphasized privatization and liberalization, with greater weight given to growth than to income distribution and social objectives. This was soon being followed in all countries of the Organization for Economic Co-operation and Development (OECD). It became the conventional wisdom of the West and later of practically the whole world, whether willingly or not.

Important exceptions were the East Asian countries that successfully took a different route to development, which differed significantly from the orthodox policy prescriptions then in fashion.

During the 1980s and 90s, a dominant view of growth based on 'globalization' and 'free markets' dismissed questions of ethnicity and culture and ignored the problems posed by nationalism, fundamentalism and terrorism. Science policy documents in many countries emphasized the economic benefits of science, along with strategic and security aspects. Public spending for higher education and research became a matter of debate, and most arguments turned on the issue of accountability and the need to reduce the size of the state. The connections between academic research and competitiveness in the first half of the 1990s, a growing literature on the 'new social contract' of science (Gibbons et al., 1994), and the continued expansion of undergraduate enrolment were part and parcel of a new understanding that wherever a large portion of the workforce had academic degrees, the rates of economic growth were persistently higher (OECD, 1996).

Within this climate of opinion, universities began to be perceived as prerequisites for the success of nations and, increasingly, of regions and cities. However, in order to deliver, they had to change their norms to become more flexible and readier to respond to social and economic demands. Knowledge increasingly came to be seen as a commodity, its practitioners became objects of trade, and higher education became a service industry included within the scope of the World Trade Organization (WTO).

Nevertheless, a different current of thought questioned this 'economicist' turn of knowledge. In the 1990s, the United Nations Development Programme (UNDP) launched the *Human Development Reports* series. These reports introduced the human development index, which tracks changes in people's quality of life. In the late 1990s, Sen, a close collaborator of the UNDP series, provided the broadest possible conception of development as freedom: a process of expanding the real freedoms that people enjoy for their economic well-being, social opportunities and political rights (Sen, 1999). Such freedoms were also perceived as being instrumental as the principal means of attaining development. Clearly, values are the leading dimension here. The question is whether society is good, fair and just, and if knowledge can improve it. The emphasis moved to attaining a higher level of public engagement in science, and widening participation in higher education among all social groups.

The growth of knowledge-handling institutions in the current process of globalization is unprecedented. Global enrolment of students has multiplied, as has the number of Ph.Ds, institutions, scientific journals, scientists and academic staff. The increase is visible in other areas as well. A scientific background today is valuable to stock analysts, science publishers and government policy experts. This shows that scientific training can be put to good use away from the laboratory bench and away from academia. However, this expansion has until recently taken place within a restricted portion of the developed world. Despite decades of efforts to implant science and knowledge in the developing world, figures show that research and development (R&D) funds, scientists, doctoral degrees, scientific publications, patents and high-quality institutions continue to be sharply concentrated within the OECD area.

By contrast, in weaker countries, efforts to put science and technology at the service of human development have yielded dismal results. Globalization as we know it today is fundamentally asymmetric. In its benefits and risks, it works less well for poor countries and for the poor institutions within developing countries.

Enrolments and institutions in some developing countries are experiencing exponential growth, although they usually start from a base so low as to be totally insufficient. This might change during this century. China, India and Brazil, to mention just the most notable examples in terms of numbers, are telling. Estimates of growth in these countries are enormous, although the stakes are also unprecedented.

Box I.6.1 Quantifying asymmetry

There are only 94.3 scientific researchers per million people in the least developed countries (LDCs), against 313 in the other developing countries (ODCs) and 3,728 in rich countries (high-income OECD). Enrolment in university-level institutions (that is, tertiary school enrolment as a share of the corresponding age group) is only 3.5% in the LDCs, against 23% in ODCs and 69% in rich countries. LDC governments are devoting only 0.3% of their gross domestic product (GDP) to research and development, against 0.8% in other developing countries and 2.4% in rich countries. Five LDCs – Haiti, Cape Verde, Samoa, Gambia and Somalia – have lost more than half of their university-educated professionals in recent years because they have moved to industrialized countries in search of better working and living conditions. Asian LDCs received more than twice from workers' remittances than from official development assistance (ODA) in 2005: $7 billion in the former case versus $3 billion in the latter. For all the LDCs, remittances amounted to some two thirds of the total ODA of $18 billion received in the same year.

Source: UNCTAD, 2007.

Today, the paradigm of 'modernity' and the Western model of development are subject to criticism from many quarters. Nevertheless, a coherent and persuasive alternative has yet to be found. It took time to realize that education is not just a consumption good that can be afforded at a certain level of development, but also an investment in human capital that is a prerequisite for attaining that level of development. Higher education and research have finally been accepted as crucial elements in the global knowledge economy, after decades of ill-fated theories and approaches by the World Bank and other institutions in the developed world that did not see them as the right priorities for developing nations. However, the treatment of higher education 'services' as merchandise, as promoted in the WTO's General Agreement on Trade in Services (GATS), does not seem the most adequate one for achieving the desired results. The lessons from the experience of science in developing countries have become embedded in both successes and failures, and are powerful reminders against non-transparent approaches that neglect the specificities of time and space. For the world to meet the challenges of the future, higher education and science must become more evenly distributed around the world and develop certain features that have largely been absent in the post-colonial and semi-colonial world.

ORTHODOX VIEW OF RESEARCH: CONSTRAINTS AND CHOICES IN THE DEVELOPED AND DEVELOPING WORLDS

One may extend to most regions in the world what Geuna (1999) describes as the governmental vision of the principal social goals for the university system in European nations. The first two goals – to reproduce the existing levels of knowledge and to improve the critical reasoning capabilities and specific skills of individuals, both as an input into their public and private work activity and into the development of a democratic, civilized, inclusive society – correspond to the traditional role of universities as institutions for the preservation and transmission through education of knowledge, culture and social values. The third social goal – to increase the knowledge base by pursuing knowledge for its own sake and for the creation of wealth – defines the action of universities in a broader sense. Scholarship and research should be pursued by universities, both for their inherent value and in order to produce a stock of useful knowledge that might be applied elsewhere for the benefit of society. This is not easily achievable in the developing world's universities, although there may be some good research groups – clearly a minority – that manage to work to solve local, regional or national problems and still be part of the international scientific community.

Unlike more mobile scientific communities in developed countries, where prestige is accumulated through the transit through various institutions, agencies and firms, successful individuals and groups in developing countries tend to spend their entire careers in a single institution, to which they show a very high degree of adherence and loyalty, despite often criticizing institutional dysfunction and inertia. Many successful research groups produce elaborate rhetoric about applied research for development but, like their less successful local colleagues, face difficulties in adapting and reconciling their discourse to the schemes of internal functioning, to national and institutional legislation, and to the explicit and tacit norms guiding careers in science. Countries besieged by corruption and inefficiency often exhibit rigid patterns of administrative control put in place at knowledge institutions as part of accountability processes, which interfere with the flexibility that scientific teams need to operate. Sources of support for applied research at the levels of investment required to push it forward significantly are also lacking. The absence or underdevelopment of local philanthropic structures is only partially remedied by the access for high-quality scientific groups to international funding (mainly from the United States and the European Union). As a result, the space for action and bargaining power is increasingly restricted and the possibility of attending to 'local needs' shrinks dramatically, since private actors clearly participate more actively in the developed countries that lead the international networks.

Geuna's fourth social goal attributes a new role to universities – one which is promoted by international actors in connection with notions of academic capitalism and managerialism. Higher education institutions come to serve specific training needs and more general research-support needs of the knowledge-based economy at the local, regional and national levels, and are seen as direct participants in the process of economic development. Numerous studies of innovation dynamics have underlined the importance of the institutional context and how it has been changing in the current techno-economic transition of developed countries. This very process, however, poses a number of problems to many developing countries' higher education institutions in their attempts to recreate themselves or to facilitate or curtail advancement towards sustainability. They do not normally cooperate with business as suppliers of applied knowledge that can be readily transformed into innovations that increase the competitiveness of national industries. This is the case precisely because, in a particular country, innovative firms may be scarce or non-existent or, when present, most often solve their knowledge problems by resorting to international applied-knowledge providers through licensing, franchising or consulting.

There is little dispute over certain important points. In conventional terms, the world made enormous economic progress during the second half of the 20th century. Over the past 50 years, the world's GDP has multiplied almost twelvefold while per capita income has more than tripled. Growth has been impressive even in the developing world. In a world more interconnected than ever, globalization has opened the door to many benefits: innovation, entrepreneurship, wealth creation, better communications, and enhanced awareness of rights and identities. The notion of the universality of science – according to which national political aims, domestic economic concerns and national boundaries should not act as constraints – has provided an ideological justification for this. The argument is that science (in fact, technology) led to rapid industrialization and economic convergence in the world economy in the late 19th century and, in some cases, the 20th century.

The dark side of this, however, is that science and technology also contribute directly to the new problems societies face today: the challenges of nuclear, chemical and biological weapons; genetically modified organisms and human cloning; and nanotechnologies. Along the way, the self-proclaimed values of science as expressed by Merton – objectivity, generosity, universalism and communism – are increasingly abandoned as knowledge institutions and researchers are subordinated to the interests of powerful private stakeholders. As things stand, the resulting global knowledge divide today is almost a mirror image of the global poverty divide. Globalization has exacerbated the existence of two worlds co-existing in space yet far apart in well-being. Inequality and deprivation persist, and poverty is everywhere. Of course, these problems existed before, but globalization seems to have accentuated exclusion and deprivation, for it has dislocated traditional livelihoods and local communities. Reducing poverty requires that poor countries upgrade their technology, master and produce knowledge, and invest in innovation. However, this is easier said than done.

UNCTAD's *Least Developed Countries Report 2007* argues that the current flow of technology to least developed countries – through international trade, foreign direct investment and intellectual property licensing – does not contribute to narrowing the knowledge divide. Sustained economic growth and poverty reduction are not likely to take place in countries where viable economic re-specialization would remain impossible in the absence of significant progress in technological learning and innovation capacity-building. The UNCTAD report suggests that national governments and development partners could meet this challenge, notably through greater attention to the following four key policy issues:

1. How science, technology and innovation policies geared towards technological catch-up can be integrated into the development and poverty-reduction strategies of LDCs.
2. How stringent intellectual property regimes internationally affect technological development processes in LDCs, and how appropriate policies could improve the learning environment in these countries.
3. How the massive loss of skilled human resources through emigration could be prevented.
4. How knowledge aid (as part of official development assistance) could be used to support learning and innovation in LDCs.

The promise for the world can no longer be that it will follow the historical trajectory of the rich West. We must reckon with the fragility of many global systems. Ravetz reminds us of that fragility, the prospects for failure and experiences of the large systems that are a common feature of the current world:

> The fates of the systems of national defense are threatened by the spread of weapons of mass destruction. Those of the management of wastes are already compromised by insidious pollutants. Our systems of maintaining health are seriously threatened by biological pathogens created by the conditions of modern technology, be they in mass over-medication, mass travel or mass food. Even the systems of communication are vulnerable to 'malware'-pathogens of information which, it now seems, can at best be kept at bay and never wiped out … Everywhere we look there are threats of failures of systems, many on a global scale. (Ravetz, 2006)

In the process of achieving sustainable, lasting development, we must solve various problems that we have never experienced in the past. Since the well-trodden paths prove increasingly unable to solve them, we must take a step into the unknown territory of creativity, discovery and invention. We must ask what mechanisms – in activities such as higher education and research, as obvious as they are resilient – block the effectiveness of science in contributing to human well-being and environmental sustainability.

The first limitation of the orthodox view of research is the unquestioned faith in unharnessed science and technology as the solution to the world's problems. There is no magic in science and research. For various reasons, the views that merely highlight the virtues of science may not hold. Countries vary greatly in their ability to absorb, diffuse, use, adapt and improve imported knowledge and in their capacity to generate original scientific and technological knowledge and innovations, although they require all three types of capacity. In Latin America, for example, nations such as Brazil, Mexico and Argentina have considerable science and technology capacity, particularly in certain industrial sectors and scientific fields. Other countries, such as Chile, Colombia and Venezuela, have a more limited, but still non-negligible, capacity in these areas. Others, such as certain small Caribbean islands and Central American countries, have little or no capacity to produce or disseminate science and technology. These particular countries in this region face various types of problems and challenges, and we need to advance our understanding of the nuances of political, cultural and social development.

Similar caveats hold for other regions and cultures. For instance, it has been argued that colonialism changed the practice of Islam such that only the pursuit of religious knowledge came to be seen as important in Islamic culture, and this led to the decline of science in Muslim society (Sardar, 2007). This could be redressed by rediscovering the spirit of scientific inquiry, reconstructing the open intellectual climate of the past and reinstating critical thinking. Clearly, the single Western canonical view of free-rein, unfettered research is not necessarily the most appropriate one. Reform measures exclusively focused on economic aspects respond to global capital interests and market needs and leave out crucial dimensions of cultural diversity. They also fail to recognize that issues of difference are closely linked to issues of power, opportunity and the specific history of groups, in addition to the experience of each individual. A great deal needs to be done in terms of cultural tolerance and mutual understanding. These changes must involve significant resources and a commitment to systemic change and education. Individual patterns of diversity might be woven together, allowing each pattern to maintain its unique character and helping them blend harmoniously to reflect the rich diversity of the whole. Meanwhile, university and research communities should concentrate on promoting debate on fundamental issues such as the future of society and the regeneration of the university mission, in favour of more inclusiveness and more openness to ideas and people.

RETHINKING RESEARCH AND HIGHER EDUCATION TO BUILD A BETTER FUTURE

Higher education and science must become more evenly distributed around the world if political tension is to be eased and the chances of economic and social development are to improve. The role of education and science in this process is taken as a given – a point of departure – and it is assumed that knowledge and skills will be at least as important for the future of the developing world in this century as they were for developed and industrialized countries in the past. Admittedly, the worldwide higher education landscape and research and knowledge production sectors are undergoing a profound transformation driven by unprecedented global social and economic forces and are embedded in an extremely complex reality, in which no self-evident choices are available and where actions have multiple effects in a dynamically interdependent environment. The size of the academic enterprise has grown tremendously in the past century. The figures for 2000 were worlds away from those for the year 1900, and the speed of change increased in the latter decades of the 20th century. Student enrolment has multiplied worldwide, as has the number of Ph.Ds. The number of institutions has multiplied twentyfold, and the number of scientific journals – not to mention the number of scientists and academic staff – has grown at a similar pace. The increase has been as rapid in industry as it has been in universities and other research organizations.

Still, this expansion has taken place within a fairly limited part of the world. Of the resources spent on science and universities in the year 2000, more than 80% were spent within the OECD area. Within the OECD, the clear majority of all activities occur in North America and Europe. If we expand this region to include the European Union with its new member states in Eastern and Central Europe, the dominance becomes even more overwhelming. A few indicators may suffice to establish the asymmetrical relationship. North America and Europe together account for 95% of the world's doctoral degrees and continue to outstrip the rest of the world combined in the production of new Ph.Ds by a rate of 10 to 1. North America and Europe are responsible for 75% of the world's scientific articles. The region is home to the great majority of the world's university faculty, as well as virtually all of the world's high-quality institutions (Sörlin and Vessuri, 2007).

In the coming century, however, this is likely to change dramatically, not just because the non-OECD world is much larger, with some 85% of the world's population, but because most projections hold that economic growth in these regions will make it possible for many countries to make a sustained investment in higher education and science. It is hard to foresee how this will play out in detail. Various scenarios are possible. If we stick to current trends and limit our speculations to a 30–40 year period, it is obvious that the growth will be huge. The growth of enrolments and institutions in the developing world is exponential, despite the fact that it is far too small to meet the needs. Both China and India are growing rapidly and have the potential to become scientific superpowers – admittedly with very large populations and a fairly low rate of citations per paper. Some Southern countries, such as Brazil, Mexico, South Korea and India, have improved their scientific standing rapidly over the past two decades. Africa, at the other end of the scale, does not reach even 1% of total scientific article production, although individual universities have grown and improved their record of teaching and research (Dakar, Makerere/Kampala, Dar-es-Salaam and a few others). Research training in African universities is still very limited, with the aforementioned institutions and several South African universities being the only exceptions (OECD, 2005).

Harnessing science and technology to contribute to human and social well-being requires a strong push to advance focused scientific research. Developments and challenges in a growing number of cognitive fields force science to take into account further knowledge systems and, in so doing, revise its own standards of efficiency and efficacy. Fields from medicine to agriculture have begun to recognize that the modern world has paid a high price for rejecting traditional practices and the knowledge, however expressed, that underpins them. The need to include other knowledges and perspectives in the scientific endeavour poses important methodological challenges to science and technology for human and social development, as it implies adopting truth and quality criteria that are more sophisticated – and better able to incorporate complexity – than those conventionally accepted by the scientific community. These criteria must be no less solid and rigorous, or else the relevance and credibility of science could be gravely damaged (Rip, 2000). A point of contention has been that traditional knowledge is often contextual, partial and localized, and difficult to translate or integrate into a more scientifically manageable conceptual framework. To what degree, in which situations, and in what type and form extra-scientific types of knowledge will need to be incorporated into the sustainable development research agenda remain open issues (Gallopin and Vessuri, 2006). Uncritically grouping together all 'non-scientific' forms of knowledge and knowledge holders into a single category and separating them from their context only invites oversimplification.

Such unhelpful generalizations jeopardize the potentially unique and worthy contributions that various social actors can make to science.

The science experience, particularly during the second half of the 20th century, provides useful lessons for redesigning strategies based on past mistakes and failures. The nature and use of scientific data and information, the conditions under which they are produced, distributed and managed, and the roles of scientists and other actors in these processes have been changing rapidly. We need a coordinated global approach that ensures equitable access to quality data and information for research, education and informed decision-making. Improved monitoring of the Earth system will allow us to detect, attribute and understand change and the future implications of change. But not only that – the international scientific community must be actively engaged in the production of socially robust knowledge within an extended participation framework.

Many people are proposing a more pluralistic view of relevant knowledge and are concerned about the fate of education and science, subordinated as they are to commercial interests. In certain regions, this situation requires immediate and profound review. The current debate about universities in sub-Saharan Africa, for example, had powerful precedents in the post-independence period of the 1960s, when most of the modernizing groups hailed the idea of the 'developmental university' as a key component of the new nation-state.

> The enormous scale of human struggle with poverty, disease, drought, famine, civil war, political authoritarianism, and decades of weakening structural adjustment programs provides obvious ground for social engagement by universities that represent resources of infrastructure, knowledge, information, expertise, agency, and activism, no matter how meager or impoverished they themselves might be. (Singh, 2007)

Today, there are attempts at university regeneration and reform in many sub-Saharan African countries (Manuh et al., 2003; Singh, 2007). But it remains to be seen to what extent these universities can develop appropriate policies and practices for engagement that do not become hostage to exclusively entrepreneurial rationales and drivers in situations of extreme paucity of funds and resource constraints. Moreover, universities are called upon to seize the opportunity to build a foundation of civic and democratic values and skills that may inspire social cohesion and purpose and enable future leaders to overcome racial and ethnic tensions, dogmatism and religious extremism. We must urgently attend to cultural diversity in higher education and research within the framework of globalization. This does not mean simply increasing the percentage of particular under-represented social groups in a campus population. Rather, diversity encompasses a network of values, policies, practices, traditions and resources that provide coping mechanisms for students and faculty from relegated or excluded groups, thus serving as a sounding board for the wider society. By their attempts to embrace the growing diversity of society and to build cross-cultural bridges with counterparts all over the globe, universities may come to reflect a basic social, institutional and scholarly commitment to freedom, democracy and justice.

Because we live in an increasingly interconnected world, we must rediscover a path that was abandoned decades ago for the sake of increasing specialization. Today's challenges require fresh generalizing capacities and an education that goes beyond the strictly technical culture of the specialist. This step opens up new windows of opportunity for science and for the world. Quality itself has to be rethought in terms of richer and more diverse forms of evaluation. Disciplines, types of research activity, research aims and objectives differ in how they decide what is good and how good something is. Many of the world's governmental agencies and universities have established undesirable administrative evaluation routines that follow criteria that are appropriate for certain research areas and institutional setups but not for others. The inclusion of under-represented groups permits higher education institutions to benefit from under-utilized pools of human talent and experience. As the global market forces industrial economies to evolve towards a knowledge-based economy, people and knowledge constitute sources of new wealth. Countries race to build well-educated and highly trained labour forces in order to acquire a competitive edge in the global economy. Higher education plays a key role in making use of the contribution of all citizens. The combination of the exploration of problems at different scales from the local to the global – starting from a strategic position to have an impact on national and international research agendas with relative autonomy – may help reorient much knowledge production and evaluation towards local needs of cohesion and social equity.

When discussing the democratization of expert knowledge, let us not forget the strong influence of international organizations. We need to better understand the realities of multilateralism and the obstacles and difficulties that new scientific and technological knowledge pose to delegates from developing countries in multilateral regimes and treaties such as those of the WTO, the United Nations System, the International Financial Institutions,

the European Union, the Aarhus Convention on Access to Information, Public Participation in Decision-Making and Access to Justice in Environmental Matters, the Framework Convention on Climate Change and so on. Delegates are increasingly forced to debate very complex issues that require sophisticated mastery of the intricacies of technology and the global market economy in order to negotiate on their country's behalf. Decision-makers in Southern countries also face growing problems with applications, due to an inadequate grasp of scientific literature, and in situations in which governmental representatives cannot tell the difference between crucial and merely interesting or banal data.

Another lesson is that prudent macro guidance and management of scientific research at the national level is both necessary and desirable. Within developed countries, there is widespread consensus that government policies should support R&D activities, whether in the public or the private sector. The associated political outcomes stem largely from business pressures, which are becoming globalized. In developing countries, government policies are even more necessary, but the process of globalization reduces the government's autonomy in formulating policies aimed at development. Like Stewart (2007), one may wonder whether the fragile democracies of developing countries, confronted by such powerful forces, can be expected to do better. The current strict international regime for the protection of intellectual property rights could pre-empt or stifle the development of domestic technological capabilities in weaker countries. Taken together, the rules and conditions of the new international agenda are bound to curb the use of industrial policy, technology policy, trade policy and financial policy as strategic forms of intervention to foster industrialization in developing countries (Nayyar, 2006). Public science policies, while secondary to the aforementioned policies, could help foster the domestic R&D activities needed to build a comprehensive national scientific and technological capacity. Under current conditions, however, it is difficult to fulfil the mission of these policies, and economic and social innovations suffer accordingly.

Any rethinking of scientific R&D must involve a balanced view of the significance of state intervention, institutions and politics in science and the critical role of good governance. Initial conditions can and should be changed to foster development. This is an unambiguous lesson that emerges from the social history of science. In countries that are latecomers to industrialization, state intervention can create conditions for the development of industrial capitalism through the spread of education in society, the development of physical infrastructure and the introduction of institutional change. This role has always been recognized. A further lesson to emerge from experience, however, is that inappropriate and excessive state intervention is counterproductive. The key issue, then, is not whether states should intervene in policy issues related to education and science, but rather what kind of interventions and policies are appropriate in different countries and circumstances. The nature, speed and sequence of change matter, and change should follow the priorities set by the particular country or society.

Another important – if less recognized – aspect is building managerial capabilities in individuals and technological capabilities in firms, for it determines technical efficiency in the short run and competitiveness in the long run. Many developing countries still have a limited understanding of the role of the productive sector in promoting innovation. This may lead to contradictory policy measures; for example, a government may make efforts to strengthen links between universities and companies without at the same time taking complementary steps to strengthen the demand for knowledge in the productive sector. Several former socialist countries underwent rapid and extensive political and economic reform in the 1990s and at the beginning of the new millennium. This involved new challenges. Mongolia, for example, had a strong competitive science base embedded in public-sector institutional structures and a weak market-driven base for adding value and applying this resource. The government currently faces the difficult task of creating favourable conditions to maximize the benefits and minimize the costs of integration with the world economy (Turpin and Bulgaa, 2004).

KNOWLEDGE INTEGRATION FOR EFFECTIVE ACTION

There is broad agreement that mankind faces three main challenges in these early years of the 21st century: freedom from want, freedom from fear and the freedom of future generations to sustain their lives on this planet. Science, technology and innovation are central both to the origins of these three millennium challenges and to the prospects for handling them successfully (Annan, 2000). They are important forces in the positive and negative trends of development. While science, technology and innovation are traditionally associated with the improvement of health, life expectancy and living standards, as well as greater opportunities for information sharing and environmental remediation in many places around the globe, they are also increasingly perceived as linked in complex ways to the current unsustainable development trajectories. Why is it so difficult to change course?

The economic drivers and financial constraints of science are huge. Despite the importance of sustainability and the centrality of science and technology in the strategies for achieving it, there is a great imbalance in the resources and attention devoted to applying research in the quest for sustainable development. So far, efforts to harness research for sustainability have had to be supported to a large extent by R&D systems built for other purposes. Financial support of science has traditionally been related to the expectations that scientific research would help achieve aims that society considered important. This basic role remains the same, but the needs and visions of very complex and heterogeneous societies have changed dramatically. Besides, visions of the future often emphasize only the opportunities for new applications of science and technology without giving due consideration to potential side effects.

The difficult adjustment and radical changes needed are illustrated by what has come to be called 'the stalemate in the energy debate' (NCEP, 2004). The inescapable linkages between energy production and use and the environment result in a vastly complicated overall picture. The risk of global climate change due to emissions released by fossil fuel combustion will exert a profound influence on the world's energy options over the decades ahead. Almost every study in recent years has concluded that current efforts in both the public and private sectors are not commensurate in scope, scale or direction with the challenges, opportunities and stakes. The gap between current efforts in energy-technology innovation and the level and quality of effort required to meet extant and looming energy challenges is very large indeed. This applies to both publicly and privately funded efforts, and it is true for the entire world, not just for the United States or Europe.

Economics is not the only thing standing in the way of much-needed change. As recently put by Ravetz (2006), reflecting on Kuhn's insight in his theory of scientific revolutions, 'the inertia of those intellectual structures that define and regulate our thoughts – be they called paradigms, frameworks or mental models – must be recognized by whoever would wish to change them'. If science is to address sustainability problems, it must be produced in a way that allows it to be linked more easily and rapidly to action communities. It is very likely that it will be reformulated and even transformed through multiple dialogues and interactions among the individuals, groups and institutions that generate and ultimately apply new scientific and technological knowledge. The implementation of new knowledge and technical capacities by different social actors – including governments, natural resource managers, industry and society in general – should not be a final phase in a research programme but rather an integral part of it, from the very early definition of the problem.

Moreover, we must insist on the critical importance of linking the various scales of interaction. Locally focused studies and actions often have limited value if they do not account for the higher-level forces affecting the immediate local dynamic. Development specialists often mention this limited understanding of multi-scale interactions as one of the main obstacles to progress. Advances in the modelling of complex systems and new integrated assessment methodologies afford new opportunities to overcome traditional disciplinary compartmentalization and to aid in decision-making under conditions of persistent uncertainty. New organizational models of international inter- and transdisciplinary assessments – such as those by the Intergovernmental Panel on Climate Change (IPCC, 2007), the Millennium Ecosystem Assessment (2005) and the Arctic Council (2004) – open up new possibilities for integrating knowledge through a wide range of disciplines and development experiences with the involvement of an extensive set of stakeholders.

These approaches are anchored in the objectives of reducing poverty, improving the human condition and conserving the systems that support life on earth. They integrate various disciplines and action communities by assuming dynamic interactions between nature and society and seeking to empower people through active participation. Emphasis is placed on the translation of knowledge into action and a focus on regionally and locally oriented solutions. These approaches encompass both basic and applied science and build upon existing initiatives. Special attention is given to 'slow' variables associated with thresholds, and to the study of vulnerability and resilience. Within an interactive framework, the creation of new scientific knowledge and technical capacities is seen as part of an experimental social process in which the producers and consumers of knowledge interact to identify R&D priorities and to translate knowledge into real actions.

In every society, economy and polity are closely intertwined. The interaction of economics and politics shapes outcomes for people. There is, however, a tendency to 'isolate' certain policy areas from the normal political processes and transfer power to special interests. Science has been assumed to be largely foreign to both economic and political concerns, although, contrary to Weber's (1919) reasoning, the results cannot be separated from the authors. In the short term, technocratic governance without politics may improve policy implementation in certain areas. In the longer term, however, it is not likely to provide a real solution, for it will induce a decline in social cohesion and generate a 'confidence gap' between

political office holders and citizens. The practice of democracy in the world today has tended to distance citizens from professionalized political instances. Excessive reliance on experts' opinions contributes to depoliticization and further removes citizens from political participation. Scientific knowledge and expertise are more crucial than ever in democracy. However, it is also true that the 'knowledge problem' has emerged as one of today's four major governance challenges, in terms of the difficulty in understanding and correctly assessing complex societal issues, as well as the causal linkages between resources and objectives. Scientists have opened Pandora's box and the powers unleashed require deft guidance and societal control to prevent irreparable damage and ensure welcome benefits to mankind. A new politics of knowledge is emerging in which political goals and economic interests have to come to terms with universal norms and values.

REFERENCES

Annan, K. (2000) *We the People: The Role of the United Nations in the 21st Century.* Strategy report submitted to the United Nations General Assembly, New York.

Arctic Council (2004) *Arctic Climate Impact Assessment Policy Document.* Issued by the Fourth Arctic Council Ministerial Meeting. Reykjavik.

Bell, D. (1973) *The Coming of Post-Industrial Society.* New York: Basic Books.

Friedman, M. (1962) *Capitalism and Freedom.* Chicago, IL: University of Chicago Press.

Funtowicz, S. and Ravetz, J. (1992) Three types of risk assessment and the emergence of post-normal science. In: Krimsky, S. and Golding, S. (eds), *Social Theories of Risk.* London: Praeger.

Gallopin, G. and Vessuri, H. (2006) Science for sustainable development: articulating knowledges. In: Guimarães Pereira, A., Guedes Vas, S. and Tognetti, S. (eds), *Interfaces Between Science and Society.* Sheffield: Greenleaf.

Geuna, A. (1999) *The Economics of Knowledge Production: Funding and the Structure of University Research.* Cheltenham, UK: Edward Elgar.

Gibbons, M., Limoges, C., Nowotny, H., Schartzman, S., Scott, P. and Trow, M. (1994) *The New Production of Knowledge: The Dynamics of Science and Research in Contemporary Societies.* London: Sage.

Herrera, A. (1971) *Ciencia y política en América Latina.* Mexico City: Siglo XXI.

Hountondji, P.J. (2006) Global knowledge: imbalances and current tasks. In: Neave, G. (ed.), *Knowledge, Power and Dissent: Critical Perspectives on Higher Education and Research in Knowledge Society.* Paris: UNESCO, pp. 41–60.

IPCC (Intergovernmental Panel on Climate Change) (2007) *Fourth Assessment Report (AR4 Overview).* World Meteorological Organization (WMO) and United Nations Environment Programme (UNEP).

Manuh, T., Gariba, S. and Budu, J. (2003) *Change and Transformation in Ghana's Publicly Funded Universities: A Study of*

Experiences, Lessons & Opportunities. Published in association with the Partnership for Higher Education in Africa. Oxford: James Currey/Accra: Woeli Publishing Services.

Millennium Ecosystem Assessment (2005) *Ecosystems and Human Well-being.* 3 vols. Washington: Island Press/London: Covelo.

Nayyar, D. (2006) Globalisation, history and development: a tale of two centuries. *Cambridge Journal of Economics* **30**(1), pp. 137–59.

NCEP (National Commission on Energy Policy of the United States) (2004) *Ending the Energy Stalemate. A Bipartisan Strategy to Meet America's Energy Challenges.* Washington.

OECD (Organization for Economic Co-operation and Development) (1996) *Technology, Productivity and Job Creation.* Document DSTI/IND/STP/ICCP (96)2. Directorate for Science, Technology and Industry, Paris: OECD.

OECD (Organization for Economic Co-Operation and Development) (2005) *OECD Science Technology and Industry Outlook 2004.* Paris: OECD.

Ravetz, J. (2006) When communication fails: a study of failures of global systems. In: Guimarães Pereira, A., Guedes Vas, S. and Tognetti, S. (eds) *Interfaces between Science and Society.* Sheffield, UK: Greenleaf.

Rip, A. (2000) Indigenous knowledge and Western science: in practice. Paper presented at the 'Demarcation Socialized' conference. Cardiff, 25–27 August.

Sábato, J. (1975) (ed.) *El pensamiento latinoamericano en la problemática ciencia-tecnología-desarrollo-dependencia.* Buenos Aires: Paidós.

Salomon, J.J. (2006) *Les scientifiques entre pouvoir et savoir.* Paris: Albin Michel.

Sardar, Ziauddin (2007) *What Do Muslims Believe? The Roots and Realities of Modern Islam.* New York: Walker & Company.

Seers, D. (1972) What are we trying to measure? *Journal of Development Studies,* **8**(3), pp. 21–36.

Sen, A. (1999) *Development as Freedom.* New York: A. E. Knopf.

Singh, M. (2007) Universities and society: whose terms of engagement? In: Sörlin, S. and Vessuri, H. (eds) *Knowledge Society vs. Knowledge Economy: Knowledge, Power, and Politics.* UNESCO Forum on Higher Education, Research and Knowledge, International Association of Universities/ New York: Palgrave Macmillan.

Solow, R. (1957) Technical change and the aggregate production function. *Review of Economics and Statistics,* **39**(August), pp. 312–20.

Sörlin, S. and Vessuri, H. (eds) (2007) *Knowledge Society vs. Knowledge Economy: Knowledge, Power, and Politics.* UNESCO Forum on Higher Education, Research and Knowledge, International Association of Universities/New York: Palgrave Macmillan.

Stewart, F. (1985) *Planning to Meet Basic Needs.* London: Macmillan – now Palgrave Macmillan.

Stewart, F. (2007) Do we need a new 'great transformation'? Is one likely? In: Mavrotas, G. and Shorrocks, A. (eds) *Advancing Development: Core Themes in Global Economics.* New York: Palgrave Macmillan, in association with the World Institute for Development Economics Research, United Nations University.

Turpin, T. and Bulgaa, G. (2004) S&T reform in Mongolia: a challenge in transition. *Science, Technology & Society,* **9**(1), pp. 129–50.

Ukoli, F.M.A. (1985) (ed.) *What Science? Problems of Teaching and Research in Nigerian Universities.* Ibadan: Heinemann Educational Books and Ibadan University Press.

UNCTAD (United Nations Conference on Trade and Development) (2007) *The Least Developed Countries Report 2007: Knowledge, Technological Learning and Innovation for Development.* Geneva: United Nations.

UNDP (United Nations Development Programme) (various years). *Human Development Report,* New York: Oxford University Press for UNDP.

Weber, M. (1919) *Politik als Beruf, Wissenschaft als Beruf.* Read in the Spanish translation (Alianza Editorial, 1972) of the French edition (1959) with an introduction by Raymond Aron. Paris: Librairie Plon.

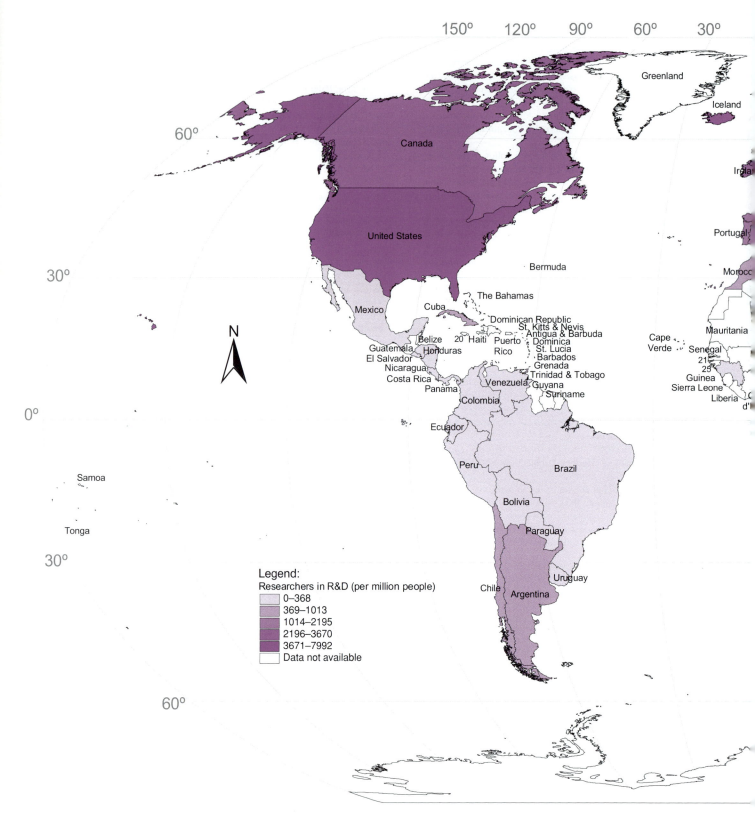

150° 120° 90° 60° 30°

Greenland

Iceland

60°

Canada

Irela

Portugal

30°

United States

Moroc

Bermuda

The Bahamas

Mauritania

Cuba

Mexico

Dominican Republic

St. Kitts & Nevis

Antigua & Barbuda

Cape

Verde

Senegal

21

25

Belize   20 Haiti   Puerto   Dominica

Guatemala Honduras   Rico   St. Lucia

El Salvador   Barbados

Nicaragua   Grenada

Costa Rica   Trinidad & Tobago

Panama   Venezuela Guyana

Colombia   Suriname

Guinea

Sierra Leone

Liberia

d'

0°

Ecuador

Samoa

Peru

Brazil

Tonga

Bolivia

30°

Paraguay

Uruguay

Legend:

Researchers in R&D (per million people)

	0–368
	369–1013
	1014–2195
	2196–3670
	3671–7992
	Data not available

Chile   Argentina

60°

Notes

This map shows the number of researchers in R&D per million people during 1990–2003. Data refers to the most recent year available during the period specified.

Classification method: natural breaks (Jenks optimization)

Source: United Nations Development Programme (UNDP) Excel sheets taken from UNDP website.

MAP 4 Number of researchers per million people

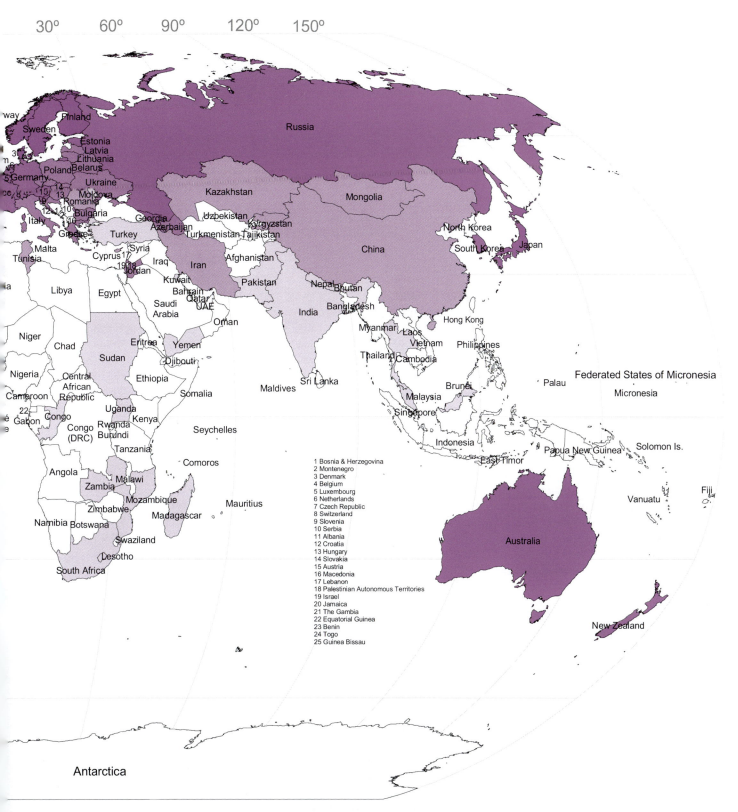

30°   60°   90°   120°   150°

way

Finland

Sweden

Estonia
Latvia
Lithuania
Poland
Belarus
Germany
Ukraine
Moldova
Romania
Bulgaria
Georgia
Turkey
Greece
Syria
Cyprus
Tunisia
Malta
Jordan
Iraq
Libya
Egypt
Niger
Chad
Nigeria
Cameroon
Gabon
Congo
Congo (DRC)
Angola
Namibia
South Africa

Russia

Kazakhstan

Uzbekistan
Azerbaijan
Turkmenistan
Kyrgyzstan
Tajikistan
Afghanistan
Iran
Pakistan
Kuwait
Bahrain
Qatar
UAE
Oman
Saudi Arabia
Eritrea
Yemen
Djibouti
Sudan
Ethiopia
Somalia
Uganda
Kenya
Rwanda
Burundi
Tanzania
Seychelles
Comoros
Zambia
Malawi
Mozambique
Zimbabwe
Botswana
Madagascar
Mauritius
Swaziland
Lesotho

Mongolia

China

North Korea
South Korea
Japan

Nepal
Bhutan
India
Bangladesh
Myanmar
Laos
Hong Kong
Vietnam
Thailand
Cambodia
Philippines
Sri Lanka
Maldives
Brunei
Malaysia
Singapore
Indonesia
East Timor

Palau

Federated States of Micronesia

Micronesia

Papua New Guinea
Solomon Is.

Australia

Vanuatu
Fiji

New Zealand

1 Bosnia & Herzegovina
2 Montenegro
3 Denmark
4 Belgium
5 Luxembourg
6 Netherlands
7 Czech Republic
8 Switzerland
9 Slovenia
10 Serbia
11 Albania
12 Croatia
13 Hungary
14 Slovakia
15 Austria
16 Macedonia
17 Lebanon
18 Palestinian Autonomous Territories
19 Israel
20 Jamaica
21 The Gambia
22 Equatorial Guinea
23 Benin
24 Togo
25 Guinea Bissau

Antarctica

Vector layer source: ESRI Data; Projection: Robinson

Societies throughout the world vary greatly in their ability to produce and use knowledge for human and social development. Today, the great expansion of knowledge and its role in globalization and economic and social development has progressively widened the knowledge gap and increased inequality among nations. Different societies undoubtedly require different sets of knowledge and research. Research as the production of knowledge must include both new-to-the-world discoveries and inventions and situation-specific inquiries in order to apply knowledge to development. Increasing the capacity of researchers and of knowledge users is an essential element of research development in developing countries. The political and social contribution of knowledge must take into consideration the uniqueness of a society and its stage of development, including the population's level of education, the knowledge capital and infrastructures, national competitiveness and indigenous values. The role of higher education institutions has to be appropriate and responsive to different societal needs.

Research relevance and utility vary with the needs of different societies. This issue is of great importance in developing countries, where wider, competing demands meet with more serious limitations. The knowledge generated by research has many different users and beneficiaries, including policymakers, action implementers, service providers and wider communities. National competitiveness is also linked to research and innovation. The benefits of research may be derived from the process rather than the products. Therefore, it is difficult to assess the relevance and utility of research. The type of research and the role of higher education institutions in different societies can be categorized to suit the specific conditions.

ESSENTIAL NATIONAL RESEARCH

The Commission on Health Research for Development devised the term Essential National Health Research (ENHR) to specify the range of health research that every country, even the poorest, needs to conduct in order to best serve people's needs, while taking full advantage of the knowledge existing in the world at the time. Each country must determine its own needs. This notion can be extended to all sectors and termed essential national research. Such research can include many goals.

RESEARCH TOWARDS LOCAL APPLICATION OF THE GLOBAL KNOWLEDGE POOL

A large amount of knowledge exists in the world. It is connected by information and communication technologies to create a global knowledge pool. Developing countries remain behind in their development partly because they cannot take advantage of existing and emerging knowledge. Reasons for not applying such knowledge range from inadequate accessibility and affordability to acceptability and feasibility.

Accessing knowledge requires both infrastructure and competencies, while sorting information requires critical appraisal and knowledge of research methodology. For instance, compiling a national drug list as a tool for benefits and reimbursement in the universal health coverage programme in Thailand requires an extensive review of up-to-date worldwide knowledge about drugs and a critical appraisal and judgment of affordability. Competencies in clinical drug trials are also essential in this process.

Intelligent choice, critical appraisal and appropriate adaptation are generally necessary when applying imported knowledge. The local situation and the detailed pattern – including the nature and extent of the problems in the specific locality, demography and environment – may be different.

To illustrate this point, people in developed countries have access to screening technology and early cancer treatment, when the disease is in a controllable or curable stage. Those in developing countries still suffer from advanced cancer with high morbidity and mortality. Technology assessment is required: cancer screening and treatment methods must be selected and adapted to suit local conditions. Infrastructure has to be put in place. Research is required to uncover the infrastructure and find location-specific solutions.

RESEARCH FOR UNDERSTANDING ONE'S OWN SITUATION AND PROBLEMS

Development efforts and solutions to problems in a particular locality must be considered holistically. Technological knowledge alone is not sufficient. An understanding of the people, the environment, and their characteristics, strengths and weaknesses is essential. Identification and prioritization of problems requires an adequate understanding of the relevant factors in the region, which can come from essential research. Situation-specific knowledge and site-specific data are essential.

One of the great mistakes in the past was to import solutions for local problems. For example, soil and water management is important when introducing new crops. Social and cultural beliefs as well as genetic and environmental conditions are essential to ensuring sustainable success and compliance with new health measures. The effectiveness, cost–benefit relationship, safety, feasibility and acceptability of a solution must be determined, as well as how to adapt it to local economic, sociocultural and political conditions.

Social science is an important area of research when using known and explicit knowledge in a new population. Research policies or actions with social science components tend to be more socioculturally relevant.

PROBLEM-ORIENTED RESEARCH

Research that starts out from a practical problem is immediately relevant and usable. Research to find new, more affordable technology may contribute to solutions. For example, oral rehydration salts, which were developed in Bangladesh, have saved the lives of many children with diarrhoea worldwide.

In the 1960s, the national family planning programme in Thailand undertook research on injectable DMPA, a longer term contraceptive, in spite of known side effects. This research was carried out because of the specific needs of remote rural people. The side effects were found to be less than expected and the drug was therefore acceptable for the local population. As a result of this study, injectable contraceptives have contributed to the success of the family planning programme in Thailand.

In response to the current energy crisis, alternative energy sources are needed. Specific research can be done on the use of such sources in a particular locality, with potential for a wider market. For instance, wind power and wind farm system and model development, including engineering such as small turbine or grid connections, can be useful in many villages. Research and development of solar energy and biomass are aimed at more abundant sources in tropical regions.

POLICY RESEARCH, SYSTEMS RESEARCH AND OPERATIONS RESEARCH

One type of essential research is aimed at supporting policy formulation, implementation and evaluation. Such research makes policies more accountable by providing evidence and sound reasoning

Knowledge from appropriate research is an essential element of all aspects of national development including economic, social, cultural and political policies and programmes. In the 1970s, populations grew at an alarming rate and food shortages were of great concern worldwide, and in developing countries in particular. As part of the 'Green Revolution', research into high-yielding crop varieties and improved agricultural practices in several developing countries such as India led to self-reliance in food production. Many countries were able to increase their export of agricultural products, which contributed to national growth and wealth.

System, service and marketing research examines the whole system and parts of it, taking into consideration the clients' specifications and the impact on society in general. The extent of and need for operations research is obvious.

RESEARCH FOR 'ORPHAN' PROBLEMS

The accumulated knowledge in the world is not evenly distributed in accordance with the magnitude and severity of the problems affecting mankind. The commercialization of science and technology has skewed the investment of capital and human resources in research and development towards projects that have a promising financial return. Many important problems have therefore been neglected. These are known as 'orphan problems'. The knowledge required to tackle them adequately is not available. International efforts are made to address these questions, but many such problems still remain. Therefore, intellectual dependency must be overcome. Countries with orphan problems must struggle to find solutions themselves, perhaps with some outside help.

The Global Forum for Health Research was established in 1996 to address the 10/90 imbalance in health research. Studies showed that 90% of the effort and investment in health research was for health problems that affect only 10% of the world's population, while 90% of the world's population – mainly in developing countries – was left with neglected health problems. Drugs needed to prevent or combat tropical diseases are in the category of orphan drugs. Companies have no interest in undertaking research and development for such drugs, as there are no incentives. Neglected health problems include tuberculosis (TB), malaria, onchocerciasis, filariasis and snake bites. TB has almost totally disappeared from the developed world. However, it has become a more serious threat in developing countries because it has evolved into multidrug-resistant TB and the even more dangerous extensive drug-resistant TB.

During the recent bird flu epidemics in Thailand, Vietnam and Indonesia, many chickens and other fowl died on farms. However, specimens had to be sent to laboratories in other countries to confirm that there was an outbreak of the disease, which can lead to human infection. This delay was probably responsible for the disease spreading out of control before appropriate measures could be implemented. Fortunately, research laboratories in Thai universities that are working on genomes, genetic mapping and viral infections were able to decode the virus and confirm that it was indeed H5N1 influenza. This demonstrates the importance of developing countries investing in research capability that enables them to cope with local problems. At present, only one drug is effective against bird flu; oseltamivir, or Tamiflu. This drug is still under patent and only produced by one pharmaceutical company. The price and availability of the drug became a problem when many countries started to stockpile it, regardless of the fact that the best response to such outbreaks is to control them as quickly as possible in the countries where they start.

A key target of the Millennium Development Goals is poverty reduction in developing countries. Research into this complex problem is not commercially attractive, since the poor do not have purchasing power. For example, research on producing shrimp as food for the rich and for export takes preference over research on producing tilapia fish as a protein source for the poor. International cooperation and philanthropic activities have led to some successes. Many success stories indicate that there is a need to empower people. National programmes for the poor must be based on recognizing this research need.

RESEARCH FOR NATIONAL COMPETITIVENESS

Many advanced countries are making public and private investments in knowledge production and innovation, in order to keep abreast of competition. Under the capitalist system, knowledge and technology become saleable commodities. Investment in research, development and production is made with expectations of high returns.

With the escalation of the cost of commodities such as drugs, supplies and services, the gap between those who own and sell intellectual property and those who buy it is rapidly widening. Intellectual property rights lead to monopolies and pricing power. Profit maximization leads to price setting based on the level of need for a product and the final consumers' ability to pay. If technology is needed, knowledge-importing countries have to use their limited resources to buy it at a high price. They become poorer or are left without the benefit of knowledge advancement.

Many developing countries are therefore trying to create dynamism and cross over the divide, if and when they have the opportunity to do so. Research and development policies reflect such inspiration. Examples of opportunities to jump-start or leapfrog can be observed in a number of developing countries. One of these involves the development of information and computer software technologies in Bangalore, India. This has transformed India from an importing to an exporting country. The development of hepatitis B vaccines in many regions resulted in more than 300 products being launched on the world market, leading to a reduction in prices.

Nanotechnology is another frontier that may be useful for many problems in developing countries. It can be applied to drug delivery devices, textile modification, energy storage, water purification, environmental sustainability and enhanced agricultural productivity. Developing countries should invest in and pursue such research leads, if they have the capability. Jump-starts can make a country more competitive. While the USA, Germany and Japan are taking the lead in the number of patents for nanoscale science and engineering, it is not surprising that China, India and South Korea are establishing national activities in nanotechnology with strong government backing. Less dramatic attempts are being made in many other countries, such as Argentina, Brazil, Chile, Malaysia, Mexico, the Philippines, South Africa and Thailand. Developing countries should try to develop their own competitive research.

RESEARCH AS AN EDUCATIONAL AND EMPOWERMENT TOOL

The benefits of research may be derived from the process itself, rather than the utility of the results. Knowledge and skills acquired through the research process can serve as a tool for cultivating scientific and critical thinking in the next generation and in the general public. Employment in technology-intensive areas requires the ability to work with knowledge and technology, critical appraisal to apply new technology, and preparation for future advances. Relevant research can aim at training future researchers or at empowering people in the community.

RESEARCH IN RESPONSE TO SOCIETAL NEEDS AND FOR THE PRESERVATION OF VALUES, SOCIAL JUSTICE AND HUMAN RIGHTS

Current society is more complex than it was in the past. Major developmental projects such as dams, large electricity-generating plants and industrial estates are considered essential for economic and social development. However, such projects can bring suffering to many people living in the locality. Dam construction aimed at electricity generation and water irrigation leads to the dislocation of many people from their homes in the flooded area. Loss of human heritage and the environmental impacts on human settlement and wildlife are downplayed. The threat to downstream villages of dam breakage, due to poor construction or earthquakes, and the possible occurrence of new parasitic diseases are some of the uncertainties of the future.

Water pollution in rivers can cause the unexpected death of many fish, health hazards for people using water taken from the river and damage to agricultural farms. Water pollution can come from industrial factories, upstream urban settlements or even certain agricultural practices. Conflicts may arise when blame is allocated and claims are made. The distribution of limited resources such as water during droughts can create conflict among those in need. At the other extreme, flood water can be diverted from urban cities to rural farms or vice versa. Equitable sharing of suffering and justified compensation for those affected have been sources of conflict. The market economy and competition aimed at profit maximization compound the situation.

Different stances and different sets of information are cited by conflicting parties. The public is given only half the truth to support each of these stances, leading to division in society. Currently, conflicting evidence and knowledge are available from many sources. Therefore, the public can easily get confused when facing controversial problems. Trustworthy sources of opinions and the critical appraisal of existing evidence and knowledge are important elements in today's society. In many societies in which public education is limited, universities are expected to serve this crucial function. Leading universities have been called upon to do research, review the situation and provide rational recommendations that are fair and sound. Academics are respected if they use their intellectual objectivity, safeguard their professional integrity and position themselves as neutral, non-partisan and trustworthy agents who are above conflicts of interest. Academic freedom remains an essential value for universities. The existence of university establishments has helped to solve many conflicts. However, improper behaviour by academics exacerbates the problems.

Besides being responsive to societal needs, higher education institutions are responsible for promoting social justice and acting against malpractice and inequity in society. This is particularly true in developing countries, where other societal mechanisms may not be fully functioning. The results of research undertaken by universities on socially relevant topics such as corruption, undemocratic activities and encroachment of human rights have helped to deter misdeeds. Together with other societal agents such as the media and non-governmental organizations, actions have been taken and corrupt politicians have been forced to resign or have been prosecuted. University authorities must keep their integrity and be able to stand firm against pressure and threats. On one occasion, a government attempt to cover up the occurrence of H5N1 bird flu in Thailand, for fear of its impact on the chicken industry and on trade, was disrupted by disclosure of scientific findings from the universities. Soon afterwards, proper measures to control the epidemics were instituted.

The trends of change in society may be inevitable. They require appropriate adjustment and adaptation. However, some changes may be undesirable and should be resisted. Changes in science and technology can create new issues requiring new sets of values or principles. Higher education institutions and academics have played a pivotal role in encouraging society to preserve values

and in setting new standards. For instance, society is now faced with ethical issues arising from new scientific advances. Such issues include brain death, organ transplantation, fertility technologies, stem cell experimentation and genetic engineering. Seminars, debates and research on these issues are organized by universities. At times, they must stand firm against powerful threats and put themselves at risk. This is particularly true of developing countries, in which universities form an integral part of society. In developed societies, political forces tend to be in balance. Different government positions towards universities can be observed. In some countries with autocratic or dictatorial governments, universities are asked to find ways to support policies that have already been established by the government. At times, universities are used to justify government actions. Many governments, however, are intelligent enough to see the benefit of allowing universities autonomy and academic freedom in order to formulate better public policies.

CONCLUSION

Some countries need to carry out essential national research, including research towards the local application of the global knowledge pool; research to understand their own situation and prob-

lems; problem-oriented research; policy research; systems research; and operations research. Many societies require research to find solutions to orphan problems that are neglected by global efforts. Some societies maintain their supremacy by investing in research and innovation. Less-advanced societies strive to produce cutting-edge knowledge in order to compete or even just to survive. In some societies, the research process is used as an educational tool in order to develop human resources and empower the community. Universities can serve as dependable agents of society and respond to societal needs. They can also be responsibly engaged in struggles for human rights and social justice. In many societies, higher education institutions and academics play a pivotal role in encouraging the society to preserve values and in setting new standards.

BIBLIOGRAPHY

Meek, V. Lynn and Suwanwela, Charas (eds) (2006) *Higher Education, Research and Knowledge in the Asia-Pacific Region*. New York: Palgrave Macmillan.

Suwanwela, Charas (2006) *Academic Freedom in Countries of Asia*. Bangkok, Thailand: UNESCO Asia-Pacific Programme of Educational Innovation for Development.

GOOD PRACTICE 1.3
The experience of the Science Shop and the Living Knowledge Network in Europe

GUNI Observatory[1]

CONTEXT
The public or social function of universities has changed over time. Currently, society requires universities to undertake knowledge transfer to society and carry out relevant research activities. In addition, universities have to train future professionals with practical knowledge that will provide them with the tools they need to function in a changing work and social environment.

In Europe, these university functions have been only partially carried out. In

general, knowledge transfer has focused on publicly communicating research results. The use of this information to society is rarely defined. Furthermore, the relevance of research has been closely linked to the needs of the production sector (and those of industry in particular), while social needs have been pushed to one side.

From this consideration of the role of research and higher education in general, it can be deduced that universities should provide solutions to the needs

and demands of civil society in a programme separate from technology transfer programmes for industry and companies. As a result, different relationships between universities and society have arisen in Europe. One of these is the science shop movement and the Living Knowledge Network, which work in the field of community-based research.

DESCRIPTION
Living Knowledge is an international network of science shops and similar organ-

izations. It is a meeting place for all individuals and organizations interested in community-based research and in the relationship between science and society in general. Living Knowledge offers a forum for exchanging information, experiences and ideas.

Science shops could be defined as offices or consultancies that link civil society with research groups that are generally based in universities and research institutions. Two main characteristics differentiate science shops from other technology and knowledge transfer programmes. First, research is community-based. Second, services on offer are either low-cost or free.

OBJECTIVES

The objectives of the Living Knowledge Network are to:

1. Create spaces for debate and discussion among science shops in their local and national contexts. These spaces should promote shared learning.
2. Provide tools for improving and perfecting the activities of every science shop.
3. Promote the activities carried out by the different science shops and expand the experience throughout Europe.
4. Establish projects and initiatives that involve international cooperation.

The general objectives of a science shop are to:

1. Provide civil society with research knowledge and skills.
2. Offer free or low-cost social consultancy services.
3. Promote and support society's access to science and technology.
4. Create equitable and stable relationships with civil society organizations.
5. Link the knowledge of the governing class and of research and educational institutions to civil society's research and training needs.
6. Link up the skills and knowledge of students, community representatives and researchers.

PROCESS

The science shop was first established in the Netherlands during the counterculture and student movements of the 1970s. A group of Dutch chemistry students decided to help non-profit organizations to use scientific research and knowledge to solve problems. This first initiative had a major impact. With the support of university lecturers, the experience was expanded to other areas of knowledge. In the next ten years, the experience spread to all universities in the Netherlands. However, Utrecht University and the University of Amsterdam are benchmarks in this area. In 1990, there were 40 science shops in Dutch universities, as all universities became required to establish a science shop.

Many European countries were inspired by this initiative and began similar programmes. Currently, science shop experiences can be found in almost all European Union countries. All these experiences aim to respond to the needs of their local society by adapting knowledge to its immediate surroundings. As a result, the experiences vary greatly according to their context.

In general terms, the process of a science shop can be described as follows:

- A request is made by a civil society organization. These organizations are usually unions or employee organizations; NGOs; professional associations; charities; popular organizations; citizen organizations linked to municipal and local life; churches and religious committees; and organizations that undertake economic activities of a markedly social nature, such as cooperatives and small companies involved in social and labour integration.
- Once the request has been received and positively assessed by science shop members, the university members who will participate in the project are identified.
- Subsequently, university researchers and students and the commissioning institution define and plan the research project with the collaboration of the science shop. The project may be carried out at no cost to the institution or for a non-commercial fee.
- The science shop is based on the idea of community-based or participative research. Therefore, the active participation of the organization that commissions the project is expected. However, this collaboration depends on different factors, such as the topic, the characteristics of the organization and the specific experience of the science shop.
- Once the project has been concluded, a communication campaign is carried out to disseminate the results.

In 2000, a network of science shops was created on the basis of previous experience and with the conviction that, despite the marked local slant of projects, practices should be disseminated on an international level. In 2003, in the framework of the European Commission programme *Training and Mentoring of Science Shops* (TRAMS), the Living Knowledge project was consolidated as an international network of science shops and similar organizations. The Network is defined as a meeting place for all organizations and individuals interested in community-based research and in the relationship between science and society. Some of the most important initiatives include international cooperation projects and the database of science shops worldwide.

International cooperation projects focus on two main areas:

1. Promoting spaces for debate, reflection and shared knowledge, such as:
   a. International conferences attended by all Network members as well as academics and researchers interested in community-based research.
   b. The *Living Knowledge Newsletter*, which contains the latest news about science shops and community-based research.
   c. The magazine *Living Knowledge:*

International Journal of Community Based Research, which gives detailed analyses of specific aspects of the science shop.

2. Joint projects that have two main objectives: to make cooperation in cross-border research viable, thus promoting learning and providing common solutions to problems; and to develop concepts and procedures for cooperation between Network members.

In addition, a database of science shops has been created: (http://www.bio.uu.nl/sspid/). This tool is useful for international projects as it can help members and collaborators to meet. It enables different organizations to contact each other and find out the main characteristics of each science shop. In addition, it is a mechanism for disseminating projects, not only in Europe, but also in other countries of the world where this experience is relevant.

RESULTS

- The Living Knowledge Network currently includes 48 science shops from 19 countries worldwide. However, many members are European. There are nine main areas of activity: agriculture, the economy, the environment, humanities, law, public health, social welfare, technology and urban planning.

- To date, three international conferences have been held. The first was in November 2001 at Paris-Jussieu; the second was held in 2005 in Seville; and the third in September 2007 in Paris.

- The publication of the *Living Knowledge Newsletter*, which comes out twice a month, and the magazine *Living Knowledge: International Journal of Community Based Research*. Between one and three editions of this magazine are published annually.

- The Living Knowledge Network has taken part in three international cooperation programmes among science shops: the Study and Conference on Improving Public Access to Science through Science Shops (SCIPAS), which targets shared knowledge by producing publications and tools that provide information about experiences in other countries; the *Interacts* programme, which is funded by the European Commission and aims to link NGOs, universities and science shops by means of a programme of democratic governance; and finally, a project to improve the International Science Shop Network (ISSNET), which is funded by the EC. Focusing on consolidating and strengthening the Network, this project ended in 2005.

RECOMMENDATIONS

The following are required to set up a science shop programme:

1. A technical team that is not necessarily scientific. This team should be in charge of managing, disseminating and making the initial contact with civil society organizations. Such a team is important as university lecturers and researchers may have difficulties with management issues and making contact with the immediate environment.

2. A campaign to disseminate the experience so that civil society organizations receive information about it. One of the most common problems is that such organizations do not have easy access to the university.

In terms of international networking, it would be advisable for all new science shop experiences to be included in the Living Knowledge Network. Thus, the knowledge of other members of the Network can be shared. This also helps to strengthen the Network.

NOTE

1 Text written by the Universities and Social Commitment Observatory with information provided by Caspar De Bok. Living Knowledge.

Sheila Jasanoff

SPECIAL CONTRIBUTION I.15
Ethical, environmental and social implications of science and technology: challenges for the future

INTRODUCTION

The 20th century saw the massive expansion and sometimes forcible intrusion of science and technology into every aspect of human life: transportation, communication, education, commerce, agriculture, human reproduction, medicine, energy, space and ocean exploration, and of course war. A pressing task for the 21st century is to foster human capacities to absorb, critically examine and reflect on these earlier developments. How to do this effectively and rigorously is a looming challenge and critical responsibility for the world's universities.

The task will not be easy. Obstacles include imperfect and continually evolving understandings of the nature of the issues; structural barriers to innovation within universities and other institutions of higher learning; and a pronounced dearth of appropriately trained human resources. These problems are compounded in many technologically advanced societies by a short-term, economically driven culture of assessment that values immediate material returns over less tangible gains, such as the production of literate, ethically aware and politically engaged citizens. Additionally, university research is increasingly tied to commercial enterprises that provide social benefits but also threaten the independence and integrity of science and create incentives for ethical misconduct. Overcoming these barriers will require skill and leadership, as well as imagination and willingness to learn from others' experiences. This paper outlines some of the opportunities along with the impediments.

AFTER PROGRESS: UNFORESEEN RISKS AND UNINTENDED CONSEQUENCES

Most of the salient implications of science and technology for human development can be grouped under one or more of the following three headings: ethical, environmental and social. Each heading, however, encompasses a diverse range of issues. Awareness of these issues has deepened and expanded along with advances in science and technology. Mapping these intellectual domains provides a foundation for considering both what universities are currently doing to enhance knowledge and education in each area and what tasks still lie ahead.

ETHICS, SCIENCE AND TECHNOLOGY

Since the destruction of Hiroshima and Nagasaki at the end of the Second World War, producing devastation and loss of life on barely imaginable scales, scientists have been actively aware of the catastrophic potential of their inquiries into nature. Just as atomic bombs prompted intense soul-searching among physicists, so the torture of prisoners by Nazi doctors and the subsequent discovery of inhumane research practices in the USA and elsewhere led biomedical scientists to reflect on ethical conduct in research on human subjects. Public responses to these events included the rise of new professional societies committed to ethical research, new governmental policies for technology assessment and, in academia, the emergence of the field of biomedical ethics.

Born in response to cases of egregious research abuse, biomedical ethics (or bioethics) focused at first chiefly on the principles that should govern doctor–patient relations. The most important achievement in this area was the principle of informed consent. However, the field took on additional issues as medical technologies advanced in the post-war period, such as: the definition of death; the technological prolongation of life; the meaning of privacy; the patenting of human tissues and novel life forms; the allocation of scarce medical technologies; the procurement of organs; and the conduct of evidence-based medicine.

The global spread of science and technology, however, has ethical implications that cannot be contained within particular disciplinary or professional enclaves, such as bioethics taught in medical schools alone. Furthermore, ethical questions cannot be limited to specific, targeted areas of science such as human subjects research. New technologies such as genetic engineering, artificial intelligence, imaging, and nanotechnologies – either on their own or together in the form of what today are called convergent technologies – present concerns that far transcend the assaults on human life and dignity that prompted earlier concerns about the ethics of science and technology. At stake now are questions about the meaning of human nature itself, and what, if anything, should be held sacred when boundaries are blurred between humans and machines, humans and animals, and living and non-living beings. Also under scrutiny is the moral status of many novel entities brought into being through science and technology, such as genetically engineered crops and animals, frozen embryos, embryonic stem cells, and robots capable of speech and learning.

Paralleling these issues are new ethical concerns about the ways in which human societies should co-exist with other species and exploit the resources of the world. Ethics, in this respect, feeds into the environmental concerns that are a second major legacy of the 20th century's massive investments in science and technology.

SCIENCE, TECHNOLOGY AND THE ENVIRONMENT

The 1960s were a decade of rising environmental consciousness, linked to growing awareness of the human-made risks of scientific and technological development. Fueled at the start by *Silent Spring*, Rachel Carson's path-breaking account of the hazards of indiscriminate pesticide use, and bracketed at the end by satellite images from the Apollo mission that vividly displayed the Earth's finiteness, the 1960s moved both science and society towards more cautious assessments of the environmental costs of economic and industrial development.

A fast-moving chronicle of environmental disasters underlined the need for foresight: mercury poisoning in Minamata, Japan; an explosive dioxin release in Seveso, Italy; a deadly methyl isocyanate leak in Bhopal, India; and a nuclear power plant meltdown at Chernobyl in the former Soviet Union, spreading contamination across Western Europe. Products and interventions once seen as entirely beneficial turned out to have unexpected adverse consequences, which were sometimes global in scope. Thus, organic pesticides such as DDT and airborne acid emissions were shown to persist and accumulate in the environment, causing severe ecological damage. Chlorofluorocarbons, impressively stable and nontoxic in consumer products, were found to be depleting the earth's stratospheric ozone layer, with long-term risks to agriculture and human health. High dams constructed to address energy problems throughout the developing world gave rise to untold numbers of environmental refugees and inequitably distributed benefits and burdens, and proved less efficient than early optimistic estimates. Furthermore, overshadowing all other dangers, the steady accumulation of greenhouse gases since the beginning of industrialization has caused demonstrable changes in the earth's climate, with potentially disastrous consequences for the world's poorest, most vulnerable populations.

By the 1970s, it became clear that university curricula needed to respond to this onslaught of knowledge. The term *environment* became an umbrella under which new research and teaching programmes began to cluster. The sciences were among the first to reorganize around this rubric, drawing support from state and privately funded programmes aimed at finding solutions to specific problems. However, other disciplines also took environmentalism on board, generating opportunities for specialized, environment-oriented study in fields such as anthropology, economics, history, philosophy, political science, sociology and law.

Impressive as these changes were, in some respects they did not go far enough. It was clear by the 1992 Earth Summit in Rio de Janeiro, Brazil, that new conceptual tools for understanding environmental phenomena on a planetary scale – such as sustainability, vulnerability, and precaution – required unprecedented collaboration among all fields of knowledge. Yet support for and receptivity towards environmental issues remained strongest in the natural sciences, with the result that humanistic and social knowledge of the environment grew at a slower pace than understanding of the earth's physical and biological systems. Hiring practices in the social sciences and humanities rarely gave top priority to environmental appointments, thus contributing to deficits in knowledge and human resources. Environmental studies took place in contexts where disciplinary perspectives predominated, and conservatism with respect to cross-cutting appointments and promotions raised barriers against scholars working on problem definitions that were not rooted in traditional disciplines. On the whole, environmental programmes were not linked to broader critical studies of science and technology.

SCIENCE, TECHNOLOGY AND SOCIETY

Despite inadequacies, the ethical and environmental implications of science and technology gained more systematic recognition within universities than their more nebulous but no less unsettling social implications. One reason perhaps is that ethical misconduct and environmental damage can both be recognized without questioning the nature or purposes of science itself. Thus, when a university researcher is discovered to have falsified data or conducted experiments on unconsenting subjects, one can judge the behaviour to be unacceptable and develop ethical norms to bar future misconduct, without asking whether the research itself is worth doing. Similarly, one can seek to prevent or mitigate the adverse environmental impacts of technological development without seriously questioning the need for particular kinds of innovation. Such black-boxing ceases to be possible when one looks at the full spectrum of science's engagements with society.

A major intellectual development of the 20th century was the recognition that science and technology are not independent of human influences but are themselves social institutions, affected by and incorporating the ideologies, enthusiasms and biases of the periods in which they are constituted. The idea that science is value-free, or that facts can be separated from values as the great German sociologist Max Weber asserted, was cast into doubt by work such as that of the philosopher Thomas Kuhn, who established in *The Structure of Scientific Revolutions* (1962) that science is always pursued within the constraints of historically specific social paradigms.

Technologies even more clearly incorporate design choices that reflect prior cultural assumptions about what is desirable or possible to achieve in society. Thus, a preference for personal mobility drove investments in the automobile and contributed to the waning of railways and public transportation systems in the USA. The Green Revolution, rightly seen as solving chronic food shortages in developing societies, carried environmental costs and distributive inequities that had not been contemplated during the technological development. Today's armamentarium of psychotropic drugs allows previously debilitating mental illnesses to be managed, but has changed societal expectations about what mental states are 'normal' and created problems of overuse in ways that the drug designers did not intend. Expensive reproductive technologies have brought solace to childless couples, but have also opened the door to treating children as designer commodities and potentially widened gulfs between the rich and the poor.

Public policies for the advancement of science and technology likewise incorporate social assumptions that are sometimes so taken for granted that they come to seem natural – that is to say, they are 'naturalized'. For example, Western intellectual property laws subscribe to the labour theory of value, and prize the contributions of individual authors or inventors in creating novel products. This legal regime leaves little space for protecting indigenous and other forms of collective knowledge that cannot be attributed to a single inventive act or moment. When generalized through global agencies such as the World Trade Organization, such region-specific policy assumptions can be superimposed on contrary, but perhaps less explicitly formulated, cultural assumptions without benefit of full deliberation.

Another example that has global consequences is the spread of 'scientific risk assessment,' especially in the regulation of environmental hazards. The insistence on the scientific nature of risk assessment masks what are now seen as deeply value-laden choices on such matters as what risks different societies view as significant, what models of risk causation are employed, how uncertainties are represented and accounted for, and who is consulted, or when, with respect to the risks of technological development. Equally, the conceptualization of risk assessment as a science tends to rule out consideration of the distribution of risks and benefits throughout society. However, perceived imbalances in just such distributive impacts account for many episodes of resistance to new technologies – from the knitting machines opposed by Luddites in the early 19th century to the genetically modified crops and foods rejected by European consumers two hundred years later.

As with the ethical and environmental aspects of science and technology, universities have responded to changing perceptions of science and technology as social institutions, and of their shaping functions in society. Responses, however, have been unsystematic, institutionally and culturally disparate, and unevenly distributed both within and among countries. To meet the challenges head on, universities will need to develop a fuller, more historically informed sense of their own institutional missions, not only as incubators for the production of new scientific knowledge and technological know-how, but also as sites of capacity building for social analysis, critical reflection and, not least, democratic citizenship. A brief review of the changing role of universities in relation to science and technology indicates why such institutional self-examination is in order.

UNIVERSITY ROLES: FROM IVORY TOWER TO SOCIAL CONTRACT, AND BEYOND

From the beginning of the scientific revolution until well into the 20th century, the university patterned first and foremost as an ivory tower – a place of retreat where science in its broadest sense could be conducted without interference from, and often with scant attention to, the mundane pressures of the world. Science was seen as the disinterested pursuit of knowledge for its own sake. Founding figures of the Enlightenment, such as Galileo Galilei, Rene Descartes, Francis Bacon, Robert Boyle and Isaac Newton, carried out their inquiries without regard for the uses of knowledge and, in Galileo's case, famously in defiance of reigning religious

authority. Scientists often taught in universities or were gentleman scholars of independent means. Their very independence was seen as a source of science's power and integrity. Writing in 1942, the pioneering American sociologist of science Robert K. Merton (1973) attributed much of the success of science to the field's ethical commitment to four principles: *communalism* in the sharing of knowledge; *universalism* in holding that scientific ideas are everywhere the same; *disinterestedness* in the sense of detachment from private gain, and *organized scepticism* through critical peer review.

Not until the maturation of the industrial revolution did scientific understanding come to be coupled with technological innovation for commercial purposes. Even then, the trajectories of the early great inventors – men like Eli Whitney, Thomas Edison, Louis Pasteur, Guglielmo Marconi and Wilbur and Orville Wright – were led by efforts at practical problem-solving rather than self-conscious efforts to apply the results of science for material gain. Higher education mirrored the perceived separation between discovery and invention. In the influential German model, technological universities founded in the 19th century offered training in engineering and applied sciences while the traditional university system provided education in pure mathematics, basic natural sciences, humanities and social sciences. Similar splits between scientific and technological education occurred in the UK, the USA, and eventually in many countries in Asia and Africa. 'IT' systems, featuring institutes of technology on the model of MIT in the US, took hold in many regions of the world. Unlike the traditional universities, these institutions generally did not offer options for systematic study in the humanities and social sciences.

Much changed with the world wars of the 20th century. The Manhattan Project and the atomic bomb, as well as the success of antibiotics, radar, computing and the Green Revolution, persuaded governments to fund university-based science in

the hopes of generating benefits for society in peace and war. In a tacit social contract with science and technology, states – and eventually private donors – undertook to support university-based scientific research, on the understanding that increasing knowledge would lead to new inventions, more employment and rising levels of health and wealth for all. Conceptually, scientists continued to insist on the division between 'pure' or 'basic' and 'applied' research. In practice, the line between these became progressively less distinct.

These developments gained impetus but also changed direction in the last quarter of the 20th century, as nations increasingly recognized that knowledge itself is a valuable economic resource to be cultivated and exploited for the common good, much as was historically the case with resources provided by nature. Industrial nations began to see themselves more and more as 'knowledge societies', and public policies for science and technology, long content with merely promoting research, also geared themselves towards speeding the transfer of knowledge into use. Among the instruments chosen for this purpose were enhanced patenting opportunities for university-based researchers, targeted funding programmes for key technological areas, such as biotechnology and nanotechnology, and funding for high-risk but potentially high-yield research. Conscious of limits on public resources, states aggressively encouraged public–private partnerships, and science-based industries sought out promising university centres in which to invest funds for breakthrough research.

By the turn of the 21st century, scientific knowledge gains were pervasively regarded as precursors to economic growth, and research funding levels were taken as a reliable indicator of a nation's future prosperity. Yet governments and the public also began to acknowledge that advances in science and technology could have unexpected and not entirely progressive consequences. Concerns centred on the emerging ethical, environmental and social implications of science and technology detailed above. Worldwide opposition to nuclear power and to some agricultural biotechnologies demonstrated the risks of failing to take public attitudes and perceptions into account. State policies accordingly strove to incorporate broader considerations within the funding portfolio for scientific research and development. Perhaps the best known of such initiatives was the widely imitated Ethical, Legal and Social Implications (ELSI) programme of the US Human Genome Project. Researchers eagerly responded to calls for investigating science's social consequences, but changes in university educational and training programmes were slow to follow.

In sum, tighter alliances with government and the private sector have eroded the classical ideal of universities as ivory towers. Instead, universities today are proactive agents in producing new knowledge and encouraging its dissemination into commerce and policy. Some applaud this development as leading to an era of what has been called 'Mode 2' scientific production, in which researchers are held accountable for meeting society's needs. Others point out that loss of independence in cash-starved universities has opened the way to personal and institut-

ional corruption, and to fashion rather than significance dictating the courses of research. By their nature, these disputes do not lend themselves to easy or definitive resolution. The important goal for universities is to maintain accessible institutional spaces in which concerns such as these can be articulated, studied and openly debated. A growing number of universities have taken up the challenge through dedicated programmes for studying science, technology and society. However, as yet there is only a trickle of such programmes, where there ought to be a flood.

STUDYING SCIENCE AND TECHNOLOGY IN SOCIETY

Universities are spaces of reflection and creation. Almost all forms of human creativity are fostered in institutions of higher learning. However, universities are also entrusted with developing the critical discourses and analytic frameworks with which human societies can continuously reflect on the products of their ingenuity. Thus, politics merits its own science and theory; economics analyses the market; sociology and anthropology examine human society and culture; and the creative arts entail their own modes of criticism. However, despite their centrality in organizing the contemporary

world, science and technology do not as yet command similar intellectual or material resources for critical reflection in the form of departments, teaching personnel, student support and research funding. Globally, less than a percent of a percent of all the resources spent on science and technology is devoted to taking their ethical, environmental and social implications seriously.

Given the wide-ranging, ambiguous and pervasive role of science and technology in human life, this gap between production and reflection is one that universities urgently need to fill. The first step is to recognize, for all the aforementioned reasons, that 'science, technology and society' is a topic of research and teaching that requires urgent attention in its own right. The second step is to make available the institutional resources for systematically studying and teaching it.

REFERENCES

Kuhn, Thomas (1962) *The Structure of Scientific Revolutions*. Chicago, IL: University of Chicago Press.

Merton, R.K. (1973) The Normative Structure of Science. In: Merton, R.K. *The Sociology of Science: Theoretical and Empirical Investigations*. Chicago, IL: University of Chicago Press.

I.7

CIVIL ENGAGEMENT IN HIGHER EDUCATION AND ITS ROLE IN HUMAN AND SOCIAL DEVELOPMENT

Rajesh Tandon

Abstract

Over the past century, the world has seen many social, economic and political transformations. A largely colonial era has given way to a largely democratic one. Yet, while the democratization of the political culture guaranteed citizens' rights and freedom, it did not result in the democratization of learning and knowledge production.

Changes in education systems have been slow in coming. Economic trends and civil society movements in the past decade have changed perceptions of what constitutes 'knowledge' and redefined the mission and mandate of higher education institutions (HEIs). With increasing demands to scale up their teaching and research functions, HEIs are facing new challenges in contributing to human and social development. The meaning and agenda of human and social development have also changed, and new civil society actors have been closely associated with this phenomenon.

This paper looks at how the engagement of civil society organizations with the world of higher education has resulted in interesting trends in social policy formation and knowledge production. It presents examples of effective engagement between HEIs and the social and human development efforts of civil society (PRIA in Asia and Mpambo Multiversity in Africa), draws lessons from these interventions and highlights future potential for HEIs. Advocating the view that the research and teaching functions of HEIs should serve the larger mission of human and social development, it looks at the gains to be obtained from such partnerships. By exploring alternative sources and modes of learning and knowledge production, the paper provides a vision of the possibilities that engagement with civil society can open up in terms of HEIs' contribution to social and human development in the coming decades.

CONTEXT

Around the world, higher education (HE) and HEIs such as universities have been experiencing the forces of economic and social transformation. The forces of globalization are affecting HEIs in many complex ways, including the supply of students and the expectations of graduates. The growth in supply of HE and the proliferation of HEIs, both public and private, has raised questions about the quality of their teaching and research functions. HE is no longer viewed as a public good, and its contribution to the labour market has been commonly advocated. Nevertheless, humanity is now facing ever-increasing challenges to its own survival. New human and social development priorities are posing new challenges for policymakers and political leaders. Societal development issues (such as multiculturalism, sustainability and so on) have become so complex that new knowledge is needed in order to address them. HEIs are expected to generate this knowledge. Further, rising expectations from growing numbers of young people in many parts of the world put pressure on HEIs to include human and social development in their teaching and extension functions. In this changing and complex context, HE is challenged to rearticulate its future relevance to society. The introductory paper of this volume very clearly and comprehensively outlines the contours of this challenge. In responding to such challenges, HEIs need to explore new forms of civil engagement. This paper attempts to address this question in some depth. It argues that human and social development should be addressed in a democratic framework and suggests that civil society, in its myriad manifestations, could become an active partner of HEIs. It then identifies ways in which HE and HEIs could explore the possibility of engaging with civil society in order to broaden and deepen their contributions to human and social development.

DEMOCRATIC SHIFTS

In various regions of the world, access to and coverage of HE has historically been limited. In India, a few elite social and economic classes had the privilege of access to HE. This historical Brahmanical[1] order legitimated the notion of stratification in human development. It was assumed, until as recently as the turn of the 20th century, that certain higher class and caste groups would inherit governing responsibilities; hence, members of such elite groups were expected to be adequately prepared for this function intellectually. Thus, through their teaching function, HEIs catered to the preparation of the ruling elites.

Over the past century, and more significantly in the 21st century, the above assumptions about the teaching and research functions of HE have been systematically challenged. Democratic political systems began to gain currency in many countries of the world, especially after liberation from colonial regimes. Ruling elites based on aristocracy, landed property or Brahmanical privilege were gradually replaced by 'mass' leaders elected on the basis of universal franchise. A new class of political leaders emerged. In many developing countries, many of these leaders did not have access to even secondary education. The role of HEIs in the intellectual preparation of these new political elites became somewhat uncertain.

Post-colonial governments opened up new possibilities of support for HEIs. Public funding of HE became more common in many post-colonial countries. Gradually, private support (largely from rulers, kings and chieftains) declined and HEIs (especially universities) became publicly funded institutions. In countries where national public resources were scarce and multiple development agendas were competing for them, public funds for HE remained limited. In some countries, like India, earlier allocations of public funds for HE were reasonably high, even in relation to allocations for primary and secondary education. By the mid 20th century, the changing nature of HE created new partnerships between states and HEIs. In many countries, HE was only available in publicly funded (governmental) universities and institutes. Political decision-makers (not necessarily with academic credentials) became the new kingmakers of 'deans' and 'vice-chancellors'.

During this period, the universalization of primary and secondary education as state policy in many countries increased the demand for greater access to HE among the masses. Many more HEIs came into being as demand increased rapidly due to both the popular aspirations of the masses and the requirements of the labour pool. With a growing economy – changing in nature from agriculture to industry and services – the labour factor changed dramatically. Employment conditions in the marketplace came to require a much higher degree of HE training. Liberal democratic aspirations for education further fuelled the demand for HE in many societies. As a result, HEIs developed new partnerships with the private sector. By the end of the 20th century, privately funded HEIs began to increase in number in many countries.

This trend towards privately funded HE further increased due to two associated phenomena. First, many national governments began to reduce their budgetary allocations for HEIs as their public resources became subjected to more egalitarian allocations in the welfare state framework. Somehow, many policymakers began to construe HE as a 'privately affordable' good. Second, the forces of globalization began to transnationalize economies and labour supplies. Migration of skilled labour, within and across countries, grew rapidly in the past decade. More service-sector and knowledge-based economies generated – and continue to generate – enormous demands for more varied and open access to HE by a growing number of young people. Demographic realities began to shift this demand for HE into the younger populations of Africa and Asia, as the European populations stabilized.

The partnership between HEIs and state institutions also included government funding and sponsorship of research. As new forms of collaboration with the private sector became more widespread, private funding of research also increased. This was particularly so in disciplines where new processes, inventions and products could be commercially exploited through patenting. Thus, in many southern countries, declining public funding for HE also affected research capabilities and outputs. Private funding did not come into the social and human disciplines with the same volume and speed as it did in the natural sciences, engineering, biotechnology, information technology and management. Thus, the quality of research on issues of human and social development at HEIs in such countries had declined substantially by the turn of the 21st century.

Due to growing democratic aspirations, the demand for 'massification' of the HE supply has increased significantly. Old, established 'Ivy League' types of HEIs (which exist in all societies) now face increasing competition from new, privately funded, career-oriented HEIs. Teaching and research on social and human development issues has therefore begun to shrink in many developing countries.

Thus, the reality of today's HEIs presents a somewhat blurred and confusing picture, when viewed from the perspective of social and human development. HE is largely viewed as a 'private good' linked to the forces of economic development. HEIs have built systems and mechanisms for engaging with governments and public authorities; they have also created linkages, interactions and partnerships with the for-profit private sector in both teaching and research functions. Nevertheless, the interactions of HEIs with civil society have been somewhat undeveloped and inadequately conceptualized. Thus, civil engagement in HE may be particularly relevant from the perspective of human and social development in the 21st century.

HUMAN DEVELOPMENT

The quest to improve life has been an ongoing human enterprise. Discourse on human and social development gained currency among policymakers and political leaders after the Second World War. The dominant human development agenda in these past few decades has focused on economic growth and associated improvements in the standard of living, as largely manifested by per capita GNP. The meaning of human and social development, however, has gradually evolved over the past three or four decades. The discourse on 'basic needs' was initiated by the International Labour Organization in the late 1960s. These needs – characterized as food, health, water, shelter and housing – became one of the early benchmarks of 'good' human development. Even today, the fulfilment of basic needs continues to be a pressing concern for nearly one billion people around the world, despite the considerable and remarkable progress that has been made. In a recent study on the conditions for a good society, conducted in 45 Commonwealth countries, citizens universally asked for the fulfilment of basic needs (Knight et al., 2002).

During the 1980s and 90s, human and social development issues became further refined. Issues of gender justice gained widespread recognition in policy circles. Environmental issues gained visibility after the UN Rio Conference in 1992, although its climate change agenda has yet to be adequately grasped by the G8 leaders. The rights of children, indigenous communities and socially excluded minorities were brought to the forefront of policymaking in the past two decades. The 'development as a human right' perspective brought new energy to the Universal Declaration of Human Rights (adopted in 1948). As democratic political processes have gained wider acceptance in most societies, new democratic aspirations – equality, justice, participation and so on – have gained ascendancy in many societies. The recent discourse on democratic governance, with its emphasis on transparency and accountability in the public sphere, has opened up another important aspect of human and social development in the 21st century. Citizenship and democratic governance are the twin pillars of human and social development; they address the phenomenon of human actualization from the demand side (participatory citizenship) while also focusing on democratic governance from the demand side of development (Tandon and Mohanty, 2002).

Thus, the key points on the human and social development agenda for the coming century are the following:

- *Inclusive globalization*
  It has been widely acknowledged that the forces of globalization have benefited some and victimized others. Growing inequalities within and across societies have generated resistance to and protest against globalization. Human and social development require new, more inclusive ways of harnessing globalization.
- *Sustainability and climate change*
  Widespread exploitation of natural resources has resulted in ecological changes which may be unsustainable, irreversible and damaging to human life. This challenge requires new approaches, technologies and lifestyles.
- *Peace and global citizenship*
  The world today is insecure. Various forms of terrorism are affecting life, livelihood and development. Global forces of violence require new solutions for peace and global citizenship based on mutual respect and shared responsibility.
- *Human rights and social inclusion*
  Despite various compacts on human rights and the rights of women, minorities, children and indigenous people, large-scale violation of basic human rights continues around the world. Unless vast sections of the world's population, hitherto excluded, receive their entitlements, they will remain unaffected by mainstream human and social development.
- *Democratizing governance*
  Despite the rise of democracy as a political form in many countries, systems of governance at local, national, regional and global levels continue to face enormous democratic deficits. New processes, forms and institutions need to be developed to address these deficits urgently.

ROLES OF CIVIL SOCIETY

It may therefore be pertinent to ask the following questions: Where has HE been in the discourse on human and social development for the past five or six decades? What roles have HEIs played in the emerging fields of human and social development?

A critical review of the processes shaping the human development agendas would suggest that HEIs have been mostly followers of this discourse, rather than its creators or champions. Of course, many individual scholars have contributed immensely to shaping these issues; their contributions must be acknowledged. Nevertheless, in national and transnational debates on these issues, the new player has been *civil* society. Citizen groups, associations, NGOs, not-for-profit research institutes and independent think tanks (as civil society actors) have been most active in identifying, analysing and articulating these issues of equity, justice, inclusion and rights. Through studies, campaigns, grassroots mobilizations and structured policy dialogues, these civil society entities and their national/global coalitions have been the most significant and central actors in ensuring that these issues of human development become part of national and global policymaking (Edwards and Gaventa, 2001).

Some HEIs have responded to these opportunities by opening new centres for the study of gender, the environment and so on. Some HEIs have started teaching these subjects in undergraduate and graduate-level courses. Some have systematically begun to conduct research on these emerging issues of human development. By and large, however, HEIs around the world have not been able to engage adequately with these central concerns of human and social development. The critical question, therefore, is: Why is this so? Why have HEIs not been at the forefront of new priorities and concerns in the human and social development of tomorrow?

Historical analysis and available experience suggest several reasons for this disconnect between HEIs and contemporary issues of human and social development. First, these issues (such as gender justice and environmental sustainability) emerged from specific social mobilizations and actions aimed at improving the conditions of the exploited and the marginalized. As this social activism progressed, hitherto hidden and suppressed human realities began to surface. The growing presence of independent media in many countries gave wider publicity to these issues, thereby bringing them to the attention of policymakers and ruling elites. For example, the reality of domestic violence against women could only be expressed in a way that challenged accepted tenets of knowledge. Likewise, the practices of local elders in water harvesting and forest protection could only be communicated with reference to indigenous knowledge frameworks. Thus, popular knowledge – indigenous knowledge – generated through the practices of countless generations became the basis for articulating these new issues. As explained by the participatory research movement, this knowledge faced negation and rejection from the dominant modes of knowledge production valued by most HEIs. The *epistemological conflict* underlying these various traditions of knowledge production, dissemination and utilization became one of the main reasons for the disconnect between HEIs and issues of human development (Tandon, 2002a).

Second, in most of the world, civil society's champi-

oning of these issues distanced it from HEIs. Historical antagonism and apathy between grassroots organizers, citizen leaders and social activists on the one hand and HEIs on the other led to a situation of disconnect. As Brown (2001) has argued, this disconnect between the world of research and the world of practice has many different roots in different regions of the world:

> Practitioners and researchers at first blush march to very different drums. Stereotypical practitioners are action-oriented, focused on immediate and concrete problems, and concerned with having direct impacts on those problems. Stereotypical researchers are theory-oriented, focused on long-term conceptual issues, and concerned with producing knowledge and conceptual results. Practitioners are embedded in institutional contexts that press them to solve practical problems; researchers work in institutional contexts that reward contributions to theory or knowledge. These differences set the stage for misunderstanding and poor communications at the practice–research boundary, even when the participants share many concerns and values.

How can the various roles of HEIs be performed through new forms of civil engagement in pursuit of the emerging human and social development agenda?

Before addressing this question, it may be worthwhile to describe what civil society means in the contemporary context. Civic associations, community-based groups and local socio-cultural organizations have existed in all societies throughout human history. Many have been based on a culture of mutual help and collective responsibility. Furthermore, all religious and spiritual traditions have called upon their followers to make philanthropic contributions for the well-being of fellow citizens and society at large. With the emergence of welfare states and the rise of the private sector in the past century, this civic phenomenon has gradually become invisible.

The reappearance of civic associations in developing countries began to be noticed in the 1970s as development issues and models began to be articulated by non-governmental organizations (NGOs). In developed countries, failures of government and excesses of the private sector gave rise to activities such as social economy and housing, on the one hand, and consumers and environmental associations, on the other. By the late 1980s, after the fall of the Berlin Wall, 'civil society' emerged as a new actor in discourse and policy circles, both in the developing countries of the South and in the developed countries of the North.

Numerous definitions of and arguments about civil

society have emerged in the past two decades. The concept of *trinity* – state, market and civil society – is useful to understanding institutional arrangements in society (Tandon, 2002b). Most societal functions and activities could be classified as predominantly emanating from, and largely based on, the state sector (from local to national governments); market institutions (the economic functions of production and consumption, organized in various ways); or civil society (arts, culture, sports, leisure, religion, welfare, civic action and so on). All individual and collective initiatives for the common public good can be considered part of civil society. Thus, welfare, service, care and mutual-help activities are included in this sector. Early conceptualizations included academia and media as part of civil society, as well (De Oliveira and Tandon, 1994). This conceptualization recognizes that education – including higher education – is a public good.

Today, millions of civil associations are active in societies around the world, addressing the entire range of issues related to human and social development. They provide welfare and charity, supply services, undertake independent research, build coalitions to address issues and make demands, and partner with governments and the private sector to develop specific solutions. They operate at the very local village/neighbourhood level and also at the transnational/global level. Salamon (1994) calls this the 'global associational resolution' and analyses the economic contributions of civil associations around the world. This phenomenon of civil action by civil associations is a new reality of human and social development in the 21st century.

ROLES OF HE

It is generally acknowledged that HE performs three sets of roles: teaching, research and extension. In the context of human and social development, the most frequently discussed role is that of extension. HEIs extend their knowledge and expertise to the communities around them, with the objective of helping these communities. While community extension (or extramural) activities of some type are prevalent in most HEIs around the world, this practice is most widespread in North American HEIs, where community-service learning programmes place students in a community (or company) to work there for a fixed period. Many students who participate in such programmes find them useful in advancing their education and careers.

Boothroyd and Fryer (2004) present a somewhat mixed picture of the popularity of these programmes in North American universities over the past two decades:

> These efforts did little to link regular curricula and research programmes with social issues. Few could conceive of education for a university degree as including learning from and with people without degrees, or of advanced research as including average citizens and officials in formulating research questions, let alone in the devising of methods and the analysis of results. Much of the professorial activism at that time was in the form of their lending to political movements their superior knowledge and intellectual credence – a kind of intellectual noblesse oblige.

Despite its growing popularity, community service has largely remained the third leg of HE, and remains overshadowed by the two core functions of teaching and research.

Despite the limited popularity of service-learning programmes at HEIs in developing countries, some large-scale examples of engagement between HEIs and civil society actors have begun to emerge in these regions of the world. The following two examples from developing regions of Asia and Africa illustrate how civil engagement can help link the teaching and research functions of HE to the advancement of the human and social development agendas.

Box I.7.1 Service-learning in ancient times

Learning from the community, and in turn contributing to it, has also been practised elsewhere. Interestingly enough, community service was the mission of some of the first universities of human civilization. Taxila, the oldest known university, functioned from the 7th century BC to the 8th century AD in what is now Pakistan. At its peak, Taxila – whose name means 'rock of reflection' – had 1,800 scholars and nearly 8,000 students in residence. The leitmotif of this university was 'service to humanity'. Its scholars and students came from Arabian, Persian and Mediterranean societies. It produced pioneering scholarship in such fields as grammar (credited to Panini), economics (pioneered by Kautilya) and medicine (Charaka was Taxila's first and most famous physician).

A later contemporary of Taxila was Nalanda University, which functioned from the 5th century BC to the 11th century AD in the eastern sub-Himalayan region of India. At its zenith, Nalanda – whose name means 'lotus of learning' – had 2,000 professors and 10,000 students. Its professors and students came from such distant places as China, Mongolia, Siam, Sumatra and Japan. Students at Nalanda University had to be sponsored by a community, with the promise of returning there to serve. It made great innovations in the fields of mathematics (the concept of zero was invented there), astronomy and metallurgy. Its most famous teacher was Buddha himself.

REVITALIZING SOCIAL WORK EDUCATION IN INDIA

From 1995 to 1999, the Society for Participatory Research in Asia (PRIA), in collaboration with the Association of Schools of Social Work in India (ASSWI), was involved in a unique development intervention with Indian social work educators. This initiative was significant in that it trained social work professionals, who comprise the potential human resource base for NGOs, government agencies and the corporate sector. More than 70 schools of social work formed part of this process, creating a sizable impact at the national level. The intervention widened its outreach by working in close collaboration with regional associations of social work educators, thus making the impact more sustainable.

The intervention included a series of interprofessional dialogues at the national and regional levels. The dialogues provided opportunities for social work educators, renowned academics and experienced practitioners of participatory development (PD) and participatory research (PR) to agree on a common platform. The dialogues examined the status of social work education, assessed the implications of PD and PR in social work education and practice, and promoted efforts to incorporate PD and PR in the social work curriculum. The dialogues were designed to be interdisciplinary, with practitioners and educators sharing and learning from each other's experience.

As part of this initiative, a fund for research on participation was created by PRIA in order to encourage faculty and students at schools of social work and other institutes to conduct field research on community participation issues.

Building on the lessons of this five-year collaboration initiative, PRIA and ASSWI initiated a new phase in 2000 in order to strengthen research and teaching on participation, democratic governance and citizenship. This intervention was intended to address the growing need for greater and more concentrated efforts to strengthen social change initiatives and the insufficient supply of trained professionals to contribute to them.

To effectively plan and implement this intervention, PRIA and ASSWI developed a strategy to strengthen five social work education institutions as regional nodal centres (RNCs). The RNCs were envisioned as becoming centres of excellence in the field of participation, democratic governance and citizenship, and offering specialized courses on civil society and citizen participation at the bachelor's, master's, M.Phil. and Ph.D. levels. In order to promote the study of participation, citizenship and governance, the libraries of these short-listed institutions were provided with many field-based documents and other knowledge resources.

PRIA's ongoing efforts to influence social science research and teaching were streamlined in the form of a programme called 'Strengthening Linkages with Academia'. These interventions now include many different disciplines of social science. The programme aims to influence the nature of academic pursuit in Indian universities, particularly in the social sciences, in order to make them:

- open to knowledge coming from the field
- adopt new research methodologies
- engage in research on contemporary issues that have the potential to influence both policy and development practice
- impart new insights to students through teaching.

What are the larger implications of this experiment in India? From a global perspective, it appears that, in many practitioner-oriented disciplines such as social work, professional education can be made more relevant and practical through creative partnerships with civil society organizations. Through civil engagement, the teaching of professionals may become organically linked to the realities in which they would function. In addition, such partnerships can enhance the HEIs' contribution to the production of socially useful and practical knowledge. A partnership of this variety can therefore mutually benefit both the HEI and its civil society partner organization.

MULTIVERSITY FOR INDIGENOUS KNOWLEDGE IN UGANDA

This second example involves an innovative research and teaching initiative in a contemporary scenario in East Africa.

The concept of Mpambo Multiversity is an outgrowth of debates and deliberations among hundreds of African scholars, social leaders and activists dedicated to the cause of building a better Africa.

The 'multiversity' concept is the antithesis of the concept of 'university'. *Uni* means one and *versity* comes from *versal*, meaning all. In other words, universities promote the prevalence of one form of knowledge everywhere. Universities promote the belief that this universal (and primarily Western) knowledge is closer to the truth than any other form of knowledge. The 'multiversity' concept challenges this understanding of knowledge by asserting the existence of 'a multiplicity of knowledges concomitant with communities, their ecology, history, language and culture' (Wangoola, 2007). It emphasizes a paradigm in which knowledge systems are seen as horizontal rather than vertical. All knowledge systems, whether indigenous African, Chinese, Indian or Western, are assigned equal relevance, space and identity in the global knowledge pool. None are seen as superior or inferior.

'Multiversity' is a space to affirm, promote, advocate and advance the multiplicity of thought and knowledges as a necessity to vitalize the world's knowledges, as well as human knowledge as a whole. It is a concrete valorization, celebration, application and popularization of pluralism at the intellectual level, and at the level of thought and knowledge. (www.blackherbals.com/Mpambo_the_African_Multiversity.htm)

In the context of Africa, this means focusing on the development of African indigenous knowledge, which was subverted through years of colonial rule.

In this endeavour, Mpambo adopts an integrated approach to promoting the development of indigenous scholars, knowledge and teaching. It does so by:

- promoting mother-tongue scholars
- providing mother-tongue higher education to help the younger generation develop a sense of respect and learn from indigenous knowledge
- collecting and documenting indigenous knowledge, thereby giving it a high level of quality and sophistication.

By providing a space for people to explore the dimensions of their own community's knowledge, Mpambo Multiversity facilitates their empowerment. This empowerment encourages a shift in the knowledge paradigm as people learn to use their own knowledge to chart their future, innovate on traditional knowledge in order to adapt to and counter the changes around them, and spearhead innovations for development.

By promoting the development of indigenous knowledge, Mpambo Multiversity seeks to bring about cognitive democracy in Africa and this helps to generate self-belief among its students and scholars and motivate the creation of indigenous social and human development paradigms that will help bring the African people out of their prevalent derelict socioeconomic conditions.

What lessons of global relevance can be drawn from Mpambo? Contestations between indigenous knowledge systems and the more modern 'scientific' enterprises are now becoming universal. The global ecological movement has reaffirmed the 'scientific' value of herbal medicines and traditional water-conservation techniques. Under the intellectual property rights regimes of the World Trade Organization (WTO), commercial patenting of such indigenous knowledge is moving ahead at a rapid pace. Gallopin and Vessuri (2006) have analysed, in some detail, the phenomenon of multiple knowledge systems in the context of sustainable development. Ironically, some HEIs are now using their research expertise to facilitate the 'privatization' of knowledge they once criticized

for being 'unscientific'. In a world of global trade and economics, private control over indigenous knowledge, through scientific enterprise, increases the importance of restoring and reviving the scholarship of indigenous knowledge. This further illustrates the possibilities of linking the research function of HE to such local practices, networks and associations within society. This form of civil engagement can broaden the contributions of HE to human and social development in areas such as multiculturalism, sustainability and inclusion.

What lessons of global relevance can be drawn from the above experiments in linking HE to the social and human development agenda? Given the largely positive outcomes of promoting civil engagement with HEIs in these examples, we should ask ourselves: Why aren't such civil engagements by HEIs common around the world? Why has innovation not been more widespread, given the challenges facing human and social development today? In examining these questions and possibilities, including the experiments in Community Service-Learning, several issues become critical. The first issue relates to the meanings and visions of knowledge, as well as its production and dissemination. Collaboration between HEIs and civil society flourishes where respect for different forms of knowledge and varied epistemological frameworks is manifest. Acknowledgement of indigenous knowledge systems and their contemporary relevance helps to build bridges across traditional divides. Boothroyd and Fryer (2004) describe the reasons for the relative success of certain experiments, such as the Learning Exchange:

The Learning Exchange is built on the premise that many different kinds of knowledge have value and legitimacy and they all need to be incorporated into attempts to resolve social problems or implement effective development strategies. The Learning Exchange tries not to privilege academic knowledge or scientific knowledge over knowledge developed through experience or wisdom gained through the navigation of difficult life situations. This perspective is at odds with the views of many, perhaps most, in the academy.

In general, HEIs and their academic culture hinder efforts to co-construct knowledge with other civil actors in order to address emerging challenges to human and social development. Where such co-construction has been stimulated, positive outcomes for human and social development have been attained.

The second issue relates to the relative power and resource differentials between HEIs and civil actors. Various efforts by HEIs towards genuine civil engagement falter due to the enormous power and resources that HEIs can bring to a partnership, in comparison with what civil actors can muster. Such power differentials contribute to the aforementioned difficulties experienced in the co-construction of knowledge for human and social development. In this respect, many HEIs need to develop innovative methods and structures that transcend these power differentials. A very interesting and recent example in this regard is the decision by the University of Victoria in Canada to make community-based participatory research (CBPR) one of its core competencies. The University has set up a CBPR office to act as a focal point for promoting such civil engagement in both the Canadian and international arenas. It has brought community leaders and academics together in decision-making structures to overcome these power differentials.

The third issue relates the different approaches to applying research to address specific local human and social development problems. A common issue faced in civil engagements by HEIs is the manner in which research questions are framed. Some HEIs have successfully contributed to actual solutions to real problems that communities face by devising a joint problem-framing and analysis process in which university experts and local residents work together to design the research process. The 'science shop' movement in continental Europe (the Living Knowledge Network) reflects some of these practices; this is especially remarkable in that many experts in these science shops are natural scientists whose general predisposition is to 'avoid any contamination' from the real world when conducting their research. Physicists, chemists, metallurgists, biologists and so on, have created outlets to jointly identify, with the community, practical problems faced in the particular locality; these outlets then bring research expertise from the HEIs and collaborate with civil actors in the community to carry out research on these practical problems.

Thus, HEIs can promote and encourage co-construction of knowledge and joint teaching of students through various approaches to civil engagement. The examples mentioned above suggest a variety of ways in which practical arrangements for civil engagement have been made by some HEIs. In the final analysis, the overarching purpose of such civil engagement is to deepen the contributions of HEIs to human and social development through the research and teaching functions of HE.

NEW FORMS OF CIVIL ENGAGEMENT

What potential new forms of civil engagement can HEIs pursue in order to deepen and widen their contributions to the future agenda of human and social development? This question can only be answered in a specific historical and political context; however, an analysis of the aforementioned examples suggests broader contours of civil engagement possibilities. The future agenda for human and social development is so vast and challenging that no social actor – be it the government, the private sector, HEIs or civil society – can address them alone. The potential for advancing this human and social development agenda increases if these actors work together to develop new ways of collaborating.

The three functions of HEI have traditionally been defined as teaching, research and extension. We need to redefine them as *education*, *knowledge* and *service*. 'Teaching' establishes the centrality of teaching and the teacher, whereas 'education' argues for the centrality of learning and the learner. Viewed in this perspective, *education* in contemporary society should be *lifelong*. HEIs in most societies need to redesign themselves to support the lifelong education of a growing number of people. In this mode, HEIs can contribute to the learning of citizens, practitioners, officials and future researchers in many different ways. Distance- and open-learning approaches can complement classroom instruction; HEIs can reach learners where they are, rather than the other way around. The contents of lifelong learning, however, cannot be based on disciplines alone; they must address the practical needs and aspirations of learners. This opens up a huge possibility for civil engagement. HEIs can partner with civil actors, community elders and practitioners to design appropriate learning curricula and facilitate such educational processes.

In another form of partnership in the teaching function, HEIs could invite civil society inside the institution. This invitation could include experienced practitioners acting as professors and teachers. In doing so, practical expertise and emerging developmental trends could be made available to students and faculty alike. The University of Victoria Faculty of Education, for example, regularly invites elders from first-nation communities to teach courses on marine ecology. In the examples presented above, similar arrangements with local practitioners and indigenous experts were effectively marshalled. Co-teaching with practitioners can help to systematize the practical insights of human and social development as new theories emerge that may have much wider applications in other societal settings. Such arrangements could also help energize and inspire students to explore their own professional contributions to human and social development.

HEIs have enormous intellectual and infrastructural resources to support increasing educational demands and aspirations. Civil engagements by HEIs would enable them to respond to such demands and aspirations in a more relevant, ongoing and effective manner.

Thus, various forms of civil engagement related to the teaching function of HEIs can contribute to human and social development.

The second main function of HEIs is research. If this function were redefined to focus on *knowledge*, then several new possibilities of knowledge production, knowledge mobilization and knowledge dissemination could be explored.

The knowledge production and mobilization function of HEIs can make immense contributions to the future agenda of creating incentives and enabling systems for students and professors to engage in socially relevant research. Civil engagement by HEIs in the promotion of knowledge production and mobilization can take several forms. HEIs can acknowledge the multiplicity of knowledge traditions and create spaces and opportunities for practitioners (from government, community and civil society) to engage with scholars in HEIs in the *co-production of knowledge*. Research problems and questions can be framed by scholars from HEIs in consultation with the community. This may help to identify a research agenda with greater societal relevance from the perspective of human and social development. By enabling scholars from HEIs to embed themselves in community problems, the Living Knowledge Network (www.livingknowledge.org) has attempted just this through its 'science shop' movement in Europe.

Joint research projects with civil society actors are another form of civil engagement in the knowledge production and mobilization function of HEIs. Scholars from HEIs and civil actors (trade unions, cooperatives, community-based organizations, NGOs, issue-based social organizations and so on) apply for joint research funding. In so doing, HEIs identify mutual responsibilities in advance; the sharing of tasks and resources is mutually negotiated at the start of the research project. Such an approach to designing research projects also helps to clarify, in advance, the manner in which research findings will be disseminated to multiple constituencies and utilized to advance the shared agendas of scholars and civil actors. In this regard, the Canadian Social Science and Humanities Research Council has a very innovative programme for funding joint research projects that has been active for more than a decade. Community University Research Alliance (CURA) funds are only available for research projects that involve both an HEI and a civil actor. Such research funding mechanisms can provide incentives for planned, long-term and enduring civil engagement by HEIs.

Partnership between HEIs and social movements and campaigns by civil actors can also be built around an ongoing need for knowledge production and mobilization. For example, the Global Call to Action against Poverty (GCAP) is presently operating in several countries around the world. It focuses on the challenge of achieving the UN Millennium Development Goals (MDGs) in all countries of the world by 2015. The GCAP therefore seeks to generate a concrete, empirical analysis of the achievement status of each MDG in each developing country, and an understanding of the causes and constraints that impede progress. In some countries, certain academics have begun to engage with the GCAP knowledge requirements. It is worthwhile to explore how HEIs can form institutional partnerships to advance the GCAP agenda globally.

Such partnerships with specific civil coalitions of campaigns or movements can be built over the medium or long term. Each coalition has a clear knowledge agenda to which HEIs can make enormous contributions. The intellectual resources of HEIs can thus be systematically mobilized towards the co-construction of knowledge for specific agendas of human and social development.

The third function of HEIs – *community service* – has already seen many innovative forms of civil engagement around the world. How can the human and social development agenda be advanced through new forms of civil engagement by HEIs? Traditional community service or extension modes of HEIs have been practised through the temporary placement of students in a local community. As has been argued elsewhere, such placements contribute more to the students' learning than to the service to community. In new forms of civil engagement towards human and social development, HEIs can explore the placement of students and scholars in national and global communities. HEI scholars and students are typically seconded or interned in various government institutions and private companies. But such placements and secondments – from a community service perspective – are rarely made towards civil actors.

One particularly exciting possibility to explore is secondment through civil engagement with new alternatives. Many experiments towards sustainable alternatives – products, services, institutions and lifestyles – are being carried out throughout the world. 'Another World is Possible' is the slogan of the World Social Forum, which has been engaged in the mobilization of such alternative visions and models over the past seven years. National, regional and global forums convened under the banner of the World Social Forum are now incubators of such alternatives. HEIs could develop partnerships with such forums, with a view to seconding their scholars and students to learn from, and contribute to, the emergence of sustainable alternatives.

Thus, HEIs can systematically explore new ways and forms of civil engagement in each of their core functions of teaching, research and extension. In so doing, their primary goal is to enhance their contributions to the future agenda of human and social development, as explained above. As Peter Taylor argues in the Introduction to this volume, HEIs have an enormous responsibility, and huge potential, for understanding this world. This social responsibility of HEIs can be more fruitfully fulfilled through meaningful and innovative forms of civil engagement.

FUTURE CHALLENGES

In light of the foregoing discussion, HEIs need to examine critically their missions in relation to contributing to the human and social development of communities in their vicinity and around the world. As the demand for human actualization increases in this century, and as a larger proportion of the population enters HEIs, society will have greater expectations for such contributions. The research and teaching functions of HEIs will have to serve this larger mission of ever-evolving human and social development. This sets up a series of strategic and practical challenges that HEIs must address in their own unique and specific manner.

1. The foremost strategic challenge that HEIs must address is the acknowledgement of other sources of contemporary and advanced knowledge on human and social development. HEIs have operated in isolation within the four walls of laboratories and academe without understanding how new forms of knowledge for human and social development were evolving. Such new knowledge emerged from the world of practice. This is particularly so for social movements, civil society coalitions and think-tanks that have focused on various aspects of human and social development. Such an acknowledgement by HEIs should be accompanied by the acceptance of alternative sources of knowledge and modes of knowledge production. The exploration of such alternative epistemologies in fact deepens contemporary challenges facing human and social development. In this acknowledgement lies the possibility of HEIs exploring new partnerships with social movements and civil society coalitions.

2. In order for such opportunities for partnerships to be made effective, many aspects of HEIs' current systems and approaches may have to be altered. There has been considerable debate in many academic cir-

cles about the non-acceptance of action-oriented participatory research as a valid methodology of knowledge production. Refereed journals and respectable academic publications do not readily provide space for the publication of such research materials, which have not gained 'scholarly respectability' in most HEIs. The University of Victoria's bold attempt to open an office of community-based participatory research as an integral part of the university's commitment is a rare exception. However, the system of scholarly recognition through publication and participation in conferences needs to be reformed in order to encourage knowledge contributions to arise out of civil engagements.

3. Other incentive systems within HEIs may also need to be adapted and modified for such partnerships to become effective. The teaching function of HEIs could be adapted to compulsorily include field practice, secondment and immersion programmes. These may be linked to local civic initiatives or movements so that students and their teachers may learn about the issues of social and human development while contributing to solving those problems. Academic rewards and research/teaching grants may need to be linked to such partnerships in order to encourage participation.

4. Finally, HEIs may need to re-examine the values associated with the social positioning of their institutions. What are the larger values that HEIs serve in society? Beyond training intellectuals and contributing knowledge, what added value do they bring to deepening democracy in societies? How can they become incubators of more empowered citizenship? What values do HEIs promote in carrying out their teaching and knowledge functions? How do these values become the reference point for new aspirations in human and social development? How can HEIs champion the larger agenda of human and social development in the 21st century?

These and many other questions need to be posed in this discourse. The possibilities and requirements for civil engagement by HEIs are huge and growing. Future human and social development agendas may be better elaborated if civil engagement by HEIs is globally encouraged.

In this perspective, HE must be viewed as a public good. Its provisions and institutions must be supported in the public spheres. Its leadership must articulate the future vision of HE in the context of the demand for deepening democracy and preparation for global citizenship in the contemporary world. In so doing, HEIs can reassert their contributions to emerging human and social development agendas through creative forms of civil engagement at the local and global levels.

NOTE

1   Brahmins are the highest priestly caste in India. They alone could study the Sanskrit language and scriptures. They were considered the intellectuals of society.

BIBLIOGRAPHY

Boothroyd, Peter and Fryer, Margo (2004) *Mainstreaming Social Engagement in Higher Education: Benefits, Challenges and Successes*, Paper presented in: Colloquium on Research and Higher Education Policy: 'Knowledge, Access and Governance: Strategies for Change'. Paris: UNESCO, 1–3 December.

Brown, L. David (ed.) (2001) *Practice–Research Engagement and Civil Society in a Globalizing World*. Cambridge, MA: Hauser Center for Nonprofit Organizations and CIVICUS, World Alliance for Citizen Participation.

De Oliveira, Miguel Darcy and Tandon, Rajesh (1994) *Citizens: Strengthening Global Civil Society*. Washington, DC: CIVICUS: World Alliance for Citizen Participation.

Edwards, Michael (2004) *Civil Society*. Cambridge, UK: Polity Press and Blackwell Publishing.

Edwards, Michael and Gaventa, John (2001) *Global Citizen Action*. Boulder, CO, USA: Lynne Reiner Publishers.

Gallopin, Gilberto and Vessuri, Hebe (2006) *Interfaces between Science and Society*. Sheffield, UK: Greenleaf Publishing.

Knight, Barry, Chigudu, Hope and Tandon, Rajesh (2002) *Reviving Democracy: Citizens at the Heart of Governance*. London, UK: Earthscan Publications.

Salamon, Lester, M. (1994). The rise of the nonprofit sector, *Foreign Affairs,* **74**(3).

Tandon, Rajesh and Mohanty, Ranjita, (2002) *Civil Society and Governance*. New Delhi: Samskriti.

Tandon, Rajesh (ed.) (2002a) *Participatory Research: Revisiting the Roots*. New Delhi: Mosaic Books.

Tandon, Rajesh (ed.) (2002b): *Voluntary Action, Civil Society and the State*. New Delhi: Mosaic Books.

Wangoola, Paulo (2007) *Learning, Culture, Language, Knowledge Production and Citizen Participation*, Paper presented at PRIA's 25th Anniversary Celebration in New Delhi, India.

SPECIAL CONTRIBUTION I.16
Practice–research engagement for human and social development in a globalizing world

L. David Brown

Universities are potentially central institutions for catalysing human and social development, especially in the knowledge-based societies that are increasingly becoming the norm around the globe. Whether universities will fulfil that potential, however, depends on how they respond to the challenges posed by certain complex and intransigent problems that do not easily yield to most current university structures and cultures (Didriksson and Herrera, 2007).

Enabling human and social development to a large extent depends on strengthening the links between university research and teaching and the problems of policy and practice. Practice–research engagement (PRE) potentially fosters improved knowledge and theory and, at the same time, catalyses innovations in policy and practice (Brown et al., 2003). However, engagement can also reinforce negative stereotypes that contribute to a continuing gulf between 'abstract theory' and 'concrete practice' that undermines university contributions to human and social development (Stokes, 1997).

In a world in which technology and communications are making it ever easier to share information and recognize interdependencies across the globe, the development and dissemination of knowledge is increasingly central to human and social development. These same factors increase the likelihood that people from very different backgrounds will become aware of their differences and their interdependencies. Citizens in developing countries, for example, will recognize that they are paying a disproportionate share of the costs of global warming, which is caused largely by the behaviour of citizens in affluent countries. Globalization is increasing international interdependence; it can also increase social learning – which creates new social perspectives and capacities based on this engagement – or social conflict, which potentially produces negative outcomes. Both social learning and social conflict can affect human and social development.

The next section identifies some emerging patterns in the relations of universities with human and social development. The following section identifies some promising developments that foster constructive engagements between researchers and practitioners. The last section suggests possibilities for the future roles of higher education institutions in promoting human and social development.

EMERGING PATTERNS AND PRE

Four emerging patterns or trends are potentially important to the role of higher education institutions as centres and catalysts for PRE that contributes to human and social development.

One important trend is the impact of *globalization on social problems and problem-solving* across countries and regions, as well as across sectors and levels. The expansion and globalization of human activities have posed a range of

Box 1   Practice–research engagement

PRE includes a wide range of initiatives that bring together practitioners (policymakers, social activists, business leaders and so on) concerned with improving practice with the researchers who are concerned with producing knowledge, so that together they are able to learn about problems of mutual interest in ways that produce both new knowledge and innovations in practice.

new problems that are either novel or exacerbated by increased interdependence. These problems range from environmental issues like climate change, to epidemics like HIV/AIDS or avian flu, to the expansion of transnational crime and terrorism. The technical possibilities for communication and engagement between practitioners and researchers, between groups in the global south and the global north, and across a wide range of values and perspectives have also increased spectacularly. These engagements can lead to mutual insight and learning – but they can also lead to misunderstanding and conflict. In a world of enormous and expanding asymmetries in wealth and power, the latter often seems the more likely result. Thus, globalization produced possibilities for transnational PRE to improve human and social development – but it also posed a new threat to human and social development.

A second pattern is the *evolving stances of universities on solving problems of policy and practice*. A narrow construction of the role of universities argues that their contributions to human and social development emerge from educating students and carrying out research, and that engaging with other practical problems may undercut their ability to carry out these primary tasks. Recent assessments of knowledge production processes have argued that key decisions in many universities and academic disciplines are dominated by researchers who focus on problems defined by their disciplines rather than by the societies in which they are embedded (Gibbons et al., 1994; Nowotny et al., 2002). Therefore, universities with narrowly construed roles may place emphasis on 'academic' rather than 'practical' problems. Researchers may be encouraged to avoid complex problems of practice that require multiple disciplines and long-term engagement, like human trafficking or persistent poverty, in favour of problems defined in terms that are more easily managed by their academic disciplines.

A broader construction of the univer-

sity's role emphasizes its potential for contributing to social as well as theoretical problems, and the importance of accountability to practice as well as research constituencies. Some universities might make real contributions to solving problems like trafficking and poverty. Pressures to account to multiple stakeholders are particularly common in professional schools and other departments with close ties to practitioners and practice problems.

A third emerging pattern is the *increased demand for research that helps deal with practical problems*. Knowledge-based societies revolve around the production of knowledge for acting on existing or emerging problems. Such problems often require multiple disciplines to work together in conditions that make the controls and time horizons of more academically rigorous investigations impractical. Whilst university-based researchers have been uninterested in these problems, other agencies – research centres, think-tanks, consulting firms, corporate research and development departments – have emerged to respond to the demand for knowledge production. Such agencies can produce knowledge that is important to social problem-solving. However, they do so in response to clients and donors who have the resources to support their work. Thus, the question of whether or not these agencies respond to problems of human and social development will depend on who has an interest in solving these problems.

A fourth pattern relevant to PRE in the service of human and social development is the *emergence of mid-career and post-retirement populations interested in development*. In many countries, universities are finding that experienced students are interested in second careers that will allow them to contribute to human and social development in various ways. The notion of 'lifelong learning' and the possibilities of 'giving back' have gained currency in many societies. As more mid-career and healthy post-retirement students seek opportunities to have an impact on their societies, they present an

opportunity for higher education institutions to affect human and social development through their education and research activities.

PRE FOR HUMAN AND SOCIAL DEVELOPMENT: PROMISING DEVELOPMENTS

The possibilities for higher education's institutional impact on human and social development have benefited from a range of substantive, methodological and institutional innovations in recent years. The examples briefly described below are intended to illustrate a few of the possibilities for expanding practice–research engagements that foster constructive social impacts.

Some innovations focus on *innovations in academic substance and research methods* that enable more effective engagements between researchers and practitioners. The products of these initiatives make it more likely that universities can contribute directly to human and social development.

- *'Citizenship' as a substantive field*. A number of universities have begun to grapple with the nature of citizenship as an active member of a society and a polity. Tisch College of Citizenship and Public Service at Tufts University, for example, provides a range of student programmes, works with local communities, supports faculty research and teaching on citizenship, and works with interested alumni to build stronger communities (http://activecitizen.tufts. edu/). It has also initiated a consortium with 23 other universities interested in renewing the civic mission of higher education. The College seeks both to create knowledge about effective citizenship and to foster innovations in citizenship practice, so that the definition of the field encourages engagement among practitioners and researchers in its development.
- *Integration and implementation sciences as methodologies*. Faculty members at the Australian National University have launched a centre to

develop the theory and practice of integrating multiple disciplines for assessing and implementing solutions to complex social problems (http://www.anu.edu.au/iisn/). They conceive this emerging set of tools as analogous to statistics, which has developed tools and techniques applied across many fields. Principles and tools for integration and implementation are relevant to many disciplines and problems. The centre is now working with an international consortium of universities to develop the integration and implementation theories and methods, which can then be applied to a range of practical problems.

- *Dissemination of action research methods*. Action research methods, which seek to simultaneously create improved theories and innovations in practice over the past decade have become increasingly recognized and practised around the world. This increased interest has been reflected in the emergence of handbooks, such as Reason and Bradbury, 2001, and professional journals, such as the *Journal of Action Research*. These initiatives help to create concepts and tools for managing the complex challenges of knowledge production at the interface between theory and practice. They likewise reflect the growing numbers of researchers and practitioners who are struggling with these challenges.

While universities are notoriously slow to change on many issues, they often provide an institutional base from which individuals can launch innovative initiatives that can be developed and elaborated in interaction with practitioners or other universities. All three of these innovations in substance and methodology are expanding through the creation of networks that involve both practitioners and researchers.

Some innovations that support higher education institutions' contribution to human and social development are focused more on *organizational and programme changes* rather than on innovations in substantive areas or in methods

of research. These initiatives can reshape both the targets and impacts of university activities.

- *Educating mid- and post-career change agents*. Many universities have tailored programmes for adults who are in the middle or latter stages of their careers. Many of these students are interested in 'making the world a better place'. For example, programmes in 'social entrepreneurship' that help students interested in working on social problems have emerged at many universities in the past decade, including Oxford, Stanford, and Harvard. These programmes enable experienced leaders from many sectors to explore new social and human development initiatives. Such programmes can support mid-career and post-retirement leaders to contribute to development initiatives. They also serve to link researchers up with practitioners so that they are able to grapple with the problems and bottlenecks of development practices.
- *University–practitioner partnerships for development*. Universities may also extend their reach and their ability to do research by collaborating with other universities and key practitioners. Harvard's Hauser Center for Nonprofit Organizations, for example, works with university and civil society partners in developing countries to build executive education programmes for civil society leaders, which enable them to carry out research on topics critical to local development and to strengthen national capacities for future PRE. In Colombia, the partnership is developing research on community empowerment and conflict management and has created several civil society capacity building programmes. A similar programme in China is building a civil society leadership development programme and is exploring several joint research initiatives. The partnerships are intended to generate new knowledge, enhance civil society capacities, and strengthen

university capacities to contribute to human and social development.

- *Transnational PRE networks*. Some universities and support organizations have created transnational networks to build new knowledge and innovative practices across many countries. The Development Research Centre on Citizenship, Participation and Accountability, for example, carries out comparative research, creates innovations in practice, and fosters policy reform with members in Nigeria, South Africa, India, Bangladesh, Mexico, Brazil and the UK (http://www.drc-citizenship.org/). In its first five years of existence, the Centre carried out joint research initiatives on several themes and supported its members' initiatives in capacity building and policy reform. While the members of the network initially struggled to build relations of mutual influence and respect through their differences, they have learned a great deal from each other and are increasingly able to use network learning in their national activities.

These examples suggest that universities are able to facilitate PRE on matters related to human and social development. Training mid- and post-career change agents can make an impact on development in a short space of time because they are in a position to exercise new knowledge and skills quickly. University–practitioner development partnerships can integrate research and practice perspectives to create widely applicable theories and practice innovations. Transnational networks can bring the resources of multiple universities to bear in order to stimulate new perspectives on shared problems as well as connecting practitioners and researchers with diverse capacities.

PRE FOR DEVELOPMENT: IMPLICATIONS

What are the implications of these examples for higher education institutions that wish to foster human and social development? The thesis of this paper is that enhancing capacity for PRE on issues of human and social development is critical. There are at least five implications of the discussion so far:

1. *A broad view of the role of universities in human and social development must be advanced*. It is true that universities that focus primarily on educating students and generating academic knowledge will contribute to human and social development. However, university contributions can be substantially expanded if they engage in key development problems more directly, as exemplified by Tisch College's efforts to understand and have an effect on citizenship and civic problems. As societies become increasingly knowledge-based, we can expect that the value of universities' commitments to a broad interpretation of their social relevance will increase.

2. *The central role of PRE must be recognized*. For universities committed to a broad construction of their social roles, the capacity to foster effective practice–research engagements becomes increasingly central. Currently, most universities do more to encourage discipline-focused research than to facilitate research that advances practice or policy goals. The explicit recognition of the importance of engaging in practices can serve to set the stage for more institutional experiments like practitioner–researcher partnerships.

3. *Substantive and methodological innovations that enable PRE must be fostered*. The rise of new substantive and methodological concepts that enable active PRE may significantly enhance the contributions of higher education institutions to development. Research and teaching in the field of citizenship can encourage joint learning by citizens, policymakers and researchers. The integration and implementation of science will facilitate cooperation among researchers and practitioners and will require their joint insights to make advances in the field. PRE will benefit from existing tools, such as action research methods, and create further useful innovations.

4. *Organizational innovations that support or facilitate PRE must be encouraged*. Organizational arrangements within and between higher education institutions can facilitate productive PRE. Creating autonomous centres that focus on policy and practice problems will encourage the integration of research and practice perspectives. Mobilizing practice constituencies for research initiatives encourages the accountability of practices as well as of research disciplines. Partnerships with practitioner organizations can balance pressures from research and practice audiences. Alliances between universities can enable information sharing and provide support for the sub-units involved in PRE, which may be difficult to attain within a single university. Attention to fostering institutional support for PRE within and between universities may enable more effective initiatives.

5. *Global linkages to foster transnational learning and impact must be built*. The patterns and forces of globalization pose new problems and challenges, but they also open new opportunities. Alliances across national and regional boundaries can catalyse innovations in both theory and practice. As globalization reduces the cost of communication, increases the importance of transnational understanding, and produces new social problems, transnational networks for sharing information, creating knowledge, and disseminating innovations may become a pervasive feature of the university institutional landscape. The capacity to build and manage global linkages is likely to be a critical resource in future knowledge production and utilization initiatives.

More generally, this analysis suggests the importance of a broader discourse about the role of universities in social development. Should universities be catalysts for innovations in the theory and practice of human and social development in knowledge-based societies? If not universities, what institutions will take on knowledge production and dissemination roles? Wide debate and discourse about the nature of 'human and social development' as well as the social roles of universities and the importance of PRE will shape the knowledge production institutions of the new century (Phillips et al., 2004). Higher education institutions potentially have much to contribute to the global processes of human and social development, particularly if they can use their common commitments to knowledge-production to bridge the widening chasms of wealth and power that separate too much of the global human family.

REFERENCES

Brown, L.D., Bammer, G., Batliwala, S. and Kunreuther, F. (2003) Framing practice–research engagement for democratizing knowledge. *Action Research,* **1**(1), pp. 85–102.

Didriksson, A. and Herrera, A.X. (2007) Universities' new relevance and social responsibility. In: *Higher Education in the World 2007: Accreditation for Quality Assurance: What is at Stake?* GUNI. Basingstoke: Palgrave Macmillan, pp. xl–xlv.

Gibbons, M., Limoges, C., Schwartzmann, S., Trow, M., Scott, P. and Nowotny, H. (1994) *New Production of Knowledge: The Dynamics of Science and Research in Contemporary Societies*. London: Sage.

Nowotny, H., Scott, P. and Gibbons, M. (2002) *Rethinking Science: Knowledge and the Public*. Cambridge, UK: Polity Press.

Phillips, N., Lawrence, T.B. and Hardy, C. (2004) Discourse and institutions. *Academy of Management Review,* **29**(4), pp. 635–52.

Reason, P. and Bradbury, H. (eds) (2001) *Handbook of Action Research: Participative Inquiry and Practice*. London: Sage Publications.

Stokes, D.E. (1997) *Pasteur's Quadrant: Basic Science and Technological Innovation*. Washington, DC: Brookings Institution Press.

For almost a century, Latin American countries have tried to develop processes that link academic training at higher education level with service to society. Diverse initiatives have emerged in this area. For example, in Mexico, university-based civic service has been made a constitutional mandate. Recent initiatives have been inspired by the service–learning model introduced in some developed countries.

Civic service offers a way for students to apply knowledge from their specialization to specific problems, particularly those of excluded sectors.

Service initiatives have developed to different degrees in Latin American countries. In general, they involve unpaid activities that students are required to undertake when they finish their degree courses, prior to receiving their qualifications.

Although most initiatives emerge from the higher education institutions (HEIs) themselves, other sectors play an increasingly important role in defining the activities and the models for linking university and society. Governments promote programmes that use the service to undertake poverty-focused activities or to involve final year students in tasks such as attending to marginalized populations. Civil society organizations carry out a variety of initiatives with the support of the university service. Such initiatives promote gender equality, sustainable production and fair-trade activities, for example. In recent years, a growing number of educational institutions have formed partnerships with companies to promote service activities in the framework of *corporate social responsibility* or to support small family companies.

There is significant variation between the objectives, practices and experiences of university-based civic service in the different Latin American countries. Countries in which some form of university service can be found include:

- *Costa Rica:* where there is a compulsory programme called University Community Work (TCU).
- *Cuba:* where service forms part of university extension activities. It is used to carry out projects linked to community development.
- *Mexico:* where service is obligatory for all higher education institution graduates.
- *Nicaragua:* where service is obligatory for all graduates. However, in practice, only graduates in health sciences have to complete service.
- *The Dominican Republic:* which has compulsory programmes for students.
- *Uruguay:* where service is compulsory for medicine, law, agronomy, architecture and dentistry graduates.
- *Venezuela:* where medicine, dentistry and nursing graduates complete a year of service.
- *Bolivia, Ecuador, El Salvador, Guatemala, Honduras, Panama, Paraguay and Peru:* where civic service is only obligatory for students of medicine.

The objectives of these HEI-promoted service activities vary. Some aim to develop the abilities of future professionals through practical work. Some try to use the experience to raise awareness of problems in our societies. Others encourage these activities in order to complete the students' ethical education. The most ambitious proposals aim to promote humanitarian student activities that respond to local needs. Such activities focus on improving the quality of learning and education to encourage responsible citizenship.

Civic service has a wide variety of objectives for graduates in terms of their knowledge base. It has several recognized educational advantages. For example, it provides opportunities to apply knowledge acquired in the classroom, to acquire new knowledge and to develop new practical abilities. It also aims to increase opportunities to adapt knowledge to the problems of excluded sectors by raising the awareness, social commitment and responsibility of university graduates as they acquire a better understanding of their reality.

There is dissatisfaction in many Latin American HEIs about the way civic service operates. Furthermore, globalization and the debate on the current role of these institutions in Latin American societies force us to reconsider the meaning and characteristics of civic service in this new context. Generally speaking, different service models coexist and compete throughout Latin America. The divergence of these models can be seen in the proposals of the many agents involved, who use civic services for different reasons.

Some experiences are focused on welfare and philanthropy. They include activities carried out from a business perspective, in which the main idea is to provide help, or at best to carry out activities that meet the needs of a population who are merely passive recipients. The aim of this type of service is to reduce some of the most negative effects of the globalization model, but the causes of the problems are ignored.

Other experiences fit the 'citizenization' model, which aims to develop collaboration based on local participation. It focuses on promoting change in technical, economic, political and social relations. It is usually adopted by higher education institutions in collaboration with those civil society sectors that promote activities to help attain the recognition of rights and responsibilities among recipients and participating students.

These two models correspond to different viewpoints on society, on how to face social problems, on responsibilities and on the political agendas of which civic service forms part. The first model represents a viewpoint in which the market regulates social life. In contrast, the second model corresponds to a viewpoint of social change in the tradition of the most progressive universities in the region. Of course, there are also some intermediate positions between these extremes. The differences in the focuses and objectives of these models can be found in the linking and intervention methods. In addition, they are revealed by the learning objectives of participating students and the type of service offered to the recipients. The development of these models in the future and the predominance of one or other of them will partly depend on the ability of HEIs to establish service programmes in collaboration with the excluded sectors. However, it will also depend on the characteristics of the more general social and political contexts in which these experiences are set, as well as on the influence of government HEI policies and the nature of the civic service.

The major challenge for the future lies in civic service becoming part of an agenda created to face the most serious problems in Latin America. Such problems have been accentuated by globalization and include inequality and exclusion; environmental damage and the rapid loss of natural resources; restricted civil and political rights and breaches of social, economic and cultural rights in wide segments of the population; and the unequal distribution of resources, power and knowledge.

Even in a context as unfavourable as that facing Latin American HEIs, the service model presents an opportunity to collaborate in solving our society's problems. Thus, the way in which global changes can be used to broaden civic service objectives should be considered.

Methodology needs to be developed on the basis of the extensive experience in Latin America. Such methodology should also use technological changes and the information society to strengthen the scientific capacities of HEIs, with an emphasis on increasing links with traditionally excluded sectors. Civic service represents an opportunity to establish new models for linking with the diverse experiences, social movements and initiatives that arise throughout the region in the search for alternative solutions to some of the most serious problems in Latin American societies. Likewise, pedagogical proposals are needed that help to develop student abilities and ensure that ethics and social commitment are the basis of their professional practice. Students should collaborate with excluded sectors in the search for alternative solutions. This is the context of the current debate on the nature of university service in Latin America.

BIBLIOGRAPHY

Tünnermann, C. Extensión universitaria a través del servicio social universitario. Mimeo.

Global Service Institute (2004) *Youth Volunteerism and Civic Service in Latin America and the Caribbean: A Potential Strategy for Social and Economic Development*. Background research paper. Washington University in St. Louis: Center for Social Development, March.

GOOD PRACTICE I.5

Educative experiences through Cooperation for Development activities (Technical University of Catalonia, Spain)

Agustí Pérez-Foguet

At the end of the 1990s, the Technical University of Catalonia (UPC) decided to embed a Development Education programme in its usual education activities, in collaboration with campus-based Cooperation for Development groups. The proposal was initially included in a four-year university strategic plan. It has since been prioritized in university policy. The origin and main characteristics of the 2000–2005 programme are presented here (Pérez-Foguet, 2006).

INTRODUCTION

Development Education is recognized as a specific tool of the international cooperation system by Spanish and Catalan laws, and the corresponding Cooperation for Development Master Plans (Spanish Ministry of Foreign Affairs and Cooperation, 2005; Generalitat de Catalunya, 2007). It can be defined as 'an active learning process, founded on values of solidarity, equality, inclusion and cooperation, [which] enables people to move from basic awareness of international development priorities and sustainable human development, through understanding of the causes and effects of global issues, to personal involvement and informed action. It fosters the full participation of all citizens in worldwide poverty eradication, and the fight against exclusion, and seeks to influence more just and sustainable economic, social, environmental, and human rights based national and international policies.' This definition was approved by the European NGO Confederation for Relief and Development (CONCORD) during the General Assembly of November 2004 (http://www.deeep.org/english/what_is_de/definitions/).

Through its Centre for Development Cooperation (CCD), www.upc.edu/ccd, UPC has been actively promoting the involvement of its community in Cooperation for Development activities since the beginning of the 1990s (mainly through competitive budget allocations for small projects, mobility grants and awareness-raising activities). In the 1990s, some introductory elective courses were introduced by the CCD in partnership with different UPC–UNESCO Chairs. However, by the end of the decade, the community was prepared to take a step further and invest supplementary efforts in more academic activities. The first priority was to promote the inclusion of cooperation and development topics within courses and educational activities, following the spirit of the cited Development Education definition.

Since the mid-1990s, UPC campus-based Cooperation for Development groups have been in contact with similar groups from other Spanish universities through the Engineers Without Borders (EWB) network. This helped the formulation of the Development Education proposal itself, as lessons learned from previous engineering-focused experiences, especially from other Spanish technical universities, were taken into account from the beginning. Previous UPC experiences in environmental awareness-raising and embedding technical studies with environmental topics have also provided essential background to the proposal (Ferrer-Balas, 2004).

LOCAL PARTNERSHIP

During the programme, UPC was able economically to support some activities and to facilitate community enrolment and participation. However, it was not possible to allocate funds for coordination, dissemination and teaching support (that is, additional staff) without affecting the established programme of grants. Neither was it possible to ask for specific public funds, as at that time this option was reserved for NGOs. This is one of the main reasons why this experience was developed in partnership with the Catalan Association of EWB. At that time, the EWB in Barcelona was a small NGO. However, it was also a campus-based organization with very active participation of students (both graduates and undergraduates), young lecturers and teachers. This was a distinctive characteristic that helped to connect classroom, campus, local civil society and in-field contexts. It was therefore an essential component of the programme.

A memorandum of understanding was signed in 2000, after implementing the aforementioned UPC strategic plan. In addition, at a general assembly in 2000, the Catalan Association of EWB approved a strategic framework that included Development Education. The following year, the Catalan government awarded its first grant to EWB to promote Development Education at UPC. Yearly grants were assigned until the end of the 2000–2005 period.

Thanks to the programme, and the empowerment conferred within it, UPC has continuously been able to introduce Development Education activities. Proposals have been adapted to the new context defined by Bologna's reform of higher education in Europe. Moreover, since 2006, the new Catalan government's Cooperation for Development grants for universities have helped UPC to go further in its commitment to promote sustainable human development. Postgraduate studies and applied research activities have been included within its academic activities.

OBJECTIVES

The final goal of the programme was for the University to permanently offer Development Education proposals specifically designed for engineers and technicians, and to coordinate such proposals in engineering schools and engineering-focused Cooperation for Development organizations. Working guidelines included in UPC's Development Education 2000–2005 programme were as follows (Pérez-Foguet et al., 2005):

- Specific elective courses dealing with cooperation and development topics with a Development Education focus, offered to all engineering studies
- Incorporation of Development Education concepts and methodologies throughout the curricula, including the development of teaching materials covering different disciplines and related to UPC in-field Cooperation for Development projects
- Training of faculty in Development Education concepts and methodologies, specifically designed for technical and scientific studies

- Promoting social volunteering, NGO participation and internships in developing countries within the framework of Cooperation for Development programmes
- Promoting final degree projects and Master's theses related to technical issues relevant in the Cooperation for Development sector
- Creating a documentation centre on Technology for Sustainable Human Development within the university library system, as a support initiative of the overall programme.

Specific activities were targeted at the teaching community rather than the students. One of the most effective ways of attaining the programme goal involved increasing the knowledge and capacities of teachers in this field. This contributed to the sustainability of the programme.

Technical Universities such as UPC have some departments with academics from social sciences and even humanities. However, numbers are low in comparison with the overall university teaching staff. Moreover, such academics have reduced lobbying capacity and no expectation of increasing their presence in a context that is extremely competitive and has limited resources. Thus, in order to promote and disseminate Development Education proposals, it is essential to involve technical and natural sciences academic staff.

RESOURCES AND RESULTS

Funds for the overall programme came from different sources, as explained in the introduction. Some came from UPC itself and others from the partnership with EWB. Grants for specific courses and teaching materials were assigned from UPC engineering schools (with amounts from €1,000 to €2,000 per annum for each course or teaching material under development). By the end of the programme, more than 20 courses (of 40 contact hours each, on average) were offered and two teaching books finished (see Pérez-Foguet et al., 2005 for details of their scope and contents). In addition, the annual UPC 0.7% campaign (which collects around €400,000 per annum of private funds) was dedicated to promoting volunteer participation in field projects and final degree projects. Funds were allocated for mobility grants and awareness-raising activities for individuals, campus-based volunteer groups and NGOs. Annually, over 200 people (students, academics and administrative staff) have directly participated in cooperation activities, as a result of these funds. Furthermore, UPC financial support was provided for faculty seminars, courses and learning materials (Boni and Pérez-Foguet, 2006), and the consolidation of the specific library collection. All activities were supported by annual grants ranging from €1,000 to €3,000 per person or initiative, depending on individual cases (see the CCD annual reports at www.upc.edu/ccd).

Finally, an annual budget of about €120,000 was provided by local government to EWB for supporting UPC Development Education activities. These funds were mainly allocated to staff contracted for coordination, dissemination and teaching support for the programme (around 75%), with the rest being dedicated to directly funding activities.

Government funding of EWB proposals started in 2001, rather than in 2000 when the programme was launched. The year 2000 proposal was focused on one engineering school, with the aim of following a bottom-up scheme. However, this proposal was not accepted. The first proposal with activities covering all of UPC was formulated and funded by the Catalan government in 2001. A second phase was implemented in 2002. After that, from 2003 to 2005, the EWB proposals were extended to all Catalan universities within the engineering field. This was done for two main reasons:

- to start training for faculty activities (which needed a broader scope than just one university)
- to start e-learning work (distance and postgraduate courses) with the Open University of Catalonia (the UOC).

Interestingly, the rector of the UOC at that time had been rector of UPC at the end of the 1980s.

At the end of 2002, the Development Education strategic programme of the Catalan Association of EWB was extended to the Spanish Federation of EWB, with the same scope but some modifications owing to the change of scale. This facilitated the fulfilment of several proposals that needed coordination between different Spanish EWB groups, mainly those relating to the Technical Universities of Catalonia, Valencia and Madrid. Notable results of this extension include the Technology for Human Development Awards for final degree projects, Master's and Ph.D. theses, and *TpDH International Review* covering the relationship of different technical areas with human development promotion (see www.isf.es for further details on EWB-Spain activities and annual reports).

RECOMMENDATIONS

The following are recommendations for other technical universities willing to include Development Education activities in their academic programmes:

- Start awareness-raising activities inside the university (campuses, schools and so on), and facilitate the collaboration of the university community in such activities. This is not an expensive working practice. In addition, community-awareness and active participation are needed to be able to undertake more in-depth proposals.
- Promote and manage a participatory network in the university (groups, NGOs and so on) in order to facilitate volunteer enrolment and the practical collaboration of the university community. The university can provide highly motivated and professional people, but it needs partners for practical and field work. It should not be, or look like, an NGO.

- The role of the university in the Cooperation for Development sector needs to be explained continuously, both inside the university itself and outside it. Activities should be non-profit making but inexpensive, if desired. Moreover, the distinction between international cooperation university activities and Cooperation for Development activities between universities has to be observed. Self-regulation of the university community is possible if information is made available.
- Teaching–learning opportunities for introducing development issues in engineering courses need to be specifically highlighted and supported. Academic staff collaborating in development initiatives should include their in-field engineering experiences in the class work. Remember that university staff will 'always' be there. They should be the major promoters of development education activities.
- Top-level lobbying, together with an active community, can help to raise specific university funds (such as from the profits from private firms, university contracts, voluntary salary reductions, donations with the payment of academic fees and so on) that can be used to promote community participation in projects.
- Value the university's involvement in the Cooperation for Development sector (provide funds, human resources, annual activity reports and so on). Look for additional financial support from local government or private corporations, as this can be more successful than expected. However, some care about which private funds are directly related with solidarity activities should be taken. The university community should demand institutional coherence.
- Liaise with those responsible for similar experiences in other universities and promote joint activities, especially those targeted at academic staff. University networking could also help, especially if specific targets are identified.

REFERENCES

Boni, A. and Pérez-Foguet, A. (2006) (eds) *Construyendo ciudadanía global desde la universidad. Propuestas pedagógicas para la introducción de la educación para el desarrollo en las enseñanzas científico-técnicas.* Colección Informes n. 32. Barcelona, Spain: Intermon-OXFAM.

Ferrer-Balas, D. (2004) Global environmental planning at the Technical University of Catalonia, *International Journal of Sustainability in Higher Education*, **5**(1), pp. 48–62(15).

Generalitat de Catalunya (2007) *Projecte del Pla director de cooperació al desenvolupament 2007–2010*, Resolution 66/VIII of the Parliament of Catalonia, DOGC 4940 – 3.8.2007, pp. 26343–64, Barcelona, Spain. http://www.deeep.org/english/what_is_de/definitions/ (1 September).

Pérez-Foguet, A. (Coor.) (2006) *Impuls de l'Educació per al Desenvolupament humà i sostenible a la UPC 2000–2005*, UPC Board of Trustees University Teaching Quality Award and Jaume Vicens Vives Award from the Generalitat of Catalonia, Barcelona, Spain.

Pérez-Foguet, A., Oliete-Josa, S. and Saz-Carranza, A. (2005) Development education and engineering: A framework for incorporating reality of developing countries into engineering studies, *International Journal of Sustainability in Higher Education*, **6**(3), pp. 278–303(26).

Spanish Ministry of Foreign Affairs and Cooperation (2005) *The Master Plan for Spanish Cooperation 2005–2008*, Madrid, Spain.

I.8

INSTITUTIONAL CHALLENGES AND IMPLICATIONS FOR HEIs: TRANSFORMATION, MISSION AND VISION FOR THE 21ST CENTURY

Teboho Moja

Abstract

In the 21st century, higher education institutions (HEIs), as well as the sector in general, face many challenges related to achieving a balance between responding to and initiating change. Their problems are further exacerbated by the necessity to serve national needs as well as to be world players who can meet global needs. Government initiatives to reform higher education systems focus on transforming institutions to meet national needs and to make their nations competitive in a global world. In contrast, most institutions focus their transformation on survival and competition with other institutions in the sector as well as outside the sector. Meeting national needs has been relatively easier to achieve because the institutions were set up with that requirement in mind. What remains a challenge is to redefine higher education and its role in a globalized world in which global challenges need global solutions. Institutional initiatives to address global problems, however limited, have been essential for linking institutions to the global development agenda, although their contribution to sustainable development at a global level has been inadequate. There is a need for new types of institutions that will tackle global issues and focus on an agenda for human and social development.

INTRODUCTION

The role of higher education in human and social development remains unchallenged. Over centuries, higher education has contributed to the advancement of industrialized countries and attempts have been made in developing countries to structure and transform higher education to play a role in development. The challenge for HEIs has been for them to find balance between the important role they play in economic development and their role in human and social development. The unbalanced focus on some forms of development has led to problems in the sustainability of those developments. Growing concerns over issues of world sustainability have been raised at world conferences on sustainability, such as the one hosted in South Africa in 2004, and by politicians such as Al Gore in the film *An Inconvenient Truth*. Thus, attempts have been made to bring to the attention of society some of the problems we face in the world and not just as individual nations.

Higher education systems, originally established to serve the needs of nation-states, are currently challenged to address needs that go beyond this framework. Through globalization, the world has become more connected, with unequal benefits to different nations. The connections are mainly economic in nature, but they have a political, social and cultural impact on all nations. It is in this sense that HEIs are challenged to address the impact of changes taking place globally and not just within the nation-states. The impact of globalization on higher education and its impact on human and social development are addressed in this report in the paper by Deepak Nayyar.

Increased economic activity between nations has pushed the critical role that higher education plays in development to the forefront. This is indicated by the increased interest of governments, individually or as a collective such as the European Union, in transforming their higher education systems to make them more responsive to emerging needs that are mainly economic in nature. The Bologna Process of restructuring qualifications and improving mobility is in line with the region's vision for major economic development. The European Union has made inroads into addressing the transformation of higher education to ensure that the sector furthers the goals set by the Union. There have been many seminars and conferences organized to address issues relating to the future of universities and their role in research and knowledge development education as part of the activities surrounding Vision 2020. The Southern African Development Community *Protocol on Education and Training* (1997) is another example of an initiative that aims to improve economic development in the region. These are just examples that indicate a revisiting of missions at regional and systemic levels that impact on higher education institutions and the role they have to play in increasing access and in developing the capacity for economic development.

REDEFINING THE ROLE OF HIGHER EDUCATION

Individual governments all over the world have embarked on major transformations to restructure their higher education systems. China, for example, has focused on improving access, improving the quality of its institutions, and improving the system's efficiency through mergers. A push to achieve efficiency at the systemic level has resulted in governments proposing mergers of institutions. China reduced the number of higher education institutions from 612 to 250 (Chen, 2002), South Africa reduced the number of institutions from 36 to 22, and Finland has a proposal to reduce its 50 institutions to 25 at most (*Eurometri*, 2007). Such reductions are happening as student numbers are increasing, and the rationale is to have fewer, good-quality, efficiently run institutions rather than a greater number of wasteful institutions. A source of concern, however, is that these changes are driven more by the need to achieve efficiency and reduce wastage, which have become primary goals, than by the desire to contribute to human and social development.

Governments are prioritizing economic development, as is evident in the case of South Africa where, out of frustration that the higher education system was not playing a decisive role in supporting an emerging economic development agenda, President Mbeki appointed, and chairs, the Presidential Working Group on Higher Education, which consists of all university leaders as well as some key government ministers. He has often raised issues related to the role of universities in development, and in the case of South Africa that role is to be framed within the context of a developmental state. The implication is that government must pay more attention to higher education's role in economic development. As a result, the Minister of Education has pushed HEIs to reduce their intake of students in the arts and humanities in order for them to increase student numbers in other fields, mainly science and business. In 2005, the US Secretary of Education Margaret Spelling appointed the Commission on the Future of Higher Education to develop a comprehensive national strategy for post-secondary education that will meet the needs of America's diverse population and also address the economic and workforce needs of the 21st century. In November 2006, Turkey hosted a high-profile conference that discussed the vision for higher education for 2023 with an emphasis on economic development. These are but a few examples of a push for an economic development agenda with little mention of human and

social development. In instances in which forms of development other than economic development are mentioned, either they are simply an addition to the main agenda or no clear strategies are put forward regarding how they are to be achieved.

There is also renewed interest among donor and development agencies in the role of higher education in development. Recent World Bank reports such as *Constructing Knowledge Societies: New Challenges for Tertiary Education* (2002) and the World Bank/UNESCO report *Higher Education in Developing Countries: Peril and Promise* (2000) refocus on the role of higher education in development. The focus, though, is more on economic development – with social development mentioned in passing. The emphasis is on how governments are to develop their human capacity in order to be able to respond to market-driven changes in their economies. There has been renewed interest in African higher education through initiatives such as the Partnership in Higher Education in Africa, which has committed millions of dollars in assistance to institutions that are being transformed. The initiatives above indicate the critical role that higher education plays in the development agenda and the steps taken to redefine that role.

INSTITUTIONAL CHALLENGES AND RESPONSES

At an institutional level, institutions are also being transformed to respond to new challenges. There is a view that these institutions are on the verge of changing so much as to be virtually unrecognizable (Drucker, 1999). An alternative view is that in past centuries HEIs have been able to change, adapt and continue to exist in recognizable form. The implications are that these institutions will survive the wave of change because they are adaptable, as made evident by their quick move to become entrepreneurial and innovative in their operations following the reduction of government funding. Survival means that that they are likely to continue with business as usual and not be responsive to the changes around them.

The question is: What challenges are likely to change HEIs? A more detailed discussion of the challenges that institutions face is presented by Philip Altbach in another paper in this report. This paper sums up some of the issues and how institutions have responded to them. What is significant about these challenges and the responses to them is that none seem to focus on ensuring that higher education pays attention to human and social development as part of the development agenda but concentrate mainly on their own survival under pressure. As a result, institutional responses have had a negative impact on social structures and have increased inequity among students and faculty members.

In the past few decades, institutions have been under pressure to expand; to be more efficient as governments cut back on spending; to become more accountable to a broad range of stakeholders; and to define their role in society. In the past two decades, higher education systems have expanded rapidly, with more students and diverse programmes. Much of this growth is attributable to their responsiveness to the demands posed by globalization for more people with high-level skills. However, direct pressure for expansion has come mainly from the greater numbers of students seeking admission to institutions of higher education. Students are in search of higher qualifications that are perceived as their means for social mobility. The pressure has also come indirectly from potential employers demanding higher qualifications for employees and putting a higher value on qualifications. HEIs have responded positively to such a challenge, as they have seen the benefit of an increased source of income from tuition fees. Expansion has been relatively easy to achieve, through the increase in numbers of students and institutions, the diversification of institutions and programmes, and the use of ICTs to reach more students.

Expansion demands have raised other issues, such as the exclusion of students, mainly from lower socio-economic backgrounds, who attend schools that do not adequately prepare them to meet the admission requirements of HEIs and the perpetuation of class distinctions in society at large. For example, increased demand for access to top institutions in the USA and the need for the production of high-level skills have pushed institutions into setting admission requirements higher. US institutions are placing greater emphasis on SAT scores and raising the bar. The number of people seeking admission, which has doubled and even tripled in the past few years, means that institutions can afford to be more selective. Harvard, Princeton and Yale rejected thousands of applicants with high scores in their admissions for fall 2007. Harvard admitted 9% of 22,955 applicants, Stanford admitted 10.3% of 23,956 applicants, and Columbia admitted 8.9% of 18,081 applicants (Dillon, 2007). Increased numbers are blamed for such practices and many reasons are advanced for this trend: baby boomers' offspring making it to college, multiple applications, increased numbers of high-school graduates heading straight to college, the value of a college degree and so on. In some developing countries, governments have set limits on the number of students they fund and that has pushed more students, often the poorer ones, to opt for private education at a higher cost or to attend low-quality institutions that are not even regulated by governments.

Because of governments' budget cuts to education, another challenge faced by HEIs is to become more efficient in their operations. Governments have used different strategies to make institutions and systems of higher education more efficient. Efficiency has been achieved through exercising austerity whilst continuing to provide the services expected from institutions, but such actions have led to problems of increasing inequities among faculty members and students. For example, there have been cutbacks on hiring whilst class sizes have increased, pressure for faculty to raise money through grants for research, and the use of cheap labour for teaching. In developing countries there is an increase in the use of temporary faculty members, particularly by HEIs expanding into other, mainly developing, countries. Because such faculty members are often the best professors employed by local institutions it is likely that their work in the base institutions will be neglected in their search for additional remuneration to supplement their low salaries.

There is a fierce battle among institutions to 'steal' the best professors from each other, resulting in competition rather than cooperation. Lack of cooperation obviously has a negative impact on working together on common agendas that could include human and social development issues. In the competitive environment in which institutions operate the race is to make institutions better and to improve rankings, but there is little reference to the development agenda, particularly by institutions in developed countries. Does the problem lie in the notion that the countries in which they operate are developed? Institutions from developing countries, for example, often mention in their mission a 'contribution to national development'. Unfortunately, those institutions do not also present clear positions on what they mean by development or plans and strategies that show how they intend to contribute to development as innovators; instead, they may be seen as being 'responsive' to an agenda that has already been set. The reforms in those institutions seem to be focused on strategies to accommodate more students and generate more income. It is in this context, I would argue, that the leaders of HEIs need to spell out a role for their institutions that defines the period in which they exist rather than being defined by it. The role of higher education in human and social development is not seriously debated but assumed.

The main task – and it is a daunting one – is to develop a new role for the 21st century. From observation, institutional leaders are working hard on leading their institutions and transforming them so that their role in the new age can become clearer. There are concerns that HEIs are hard to transform and that the change process is generally very slow and often resisted by those affected. There is a body of literature that points out that institutional culture plays a role in how change takes place. Leadership plays a role in transformation and in leading institutions to buy into their vision for institutional transformation. Responses to global challenges have been varied among the leaders in the higher education sector.

GLOBAL CHALLENGES TO HIGHER EDUCATION

The role that higher education plays in human and social development has been addressed in this report mainly in Part II. The papers present a regional perspective on the role that higher education plays in regional development. There are overlaps and similarities in some areas, such as human capital development, but other roles are region-specific. The role as presented in Part II is not exhaustive but rather sums up some of the roles played by higher education and indicates a need for global solutions.

Higher education contributes to development nationally and globally and is expected to ensure that development is sustainable and that the environment is preserved for future generations. There is some recognition of the part that higher education could play but the strategies and discussions often exclude the higher education sector. For example, calls have been made by international organizations such as UNESCO and the G8 for the sector to play a role in sustainable development. At the recent G8–UNESCO World Forum on Education, Research, and Innovation in Trieste, higher education was represented by individuals, rather than organizations that would take the agenda further with their member institutions. What is disturbing is the absence, or minimal involvement, of higher education leadership in those seminars working out strategies to involve the sector. Another example was the notable absence of higher education participation at the World Summit on Sustainable Development hosted in South Africa in 2002. Academics participated as individuals interested in sustainability issues but there was no formal sector representation. The higher education sector is often left out in discussions on the world's transformation and in setting the development agenda. Another example is that of the New Partnership for Africa's Development, which did not include higher education initially, although it was later included when the sector raised concerns about being left out. Perhaps the reason why the sector gets left out is that there is no formal structure that focuses on sustainability issues in higher education other than individual researchers and small centres within institutions.

One of the criticisms worldwide is that HEIs are often isolated from the communities within which they are located – the accusation of 'ivory-towerism'. Governments are often unsure how to relate to institutions and will, out of frustration, violate their academic freedom by stepping in and interfering with institutional operations for political reasons or genuine development concerns. The role of institutions worldwide receives the lowest priority, even in institutions that regard themselves as developmental institutions. Research is still prioritized for promotions and advancement, followed by teaching and lastly community involvement or development. Academics sometimes report that they are instructed to curb their community involvement if they are on tenure track and to focus on research, because community involvement activities will not contribute to their advancement. What is needed, therefore, are institutions that are set up specifically with the mission to become involved with the community to ensure human and social development. The definition of community here is understood to be broad and includes other levels of education to which higher education could make a critical contribution.

The last issue I would like to discuss is that of the role of human capacity, with a focus on skills development. In some quarters the focus has been on the technology aspects of this and the skills required have been broken down into manual skills. There are institutions focusing on providing students with demonstrable skills and competencies needed by industry. In other quarters the focus has been on the knowledge aspects of the economy, raising concerns about developing skills for generating, accessing, configuring and using knowledge. There is concern that some of the values that are important in human and social development have been lost as institutions become responsive to the needs of the market. Values, behaviour and lifestyles that promote sustainable development are said to be receiving less attention. It is in this sense that higher education is called upon to rethink its role in social development too.

In relation to the above issues, another criticism is that there is more focus on skills that limit creativity and the development of the mind because students are only interested in acquiring skills that will render them employable. The value of learning for learning's sake has been lost, and that of pursuing knowledge for the sake of knowledge that might not seem to have an immediate use is not encouraged. Such criticisms and the ones in other papers call for a rethink of higher education's role and for a vision that is relevant in this century to the needs of a changing world.

TOWARDS A MISSION AND VISION FOR THE 21ST CENTURY

Higher education institutions are being transformed, both as individual institutions and as part of a system that is redefining its role and vision in the 21st century. At the turn of the century, many scholarly papers were produced in an attempt to chart the path that institutions would need to follow in order to remain relevant in a changing world order. The World Conference on Higher Education was one forum where such papers were produced and shared with experts and leadership in the sector. Earlier work signalled directions that could be taken to transform the sector. Presentations at an event, however, are not sufficient to transform institutions or the sector, although they are a step in the right direction. The process of change in higher education worldwide is affecting individual institutions, national systems and regional collectives. As a result, different views are articulated by leaders within and outside institutions as to what role the sector should be playing. The initiative to host a conference on the diversity of missions in Dublin in June 2007 was a step in the direction of collectively articulating a mission for the sector.

Global initiatives to transform higher education craft their thinking and vision within a framework of national institutions. This happens despite the awareness that their influence is global in terms of activities such as research and teaching. Government initiatives for the transformation of higher education systems are limited to national systems, and institutional transformation efforts are mainly limited to individual institutions. World transformation has had an impact on HEIs and the role they play in transforming the world order. Therefore, higher education's role needs to be expanded beyond national development and to be articulated in terms of global development in a collective way. The interconnectedness of developments and the effects they have in the world need to be tackled from a global perspective. I would argue that there is a need for a form of global higher education that addresses the needs of a global world.

Central to this paper is the argument that a new vision is needed to articulate the role that higher education should play to ensure balanced economic, human and social development. As argued in the earlier part of this paper, the current vision and role of higher education is articulated within the current structure of how higher education is organized, that is, within national systems of higher education or within individual institutions, and to a limited extent in a move towards more regional cooperation between HEIs.

Institutions are influenced by the world around them as much as they are able to influence the world around them. Spies (2000, p. 22) traces the history of universities and argues that they are products and co-producers in each age in which they exist and that there is a connection between shaping that age and being shaped by it. Over the years, universities have been concerned about their relevance and responsiveness to wider society, and it is because of that concern that institutions are shaped by societal changes. It is in their search for relevance and responsiveness to external pressure that institutions are shaped.

The main challenge for institutions becomes that of being shaped by the world around them whilst also being the initiators of change. There is a tendency to focus more on being responsive to change rather than initiating it. There is a long list of global problems, some of which are highlighted by higher education scholars in their research, but little in terms of positioning the institutions to play a role in finding solutions. Part of the difficulty is that the problems are global in nature and global solutions are therefore needed. The question is how global problems should be researched and solutions found to address them.

The fundamental mission of HEIs as they are currently structured is to serve national needs, but issues such as poverty reduction, environmental issues, global terrorism, equity, diseases and continuing national conflicts cut across national borders and thus need to be addressed through strategies that are more global. There is a need for both institutions that serve national needs and those that serve global needs. The vision needs to be articulated from both perspectives, but the latter is often omitted.

The vision of the role that higher education needs to play in the 21st century is informed by earlier thoughts of great thinkers such as Tagore, who, as quoted in Sanyal (2007), claimed that too great an emphasis on nationalism in education is one of the reasons for conflicts among nations and the human race in general. Tagore's ideas led to the setting up of Visva-Bharati in 1918, a university that was regarded as a world university. This signalled a need to shift from nationalism to developing some form of 'globalism'. Typologies, such as the one presented by Duderstadt (2000), president emeritus of the University of Michigan, also signal a need for new types of institutions based on the emerging focus and activities of universities.

GLOBAL VISION FOR HIGHER EDUCATION

Establishing a different type of HEI that would address global issues such as those mentioned above is a possibility that must be considered. For the purpose of this paper I will refer to such an institution as a 'global university'.

First, an institution whose core mission is global, such as the United Nations University, must be set up, which differs from an institution whose mission is national but that is trying to address global needs. Second, its mission would have to be human and social development globally. Third, the university needs to be committed to social issues and involve various levels of society. Engaging in this way will give the institution an opportunity to rewrite its social contract, as suggested by Frederico Mayor Zaragoza in his speech on the UN Plan for Human Settlements, as quoted by Berit Kjos (2004). The proposal is put forward because it would be hard to make fundamental changes to current institutions for them to operate completely differently to the way in which they currently operate in order to meet new global needs.

Current initiatives involve setting up global centres within existing institutions in partnership with other institutions; such initiatives are good as nodes for linking national institutions to global institutions and global networks of scholars and practitioners. The setting up of global institutions should be considered the intellectual project that will define the contribution of higher education in the 21st century. There have been calls for higher education to get involved in an intellectual project. One such example is the commitment by the vice-chancellor of the University of Cape Town to 'maintaining the University of Cape Town's momentum towards building a global profile', and using research as a means to develop a link between intellectual work and commercial and social development is an illustration of the point made above (Ndebele, 2001). In various speeches, the vice-chancellor has referred to the need for an intellectual project by HEIs to address development needs. The setting up of an intellectual project that links global society to research for development could be achieved by setting up global HEIs, as suggested. This line of thought is supported by Spies (2000), who also argues that institutions need to develop a new kind of intellectualism that addresses global problems.

There is a place in the sector for both national and global institutions that would be complementary to each other for ensuring sustainable development. National institutions could develop nodes or centres that link the institutions with immediate communities as well as with global institutions. Examples of such initiatives are projects within institutions that attempt to link communities of scholars and the public across institutions and disciplines, such as the H2O project set up by the Berkman Center for Internet and Society at Harvard University. The project aims to use internet technologies for the creation and exchange of ideas and the communities around those ideas both within and beyond the confines of the tradit-

ional university setting (for more information on the project see http://h2o.law.harvard.edu/about/about.jsp). Another example of an intellectual project that brought together scholars across disciplines was the project at the Fernand Braudel Center that sought to bridge the gap between humanities and social sciences in finding an explanation for the development of the modern world system (for further information see http://www.binghamton.edu/fbc/fbcintel.htm).

GLOBAL UNIVERSITIES FOR GLOBAL NEEDS

The higher education sector must take the lead in addressing global issues in a way that will contribute to human and social development. There has been a call by higher education leaders for HEIs to set up intellectual projects that address issues of social and human development. I would argue that there is a place for such projects within countries but also a need for a global intellectual project. To tackle problems on a global scale would require the establishment of global universities as new institutions – rather than trying to transform existing institutions that are deeply entrenched in the current higher education culture – to serve a new mission. Global universities as envisioned here are not to be confused with what have been referred to in the past as world-class universities. In his typology of universities, Duderstadt (2000) acknowledges a need for such institutions and refers to them as world universities. He argues that those institutions would need to be funded largely from international funds rather than by nation-states, and that their faculty, students and programmes would need to be diverse and global in nature.

Global universities in this paper refer to universities that serve as spaces for intellectual creativity beyond what current universities are doing. Creativity needs to be unleashed in the way knowledge is created and disseminated, and that has implications for how classes are taught, how research is conducted, how service is delivered and how qualifications are structured. The mission of such institutions should be to tackle global issues such as global warming and global poverty from inter- and intradisciplinary perspectives. Current global centres set up within universities are a move in the right direction, but they are constrained by hard-to-change university cultures. New spaces outside HEIs are needed for generating knowledge and packaging it for delivery and use in new ways.

There is a need for a global community organized within an institution to work together on global solutions for sustainable human and social development. A community of scholars and students would work together in the development of a shared vision from a global perspective. Such institutions need to be established regionally, one per region, but with a global agenda in order to meet both regional and global needs, to link regional issues to global issues, and to serve as a base for a network of scholars working on common issues. The idea of a university has been used for lack of a better concept, but the proposed institution is unlikely to operate in the same manner as a traditional university. A university's additional activities, such as teaching research and community service, would be retained, but the operation mode would be different.

The mission would be twofold. First, the institution would serve local needs whilst addressing global issues. Second, it would serve as an initiator of change rather than being responsive to changes that are already taking place.

GOVERNANCE AND FUNDING

The governance structure of such an institution needs to be made up of a body that is globally representative; the majority of the members of this body, however, should be from the region in which the institution is located.

Global funds should be made available to supplement funds provided by the region. The institution should be financially independent but accountable to a governing body rather than to one particular government. Financial independence would allow the institution to set up its own priorities without the constraints of aligning them to the priorities of one particular government. Accountability should be expanded beyond financial accountability to being accountable to members of society by serving their needs and delivering solutions that will be of benefit to them.

Funding structures would need to be adapted and made more flexible to accommodate the needs of faculty that spend part of their year at such institutions, students who need to study there and for the type of activities to be conducted at such institutions.

FACULTY AND STUDENTS

Faculty at such institutions could consist of a diverse core faculty and faculty members who spend short periods of time working there away from their base institutions during their sabbatical leave or as seconded by their institutions for short or long periods. Such professors would be global professors who are not necessarily attached to one institution but rather spend time at different institutions for the benefit of more students and faculty colleagues

than those based at one institution. Such faculty could work side by side with members of the public who are knowledgeable in the area that they are working in and experts from related disciplines. Such cooperation arrangements would promote the exchange and creation of ideas on addressing global issues from different perspectives. Discipline boundaries could be crossed and traditional university pressures and restrictions that inhibit creativity could be modified, because the members working at such institutions would not be under pressure to meet the demands of qualifying for tenure. These demands often become an obstacle to focusing on community service, and under these circumstances research for publications is valued more than research with outcomes that provide practical solutions.

Students at such an institution would be a group of diverse students from the region or outside the region who are interested in learning rather than chasing after qualifications. The institution would be their learning laboratory, where there is no pressure to obtain qualifications. Creative teams consisting of faculty, students and members of the public would work side by side on topics of interest to them in order to find solutions that could be applied in the region or globally. The overall goal would be to promote the unconstrained creativity that is to some extent inhibited in traditional institutions.

LEADERSHIP

Institutional leadership does not have to come from the traditional leadership in traditional universities, which is often drawn from faculty within or outside the institution. Leaders should be drawn from the wider public, including members from the private sector and ex-politicians, for example. There is a need for global leadership that would link the institution to the global agenda. The criteria for selecting leaders should be broader and not just based on disciplinary expertise. Higher education institutions should seek people with a global vision for the institution rather than an institutional vision, and an interest in driving a global agenda.

Another characteristic should be that of being transformative, so that the institution is continuously being transformed to meet emerging needs rather than being steeped in tradition. Transformational leadership is defined in Northouse's framework (2001) as leadership that provides a vision of the future that followers are persuaded to follow, that manages the interplay between leadership and followers, and that pays attention to the needs of the followers. Higher education needs transformational leadership that will articulate a vision that redefines and articulates the role of higher education systems in the 21st century. Drucker (1994), in his article entitled 'The Age of Social Transformation', argues that massive social transformation needs to be addressed by a critical mass of transformational leaders, as quoted in Berit Kjos (2004). Such transformational leaders would need to be located in a global university and concentrated at those institutions in the different regions.

PROGRAMMES

Programmes need to be structured differently from those of traditional HEIs, most of which are organized around disciplines. There is a need for new interdisciplinary programmes and new fields of study developed to meet new needs. Some non-traditional courses are already emerging at traditional universities and could be developed further and expanded in areas such as knowledge management, peace studies, global warming, poverty reduction studies and the study of new diseases. A more detailed paper on curricula that would address human and social needs would contribute to an understanding of the kind of curriculum transformation that is needed in higher education in general. Qualifications would need to be restructured because the focus would not be on the acquisition of traditional qualifications but on the acknowledgement of some form of expertise, or an update of one's qualifications, or even a reskilling process.

Lastly, I would like to comment on research, knowledge production and dissemination. New modes of knowledge production should be used, once again bringing practitioners and scientists together. Certain models of this mode of knowledge production, such as mode 1 and mode 2, could be used in HEIs. Scholars such as Gibbons et. al. (1994) and Kraak (2000) have argued and made a case for a need for both applied and basic research and show that the two modes of knowledge production are interdependent.

CONCLUSION

Higher education institutions play multiple roles in society. The paper by Philip Altbach in this report lists some of those roles. The vision proposed in this paper is that of transforming HEIs so that they become initiators of change rather than just responding to external pressures and external needs. It is hard to play this role, given the traditional cultures of universities, their modes of operation and practices, which are hard to change. The very structure of an institution that has been set up to serve national needs is hard to modify to serve global needs.

Institutions have been set up by governments and are mostly funded by those governments, which expect them to serve their national needs. As a result, some institutions become instruments of government and find it hard to operate independently, particularly in developing countries, where the bulk of funding comes from governments.

There are institutional, sectoral and global expectations that need to be met through a combination of different types of institutions. The establishment of new types of institutions is not to be seen as replacing existing institutions but rather as an addition to the sector. Existing institutions need to transform themselves so that they are in a position to tackle global issues within their agenda too. The current visions and actions of institutions indicate their attempt to be relevant in a global context by shifting from internationalization to globalization. Several researchers, such as Peter Scott (1999, 2000, 2005) and Van Vught et al. (2002), have drawn a distinction between internationalization and globalization.

The proposal for the establishment of global universities is aimed at finding global solutions to global problems for human and social development. Setting up new types of institutions provides the opportunity to focus attention on human and social development needs on a global scale. Peter Drucker, the management guru, was optimistic that we are on the verge of change and that our institutions will change into an unrecognizable form. I would argue that institutions shifting away from being responders to change towards becoming the initiators of change would be a step in the right direction.

REFERENCES

Chen, D.Y. (2002) The amalgamation of Chinese higher education institutions. *Education Policy Analysis Archives*. **10**(20) 14 April.

Dillon, S. (2007) A great year for Ivy League colleges, but not so good for applicants to them. *New York Times*, 4 April, p. 7, section B.

Drucker P.F. (1994) The age of social transformation. *Atlantic Monthly*, Vol. 274, November.

Drucker P.F. (1999) *Management Challenges for the 21st Century*. New York: Harper Business.

Duderstadt, J.J. (2000) A choice of transformation for the 21st century university. *The Chronicle of Higher Education – Opinion and Arts*. 4 February, 2000.

Eurometri (2007) Positive vision for Finnish higher education in 2020. http://www.suomeneurooppaliike.fi/eurometri/1eurometri2007/sivu10.pdf (accessed 05/21/2007).

Fischer, S. (2003) Globalization and its challenges. *American Economic Review*, **93**(2).

Gibbons, M., Limoges, C., Nowotny, H., Swartzman, S., Scott, P. and Trow, M. (1994) *The Production of Knowledge: The Dynamics of Science and Research in Contemporary Societies*. Thousand Oaks, CA: Sage Publications.

Kjos, Berit (2004) *Creating Community, Part 1: Purpose-driven Change Through Transformational Leadership*, http://www.crossroad.to/articles2/04/community-1.htm#1

Kraak, A. (2000) (ed.) *Changing Modes: New Knowledge Production and its Implications for Higher Education in South Africa*. Pretoria: HSRC.

Ndebele, N. (2001) *The Way Forward for the University of Cape Town*. Introduction to Vision 2001 and Beyond. A strategic planning document of the University of Cape Town. www.uct.ac.za/downloads/uct.ac.za/about/management/vc vision2001andbeyond.pdf (accessed 05/18/07).

Northouse, P.J. (2001) *Leadership Theory and Practice*. New York: Sage Publications.

Sanyal, B.C. (2007) *Tagore and Higher Education*. France: Maison de l'Inde.

Scott, P. (1999) *The Globalization of Higher Education*. London: Taylor and Francis.

Scott, P. (2000) *Globalization and the University: Challenges for the Twenty-First Century*. Report: Internationalization Forum of Change Projects – Internationalization and Globalization. Conference hosted jointly by American Council on Education and Center For Higher Education Transformation. 19–21 August 2000, San Lameer, Durban, South Africa. Website: www.chet.org.za/download/2291/archive_intl_forum_report.doc.

Scott, P. (2005) Cross-Border Higher Education and Internationalization. Overview of Concepts, Trends, and Challenges. IAU International Conference, Alexandria, Egypt, 15–16 November, 2005.

Spies, P. (2000) University traditions and the challenge of global transformation. In: Inayatullah, S. and Gidley, J. (2000) *The University in Transformation: Global Perspectives on the Futures of the University*. Westport, CT: Bergin and Garvey.

The Southern African Development Community *Protocol on Education and Training* (1997) Adopted on 8 September 1997 in Blantyre, Malawi and entered into force on 31 July 2000. The original languages are English, French and Portuguese, all equally authentic. Available at www.iss.org.za and www. sadc.int.

UNESCO (1993) Recommendations on the Recognition of Studies and Qualifications in Higher Education. 27th Session of the General Conference in Paris, November.

Vught, F. van, Wende, M.C. van der and Westerheijden, D.F. (2002) Globalisation and internationalisation: Policy agendas compared. In: Enders, J. and Fulton, O. (eds.) *Higher Education in a Globalising World*. Dordrecht: Kluwer Academic Publishers, pp. 103–21.

World Bank/UNESCO (2000) *Higher Education in Developing Countries: Peril and Promise*. Report of the Independent World Bank/UNESCO Task Force. Washington, DC.

World Bank (2002) *Constructing Knowledge Societies: New Challenges for Tertiary Education*. Washington, DC.

SPECIAL CONTRIBUTION I.17

The role of the universities in constructing an alternative globalization

Boaventura de Sousa Santos

INTRODUCTION

What has happened in the past ten years? How can we define the current situation? What potential solutions can be found to the problems now facing universities? The following paper aims to answer these questions.

The first section contains an analysis of recent changes in the higher education system and the impact of these changes on public universities. The second section describes and justifies the basic principles of a reform that would enable public universities to respond creatively and effectively to the challenges faced at the beginning of the 21st century. It also includes some reflections on the role that universities should play as agents of social change in constructing an alternative globalization.

THE UNIVERSITY CRISIS

The financial crisis in universities is closely related to their institutional crisis. Public universities have lost priority in states' public policies. This is due, above all, to the general decrease in the priority of social policies (education, health, social security), caused by a model of economic development known as *neo-liberalism* or *neo-liberal globalization*. This model has been spread around the world since the 1980s. In public universities, the imposition of this model meant that existing institutional weaknesses – of which there were many – were not used to create a pedagogical, political programme of university reform. Instead, the problems were judged insurmountable and used to justify opening up universities – a public good – to commercial exploitation. Likewise, these weaknesses were used to explain the decapitalization and destructuring of public universities in favour of an emerging university market where human resource transfers sometimes involved a rudimentary type of accumulation by private universities to the detriment of the public sector.

Another contradiction also emerged in this area between the rigidity of university education and the changeability of the qualifications required by the market. The university became a service that you could access as a consumer, by paying for it. Thus, a citizen's right to education was drastically diminished. The number of free university education systems fell and most grants were replaced by loans. As a result, students were transformed from citizens to consumers. The other main factor in the neo-liberal project for universities is the transnationalization of university services.

As mentioned above, this neo-liberal project is linked to a reduction in public funding. However, other factors are equally significant, such as a general deregulation of commercial exchanges; the defence, or even imposition, of the commercial solution by multilateral financial agents; and the high concentration of the potential benefits of new information and communication technologies (ICTs) in the North.

Public universities – and the education system as a whole – have always been linked to the project of nation-building. This project is now in crisis due to the progress of neo-liberalism.

WHAT CAN BE DONE?

The only effective, liberating way to face neo-liberal globalization is to challenge it with an alternative, counter-hegemonic globalization. *Counter-hegemonic globalization of universities* as a public good involves the following in particular. National public university reforms should reflect a project of nation-building. This project has to be focused on political preferences that mark the integration of the country into contexts of knowledge production and transfer that are increasingly transnationalized and polarized between contradictory transnationalization processes: neo-liberal globalization and counter-hegemonic globalization. Nation-building should be the result of an extensive political and social contract, specified in several sectorial contracts. One of these is the educational contract, which includes the idea of universities as a public good. The main aim of the reform is to respond to social demands for the radical democratization of universities. This should bring an end to the exclusion of social groups and their knowledge. Universities have played a key role in this process of exclusion for many years, even before the current phase of capitalist globalization. Responses to such demands are currently limited, since capitalist globalization makes any opportunity for democratization unfeasible.

The global context is now strongly dominated by neo-liberal globalization. However, there is still room for national and international coordination based on reciprocity and mutual benefit. In universities, such coordination renews and expands on long-standing internationalism.

The new alternative, humanitarian transnationalization is supported by ICTs and by the formation of national and international networks for sharing new pedagogical methods; new processes for the production and dissemination of scientific knowledge and other knowledge; and new social, local, national and global commitments. The aim is to restore the role of public universities in collectively defining and solving social problems.

Although such problems may be local or national, they can now only be resolved by considering their global context. Thus, the new university contract is based on the premise that universities play a crucial role in constructing a country's place in a world that is polarized by contradictory globalizations.

Neo-liberal globalization involves the systematic erosion of national projects. As universities and university staff were actively involved in designing many such projects, it follows that public universities have to be revolutionized, as they are not in complete harmony with the objectives of this kind of globalization. However, public universities should not be isolated from the pressures of neo-liberal globalization. This would be impossible to achieve. In addition, such isolation could give the impression that universities enjoy a status that is relatively independent from such pressure. Although it is not exactly the case, we could say that part of the university crisis is due to having been co-opted by hegemonic globalization. The question is whether universities can actively respond to this co-option, in the name of counter-hegemonic globalization.

The counter-hegemonic globalization of universities as a public good, as proposed in this paper, upholds the idea of national projects. However, such projects are conceived of in a non-nationalist, non-autarkic way. In the 21st century, nations will only exist in so much as national projects exist for qualifying incorporation into globalized society. For peripheral and semi-peripheral countries, this qualification will not exist unless resistance to neo-liberal globalization is channelled into alternative globalization strategies. The difficulty – and at times the drama – of university reform in many countries lies in the fact that the national project has to be reworked before reforms can take place. Public universities are aware that without a national project there are only global contexts. These global contexts are too powerful for university criticism of them to lead to the decontextualization of universities.

Counter-hegemonic globalization of universities as a public good is therefore a demanding political project. To attain credibility, it must quash two deeply rooted, conflicting, preconceived ideas:

1. that universities can only be reformed by university staff
2. that universities never reform themselves.

The main protagonists are public universities themselves, that is, they are the ones interested in alternative globalization. Currently, public universities represent a very fragmented social field, at the heart of which lie conflicting sectors and interests. In many countries, particularly peripheral and semi-peripheral countries, such conflicts appear to be latent, as the focus is on maintaining the status quo. This is a conservative stance: not only is the status quo defended, but no realistic alternatives are offered. Universities in these countries will therefore end up being swallowed up by neo-liberal globalization. University staff who condemn this conservative position and reject the inevitability of neo-liberal globalization will play a leading role in the progressive reforms proposed in this paper.

The *second protagonist* capable of responding to these challenges is the *nation-state*. However, this is only the case when it opts politically for the humanitarian globalization of universities. If the nation-state does not choose this option, it will end up accepting the pressures of neo-liberal globalization more or less unconditionally, or at least yielding to these pressures with little resistance. In either case, the nation-state will become the enemy of universities, regardless of any declarations to the contrary. The options tend to be dramatic, due to the close, love–hate relationship between the state and universities during the 20th century.

Finally, the *third protagonists* of the reforms proposed in this paper are *citizens*, organized either individually or collectively, as social groups, unions, social movements, non-governmental organizations and their networks, and progressive local governments. These bodies become protagonists when they are interested in encouraging cooperation between universities and the social interests that they represent. In contrast to the state, this third group of protagonists has had a distant and sometimes hostile relationship with universities in the past. This arose because of the elitism of universities and the resulting distance this caused for many years in relation to social sectors that were considered uneducated. This group needs to be won over by a response to legitimacy, that is, by non-classist, non-racist, non-sexist and non-ethnocentric university access and by initiatives that strengthen the social responsibility of universities in the area of multi-university, humanitarian knowledge.

In peripheral and semi-peripheral countries there is also a *fourth group*. Although this group does not meet the general requirements for a protagonist of the reforms proposed here, it can introduce the social contract that will give legitimacy and sustainability to the reforms. This fourth group involves *national capital*. The most dynamic national capital sectors – the sectors that are potentially best-equipped to construct the social contract – are transnationalized. Therefore, they form part of neo-liberal globalization, which is opposed to the social contract. However, the process of transnationalizing these sectors in peripheral and semi-peripheral countries does not take place without conflict. The search for conditions to improve the inclusion of these countries in the global economy depends on the scientific, technological and managerial knowledge produced in the universities. Thus, there could be interest In being associated with a reform that defends public universities, particularly in cases in which only universities produce knowledge of excellence.

The following guiding principles are related to this general idea of public university reform and its protagonists:

1. *Face new with new*
   Resistance should involve promoting alternatives for research, education, extension activities and organization that aim to democratize universities as a public good, that is, to promote the specific contribution of universities to the definition and collective solution of social, national and global problems.
2. *Fight to define the crisis*
   In the past 20 years, the hegemony of universities has suffered damage that is perhaps irreparable. This is due to changes in knowledge production and the transition that is underway: from conventional university knowledge to knowledge that is multi-university, transdisciplinary, contextualized, interactive, produced, distributed and consumed on the basis of the new ICTs. This has changed the relationship between knowledge and information and between education and citizenship.
3. *Fight for the definition of university*
   Reforms should be based on the assumption that in the 21st century a university only exists when three factors are present: graduate and postgraduate courses, research, and extension activities. If any of these factors are missing, there will be higher education but no university.
4. *Regain legitimacy*
   Universities must overcome a *threefold crisis*, which they have been facing since the 1990s: a *crisis of hegemony* (it no longer has a monopoly on research), a *crisis of legitimacy* (it is perceived as an institution that is inaccessible to underprivileged people), and an *institutional crisis* (due to the difficulties it has in maintaining its independence in the face of pressure from market demands and the view of universities as companies). Therefore, a new reform should be undertaken, in accordance with a viable national project that considers education to be a public good and trains its graduates to work on sustainable development and equity.

Miquel Barceló and Didac Ferrer

GOOD PRACTICE 1.6

Institutional learning: Participatory design of the 2015 UPC sustainability plan (Technical University of Catalonia, Spain)

CONTEXT

Sustainable development can be understood as a process of social (individual and collective) learning aimed at reorienting a development model over the long term. The introduction of sustainable development at any university or other institution usually involves an in-depth redefinition of the institution's practices, attitudes and foundations in a process known as *institutional learning*. In this process, the various agents of the institution (that is, the various university bodies) commit to changing their behaviour, and the institutional structure is transformed in keeping with the new knowledge acquired by the institution. When an institution adopts a structure that is appropriate to new practices and its agents accept this new structure, it is easier to promote the practices in question. Institutional learning can be understood as a 'paradigm shift' that facilitates practices that are consistent with the principle being introduced – in this case, sustainable development – and presents obstacles to practices that run contrary to the principle.

The direct participation of the institution's agents can facilitate the process of introducing sustainable development at a university. This is done through a participatory process in which the design of the plan for change is discussed collectively. Thus, each institutional agent becomes jointly responsible for the plan and undergoes a learning process that favours a change in attitudes and practices.

Certain general characteristics of universities can hinder the process of institutional learning and therefore also hinder the introduction of sustainable development. These characteristics include the following:

- The lack of a culture of sustainability at the institution (which reflects the attitudes of the wider community)
- The complexity of the organization
- The complexity and uncertainty associated with the concept of *sustainable development* (which, at the same time, affords the opportunity to join forces with groups dedicated to development cooperation, values education and so on)
- The dispersion of isolated efforts with limited impact
- General resistance to change at universities
- The difficulty of working in organizations where the indirect impacts (on education, knowledge generation and so on) are much greater than the direct impacts (waste, energy and so on); the indirect impacts are also much more difficult to evaluate using proper indicators.

The fact that the Technical University of Catalonia (UPC) is strictly a technological university presents additional challenges with regard to interdisciplinary issues like sustainable development, which include socioeconomic and cultural aspects and so on.

In 2005, UPC began the process of defining the 2015 UPC Sustainability Plan. The University, taking a global approach to this process, began by identifying some of the weaknesses that might affect the introduction of sustainable development at the institution.

DESCRIPTION

After two consecutive environmental plans during the periods 1996–2001 and 2002–2005, as well as the development of various sustainability and social-commitment initiatives both inside and outside the framework of these plans, the University proposed the 2015 UPC Sustainability Plan, which combines internal efforts with external alliances.

One of the most innovative aspects of this plan is the design of the development and definition process. This process seeks both the legitimacy afforded by collaboration with internationally recognized authorities on sustainable development and the active participation of the various bodies within the University.

The project has a mixed financing scheme that involves UPC, government agencies and private entities. The 2015 UPC Sustainability Plan's overall budget is €150,000 per year. The Plan enjoys the support of various internal and external bodies, including the Barcelona City Council, the Catalan government, NGOs, professional associations, the entire university community (teaching staff, technical staff, administrative personnel and students), and national and international networks and associations. The United Nations University and the European Union are also cooperating with the Plan. These agents collaborate in different ways and with varying degrees of involvement.

GOALS

The overall goal is to develop a strategic sustainable development plan that establishes priorities and determines the activities to be carried out during its implementation period.

The goals of the participatory process are to:

- Encourage the participation of all parts of the university community
- Raise awareness of sustainability among the university community
- Make all members of the University jointly responsible for the actions defined in the Plan.

The strategy involves facing four challenges, one for each area of the Plan. One of these challenges is global in nature – linked to the areas of interaction and social commitment – whereas the other three are sector-related – linked to the areas of research, education and internal management.

The four challenges included in the Plan are:

- UPC will participate in and commit to the challenges of sustainability at the local, regional and international levels
- UPC's research activity will respond to social challenges by integrating sustainability criteria
- All UPC graduates will apply sustainability criteria in their professional activity and area of influence
- UPC will operate as a sustainable organization.

PROCESS

Based on the lessons learned in the previous sustainability plans, the process of developing the 2015 UPC Sustainability Plan consists of the following stages:

1. *International external assessment.* Towards the end of the second environmental plan (2002–2005), UPC's sustainability situation was assessed in order to make strategic recommendations. In July 2005, the chairman of the UPC Board of Trustees entrusted a committee of three independent international experts with the task of carrying out this assessment. The Board of Trustees is the UPC body responsible for participation in society. Its function is to integrate and relate the University's activities with the public sector, civil society and industry.

2. *Participatory assessment and diagnosis.* A six-month participatory assessment and diagnosis process was carried out involving more than 120 people from UPC and various interest groups.

In an initial stage (virtual forum), the entire university was invited to participate. A later stage (face-to-face meetings) involved intensive work with a smaller group.

- Online forum and questionnaire: The entire university community was invited to participate in an open online forum, and a subgroup of the university community was asked to fill out an online questionnaire. In both cases, discussion focused on the second environmental plan (2002–2005).
- In November 2005, once this information had been collected and processed, a series of assessment meetings were held. Sixty-one people representing various parts of the university community (teaching staff, students, support staff, administrative personnel and so on) and members of related groups (NGOs, professional associations, active professionals and so on) participated in these meetings. Over the course of three sessions, the participants made a total of 112 proposals, which were integrated into the four areas of the 2015 UPC Sustainability Plan (education, research, university life, and social commitment and community). The participants concluded by identifying 40 high-priority proposals, which served as the starting point for the next stage in the process.

3. *Participatory design of the new Plan*. In this part of the process, held in February 2006, 41 participants made proposals and prioritized actions to be included in the new Plan. The participants worked in groups corresponding to the four areas of the Plan (education, research, university life, and social commitment and community). The process resulted in a strategic structure made up of four areas and five high-priority challenges. Thus, the actions defined in the 2015 UPC Sustainability Plan are based on the proposals and decisions reached during this participatory process. This fact sets the new Plan apart from its predecessors.

4. *Organizational structure*. While this process was being carried out, UPC consolidated its Sustainability Centre (CITIES), the body responsible for promoting the various dynamics and strategies of the Plan. Today, the CITIES team consists of eight specialists and seven students. Since 2006, UPC has also had a commissioner (equivalent to a vice-rector) dedicated exclusively to the issue of sustainable development.

5. *Approval of the Plan*. The Plan was submitted for approval by key internal committees, including the Board of Governors, UPC's top executive body.

6. *Execution and implementation*. The various actions included in the Plan have been progressively implemented since it was approved in May 2006.

7. *Assessment*. UPC will carry out an annual assessment of the Plan's progress by means of a participatory process involving the Sustainability Committee. A progress report will be published at the end of the first stage of the Plan (2010).

RESULTS

Results of the participatory process:

- A total of 209 members of the university community participated in the online forum and questionnaire
- A total of 61 people representing the areas of education, research, university life and social commitment participated in the work meetings
- The best result of the process is the fact that all the actions included in the Plan were developed by means of a participatory deliberative process.

Other results of the Plan:

- UPC has joined forces and established synergies with various complementary agents, such as experts in sustainable and human development
- The actions set out in the Plan for the period 2006–2007 have been implemented successfully. These actions include the following:

- The creation of a Regional Centre of Expertise in Education for Sustainable Development (RCE Barcelona, www.rce-barcelona.net)
- The organization of a conference of the Alliance for Global Sustainability (www.ags-event.org)
- The introduction of the EURO PEAN ECO-MANAGEMENT AND AUDIT SCHEME (EMAS) environmental management system on the UPC campus
- The launch of the UPCO2 programme to reduce greenhouse gas emissions
- UPC has strengthened its image as a leader in sustainability issues. For example, UPC was placed fourth in a ranking of European technological universities for commitment to sustainable development in education (www.upc.edu/eesd-observatory)
- UPC has contributed to a cultural change that favours sustainability
- The University is garnering national and international recognition
- The 2015 UPC Sustainability Plan is now recognized internally, not only by the body responsible for promoting the framework but by many other university bodies
- A specific communication plan is being developed to raise awareness about the 2015 UPC Sustainability Plan and encourage a cultural change.

RECOMMENDATIONS

To carry out an institutional transformation project aimed at introducing sustainability, we recommend the following:

- A technical team of at least two or three people should be created and dedicated exclusively to the project
- A basic commitment should be obtained from the rector's team
- The university community and other interest groups should be encouraged to truly participate in the process, especially in the definition of the strategy
- The process should be made as transparent as possible

- Enough money should be made available to implement the planned actions. A mixed (internal/external) financing scheme is advisable
- Invite experts to carry out an external

assessment beforehand and at regular intervals throughout the process.

Even if the project has not yet reached an advanced stage warranting an assessment of the results, reviews form part of

the process of planning such an assessment. At UPC, a committee of international experts will carry out this function in two stages: during the implementation of the Plan (2010) and upon its completion (2015).

Four experiences of including social commitments in the role and organization of Latin American universities

GUNI Observatory

GUNI's Universities and Social Commitment Observatory has sought university experiences that not only develop social-commitment initiatives and experiences, but also design their institutional models based on ethical criteria, community ties or a reformulation of the knowledge generation and transfer model. Such universities put greater emphasis on their institutional role of linking higher education with the social, political and economic context in which they operate. Social commitment forms a constituent part of these institutions.

It is no doubt possible to identify university experiences with institutional models based on social commitment in many regions of the world and in different cultural and socioeconomic contexts. Our intention is to illustrate what is happening in Latin America. We will look at four examples.

COOPERATIVE UNIVERSITY OF COLOMBIA (UCC)

The cooperative and solidarity-based economy is deeply rooted in Colombian society. According to data provided by the UCC, 4.5 million Colombians participate in cooperatives. Most cooperatives (61.84%) are micro-enterprises, with only 2.14% classed as large enterprises. This system of small cooperatives makes it possible for large sections of society with limited resources to participate in them, thus boosting economic and social development in the community.

The UCC is viewed as the university of the solidarity sector, since its main purpose is to provide training, support and advice for cooperatives and professionals in the sector. There are currently 23 UCC campuses in the country. The University is therefore able to carry out its mission in a decentralized way and adapt to the context of the local community.

Founded in 1958, the UCC was originally an organization for the training of members of cooperatives; it was not until 1964 that it became a higher education institution. The origins of the institution have left their mark on its current functions and structure.

The key institutional body of the UCC is an assembly formed by the cooperatives that founded the University and various federations of cooperatives. The assembly ordered the creation of a higher council, which establishes and implements the University's policies.

Another unique feature of the UCC is the central role it plays in training and supporting institutions and professionals in the cooperative economy. Senior managers, civil servants and members of cooperatives receive undergraduate and postgraduate education, and skills training. The University's research focuses on the quality and efficiency of the socioeconomic management of cooperatives, employee funds and mutual associations. Through extension programmes, professionals in the solidarity economy are given continuing education.

The UCC is a general university. Its syllabuses, which all include specific subjects directed towards the solidarity economy, as well as special modules that also focus on this area, provide the skills and knowledge necessary for professionals to work in the solidarity economy, towards which all its activities are directed. UCC graduates receive training directed towards drawing up political, creative and solidarity criteria, as well as providing them with basic knowledge for their professional futures.

NATIONAL UNIVERSITY OF GENERAL SARMIENTO (UNGS)

Founded in 1993, the UNGS is a public institution with an innovative institutional vision and structure. The three key values of the institution are: relating applied research to education to provide a complex approach to real problems; structuring courses from an interdisciplinary perspective; and widening access to university education.

To meet the demands of society and fulfil its strategic priorities, a basic principle of the UNGS is the linking of professional training, relevant research, community service and the quest for alternative solutions for comprehensive development. It defines its frame of reference as the surrounding urban area and the Buenos Aires Metropolitan Region as a whole.

The academic structure of the UNGS is based on the needs and problems of the community, rather than areas of knowledge. The University therefore has four academic units:

1. *Institute of Sciences (ICI)*. This unit is responsible for the first cycle of studies for all students. It provides training and basic research programmes to enable students to use comprehensive knowledge to tackle any specific problem. Students then complete their undergraduate studies in one of the following three specialized institutes.
2. *Institute of Conurbation (ICO)*. This institute deals with urban problems from a comprehensive perspective. It focuses most of its training and research work on the Buenos Aires Metropolitan Region, thus enabling a practical approach.
3. *Institute of Human Development (IDH)*. This institute organizes university preparation courses and trains teachers of different educational levels (including higher education) in areas such as culture, politics and communication.
4. *Institute of Industry (IDEI)*. This institute trains students in technical and industrial engineering, and in industrial and political economics.

This academic structure facilitates interdisciplinary work and interaction between research, teaching and professional services to the community.

The University's cross-disciplinary perspective on research takes into consideration the problems and challenges identified in the four institutes. It promotes the consolidation of cross-disciplinary research groups and adapts its teaching to research needs.

Finally, the UNGS promotes university access through free undergraduate degrees, grants and teaching models that focus on individual tutoring and monitoring.

BOLIVARIAN UNIVERSITY OF CHILE
Founded in 1987, the Bolivarian University operates on 13 campuses in different parts of the country. The University's mission is to 'contribute to socially sustainable cultural change by institutionalizing an innovative university practice in the social sciences that integrates three strategic aspects: training, research and socio-community intervention'.

Based on these foundational principles, the Bolivarian University aims to develop the idea of the 'extended' university. It believes that universities are places for knowledge building, critical thought and generating action through intense interaction with the community. The University's institutional model defines the necessary tools and policies to identify the needs and the diversity of the surrounding communities. In this model, the University is also responsible for reflecting on problems in the community and proposing solutions. It must also generate the tools (theoretical, analytical and technical) expected by stakeholders and the wider social community.

In 1994, based on this twin perspective, the Bolivarian University created the Yungay Centre, an independent unit for community service. This open, educational, cross-disciplinary unit aims to empower and support the development of local communities and promote respect for human rights, self-management, identity and diversity.

The Centre has two roles: first, to complement the theoretical training students receive from the University, since the institution's principles include the application of Polanyi's theories to develop a learning model focused not only on explicit learning (that is, the transfer of theoretical knowledge) but also on tacit learning, which can only be acquired through praxis (that is, participation or the observation of others). All students at the University do part of their work placement at this Centre. Second, the Centre serves the Yungay community through a legal clinic, a psychological support centre, a local library and various other centres. This means that the Centre actively participates in the cultural

network of the Yungay neighbourhood and promotes human and social development in the area.

THE MULTIVERSITY *MUNDO REAL EDGAR MORIN*

The University *Mundo Real Edgar Morin* intends to be an important centre for appropriate knowledge. This knowledge helps to understand people, their local and national problems, as well as the planet's difficulties. It is indeed this understanding that helps to take action in different fields. This is the mission of the University *Mundo Real Edgar Morin*. (Edgar Morin)

This University is conceived of as a world institution, with a clear awareness of its reality and its social environment. For this reason, the University seeks to produce people who are aware that their 'Multiversity' education is linked to life – theirs and everybody else's life. What gives sense to knowledge is understanding it in context – that is, living, thinking and feeling reality.

Taking this into account, it is important that students learn not only from great specialists and theoretical experts, but also from workers, technicians and craftspeople, or even from people lacking in formal education.

As a social academic entity, the Multiversity's purpose is to generate, promote and spread throughout the economic and social environment, at all levels, the ability to identify options for solving problems and designing routes that lead to change and innovation.

Edgar Morin's oeuvre inspired this initiative. He created the concept of 'complex thought' and proposed using this in a transdisciplinary way to reconstruct knowledge and generally make possible the reform of thought and education.

The methodology of this University starts with the premise that society requires more dynamic, flexible, pertinent and significant educational institutions. Thus, a new approach is required to produce models that can sustain the new educational purposes. This approach should include:

1. New relations in all components of the University.
2. Overcoming traditional and artificial divisions between administration, investigation, teaching and the spreading of knowledge.
3. Changing the educational point of view based on the teacher and his/her subject, to a point of view more focused on the student.
4. Changing the traditional concept of standardized groups of students (with time, place, contents and so on) to learning communities.
5. Overcoming the limitations of predefined modalities of teaching, opening them up to a wide range of possible ways to learn.
6. New ways to evaluate and certificate what has been learned.
7. New curriculum proposal based on transdisciplinarity.
8. New methods of management, organization and institutional administration, aimed at non-lineal and distributed nets (heterarchies), based on education and learning, not bureaucracy.

SPECIAL CONTRIBUTION I.18
Social responsibility of universities

Alma Herrera

The notion of the social responsibility of universities has acquired a different meaning in the 21st century and has come to signify the relationship between the role of higher education institutions in teaching multidisciplinary courses – generating knowledge in the context of its application and developing organic links with the environment – and the demands of society for the benefit of the majority.

The result is the design and implementation of sustainable human development projects and strategies that aim to reduce the cognitive divides between sectors, institutions and countries. This leads to changes in institutional structures and in the nature of the basic functions of higher education institutions. Further changes are brought about by implementing new ways for higher education institutions to effect international cooperation, set up networks and create links with diverse social and economic sectors with which collaboration was unimaginable until a few years ago.

The new profile of the social responsibility of universities, which transcends what has commonly been termed *relevance*, is reflected in the design of educational policies that are intended to encourage greater correspondence between the fundamental objectives of universities and the environment in which they operate. In general terms, as stated by Tünnermann (2000, pp. 190–5), it is linked to the commitment of higher education to the needs of all sectors of society and is based on 15 fundamental principles, which include the following:

1. Knowledge and higher education constitute a social asset that is generated, transmitted and recreated for the benefit of society ...; higher education institutions must therefore undertake a public commitment to the general interests of the society of which they form part.
2. Access to higher education must be equal for everyone, according to their respective merits ...; equal opportunities must be extended to the possibility of permanence and success in higher education.
3. In contemporary society, higher education is taking on increasingly complex functions that may add new dimensions to its essential mission of searching for truth ...; it serves as a centre for critical thought because it exercises a kind of intellectual power that society needs if it is to reflect, understand and act.
4. The ethical dimension must form the basis for reflection on the impact of the rapid transformations that are affecting almost all levels of individual and collective life and which threaten to destroy the moral foundations that will enable the new generations to construct the future.
5. Universities must help to create the future ... by anticipating events in order to guide them and give them meaning ...; they must direct their critical analyses towards future scenarios and the formulation of alternative proposals.
6. Universities must maintain their cultural mission because ... globalization threatens to impose a damaging cultural uniformity if different peoples do not strengthen their own identities and values ...; the cultivation and dissemination of these values must be closely linked to the local, regional and national community in order to use this base to open up to the world and, by adopting a universal outlook, create citizens of the world who are capable of committing themselves to the world's problems and appreciating and valuing cultural diversity as a source of enrichment of world heritage.
7. Higher education institutions must take part in training citizens who are aware and responsible, that is, citizens for the 21st century who are critical, participative and who show solidarity ... in a context of sexual equality ...; it is also necessary to promote the principle of an appropriate balance

between the basic functions of higher education in such a way that teaching, research and dissemination are mutually enriching.

8. Higher education institutions must enjoy complete freedom to fulfil their missions ...; they should have autonomy not only from the state but also from other social, political and ideological forces that may seek to exert control over them.

9. Higher education must be creative and use multidisciplinary strategies in assimilating the basic principles of a culture of peace that are essential to the future of humanity and the sustainable development of peoples.

In this regard, the social responsibility of universities constitutes the link between the knowledge generated in the context of its application (scientific, technological, humanistic and artistic knowledge) and local, national and global needs. Its fundamental objective is to promote the social usefulness of knowledge, thus contributing to improving quality of life. It consequently requires a two-way perspective between universities and society, which involves directly multiplying the critical uses of knowledge in society and the economy.

Furthermore, there is an increasing interest in setting up methods of analysing the social responsibility of universities. This is illustrated by the Social Responsibility of Universities Network, which is based at the National University of Colombia and which organized the first Regional Forum on the Social Responsibility of Universities. This network was set up to pursue the objectives proposed by the World Declaration on Higher Education for the Twenty-First Century. It set out to establish the need for a vision of socially responsible universities with the following objectives:

- To conserve and create the social capital of knowledge and thought through reflection and multidisciplinary research and to disseminate it via different media
- To support the design of public and private development policies and to take into consideration the needs of different sectors in order to define its contribution to sustainable development and to the improvement of society as a whole
- To create a vigorous policy that promotes staff development and curricular innovation
- To train highly qualified, integrated men and women of integrity who are committed to values that they actively defend and disseminate. These men and women should view their profession as an opportunity to serve others and who are able to use their role as citizens to help build society and provide creative solutions to the challenges of a nation-building project
- To include a cross-disciplinary curriculum that adopts a global vision of the reality of the country in all its richness and that creates opportunities to offer services to individuals and groups who have no access to the benefits of development
- To provide permanent training and facilitate re-entry into higher education for updating and complementing training in order to provide civil education and encourage active participation in society. This process should take into account current trends in the world of work and in the scientific and technological sectors
- To remain open to change; to assess and incorporate knowledge and experience of the environment; to generate and maintain discussion forums within higher education institutions; to search for the truth, express it and act in accordance with it.

As has been discussed, the social responsibility of universities includes a wide range of actions and processes that endeavour to respond to the needs of their environment in an appropriate and effective manner and with a strong sense of ethics. This approach is of great importance because globalization and the application of neo-liberal models of economic development have led to social crises to which universities must respond by providing innovative solutions to the complexity of the current problems at the national and regional levels.

Such innovative solutions will require universities to establish organic links between their substantive functions and reconsider their role in solving the complex problems of society in the 21st century.

REFERENCES

Tünnermann, C. (2000) *Universidad y Sociedad*. Caracas: Comisión de Estudios de Postgrado. Facultad de Humanidades y Educación. Universidad Central de Venezuela. Ministerio de Educación, Cultura y Deportes.

PART II

REGIONAL PERSPECTIVES ON THE ROLE OF HIGHER EDUCATION FOR HUMAN AND SOCIAL DEVELOPMENT

Abstract

In Part I this report studied selected global issues on higher education's role in social and human development. This overview is a synthesis of the regional perspectives on higher education's role for human and social development based on the contribution of the authors in four key areas – one of which is the state of higher education in each region since the World Conference on Higher Education (WCHE) held in 1998, the other is possible future roles, strategies and actions of higher education in order to foster social and human development – for the regions classified as: Sub-Saharan Africa, Arab States, Asia and the Pacific, Europe, North America (USA and Canada) and Latin America and the Caribbean.

INTRODUCTION

The role of the higher education institutions (HEIs) has been changing over time from custodians and transmitters of culturally respected forms of knowledge through producers of skilled human resources to a more recent role as agents of social transformation through social and human development. This role, although it had been there in the past, has been receiving new emphasis in today's world of overemphasized market friendliness and material well-being. In Part I, the present report has analysed selected global issues on higher education's role in social and human development. The present overview attempts to synthesize the regional perspectives on higher education's role for human and social development based on the contributions of the authors in the following four areas.

- What has been the state of higher education in the region since the World Conference on Higher Education (WCHE) held in 1998?
- What has been the impact of political, social, economic and technological challenges of globalization in the region in relation to social and human development?
- What could be the contribution of higher education to social and human development in the region?
- What could be the future role, strategies

and actions of higher education in order to foster social and human development?

We shall deal with each of these issues for the regions classified as: sub-Saharan Africa, Arab States, Asia and the Pacific, Europe, North America (USA and Canada) and Latin America and the Caribbean. Except for the statistical part, our overview reflects, as a rule, the authors' point of view – in some cases almost verbatim. Nevertheless we have constructed some joints with our own inputs. We strongly recommend the reader to make a careful reading of the authors' original papers, in order to appreciate all the richness and nuances within them. In a brief synthesis like this one only some relevant points appear, but not the enlightening picture given in the whole article by the authors.

Obviously countries in each of these regions vary significantly in their status for each of these areas. The authors have had to aggregate for simplicity and for interregional comparison. Variation exists not only in geo-political and socioeconomic contexts but more so, in the size of their population, their status in human development as defined by the UNDP and also in the size of their higher education sector. We give below the magnitude of the intra-regional variation for the year 2004 from the UNESCO (population and enrolment)[1] and the UNDP (human development index)[2] statistics for the reader to have an idea of the nature and extent of this variation.

In sub-Saharan Africa's 45 countries, total population varied from 80 thousand in Seychelles to 129 million in Nigeria; in the Arab States' 20 countries, it varied from 716 thousand in Bahrain to 73 million in Egypt; in Asia and the Pacific's widely varied 51 countries it varied from a meagre 1 thousand each in Niue and Tokelau to 1308 million in China; in Europe's 44 countries (including Israel) it varied from San Marino's 28 thousand to Russia's 144 million, in North America's two countries it varied from Canada's 32 million to the USA's 295 million and in Latin America and Caribbean's 41 countries it varied from Montserrat's 4 thousand to Brazil's 184 million.

The human development index varies from

Bikas C. Sanyal and Francisco López Segrera

TABLE II.1.1
Regional average of enrolment, GER and GPI (1999 and 2004)

Region	1999 Enrolment Total		1999 Enrolment Female		2004 Enrolment Total	2004 Enrolment Female		GER Total 1999		GER Total 2004	GPI 1999		GPI 2004	
Arab States	5,165,102		2,146,236	**	6,519,997	3,104,275	**	19		21	0.74	**	0.94	**
Central and Eastern Europe	12,960,439	**	6,930,388	**	18,517,288	10,137,470		39	**	54	1.18	**	1.24	
Central Asia	1,278,741	**	609,876	**	1,883,736	956,126		19	**	25	0.91	**	1.04	
East Asia and the Pacific	22,809,230		9,493,132	**	39,397,161	17,882,449		14		23	0.74	**	0.88	
Latin America and the Caribbean	10,662,525		5,619,533		14,869,644	7,973,367		21		29	1.12		1.17	
North America and Western Europe	28,240,250		15,304,602		32,951,513	18,359,176		61		70	1.23		1.31	
South and West Asia	...		...		15,390,226	6,091,718		...		10	...		0.7	
Sub-Saharan Africa	2,133,275		858,935	**	3,338,427	1,271,189		4		5	0.67	**	0.62	

Note: (**) UIS estimation; (...) Data not available.
Source: UNESCO Institute of Statistics website.

0.311 in Niger (the lowest in the world with a rank of 177) to 0.842 in Seychelles (rank: 47) in sub-Saharan Africa; from 0.492 in Yemen (rank: 150) to 0.859 in Bahrain (rank: 39) in the Arab States; from 0.527 in Nepal (rank: 138) to 0.957 in Australia (rank: 3) in Asia and the Pacific; from 0.694 in Moldova (rank: 114) to 0.965 in Norway (rank: 1) in Europe; from 0.950 in Canada (rank: 6) to 0.948 in USA (rank: 8) in North America and from 0.482 in Haiti (rank: 154) to 0.879 in Barbados in the Latin America and Caribbean region (rank: 31).

The size of enrolment varies in sub-Saharan Africa from 1500 in Gambia to 633 thousand in South Africa; from 1100 in Djibouti to 2.5 million in Egypt in the Arab States; from 500 in Palau to 19.4 million in China in Asia and the Pacific; from 300 in Andorra to 8.6 million in Russia in Europe; from 1.3 million to 16.9 million in the USA in the North American region and from 700 in Belize (only 10 in Turks and Caicos Islands) to 4 million in Brazil in the Latin America and the Caribbean region.

WHAT HAS BEEN THE STATE OF HIGHER EDUCATION IN THE REGION SINCE THE WORLD CONFERENCE ON HIGHER EDUCATION (WCHE) HELD IN 1998?

One of the recommendations of the WCHE was increased provision of access. This has been realized at different rates in different regions. Development of higher education is the most important element for human and social development. Its distribution between male and female

provides an important social aspect of development. We start our analysis with these two aspects.

World enrolment has increased from 92 million in 1999, with 44.2 million female, to 132 million in 2004, with 65.3 million female.[3] World participation rate measured by gross enrolment ratio (GER, total enrolment divided by total population in the relevant age group) in higher education has increased from 18% to 24% during 1999–2004 with an increase in gender parity index (GPI = female GER/male GER) from 0.97 to 1.03, female overtaking males in participation.

It can be observed that higher education at the world level has achieved 'mass' stage (GER, more than 15%) at 24% whereas in sub-Saharan Africa and South and West Asia it is still elitist (GER less than 15%) with a meagre participation rate of 5% and 11% respectively. In North America and Europe it has achieved universal stage with higher than 50% GER whereas in Arab States, East Asia and the Pacific, and Latin America and the Caribbean higher education is at the 'mass' stage with 21%, 23% and 28% GER respectively.

In respect of gender parity significant improvement can be noted at the world level where females have taken over males. Women are most favoured in Iceland with a gender parity index of 1.78 followed by the Caribbean sub-region at 1.70. Region-wise, they are most favoured in North America and Western Europe combined, where the index is highest at 1.32, followed by the Pacific sub-region (1.27), Central and Eastern Europe (1.25), Latin America (1.16) and Central Asia (1.05). In all the other regions males dominate. In sub-Saharan Africa women are least favoured with an index of 0.62 below South and South West Asia at 0.70. Among the regions, significant improvement has been achieved by the Arab States with an increase in the value of the index from 0.74 to 0.95.

There have also been other developments in the regions, which are discussed below.

In the sub-Saharan region, a large number of initiatives have been launched to revitalize higher education. The US$200 million programme of 'Partnership for Higher Education in Africa' launched in 2000, US$5 billion ten-year partnership project called 'Renewing the African University' launched in 2005, a four-year US$7 million programme called 'Regional Capacity Mobilization Initiative' funded by the United Kingdom, and the Association of African University's four-year US$20.4 million 'Core Programme' launched in 2005, to mention only a few, are mobilizing development partners in Africa to bring about reforms in higher education to promote human and social development in the region. Nevertheless, the deterioration of the infrastructure, the 'brain drain' and the high number of vacancies in university positions are among the main factors hindering higher education development in this region.

In the Arab region, although access has been widened as noted above, the development after WCHE is characterized by reduced public expenditure in higher education with emphasis on market mechanism, deterioration in quality, gender inequity in teaching posts, proliferation of diversified providers, and less emphasis on research and innovation. Indeed, it is apprehended that if the current state of affairs continues human and social development will be inhibited.

The WCHE has experienced the following changes in Asia and the Pacific, in addition to the issue of access mentioned above: a polarized transition from 'elite' to 'mass' higher education, a rise in private higher education, corporatization, and cross-border mobility raising concern for social equity and broader issues of human development.

Europe has shown concern for many of the WCHE issues in working together through a diverse range of international organizations and initiatives including the European Union (EU), the Council of Europe and, above all, the Bologna Process. The mechanisms of the Bologna Process provide a model for collaborating and for developing a community of practice.

The change in the political perception of universities is the most striking fact about European higher education in the decade after the WCHE, according to Anne Corbett. At the beginning of the 1990s, universities were considered by national governments to be difficult to manage and fund and, apparently, they seriously lagged behind the universities of the US and Japan. Yet ten years on from the WCHE, universities have achieved an uncommon and exceptional level of political importance at European and national level. According to the author 'they form part of normal experience for around half of the European population of conventional student age, with the complexities of funding and governance that this implies at national level. They are clearly identified by the EU and many national governments as a critical part of the solution to the economic challenges that face Europe as a whole, as profitable activity becomes increasingly tied to the wealth that knowledge exploitation can generate on a global scale. All organizations, and especially the Council of Europe, look to them to advance democracy' (Corbett, 2008).

Even if Europe is closer than many developed countries to the social and equity in access aims of the WCHE, a more explicit link between the Bologna Process and the WCHE agenda is needed.

In North America, as a response to the WCHE recommendations, clear guidelines were given in support of a humanistic perspective of higher education where ecological, cultural and ethical dimensions of human and social development received as much importance as economic ones. Increased access for underprivileged and non-traditional students, such as aboriginals, people with disabilities, minority groups, programmes offered in minority languages, emphasis on adult and continuing education programmes and interdisciplinary research combining social and natural sciences and science and engineering are facilitating the achievement of the WCHE goals. The use of ICT in the institutions of higher education is promoting transparency and accountability as well as off-campus outreach activities while making higher education accessible to the 'unreached'.

In Latin America and the Caribbean, the WCHE had as a central impact the offering – beginning from what was expressed in the Regional Conference of LAC (1996) and in the Action Plan, as well as in the WCHE – of a theoretical frame with consensus to transform higher education in the region. At a higher level, this implied a shared general vision about how to carry out the transformation processes of public – and even private – HEIs through institutional evaluation, with the goal of improving management and financial systems as well as equity in access as a key priority. But also it implied much more: that the university should be a key agent in transforming society by building viable alternatives in the middle of complexity and uncertainty. According to Axel Didriksson (2008), author of the regional perspective of Latin America and the Caribbean, international cooperation and building of networks has been one of the greatest inputs of the WCHE in the region as along with innovation and the internationalization of HE. IESALC-UNESCO has played a leading role in this sense. Didriksson also points out the challenges for HE: the rapid increase of privatization, the lack of access for the poorest and the low GER – despite its improvement – in comparison with developed countries.

WHAT HAS BEEN THE IMPACT OF POLITICAL, SOCIAL, ECONOMIC AND TECHNOLOGICAL CHALLENGES OF GLOBALIZATION IN THE REGION IN RELATION TO SOCIAL AND HUMAN DEVELOPMENT?

In his paper on sub-Saharan Africa, Goolam Mohamedbhai gives a picture of the effects of globalization arguing that, although globalization has improved growth and development in many developing countries, there is genuine concern that the poorer countries of sub-Saharan Africa have not benefited from this processes.

'There is now worldwide agreement that global sustainable development cannot exist if sub-Saharan Africa remains underdeveloped, that the region needs to be assisted, and that higher education can play a significant role in improving the situation' (Mohamedbhai, 2008).

In the Arab States region, according to Mohaya Zaytoun (2008), 'the Arab economy under globalization lacks many of the features of a knowledge-based economy that can develop, promote and reward high productivity, scientific research and innovation. Moreover, Arab economies have not attained expectations of a high and sustainable growth rate.'

Concerning globalization, one dilemma for the Asia and Pacific region is how to make value and moral education serve the two complementary purposes of modernization and preservation of national identity and culture. Reduction of poverty and economic growth have been accompanied by growing inequality; increased consumerism by environmental degradation; and great economic success has been accompanied by increased competition for resources and for potential for conflicts affecting human and social development.

The author of the European regional paper considers that globalization is a highly controversial topic across Europe. Dispute is fuelled by the uncertainties generated by globalization – the interdependence of economies worldwide, driven forward by liberalizing market economies and rapidly falling costs of transport and communication – and the ambiguities as to where cause and effect lie. 'The case for globalization is that Europe – and the world – has got richer in this period; human welfare, broadly defined, has been promoted since the late 1980s

and the number of people in poverty has declined. However, opponents of globalization have had a significant political impact within the past few years and widespread public support. In Europe, globalization is blamed variously for the disappearance of traditional industrial jobs; the emergences of new consumer demands as successful societies get richer; the necessity for a highly educated society to keep such an economy expanding, perhaps at the expense of other educational needs; and the emergence of disparities which are geographical and income-relate' (Corbett, 2008).

In North America, globalization is perceived to have changed communicative culture. Institutions have been recommended to adapt to the demands of the knowledge-based economy to survive in the globalize world. Globalization leads to 'lifetime fluidity' between school and work. Institutions of higher education are in the best place to take advantage of that. However there are also challenges facing higher education due to globalization in the North American context. These include more emphasis on economic values of education, priority to business and industry, 'corporatism' and 'academic capitalism', which is perceived as not harmonious with social and human development (Hall and Dragne, 2008).

According to Didriksson's (2008) data and analysis, globalization has had a very negative effect on higher education in the Latin America and Caribbean region. Globalization benefited some countries of LAC but imposed new asymmetries that, instead of stimulating the development of local capacities in the area of creation and diffusion of knowledge, and of extending the possibility of development with equity, blocked them, thereby strengthening privatization, inequity and backwardness in higher education and scientific research. The impact of globalization has not implied a positive reform, but rather the deformation and alteration of the universities.

One can observe marked difference in the perception of the impact of globalization in the different regions. The industrialized countries of the North and West observe a more or less positive impact of globalization; sub-Saharan Africa, the Arab States and Latin America and the Caribbean observe a predominantly negative impact of globalization whereas the Asia and Pacific region observes mixed results according to sub-regions and countries.

WHAT COULD BE THE CONTRIBUTION OF HIGHER EDUCATION TO SOCIAL AND HUMAN DEVELOPMENT?

In sub-Saharan Africa, the most important contribution of higher education to human and social development would be human capital formation followed by capacity building in coping with globalization, addressing gender issues, meeting the goals of the 'Education for All' programme and of the Millennium Development Goals (MDGs), providing the necessary skilled human resources especially teachers, facing the challenge of HIV/AIDS through relevant means including outreach programmes and alleviating poverty through rural development programmes.

In the Arab states, higher education would contribute to human and social development by promoting socially relevant non-university education, open and distance learning, focusing on the issues related to quality of higher education, emphasizing research and knowledge creation, focusing on better working conditions for faculty in order to control brain drain, designing employment-oriented higher education strategies and regulating new providers of higher education.

In Asia and the Pacific, the challenges facing higher education are the idea of higher education as a public good, inadequate operational mechanisms to respond to the changing external environment because of the lack both of institutional autonomy and of interaction between institutions, commerce and industry, and a polluted academic and campus culture. According to Wang Yibing (2008), for higher education to contribute to social and human development, transformative measures are needed in these areas.

In Europe, higher education's contribution to social and human development is noted through its meeting the new demands imposed on it by globalization. Higher education holds many of the keys that will make the difference between an active and a passive response to the challenges, and European countries have high standards of higher education. However, for higher education to contribute to social and human development there is need, according Corbett (2008), for attention 'to the uncertainties and options which relate to knowledge in a context in which universities are ever more conscious of globalization, knowledge as exemplified by student mobility, knowledge in terms of production and knowledge as legitimated by a universal model'.

One important contribution of European higher education to social and human development is the growing debate in universities around issues such as the social dimension of European higher education, the nature of the 'public good' and the international role of European universities. Other issues under debate include how universities can contribute to North–South solidarity, sustainable development, climate change and personal development priorities. Nevertheless, this debate should be widespread to all European universities, and also take into account reform strategies and the multiple roles of universities; roles as both reproductive – of elites, and of knowledge – and transformative agents.

Higher education in North America is contributing to social and human development through civic engagement (engaging community by taking activities off campus, enhancing civic literacy and promoting the value of community engagement among students, faculty and staff, supporting community-based research initiatives and links with community groups, promoting opportunities for knowledge transfer and technology transfer), curricular reform, multiculturalism, increased continuing education access, internationalization and finally addressing the issue of global warming through implementation of plans for specific actions.

In North America, multiculturalism and fostering diversity have an important place in social and human development through higher education. Diversity has been raised as an issue in post-secondary institutions, with attention being paid to exclusion, discrimination, inequities, and harassment. HEIs have been roused to action to provide organizational responses to diversity by demands, pressures and normative expectations originating in their external world.

The major contribution higher education might have to human and social development in Latin America and the Caribbean, would imply that the diverse forms of education and higher education, the science and the technology, are evaluated by their capacity to improve the distribution of income and the eradication of poverty.

The region is characterized by indifference towards the MDGs, stagnation, growing poverty and inequality, and by not fulfilling the proper features of knowledge society. This crisis of transition could be overcome by constructing an alternative scenario in which governments and institutions would consider higher education to be a public good and a strategic instrument in the elimination of poverty and inequality.

WHAT COULD BE THE FUTURE ROLE, STRATEGIES AND ACTIONS OF HIGHER EDUCATION IN ORDER TO FOSTER SOCIAL AND HUMAN DEVELOPMENT?

SUB-SAHARAN AFRICA

In sub-Saharan Africa the future role, strategies and actions that would be considered as options by governments and institutions – in order to foster social and human development, according to Mohamedbhai (2008), author of the regional paper – are the following:

- Higher education may be reformed with quality assurance as the driving force at both system and institutional levels with emphasis on higher participation rate, with multidisciplinary programmes incorporating elements for social and human development, with participative and problem-based teaching and with the development of analytical skills and critical and independent thinking that fosters team work.

- Higher education would try to achieve the MDGs.
- Higher education would resist the commercialization and commoditization of higher education. Private and cross-border higher education would be welcomed but regulated.
- The state would differentiate the country's institutions capable and suitable for carrying out research while research in science and technology will be given priority. Universities could emphasize developmental research. Fundamental research should also be emphasized in selected relevant areas.
- Higher education in Africa would have to place greater emphasis on community engagement.
- Higher education in Africa should be relevant to both the local community and the global society. There would be recognition of community service on equal terms with teaching and research involving students and staff in developmental problems of rural areas, with appreciation for rich indigenous knowledge.
- Resources would be pooled and collaborative partnerships created with institutions and through associations at the national, regional and international levels involving the African Diaspora academics.
- The government would have the primary responsibility but institutions can and should assist in performing the future role of the sector effectively by operating democratically, by promoting fairness and justice and by setting appropriate machinery for dialogue and for resolving disputes and differences.
- The future role of higher education to achieve human and social development in Africa would need institutions to operate in a peaceful and democratic environment with transparency and accountability, free from conflict, political interference and persecution and in an environment conducive to learning.

THE ARAB STATES

In the Arab States, the future role, strategies and actions that would be developed by higher education in order to promote social and human development according to Zaytoun (2008) could be the following:

- Higher education would focus on achieving the MDGs.
- Higher education would promote research activities.
- Higher education would have to upgrade curriculum and pedagogy.

- Higher education would have to enjoy autonomy and academic freedom, and foster social responsibility.
- Higher education would develop research directed towards: enhancing the levels of education; graduating qualified and socially committed teachers; appropriate curriculum design; periodic evaluation of the educational process and staff development.
- Higher education would generate political will to address local problems, developing intra-regional cooperation, emphasizing industrial progress to create effective demand for R&D, recognizing traditional knowledge, performing research on formulation of sound public policies, implementing strategies and evaluation procedures for human and social development and developing strategic alliances among the stakeholders of research.
- Higher education would promote the integration of selected disciplines and creation of new disciplines, the introduction of active and participative learning and a right balance of 'general' and 'professional' education to facilitate development of the whole individual.
- Higher education would ensure faculty members, students and public the right to information and internet connectivity, empowering the academic community to resist foreign pressures and interests and enabling them to identify a unified vision and agenda.
- Higher education would design and implement an employment-oriented strategy, which may combine entrepreneurship skills with skills for social and human development.
- Higher education would contribute to overcoming inequality in its different forms and to fostering equal opportunity within the entire society through female empowerment; promoting human rights; broadening access to quality higher education, knowledge and information; regulating privatization and commercialization of higher education; controlling 'monoculture' and foreign language domination; balancing financial motivations with social and human development motivations and last, but not least, managing the phenomenon of globalization to the advantage of the country.

ASIA AND THE PACIFIC

In Asia and the Pacific, the future role, strategies and actions that would be developed by higher education in order to encourage social and human development according to Wang (2008) are the following:

- Higher education would be the builder of a 'culture of peace' and the major partner in the 'dialogue of civilizations'.

- Higher education would foster political awareness in the public by training future leaders and educators.
- Higher education may provide solutions to problems facing human, social and environmental development.
- Higher education would redefine its role and reposition itself through a rational analysis of the principle of cost-sharing, reinstating its fair share in national budget, balancing its economic role with the role of social and human development, alerting the major lending and donor agencies about the negative effects of ignoring higher education and enacting new legislation or revision of present laws to ensure institutional autonomy and other requirements to achieve the new role for social and human development.
- Higher education institutions would have to readjust their vision, mission and the 'nurture of the uniqueness' keeping in view their comparative advantage due to location, context or historical and cultural traditions and their commitments for social and human development.
- They would go through a process of reengineering for adoption of one or more learning models for the future such as, 'single mode', 'open and distance model', 'dual' and 'mixed mode' of universities, and the model of entrepreneurial universities.
- They would go through renovation and development of curricula to meet social and human developmental needs.
- They would create the political will and institutional framework, and mobilize resources to develop the research capacity in the countries for economic, social and human development.
- Higher education institutions of the region would promote international cooperation, especially working with international and regional organizations and agencies, and establish bilateral cooperation with foreign institutions to perform the role higher education has assigned itself as described above.

EUROPE

In Europe, the future role, strategies and actions that may be developed by higher education in order to foster social and human development according to Corbett (2008) are the following:

- The rights of individuals to exercise real choice over various types of higher education would be vastly increased.
- In the European higher education area there would be many signs of common practice such as, compatible national systems of qualifications, common use of credits both for transfer and accumulation and so on.
- European universities would play an important role

on the international scene because of their intrinsic democratic and human rights values and their humanistic tradition so important for human and social development.

- Questions such as the social dimension of higher education, the nature of the 'public good' and the international role of the universities would be priority issues.
- European universities would contribute to North–South solidarity, sustainable development, climate change, and personal development of citizens.
- The Council of Europe, networked with Magna Charta and Bologna members, would encourage and accelerate implementation of higher education strategies to contribute to social and human development.
- 'A new international strategy' would bring governments, academics, students and other stakeholders together to explore and identify affordable strategies for higher education including internationalization for a more sustainable world which could be supportive of human and social development. The internationalization strategies would be determined not solely on European terms, but also include capacity development in developing countries in areas such as democratization process, managing cross-border higher education, finance, and gender and brain drain issues.
- The implementation strategy has to be collaborative and not imposed from top to bottom; the policy aims would be not to harmonize systems but to develop a community of practice.
- Finally, universities would engage in their traditional tasks of teaching and research by combining 'consciousness raising and solid knowledge accumulation' in support of social and human development.

NORTH AMERICA

In North America, the future role, strategies and actions that may be developed by higher education in order to promote social and human development, are perceived to be different in the USA from those in Canada in various aspects. Nevertheless, in a synthesis of this sort we will try to show analogies more than differences. For a full picture of the current situation, see Hall and Dragne's paper later in this report.

- Public HEIs would have to face the difficulties in providing wider access and necessary supports from poor, black, Hispanic, Native American and other socially challenged groups within their neighbourhood communities.
- Higher education would also have to face challenges of climate change, civic engagement, global harmony, inclusion, and the reduction of violence in the lives

of people as useful elements for social and human development.

- Concern has already been expressed about the crucial role of higher education in improving social cohesion and inclusion with priority given to under-represented groups including aboriginal peoples.
- Universities would expand their outreach efforts to develop a research and science culture.
- Universities would promote international solidarity through graduate scholarships.
- Higher education would incorporate 'robust language' on civic engagement into the strategic plans of all institutions and create university-wide offices, programmes or centres of civic/community engagement and Chairs of Community Engaged Studies as well as places for Community Scholars in Residence.
- Higher education would create institutional and national working groups on the implications for merit, tenure and promotion of community-engaged programming.
- Higher education would create/consolidate a national network of community-engaged practices.
- Higher education would support the creation of an open-source database for relevant knowledge.
- Higher education would promote the revitalization and recovery of relevant dying languages.
- Higher education would promote internationalization through curricular reforms focusing on inclusion of a truly global knowledge base and linking institutions of the South with the idea of mutual development.

LATIN AMERICA AND THE CARIBBEAN

In Latin America and the Caribbean, the future role, strategies and actions that could be considered as options by governments and institutions in order to foster social and human development, according to Didriksson (2008), are the following:

- To assume their social responsibility for fostering democratization and the broader participation of civil society and for recommending policies benefiting the whole society.
- To emphasize the need for national, regional and local policies articulating different levels of education.
- To recommend and put in place policies in order to avoid and eliminate existing inequalities in gender, colour, ethnic origin and social class.
- Higher education could broaden and diversify the institutional offer and the curricula, offering knowledge with social relevance. This action would help to include marginalized youth and adults previously excluded from access to higher education.
- To recommend policies in order to foster investment

in technological and scientific research and to consider science and technology to be the strategic components of the knowledge society.
- The universities would strengthen, update and introduce capacities of research according to their social needs.
- To recommend policies to avoid massive migration of the labour force, and brain drain in particular.
- Higher education would be predominantly of public character, free and with high relevance (pertinence) and social responsibility.
- Higher education could be an object of state policies with a prospective vision and the aim of constructing a knowledge society with equity.
- The knowledge produced and transferred from the universities would be oriented to (a) eradicate poverty and inequality, (b) diminish the gap between developed and less developed countries, and (c) strengthen the competitiveness and productivity of the Latin America and the Caribbean region in order to foster regional and international cooperation.
- Higher education would encourage diversification of financial sources.
- Higher education would promote its own democratization in order to give access to those with merit who have previously been excluded.
- Higher education would realize a process of reform and change in order to achieve a common space of human and social development, of construction of equity and citizenship, as well as of scientific and technological development.

CONCLUDING REMARKS

We have noted above that in respect of the past roles higher education played in social and human development the experiences differ among the regions.

1. Concerning the state of higher education since the WCHE, we can see that it had less impact in Europe and North America and in developed countries of Asia, and more impact in the rest of the regions. This could be explained by the fact that many of the recommendations of the WCHE had already been achieved by developed countries.

2. Differences among regions have been most significant in the area of the impact of globalization. In the developed countries of Europe and North America, the trends of globalization are perceived in a very optimistic way. However, in regions hosting less developed countries – sub-Saharan Africa, the Arab States, Latin America and the Caribbean – you can

find a rather worrisome view of the problems and challenges posed by globalization, whereas the Asia and Pacific region has an eclectic view concerning the impact of globalization in relation to social and human development.

- In sub-Saharan Africa, even if globalization has improved growth and development in some countries, a general perception exists that the income gap with developed countries has increased and that globalization has posed challenges such as growing poverty in some countries and brain drain.
- In the Arab States, globalization has had an impact on social and human development, leading to dualism in the world of work in many countries. High-productivity, technologically advanced enclaves co-exist with a low-productivity, technologically traditional sector. A perception exists that globalization may create problems in relation to issues such as: equity; funding; and economic, social and human development. Challenges of globalization to national and regional sovereignty are also at stake.
- In Asia, challenges of globalization to social and human development include 'rapidly growing economies; the accelerating pace of economic globalization; the transition towards a knowledge society; and the mistrust, tension and potential for conflict caused by competition for markets, recourses and influences between and within nations in the region, which has a severe impact on human and social development and on the role of higher education in literacy campaigns, poverty alleviation, environmental protection and sustainable development' (Wang, 2008).
- The perception of globalization in Europe, according to the author of the regional paper, is that Europe – and the world – has got richer in this period: human welfare, broadly defined, has been promoted since the late 1980s and the number of people in poverty has declined. Nevertheless, in Europe, globalization is criticized for the elimination of traditional industrial jobs; consumerism; elitism in education and higher education; and the emergency of disparities affecting access to education and to higher education.
- Research developed in the USA and Canada suggests that globalization faces important challenges (Hall and Dragne, 2008):
  – Instruction tends to be valued for and carried out with economic ends in mind ('economizing');
  – Education is more sensitive to the needs of business and industry ('the new vocationalism');

  – In a more competitive environment, HEIs tend to emulate corporations' behaviour ('corporatism');
  – With the diminution in state funding, universities may seek and favour research contracts that lead to substantial revenue ('academic capitalism').
- In Latin America and the Caribbean, globalization imposed new asymmetries and conditions that instead of promoting and benefiting the development of the local capacities of creation and diffusion of knowledge, and of higher education, leads to stagnation in many aspects. Nevertheless, in some countries and institutions innovation and excellence in various fields developed.

3. Higher education can play a key role in the social and human development in the different regions of the world according to their peculiarities, as well as at world level, contributing in the solution of unresolved problems such as: poverty; abuse and lack of respect for human rights; improving democracy; conflict resolutions; peace keeping and peace building; environmental protection; and preserving and developing human values. Universities and HEIs have the capacity to study all these complex problems and also to help shape new solutions to them. HEIs need to develop a prospective vision of the scenarios and alternative solutions to ongoing problems, as well as the political will and the capacity to reach out towards an uncertain and unknown future by working in concert in global networks at world level.

Let us now turn to how higher education is contributing to social and human development at the regional level. The main concerns, as well as those voiced in the contributions on sub-Saharan Africa, the Arab States, and Latin America and the Caribbean, are around the following issues: human capital formation; capacity building; MDGs; gender issues; improving quality and incorporating the newest ideas of higher education; fostering state financing of higher education; better working conditions for faculty; and helping to deal – especially in Africa – with the challenge of HIV/AIDS.

- In Asia, there is strong criticism concerning the vision that only through higher education as a public good can social and human development be reached. Higher education is contributing in literacy campaigns, poverty alleviation, environmental protection and sustainable development as well as in fostering the trends of the knowledge society.
- In Europe, important contributions are developing around the following issues: the social dimension of higher education as a public good and how universities can contribute to democracy; human

rights; North–South solidarity; sustainable development; climate change; and personal development priorities.

- In North America, the main concerns are around specific issues such as: student mobility; civic engagement; curricular reform; diversity and multiculturalism.

- In Latin America and the Caribbean, in addition to what we said above concerning some common features with sub-Saharan Africa and the Arab States, the contribution of higher education to social and human development lies mainly in their role of improving the distribution of income and the eradication of poverty.

4. In respect of the future role for higher education in social and human development, the main demand in sub-Saharan Africa, the Arab States and Latin America and the Caribbean is that higher education should give answers and recommend policies in order to achieve sustainable human development with equity. In Asia, in spite of differences in sub-regions, the priorities concerning the future role of higher education are to provide solutions to development problems and to foster institutional autonomy. In Europe and North America, HEIs will play a leading role in fostering democracy and human rights values through international cooperation and elaborating adequate responses to growing diversity as well as to multiculturalism.

Concerning future strategies and actions, all the regions are unanimous in devising ways and means to make higher education oriented towards a balance between economic developments on the one hand and social and human development on the other. There is universal agreement among the authors that without human and social development there cannot be sustainable development in the world.In addition to the specific regional strategies already summarized, global strategies recommended by authors of regional papers, and with consensus among them, in order to foster social and human development through higher education are, among others, the following:

- to develop an equally accessible higher education on the basis of merit
- to reinforce its critical function
- to promote academic freedom and autonomy

- to develop systems of higher education adapted to the needs of society
- to promote the contribution of higher education to the whole education system
- to diversify the models of higher education
- to develop research oriented towards sustainable development
- to achieve equity in the gender issue
- to foster the status of higher education as a public service and as a public good even if considering that private higher education could play a positive role
- to develop internationalization of higher education as an important tool for reinforcing international cooperation and building peace as well as global harmony.

The following chapters give the details of the perspectives for the regions as perceived and experienced by the authors.

NOTES

1   UNESCO Institute for Statistics.
2   UNDP (2006) The Human Development Report, 2006, Table 1 UNDP, New York.
3   See Statistical Tables in this volume.

REFERENCES

Corbett, Anne (2008) The role of higher education for human and social development in Europe (this volume).

Didriksson, Axel (2008) The role of higher education for human and social development in Latin America and the Caribbean (this volume).

Hall, Budd L. and Dragne, Cornelia (2008) The role of higher education for human and social development in the USA and Canada (this volume).

Mohamedbhai, Goolam (2008) The role of higher education for human and social development in sub-Saharan Africa (this volume).

Wang, Yibing (2008) The role of higher education for human and social development in Asia and the Pacific: new challenges and changing roles (this volume).

Zaytoun, Mohaya (2008) The role of higher education for human and social development in the Arab Sates (this volume).

Abstract

This paper first examines the current state of human and social development in sub-Saharan Africa. All indicators show that, of all the world's regions, sub-Saharan Africa is the worst from a human and social point of view.

The paper then examines the state of higher education in Africa. Although they made a significant contribution to national development after independence, higher education institutions went into crisis in the 1980s and 1990s as a result of high student enrolment, shortage of funds, poor quality, lack of relevance and campus upheavals. The 1998 UNESCO World Conference on Higher Education helped to focus attention on their plight, but several years passed before significant resources were mobilized for their revitalization.

The rest of the paper concentrates on the contribution of African higher education institutions in seven areas that have a significant influence on human and social development: human capital formation, globalization, gender issues, 'Education for All', HIV/AIDS, poverty and rural development, and peace. In each case, the current situation is examined, weaknesses are identified and suggestions for greater involvement of higher education are made.

The paper ends by identifying the future challenges facing African higher education institutions and highlighting the need for them to be responsive to local development problems in all of their activities while also forming part of the global higher education community. The paper emphasizes the importance of African higher education institutions operating in a democratic and peaceful environment.

INTRODUCTION: THE STATE OF HUMAN AND SOCIAL DEVELOPMENT IN SUB-SAHARAN AFRICA

Before discussing the role that higher education plays in the human and social development of sub-Saharan Africa, let us examine the state of development in the region, while keeping in mind that the 46 countries of sub-Saharan Africa do not form a homogeneous block and have experienced different levels of development.

All indicators show that, of all the world's regions, sub-Saharan Africa is the worst in terms of human and social development. The UNDP's Human Development Index (HDI) measures the average achievement of a country in three basic aspects of human development: long and healthy life, knowledge, and a decent standard of living. In 2004, sub-Saharan Africa accounted for 36 of the 40 countries with the lowest HDI (UNDP, 2006).

Education is perhaps the most important indicator of human development. In 2004, barely two-thirds of the children eligible to attend primary school were doing so. In the same year, the enrolment rate was 24% at the secondary level and a dismal 5% at tertiary level. At all education levels, the participation rate of females was lower than that of males (UIS, 2007).

Poverty is an equally important indicator. Poverty reduction is the highest-priority goal of the United Nations Millennium Development Goals (MDGs). The latest available figures indicate that, in sub-Saharan Africa in 2002, 44% of people were still living on less than US$1 a day (United Nations, 2006). The poverty rate is even higher in rural areas, where most of the population lives. Poverty inevitably leads to malnutrition and poor health. No less than 31% of the population of sub-Saharan Africa was living with insufficient food, and the under-five mortality rate was 165 per 1000 live births, nearly double the rate in developing countries. Access to clean water and satisfactory sanitation also has an impact on the quality of life. Only about 56% of the population in sub-Saharan Africa had access to improved water in 2004, and only 37% had adequate sanitation.

Sub-Saharan Africa is also afflicted by the HIV/AIDS pandemic like no other region of the world. At the end of 2005, there were 24.5 million people living with the disease in sub-Saharan Africa, and 2 million people died of AIDS during that same year (UNAIDS/WHO, 2006). AIDS has resulted in 12 million children being orphaned, and it is believed that 9% of all children in sub-Saharan Africa have lost at least one parent to AIDS. The epidemic is currently placing serious pressure on the health, education, social and governance structures and facilities of the afflicted countries, but it will have even greater and farther-reaching consequences for the human and social development of the region in the long term.

The development of sub-Saharan Africa has also been seriously hampered by armed conflicts, which have undermined countries' efforts to attain economic prosperity and social stability. The worst period was perhaps the mid-1990s. The situation has improved at the beginning of the 21st century, but the conflicts have left long-lasting scars of human suffering, human rights abuses, physical destruction, social and political upheavals and economic setbacks, from which the affected countries will take decades to recover. Armed conflicts still persist in sub-Saharan Africa. It is estimated that, in 2003, armed conflicts affected 4.6 million people in Africa, mostly refugees but also internally displaced persons, returning refugees, asylum seekers and stateless persons (Faria, 2004).

Although globalization has improved growth and development in many developing countries, there is genuine concern that the poorer countries of sub-Saharan Africa have been marginalized by the process; that the income gap between those countries and the richer ones, and even other developing countries, has increased; that they have not fully benefited from the information and communication technology revolution; and that globalization has in fact caused an increase in poverty (Ajayi, 2003). Also, brain drain, a direct consequence of globalization, is depleting Africa of the very people the continent needs for its development. It is estimated that, since 1990, roughly 20,000 doctors, university lecturers, engineers and other professionals have left Africa every year, mainly for industrialized countries.

There is now worldwide agreement that global sustainable development cannot exist if sub-Saharan Africa remains underdeveloped, that the region needs to be assisted, and that higher education can play a significant role in improving the situation. The state of higher education in sub-Saharan Africa is examined in the next section.

THE STATE OF HIGHER EDUCATION IN AFRICA

Over the post-independence period of the 1960s and 1970s, higher education institutions (HEIs) made an important contribution to national development in sub-Saharan Africa. They trained professionals to staff and manage public and private enterprises; they produced teachers for the growing numbers of children attending schools; and, through research and publication, they created an intellectual community. However, the structure,

mode of operation, curriculum and even research activities of almost all HEIs in sub-Saharan Africa were patterned on universities in the colonizing countries. This was part of the reason for the eventual alienation of African HEIs from the African societies they were meant to serve.

About a quarter of a century after independence, African HEIs were facing serious problems. First, student enrolment had dramatically increased. In 1960, there were only about 21,000 university students in sub-Saharan Africa; by 1983, that figure had increased to 437,000 (World Bank, 1988). The institutions had never planned for, nor could they cope with, such massive increases. There was also considerable gender inequity. In 1983, females accounted for no more than 21% of total tertiary enrolment.

Second, the institutions were short of funds. Because of the financial crisis they were facing, African governments could no longer meet the increasing financial needs of the institutions. As a result, the quality of higher education deteriorated.

Third, the relevance of the institutions came under question. The universities were mainly providing training in the humanities and social sciences and had not placed sufficient emphasis on science, technology and market-oriented programmes. Graduate unemployment was soaring, and the institutions were hardly undertaking any research that was relevant to their countries' development needs.

Fourth, there was increasing tension in the relations between higher education and governments. Student strikes, whether for political reasons or in protest against living conditions, were common on most campuses, which caused the institutions to close down for extended periods. Academic staff were often persecuted on political grounds, and there was growing interference by governments in the day-to-day running of the institutions (Saint, 1992).

In short, by the end of 1980s, higher education in sub-Saharan Africa was in crisis. The lamentable state of African universities over that period is vividly described in a book published by the Association of African Universities (AAU) (Ajayi et al., 1996).

Then came another blow. The international development community, led by the World Bank, published studies that showed that the economic and social returns of investment in higher education were poor, and encouraged African governments to invest more in basic and primary education. The effect of this policy can be gauged from the fact that the World Bank's worldwide education-sector spending on higher education, which was 17% between 1985 and 1989, dwindled to just 7% from 1995 to 1999 (Bloom et al., 2006).

Throughout the 1990s, HEIs in Africa suffered from neglect at a time when they needed assistance most. Nevertheless, they displayed remarkable resilience and managed not only to survive but also to do more with less. Only in the late 1990s did the World Bank rectify its stance. UNESCO played a crucial role in mobilizing world attention to higher education by convening the World Conference on Higher Education (WCHE) in 1998.

In preparation for the 1998 WCHE, an African Regional Consultation was held in Dakar, Senegal, in 1997. This event produced the 'Declaration and Action Plan on Higher Education in Africa', which was subsequently adopted at the WCHE (UNESCO, 1998). The Dakar Declaration identified the aforementioned structural problems of HEIs and proposed new guidelines focusing on four key issues: relevance, quality, management/finance and cooperation. It emphasized the importance of relevance as it relates directly to the role of higher education in solving development problems, although the other three issues are also important because they underpin the achievement of relevance in any institution.

In 2003, five years after the 1998 WCHE, UNESCO convened a meeting to evaluate the progress made in implementing the WCHE recommendations. It was observed that, although some improvements had taken place in terms of quality, access, relevance, management and financing of the institutions, a lot more needed to be done in sub-Saharan Africa. Moreover, new challenges had emerged, including achieving the 'Education for All' (EFA) targets and the MDGs; ensuring that Africa was not marginalized in the global knowledge economy; promoting peace and assisting in conflict resolution; and supporting development in rural areas (UNESCO, 2003). It became clear that vast efforts were required to revitalize higher education in Africa to better equip it to meet the challenges of promoting the region's development.

A number of initiatives have since been launched to support higher education in Africa. In 2005, the 'Partnership for Higher Education in Africa', comprising the Ford, MacArthur, Rockefeller, William and Flora Hewlett, and Andrew W. Mellon Foundations, as well as the Carnegie Corporation, announced a commitment of US$200 million over the following five years to strengthen higher education in selected African countries (Foundation Partnership, 2007). The Partnership, which was launched in 2000, contributed over US$150 million from 2000 to 2005, mainly for developing the physical infrastructure of African universities and reinforcing the use of ICTs.

The most ambitious recent initiative for revitalizing higher education in Africa is a 10-year partnership programme (2005–2015) developed by the AAU, the Association of Commonwealth Universities (ACU) and SAUVCA (now Higher Education South Africa), and called Renewing the African University. The programme, endorsed by the Africa Commission and submitted to the G8 Summit for funding to the tune of US$5 billion, aims to address all the major problems faced by African higher education and seeks to promote collaboration between African HEIs and all relevant stakeholders – local and regional, North–South and South–South.

Another major initiative is a four-year programme (2006–2010) known as the Regional Capacity Mobilization Initiative, to be funded by a US$7 million grant from the Department for International Development of the UK. One key feature of the programme is the creation of a Challenge Fund, to be led and managed by the AAU. This fund will be used to renew and strengthen African HEIs in order to enable them to serve as catalysts for poverty eradication and sustainable development (AAU, 2006).

The AAU itself launched a four-year Core Programme at its General Conference in February 2005. The programme, requiring an estimated funding of US$20.4 million, covers all the pressing problem areas facing African higher education: quality assurance, HIV/AIDS, ICTs, gender equity, research capacity development, and graduate training in conflict prevention, management and resolution (AAU, 2005).

The African Union (AU) has also acknowledged the key role played by higher education in achieving the MDGs in Africa. Higher education and teacher training both feature prominently in its Plan of Action for the Second Decade of Education for Africa (2006–2015). The identified priorities for higher education are original knowledge production, quality assurance and advocacy for increased funding (AU, 2006). This plan would be funded mainly by the AU member states.

At the sub-regional level, the West African Economic and Monetary Union has embarked on a project to revitalize the HEIs in its eight francophone West African member countries. The project, to be funded mainly by the African Development Fund from 2006 to 2011, will provide support for institutional reform, improve the effectiveness of management and strengthen research capacity (ADF, 2006).

In the Southern African sub-region, the Southern African Regional Universities Association (SARUA), set up in 2005 with a membership of 58 public universities in the 14 countries constituting the Southern African Development Community (SADC), will strengthen university collaboration and assist higher education in promoting regional development. For the period 2007–2012, SARUA has identified four areas of activities: institutional governance and leadership, ICTs, science and technology, and HIV/AIDS. It has received start-up funding from the Dutch government (IEASA, 2007).

The above list is by no means exhaustive, but it clearly illustrates the mobilization of development partners and major stakeholders in Africa to bring about reforms in higher education. However, in implementing the reforms, the different needs and expectations of the various sub-regions should be taken into account. Furthermore, it must be ensured that, although the funding is external, the agenda is set locally by African countries and institutions and that the activities are home-driven. Every effort should be made to involve the African Diaspora in the process.

CONTRIBUTION OF HIGHER EDUCATION TO HUMAN AND SOCIAL DEVELOPMENT IN SUB-SAHARAN AFRICA

This section surveys the contribution of higher education to human and social development in sub-Saharan Africa in the light of the key development indicators identified above and the recommendations of the Dakar Declaration at the WCHE.

PROMOTING HUMAN CAPITAL FORMATION

A nation's competitive advantage is no longer judged by its natural resources or the availability of cheap labour, but rather by its human capital. To that effect, in spite of all the difficulties they have faced, African HEIs have managed to increase their enrolment. Tertiary education enrolment in sub-Saharan Africa has more than tripled over the past two decades. A significant amount of this increase has taken place either in existing public HEIs, albeit to the detriment of their quality, or in newly created ones. The use of distance education has also made an important contribution. In addition to UNISA in South Africa, open universities now exist in Nigeria, Sudan, Tanzania and Zimbabwe, and their enrolment has rapidly increased since their creation. Distance education has made it possible to enhance participation of mature and disadvantaged students, to promote continuing professional education and lifelong learning, and to reach out to distant and rural areas. Nevertheless, the tertiary enrolment rate, currently about 5%, is the lowest of any region in the world. That figure would need to increase to at least 30% for it to have any effective impact on growth and development. Clearly, African governments are unable to provide for such increases from their education budgets.

Although the importance of having highly skilled personnel in science and technology (S&T) to promote tech-

nological and socioeconomic development has long been acknowledged, student enrolment rates in S&T in African HEIs are quite low. In fact, the Dakar Declaration identified the imbalance in student enrolment between S&T-based programmes and the humanities as a problem to be resolved. Table II.2.1 compares the tertiary enrolment rates in S&T fields in some African countries for which data is available over the period 1980–2004. With the exception of Namibia, the percentage of S&T has consistently decreased in all cases.

TABLE II.2.1
Tertiary enrolment in S&T fields in certain African countries

Country	Enrolment rates in S&T fields			
	1980[1]	1987/90[1]	1994[2]	2004[2]
Ethiopia	57%	40%	32%	30%
Ghana	46%	42%	35%	34%
Mauritius	–	–	12%	9%
Namibia	–	–	16%	19%
Swaziland	41%	33%	27%	22%
Uganda	46%	21%	21%	16%

Sources: [1] Mohamedbhai, 1994; [2] Statistical Tables, UIS, 2007.

This is a matter for concern. Through appropriate policies, governments and HEIs in Africa must make a concerted effort to increase enrolment in higher education in S&T. It has been suggested that enrolment in S&T should be in the order of 55% to 60% (Mohamedbhai, 1994). It would be near impossible for most African countries to reach that target over the next decade, but an effort should be made to achieve at least 40% to 50%. Conscious of this problem, in 2006 the African Development Bank created a new division that focuses on skills creation in S&T at the tertiary education level. In doing so, this new division aims to help African countries develop a skilled human capital base so as to achieve the MDGs and position themselves to face globalization and become competitive (Knowledge for Development, 2006).

Because of the heavy demand for higher education in sub-Saharan Africa, private institutions have started to appear and proliferate rapidly. It is reported that, in 2003, there were over 100 private HEIs in sub-Saharan Africa, nearly 65 of which were established between 1991 and 1999 (Varghese, 2004), the decade during which public institutions were in distress. Nevertheless, most of these private institutions enrol small numbers of students. The nature of these institutions varies considerably. Some are for-profit. Others, often religious-based, are not-for-profit. Some are recognized and registered by public authorities. Others operate illegally. Some function as universities, offering degrees, while still others are mere colleges running only diploma and certificate courses. Several African countries, such as South Africa, Nigeria and Mauritius, have put in place regulatory frameworks to control the quality of private institutions, but many other countries have yet to follow their lead. There is no doubt that private higher education will continue to expand in Africa. It is therefore important to set up appropriate quality control mechanisms in all countries. Perhaps a regional or sub-regional effort would be more appropriate for this purpose.

COPING WITH GLOBALIZATION

The era of globalization has ushered in another aspect of private higher education. The excess demand that cannot be met by local institutions and the liberalization of trade in education services (including higher education) through the World Trade Organization's General Agreement on Trade in Services (GATS) have encouraged enterprising providers of higher education from developed countries to move into Africa. Cross-border higher education (CBHE), as it has come to be known, is delivered by establishing a local branch or satellite campus – using a local partner – or through distance education and e-learning.

There has been some ambiguity in the reaction of African countries to CBHE. In most cases, providers have not been barred from entry, as it is recognized that they provide a means of increasing access without additional public funding. Nevertheless, their presence is viewed with scepticism. In other cases, their entry has been facilitated. In a few cases, such as in South Africa, their presence has been strictly regulated. Most African countries have made no commitment to higher education under GATS, and are perhaps unaware of its full implications (AAU, 2004a).

While CBHE has many positive aspects, not the least being an increase in access, it also has several negative aspects. First, programmes developed by foreign providers are not always sensitive to the local social, economic and cultural environment. Most providers are profit-motivated, run market-driven courses designed for the global market, and hardly undertake any research. The programmes are often of dubious quality. The providers usually are not accountable to any national body and operate outside of national control and planning of higher education. There is also the danger that a large number of foreign providers could increase the social divide in African countries, favouring affluent and middle-class students in terms of both access to higher education and employment in the private sector. But perhaps the real danger is that CBHE could weaken existing public institutions. By offering enticing salaries, many foreign providers attract the best-qualified faculty from local institutions, which are already facing a severe staff shortage. They also outsource faculty from local institutions on a part-time basis, which undermines the ability of those staff to be more active in research and development (Mohamedbhai, 2003). Moreover, they compete with local institutions on a non-level playing field. This has prompted UNESCO and the OECD to draw up CBHE guidelines (UNESCO, 2005). A number of university associations jointly prepared a statement on 'Sharing Quality Higher Education Across Borders' (IAU, 2005). So far, there has been little collaboration between foreign providers and local HEIs. For CBHE to thrive in and respond to the development needs of Africa, it must establish close partnerships with local institutions.

Meanwhile, in response to globalization, public institutions have started operating much like business enterprises, serving their 'clients' (students) and being accountable to their 'stakeholders' (government, business community). At many such institutions, managerialism has replaced academic collegiality. These institutions, too, have started to run programmes according to private market needs. This could lead to the abandonment of less-popular subjects in arts, humanities and sciences, which are vital to a country's overall development. Similarly, their research and development activities are largely influenced by the source of funding, which increasingly comes from the private sector. Higher education to meet real human and social development needs, in both teaching and research, gets lower priority. Indeed, globalization has brought in concepts of commercialization and competitiveness in higher education, which until recently were considered anathemas.

ADDRESSING GENDER ISSUES

The major role played by women in the development of Africa is highlighted in the Dakar Declaration, with a recommendation that African countries and HEIs should develop well-articulated policies to remove gender inequity in education and promote the advancement of women throughout society. Specifically, the Declaration recommends that measures be taken to double the number of women (students, teachers and decision-makers) in higher education over the next decade, with particular emphasis on orienting women towards S&T disciplines (UNESCO, 1998).

Table II.2.2 shows female student enrolment and female teaching staff at the tertiary level in sub-Saharan Africa in 1999 and 2004. Although both female enrolment and female teaching staff have actually increased over this period, gender inequity has not changed. Also, the proportion of women in senior teaching positions (professor or associate professor) is even smaller. There are, of course, considerable variations in individual countries and institutions. For example, women make up 7% of the higher education teaching staff in Ethiopia, 14% in Ghana and 50% in Lesotho (ADEA/WGHE, 2006a).

TABLE II.2.2
Female enrolment and teaching staff at the tertiary level in sub-Saharan Africa

Enrolment/teaching staff	1999	2004
Total enrolment (x10³)	2,133	3,303
Female enrolment (x10³)	856	1,250
% female enrolment	40%	38%
Total teaching staff (x10³)	116	141
Female teaching staff (x10³)	33	40
% female teaching staff	28%	28%

Source: UIS, 2007.

Table II.2.3 shows female enrolment in tertiary education in S&T fields in 1999 and 2004 in certain sub-Saharan countries. Although there has been a marked increase in actual female enrolment in S&T fields in some cases (fourfold in Ethiopia and twofold in Uganda), the gender imbalance in S&T enrolment is quite significant and has hardly changed from 1999 to 2004.

TABLE II.2.3
Female enrolment in S&T fields in certain African countries

Country	Female S&T enrolment		Women as % of total S&T enrolment*	
	1999	2004	1999	2004
Ethiopia	2,344	9,656	14%	19%
Ghana	2,965	4,957	5%	7%
Mauritius	911	1,521	12%	9%
Namibia	840	940	9%	8%
Swaziland	568	634	12%	10%
Uganda	1,886	3,776	5%	4%

Note: *expressed as percentage of total S&T enrolment.
Source: Statistical Tables, UIS, 2007.

However, gender inequity in enrolment and staffing is just part of the overall gender problem. To empower women to play an important role in the development of their countries, HEIs would need to adopt a holistic approach and incorporate gender issues in all their major activities – teaching, research and community engagement. Several institutions have successfully done this. Makerere University in Uganda and the University of Cape Town in South Africa have both established gender institutes for this purpose. The University of Bakhat Alruda in Sudan promotes the education of rural women (see Box II.2.1).

However, most institutions approach the gender problem in a rather uncoordinated manner. To assist these institutions, the Working Group on Higher Education (WGHE) of the Association for the Development of Education in Africa (ADEA) produced the excellent *Toolkit for Mainstreaming Gender in Higher Education in Africa*, which covers such topics as forming policies and strategies, the role of human resources development and management, mainstreaming gender in the curriculum, research and gender-sensitive methods, female student access and retention, and gender violence and sexual harassment (ADEA/WGHE, 2006a).

At a time when many African institutions are going through a revitalization process, this toolkit is a valuable instrument that can help them address the gender problem both in their institutions and in their communities. The Forum for African Women Educationalists (FAWE), a pan-African, non-governmental organization headquartered in Kenya with chapters in a number of African countries, is another excellent source of material. One of its main objectives is to promote girls' and women's education in sub-Saharan Africa in line with EFA goals. It has published programme tools and handbooks on best practices for educating girls. These instruments are very valuable to faculties and colleges of education (FAWE, 2007).

MEETING EFA TARGETS

Higher education can make an important contribution to achieving EFA by training teachers for other education

Box II.2.1 University of Bakhat Alruda, Sudan: educating rural women

In October 2005, the University of Bakhat Alruda created the Faculty of Community Development with the main mission of promoting education and training for women in rural areas of the White Nile.

The faculty has set up 11 community colleges in rural areas, often located in old, under-used buildings or buildings donated by individuals or the local government. The colleges, which are jointly managed by the community and the university, offer training exclusively to women in each community. There are no age restrictions (the students range from age 15 to 50) or educational level (from secondary education to illiterate). The maximum number of students per course is 50.

Courses are offered in health, environment, food and nutrition, religion, and craft-work. Each course lasts about six months. The students choose a timetable that fits with their other commitments, but they are required to take at least three hours of classes a day, one hour of theory and two hours of practical work. Students who complete the course receive a certificate from the college.

Source: GUNI website: http://www.guni-rmies.net/info/default.php?id=77.

levels. From 1999 to 2004, the increase in the number of teachers at the pre-primary, primary and secondary levels in sub-Saharan Africa was 18%, 20% and 28%, respectively (UIS, 2007). The major challenges for higher education are to produce even more teachers and to retrain the existing ones. According to the 2007 EFA Global Monitoring Report, sub-Saharan Africa would need an additional 1.6 million teachers merely to achieve universal primary education by 2015 (UNESCO, 2007). This is a mammoth task, and it would be impossible to attain the targeted numbers using traditional face-to-face education. Institutions have realized that distance education and e-learning will have to be used. Several open universities in Africa, including UNISA, run a large variety of teacher training programmes using distance education and open learning. The African Virtual University has received funding from various sources and partners a number of organizations, both within and outside Africa, to train teachers through e-learning (eLearning Africa, 2007).

UNESCO has recognized the enormous challenge of teacher training in Africa and launched two important initiatives. The first is the International Institute for Capacity Building in Africa (IICBA), whose mandate is to strengthen the capacities of teacher education institutions in Africa. Its numerous activities include creating a network on teacher education, running postgraduate programmes, mainly through distance education, in order to upgrade the skills of teachers, and encouraging the cost-effective use of ICTs. The second is the Teacher Training Initiative for Sub-Saharan Africa (TTISSA), a 10-year project (2006–2015) aimed at improving national teacher policies and strengthening teacher education in 46 sub-Saharan countries (UNESCO, 2006). It is imperative that higher education be closely associated with the activities of IICBA and TTISSA.

But teacher training is just one of the means of meeting the EFA targets. There has long been a perception that EFA deals mainly with basic and primary education, which fall under the responsibility of ministries of education and are therefore of little concern to higher education. This was partly reinforced by the fact that the 1990 Jomtien Conference on Education did not identify higher education as an important actor in promoting EFA. However, the proclamation of the 1998 WCHE emphasized that a primary mission of higher education is to contribute to the development and improvement of education at all levels. The final report of the WCHE+5 in 2003 re-emphasized that higher education should be intimately associated with all education programmes, especially EFA. A year later, in response to the need for universities to have a greater and more structured involvement in EFA, UNESCO convened an international meeting

entitled University Community and EFA: Creating and Sustaining Improvements. One of the working groups of that meeting reported that, in some countries, universities are completely unaware of EFA and, in others, there is a conflict between higher and basic education.

The latest evidence seems to indicate that higher education is still not fully committed to EFA. In 2005 and 2006, the IAU conducted a pilot study to determine the contribution of higher education to EFA. Higher education institutions and donor agencies that fund higher education were surveyed. Thirteen agencies and 33 institutions (16 of which were in sub-Saharan Africa) responded. Nearly half the agencies reported that less than 10% of their funding was allocated to EFA. Two-thirds of the agencies and three-quarters of the institutions felt that higher education involvement in EFA was insufficient or non-existent. The institutions' main area of involvement was teacher training, and related topics, with only a handful mentioning non-formal education, promotion of literacy and research on EFA. The overwhelming majority of the institutions felt that government policy needed to change in order to improve the participation of higher education in EFA (IAU, 2007).

In March 2007, the African Regional Committee of the UNESCO Forum on Higher Education, Research and Knowledge organized a seminar entitled 'The Contribution of Higher Education to Other Education Systems'. Of the 115 proposals received from African academics in response to a call for papers, the vast majority failed to address the issue of linkages between higher education and other levels of education. Moreover, of the 18 papers selected for presentation, most did not really do full justice to the topic.

It would seem that very few HEIs in sub-Saharan Africa are fully aware of the EFA goals and are incorporating them institutionally in their teaching, research and community service activities. There are some examples of higher education's involvement in basic education, literacy, educational research, use of ICTs in non-formal education, and so on (Sanyal, 2005), but these are relatively few. This is a matter of concern. The 2007 Global Monitoring Report warns that it is unlikely that the six EFA goals will be met in sub-Saharan Africa. There is an urgent need to establish real partnerships between higher education, ministries of education, donor agencies, civil society, and international and regional organizations in order to address the critical issue of EFA in sub-Saharan Africa.

RESPONDING TO HIV/AIDS

It is quite revealing that the 1997 Dakar Declaration failed to mention HIV/AIDS as a challenge facing Africa or list the issue in the actions to be taken by higher education.

The same applies to the 1998 World Declaration for the 21st Century. Nevertheless, by the end of the 20th century, it was obvious that the scourge of HIV/AIDS in sub-Saharan Africa was similarly affecting its higher education sector. What was not obvious was the extent of its effect on the institutions and the response of the latter.

A number of reports on HIV/AIDS and higher education started appearing at the beginning of the 21st century. One such report, published in 2001, documented seven case studies of universities in six African countries, described the seriousness of the impact of HIV/AIDS on higher education and highlighted the absence of an institutional response to the problem (Kelly, 2001). This prompted the AAU to place HIV/AIDS high on its agenda. In 2004, the AAU published a comprehensive toolkit to help HEIs tackle the problem (AAU, 2004b).

At the same time, from 2003 to 2005, the WGHE sponsored an extensive survey of universities, teacher training colleges and polytechnics in Africa to determine their responses to HIV/AIDS. The results of the survey, which covered 339 institutions, were published in 2006 (ADEA/WGHE, 2006b). One revealing finding was that most institutions did not collect institutional data on HIV/AIDS. The impact of the disease on the institutions could thus only be gauged by the observations and perceptions of the respondents. Few institutions felt that the impact of HIV/AIDS was serious, which does not reflect the true picture. Not many institutions reported having a written policy on HIV/AIDS, although a larger proportion in all three categories had developed guidelines. Less than half the institutions had a specialized unit for coordinating HIV/AIDS activities or had integrated HIV/AIDS into their curricula. Very few institutions were actually undertaking research on HIV/AIDS or had community outreach programmes. Almost all the institutions mentioned a lack of financial resources as a major constraint in addressing the HIV/AIDS problem.

The general picture that emerges is that while many HEIs are now breaking the silence on HIV/AIDS and some are taking responsive action, much more needs to be done. Even if HIV/AIDS starts abating in Africa now, the serious social and economic repercussions would be felt over the next generation. It is therefore imperative for higher education to first address the impact of HIV/AIDS on its own institutional community and then, through its teaching, research and outreach programmes, respond to national needs. The AAU toolkit (AAU, 2004b) provides excellent guidance to institutions in all these aspects, and higher education leadership may consider making its application mandatory for their respective institutions. The institutions, however, need adequate resources in order to respond effectively to the pandemic.

Another very important and useful resource is the free, internet-based training programme for teachers at the primary, secondary and higher education levels developed by the Virtual Institute for Higher Education in Africa, a joint venture between the UNESCO Harare Cluster Office and the National Universities Commission of Nigeria (VIHEAF, 2007). All teachers of African HEIs should be encouraged to register for the programme.

The creation of UNESCO Chairs at African universities, specifically in relation to HIV/AIDS, can be an effective way for higher education to coordinate the institutional and national responses to the problem. An interesting example exists at the University of Zimbabwe. A UNESCO Chair on HIV/AIDS and Education was established there with the support of a two-year grant made to UNESCO in 2005 by the UK's Department for International Development. The main objective of the Chair is to assist the University of Zimbabwe in facing challenges posed by HIV/AIDS. But a sub-regional or even regional approach may prove to be more effective. In the West Indies, a UNESCO-Commonwealth Regional Chair in Education and HIV/AIDS was launched in 2004 at the University of the West Indies, supported jointly by UNESCO and the Commonwealth Secretariat, to coordinate the contribution of higher education to HIV/AIDS. This initiative could be emulated in Africa.

ALLEVIATING POVERTY THROUGH RURAL DEVELOPMENT

About 70% of the population of sub-Saharan Africa currently lives in rural areas, where poverty is at its most extreme and the main development challenges in Africa are found. Thus, by promoting rural development, higher education should be able to help alleviate poverty and achieve the first MDG.

Agriculture is the main rural activity. University agriculture faculties, agricultural colleges and agricultural universities can play a key role in promoting rural agricultural development. The problem is that most agricultural HEIs focus on production agriculture – mainly crop and animal production – and hardly deal with the problem of rural development and food security (Maguire and Atchoarena, 2003). Agriculture graduates tend to seek employment in urban rather than rural areas, which results in high graduate unemployment in agriculture. Many HEIs are under pressure to merge their agricultural education activities with other scientific disciplines, which further limits their scope of promoting rural development. Agricultural institutions need to refocus their teaching, research and community outreach activities on the needs of rural communities, including a greater involvement in the lifelong learning of farmers and agricultural extension workers. The issue of gender also needs to be addressed. Roughly 70–80% of the agriculturalists in Africa are women, yet in Ethiopia, Ghana and Uganda, for example, enrolment of female tertiary students in agriculture in 2004 was no more than about 20%. It is equally important to re-valorize agriculture by introducing it in secondary and even primary schools, especially those in rural areas. Higher education institutions have a role to play here in designing curricula and training teachers (Maguire and Atchoarena, 2003).

The emphasis on rural development should be mainstreamed in all areas of higher education. In engineering, for example, students should be made aware of rural technological traditions and innovations, and medical students should be familiar with traditional medicine and understand the practices of sorcery and witchcraft (Mohamedbhai, 1994). Technological, health and socioeconomic challenges related to water supply and sanitation should also receive special consideration.

One excellent way of linking higher education to the rural community is to post students in rural areas for practical training during their courses. This exposes the students to rural challenges and helps bring problems to the university for possible solution through projects. Every year, the University of Cheikh Anta Diop in Senegal runs a vacation camp that sends some 500 students in various disciplines to rural communities, where they participate in reforestation activities, educate illiterate women and provide medical consultations. Some African countries require graduates to work in rural areas for about a year upon completion of their studies in order to expose them to indigenous practices and skills.

Several African countries have set up universities in rural areas to facilitate the access of rural students to higher education and ensure that the institutions' teaching, research and community service activities are aligned with rural development requirements. Some universities have created institutions or centres for rural development. Ghana has even created the University for Development Studies, 'a pro-poor community-based university' (see Box II.2.2). This is commendable. The danger, however,

is that a university degree may become a passport for migrating to an urban area. Instead, it might be desirable to run programmes leading to certificates and diplomas, or even non-award programmes, as these are more pertinent to rural areas.

PROMOTING PEACE AND ASSISTING IN CONFLICT RESOLUTION

In 1997, there was evidence that HEIs in several parts of Africa had embarked on peace-related programmes. A couple of UNESCO Chairs had been created; Moi University in Kenya had established the Centre for Refugee Studies; and the then-University of Durban-Westville had set up the Gandhi-Luthuli Institute to promote peace. In particular, the African Centre for the Constructive Resolution of Disputes (ACCORD) was quite active in the Southern African region (Mohamedbhai, 1998). However, these activities were not well documented, and use of and access to the internet was then limited.

Significant progress has since taken place. Additional centres and institutes have been created, for example at the University of Khartoum in Sudan, the National University of Rwanda and the University of Ibadan in Nigeria. In almost all sub-regions of Africa, postgraduate peace-related programmes or undergraduate modules now exist in HEIs. South Africa alone has more than forty institutions and organizations running such programmes. ACCORD is now a dynamic African, non-governmental, conflict management organization running short training courses and undertaking research. Its activities go beyond the SADC region to the Great Lakes region, the Horn of Africa and West Africa. To date, ACCORD has trained 12,000 people in conflict management and conflict resolution skills. In 1998, it started *Conflict Trends Magazine*, which reports on and analyses trends in current and emerging conflicts in Africa. A year later, in 1998, it launched the *African Journal on Conflict Resolution*, thereby providing an avenue for scholarly publications in the field (ACCORD, 2007).

In 2002, the United Nations-affiliated University for

Box II.2.2 University for Development Studies, Ghana

Date of creation: 1992
Vision: To be the home of world-class pro-poor scholarship.
Mission: To promote equitable socioeconomic transformation of communities through practically oriented, community-based, problem-solving, gender-sensitive and interactive research, teaching, learning and outreach programmes.
Location: Campuses located in four of the most deprived areas of Ghana.

Student population: 5200 (2005–2006).
Faculties: Agriculture, Integrated Development Studies, Applied Sciences, and Medicine and Health Sciences.
Centres: Interdisciplinary research and French language.
Units: Gender Programmes Unit, with the objective of mainstreaming gender in university policies, programmes and community relations.
Special features: (a) Special admission provis-

ions for female applicants and those with poor secondary school qualifications, and (b) In all programmes, students spend one term each year for three years doing practical, community-based fieldwork.

Source: Information pamphlet published by the UDS University Relations Section, 2006.

Peace, located in Costa Rica, launched its Africa Programme. The objective of this programme was to 'strengthen African capacity for education, training and research on issues of peace and security, including the prevention, management and resolution of conflicts' (UPEACE, 2007). The Africa Programme is now based in Addis Ababa, Ethiopia. It runs training workshops and short courses on peace, human rights and conflict resolution. It also organizes conferences and workshops. So far, the Africa Programme has organized 24 events involving nearly 1000 peace practitioners, academics, policymakers, civil society members, and so on. It has also developed and disseminated Africa-specific teaching and resource materials. Of particular interest is its module 'Teaching Model: Non-Violent Transformation of Conflict', designed for final-year undergraduates and available to all HEIs.

However, no studies have been undertaken to determine the effectiveness of these initiatives. In afflicted countries such as Sudan, Rwanda and Côte d'Ivoire, such studies would yield useful results. Insufficient information is available on efforts to train teachers in Africa, especially at the primary school level, to inculcate values and attitudes that foster tolerance, understanding and respect for diversity among students. The early years of childhood are the most significant in the development of attitudes and skills that can later influence an adult's approach to conflict resolution. Similarly, limited evidence is available on the involvement of higher education students in community engagement in conflict-ridden areas. In particular, students in countries with refugees could, during their vacation, provide assistance and comfort to the refugees in the form of education, health, nutrition, water supply or sanitation, depending on their areas of study. Such activities create awareness of the refugee crises and even encourage students to bring some of the problems to the campus for resolution through projects (Mohamedbhai, 1998). Both ACCORD and the UPEACE Africa Programme should be involved in these areas.

The UNESCO website currently shows ten Chairs on peace, democracy and human rights in nine sub-Saharan African countries. However, little information is available on the activities of these Chairs or even on whether some of them are still active. UNESCO should undertake a study of these Chairs and document their activities and effectiveness.

CONCLUSIONS: FUTURE CHALLENGES FACING AFRICAN HIGHER EDUCATION

In order to adequately respond to the human and social development needs of their countries, public HEIs in sub-Saharan Africa must first be reformed. The institutions' major weaknesses are known. African governments are now committed to supporting higher education and donor agencies are ready to provide funding in order to revitalize the sector. The institutions must seize the opportunity – it is now or never. Quality assurance must be the driving factor in all reforms, at both the institutional and system levels, as a high-quality higher education sector will attract students and limit brain drain. A number of institutions have already embarked on the reform process and achieved impressive results (ADEA/WGHE, 2004).

A major challenge facing African higher education is to transform institutions so that they cater not only to the elite few but to a far greater proportion of the population. This requires differentiated institutions and diversified programmes within the institutions. They must cater to learners at different stages in life with different educational backgrounds. In particular, higher education must reach out to rural areas and help overcome gender inequity. The approach to curriculum and teaching must also change. Programmes must be multidisciplinary in order to equip graduates to tackle the complex problems of society. Teaching must be more participative and problem-based, with an emphasis on developing analytical skills, encouraging critical and independent thinking and learning through teamwork. All of this, however, requires staff training and lower student/staff ratios, which should form part of the reform process.

Another challenge for higher education is to resist the wave of commercialization and commodification brought about by globalization. Of course, institutions must respond to market manpower needs as part of their objective of being relevant, but this should not be their sole mission. They must also address the human and social development needs of society. Private higher education and CBHE are inevitable and necessary; they should be welcomed but regulated. Furthermore, it must be recognized that their operations will be governed by market forces and, in most cases, will be profit-driven. It is then incumbent on African public institutions to address the broader development objectives of higher education. To this end, they require the support of their governments, which must acknowledge that higher education is a public good.

Research is currently at low ebb in most institutions because of the heavy concentration on teaching and lack of resources. However, research in all areas is fundamental to the future development of Africa. While emphasis must necessarily be placed on developmental research, African higher education must also be in the forefront of fundamental research in certain areas. It must be accepted that not all HEIs in a country will be able to excel in research. A country's institutions must differentiate themselves, with some placing greater emphasis on research than others. Research in areas of S&T must be given priority, as without scientific and technological innovation, Africa risks being marginalized in the global knowledge society.

African HEIs also need to place much greater importance on community engagement, although several of them are already doing so (ADEA/WGHE, 2004). This requires the recognition of community service on equal terms with teaching and research. Students offer an enormous potential for community service that has not been fully tapped. Their involvement in rural areas can help identify developmental problems to be solved at the institutions and bring students into direct contact with Africa's rich indigenous knowledge.

Perhaps the greatest challenge facing African HEIs is that they must – through their teaching, research and community engagement – address pressing local development problems while also understanding the global issues facing humanity, such as sustainable development and climate change, and participate in international efforts to address these challenges. They must help promote an African cultural identity while learning to operate in a multicultural environment. They need to inculcate nation-building consciousness, but also promote the concept of world citizenship. In other words, they must be relevant to both the local community and global society. This can only be achieved by pooling resources and creating collaborative partnerships with institutions and through associations at the national, regional and international levels. The assistance of African Diaspora academics can be immensely useful in this process.

Finally, for African HEIs to be effective in promoting development, they need to operate in a peaceful, democratic and conflict-free environment, on campuses devoid of political interference and persecution and conducive to learning for both staff and students. Primary responsibility for this rests on the respective governments, but institutions can and should assist in achieving these conditions. By operating democratically, by practising consultative and participative governance, by promoting fairness and justice in all dealings, by ensuring accountability and transparency in all transactions, and by setting up appropriate machinery for dialogue and for resolving disputes and differences, African HEIs can not only familiarize their students with such practices, which the latter can emulate later in their professional lives, but also become an example for society to follow – yet another daunting challenge.

REFERENCES

ACCORD (2007) African Centre for the Constructive Resolution of Disputes. Accessed from http://www.accord.org.za/web/home.htm.

ADEA/Working Group on Higher Education (WGHE) (2004) *Higher Education Innovations in Sub-Saharan Africa with Specific Reference to Universities*. Accra, Ghana: Association of African Universities.

ADEA/Working Group on Higher Education (WGHE) (2006a) *Toolkit for Mainstreaming Gender in Higher Education in Africa*. Accra, Ghana: Association of African Universities.

ADEA/Working Group on Higher Education (WGHE) (2006b) *Higher Education Institutions in Africa Responding to HIV/AIDS*. Accra, Ghana: Association of African Universities.

Association of African Universities (AAU) (2004a) The implications of WTO/GATS for higher education in Africa. *Proceedings of Accra Workshop on GATS*. Accra, Ghana.

Association of African Universities (AAU) (2004b) *An HIV/AIDS Toolkit for Higher Education Institutions in Africa*. Accra, Ghana.

Association of African Universities (AAU) (2005) *Core Programme of Activities 2005–2009*. Accra, Ghana.

African Development Fund (ADF) (2006) *Appraisal Report: Multinational Support for Higher Education in WAEMU Countries*.

African Union (AU) (2006) Second decade of education for Africa (2006–2015). *Draft Plan of Action*. Addis Ababa, Ethiopia.

Ajayi, Ibi (2003) Globalization and equity in sub-Saharan Africa. Paper presented at the Fourth Annual Global Development Conference. Cairo, Egypt.

Ajayi, J.F.A., Goma, L.K.H. and Johnson, A.G. (1996) *The African Experience with Higher Education*. Accra, Ghana: Association of African Universities.

Association of African Universities (AAU) (2006) *Planning Consultation Report: Regional Capacity Mobilization Initiative (RCMI) for Revitalizing Higher Education in Africa*. December 5–6. Accra, Ghana.

Bloom, David, Canning, David, and Chan, Kevin (2006) *Higher Education and Economic Development in Africa*. Harvard University. Study commissioned by the World Bank. Washington, DC.

eLearning Africa (2007) News Portal. The African Virtual University: Interview with the Rector. Accessed from http://elearning-africa.com/newsportal/english/news5.php.

Faria, Fernanda (2004) *Crisis Management in Sub-Saharan Africa: The Role of the European Union*. European Union Institute for Security Studies. Occasional Paper No. 51, Paris.

Forum for African Women Educationalists (FAWE) (2007) Accessed from http://www.fawe.org/home/index.asp.

Foundation Partnership (2007) Accessed from http://www.foundation-partnership.org/.

IEASA (2007) From ivory towers to poverty eradication: SARUA gets wings. IEASA Online Newsletter, 7 February. Accessed from http://www.nu.ac.za/ieasa/SARUA.asp.

International Association of Universities (IAU) (2005) *Sharing Quality Higher Education Across Borders: A Statement on Behalf of Higher Education Institutions Worldwide*. Accessed from http://www.unesco.org/iau/p_statements/index.html.

International Association of Universities (IAU) (2007) *IAU Pro-*

ject Methodology and Results. Presented at the IAU Experts' Seminar on 'Higher Education and EFA: The Case for Two Solitudes?' Maputo, Mozambique. Accessed from http://www.unesco.org/iau/conferences/maputo/pdf/Turmaine.pdf.

Kelly, M. (2001) *Challenging the Challenger: Understanding and Expanding the Response of Universities in Africa to AIDS*. ADEA Working Group on Higher Education. Washington, DC.

Knowledge for Development (2006) Accessed from http://knowledge.cta.int/en/content/view/full/3771.

Maguire, C. and Atchoarena, D. (2003) Higher education and rural development: a new perspective. In: Atchoarena, D. and Gasperini, L. (eds) *Education for Rural Development: Towards New Policy Resources*. Joint study conducted by the FAO and UNESCO-IIEP.

Mohamedbhai, G.T.G. (1994) The emerging role of African universities in the development of science and technology. Paper prepared for the DAE Working Group on Higher Education. Accra, Ghana: Association of African Universities.

Mohamedbhai, G. (1998) The role of higher education in developing a culture of peace in Africa. In: *Higher Education in Africa: Achievements, Challenges and Prospects*. Dakar: UNESCO-BREDA.

Mohamedbhai, G. (2003) Globalization and its implications for universities in developing countries. In: Breton, G. and Lambert, M. (eds) *Universities and Globalization: Private Linkages, Public Trust*. Paris: UNESCO/Université Laval/Economica.

Saint, William S. (1992) Universities in Africa: strategies for stabilization and revitalization. World Bank Technical Paper No. 194. Washington, DC.

Sanyal, B.C. (2005) The role of higher education in obtaining EFA goals with particular focus on developing countries.

Paper prepared for the UNESCO Forum on Higher Education, Research and Knowledge. Paris: UNESCO..

UNAIDS/WHO (2006) *AIDS Epidemic Update: December 2006*. Geneva.

UNDP (2006) *Human Development Report 2006: Beyond Scarcity: Power, Poverty and the Global Water Crisis*.

UNESCO (1998) *Higher Education in the Twenty-First Century: Vision and Action*. Final report, World Conference on Higher Education. Paris: UNESCO.

UNESCO (2003) Recent Developments and Future Prospects of Higher Education in Sub-Saharan Africa in the 21st Century. Meeting of Higher Education Partners, Paris, 23–25 June 2003. Paris: UNESCO.

UNESCO (2005) *Guidelines for Quality Provision in Cross-Border Higher Education*. Accessed from http://www.unesco.org/education/guidelines_E.indd.pdf.

UNESCO (2006) *Teacher Training Initiative for Sub-Saharan Africa (TTISSA)*. Accessed from http://www.unesco.org/education/TTISSA.

UNESCO (2007) *EFA Global Monitoring Report 2007*. Paris: UNESCO.

UNESCO Institute for Statistics (UIS) (2007) Data accessed from http://www.uis.unesco.org/.

United Nations (2006) *Millennium Development Goals Report 2006*. New York.

UPEACE (2007) University for Peace. Africa Programme. Accessed from http://www.africa.upeace.org.

Varghese, N.V. (2004) *Private Higher Education in Africa*. Paris: UNESCO-IIEP.

Virtual Institute for Higher Education in Africa (VIHEAF) (2007) Accessed from http://www.harare.unesco.org/viheafmodules/m1-hivaidseduc/index.htm.

World Bank (1988) *Education in Sub-Saharan Africa: Policies for Adjustment, Revitalization and Expansion*. Washington, DC.

SPECIAL CONTRIBUTION II.1

Science and technology for human and social development in Africa

Paul Tiyambe Zeleza

Africa has been grappling with the question of human and social development for a long time. Africa's awareness and concerns about its relative levels of economic, technological and social development have been heightened since the continent's tragic encounter with an increasingly imperial and industrializing Europe in the 15th century. This encounter made modernity and modernization urgent practical and intellectual issues. The issues of 'African regeneration' and 'African renaissance' have engaged African intellectuals since the middle of the 19th century. African development and modernization have been seen in terms of continental societies that acquire the scientific and technological tools required to improve the human condition; increase social development; and bring Africa into global prominence and parity (Zeleza, 2003).

This global yet distinctly African quest for modernity and development intensified in the 20th century, a period in which Africa was marked by colonialism, decolonization and independence, and across the world by imperialism, ideological rivalries and globalization. At the centre of this quest were education, science and technology, which were seen as vehicles for intellectual enlightenment, social engineering, cultural production, political participation and, above all, economic and social development. Education and science were treated as processes and projects through which social, cultural, technological, and economic capital is acquired and reproduced, and by which the nation and the world are productively imagined. This concept has dominated African discourses about development, nationalism and globalization for a long time.

Ultimately, Africa's search for human and social development and for modernity revolves around the question of developing, to quote Abiola Irele (1999, pp. 7–8), 'a workable and effective social and political organization of our national communities, and the productive management of our physical environment and material resources, all this in a world dominated by "instrumental reason" and controlled from ever fewer centres of power and decision.' This project poses challenges that are simultaneously political and philosophical, in addition to being concrete and conceptual. Such challenges involve renewal in economic and epistemic terms; modifications to social and structural conditions; and the development and democratization of African institutions in a world that rewards technological and scientific progress and punishes those that lag behind.

These issues have given African thinkers and policymakers grounds for serious reflection. The eminent Kenyan scholar, Ali Mazrui (1999) contends that 'Modernization is change which is compatible with the present state of human knowledge, which seeks to comprehend the legacy of the past, which is sensitive to the needs of the future, and which is increasingly aware of its global context.' In his formulation, modernization minus dependency equals development. He argues that African modernization needs three major revolutions: in skills, values, and gender relations. In an increasingly knowledge-based global economy, the power of skills is self-evident. Skills often need science and technology at different levels. Science and technology, in turn, are conditioned by culture. He also suggests several strategies for reducing and transcending dependency. Among them are indigenization, domestication and diversification. Indigenization requires a greater utilization of indigenous techniques, personnel and approaches for purposeful change, while domestication involves making imported institutions more relevant to Africa in their organization and functions. As for diversification, he recommends that Africa must diversify the foreign cultures from which it seeks to learn and stop its 'excessive reliance on the West as the only Other.'

One of the distinguishing characteristics of science is its systematicity in terms of how it describes and explains phenomena, establishes knowledge claims, and expands and represents knowledge. However, this very systematicity sometimes leads to extravagant neo-positivist claims about science's explanatory and predictive power, which post-positivists – especially post-modernists, with their anti-foundationalist and constructionist views – have done much to debunk (Galavotti, 2000). While these critiques are pertinent, we must be careful not to throw the baby out with the bathwater. Irele (1999, pp. 7–8) insists that while we must indeed recognize the limits of science, there is no reason to jettison its real triumphs and the keys it holds for 'advancing our interests in the modern world.'

Science is ultimately a social and political enterprise. It needs political will in terms of funding, structured support, effective regulation and application. In turn, this entails that science must respond to the needs of society, find practical solutions to pressing problems and make inspired innovations to realize society's collective dreams of the future. As Federico Mayor (2000, pp. 26–7), then UNESCO Secretary-General, put it at the opening of the World Conference on Science in June 1999, 'science is too important to be left to the markets'. Public support for science is critical with the rapid expansion of proprietary science, which is spreading as private, profit-seeking corporations assume a greater share of scientific research.

If Africa is to become a major producer of scientific products, a massively increased investment in basic or fundamental science is imperative, as there are no technological products – applied science – without basic science. Since the industrial revolution in the 19th century, the links between science and technology have become increasingly close. Almost all the significant technological advances made since the beginning of the 20th century have been by-products of scientific research. Of course, the relationship between science and technology is not unilinear. There are multiple feedback loops between and among them, which also applies to markets and national economic and social well-being (Gibbons, 1995).

Science and technology are of course not a panacea for all the challenges to human and social development. They have an equal capacity to bring progress or destruction, whether we consider the power of nuclear energy, the impact of the automobile, the effects of ubiquitous information and communication technologies, or the potential of genetically modified foods and organisms. They have a great capacity to influence, for better or worse, the spatial and social divides between and within countries (Sagan, 1999). Science and technology alone will not solve Africa's stubborn legacies of underdevelopment. However, underdevelopment cannot be solved without them. Africa's scientific and technological literacy must be raised. In the developed world, science has become a major, or sometimes leading, productive force. References to the new knowledge economy and knowledge society are essentially tributes to the pervasive role of science and technology in contemporary life.

Africa's science policy should entail both the appropriation of the existing huge stock of scientific and technological innovations, and an active participation in the production of new scientific knowledge. Existing knowledge should be considered an international or global public good. Strategies need to be developed to systematically collect scientific and technical information from around the world. This may be cheaper than conducting research locally. However, it is not a substitute. In addition to catching up with the old frontiers of science and technology, Africa must be actively engaged in the emerging scientific revolutions of our times – the gene revolution (genomics, bioinformatics, molecular breeding, diagnostics, vaccine technology, and so on), the ecotechnology revolution (in the fields of economics, ecology, equity, employment and energy), the nanotechnology revolution (the miniaturization of physical and biological objects), and the information and communication revolution (the internet, computing, software, remote sensing, and so on). The challenges cannot be underestimated in a world in which scientific knowledge is increasing so rapidly.

African countries must pursue a multipronged agenda. They must strengthen their national systems of science and technology by building strong education systems and establishing productive scientific networks with developing and developed countries, and with African scientists working abroad. Such activities should form part of a systematic, sustainable drive to generate, import, adapt and disseminate scientific knowledge and new technologies. Enabling conditions must be created for Africa's own scientists and to attract foreign research and development. Even in the scientifically and technologically well-endowed USA, foreign R&D plays an increasingly important role. The US expenditure on foreign research rose from US$700 million in 1987 to over US$17 billion in 1995. This provoked bitter debates between the techno-nationalists and techno-globalists (Florida, 1995).

Clearly, African governments have a responsibility to identify the problems, harness the progress, and explore the possibilities of science and technology in both general and specific fields, such as information technology and biotechnology. This can be achieved by developing and implementing appropriate policies for relevant sectors; mobilizing the required investment, especially in education; and by creating an enabling environment for entrepreneurship in the technology sectors. There is also a need for greater coordination between governments, civil society, the intelligentsia, businesses and entrepreneurs to promote the development of science, technology, culture and enterprise. Particular attention needs to be paid to the mobilization of African scientists and entrepreneurs in the diaspora. These individuals constitute a vast reservoir of scientific and technical skills, as well as intellectual and social capital.

As Mohamed Hassan (Hassan, 2003; Gaillard et al., 2005), the renowned Sudanese scientist and head of both the African Academy of Sciences and the Academy of Sciences for the Developing World (formerly the Third World Academy of Sciences) has passionately argued, the challenges are as daunting as the opportunities are immense. Local capacities and leadership need to be developed, sustained and utilized in efforts to advance science and technology. The best and most relevant science and technology in Africa should be mobilized, and institutional networks established to address the critical social and economic problems that face the continent. Centres of excellence in science and technology need to be to established and strengthened among African universities and research institutions. Strong political will at national and regional levels should be developed to support science and technology. Finally, expenditure on science and technology, and on research and development must be substantially increased.

African expenditure on science and technology is grossly inadequate, even in comparison to other developing regions. According to the *UNESCO Science Report 2005* (UNESCO, 2005, pp. 4–16), in 2002 Africa accounted for a mere 0.6% of the world's gross expenditure on research and development (GERD). In addition, it had only 1.1% of world researchers, which was the lowest figure in the world – below Oceania with 1.1% and 1.4%, respectively, and Latin America and the Caribbean with 2.6% and 2.5%. Asia has overtaken Europe, fuelled in part by China's explosive growth (its share of the world's GERD rose from 4% in 1997 to 9% in 2002). In 2002, Asia accounted for 31.5% of the world's GERD and 36.8% of world researchers, compared with Europe's 27.3% and 33.4%, respectively. Remarkably, Africa's share of world GERD is lower than its share of world GDP (3.7%). Therefore, GERD as a percentage of GDP is a dismal 0.3%, compared with a world average of 1.7% (0.6% for Latin American and the Caribbean, 1.4% for Oceania, 1.5% for Asia, 1.7% for Europe, and 2.7% for North America). In actual dollars, Africa's GERD per inhabitant is a measly US$5.6, compared with a world average of US$134.4 (US$40.9 for Latin America and the Caribbean, US$71.3 for Asia, US$274.2 for Oceania, US$284.6 for Europe and US$960.5 for North America).

Not surprisingly, Africa's share of patents granted by the United States Patent and Trademark Office, the European Patent Office and the Japan Patent Office in 2000 was a negligible 0.1%, the same as in 1991 (altogether the developed countries accounted for 92.9% and 92.7% of the patents granted in 1991 and 2000, respectively). Africa's share of world scientific publications was slightly higher. It stood at 1.6% in 1991 and 1.4% in 2000, compared with 1.8% and 3.3% for Latin America and the Caribbean, 2.9% and 3.3% for Oceania, 16.2% and 22.5% for Asia, 43.9% and 36.2% for North America, and 41.2% and 46.1% for Europe over the same period. The low levels of scientific and technological knowledge production are reflected in Africa's equally low share of high tech imports and exports, which in 2002 stood at 0.9% and 2.5%, respectively, (compared with 1.3% and 0.3% for Oceania; 4.5% and 3.4% for Latin America and the Caribbean; 21.7% and 15.7% for North America; 36.2% and 38.6% for Europe; and 35.4% and 39.5% for Asia). Needless to say, there are vast differences in these indicators among African countries. South Africa and Egypt tend to have the highest numbers of researchers and scientific publications (accounting for 46% of the total in 1998, followed by Kenya, Morocco, Tunisia and Nigeria, in that order). In 2002, South Africa accounted for 90% of the sub-regional GERD for sub-Saharan Africa.

It is quite clear that Africa's science and technology expenditure and capacities lag behind the continent's economic potential and are well below the levels needed to meet the challenges of globalization. However, as Akin Adubifa (2003) suggests, rising levels of literacy, entrepreneurial activities, democratization and new wireless technologies offer new possibilities for the development of science and technology in the continent. Besides developing the capacities of their universities and research centres, African countries need to explore the full potential of industrial manufacturing as a vehicle for building scientific and technological capacity. Indeed, greater coordination between the different stakeholders – government, industry, donors and universities – is needed to build a capacity that is relevant to local needs and sustainable in the long term. For this to be achieved, public awareness and an advocacy of the importance of science and technology in modernizing national economies, improving national security and participating competitively in international trade must be promoted. Science and technology research capabilities and coordinated systems need to be developed by establishing academies of science and encouraging the production and dissemination of scientific knowledge.

Globalization is a process in which there are rapid flows of capital, labour, communications and culture, as well as the closer integration of markets and economies. It is also a project of neoliberal ideology that is transforming the importance and context of science and technology development. Africa is particularly vulnerable in this brave new world of highly competitive, global, knowledge-intensive economies that are dominated by transnational corporations. These companies scour the planet for creative and skilful talent to generate new products and production processes. The considerable scientific infrastructure that Africa had built by the 1970s was eroded by the structural adjustment programmes of the 1980s and 1990s that devastated African universities (Zeleza and Olukoshi, 2003, 2004). The continent's access to sophisticated science and technology has also frequently been curtailed by racist donors who push for so-called 'appropriate technology'. Africa's development and competitiveness can no longer simply depend on its richly endowed natural resources. Instead, development should be based on Africa's ability to mobilize

science and technology, so that it is able to establish new comparative advantages in the global economy.

The developmental and democratic implications of new technologies are already quite evident. For example, the explosive growth in mobile telephones has had an empowering effect on rural farmers by improving access to market information, while the internet has had a liberating impact on Africa's often beleaguered journalists and information-hungry masses. Africa has emerged as one of the most dynamic telecommunication markets in the world, thanks to economic liberalization, the introduction of competitive markets, and increased investment in the sector. According to the *World Telecommunications/ICT Development Report 2006* (ITU, 2007, p. 11), telecommunications services have grown fastest in Africa. They accounted for 5% of GDP by 2004, compared with 4.5% in Oceania, 3.8% in Asia, 3.3% in Europe, and 2.9% in the Americas. Mobile phones began to outstrip landlines in 2000. By 2004 there were 8.8 mobile phone subscribers per 100 inhabitants compared with 3.1 landline subscribers. In 1994 the ratios were 0.06 and 1.7, respectively.

The growth of information technology has been as spectacular as its impact is far-reaching. The information-producing service and manufacturing sectors directly generate jobs and revenue. Indirect benefits include improved productivity, efficiency, information flow and transparency. Among the services facilitated by information technology are e-commerce, teleworking, e-government, e-health (telemedicine), and e-education (e-learning). However, the vast infrastructural investments needed to develop information technology often engender spatial and social inequities in terms of access between rural and urban areas and among people of different social classes. The digital divide also has a gender dimension. In so far as technology is both socially embedded and engendered, it reflects and reproduces hierarchies and

inequities between men and women. Therefore, it is important to address the intersections between gender, technology and development when science and technology policies are drawn up.

The challenge facing Africa is to narrow or even close the digital divide that exists with other world regions. A further challenge is to reduce the digital divide in the continent. This divide can be observed between and within countries and among telecommunication sectors and products – internet use lags far behind that of mobile phones, for example. In addition, Africa needs to train both informed consumers of technology-driven products and efficient producers of information technology who are able to contribute to the design and/or manufacture of technology-oriented products such as software and internet services. Khaled Ismail (2003) argued that to attain these goals, the education system must be reoriented to produce graduates specialized in technology areas. Technological literacy should be translated into entrepreneurship. The establishment of close, mutually beneficial relations between industry and academia is critical to the development of productive technological skills.

Africa cannot afford to be left behind in the new scientific and technological revolutions as it was left behind during earlier industrial revolutions. Science and technology will not make any headway without massive investments in the continent's universities and other research infrastructures. The continent would also benefit from mobilizing its scientific diaspora; exploiting its comparative advantages in biodiversity; harnessing the leap-frogging possibilities offered by the new information technologies; and collaborating with developing countries such as China that have made scientific and technological advances. The gap between prescription and implementation is of course filled with political calculations, struggles and uncertainties. African leaders are known for their flowery rhetoric about the importance of science and technology for development.

However, there is often a lack of political will to translate rhetoric into reality. Political will is also needed for Africa to forge a new developmental paradigm for the 21st century. This paradigm should prize science and technology for their instrumental value in the quest for human material fulfilment.

REFERENCES

Adubifa, O. Akin (2003) An assessment of science and technology capacity building in Africa. In: Zeleza, P.T. and Kakoma, I. (eds) *In Search of Modernity: Science and technology in Africa*. Trenton, NJ: Africa World Press, pp. 51–70.

Florida, R.L. (1995) Technology policy for a global economy. *Issues in Science and Technology* **11** (Spring), pp. 49–56.

Gaillard, J., Hassan, M. and Waast, R. (2005) Africa. In: *UNESCO World Science Report 2005*. Paris: UNESCO, pp. 177–201.

Galavotti, M.S. (2000) What makes science unique in the experience of mankind? The specificity of the scientific approach. In: *UNESCO, World Conference on Science: Science for the Twenty-First Century: A New Commitment*. Paris: UNESCO, pp. 80–2.

Gibbons, J.H. (1995) Science and technology in post-cold war era. *Forum for Applied Research and Public Policy* **10** (Spring), pp. 119–22.

Hassan, Mohamed (2003) Science and technology in Africa: pathways to Success. In: Zeleza, P.T. and Kakoma, I. (eds) *In Search of Modernity: Science and Technology in Africa*. Trenton, NJ: Africa World Press, pp. 35–49.

International Telecommunications Union (ITU) (2007) *World Telecommunications/ICT Development Report 2006*. Geneva: ITU.

Irele, Abiola F. (1999) *The Political Kingdom: Toward Reconstruction in Africa*, <wysiwyg://39/http://www.africahome.com/scholar/stories/irele_reconstruct.shtml>, accessed June 19, 1999.

Ismail, Khaled (2003) Development and retention of technology skills in Europe. In: Zeleza, P.T. and Kakoma, I. (eds) *In Search of Modernity: Science and technology in Africa*. Trenton, NJ: Africa World Press, pp. 257–65.

Mayor, F. (2000) Opening address. In: *UNESCO, World Conference on Science: Science for the Twenty-First Century: A New Commitment*. Paris: UNESCO: 26–8.

Mazrui, Ali A. (1999) *The African Renaissance: A Triple Legacy of Skills, Values and Gender*, <http://africacentre.org.uk/renaissance.htm>, accessed November 23, 1999.

Sagan, C. (1999) Science and technology in the 20th century: good and bad. *New Perspectives Quarterly* **16**(2), pp. 25–30.

UNESCO (2005) *UNESCO World Science Report 2005*. Paris: UNESCO.

Zeleza, Paul T. (2003) Africa's search for modernity in the internet age. In: Zeleza, P.T. and Kakoma, I. (eds) *In Search of Modernity: Science and technology in Africa*. Trenton, NJ: Africa World Press, pp. 1–31.

Zeleza, Paul T. and Olukoshi, Adebayo (2003) (eds) *African Universities in the Twenty-First Century*. Vol.1: Liberalization and Internationalization. Dakar: Codesria Book Series.

Zeleza, Paul T. and Olukoshi, Adebayo (2004) (eds) *African Universities in the Twenty-First Century*. Vol.2: Knowledge and Society. Dakar: Codesria Book Series.

Zeleza, Paul T. and Kakoma, Ibulaimu (2003) (eds) *In Search of Modernity: Science and Technology in Africa*. Trenton, NJ: Africa World Press.

GOOD PRACTICE II.1

Setting up an opencourseware project (University of the Western Cape, South Africa)

GUNI Observatory[1]

CONTEXT

OpenCourseWare (OCW) is digital teaching material that is openly available to the community free of charge. It is generally produced by higher education institutions as it consists of course material for the subjects they teach.

The first university to design and plan an OCW system was the Massachusetts Institute of Technology (MIT), in 2002. The system is a large-scale electronic publishing initiative based on the internet and was set up jointly by the William and Flora Hewlett Foundation, the Andrew W. Mellon Foundation and MIT, with a budget of US$4 million. There are already 1,550 courses from 34 departments in MIT's five faculties in OCW format. As well as general course content, self-learning materials are also provided. These include exams and exercises, additional reading material and even video lectures. Some courses also include interactive tools in different formats or programs and digital books written by MIT professors. Materials for all courses are scheduled to become gradually available in 2008. The OCW system allows the general public to acquire the same training as university students at no cost, though there is no official recognition of these studies.

Currently, universities throughout the world are initiating similar programmes. MIT has helped create the OpenCourseWare Consortium (OCWC), which is made up of more than 100 higher education institutions and associated organizations. The mission of the Consortium is to make progress in educating and training people throughout the world using OCW.

This shows that increasing numbers of higher education institutions are acknowledging that sharing syllabuses and educational course materials freely is worthwhile. However, in developing nations very few higher education institutions are making an active contribution in this field. In this type of project, knowledge flows from developed nations to less developed ones. This means that the educational material available is not entirely adapted to the specific needs and demands of developing nations and that in these nations its contribution to society in general will be less.

DESCRIPTION

The aim of the OCW project of the University of the Western Cape (UWC), South Africa, is for students and lecturers to make free use of the resources developed for teaching and learning at UWC. This serves the double purpose of providing the university community with easy access to the educational resources that the institution produces and of allowing the local and regional community to benefit from the wealth of knowledge at UWC. The project is an extension of the social role that UWC played in the past during the struggle to achieve political freedom in South Africa. Its ultimate aim is to bring the political ideals of the past up to date. Today, access to knowledge is crucial, not only to the socioeconomic development of a country but also to its human development; universities have an important role to play in this.

The OCW project was set up in August 2006 and the first phase of development and implementation is scheduled to finish in August 2008. In the first year, work was carried out on developing the infrastructure (the software and internet platform). The second year will be dedicated to disseminating the OCW (publication of courses). Annual funding for the project amounts to €40,000.

OBJECTIVES

The objectives of the project are as follows:

- To encourage UWC lecturers and stu-

dents to benefit from the free open-access educational content of the OCW

- To share the wealth of the educational resources developed at UWC with the local community
- To create a repository of high-quality OCW material that is particularly relevant in the local context
- To create the legal infrastructure needed for publishing the UWC courses using licences for free, open-access distribution
- To raise awareness about the importance of free, open access to knowledge within higher education institutions in Africa
- To work with individual lecturers and departments to identify and publish course material that is relevant to and appropriate for the local environment.

PROCESS

The project is in the first of the two phases of implementation and consolidation. The following actions were carried out in the first year:

1. *Setting up a work team to begin publishing courses*
   All the university departments were invited to participate in order to involve the largest possible number of members of the university community and thus consolidate the project, even though the team currently running the project is small.
   One of the groups most closely involved in the project is the e-learning team, which provides support to all participating lecturers. This team organizes workshops and provides individual assistance in order to answer queries from lecturers and students. Seminars on different themes are also organized every month. The Free Software Innovation Unit also makes a major contribution by helping to develop the e-learning platform, publish the contents and promote the project for users outside the university.

2. *Development of the technical infrastructure*
   Knowledge of copyright law is essential for developing a project of this nature. The team backing the project therefore trains in this field and disseminates its knowledge throughout the university community in the form of support material on how to produce free, open-access contents.
   The technical development of the internet platform and the software is achieved through the cooperation of the UWC Free Software Innovation Unit, the OCWC and other international partners.

3. *Awareness-raising among lecturers and students*
   Awareness in the university community is raised by means of a blog that disseminates the ideas behind the OCW. Other mechanisms used for raising awareness include email distribution lists and articles in free-access journals.

4. *Identifying courses and lecturers likely to contribute to the project*
   The first step in obtaining the cooperation of the members of the university community is to hold meetings with the faculty heads. Lecturers who show an interest in the project receive support and all the information they need to take part in it. A special effort is made to encourage the participation of staff who already have some knowledge of e-learning or who have worked with free software. This is done to reduce the number of problems that may arise while adapting to the technological tools used on the project.

In this first phase, three areas of knowledge were identified as being highly relevant to local circumstances and in which UWC has a great deal of experience. These are *public health, constitutional law and biocomputing*. Staff responsible for teaching these disciplines are encouraged to take part in the project by giving pilot OCW courses at the University.

A great deal of work was likewise done

in the project's first year of development to promote links with other institutions at international, regional and local levels. At the international level, the aim was to collect information on successful OCW experiences at other universities. At the local and regional level, the objective was to establish a network of universities interested in developing similar programmes.

UWC is the first African university to join the OCWC, in which it plays a very important role as it expresses the point of view of developing nations in the region. The OCWC's specialized support and assistance strengthens the UWC project, particularly in terms of technical infrastructure.

As this is a pioneer initiative in Africa, UWC has signed an agreement with UNESCO's open education division to cooperate in developing and publishing specific materials for higher education institutions in developing nations. Other examples of international cooperation include the forthcoming publication in iCommons of a strategic document on open education and on links with NGOs participating in the Creative Commons organization.

Looking to the future, the OCW project is promoting a programme that creates links with 14 other African universities. The project is called the African Virtual Open Initiative and Resource (AVOIR), and is directed and funded by UWC.

Further collaboration is being established with civil society at national and regional levels, in particular with the group working in open education at the Shuttleworth Foundation.

RESULTS
DEVELOPMENT OF INFRASTRUCTURE
- The project's website went into operation in April 2007 at (http://elearn. uwc.ac.za/index.php?module=splash screen#)
- A blog and general information portal were set up
- A local mirror site for MIT OCW courses was created to overcome

problems of access from African servers
- A repository, or central database, of OCW course materials was set up for publishing UWC courses.

PUBLICATION OF COURSES
- The first pilot course in OCW format was published in June 2007 after an agreement was reached with the School of Public Health. A total of 10 courses were published in 2007.

AWARENESS-RAISING, TRAINING AND DISSEMINATION
- A community of practice has been set up, with an email distribution list that currently has 30 members
- Individual and group meetings are held to provide information and raise awareness in an effort to create the best possible reception for the OCW project
- Support material for using and producing free, open-access educational content is created at UWC and is published on the project's blog
- One unexpected spin-off of the project was the increase in participants' skills and knowledge in the area of open-content licences and copyright law within the context of higher education in South Africa
- The project was presented at a seminar on e-learning and at the UWC symposium on teaching and learning – both in 2007
- An article on Education 3.0 was published in the journal *First Monday* **12**(3) in March 2007, with the title 'The genesis and emergence of Education 3.0 in higher education and its potential for Africa'
- A course was given at UWC on free, open-access licences by the e-learning team and the Digital Media Studio
- The project expressed the point of view of African universities at the 2007 OCWC meeting
- It has proposed and developed research assignments and received consulting contracts for the coming years from institutions such as the

International Development Research Centre, UNESCO and the Shuttleworth Foundation.

RECOMMENDATIONS
The following practical recommendations have arisen from the activities carried out so far:

- *Making use of synergy:*
  A small team should be set up to carry out the project and identify initiatives that already exist within the institution in order to work with them. If there is already an e-learning group in the institution, many advantages can be gained by combining synergies. The e-learning team can help to raise awareness within the university community and identify members of this community who are especially interested in the project.
  It is also advisable to establish a close relationship with the law department, particularly if this department has experience in copyright legislation. It is important to bear in mind that the use and publication of free, open-access course materials in the university has complex legal implications.
- *Institutional support*
  The institutional support of university managers is essential for ensuring the continuity of the project and the involvement of the university as a whole. It is therefore of the utmost importance to establish good communication channels and to take the necessary time to convince this sector of the importance of the project.
- *Groundwork and support for lecturers*
  When materials are published, staff must be sufficiently grounded in legal and technical matters. Lecturers may have doubts about how the information they provide will be used and it is important to make it clear that there is considerable legal support in this matter.
  It is also advisable to keep up-to-date with technological advances in software and standard content management. In the case of UWC, the

eduCommons repository system, and especially the learning object metadata (LOM) system of the Institute of Electrical and Electronic Engineers (IEEE), was used as a standard exchange package.

It is important to facilitate the task of participating lecturers as much as possible by providing them with support in updating their online course material and in implementing control mechanisms to ensure that the steps taken are correct. The energy and support that lecturers give to the project are essential for maintaining the system and the courses.

NOTE

1 Text written by the Universities and Social Commitment Observatory with information provided by Philipp Schmidt, University of the Western Cape.

GOOD PRACTICE II.2

Achieving sustainable development through curriculum transformation in higher education institutions of Southern Africa

GUNI Observatory

THE ROLE OF HIGHER EDUCATION INSTITUTIONS

Six universities in Southern Africa participate in a network of 13 institutions aiming to include sustainable development aspects in their curricula. The weight of these universities within the network shows the importance of higher education in contributing to the improvement of sustainability in general, including factors affecting the development of Southern Africa in particular, such as the region's marginal economic position in the global context, the close relationship between poverty and environmental degradation, and HIV/AIDS. These factors not only have a devastating impact on social, economic and health systems, but also on education.

Given its complexity, sustainable development requires an interdisciplinary response. Academics are thus asked to engage critically and proactively on this issue. Changing curricula is more than a way of teaching environmental issues; it can contribute to the broader issue of making new policies by effecting changes in thinking and practice. In this sense, higher education institutions (HEIs) have a double role: teaching development issues through curriculum transformation, and contributing to policy changes.

However, practice shows that existing national needs and policies are the main motivation for engaging in curriculum reform, leading to mere policy implementation with little policy critique.

The experiences of the Course Development Network highlight the problems that HEIs face when implementing new curricula.

A SPECIFIC PROGRAMME FOR ENVIRONMENTAL EDUCATION

In 1997, the Southern African Development Community (SADC) initiated its Regional Environmental Education Programme (REEP) to strengthen environmental education processes in the region's 14 countries.

Coordinated from a regional centre based in Howick, South Africa, the programme is mainly financed by the Swedish development cooperation agency Sida and the Danish development agency Danida.

The REEP consists of four major areas with different sub-projects:

1. Training environmental educators for sustainability.
2. Developing resource materials: improving capacity to access, use and develop appropriate environmental education resource materials.

3. Supporting policy initiatives: creating an environment for regional and national environmental education policy and supporting the development and implementation of local-level environmental and environmental-education policy within the SADC region.
4. Networking: setting up a broad, decentralized regional environmental education network consisting of the SADC Food, Agriculture and Natural Resources Directorate, national network representatives, the Regional Environmental Education Centre and other practitioners in the region.

TRAINING EDUCATORS FOR SUSTAINABILITY

An important part of the REEP is undoubtedly the training component, which aims to increase the capacity to respond to environmental issues through improved education processes and training activities. It provides:

1. Courses, such as the Rhodes University/SADC International Environmental Education Certificate Course.
2. The Attachment Programme: practical stays lasting an average of 10 days, which provide the opportunity to work and exchange experiences with

other educators and make it possible to combine all four areas of the REEP, adding aspects of networking, policy issues and the development of resource materials.

3. The Course Development Network, composed of universities, NGOs, polytechnics and other organizations responsible for developing environmental education programmes. This was the first formal network to be set up, in 2001, and aims to broaden and strengthen environmental education capacity and professional development in the region. Out of the 13 institutions that make up the network, six are universities: University of Botswana, University of Malawi, University of South Africa, University of Swaziland, Rhodes University in South Africa and the National University of Lesotho. This formal network is linked to a more informal network consisting of over 28 course development initiatives.

In the course development process, the networking institutions meet at course development workshops twice a year over a period of thirty months. Through these regional workshops, network members share skills, experiences and resources in order to enable the development of environmental education courses in their own institutions, drawing on their local context. The network has been compiling a course developer's resource kit called 'the toolkit'. This is a collection of course development materials and case stories from members and partner institutions. The toolkit is seen as a resource that will enable the developing work of the network to unfold as a coherent capacity development programme.

One of the most notable achievements of the network has been the development and implementation of at least 12 new courses in environmental and sustainability education.

IMPACT OF CURRICULUM REFORM

In 2005, an external team evaluated the first eight years of the REEP and published its recommendations. While the impact of the curriculum reforms in HEIs and the new teaching content are still difficult to measure, the overall assessment of the Course Development Network is positive. Interaction among course developers, which creates long-term synergies, is seen as helpful towards achieving the desired impacts.

Although the networking benefits are more important, pedagogical transformations are also seen in some cases. In one of the participating HEIs, new partnerships involving university, government and civil society were created and multidisciplinary approaches were established.

This encouraging regional experience also led to involvement in a pan-African initiative to improve course development competences and hence had a certain snowball effect.

CHALLENGES INVOLVED WITH DESIGNING AND IMPLEMENTING NEW CURRICULA

In HEIs, curriculum development is a difficult, hierarchical process to which the contribution of individual lecturers is very limited. However, development issues are complex and require not only the participation of a broad range of academics, but also a clear interdisciplinary approach. The curriculum transformation process should seek interaction and discussion with all stakeholders involved in an issue. Unfortunately, the current processes are too rigid to include a broad range of experiences.

Other institutional difficulties are the structural constraints of accredited curriculum development processes and the length of the procedure due to heavy bureaucracy. These factors hinder a fast and flexible adaptation of curricula to new social circumstances. Broader national policies usually stimulate changes within HEIs, but the above-mentioned restrictions hinder the successful integration of new policy-responsive initiatives.

As for course contents, the challenge lies in developing a course for a wide-ranging target audience including, among others, teachers, conservation officers and industry representatives. This requires introducing multidisciplinary perspectives, while at the same time addressing the specific needs of each learner group.

On the individual level, academics involved in the Course Development Network believe that curriculum reform is time-consuming, but state that they receive individual and collective rewards and recognition. For instance, they get the opportunity to present their work in congresses and publish papers on the matter, thus contributing to their personal professional academic career.

THE WAY FORWARD

The positive results of the Course Development Network cannot hide the obstacles HEIs face in engaging in a much-needed change process, which would make it easier to adapt to new social requirements and make it possible to influence broader policies. In this sense, effective environmental education should be seen in a wider context, reaching from the specific problems of curriculum transformation to the need for reforms on an institutional level.

Abstract

This paper is divided into three main sections on the three broad objectives of the analysis. The globalization context within which the Arab higher education (HE) systems function is taken into consideration.

- The first section examines and evaluates the present state of the Arab HE system by focusing on (a) the main developments that have taken place since the 1998 World Conference on Higher Education (WCHE), including the level of achievement of the Millennium Development Goals (MDGs) for education; and (b) aspects of globalization that have a significant economic, social and political influence on Arab societies and which may directly or indirectly affect the current features of the HE systems in the region.

- Taking into consideration the developments discussed in the first section, the second section examines their impact on shaping public HE policies, demonstrates the main problems and challenges facing the Arab HE systems in this context, and discusses implications for social and human development.

- The third section recommends the future actions and policy measures needed to sustain and empower the Arab HE systems and to promote their capacity to respond to the needs of human and social development in the region.

INTRODUCTION

The Arab world is composed of countries of varying population size, wealth, educational history, and level of social and economic development. Out of 19 Arab countries, 11 fall within the medium human development (HD) range, 5 are within the high HD category and 3 are in the low category. Disparity related to gross domestic product (GDP) per capita is high; the average GDP for the Gulf countries is 4.4 times the average for the rest of the Arab countries (UNDP, 2006). In spite of these undeniable discrepancies, the Arab HE systems share many common features and face similar challenges. Therefore, the region can be coherently analysed as a whole. This paper focuses on the issues that affect most of the Arab countries. There may be some exceptions, but they should not significantly affect our analysis.

This analysis is based on the proposition that highly educated people are indispensable to the social, human and economic development of any modern society and to the development of Arab countries in particular. Therefore, HE is considered an activity that benefits the entire society; it does not only confer private benefits to the educated population segments. In other words, this analysis regards HE as a public good. Its function and mission are much broader than the neo-classical concept that limits the value of HE to its impact on the labour market and on increasing productivity, output and earnings – although this function is also crucial.

The present analysis will be guided by the social and human dimensions endorsed by the World Conference on Higher Education (WCHE) (UNESCO, 1998a) and the Arab Regional Conference (ARC) (UNESCO, 1998b). In addition to providing highly trained personnel to meet the requirements of various sectors of the economy and promote its productivity and competitiveness, HE in Arab states should aim to achieve the following:

- Broaden access and the opportunity for participation on the basis of merit, in line with the Universal Declaration of Human Rights, which states that 'everyone has the right to education', and that 'higher education shall be equally accessible to all on the basis of merit' (UNESCO, 1998a). This will enable HE to work for both widespread knowledge acquisition and for upward mobility.

- Educate aware, responsible citizens who are prepared to become full participants and promoters of the changes that lead to the development of a truly democratic society. Increase the commitment of these citizens to the crucial issues and challenges facing their societies and humanity at large, for example, poverty, human rights, social equity, environmental protection and cultural diversity.

- Undertake research activities that can contribute to the understanding, anticipation and solving of the most serious problems in the Arab region (UNESCO, 1998b). Knowledge derived from relevant research is an essential component of all aspects of human and social development.

AN OVERVIEW OF THE PRESENT SITUATION

ACCESS TO HE AND MILLENNIUM DEVELOPMENT GOALS (MDGs) ACHIEVEMENTS

Increasing access to HE is one of the key objectives of human and social development advocated by the 1998 WCHE and the ARC. Arab researchers and educational experts agree that most Arab countries have achieved significant progress over the past few decades in widening access to HE. From 1990 to 2006, the number of HE students in the Arab region increased almost threefold, from 2.4 million to 6.8 million. This expansion was triggered by several factors. The most important of these are the very high population growth rate (the second highest of all world regions) and the rapid increase in secondary enrolment. Globalization and the growing awareness worldwide of the importance of knowledge, skills and female participation also had a significant influence.

Statistics from the period following the WCHE reveal similar quantitative progress. Table II.3.1 shows that the rate of growth of total HE enrolment in the Arab region (1999–2005) reached 31.3%. Female enrolment had an exceptionally high rate (55.2%), which was much higher than the corresponding rate for male students (14.3%). Currently, the majority share of the increase in enrolment (73.3%) over this period is due to the massive increase in female students. The number of female students out of the total number of HE students rose significantly over the same period, from 41.5% to 49.1%.

TABLE II.3.1
Indicators of HE access in the Arab world (1999–2005)

	1999	2005	Enrolment growth rate (%)
Total enrolment	5,165,102	6,782,489	31.3
Male enrolment	3,018,866	3,451,343	14.3
Female enrolment	2,146,236	3,331,506	55.2
Female share in total enrolment	41.5%	49.1%	–
Gross enrolment ratio	19%	21%	–
Male	22%	21%	–
Female	16%	21%	–

Source: UNESCO Institute for Statistics, 2005.

The same trend can be identified in the gross enrolment ratio (GER). Following the WCHE, the total GER increased from 19% to 21%, marking an enrolment growth rate that was higher than population growth, and giving the Arab region a favourable GER in comparison with other less developed countries (LDCs). However, the GER is still much lower than in developed countries. The prominent increase in female participation was also obvious. The female GER increased by five percentage points, whereas the male GER declined by one percentage point over the period.

SHORTCOMINGS

In spite of the outstanding quantitative progress and the impressive increase in female participation in HE, the following shortcomings may cause concern:

- There is great disparity in the average GER for individual countries, ranging from 2.5% in Djibouti to 51% in Lebanon in 2005
- The fact that the Arab region achieved complete gender equality in HE enrolment in 2005 (gender parity index = 1.01) conceals the unfortunate situation of some Arab countries that still have a high rate of gender inequality, such as Djibouti, Iraq, Mauritania and Yemen.
- The distribution of HE students in different fields of study is highly skewed towards social science and the humanities. The percentage of students enrolled in engineering and natural sciences is generally low. The total enrolment rate in the humanities and social sciences is estimated to be 72%. The corresponding rate for females is much more skewed (ALECSO, 2003).
- The accelerated increase in student enrolment has not been matched in many cases by a corresponding increase in the number of teaching posts or by a significant improvement in working conditions and level of earnings. Furthermore, women are still under-represented in HE teaching posts (33%) compared to their representation in primary (57%) and secondary education (47%) (UNESCO Institute for Statistics, 2005).

MDG ACHIEVEMENTS

The region's performance is rather modest; for example, primary net enrolment rate (NER) did not exceed 83% until 2005. Furthermore, none of the Arab states for which information is available were able to achieve universal primary education in 2005 (UNESCO Institute for Statistics, 2005). It will probably be difficult to achieve this goal even by 2015 in countries such as Djibouti, Mauritania, Oman and Saudi Arabia. The first two of these countries are among the least developed in the world, whereas the other two are rich Gulf states. This indicates that cultural factors as well as income availability may influence the attainment of MDGs.

However, the most extraordinary result is the decline in primary NER in some Arab countries between 1999 and 2005 (Jordan, Lebanon, Oman and the Palestinian Territories). The worst hit were the Palestinian Territories.

Among the MDGs for education is the achievement of gender equality in primary and secondary education, preferably by 2005 and no later than 2015. Although HE gender equality in the Arab region as a whole had been achieved by 2005, a certain degree of gender inequality still prevails in primary and secondary education. In addition, there is a significant gap between the male and female literacy rates in the young population (UIS, 2005).

GLOBALIZATION AND ARAB SOCIETIES

This section focuses on global issues related directly or indirectly to the Arab HE sector and influence its capacity to promote human and social development.

THE CONCEPT OF GLOBALIZATION

Our definition of globalization is based on the following two quotations (Held et al., 1999):

> Globalization is associated with an evolving dynamic global structure of enablement and constraint. But it is also a highly stratified structure since globalization is profoundly uneven: it both reflects existing patterns of inequality and hierarchy while also generating new patterns of inclusion and exclusion, new winners and losers.

> Power is a fundamental attribute of globalization. In an increasingly interconnected global system, the exercise of power through the decisions, actions or inactions of agencies in one continent can have significant consequences for nations, communities and households in other continents.

The authors also draw attention to the dangers of confusing globalization with other concepts such as interdependence, integration and universalism. Unlike globalization, these concepts imply symmetrical power relations between various nations.

Taking the above definition, we will demonstrate that most Arab countries have been vulnerable to the constraints created by globalization and have benefited much less from its opportunities.

THE INFLUENCE OF NEO-LIBERALISM

Globalization embraces neo-liberalism, whose concep-

tions and principles have been taken on by policymakers, politicians and many intellectuals in Arab countries (and in LDCs). The narrow concept of economic growth, or the rate of increase of national income, has tended to replace the broad 'development' concept, which is concerned with enhancing the lives people lead and the freedom they enjoy (Sen, 1999). Focusing on economic growth alone leaves little or no room for vital issues related to human and social development such as how income is distributed; who benefits most from economic growth; to what extent economic growth creates more jobs or more unemployment; the influence of the pattern of economic and political power on the growth pattern; and the impact of growth on HD.

If level of income is considered a good indicator of the achievement of human and social development, the ranking of various Arab countries will be similar, or at least not widely divergent, under the human development index (HDI) and GDP per capita. However, out of 19 Arab countries, 12 countries have a lower HDI ranking than GDP per capita (UNDP, 2006). In all the Gulf countries except Kuwait, the divergence between the two indicators is substantial.

The global governance organizations, particularly the World Bank, the International Monetary Fund (IMF) and the World Trade Organization (WTO), have also enforced conformity in social and economic management through the application of the Structural Adjustment Programme (SAP) and the WTO agreements in most Arab countries. This tendency has guided public policies towards restraining public expenditure, increasing privatization and liberalizing trade. The global governance organizations see these policies as the only viable alternative for efficient macro-economic management.

WEAKENING THE ROLE OF THE STATE

Globalization – which has stretched across borders and enabled market forces to transform national systems of governance – has strongly challenged the role of the state. In most Arab countries, the state's participation in direct production has been severely reduced and its responsibility for social sectors has been restricted. National economic and social management has therefore become less influential, thus limiting the scope for government intervention. For instance, public expenditure used to be a powerful instrument of Arab governments that could influence income distribution, promote social sectors, alleviate poverty and strengthen investment towards more job creation. However, there has been a significant decline in public expenditure. From 1987 to 2005, it dropped from 50.2% to 29.2% of GDP (Arab League, 2006a).

In addition, from 1987 to 2002, public revenue as a

percentage of GDP declined from 32.41% to 28.88% (Arab Monetary Fund, 1999, 2003). Currently, the taxation level in the region is considered low in comparison to world levels. In many cases, the proportion of tax receipts does not exceed 20% of the GDP. Some Gulf countries do not even impose any taxation (ESCWA, 2006). Therefore, in most countries in the region, the role of the state and its public policies are significantly restricted, since the burden of adjustment falls largely on the expenditure side of public budgets, leaving the revenue side to grow negatively.

THE ARAB ECONOMY AND ADVANCES IN SCIENCE AND TECHNOLOGY

The economies of most Arab countries have not satisfactorily responded to the science and technology (S&T) advances brought about by globalization. Worldwide, there has been a dramatic shift from production that relies mainly on labour or capital intensity to production based on knowledge, innovation, creativity and their technological applications. Under globalization, the Arab world has become an enormous market for the sales of information and communication technology (ICT) and investment in various economic sectors, particularly the oil and gas sector. However, there has been no corresponding enhancement in innovation and knowledge creation, or a visible tendency to build the endogenous capabilities of the region (Zahlan, 2007). Although several research centres have been established in Arab countries, most of them have not made any noteworthy scientific research contributions or innovations.

Two indicators reflect the weak response of the Arab economies to global S&T advances. The first relates to exports, which are generally concentrated in the category of non-industrial products (mostly energy and raw materials). Moreover, within the industrial category, the share of high-technology exports is very low (2% at the most) compared to that of LDCs in general (23%) (Arab Planning Institute, 2006). The other indicator is the Technology Achievement Index, which was introduced by the Human Development Report (HDR). This index marks the relatively low status of Arab countries in the sphere of invention and product development (UNDP, 2001).

In brief, the Arab economy under globalization lacks many of the features of a knowledge-based economy that can develop, promote and reward high productivity, scientific research and innovation. Moreover, Arab economies have not reached expectations of a high and sustainable growth rate under the SAP. In fact, the percentage of the population living on less than US$2 a day increased from 24.8% in 1990 to 29.9% in 1998 (ESCWA, 2006).

GLOBALIZATION AND THE WORLD OF WORK

The state of the Arab economy is reflected in the world of work. Thus, while the agricultural and services sectors absorb 83.1% of the Arab labour force, industry – which has the potential for both technological progress and productive job creation – employs only 16.9% (Arab League, 2006a). Moreover, productivity gains in the region have been low compared to those seen in other regions, especially Asia. In fact, a slight majority of Arab economies failed to reach the labour productivity level they had achieved in 1980, with the exception of the United Arab Emirates, which far exceeded its 1980 labour productivity level (ILO, 2004–05).

Globalization has also led to dualism in the world of work in most Arab countries. High-productivity, technologically advanced enclaves coexist with low-productivity, technologically traditional sectors. The enclaves are mainly dominated by subsidiaries of transnational companies (TNCs) and joint ventures. Such companies provide highly paid jobs, employment security, social and health insurance, and opportunities for training and promotion. Yet the number of employment opportunities created by this sector is almost insignificant. The traditional sector, which is dominated by what is known as the informal sector, includes a large number of small enterprises and has exactly the opposite characteristics. This sector absorbs a large proportion of the labour force in the region (Wadiee, 2005).

Labour demand falls short of labour supply in most countries, due to the substantial decline of public investment; the slackness of private sector growth induced by the SAP-created contraction; high, capital intensive investment by foreign enterprises; and the import impact of trade liberalization, which has become a threat to domestically produced goods and services in several countries.

Unemployment, especially among the educated, has therefore become a major problem in most Arab economies. Even in the Gulf countries, which rely on imported labour, unemployment is an increasingly visible problem caused by overstaffing and underemployment in the government sector, and the rejection of private sector employment by most Gulf nationals.

INVASION AND OCCUPATION

Globalization may create problems in relation to issues such as equity, funding, and economic and human development. More seriously, it also tends to challenge national and regional sovereignty and threaten the ability of smaller states to defend their independent political will. The Arab region is perhaps the most vulnerable in the world to this ugly face of globalization. The invasion of Iraq by the American and allied forces is a startling example. The result of the invasion has been the destruction of Iraqi human and physical resources and the exploitation of oil production and exports. The occupation of the Iraqi territories, which has lasted for almost five years so far, has resulted in the death of hundreds of thousands of civilians; the emigration of millions of Iraqi people to remote areas and neighbouring countries to seek refuge and avoid death or unbearable living conditions; and the spread of fear and unrest, not only in Iraq but throughout the region. Many Iraqis now suspect that their country will be partitioned.

Inaction; the international community's lack of involvement in establishing a just and effective peace settlement; serious discrimination against the Palestinian cause in world politics; and the utter silence about the aggression towards and the daily suffering of the Palestinian people inside and outside of the territories is another ugly side of globalization that also indicates the weakness of the nation-states in the region. As the next section will show, the HE sector and its human and social development mission have been harshly affected by the above circumstances in the region.

HE POLICIES AND CHALLENGES IN THE CONTEXT OF GLOBALIZATION

CHANGES IN HE POLICIES

To accommodate the accelerated growth in the demand for HE under the constraints and influences of globalization, most Arab countries have introduced significant changes to their public policies. Such changes were implemented within the context of globalization described above, and are oriented towards considering HE a private rather than a public good. The notion of HE as a private good was widely publicized and promoted by several of the World Bank's publications and reports.

In its recent publications, the World Bank has tended to acknowledge the importance of HE and its crucial role as a pillar of the competitive economy. Nevertheless, it continues to recommend the market-oriented approach as the most effective mechanism for supporting the expansion of HE. It emphasizes the idea that public spending and state intervention impede the market mechanism and result in economic inefficiency. Thus, many Arab governments (and LDCs in general) have been encouraged to change their current HE policies, limit public expenditure and promote private sources of funding.

LIMITING PUBLIC EXPENDITURE

In most Arab countries, HE funding strategies and the responsibility of the state have undergone significant changes, not only as a result of external pressure but also due to sluggish economic progress and other domestic circumstances. The trend towards limiting public expenditure on HE cannot be gauged precisely, due to the scarcity of information on HE expenditure in most countries of the region (Charafeddine, 2006). However, according to ALECSO (2003), in the 1990s, most Arab countries reached a ceiling of public expenditure as a proportion of their state budgets. In addition, a reduction in financial resources allocated to HE has been observed. The Arab Human Development Report (UNDP, 2003) reveals a declining trend in public expenditure on education. In addition, ESCWA (2006) indicates that the public expenditure allocation pattern is not likely to lead to growth or improvement because governments in the region do not spend enough on education, health and research and development (R&D) activities.

THE DIVERSIFICATION OF HIGHER EDUCATION INSTITUTIONS (HEIs)

The accelerated demand for HE, together with increasing restraints on public spending, has compelled decision-makers in many Arab countries to diversify their HE systems. This diversification process involves the establishment of non-university education, open education, private universities and cost recovery schemes.

NON-UNIVERSITY EDUCATION

The institutional structure of HE in the Arab countries has long been dominated by university education. The trend towards the expansion of technical and vocational institutions in several countries did not take off until the early 1990s. The following four factors may explain the reasons behind this expansion:

- The need to train technicians and applied specialists to meet the requirements of the world of work. In the case of Gulf countries, another objective is to increase the nationals' participation in the workforce
- The need to absorb the increasing number of upper secondary vocational school graduates
- The need to replace high-cost university education with low-cost vocational education and reduce the pressure of demand on public universities
- The relatively low investment cost of these types of HEIs, in comparison to university education, which makes it possible for the private sector to carry the main responsibility for this investment.

All of the above objectives have been met except for the first one, which relates to the preparation of technically trained graduates to meet the requirements of the world of work. This objective has not been achieved because expansionary policy has been concerned with financial considerations at the expense of providing modern, high-quality technical and vocational training.

OPEN EDUCATION

Another way of diversifying the Arab HE system and adjusting to the global environment has involved developing certain patterns of open education. Several Arab countries, including Egypt, Libya, Tunisia, Algeria, Sudan, the United Arab Emirates and the Palestinian Territories, have already launched (or expanded) open education programmes. In 2002, the Arab Open University started its activities as a non-profit institution with headquarters in Kuwait and branches in several other Arab countries. It is perhaps the first well-equipped, planned open university in the region. The university derives its marketing and publicity from its connection with the UK's well-known Open University, whose programmes and instructional materials it also adopts. This excessive foreign dependence, however, has been criticized on the grounds that it tends to obstruct the development of Arab experience in this new technological field (UNESCO, 2003). Most of the Arab students who are enrolled in open education institutions pay tuition fees.

PRIVATE UNIVERSITIES

The establishment of private universities is the most pronounced recent policy in the Arab HE system. The number of these institutions increased rapidly in a relatively short period: from 26 to 77 universities between 1993 and 2003. Many other private universities have been established since 2003. In fact, the exact scale of expansion of these institutions and the number of students they absorb cannot be precisely determined, since the number of newly established universities in the Arab states is rapidly increasing from one year – and even one month – to the next. In addition, UNESCO statistical agencies do not cover private HEIs.

Privatization was not only confined to encouraging new, private providers within national or regional boundaries. In the era of globalization and trade liberalization, HE became one of the service sectors included in the General Agreement on Trade in Services (GATS). Therefore, a global market for HE has begun to materialize in several Arab countries since the middle of the 1990s. This trend has intensified recently, as an increasing number of Arab governments believe that cross-border institutions represent an easy, ready-made solution to their HE problems of participation, finance and educational quality. American education is becoming the most preferred model for foreign collaboration in HE in several Arab countries. The Gulf countries in particular have wholly adopted the American university model. It is maintained

that all the many private universities established in this sub-region publicize their partnerships or affiliations with American universities (Coffman, 2003).

The new private universities in the Arab region have some specific features:

- They are different from the few private universities that used to exist in some Arab countries (especially Lebanon) before restructuring began. The new private universities are basically for-profit institutions, even if the laws authorizing such universities are not explicit about this issue
- They depend almost completely on tuition fees to cover the cost of education, that is, they have no complementary sources of financing
- They are basically teaching universities, that is, they are not involved in research activities or postgraduate studies.

In addition, regardless of whether private universities are domestic or affiliated with foreign institutions, they generally use English as the main medium of instruction. In fact, in most Arab countries, teaching staff who are native English speakers are a great asset and convey competitive advantage to the institution concerned. For instance, in Morocco – one of the main Francophone countries within the Arab region, where French is the dominant foreign language in the HE sector – the only private university was founded as an American-style English-language university (Clark, 2006). In Egypt, the German university founded in 2002 uses English rather than German as the medium of instruction in order to attract a larger intake of students.

FEES AND COST RECOVERY SCHEMES

Private funding of HE has also been fostered in several Arab states (for example Egypt, Jordan, Yemen, Lebanon and Morocco) within the framework of publicly owned HEIs by imposing tuition fees, introducing cost recovery schemes or reducing student scholarships. Two cost recovery schemes are worth mentioning here. The first targets a wide student base: the number admitted is usually large; the fees are not too high (though subject to increase at any time); admissions are limited in some countries to the humanities and social sciences (low-cost education); and the language of instruction is Arabic. The other scheme targets the elite and is called a special or international programme: the number of students admitted is very small; tuition fees are much higher; the disciplines are varied; and – most importantly – the instruction language is English (or French in a few cases).

With more countries following suit, the number of Arab students who pay for their education within public HEIs is expected to increase significantly.

CHALLENGES FACING HIGHER EDUCATION

Changes in public policies, in addition to some inherent deficiencies in the Arab HE systems, tend to create crucial challenges that are likely to undermine the role of HE in meeting the human and social development needs of the Arab society. The most significant of these challenges are:

- Issues related to the quality of HE
- Challenges related to invasion and occupation
- Research activities and their tendency to be marginalized
- Imbalances in the world of work
- Renewed challenges by the new providers.

QUALITY OF HE AND RELATED ISSUES

The quality of HE was not considered an issue in itself during the various phases of its development in Arab countries. This may be because education was perhaps taken – even internationally – to mean quality education. However, the increasing importance of knowledge and innovation in the past few decades has positioned quality as a global priority issue. Arab societies have therefore become concerned about the output of their HEIs, and interest in issues of quality and quality assurance has begun to increase (Babiker, 2007). However, these issues have not been translated into effective policies for quality evaluation and assurance. Instead, since the early 1990s, financial considerations have become the dominant force driving HE policies in most Arab countries (and many LDCs), regardless of their impact on the quality of education. Expansion under these conditions has taken place as described above within public funding restraints. It has been motivated by the quest for social and political gains rather than equity for its own sake.

As a consequence, most HEIs have suffered from inadequate infrastructure, a shortage of education materials and equipment, the degradation of libraries and laboratories, and the existence of unmotivated teaching staff with declining real earnings. More critically, insufficient funding in many Arab universities (except some universities in the rich Gulf countries) has constrained the adoption of ICTs. Internet connectivity, where it exists, remains in the early stages of development. An interesting contrast has been observed by the UNDP (2003): whilst the Arab region has more PCs than any other developing region except Latin America, it has the lowest rate of internet access and usage. Therefore, the capacity of most Arab public universities to integrate ICTs into their study programmes has been limited. In addition, the role of universities as the main actors in laying the national foundation for scientific and technological skills within the Arab economy and society at large has also been severely hindered.

Moreover, in order to accommodate the increasing number of students without having to invest in new campuses, several Arab states have extended the administrative structures of their universities, which have been facing serious management difficulties. This has opened the way for a highly centralized system and bureaucracy to dominate the decision-making process. It has further suppressed innovation and creation. This development has also diverted attention from upgrading the main functions of the university, that is, teaching, research and community service. Instead, time is spent solving the many administrative problems resulting from the complex structures.

Another factor that contributes to the modest quality of HE in Arab countries is that most university and HEI curricula are outdated and relatively dependent on theoretical materials that have little relevance to the social and economic realities of Arab communities. Curricula are also far from interdisciplinary. Moreover, the issues that are considered most valuable to humanity are excluded from them. Such issues include the environment, human rights, citizenship, democracy, social participation, equity and cultural diversity. The result is a widening gap between HEIs in the Arab world and their counterparts elsewhere.

In the globalization era, there is a vital need for new modes of learning that prepare students to be responsible citizens in their societies. However, the mode of HE delivery in most Arab universities remains traditional. It depends heavily on rote learning, a fanatical exam culture and a lack of extracurricular activities. A teacher-centred culture has further impeded students' capacity to debate crucial issues, to think critically and to work collaboratively with peers.

Challenges concerning the quality of HE in the Arab world are therefore multifaceted. They create concern and heated debates within various Arab countries.

CHALLENGES RELATED TO INVASION AND OCCUPATION

Occupation and aggression, particularly in Iraq and the Palestinian Territories, have had seriously detrimental impacts on HE. In Iraq, it is maintained that:

> The war has inflicted heavy casualties and losses on a weakened Iraqi civilian population. The occupying authorities hastened to control universities and other state institutions, implementing a wide-scale 'de-Baathification' policy. Thousands of professors and all university deans and presidents were dismissed from their positions by occupation authorities. (Mazawi, 2004)

In the West Bank and the Gaza Strip, evidence indicates that Israeli military aggression has caused heavy human and material losses, thus hindering teaching and research activities (Nakhaleh, 2005). As indicated above, in 1999, Palestine approached the level of universal primary education (NER = 97%). However, this magnificent achievement had been eroded by 2005, with a sharp decline to an NER of 80%. Moreover, the educational authorities in Israel severely discriminate against Palestinian people. According to Human Rights Watch (www.hrw.org), 'Palestinian Arabs seeking admission to university are rejected at a far higher rate than are Jewish applicants'.

Continuous aggression and occupation are therefore likely to result in huge losses, creating further challenges for the countries involved and for their HE systems.

RESEARCH AND KNOWLEDGE CREATION

Research and knowledge creation can be considered the most important indicator of university performance and can be used to rank universities at the global level. It is also a key element in linking HEIs with the development needs of an entire society. In addition, research is undertaken in HEIs not only for its own sake, but also for educational benefits: it helps develop and renew the learning process, as research findings are included in curricula. It also opens opportunities for students to participate in research and trains them to work collaboratively in research teams (UNESCO, 1995). The volume of research produced in the Arab states is modest. This is clearly evident when considered within an international context (Zaytoun, 2006). R&D expenditure is another indicator of the low priority that the Arab states give to research activities. Most Arab countries allocate insignificant financial resources to research (ESCWA, 2006). In fact, it has been estimated that the rate of expenditure on R&D in Arab states is the lowest of all world regions, with the exception of sub-Saharan Africa.

The source of funding for research is a third indicator of the priority given to such activities. In the Arab region, the government is the main and sometimes sole source of R&D funding. Private sector participation is almost negligible. Therefore, the involvement of the productive sector in joint research with HEIs is quite insignificant. Thus, a vicious circle emerges in which investors in the productive sector have no confidence in HEIs and in their capability to provide the sector with scientific consultancy, research output, and solutions to their production problems. University academics believe that the private sector depends heavily on the outside world for technology and knowledge transfer, and hence it has no intention of collaborating with Arab state universities in the field of research, even if the universities are capable of undertaking this task.

Except for some foreign-funded research projects, the main motivation for carrying out research in the region is either to attain promotion to a higher academic post or to obtain a higher academic degree that is a prerequisite to becoming a member of teaching staff.

The marginalization of research activities in Arab universities poses very serious challenges. It tends to confine academics to a narrow, undeveloped teaching context, reduces their ability to keep up with new international developments in their scientific fields, and decreases their capacity to produce new knowledge and to solve the nation's most pressing problems.

STAFF MOBILITY AND BRAIN DRAIN

In many Arab universities outside the gulf countries, teaching staff suffer from poor working and living conditions. This lowers the prestige of university employment and encourages new generations to seek work in sectors of the economy that are better paid and have more attractive working conditions (for example working for TNCs). Many teaching staff move within the Arab region from low-income countries to Gulf universities. To a certain extent, this has helped alleviate the low quality of life of many Arab lecturers.

However, the critical issue is that both push and pull factors induce highly qualified Arab scientists and engineers to migrate to Western countries. Recently, there has been a significant rise in the proportion of highly educated people among those who have emigrated from the Arab region. More than one million Arab emigrants to countries of the Organization for Economic Co-operation and Development (OECD) hold university degrees. An estimated 5,000 Arab doctors emigrate annually to Europe. The number of Arab emigrants holding university degrees is 70,000 out of 300,000 annual graduates from Arab colleges (Arab League, 2006b). The seriousness of the brain drain problem confronting the Arab world is also revealed by the estimate that out of 20,000 Arabs obtaining Ph.Ds abroad annually, 85% remain abroad (Zahlan, 2007).

HE AND IMBALANCES IN THE WORLD OF WORK

Access to employment is a key factor in enhancing human and social development. Unemployment can have disastrous repercussions, especially when it is widespread among the educated and the vulnerable. The real danger of unemployment in such cases is not just economic considerations but also the waste of human resources, which hinders social integration, aggravates poverty and increases social tensions and political instability. Furthermore, being unemployed for long periods of time is considered by several social scientists to be responsible, at least in part, for crime and extremism.

In many Arab countries, the unemployment rate exceeds 10%. The average for the entire region is estimated to be 14%, while a much higher rate (20%) is predicted by unofficial sources (Wadiee, 2005). The Arab region has the highest unemployment rate among all world regions (ILO, 2004–05).

Three other aspects of unemployment in the Arab region accentuate the seriousness of this problem:

- Unemployment is concentrated among the young population. The rate of unemployment for young people is more than three times that of adult unemployment (ILO, 2006)
- The unemployment rate is much higher among educated people than among non-educated people
- Unemployment is higher among the female workforce (17%) than the male workforce (10%) (ILO, 2007).

It is usually claimed that unemployment is the result of the HE sector's tendency to produce numbers of graduates that far exceed the requirements of the Arab world of work. The sector is also accused of not producing graduates with the skills needed by the economy, particularly due to the imbalance between the social and natural sciences. For these two reasons, unemployment in the Arab region has been labelled 'educated unemployment'.

The exceptionally high rate of female unemployment can partially be explained by the status of women in HE. Women are over-represented in the humanities and social sciences, which have limited and low-productivity work opportunities.

Another serious social consequence of the persisting level of unemployment, particularly among young males in some low-income Arab countries, is their attempt to escape poverty and despair via illegal migration channels. This often turns out to be a cause of death or humiliation.

NEW PROVIDERS CREATING NEW CHALLENGES

The increasing trend towards the privatization of HE is expected to have grave consequences on crucial human and social factors such as access, equal opportunities, equality in the world of work, and upward mobility.

While Arab governments have enthusiastically encouraged private HEIs to share responsibility for access and for relieving pressure on public institutions, the continuous expansion of private institutions is likely to threaten overall access. In fact, most of these institutions have been established as private companies and licensed accordingly. They therefore have complete freedom to determine their tuition fees. Despite a lack of information, evidence from Egypt, Lebanon, Morocco, Oman and even Kuwait and the United Arab Emirates (Zaytoun, 2005) indicates that fees are too high given the average per capita income in Arab societies. The very high tuition fees exclude the majority of the student population from admission, on the grounds of the ability-to-pay principle.

Another important reason for encouraging private universities is that they are likely to introduce new, modern disciplines and syllabuses that do not exist in public universities. However, to date, private universities have generally offered the same subjects – namely those that have the highest prestige in the Arab market. Such subjects include pharmacy, medicine, engineering, information technology and business studies. The same disciplines exist in public universities and in other private institutions. Therefore, although responding to the requirements of the world of work may be considered an advantage, it can turn out to be a disadvantage when there is an over-response and a glut of graduates from particular disciplines that the market cannot absorb. Furthermore, many private HEIs depend heavily on human resources from public universities. This makes deteriorating conditions in the public universities even more likely.

Other more serious challenges to social equality and Arab culture include the following:

- First, privatization and cost recovery schemes are likely to affect Arab women's access to HE to a greater extent than that of men. Traditional Arab culture usually discriminates against girls when it comes to paying fees, particularly at the HE level. In Egypt, for instance, while the proportion of female students in public universities is 48%, the corresponding rate for private universities is 35% (CAPMAS, 2004–05).
- Second, a new and more serious segmentation in the Arab world of work arises between graduates with the same level of education and academic specialization who have graduated from different types of institutions. Thus, jobs that are well paid and have good working conditions (see earlier sub-section entitled Globalization and the world of work) are largely the preserve of graduates from private universities, especially foreign subsidiaries.
- Third, the spread of English as a medium of instruction in the Arab HE system has increased recently, particularly with the expansion of private and cross-border institutions. Arab people in the context of globalization need to learn English as a global language. However, the situation becomes serious and threatens Arab identity and culture when English advances at the expense of the Arabic language, and when Arabic is relegated to secondary status (Zughoul, 2003), to the extent that good-quality and

poor-quality education have become synonymous with English-language and Arabic-language institutions or programmes, respectively.

VISION AND POLICY MEASURES

The main issue to be addressed in this concluding section relates to the vision and policy measures needed to sustain and empower the Arab HE system in order to meet the human and social development requirements of the region. Some reform measures and legislation are expected to be introduced in various Arab countries, particularly in the field of accreditation and quality assurance, which currently occupy the attention of many Arab policymakers (Babiker, 2007). However, the limited scope of these measures, and sometimes the lack of proper mechanisms for their implementation, may render them somewhat ineffective. As a result, the core problems and challenges facing the Arab HE systems may remain unsolved or even become more complex. The following components of the proposed vision do not represent a comprehensive list. Nevertheless, they deal with some of the important realities, problems and challenges facing the Arab HE systems, as examined above.

ENHANCING THE HE ROLE IN OTHER EDUCATIONAL LEVELS AND IN ATTAINING THE MDGs

Primary and secondary education are the foundations that can help to improve HE. Even pre-primary education is an essential first step to alleviating the dropout rates in primary education. Furthermore, the region's performance in achieving the MDGs on primary education is rather moderate. It is unlikely that universality of primary education will be attained by 2015, at least in several countries in the region. In this respect, the interaction between HE and other levels of education is likely to trigger a virtuous circle of capacity building that benefits all levels of education (World Bank, 2002). It is also believed that although HE is not explicitly mentioned as a device for achieving any of the eight MDGs, the attainment of each of them will be greatly facilitated if a country has a strong HE system that produces committed citizens who are aware of the social and economic problems of their societies and are willing to participate in solving them (Bloom, 2002).

Therefore, HE should be reformed in order to become a key sector that participates in achieving the MDGs. HE should be responsible for promoting interaction between the different levels of education via research directed at enhancing the level of education at all stages. It should train highly qualified and socially committed teachers;

participate in improving curricular design; undertake periodic assessments of educational process and programmes; and carry out teacher training and retraining.

PROMOTING RESEARCH ACTIVITIES IN UNIVERSITIES

Given the modest conditions of scientific research in most Arab universities (see section HE policies and challenges in the context of globalization), improving and stimulating research activity could work as an important catalyst for promoting the quality of the whole HE system. It could also break the vicious circle of mistrust between university academics and the productive sector, which obstructs collaboration. Above all, such improvements could strengthen the relationship between the university and social development.

A research strategy has to be planned that mirrors the development needs of the Arab population and is compatible with the structure of human and material resources in the entire region. To properly design and successfully implement such a strategy, the following key aspects should be taken into consideration.

First, political will to initiate the required changes is a necessary prerequisite. This implies the need to overcome what is considered the 'defeatist attitude' of some policymakers, who believe that research is a luxury that only advanced countries can afford. However, research is not a luxury when, by addressing local problems, it becomes beneficial to Arab society as a whole and perhaps to humanity as well (for instance, the salt powder developed in Bangladesh has saved the lives of many children suffering from diarrhoea in LDCs). This is vital, given the fact that international technologies are often created in response to market pressures rather than to the needs of poor people in LDCs (UNDP, 2001).

Second, the Arab societies share a wide range of key scientific and technological problems. Research into these issues could have a direct impact on the state of human and social development in the region. Some important research areas include water desalination and management; energy; common health problems in the region; improving the yield of agricultural products and their nutritional values; reducing the need to use pesticides that damage soil and harm farmers' and consumers' health; and vaccines for HIV and bird flu.

Third, no successful strategy will ever materialize unless there is parallel economic and industrial progress that increases the international scope of the production sector and creates effective demand for R&D (Zaytoun, 2006).

Fourth, research serving human and social development should be oriented by the following factors:
- Research should be directed towards finding new and

more affordable technology and adapting transferred technology to local conditions. This could save Arab countries some of the huge financial resources usually spent on importing products and technology (Zahlan, 2007).

- Indigenous and traditional knowledge should be considered a socially beneficial area for research activity that can solve local problems by local means. Identifying such knowledge, examining its worthiness and developing its potential can be an effective way to increase the prosperity of the rural and urban populations.

- Research should be undertaken that reinforces the formulation of sound public policies, investigates ways to facilitate their implementation and makes objective and neutral evaluations of the human and social impacts of these policies.

Several factors affect the problem of funding research in Arab universities. In addition to its positive impact on education and the economy, the social benefits derived from research should induce Arab governments to give it more priority in the allocation of public funds. Research efforts are fragmented in individual Arab countries. Establishing a regional research network would promote cooperation and resource sharing and reduce duplication of research, hence ensuring better use of scarce financial resources (ESCWA, 2005). Lastly, the Arab private sector needs to increase its support for research. However, this will not occur unless the dynamism of private industry increases, thus enhancing its knowledge component and reinforcing its relationship with the university sector.

The establishment of the Arab Science and Technology Foundation is an example of a good practice that provides hope for scientific research and research funding in the Arab states. More information about this foundation is given in Box II.3.1.

CURRICULA AND PEDAGOGICAL IMPROVEMENT

Many HEIs in Arab countries occasionally review their curricula. However, from a societal and developmental perspective, these reviews are usually inadequate. Curricula must be periodically and thoroughly reviewed on a comprehensive and integrated basis. The mission of the reform process should be to incorporate the most recent developments and breakthroughs in different fields, and to make the contents more compatible with the human and social development issues that are most important to Arab societies. Curricula should generally satisfy the Arab people's expectations For instance, they should respond to public opinions that express strong support for democracy and reject authoritative rule (UNDP, 2004b). They should transmit the values that are indispensable for democratic practice and necessary for learning and knowledge, such as tolerance, equity, critical thinking, civil participation and reasoned argument.

The reform process should also take into consideration two key aspects that are relevant to HE in the Arab region and to the global context:

- issues and values appraised by humanity as a whole, such as those related to the environment, poverty, gender equality and human rights
- competences that the knowledge economy worldwide greatly values, including creativity, broadmindedness, oral and written communication, problem solving and the ability to adjust to change.

The above factors may lead to some separate disciplines being combined (for example natural and social sciences) or to new disciplines being adopted. The traditional divide between different disciplines and departments may have to be relaxed. The skew of the Arab HE structure away from scientific and technological specializations can also be adjusted within this framework.

Another essential and complementary reform relates to the long-standing Arab learning system described in above section on HE policies and challenges in the context of globalization. This system should give way to a new pedagogical model. Such a model was investigated by a pioneering study in the early 1990s. The study proposed a new approach based on the active engagement of the students rather than passive reception of information; learning as a collaborative activity rather than an individ-

Box II.3.1 The Arab Science and Technology Foundation (ASTF)

The ASTF is an independent, non-governmental, non-profit regional and international organization. It was established by scientists and researchers from both inside and outside the Arab world, as well as representatives of Arab and international science centres and organizations. It is based in Sharjah, the United Arab Emirates, and is seeking to set up branches and links in Arab and world capitals that have scientific entities willing to participate in its activities.

Since its establishment, the ASTF has worked to support, promote and facilitate scientific R&D in the Arab world.

The ASTF promotes the dissemination of know-how by coordinating the efforts of collaborative research centres throughout the Arab world. The main aim is to obtain international-standard research results at a cheaper cost, by creating simple solutions to common Arab problems. Collaborative research projects include water desalination by solar energy, and water desalination and purification in the Arab world.

Source: www.astf.net.

ual act; and the representation of concepts and knowledge in multiple ways, not just with text. The study also emphasized the need to incorporate ICTs into educational programmes in order to enrich the teaching and learning experience (World Bank, 2002).

Given this new vision, Arab educators and policymakers need to examine in depth the benefits (and costs) that can be derived from the application of what is known as general education (GE). GE is the educational approach that stresses the development of the whole individual, not just occupational training. It also stresses breadth of knowledge across a number of disciplines and seeks to develop important student abilities and competences such as those defined above. GE is enthusiastically supported for its clear and practical impact on society. It is thought to promote responsible citizenship, foster tolerance, encourage civil society and help countries to develop an intellectual identity by defining curricular content that can satisfy national- and regional-specific needs (UNESCO/World Bank, 2000).

AUTONOMY, ACADEMIC FREEDOM AND SOCIAL RESPONSIBILITY

Radical changes such as those described above cannot be successfully implemented without Arab HEIs experiencing autonomy and academic freedom. These institutions must be autonomous and democratically self-governed by the academic community itself. Teaching staff should be guaranteed basic academic freedoms such as freedom of inquiry, research, teaching, expression and publication. These freedoms empower universities to advance knowledge, to transmit it effectively to their students and the public at large, and to be a catalyst for new and constructive ideas.

Academic freedom and the university's social responsibility cannot be significantly enhanced without ensuring the right of teaching staff, students and the general public to communicate and to access information. Given the weakness of internet connectivity in the region, promoting access would be a powerful instrument that would help to achieve the objectives of academic freedom and social responsibility.

In a globalized environment, private for-profit and cross-border institutions, which have flourished recently in many Arab countries, consider that generating a surplus is a key target of their activity. This tends in different ways to undermine academic freedom. Therefore, autonomy and academic freedom include not only freedom from political interference, but also freedom from private stakeholders' or patrons' influences. The academic community in the context of globalization should also be empowered to resist the foreign pressures and interests that seek to impose a market-oriented agenda on HEIs.

In the Arab world, the fragmentation of the academic community and the absence of a unified vision and agenda may be one of the most serious weaknesses obstructing academic freedom and autonomy and limiting the social responsibility of HEIs. An important step towards eliminating such weakness has already been taken in Egypt. The emergence and success of the 'March 9' academic group, described briefly in Box II.3.2 by one of its prominent members, represents a good practice that should be followed in other Arab countries.

ALLEVIATING YOUTH UNEMPLOYMENT

In many Arab states, young people, and particularly the educated, are losing the sense of belonging to their societies. Some major reasons behind this despair include the excessive differentiation among HEIs, the unusually high rate of unemployment, the many difficulties encountered in getting a decent job, the social and gender discrimination in the world of work, and the defeatism caused by military aggression and destruction in many parts of the region.

To relieve this situation, the output of the education system, and particularly that of the public universities and technical institutes in which most Arab youth are enrolled, should be made more relevant. Well-designed

Box II.3.2 The March 9 academic group

March 9 is a group of university teaching staff interested primarily in defending and working to achieve university independence against government interference and the influence of security. The date 9 March refers to a historic event at which the president of Cairo University resigned in protest against government interference in academic issues. The group was initially formed at Cairo University from a small group of staff members. Gradually the numbers increased, and numerous members from other universities joined.

The group stands firmly against any action that does not comply with the international rules and agreements of academic freedom. It tries to protect the rights of professors and students through articles in the press, protests, and negotiations with university management.

The group is not only interested in defending academic freedom, but also in the social aspect of university education. It stands firmly against the privatization of university education in Egypt.

Although none of the group members has any authority inside or outside the university other than being members of teaching staff, they have managed to put a lot of pressure on university management. Despite continuous government opposition to the group, so far, March 9 (now in its fourth year) has been very influential at most Egyptian universities. It has succeeded in making a difference and increasing awareness of the importance of academic freedom.

Source: Mohamed Aboughar, Professor, Cairo University.

S&T curricula need to be introduced. The scientific, technological and ICT capabilities of students have to be fully developed.

Whatever improvements can be introduced in the HE sector, the youth unemployment paradox will not find adequate solutions as long as economic development in the region remains disappointing. In spite of economic restructuring – carried out under SAP or otherwise – government employment still dominates in most Arab countries. As described in the first section, An overview of the present situation, the region has some modern private investment enclaves that create good jobs, but very few employment opportunities. In addition, the region has a wide range of small and medium-sized enterprises that have not been able to adapt to knowledge advances.

Given that small and medium-sized enterprises dominate the production sector in most Arab economies, HE should transmit knowledge and skills that are more suitable to these kinds of enterprises and can raise their productivity. Students also need to learn entrepreneurial skills and practices, which help them to become job creators, not just job seekers (UNESCO, 1995).

It should be clear, therefore, that solutions to unemployment cannot be found in the education sector alone. A more comprehensive and collaborative development strategy is urgently needed in many Arab countries. Such a strategy should make job creation the highest priority and take advantage of the opportunities offered by globalization.

ERADICATING SOCIAL INEQUALITY

Globalization and the market approach may enter a new and a more intense phase in the Arab world in the future, given the following prospects:

- The high rate of population growth predicted for the Arab region until 2015, combined with the high proportion of young people in the population, is likely to maintain excessive pressure on HE in the coming years, thereby creating an excuse for the application of stricter market measures
- Further withdrawal of the state from HE responsibilities is also expected, as is a growing conceptualization that HE is a private good rather than a social investment. Thus, HE delivery by private institutions will increase
- In order to facilitate the smooth corporatization of public universities, some governments may seek to introduce private university management practices
- The global market for HE is expected to grow in the future. Thus, HE will be more controlled by the GATS measures and be further targeted by advanced economies that have the ability to trade and export

their HE programmes. Thus, pressure to liberalize Arab HE systems is likely to be more influential.

Under these conditions, there is a risk that HE systems in the Arab world could gradually be transformed from mechanisms for social integration, upward mobility and the development of a solid and sizeable middle class into mechanisms for social stratification, greater inequality, and more discrimination against the poor.

Therefore, to promote human and social development in the Arab world, inequality in its various forms should be overcome and equal opportunities – whether in the HE sector or throughout society – should be fostered. The following proposals should be taken into account to achieve this:

- The Arab world must adopt and reinforce positive concepts of globalization such as the empowerment of women, human rights and democracy. Simultaneously, it should control negative aspects such as commercialization, the weakness of the nation-state, unfettered trade liberalization, monoculture and foreign language domination
- The creation of a more equitable Arab society should be a yardstick for measuring the quality of development. Economic growth may be a necessary condition for human and social development, but it is not enough on its own. Broadening access to HE, knowledge and information can be a powerful instrument for achieving a more equitable society
- HE should be a means for alleviating – rather than reinforcing – the structured segmentation of the Arab labour market. The following proposals should be implemented to achieve this objective:
  - Access to quality education should be available for all on the basis of merit. Access should not be dependent on socioeconomic group, rural/urban area, gender or the ability to pay
  - The policy of using foreign languages as the main media of instruction should be reconsidered. In most Arab countries, this policy works as a tool for transforming differentiation in the HE sector into discrimination in the labour market. It should also be taken into consideration that language 'symbolizes respect for the people who speak it, their culture and their full inclusion in society' (UNDP, 2004a)
- Private HEIs should not be developed at the expense of public universities and institutions. Currently, strengthening and expanding the public institutions may be the best guarantee of serving the public purpose, fostering equality of opportunity, improving the quality of education, supporting research and scien-

tific education and exerting a positive competitive influence on private and cross-border institutions

- HE strategy in the Arab world should not be based on financial motives but on educational, social and human development aims. This does not imply that funding is not a problem or a challenge facing HEIs, particularly in low-income Arab countries. Rather, it means that funding problems should not be resolved at the expense of quality and equal opportunities. Currently, several channels are open to Arab countries to promote public funding of HE, in addition to widening the tax base, raising tax rates and increasing the progressiveness of the tax system (Zaytoun, 2005).

We end this paper with a word about globalization. The above analysis clearly shows that globalization has to be considered one of the factors that have affected HE and Arab societies. It has increased the divide between the richest and the poorest countries and the growing inequality within most countries. Therefore, as Stiglitz (2006) maintains, 'unless we recognize and address the problems of globalization, it will be difficult to sustain'.

REFERENCES

ALECSO (Arab League Education, Culture and Science Organization) (2003) *A Proposed Arab Strategy for the Development of Higher Education*. 9th Conference for the Ministers Responsible for HE and Research in the Arab World, Damascus, 15–18 December (in Arabic).

Arab League (2006a) *Joint Arab Economic Report*. Cairo, Egypt.

Arab League (2006b) *Regional Report on Arab Workers' Emigration*. Series on Population and Development in the Arab Region, Cairo.

Arab Monetary Fund (1999) *Joint Arab Economic Report 1999*. Abu Dhabi: Arab Monetary Fund.

Arab Monetary Fund (2003) *Joint Arab Economic Report 2003*. Abu Dhabi: Arab Monetary Fund.

Arab Planning Institute (2006) *Arab Competitiveness Report*. Kuwait.

Babiker, A.G. (2007) Quality assurance and accreditation in the Arab region. In: *Higher Education in the World 2007. Accreditation for Quality Assurance: What is at Stake?* Basingstoke, UK: Palgrave Macmillan.

Bloom, David E. (2002) *Mastering Globalization: From Ideas to Action on Higher Education Reform*. Cambridge, MA: Harvard University.

CAPMAS (Central Agency for Public Mobilization and Statistics) (2004) *University Education in Egypt 2004/05*. Arab Republic of Egypt.

Charafeddine, F. (2006) Financing higher education in Arab countries: problems and challenges. In: *Higher Education in the World 2007. The Financing of Universities*. Basingstoke, UK: Palgrave Macmillan.

Clark, N. (2006) Education in Morocco, *World Education News & Reviews*, **19**(2), April.

Coffman, J. (2003) *Higher education in the Gulf: privatization and Americanization, International Higher Education.*

Boston, MA: Boston College Center for International Higher Education, autumn.

ESCWA (Economic and Social Commission for Western Asia) (2005) *Networking Research, Development and Innovation in Arab Countries*. Lebanon: United Nations.

ESCWA (Economic and Social Commission for Western Asia) (2006) *Survey of Economic and Social Development in the ESCWA Region 2005–2006*, E/ESCWA/ EAD/2006/2. United Nations.

Held, D., McGrew, A., Goldblatt, D. and Perraton, J. (2000) *Global Transformations*. Cambridge, UK: Polity Press.

ILO (International Labour Organization) (2004–05), *Employment, Productivity and Poverty Reduction*. World Employment Report.

ILO (International Labour Organization) (2006) *Global Employment Trends for Youth*. Geneva.

ILO (International Labour Organization) (2007) *Global Employment Trends for Women*. Brief.

Mazawi, A. (2004), Wars, geopolitics, and university governance in the Arab States, *International Higher Education*, summer.

Nakhleh, K. (2005) *Palestinian tertiary educational system: overview, challenges and possible responses*. Beirut: Institute Français du Proche-Orient, 17–18 March.

Sen, A. (1999) *Development as Freedom*. New York: Alfred Knopf.

Stiglitz, J. (2006) *Making Globalization Work*, Global Policy Forum, 8 September.

UIS (UNESCO Institute for Statistics) (2005) www.uis.unesco. org/ev.php?ID=2867_2018ID2=20_TOPIC.

UNDP (United Nations Development Programme) (2001) *Making New Technologies Work for Human Development*. Human Development Report. Oxford: Oxford University Press.

UNDP (United Nations Development Programme) (2002) *Arab Human Development Report* (AHDR).

UNDP (United Nations Development Programme) (2003) *Building a Knowledge Society*. Arab Human Development Report (AHDR).

UNDP (United Nations Development Programme) (2004a) *Cultural Liberty in Today's Diverse World*. Human Development Report.

UNDP (United Nations Development Programme) (2004b) *Towards Freedom in the Arab World*. Arab Human Development Report (AHDR), Arabic version.

UNDP (United Nations Development Programme) (2006) *Human Development Report*.

UNESCO (United Nations Educational, Scientific and Cultural Organization) (1995), Policy paper for change and development in higher education, Paris.

UNESCO (United Nations Educational, Scientific and Cultural Organization) (1998a), World Declaration on Higher Education for the Twenty-First Century: Vision and Action, 9 October, Paris.

UNESCO (United Nations Educational, Scientific and Cultural Organization) (1998b), Arab Regional Conference, *Beirut Declaration on Higher Education in the Arab States for the XXIst Century*, Beirut, Lebanon.

UNESCO (United Nations Educational, Scientific and Cultural Organization) (2003) Regional Bureau for Education in the Arab States, Higher Education in the Arab Region, 1998–2003, Paris.

UNESCO (United Nations Educational, Scientific and Cultural Organization) Institute for Statistics (2005), database.

UNESCO (United Nations Educational, Scientific and Cultural Organization)/World Bank (2000) *Higher Education in Developing Countries: Peril and Promise*. Task Force on Higher Education and Society, Washington, DC: World Bank.

Wadiee, M. (2005) *The role of education in employment and enhancing the level of living in Arab countries*, Arab Societal Workshop on MDGs Towards 2015, Arab League and the United Nations Development Programme (UNDP), Cairo, 28–29 June.

World Bank (2002), *Constructing Knowledge Societies: New Challenge for Tertiary Education*. Washington, DC: World Bank.

Zahlan, A. (2007) *Higher education, R&D, economic develop-*

ment, regional and global interface, UNESCO Forum on Higher Education, Research and Knowledge, Second Regional Research Seminar for the Arab States. Rabat, Morocco, 25–26 May.

Zaytoun, M. (2005), *Education in the Arab World Under Globalization and Market Culture*. Beirut, Lebanon: Centre for Arab Unity Studies.

Zaytoun, M. (2006), *Condition of Research and Development in Arab Countries*, UNESCO Forum Occasional Paper Series no. 13, Organization, Structure and Funding of Research. Alexandria, Egypt, 12–13 September

Zughoul, M. (2003), Globalization and EFL/ESL pedagogy in the Arab world, *Journal of Language and Learning*, **1**(2).

Abstract

Higher education in Asia and the Pacific is unique with regard to its origin, uneven development, and different cultural and political environments. The progress made following the 1998 UNESCO World Conference on Higher Education (WCHE) is quite impressive and dynamic, but not sufficient to meet the new challenges that have emerged and intensified in the region since then. These challenges include rapidly growing economies; the accelerating pace of economic globalization; the transition towards a knowledge society; and the mistrust, tension and potential for conflict caused by competition for markets, resources and influences between and within nations in the region, which has a severe impact on human and social development and on the role of higher education in literacy campaigns, poverty alleviation, environmental protection and sustainable development, and so on. Most higher education institutions, and those in developing nations in particular, are ill-prepared for these challenges. To set a course for human and social development, new strategies should be formulated and new actions should be taken at the institutional, national and regional levels.

SOME FEATURES OF HIGHER EDUCATION IN ASIA AND THE PACIFIC

Asia and the Pacific is the largest and most diverse region in the world. It is home to some of the oldest civilizations and fastest-growing economies, as well as the largest number of illiterates and poor people on earth. Today, it is the site of numerous tensions and conflicts. Let us review some basic features of its past before analysing the impact of globalization and its role in the region's human and social development.

MIXTURE OF ORIGINS FROM THE WEST: A HISTORY OF ADOPTION AND ADAPTATION WITH IMPACTS UP TO THE PRESENT DAY

In Asia and the Pacific, higher education in the modern sense is an imposition of the West over the past two centuries. Its origin is a mixture of almost all major Western university models. Its

history is, therefore, one of adoption in and adaptation to various national contexts.

POLARIZED TRANSITION FROM ELITE TO MASSIFIED HIGHER EDUCATION

Higher education in Asia and the Pacific has been the privilege of an elite for hundreds of years. The massification of higher education is a very recent phenomenon in the majority of countries in this region. The present expansion of higher education has been polarized, with several remaining at the elite stage and others, such as Japan and South Korea, facing a surplus of places at their higher education institutions (HEIs) that must be filled by a declining age cohort. This comes at a time when most developing nations are under increasing pressure to expand their higher education systems to accommodate growing demand.

UNIVERSITY AUTONOMY: STILL A LUXURY IN MANY COUNTRIES

University autonomy has been a weak point in the region's higher education from the very beginning. Colonial universities did not have all of the characteristics of the metropolitan model (Altbach and Umakoshi, 2004). The historical tradition of subservience and the lack of full autonomy and academic freedom created problems for the emergence of modern universities in post-independence Asia. The worst situation was found in the Asian countries that adopted the Soviet 'planned economy' model. There, universities formed part of the government and enjoyed little autonomy. This issue remains unresolved in many such countries even today.

UNESCO WCHE+10 IN THE REGION

QUANTITATIVE EXPANSION AND MASSIFICATION

Merit-based higher education for all is one of the major goals set in both the 1997 Declaration about Higher Education in Asia and the Pacific and the Declaration of the 1998 World Conference on Higher Education (WCHE). Since then, most member countries in the region have seen a rapid and impressive increase in student enrolment rates. In China, expansion of higher education has caused total student enrolment figures to increase from 6.4 million in 1998 to 19.4 million in 2004 (GUNI, 2006), thereby making China's higher education system the largest in the world. Meanwhile, in India enrolment figures increased from 4.9 million in 1995 to 11.3 million in 2003, in Kazakhstan from 494,152 in 1994 to 664,449 in 2004, and in Bangladesh from 434,309 in 1990 to 877,335 in 2004 (GUNI, 2006).

THE ROLE OF PRIVATE HIGHER EDUCATION

The role of private higher education in countries such as the Philippines, Japan, South Korea and Thailand has been crucial from the very beginning. However, many other countries in the region, including a number of countries transitioning from a centrally planned economy to a market economy, have taken important steps to create a private sector as a means of easing growing pressure for student access and making up for the government's inability to meet higher education funding demands. In the past 10 years, the number of private colleges and universities in Malaysia has increased from around 100 to 690. From 1998 to 2001, Bangladesh, Mongolia, Nepal and China saw the creation of 100, 46, 20 and 1000 new private HEIs, respectively (UNESCO, 2005).

The development of private higher education sectors has presented governments with major policy dilemmas. The most challenging of these is how to deal with higher education as a public good for social equality while relying on the private sector for growth, and at the same time taking increasing responsibility in providing legislative and policy frameworks, attracting private investment, and protecting consumers' interests through effective quality assurance, monitoring and accreditation arrangements, and so on.

DIVERSIFICATION OF FUNDING AND CORPORATIZATION

The dilemma of increasing pressure for expansion combined with dwindling financing has forced many governments to reform funding systems and readjust their relationships with universities as a way out. Funding diversification is a key area of this reform.

Due to the legacy of the Soviet model, almost all Chinese universities, especially those with engineering and technical programmes, are affiliated with experimental factories. This has led to the emergence of a number of businesses that were originally owned and run by universities, but which have eventually been corporatized. Some of these companies have produced success stories. For example, the Founder Group, created by Peking University, has become an international giant with an annual income of CNY30 billion in 2005 and more than 20,000 employees. The company has around a 90% domestic market share and a 95% global market share in Chinese laser printing (Founder, 2006). Key national universities earn 50% or more of their total budget through a wide range of other measures, such as increasing tuition fees, bidding for research grants, offering a variety of training programmes, providing consultancy services, and so on.

In Malaysia, the University and University College Act was amended in 1995 to create a framework for the corporatization of public universities. Corporatized universities are empowered to engage in market-related activities such as entering into business ventures, building endowments and setting up companies. Each university was expected to generate 20% of its own budget. This target turned out to be difficult to achieve, due to student resistance to increased tuition fees, among other factors. Therefore, the public universities were 'corporatized by governance only, and not financially' (Lee, M.N, 2004). However, Malaysia's idea and practice of corporatization has had a clear impact on Thailand and Indonesia, both of which have adopted similar changes in their university-related laws to push their HEIs in the same direction, but with varied outcomes due to different national contexts.

Australia has moved down the same path towards decreased government support as a percentage of total revenue for public higher education. Australian universities now generate almost 50% of their total operating revenue through tuition fees charged to domestic and international students; external research grants; student contributions through the Higher Education Contribution Scheme (HECS); commercial activities; revenue from investment; and endowments and donations.

GOAL OF AND EFFORTS TOWARDS BECOMING 'WORLD CLASS'

In China, efforts towards developing 'world-class' HEIs started with two national projects that received special funding from both the central and local governments. One is the 211 Project, created in 1995, which aims to build 100 HEIs or national academic centres of excellence. The other is Project 985, thus named because it was launched in May 1998 (month 5). This project selected nine top research universities to be built into world-class institutions and received substantial government funding (Chinese Ministry of Education website). In 1996, the Prime Minister of Singapore announced the government's intention to turn Singapore into the 'Boston of the East', with Harvard University and the Massachusetts Institute of Technology serving as role models for transforming the National University of Singapore and Nanyang Technological University into world-class institutions (Tan, 1999). In 2001, the Japanese Ministry of Education proposed a structural higher education plan that recommended designating thirty leading research universities as Japanese centres of excellence under international standards. The plan was revised as the 21st Century Centres of Excellence Plan, which calls for assistance and financing for about two hundred centres of excellence in ten research fields at national and private universities (Kaneko, 2004). South Korea has adopted a policy called Brain Korea 21, which aims to raise the quality of Korean higher education in the 21st century to world-class standards, particularly in selected schools and fields of the natural sciences (Lee, G.E.J., 2000).

These efforts have sparked debate on the feasibility of the projects, the selection process, and the way in which target institutions are funded. However, these initiatives have also shown that Asian leaders are increasingly aware of the strategic importance of universities in the creation and utilization of knowledge and technologies today and in the future. These efforts also illustrate Asian countries' ambitions to catch up with the most developed nations.

MOBILITY, CROSS-BORDER PROVISION AND MUTUAL RECOGNITION

China and India send more higher education students to study abroad than any other country in the world. Some countries in the region, such as Australia, are also emerging as competitive exporters of higher education. In 2005, the 239,495 overseas students enrolled in Australian universities accounted for around 25% of total enrolment (AEI, 2007). While the number of foreign providers of higher education has been increasing in the Central Asian Republics, ICT-driven distance learning, open learning and e-learning programmes are new forms of cross-border provision. The number of online courses offered from within the region is also growing. The Indira Gandhi National Open University (IGNOU) in India now offers English-language academic programmes in 30 countries in Asia, the Arab region and Africa (IGNOU website).

The UNESCO Regional Office plays a key role in the mutual recognition of academic and professional qualifications in the region, a role which rests on the Regional Convention on the Recognition of Studies, Diplomas and Degrees in Higher Education in Asia and the Pacific, adopted in 1983 in Bangkok. With the ratification of India, Laos and the Philippines after the 1998 WCHE, twenty states are now parties to the Convention. Impressive progress has been made through the convention mechanism. Examples include the establishment of the Asia-Pacific Academic Recognition Network for the exchange of information, the UNESCO-APQN *Toolkit*

on Regulating the Quality of Cross-Border Education, and the updated version of the *Handbook on Diplomas, Degrees and other Certificates in Higher Education in Asia and the Pacific*.

POLITICAL, SOCIAL, HUMAN, ECONOMIC, ENVIRONMENTAL AND TECHNOLOGICAL CHALLENGES OF GLOBALIZATION IN THE REGION

When John Naisbitt predicted the coming of the 'Asia Age', China's foreign exchange reserves totalled US$76 billion and India's yearly earnings from software exports was just US$325 million (Naisbitt, 1995). By 2004, just one decade later, these two figures had reached US$1,200 billion (number one in the world) and US$17.4 billion, respectively (Mittal, 2005). These figures convincingly reflect the features of the 'Asian growth model': relying on foreign investment by offering cheap land, low-cost labour, tax relief and simplified procedures for approval, thereby benefiting from brain gain rather than brain drain and developing fast-growing, export-oriented countries. However, this growth has been achieved in the international environment of economic globalization, and has not been without heavy long-term costs. In fact, the implications and impacts, both positive and negative, on human and social development and on the role of higher education in particular, have been tremendous.

THE CRISIS OF VALUES

Many of the region's policymakers – in particular, those in charge of culture, education, media, sports and religion – are more concerned about these aspects than about the trade surplus or deficit. The debate on values, including warnings against losing national or indigenous cultural identities or Asian values, began as soon as governments started adopting liberal policies to face economic globalization. However, this debate always sparks controversy between the East and the West, and between different countries in the region itself, regarding core issues such as how to define Asian values, Western values or a specific national identity; modernization vs. Westernization; positive and negative sides of both values; and so on. The debate in transitioning economies (that is, in socialist or formerly socialist countries) seems more acute. This may be due to the fact that some ideological vacuums need to be filled in the post-Soviet era, or to the enormous gap between completely different values when a socialist country opens its doors to economic globalization, a process dominated by Western powers and values. This crisis of values in economic globalization poses a challenge and a dilemma for all education authorities –

at both schools and universities – regarding what values should be taught and nurtured, and how to make values and moral education serve two complementary purposes: the modernization of the country and the preservation of the national identity and cultural tradition.

SOCIAL INEQUALITY IN TANDEM WITH HIGH GROWTH

Despite significant progress in economic growth and poverty reduction, the region still shows considerable disparity and inequality, with approximately 679 million people living in poverty (one dollar a day). Between 1992 and 2002, unemployment figures rose from 4 million to 9 million in East Asia and from 5.5 million to 14.6 million in Southeast Asia and the Pacific. In South Asia, total unemployment increased by 7 million during the same period. Within countries, there is ample evidence of high growth rates accompanied by growing inequality. For example, inequality is increasing in the large and rapidly growing economies of China and India, in middle-income developing economies such as South Korea, Thailand and Georgia, and in the Philippines, Nepal and Sri Lanka. Social inequality, especially in access to healthcare and education, still exists in many countries. At the current rate of progress, achieving the Millennium Development Goal of 'Education for All' and eliminating gender disparity in education by 2015 will be a great challenge (UNESCAP, 2006).

THE COST OF GROWTH TO THE HUMAN ENVIRONMENT

The UNEP assessment report *Climate Change 2007: Climate Change Impacts, Adaptation and Vulnerability* paints a very gloomy picture of Asia regarding the consequences of changing ecosystems. According to this report, the resilience of many ecosystems is likely to be exceeded this century by an unprecedented combination of climate change and associated disturbances. The report predicts that glacier melt in the Himalayas will increase flooding and rock avalanches from destabilized slopes and affect water resources within the next two to three decades. It also projects that fresh water availability in Central, East, Southeast and South Asia, particularly in large river basins, will decrease due to climate change. Combined with population growth and increasing demand arising from higher living standards, the report predicts that these changes could adversely affect more than one billion people by the 2050s (UNEP, 2007).

GLOBALIZATION IN HARMONY?

Despite great economic success and huge potential, the Asia-Pacific region still faces a fluid and volatile security situation and lacks a sense of community. Deep-rooted differences over history, border demarcation, political and economic systems and ethnic, religious, and cultural traditions have prevented countries in the region from seeking a shared destiny. Increasing competition for resources, energy, markets, and control of and influence over strategic areas make many of the region's bilateral relationships sensitive and tense. Asia and the Pacific is the region of the world with the greatest number of hot spots – that is, areas with the potential for conflicts, terrorist attacks and even war.

LESSONS GAINED FROM EXPERIENCE

One lesson from the experience of many of the region's countries is that economic growth alone does not necessarily enhance human and social development or lead to social harmony. Reasons for this include the thirst for GDP growth without a human-centred objective; the dominance of new liberalism as the guiding philosophy of economic reform; too much money spent on infrastructure; political motives in recourse allocation; lack of proper social policies to prevent the widening of gaps between social groups; failure to fight corruption, and so on. With specific reference to higher education, one reason is the fact that the critical voices of universities seem too weak to make a difference to national political processes.

IMPLICATIONS FOR HIGHER EDUCATION REGARDING ITS CONTRIBUTION TO HUMAN AND SOCIAL DEVELOPMENT

CHALLENGES TO THE IDEA OF HIGHER EDUCATION AS A PUBLIC GOOD

The idea of higher education as a public good has faced serious challenges in the Asia-Pacific region in the context of globalization. First, the idea is at odds with the internationally dominant ideology of neo-liberalism, in which privatization, marketization, commodification and corporatization are increasingly seen as policy tools for transforming public management and social delivery. In order to offload the cost of public services such as education, states force citizens to buy these services at market value. The reduction of the government's share of higher education funding, the allocation of financial resources through competition, changes in personnel policies, and so on, have been adopted under the influence of this doctrine (Mok, 2007). As a developed nation and member of the OECD in this region, Australia surpassed its European counterparts in the early 1990s by adopting the Higher Education Contribution Scheme (HECS), under which Australian students pay tuition fees of around 20% of the full cost per student while overseas students pay full fees.

Second, in a region in which developing countries

are a majority, the idea of higher education as a public good is attractive and could be a long-term goal, although it is not an affordable policy choice at the present stage. Therefore, to relieve the growing pressure for the expansion of higher education opportunities, governments have adopted the strategies of relaxing control policies, encouraging the private sector to join the massification process, charging or increasing tuition fees, and corporatizing university governance and management in order to push universities to generate additional income. Internationally, the inclusion of higher education as a tradable good in the agenda of the World Trade Organization's General Agreement on Tariffs and Trade, 2000, although still very controversial, reinforces the aforementioned trend.

However, the lessons and consequences of such doctrines and practices – such as growing quality and social-equity issues, corrupt campus cultures and graduate unemployment – already seem significant enough to warrant reflection. Unfortunately, these issues do not seem to be problematic enough to draw the attention of policymakers. This may itself be a challenge for the region.

CURRICULUM, TEACHING AND QUALITY TESTING

Many countries in the region face both rapidly increasing enrolment rates and high rates of graduate unemployment. This dilemma provides strong evidence of the impact of economic globalization, the inability of HEIs to respond to this challenge and the sharp mismatch between employers' requirements and the quality of graduates. Outdated curricula and teaching content fail to provide graduates with the knowledge, competence and skills they need to meet the changing demands of the labour market. China's transitioning, export-oriented economy – the fastest-growing economy in both the region and the world – provides a good example of this point. Each year, around 5 million Chinese graduates seek jobs in the labour market. According to the Chinese Ministry of Education, around 30% of these graduates fail to find employment. This places increasing social and political pressure on the government, HEIs, graduates and their families. Meanwhile, surveys reveal that employers, including joint ventures and foreign firms, are unable to find graduates of satisfactory quality (Wang, 2006).

HIGHER EDUCATION'S INADEQUATE OPERATIONAL MECHANISM FOR RESPONDING TO CHALLENGES

The aforementioned mismatch and related problems with curricula, teaching and quality are superficial problems. The operational mechanisms of national higher education have been unable to respond to the challenges of rapidly globalizing economies – due to lack of capacity, motivation, dynamism and potential. This reveals a deeply rooted conflict between the changing environment and the demand for reform and innovation in several of the region's national higher education systems. First and foremost is the HEIs' lack of autonomy in many transitioning economies where the state has a strong legacy of rigid and direct control of universities and colleges. Autonomy is still quite limited in, for example, restructuring and renewing programmes and curricula, admitting students, and recruiting teachers (Wang, ibid.). In some non-transitioning economies, such as Malaysia, Thailand and Japan, increased university autonomy is a recent phenomenon and a by-product of corporatization campaigns.

In most of the region's national higher education operational mechanisms, there is a lack of interaction between HEIs and industry and commerce. Dialogue between industry, commerce and universities is rarely reported. University students often find it difficult to contact firms regarding internships, even if these are without pay. The mismatch between the quality of higher education graduates and rest of society will definitely continue if sound interaction remains absent in national higher education macro-operational mechanisms.

HIGHLY CORRUPT ACADEMIC AND CAMPUS CULTURES

In the changing and globalizing economic environment of the past decade, academic and campus cultures in the region have become highly corrupt. Academic corruption cases have been periodically reported and criticized in the media. This phenomenon is not limited to transitioning or booming economies such as the Central Asian Republics and China; it also affects advanced economies such as South Korea, where professors are quite well paid and ethical practices in the academic profession have become a major concern.

Academic corruption is quite common in the region, although it varies in form depending on the national context. In Kyrgyzstan, for example, forms of corruption include the selling – or providing through connections – of admission places, grades and academic degrees, as well as the theft of valuable resources, falsification of academic credentials, and awarding of contracts in return for kickbacks (Wolanin, 2002). In South Korea, academic corruption mainly takes place in the areas of contract research, teaching staff recruitment and consulting services, and may involve cheating on the part of universities and students, the falsification of research data, the hiring of teaching staff through bribes or social connections without a truly open competition, or teaching staff giving top priority to well-paid consulting jobs while neglecting their main responsibilities (Lee, S.H., 2001).

In a few cases in China, campus corruption has even involved presidents and vice-presidents receiving bribes in exchange for awarding contracts for campus construction or renovation projects. In other cases, public funds earmarked for particular purposes have been lost on the stock exchange.

It will not be easy to cure the social disease of academic corruption and restore society's respect for the academic community. Academia's role as a social critic and the role of higher education in human and social development will be diminished and damaged if corruption is not corrected through the collective effort of the academic community, the government and society as a whole.

VISIONS OF THE FUTURE ROLE OF HIGHER EDUCATION IN HUMAN AND SOCIAL DEVELOPMENT IN THE REGION

BUILDING A CULTURE OF PEACE AND ACTING AS A MAJOR PARTNER IN THE DIALOGUE AMONG CIVILIZATIONS

The sustainable development of all of the region's nations requires a peaceful environment, mutual understanding and trust, in particular among nations with disputes and among stakeholders in hot spots. Without this, the development process could be set back or halted at any time. Such an environment requires the wisdom of national leaders, the right and proper intervention of international agencies, the building of a culture of peace, and the nurturing of mutual understanding and respect for different civilizations, religions and traditions among the peoples of the various countries, and among young people in particular. In this regard, higher education will play an essential role as a builder of a culture of peace and a major partner in the dialogue among civilizations through the creation of new curricula, the exchange of viewpoints on textbook disputes between nations, the development of exchange programmes for students and professors, and the organization of and participation in dialogue between different civilizations.

TRAINING FUTURE LEADERS AND EDUCATORS FOR POLITICAL AWARENESS

The challenges imposed by rapid economic globalization and the transition towards a knowledge society require at least the following:

- That new programmes of higher education be developed to train future leaders and politicians at different levels. Such leaders should not only be knowledgeable and competent, but also open-minded; under-

standing and respectful of different civilizations, cultures and religions; and sensitive to changes in ecosystems and human sustainable development.

- That higher education maintain its educational role to raise the public's awareness of ongoing political, economic, social, cultural and environmental processes, as well as its critical role in disclosing and analysing unhealthy, unjust or harmful social phenomena in national political life.

These two roles are particularly important in the Asia-Pacific region, where most countries are young or transitioning democracies with a long legacy of colonial or feudal rule.

PROVIDING SOLUTIONS TO CHALLENGES RELATED TO HUMAN, SOCIAL AND ENVIRONMENTAL DEVELOPMENT AND COLLABORATING IN THEIR IMPLEMENTATION

The widening gap in economic growth is, in fact, a gap in productivity and trade, in producers' knowledge and technologies, in people's education, and in the quality, relevance and vitality of national education systems and higher education systems in particular. Higher education institutions should therefore be one of the region's major providers of solutions to poverty and to the many problems related to sustainable human, social and environmental development through their research, teaching, service and close links with the national development process and surrounding communities. These roles are definitely desirable, since most developing countries in the region started the development process with little intellectual and technological strength, a low degree of competitiveness and an uneducated labour force; moreover, the heavy cost of growth related to this development process is increasingly being felt today.

FUTURE STRATEGIES AND ACTIONS TO BE CONSIDERED: THE ROLE OF THE STATE

The recommendations made in this section are based on general global trends in higher education, which, sooner or later, will be followed by all. Similar innovative initiatives have already emerged at some of the region's universities and colleges. The recommended strategies and actions are regarded as essential minimums for nations that want to see their HEIs play the aforementioned visionary roles in facing the globalizing world and transitioning towards a knowledge society. Emphasis is placed on recommendations regarding how to build a legal environment that protects and ensures the strategic status of higher education, a dynamic mechanism that interacts proactively with societies, innovative and future-oriented models of universities and HEIs, healthy campus cultures, and so on. These recommendations will guide, encourage and pressure HEIs to be sensitive and responsive to changes and challenges related to human and social development at the regional, national and local levels, rather than just in immediate and direct projects, although these are absolutely necessary, as well. In fact, some such specific projects have already emerged and spread throughout various parts of the region as individual actions rather than as a rule, a common trend or a culture in HEIs.

THE NEED TO REDEFINE AND REPOSITION HIGHER EDUCATION

When higher education is required to play a central role in facing challenges related to economic globalization and the transition towards a knowledge society, the signals given by governments and international agencies are often confusing. These signals can even embarrass people at HEIs: they face increasing pressure in their crucial role in addressing challenges related to economic, technological, social and human development, yet at the same time, they face declining government funding and support, and the danger of becoming marginalized. The following are just a few reasons that higher education needs to be redefined and repositioned:

- Under the impact of neo-liberalism and economic globalization, some governments see the sharing of higher education costs between the government, the universities, the students and their families as a way out, that is, a way of reducing the 'burden' of funding higher education, and as a major strategy for the massification of higher education (Tilak, 2002).
- Today, 'Education for All' is a top priority on the agenda of all developing countries. In order to achieve this goal, many countries increase the budget of basic education by decreasing that of higher education. This strategy is often justified using the argument that basic education is compulsory, while higher education is not, and users should therefore have to pay for higher education.
- Some politicians and policymakers take a short-sighted view of higher education. When making policies, they see only the economic role of higher education and neglect its role for human, cultural and social development. Rather than seeing higher education as a public good or a human right, some Chinese politicians have seen the potential to boost consumerism as a major reason for increasing enrolment in higher education over the past seven years.
- Higher education's problems have been exacerbated in poorer parts of the Asia-Pacific region by the idea –

popular over the past several decades and stressed by some agencies – that investment in basic education is more cost-effective than investment in higher education. As a result, higher education has been ignored by major lending and donor agencies. In the past, this conclusion has also had a negative impact on national higher education policies in the region.

STRATEGIES AND ACTIONS FOR REDEFINING AND REPOSITIONING HIGHER EDUCATION

Due to the lack of autonomy and embarrassing situations facing higher education in a number of countries in the region, states should shift away from rigid bureaucratic control of HEIs and instead focus on the following:

- Passing new legislation or revising current laws to ensure institutional autonomy, incrementally increase funding, protect higher education's status as a public good, and prevent commercialization and social inequality in the higher education reform and innovation process.
- Establishing clear-cut strategies and priorities for the allocation of state funds. These include protection of social equity, equal treatment of students in awarding state grants and scholarships for both public and private HEIs, support for programmes that have less immediate market value but which are necessary for human and social development, and the establishment of centres of excellence in various fields of strategic importance in the transition towards a knowledge society and a globalized world.
- Adopting a national strategy for the restructuring of HEIs, including encouraging institutional models that are future-oriented, open, flexible, dual- or mixed-mode, lifelong, entrepreneurial and responsive to changing needs, including human and social issues.
- Shifting away from the role of quality assurance organizer and instead establishing an authoritative, fair and transparent national mechanism; using quality assurance as a strategic instrument for guiding HEIs in future-oriented reform and innovation with a focus on institutional capacity-building for innovation; assessing the quality of graduates in terms of necessary knowledge, competence and skills; assessing the plans, actions and effectiveness of institutions in addressing present and emerging challenges related to social and human development; establishing internal quality control systems, mechanisms and incentive policies; nurturing a campus culture that favours quality control for the aforementioned purposes and so on.

FUTURE STRATEGIES AND ACTIONS TO BE CONSIDERED: INITIATIVES FROM WITHIN HEIs

THE NEED FOR INITIATIVES FROM WITHIN HEIs

Globally, the explosive growth of new knowledge – and its organization in increasingly specific disciplines and ever-more complex and decreasingly hierarchical knowledge networks – is calling into question the viability of universities (UNESCO, 2005). In the Asia-Pacific region, this phenomenon includes the negative impact of the 'ivory tower' legacy, the lack of motivation to respond to a changing environment, and resistance to change. The old-fashioned control of higher education formulated under planned economies – which, in some transitioning economies, has seen no substantial renovation – means that many constraints on universities and colleges remain unchanged. Under these constraints, HEIs lack autonomy, dynamism, motivation and the potential to respond to the changing context (Wang, op. cit.). Any attempt at higher education reform will fail if no initiative is taken from within the HEIs themselves.

AREAS FOR ACTION
READJUSTING MISSION AND VISION AND NURTURING UNIQUENESS

Alan Wagner (2001) has noted that the problems faced by mass higher education are due to the fact that the system has become mass in its size but remains elite in its values. Both public and private institutions in the region should take into account emerging challenges related to human and social development in their countries or surrounding communities when readjusting their missions, visions and strategies, which, to varying degrees, have been influenced by the legacy of colonial rule or planned economic systems. In this new round of exercises, HEIs should also review their practices to identify their strengths, their unique characteristics and the challenges they face in the context of globalization and the transition towards a knowledge society, in order to adopt a new vision for their future. No university in the world can claim to be the best in all disciplines – just strong in some fields. When developing strategies, universities in developing countries in the Asia-Pacific region should keep in mind that catching up and becoming world class may not be realistic. However, it may be feasible to become strong and unique in certain disciplines, especially those for which location, context or historical and cultural traditions offer a competitive advantage.

REENGINEERING TO ADOPT THE LEARNING MODELS OF THE FUTURE

Many of the world's existing educational systems were designed to suit the requirements of the passing industrial revolution. Worse, some still fit the agrarian society. All higher education systems and institutions in the region face the challenge of adapting to a rapidly changing world marked by contrast and characterized by division, extremism and even irony, where, amid breathtaking advances in science and technology and economic miracles, there is massive poverty, socioeconomic inequality and political marginalization (Khan, 2006). Accordingly, the simple question to be answered by all policymakers and educators in the region is the following: Should higher education be for the few, for the majority or for all? How can we make education, including higher education, a practical tool for all, one with new learning models capable of reaching everyone – rich or poor, urban or rural, young or old – with information, knowledge, skills and training for various purposes? Making access to colleges and universities open to all qualified individuals who wish to learn, or learn further, is a fundamental protection of human development. This restructuring is extremely crucial for social mobility in the region that still has the largest number of people living in poverty and wishing to change their social status. Fortunately, we in the Asia-Pacific region do not need to start from scratch. Several learning models that have already been functioning for some time have great potential to expand and develop into the learning models of the future.

- *Single-mode open and distance model.* The Asia-Pacific region is home to around 70 open universities and numerous open and distance secondary vocational and technical schools, including some agricultural schools. Eleven of the world's 17 mega-universities are located in this region. Practices in Bangladesh, China, India, Indonesia, Iran, South Korea, Pakistan, Thailand, Vietnam, the Philippines and the South Pacific have provided convincing proof that this learning model is the best for reaching a variety of disadvantaged groups. Of all the existing educational forms, it is also the most practical and powerful, with short, flexible training courses for alleviating poverty, overcoming social inequalities and meeting lifelong learning needs in emerging knowledge societies. However, the bias of conventional universities and society as a whole remains a barrier to further development. Nevertheless, the vitality, dynamics, openness, flexibility and convenience of open and distance learning will make this the most acceptable, accessible and effective learning model of the future.
- *Dual- and mixed-mode universities.* Changing and growing educational demands have forced all conventional institutions, including universities, to become open and flexible in order to meet the needs

of numerous categories of learners of different age groups and social backgrounds. In this regard, Australia provides a very relevant model. With the amalgamation of universities and other types of HEIs in the late 1970s and 1980s, all Australia's distance learning centres – the result of the country's long tradition of education in a vast land with a small population – were merged into conventional universities. In other words, all conventional universities became dual-mode after the exercise. Students who register for distance learning get the same courses, teachers and diplomas as on-campus students. This restructuring was a critical step towards guaranteeing the quality of distance learning and helping off-campus students gain better recognition of their qualifications. It also served to create a national dual-mode higher education system, which has proved to be open and flexible enough to suit the learning demands of all people in the transition towards a knowledge society, and has enhanced national competitiveness in a globalizing world.

- *Entrepreneurial-mode universities.* Some universities in Europe, North America and Asia have successfully been converted into entrepreneurial universities. This transformation has left the universities in a better position, nurtured a proactive capacity and created a culture conducive to addressing challenges related to growing knowledge economies, clients, governments and globalization. Today's entrepreneurial universities represent a new philosophy, a new model, a new way of managing scholarship, a new campus culture, a new outlook on quality, a new image of the teaching staff, and a new generation of graduates. For HEIs, becoming entrepreneurial is not a choice – it is a future model that must be explored. This could mean a revolution at some universities in the region, where the 'ivory tower' tradition remains strong. Therefore, creating entrepreneurial programmes and organizing successful entrepreneurial activities is one thing; completely transforming a university in accordance with an entrepreneurial model could be something else entirely, depending on the chosen purpose.

CURRICULUM RENEWAL AND DEVELOPMENT

The extent to which HEIs develop and renew their curricula is a good measure of how well they serve the changing needs of human and social development at the national and local levels. If HEIs are to address all human and social challenges in their teaching and provision of services, then the structure, content and methodology of the present curricula must be adjusted, new requirements must be established, staff must be trained and research

capacity must be developed. With almost all developing countries in the region facing increasing graduate unemployment, there is an urgent need to renew curricula in order to improve students' general competence, social and communicative skills, entrepreneurship, and flexibility in order to prepare for changing and challenging labour markets. Graduates are expected to cope with uncertainty, be interested in and prepared for lifelong learning, have acquired social sensitivity and communicative skills, be able to work in teams, be willing to take on responsibilities, be entrepreneurial, be prepared for the internationalization of labour markets through an understanding of various cultures, be versatile in generic, interdisciplinary skills, and be literate in areas of knowledge that form the basis of various professional skills, such as new technologies (WCHE, 1998a).

Higher education institutions may not be able to accomplish this task on their own. They require strong support from the government; sound partnerships between the university, industry, commerce, and civil society, and between the disciplines within universities; and wise use of ICTs as a revolutionary tool. In response to concerns over deteriorating quality and rapid expansion of enrolment since 1999, and inspired by the open courseware developed by MIT, in 2003 the Chinese Ministry of Education launched the national Creation of Classic Courseware Project, which aimed to create 1500 classic courses by 2007. The general strategy is to ask professors and universities if they would be willing to offer courseware now in use and submit it to the Ministry of Education for peer review. If selected, the courseware is declared 'approved classic courseware'. Teaching notes, extra reading materials, and so on, are developed and the package is made available online, without copyright, for five years. It may be used freely, without the need to register or obtain a password, but may not be used for business or profit-making purposes. Each accepted course receives a grant of CNY100,000 from the Ministry of Education to subsidize the cost of developing and maintaining the website. The project proved to be a success and was thus extended to 2010. In 2007 alone, 650 new classic courses are expected to be created as part of this project.

Mutually beneficial international collaboration is a necessary part of upgrading and updating curricula. The modality, strategy and outcomes of the EU Asia-Link Programme provide an example of regional and international cooperation. This European Commission initiative promotes regional and multilateral networking between HEIs in Europe and developing countries in Asia. Since 2002, the programme has funded 155 partnerships that together involved over 700 HEIs from Asia and Europe.

Curriculum development is one major area of the partnership projects (www.ec.europa.eu/asia-link/).

In today's increasingly competitive and globalizing economies, capacity building in science, technology and innovation (STI) is no longer a luxury for the few but rather an absolute necessity for poor countries that wish to become richer or avoid falling further behind (World Bank, 2002). Research should not be the exclusive privilege of research universities. Rather, a certain research capacity is necessary for all HEIs today. Not all will become research universities, but all should be competent at providing timely solutions to human and social challenges, at the local level in particular. The key issue is what type of capacity HEIs should build, given their economic constraints, category and nature; the unique human and social problems facing particular localities; and how best to implement capacity-building action plans. Without a doubt, research capacity building in HEIs is the key to STI capacity building in any developing nation. This requires, first of all, political will and government initiative to create a social and cultural environment that nurtures scholarship, and to provide a reasonable percentage of the GNP to promote quality higher education and research capacity. This includes improving infrastructure and attracting talented scientists from home and abroad (WCHE, 1998b). Successful experiences show that HEIs will continue to receive public funding only if their research proves relevant and crucial to facing the country's pressing challenges and problems related to economic, political, environmental, technological, human and social development. Higher education institutions, therefore, should define the priorities of their research programmes carefully, paying particular attention to urgent regional issues such as development theories, modalities and practices in national or local contexts; poverty alleviation; and human and social challenges such as illiteracy, gender equality, child mortality, malnutrition, access to clean water, access to sanitation and the spread of HIV/AIDS. Research outcomes can assist the creation and renewal of curricula, provide solutions to challenges facing the country and local communities, and guide the development process.

INTERNATIONAL COOPERATION AND THE ROLE OF INTERNATIONAL ORGANIZATIONS

Effective international cooperation is essential to achieving the objectives of higher education in developing nations and – in low-income and least-developed countries, in particular – to making contributions to human and social development.

MAJOR INTERNATIONAL AND REGIONAL AGENCIES AND ORGANIZATIONS CONCERNED WITH HIGHER EDUCATION COOPERATION IN THE ASIA-PACIFIC REGION

- *UNESCO Asia and the Pacific Regional Bureau for Education, Bangkok*
  The strengths of this organization lie in its expertise as the only specialized UN agency for education and higher education; its direct links to and dialogue with governments and universities; its secretariat's role in the Regional Convention on the Recognition of Studies, Diplomas and Degrees in Higher Education in Asia and the Pacific; its 12 UNESCO Chairs and UNITWIN (university twinning) networks dedicated to higher education; its workshops and conferences aimed at providing new ideas, trends, practices, experiences and lessons; and its close working ties with other IGOs and NGOs in the region.
- *Asian Development Bank (ADB) and World Bank*
  These two banks are vital sources of financial and technical assistance to developing countries in the region. Their mission is to help their developing member countries in the region to reduce poverty and improve their citizens' quality of life, and to increase attention to the role of higher education in human and social development in developing countries.
- *Southeast Asian Ministers of Education Organization (SEAMEO)*
  This body was established on 30 November 1965 as a chartered international organization aimed at promoting cooperation in sustainable human resource development, science and culture through its 12 academic centres (including a higher education centre) in Southeast Asia.
- *Asian Association of Open Universities (AAOU) and Association of Universities of Asia and the Pacific (AUAP)*
  These two NGOs were established with the initiative and support of UNESCO, in collaboration with the ADB, the International Association of Universities (IAU) and the government of Thailand.

NEW STRATEGIES TO BE CONSIDERED

Experience shows that every organization will try to reinvent the wheel for its own creditability and brand. Effective coordination and partnership between organizations will be lacking, even though the objectives of many activities launched by different organizations in a given country or region are similar or overlapping. To make regional and international cooperation more effective for target countries or communities, each organization should be aware of its own strengths and weakness, as well as its target for assistance. If an organization is dedicated to capacity building, for example, it should choose an area of activity in which its catalytic role can be maximized and the receiving country has the greatest capacity-building needs. There should be continuity in activities. Success stories from similar geographical areas or contexts may be more effective than theoretical analysis in establishing policy preferences. Moreover, instead of competing with one another, organizations should recognize the simple fact that they are working towards the same targets in the same region. Cooperation between aid organizations increases effectiveness, while competition wastes limited resources. The adoption of many of the aforementioned strategies and principles will depend largely on whether the leaders of these organizations have vision, will, wisdom and courage.

REFERENCES

Altbach, P.G. and Umakoshi, T. (2004) *Asian Universities: Historical Perspectives and Contemporary Challenges*. Baltimore, MD: Johns Hopkins University Press.

Australia Education International (AEI), Australian Department of Education, Science and Training (2007) Country Report submitted to the 9th Session of the Regional Committee of the Regional Convention for Mutual Recognition, 22–23 May 2007, Seoul, South Korea.

GUNI (2006) *Higher Education in the World 2007. Accreditation for Quality Assurance: What Is at Stake?* Basingstoke: Palgrave Macmillan.

Kaneko, M. (2004) Japanese higher education: contemporary reform and the influence of tradition. In: *Asian Universities: Historical Perspectives and Contemporary Challenges*, pp. 115–44, Baltimore. MD: Johns Hopkins University Press.

Khan, A.W. (2006) Distance education for development. Paper presented at the ICDE SCOP Conference, Norway, 2006.

Lee, G.E.J. (2000) Brain Korea 21: A new national policy initiative. *International Higher Education*, Boston College Center for International Higher Education, (19), spring.

Lee, M.N. (2004) 'Restructuring higher education in Malaysia'. School of Educational Studies, University Sains Malaysia, Penang, Malaysia.

Lee, S.H. (2001) Ethics and the Korean academic profession. *International Higher Education*, Boston College Center for International Higher Education, (25), fall.

Mittal, S. (2005) National Association of Software and Service Companies (NASSCOM), http://it.sohu.com/20050228/n224457313.shtml.

Mok, K.H. (2007) When neo-liberalism colonizes higher education in Asia: bringing the 'public' back in the contemporary university. Paper submitted at an international conference held at Zhejiang University, 2–4 April 2007.

Naisbitt, J. (1995) *Megatrends Asia*, London: Nicholas Brealey Publishing Ltd.

Tan, J. (1999) Recent developments in higher education in Singapore. *International Higher Education*, Boston College Center for International Higher Education, (14), winter.

Tilak, J.BG. (2002) Privatization in India. *International Higher Education*, Boston College Center for International Higher Education, (29), fall.

UNEP (2007) *Climate Change 2007: Climate Change Impacts, Adaptation and Vulnerability*. www.unep.org.

UNESCAP (2006) *Economic and Social Survey of Asia and the Pacific*. www.unescap.org.

UNESCO (2005) *Towards Knowledge Societies: First UNESCO World Report*. Regional report of the Asia and the Pacific Regional Bureau for Education submitted to the Meeting of Higher Education Partners, Paris, 2003.

Wagner, A. (2001) From Higher to Tertiary Education. *International Higher Education*, Boston College Center for International Higher Education, (22), winter.

Wang, Y. (2006) Chinese higher education on an overpass of fourfold transitions. *Higher Education Research*, (11), 2006, and *Xinhua News Digest*, (6), 2007.

Wolanin, T. (2002) Changes in Kyrgyzstan. *International Higher Education*, Boston College Center for International Higher Education, (26), winter.

World Bank (2000) *Poverty in an Age of Globalization*.

World Bank (2002) *Constructing Knowledge Societies: New Challenges for Tertiary Education*.

WCHE (1998a) *The Thematic Debate: The Requirements of the World of Work*. Paris: UNESCO.

WCHE (1998b) *The Thematic Debate: Higher Education and Research: Challenges and Opportunities*. Paris: UNESCO.

WEBSITES

www.unescobkk.org, UNESCO Asia and the Pacific Regional Bureau for Education

www.unescap.org, United Nations Economic and Social Commission for Asia and the Pacific

www.unep.org, United Nations Environment Programme

www.moe.gov.cn/english, Chinese Ministry of Education

www.apqn.org, Asia-Pacific Quality Network

www.seameo.org, Southeast Asian Ministers of Education Organization

www.founder.com, Founder Group, China

www.ignou.ac.in, Indira Gandhi National Open University

http://ases.stanford.edu/, Asia-Pacific Student Entrepreneurship Society

http://ec.europa.eu/europeaid/projects/asia-link/index_en.htm, EU Asia-Link Programme

In today's world, education has become part of a development discourse that seeks to 'pull' people out of poverty and backwardness and enable them to enjoy the fruits of progress and civilization. This 'modernizing' mission of education can be seen to follow from the 'civilizing' mission that characterized 19th-century colonial approaches to education. In both cases, an interesting debate ensues on the purpose of education and the uses that are made of it as educational institutions are set up and people learn to use concepts and skills for themselves.

This paper will explore how tertiary education is seen within the globalized arena, to what extent it is driven by 'instrumental' concerns of development (a follow-on from the civilizing mission), and whether it provides space for its subjects, or clients, to engage in knowledge production, forge new worldviews and take the lead in global programmes and processes. The establishment of BRAC University is an example of how the tertiary education sector in Bangladesh has been opening up and experimenting with new organizational methods.

HISTORICAL BACKGROUND

Before looking at BRAC University itself, let me review the context in which modern tertiary education began in this region. The 19th-century colonial interventions provide the background for contemporary experiments in tertiary education.

Macaulay's *Minutes on Indian Education*, written in 1835, can be seen as the founding document of the 'modern' and, significantly, secular educational tradition in South Asia. He emphasizes using English as the language for education. This emphasis was guided by strong colonial considerations: Macaulay was engaged in the task of providing the British government in India with an army of administrators, employees and clerks. He also felt that the English language – with the strength of English literature – would 'impress' the colonial subjects with the glories of English civilization. So not only would English-educated Indians and Bengalis carry out some of the administrative and governing tasks of the British government, they would also act as a conduit for British values and ideals.

However, even as the new English educational system was being put into place, there was much debate on how this was to be organized. The native elite asked for scientific education in English, arguing that the 'wisdom' and progress of the West lay in the development of science and technology, but that language and literature could easily be taught in Bengali.

Hence, as colonial education was introduced in this bifurcated arena, both sides debated the function and purpose of education, as well as what constituted progress and modernization.

In the 19th century, progress and development were debated within colonial and nationalist considerations. Today, the notion of progress is considered through the lens of globalization. The emphasis of education has shifted from language and literature to technology and business. This is illustrated in the educational curricula of the newly emerging private universities in Bangladesh. However, these new universities also need to consider knowledge production and new ways of thinking in the globalized world. The World Bank, for example, in 2002 published a document entitled *Constructing Knowledge Societies: New Challenges for Tertiary Education*. The first part of the title adequately points to the challenge facing tertiary education today: not only to impart skills, but also to create a skilled population with an innovative thinking capacity that can adapt new knowledge for its own needs and forge new ways of thinking and organizing for the future.

TERTIARY EDUCATION IN BANGLADESH

Upon gaining independence in 1971, Bangladesh based itself on the notion of linguistic nationalism. It traced the origins of its independence struggle to the language movement of 1952. The establishment of Bengali as its only official language seemed to be the raison d'être of the nation. With this in mind, Bengali was established as the language of education soon after independence in 1972. The English language remained in a somewhat anomalous position. Higher education and research necessarily had to be conducted in English, as there were no books or tradition of tertiary education in Bengali. The result was that students coming into the tertiary level lacked language skills and were therefore ill-equipped to study. This was felt especially in science and technology, but also in the arts and humanities. Another aspect became noticeable soon after independence: with the proliferation of primary and secondary education, larger numbers of students found themselves knocking at the doors of a very limited number of tertiary and technical educational institutions. This demand led to a proliferation of ill-equipped 'colleges', which in reality churned out general – that is, unspecialized – BA degrees.

Only since the 1990s has the state started opening up new avenues for the development of tertiary education. Foreign aid for education had been concentrated in the primary sector. Given the lack of resources, both within and outside the country, the government of Bangladesh enacted the Private Universities Act in 1991, thus paving the way for the establishment of new universities. These universities, set up by private funds, were largely market-driven, typically offering courses in business administration and computer science. While certainly a change from the largely humanities-based offering of the colleges, these courses could still be seen as skills development rather than tertiary education.

BRAC University was established against this backdrop. In its initial consultative process, led by Professor David

Fraser, former president of Swarthmore College in the USA, and Dr Riaz Khan, BRAC opted to follow the liberal arts tradition of US universities and colleges.

This decision posed certain challenges for the proposed university. First, as mentioned above, liberal arts and the humanities had traditionally become the purview of a 'cheap' education, where large numbers of Bengali students followed a course of studies leading to a BA at a college. Even at the universities, such as Dhaka and Chittagong, arts departments were characterized by huge classes and rudimentary teaching aids. Private universities focused on the market needs of the country, concentrating on business and computers as their mainstay. BRAC decided to address these demands within a liberal arts framework.

A second consideration was how to incorporate BRAC's experience with development and poverty alleviation into the university curriculum. In the field of knowledge production, BRAC itself was seen as a huge laboratory from which students could learn and a new knowledge base could be created.

The third was deciding on a language of instruction. English was ultimately chosen, making BRAC University a new global hub for education. However, this put a large group of students at a disadvantage. Given the vision that BRAC was pursuing, these disadvantaged students were the very people the university would have liked to incorporate into its student body.

BRAC UNIVERSITY

BRAC University finally began its journey in April 2001. It started with the usual departments of Computer Science and Business Administration. The English department was also established, but more as a service department than a department in its own right. Courses clustered under 'general education' and compulsory courses from outside the major area remained part of the curriculum. As the university progressed, other departments were created, such as Eng-

lish and Humanities, Economics and Social Sciences, and Architecture.

As each department developed its own course curriculum and pedagogical practices, the University as a whole established some defining characteristics. A planning process called BRAC University Initiative for Learning and Development (BUILD) was instituted. Junior and senior teaching staff and other BRAC stakeholders debated and discussed the best ways for the University to progress.

Perhaps the most significant innovation that came out of this process was the establishment of a residential semester. General courses were made part of this semester, with a special emphasis on English. The general courses that students take during the residential semester include Bangladesh Studies, Computer Science, English, and Ethics and Culture. The Bangladesh Studies course, for instance, includes field visits to Bangladeshi historical sites and BRAC projects. During this semester, students live and work together, interact with other people using the training facilities where the residential dormitories are located, and acquire more intimate knowledge of the realities of Bangladesh. Living away from home, students become more independent and acquire a sense of self and purpose.

The University aims to foster independent thinking habits in students. With this goal in mind, each department debates pedagogical methods and introduces innovations. The English department, for instance, emphasizes making the study of English literature relevant and interesting to 21st-century men and women in Bangladesh. Post-colonial and feminist approaches are emphasized, so students learn to relate even 19th-century novels to their own realities. Literary studies are given a practical application through courses on media, language teaching and linguistics. The status of English in Bangladesh and around the world is debated in classrooms, term papers and dissertations. The School of Business Studies emphasizes learning through case studies, and students are encouraged to

think on their feet as they prepare to enter the commercial field in Bangladesh.

BUILD conducted research into what employers expect from new university graduates. It found that employers expect graduates to be competent in their specialized fields. Even more than that, however, they expect graduates to think independently, be flexible in the tasks they perform and have good communication skills.

Since BRAC University expects a more interactive classroom, teachers need to be trained towards this end. Many members of the senior teaching staff at BRAC University have been attracted from the public university system. While drawing on their teaching experience and expertise, they must also change some of their teaching habits. A core group of teachers was created to train new entrants into the profession. As a small university, BRAC can constantly monitor and innovate in order to make classrooms livelier and encourage student participation.

Two decades have now passed since private universities were introduced in Bangladesh. We have had a period of time in which to think and plan for the higher learning needs of the 21st century. The proliferation of private universities has also had an effect on public universities, which have been revising and reviewing their curricula and opening new departments.

CHALLENGES FACED AND LESSONS LEARNED

BRAC University's experience is unique among Bangladesh's private universities. Its first challenge was and remains the introduction of a liberal arts university in Bangladesh. Students enter university education with the idea that they are going to specialize in a particular area, such as architecture. Being made to read philosophy or take history courses is therefore a real challenge. The establishment of a broad-based liberal education at the tertiary level is difficult, but BRAC University is committed to this concept and working hard to establish it.

The second challenge involves students' language skills. Teaching and learning takes place in English, which can prove both difficult and alienating to students whose language of instruction up to this level has been Bengali. Making learning English student-friendly and drawing students into thinking and debating in the language require special attention and concentration. However, the University feels that, given the educational heritage and practices in our region, education in English is necessary. Both globally and regionally, English proficiency is necessary for the job market and for forging new knowledge.

The University is also facing the usual practical difficulties, such as building up a library. Physical facilities are limited in this high-rise urban university. Students, staff and lecturers need a proper campus area and building. However, in some ways BRAC University is very well equipped. Students have ready access to computers and online journal facilities.

Drawing on BRAC University's experience, I offer the following suggestions for new universities in Bangladesh:

1. A proper planning process should be implemented. When the country's first private university (North South University) was set up in 1991, its main focus was on equipping graduates to enter the business world. As a result, its business graduates are highly valued in the job market. Since then, most private universities have followed on from this experience. BRAC University drew on this experience in setting up its own business school, but has also been innovative in looking at the other gaps in Bangladesh's educational and development-related needs. As such, its progress has been slow, in the sense that it does not have a huge influx of students. As time passes, however, the liberal arts features of the university are becoming more attractive to both students and their guardians.

2. The planning process should be continuous and intense. As the university develops and new areas of priority open up, there must be room for innovation and change.

3. Based on the experience of the residential semester at BRAC University, I feel that Bangladesh needs small residential campuses. The BRAC University experience of one residential semester could be followed, or a full residential year could be considered. In any case, I recommend the combination of an urban campus with a residential campus.

4. The typical Bangladeshi student needs a lot of language training, both in the English language and in general communication skills. Innovative language programmes are very important in this context.

5. Perhaps surprisingly, students also need to become acquainted with the realities of Bangladesh, as tertiary education has historically been a source of disconnect in our region. Universities therefore need to incorporate cultural and development issues into the curriculum and devise methods for keeping the learning process grounded.

6. Finally, freedom of thought and expression can only be fostered through an open and friendly learning environment. We must wean ourselves away from the hierarchical pedagogical practices to which most of us are accustomed.

REFERENCES

Macaulay, Thomas Babington (1835) *Minutes on Indian Education*.

World Bank (2002) *Constructing Knowledge Societies: New Challenges for Tertiary Education*.

II.5

THE ROLE OF HIGHER EDUCATION FOR HUMAN AND SOCIAL DEVELOPMENT IN EUROPE

Anne Corbett

Abstract

This paper is an analysis of the way in which the two UNESCO European regions have taken up the call of the 1998 World Conference on Higher Education (WCHE) to support human and social development. It draws on a range of recent documentation to suggest that nations of the two 'Europes' have shown some concern for most of the WCHE issues in working together through a diverse range of international organizations and initiatives including the European Union (EU), the Council of Europe and, above all, the Bologna Process. The mechanisms of the Bologna Process provide a model for collaborating and for developing a community of practice. However, this paper suggests that the globalization challenge of a more interdependent, interconnected world makes it urgent to do more, and in particular to rethink not just what universities do, but what they are, so that they can react in the most effective ways to these challenges. Linking the agendas of the Bologna Process and the World Conference on Higher Education could be an appropriate first step.

INTRODUCTION

Universities in Europe live with the idea that they have a history which goes back 900 years and have provided a model for the world. The European concept of an institution of teaching and research has been exported successfully on a global scale. In many ways, European universities deserve the accolades. They attract more students and run more diverse activities than at any time in their history. They are assuming more social responsibilities. However, despite – or perhaps because of – such success, European universities are under stress (Olsen, 2007). Their performance is regularly compared unfavourably with universities in the USA and Japan, and they are seen as potentially disadvantaged in quantity and perhaps in quality with what is being developed by India and China. The European Commission, which can support but not control universities, consistently paints a picture of crisis. It is among the loudest voices urging modernization. It and

some governments argue that modernization must imply, at the minimum, a three-pronged strategy: the reform and diversification of curricula, more efficient governance, and more private funding to take account of globalization and the knowledge economy.

However, the Declaration of the 1998 WCHE raises some different questions for universities in Europe. It states that universities should respond to the challenge to make human and social development criteria integral to their activities. This does not mean providing the human capital to succeed in economic competition. The question is how universities, in the words of the United Nations Development Programme (UNDP), enhance *'the education, the knowledge and the capabilities'* which *'enable individuals to be active citizens with the opportunities to make choices which affect their daily lives'* and enable *'people to develop their full potential and lead productive, creative lives'*. Translated into criteria which fit universities, as institutions whose core activities are transmitting and creating knowledge and the exercise of critical skills, the UNDP vision has two main implications. It implies more effective learning by students whatever their age, status, race or religion. European research overwhelmingly suggests that this means more active and autonomous learning. The UNDP criteria also imply that teaching and research should be more responsive to context. Students and their teachers need to be much more aware of the challenges of an interdependent and environmentally threatened world. They need to be at the forefront of the search for solutions. Thus, active citizenship implies an awareness of the links between environmental and social sustainability and the dislocations, or inequalities, manifested in such scourges as terrorism and wars over resources (including land and water) and over religious or other beliefs.

In pursuing the theme of how universities can help provide for human and social development, this paper makes two assumptions. The first is that universities, whatever their geographical situation within Europe and whatever the diversity of size and scale or their dominant language and culture, interpret their core mission in similar terms of teaching, research, legitimizing knowledge and the social responsibility for educating highly qualified graduates and responsible citizens. The second assumption is that change is driven by political processes and shaped by institutional resources (March and Olsen, 1989).

The argument in this paper is presented in three parts. First, there is a brief account of how the ideas of the WCHE have been pursued within European institutional frameworks over the past decade. The second part considers the particular challenges of globalization to universities wishing to fulfil human and social development criteria. The third part takes up the challenge of turning WCHE ideas into action, in suggesting how policies that are more sensitive to human development criteria and appropriate to universities might operate within Europe.

DEFINING THE 'EUROPES' OF HIGHER EDUCATION

In applying human development criteria, UNESCO divides Europe into two, along lines that largely reflect Cold War Europe's divisions. The culturally, linguistically and generally rich Western European region, classified by UNESCO alongside North America (Canada and the USA), consists of 27 states, five of them microstates. Twenty-six are geographically part of the European continent, the 27th is Israel.[1] UNESCO's Central and Eastern Europe (CEE) consists of 20 states, almost all of which in the past were part of the Communist bloc. It also includes Turkey (Table II.5.1).

Some of the most informed commentators support this division (Sadlak, 2003, Tomusk, 2006). The CEE is seen as not only poorer, but culturally still different. It also has the practical problems which the changes since 1989, and the fall of the Berlin Wall, have uncovered: these states have needed to transform their public institutions to respond to the new democratic demands. However, they have also had to digest an influx of private and transborder higher education providers. Some of this provision is unregulated and inadequate, and there are problems of corruption. The new situation has also given rise to a brain drain, much of it to Western Europe (Sadlak, 2003). In UNESCO's Western Europe, the most vociferously expressed issues concerning higher education are, in contrast, essentially ones of efficiency, fairness and modernization. This is not to say that other problems do not exist. However, they have not been on the political agenda.

There is more diversity within and between these European regions than widely thought. This diversity is not just linguistic and cultural, but also reflects disparities of GDP and of political choice, the size of the higher education system and the extent of private education (see Statistical Appendix Part IV of this report). At the same time, the strong international institutions which characterize Europe have their own agenda and legislative and financial resources, and membership criteria.

The EU operates under the Treaty on European Union, which gives it some supranational powers. None of these apply directly to education. The EU Treaty explicitly states that education is a matter for 'subsidiarity' or national control. The EU's role is limited to support and adding quality. It is in this light that the EU works for large scale transformations of university and training systems through the Lisbon Strategy for Growth and Jobs.[2] The ambition to ensure Europe's wealth and growth by developing and expanding a highly competitive knowledge economy has many implications for universities.

European educational systems – and the lives of citizens – are also affected indirectly by 'spillover' from the EU's core powers relating to the four freedoms of movement of capital, goods, services and labour. The EU at summit and ministerial level, as well as through the Commission, is explicitly concerned with the livelihoods of European populations. It has consistently promoted a social dimension alongside its economic policies, in its funding of impoverished regions, its employment and gender policies, and its multicultural initiatives. Its increasing concern with threats to Europe, including environmental issues and the security threats of organized crime and terrorism, is positively reflected in areas as diverse as climate change research, and a more active 'neighbourhood' policy of cooperation and support for the countries which align Europe's eastern and southern borders.

The Council of Europe has no supranational powers. Nevertheless, it has an important role in supporting human and social development issues, through its promotion of democratic values and human rights by demanding its members' adherence to the European Human Rights Convention and by the operation of the European Court of Human Rights. It has a permanent secretariat.

The extent to which the Bologna Process is an active player in human and social development issues is considered in some detail below. To participate in the Bologna Process, countries are required to have signed the European Cultural Convention, which sets out the Councils' educational and cultural ambitions, and to be committed to the Bologna principles (European Ministers Responsible for Higher Education, 2003). The Process operates by agreement between its participants, with the objective of creating a European Higher Education Area (European Ministers Responsible for Higher Education, 1999). It has no legislative underpinning, nor its own resources. Indeed, its resources include having the European Commission as a special member, and a process which engages an active range of stakeholders as consultative members.

The Magna Charta Observatory also contributes to human and social development values. It is the guardian of the *Magna Charta Universitatum* (1988), a statement of the fundamental rights and responsibilities of a university, which individual institutions may sign. It now has signatories from many regions of the world to support it in its work.[3]

Overall we can envisage this kaleidoscopic, yet organized, Europe as having between 20 and 32 million students, depending on which setting we are talking about. Western Europe has around 15 million students; the CEE of UNESCO has 17 million. The EU-15 had around 15 million students. The EU-27 has around 20 million students, and Russia, the Ukraine and Turkey between them have 12 million students.[4]

The diversity of students' lives in UNDP terms is underlined by looking at the Human Development Index (HDI) scores of these 'Europes' of the EU and the Bologna Process, which contain members that are not in the UNESCO definitions.

THE EUROPEAN HIGHER EDUCATION SCENE WCHE+10

The most striking fact about European higher education in general in the past decade is the change in the political perception of universities. In the early 1990s, uni-versities were seen by national governments as a problem. They were considered difficult to manage and to fund and, apparently, they seriously lagged behind the universities of the USA and Japan. Yet ten years on from the WCHE, universities have achieved a rare level of political importance at European and national level. They form part of normal experience for around half of the European population of conventional student age, with the complexities of funding and governance that this implies at national level. They are clearly identified by the EU and many national governments as a critical part of the solution to the economic challenges that face Europe as a whole, as profitable activity becomes increasingly tied to the wealth that knowledge exploitation can generate on a global scale. All organizations, and especially the Council of Europe, look to them to advance democracy.

In evolving the strategies that have helped to hoist universities to prominence, the policy actors in these different institutions are preoccupied by many of the same issues. Pavel Zgaga, the rapporteur for a major study of Bologna's external dimension entitled *Looking Out: The Bologna Process in the Global Setting*, lists as common reform issues: access; curriculum diversification in study programmes; employability; links to the economy; mobility; international students; and recognition (Zgaga, 2006). The list from the WCHE in 1998 was somewhat different (Table II.5.3).

TABLE II.5.1
The Europe of higher education: membership of selected international organizations

UNESCO Western Europe region – 27
Andorra, Austria*, Belgium*, Cyprus*, Denmark*, Finland*, France*, Germany*, Gibraltar, Greece*, Holy See, Iceland, Ireland*, Italy*, Liechtenstein, Luxembourg*, Malta*, Monaco, Netherlands*, Norway, Portugal*, San Marino, Spain*, Sweden*, Switzerland, UK*. Also Israel

UNESCO Central and Eastern Europe region – 20
Albania, Belarus, Bosnia Herzegovina, Bulgaria*, Croatia, Czech Republic*, Estonia*, Hungary*, Latvia*, Lithuania*, Poland*, Republic of Moldova, Romania*, Russian Federation, Serbia and Montenegro, Slovakia*, Slovenia*, the former Yugoslav Republic of Macedonia, Turkey, Ukraine

European Union member states – 27
All asterisked countries*
Council of Europe members – 47
Andorra, Albania, *Armenia*, Austria*, *Azerbaijan*, Belgium Flemish, Belgium French* , Bosnia Herzegovina, Bulgaria*, Croatia, Cyprus*, Czech Republic*, Denmark*, Estonia, Finland*, France*, *Georgia*, Germany*, Gibraltar, Greece*, Holy See, Iceland, Ireland*, Italy*, Latvia, Liechtenstein, Lithuania, Luxembourg*, Malta*, Republic of Moldova, Montenegro, Netherlands*, Norway, Poland, Portugal*, Romania*, Russia, Serbia, Slovakia, Slovenia, Spain*, Sweden*, Switzerland, The former Yugoslav Republic of Macedonia, Turkey, Ukraine, UK – EWNI (England, Wales and Northern Ireland) and UK – Scotland*
Italicized countries outside UNESCO European regions
Belarus suspended

Bologna Process participants – 47 (46 national members; 1 special member); 8 consultative members
Members: 46 signatories of the Council of Europe Convention on Human Rights
Special member: the European Commission
Consultative members: the Council of Europe; the Education International Pan-European Structure (EI), representative of academics; the European Association for Quality Assurance in Higher Education (ENQA); the European Student Union (ESU) representative of national student unions; the European University Association (EUA), representative of university leadership; the European Association of Institutions in Higher Education (EURASHE),representative of professional higher education institution leadership; UNESCO Centre for Higher Education (UNESCO-CEPES); BusinessEurope

TABLE II.5.2
Human Development Index (HDI) ratings in Europe, as it is variously defined

HDI global ratings	1–27	28–50	51–100	101–150	151–177
Council of Europe/ Bologna 46	16	14	12	1	0
EU-27	13	12	2	0	0
EU-15	12	3	0	0	0

HDI global ratings	1–27	28–50	51–100	101 150	151–177
EU-15	Austria Belgium Denmark Finland France Germany Greece Ireland Italy Luxembourg Netherlands UK	Cyprus Malta Portugal			
EU-27	Slovenia	Croatia Czech Republic Estonia Hungary Latvia Lithuania Poland Slovakia	Bulgaria Romania		
Council of Europe/Bologna in UNESCO Europe	Iceland Norway Switzerland	Croatia Russian Federation	Albania Bosnia Herzegovina Former Yugoslav Republic – Macedonia Turkey Ukraine	Republic of Moldova	
Council of Europe/Bologna outside UNESCO Europe -3			Armenia Azerbaijan Georgia		
Totals*	16	14	12	1	0

Note: *No information for Serbia and Montenegro; Belarus suspended from the Council of Europe; Belgium (Flemish and Walloon). Total = 46.

Source: derived from the United Nations Development Programme, Human Development Report 2006.

TOOLS: MOBILITY, RECOGNITION, QUALITY, CREDIT TRANSFER AND A COMMON STRUCTURE

The best known of the reform ideas for European universities over the decade relate to measures that provide governments with incentives to make their systems compatible with a European framework: the European Higher Education Area (EHEA). All governments in the Bologna Process have reacted in some measure to this idea.

These tools to strengthen European higher education within a wider and more global system have been brought together and packaged by the Bologna Process. The *Trends* report to Bologna ministers in May 2007 said that 82% of higher education institutions had adopted a three-cycle system of bachelors–masters–doctorates; up from 53% four years earlier (Crosier et al., 2007). Furthermore, 75% were using a credit transfer system.

However, a Bologna ministerial commitment to multi-dimensional quality assurance – as the WCHE had proposed – had not yet seen much evidence of institutions using the strategy 'holistically' (Crosier et al., 2007). This strategy makes higher education institutions themselves key actors, responsible for internal evaluation, and expects that agencies, responsible for external evaluation, will work to a European framework of standards and guidelines for quality assurance, as agreed in 2005 (European Ministers Responsible for Higher Education, 2005). Recognition is also being interpreted somewhat ambivalently. Many institutions and/or governments have accepted credit systems and the diploma supplement, which is given to every student on graduation. However, institutions responding to the *Trends* survey are confused about the type of qualifications frameworks that the

TABLE II.5.3
The policy agendas of the WCHE and 'Europe of Higher Education' organizations

Zgaga report 2006	WCHE 1998
Access	**Improve access** No discrimination on account of class, age, gender
	Strengthen and expand core missions Teaching, training, research Educate highly qualified graduates and responsible citizens
	Enable the exercise of critical functions Protect academic freedom and university autonomy
Employability Links to economy /relevance	**Create greater relevance** Reinforce relations with the world of work
Curricular diversity	**Create a seamless system** Links with secondary education and lifelong learning Diversify institutions and programmes of study
	Develop a **multidimensional concept of quality**
	Develop research
	Develop staff status
	Place students at the centre of concern
	Provide for partnership among stakeholders See above
	Ensure **sustainability**
	HE as a public service Whatever the funding, ensure management aims are for the improvement of quality and relevance
International students	**Strengthen international dimension** Extend networking, sharing, solidarity
Recognition	

Sources: Zgaga, 2006; UNESCO, World Conference on Higher Education Declaration 1998.

Bologna Process and the EU are working on. Such frameworks are geared to learning outcomes.

The principle of *fair* Europe-wide recognition is well accepted. Thirty-eight members of the Bologna Process, including the newest, Montenegro, have signed the Council of Europe/UNESCO Lisbon Convention on the Recognition of Qualifications. The major components of the convention are that holders of qualifications issued in one country shall have adequate access to an assessment of these qualifications in another country, without any discrimination. Significantly, the responsibility for demonstrating that an applicant does not fulfil the relevant requirements lies with the body undertaking the assessment and not with the applicant (Reinalda and Kulesza, 2005).

The core ideas – with one exception – were developed within the EU over 30 years. Mobility and exchange have been seen as essential ever since the European Community's foundation in the 1950s (Corbett, 2005). Community-aided mobility became a reality in the 1980s, with the creation of Erasmus and other programmes. A European credit transfer system was pioneered under the wing of the Erasmus programme. From the 1990s, the Commission was also working actively on

quality assurance. However, it was not able to devise a model that satisfied member states.

It is significant that it was under the Bologna Process, rather than within EU structures, that national governments committed to these reforms. It may well be, as some (including Zgaga, 2006) suggest, that the membership of the CEE countries and Russia has been a driving force for common policy ambitions. It is clearly the case that only national governments can advance the reform which provides the 'glue' for much of the reform process, starting with the adoption of a three-cycle approach.

MEASURES: ACCESS, CURRICULUM, RELEVANCE, THE SOCIAL DIMENSION AND LIFELONG LEARNING

The Bologna Process, like the WCHE, is concerned with fair access to higher education and putting the student at the centre of the learning process. The aforementioned measures offer new opportunities. A further package of measures, based around the Bologna Process and the EU, encourages national governments to take the steps to make a reality of such opportunities.

Lifelong learning has long been seen as a necessity by the EU. The EU in fact took on ideas developed in the 1970s and 80s at the OECD under the name of recurrent education. Its motivation is to equip people to respond and develop in a knowledge economy where knowledge and skills become outdated. A demographic shift of population adds force to this argument: the old have outnumbered the young since 2007. In addition, there are also signs of a growing demand from motivated individuals to renew or recycle themselves. The EU has taken the initiative to group most of its exchange and mobility programmes under the banner of the integrated Lifelong Learning programme (2007–13). Its version of a qualifications framework is seen as part of a larger lifelong learning strategy, which includes vocational education and training. In 2007, Bologna ministers found that some elements of flexible learning now exist in most countries. However, few national structures treat the recognition of prior learning in a systematic way, whether for access to higher education or in the calculation of credits (European Ministers Responsible for Higher Education, 2007).

The social dimension is another area in which strong statements have not been followed by much action. 'We share the societal aspiration that the student body entering, participating in and completing higher education should reflect the diversity of our populations.' To achieve this, adequate student services and flexible learning pathways into, and within, higher education need to be developed (European Ministers Responsible for Higher Education, 2007).

Ministers encourage joint courses and university collaboration but do not have anything specific to say on the curriculum. However, a potentially changed curriculum is implicit in many of the decisions. The restructuring of university courses into cycles in countries where the bachelors–masters–doctorates structure was not the rule, and the introduction of credit accumulation systems, in theory at least, means adaptation. The commitment to accessible systems also implies curriculum diversity. Probably the main curriculum initiative comes from the European Commission, in order to encourage convergence. Under the Tuning project, the EU has backed a number of discipline-related development studies in which academics draw from the work of different countries to define common reference points based on competences (European Commission, 2007).

RESEARCH

Research is an area where the Bologna Process and the EU play complementary – but competitive – roles. Both institutions recognize the value of a closer alignment of the EHEA with the European Research Area (ERA). For the EU, the main driver is the Lisbon Strategy: a ten-year strategy designed to advance Europe's knowledge economy dramatically and strengthen social cohesion (European Council, 2000). The EU would like to translate this into a number of world-beating initiatives. These include targeting leading research institutions for special treatment and setting up new strategic institutions in which university researchers and business interests are in partnership. However, the EU has had to listen to the academics on whom the results depend. It has accepted that a European Research Council is likely to be most effective if the council members are themselves widely respected researchers. It has modified its initial proposal to create a European version of the flagship Massachusetts Institute of Technology – the European Institute of Technology (EIT). It has also taken a number of measures which complement the Bologna concern to create better synergies between higher education and research. An example is the development of a Europe-wide code defining the status of the early career researcher (European Commission, 2006b, 2006c).

VALUES: UNIVERSITY AUTONOMY, GOVERNANCE AND FUNDING, ETHICS, PARTNERSHIP, A PUBLIC GOOD

The inter-governmental Bologna Process has kept out of the issue of autonomy, other than declaring that it adheres to the fundamental principles of academic freedom, including autonomy, laid down in the *Magna Charta Universitatum*. In contrast, the European Commission, in its supporting role, has fewer qualms about being specific. Since 2001, it has issued a stream of communications delivering an unambiguous message of the crisis to come unless there are management and funding reforms. To implement such reforms, universities need the freedom to manage their affairs. Recent examples of these communications are *Efficiency and Equity in European Education and Training Systems* (European Commission, 2006a); and *Delivering on the Modernisation Agenda for Europe: Education, Research and Innovation* (European Commission, 2006b).

University organizations – and notably the EUA that represents university leadership – support the Commission. However the proposals have been viewed sceptically within the academic profession as they represent a strategy that is not evidence-based. Johan Olsen, for example, sees that the Commission's modernization approach for universities is more appropriate to the steel industry, as it ignores the specificities of academic production and threatens to sweep away what remains of universities as communities of self-governing scholars, organized around strong faculties. He considers that the strategy is based on weak evidence about the need for entrepreneurial management and a significant amount of private funding. He is a widely respected scholar and his view carries authority (Olsen, 2007).

Recently, the Magna Charta Observatory and the Euro-

TABLE II.5.4

Delivering on a modernization agenda for Europe: The Commission's nine action points

1. Break down barriers around universities in Europe; mobility and achievement of core Bologna reforms by 2010; comparable qualifications, flexible curricula and trustworthy quality assurance systems.

2. Ensure real autonomy.

3. Provide incentives for structures, partnerships with the business community.

4. Provide the right mix of skills and competencies for the labour market. Universities should be structured to directly enhance the employability of graduates as well as offering broad support to the workforce through lifelong learning.

5. Reduce the funding gap, and make funding work more effectively in education and research. The Commission proposes to devote at least 2% of GDP (public and private) to a modernized higher education sector.

6. Enhance interdisciplinarity and transdisciplinarity.

7. Activate knowledge through interaction with society.

8. Reward excellence at the highest level. Support initiatives such as networking, the European Institute of Technology and the European Research Council.

9. Make the European Higher Education Area and the European Research and Innovation Area more visible and attractive to the world.

Source: European Commission, 2006b.

pean Centre for Higher Education (UNESCO-CEPES) – institutions with experience of CEE countries – have stepped into the debate with a line which supports WCHE aspirations that are not reflected in other forums for reform. They want to see universities allowed forms of governance that are driven primarily by a concern to improve institutional quality and relevance. These organizations have been concerned about corruption in academic life. CEPES gives examples such as degrees being sold and the unethical exploitation of research. In 2006, the Council of Europe and the Magna Charta Observatory promoted the idea that support for institutional autonomy and academic freedom can strengthen the core missions of the university. The Council of Europe resolution also urged the Council's Committee of Ministers to make the recognition of academic freedom and university autonomy a condition of membership of the Council of Europe, since it is fundamental to a democratic society:

> The social and cultural responsibilities of the universities mean more than mere responsiveness to immediate demands of societies, to the needs of the markets, however important it may be to take these demands and needs into account (Council of Europe, 2006).

INTERNATIONAL DIMENSION

The last area considered here that reflects and reinterprets a WCHE concern is the international dimension of universities. The WCHE saw this in terms of networking, sharing and solidarity between universities in different regions of the world. The EU sees such linkages primarily in terms of global competition, and a way of promoting the personal development of those involved. Its

Erasmus Mundus programme, a sort of European 'Fulbright' scheme, pays the brightest and best handsomely to work in two or three European universities. In 2007 the Bologna Process ministers approved a five-part strategy on the international dimension. This satisfies the range of opinion amongst governments and other stakeholders by leaving options open as to whether they wish primarily to adopt the measures that back cooperation or whether – as in the UK – they see higher education as a trade which delivers billions of pounds to the national coffers.[5]

TABLE II.5.5

The strategy for the European Higher Education Area in a global setting, adopted by European Ministers for Higher Education, London 2007

1. Improving information on the EHEA.

2. Promoting European higher education to enhance its worldwide attractiveness.

3. Strengthening cooperation based on partnership.

4. Intensifying policy dialogue.

5. Furthering recognition of qualifications.

Source: Bologna Process official website. Working papers 2007.

In sum, WCHE issues are all receiving attention from one or more of the high-level European bodies. However, as the Bologna communiqués illustrate, many initiatives are only in the early stages of implementation. Nevertheless, contemporary European processes encourage a plurality of voices, which has been to the benefit of some of the most crucial human and social development issues. Ethics, for example, is an issue which is being raised outside the more powerful organizations in those institutions which play a major role in CEE countries. Yet the issue is surely relevant across the whole European region.

TABLE II.5.6
The trajectory of the Bologna Process 1999–2007

Creating the EHEA
Agreeing action lines
● Adopt a system of easily readable and comparable degrees
● Adopt a system that is essentially based on two cycles
● Establish a system of credits
● Promote mobility
● Promote European cooperation in quality assurance
● Promote the European dimension in higher education
● Develop lifelong learning
● Higher education institutions and students.
● Promote the attractiveness of the European Higher Education Area
● Support doctoral studies and the synergy between the EHEA and ERA
● Assume the social dimension as an overarching and transversal action line
Sources: Bologna Declaration 1999; Prague Communiqué 2001; Berlin Communiqué 2003.
Deciding and acting on priorities
● *Quality assurance:* develop mutually agreed criteria and methodologies
● *The two-cycle degree:* develop an overarching framework of qualifications
● *The recognition of degrees and periods of study:* ratify the Lisbon Recognition Convention. From 2005, provide graduating students with a Diploma Supplement
Sources: Berlin Communiqué 2003; Bergen Communiqué 2005.
● Complete ongoing priorities
● New priority for mobility, the social dimension, data collection, employability, the EHEA in a global context
Source: London Communiqué 2007.
Introducing evaluation
● National stocktaking to be presented
Sources: Berlin Communiqué 2003; Bergen Communiqué 2005; London Communiqué 2007.
To consider vision and structures for EHEA in 2010 and beyond
Foresee an EHEA based on quality and transparency that is committed to public responsibility for higher education; a belief in higher education as the key to Europe's competitiveness; higher education institutions to enjoy autonomy to implement the agreed reforms; recognition of the need for sustainable funding of institutions.
Source: Bergen Communiqué 2005.
To reformulate the vision that motivated us.
To consider a BFUG proposal for appropriate support structures, bearing in mind that the current collaborative arrangements are working well and have brought about unprecedented change.
Source: London Communiqué 2007.

HIGHER EDUCATION AND THE HUMAN AND SOCIAL CHALLENGES OF GLOBALIZATION

Globalization is a highly controversial topic across Europe. Dispute is fuelled by the uncertainties generated by globalization – the interdependence of economies worldwide, driven forward by liberalizing market economies and rapidly falling costs of transport and communication (Wolf, 2005) – and the ambiguities as to where cause and effect lie. The case for globalization is that Europe – and the world – has got richer in this period; human welfare, broadly defined, has been promoted since the late 1980s and the number of people in poverty has declined. In a widely admired book, Martin Wolf makes the case that the world needs more, not less, globalization because it helps human and social development in general (Wolf, 2005). However, opponents of globalization have had a significant political impact within the past few years and widespread public support.[6] In Europe, globalization is blamed variously for the disappearance of traditional industrial jobs; the emergence of new consumer demands as successful societies get richer; the necessity for a highly educated society to keep such an economy expanding, perhaps at the expense of other educational needs; and the emergence of disparities which are geographical and income-related. Every state within UNESCO and the European regions can recognize the tensions within its own society between the culturally 'cosmopolitan' and those whose communities are fragmenting in the face of economic change, industrial collapse and some of the stresses of mass migration. Racism and religious intolerance have become salient issues, fuelled by cross-border crime and terrorism. Not least, globalization has alerted Europeans to the looming threats of climate change and reinforced the need for a more sustainable economy (Giddens, 2007; Liddle and Lérais, 2007).

In policy circles where the issue is how to manage change, there is widespread appreciation that there are different ways to respond to globalization. A recent fact-filled paper from policy advisers to the European Commission, *Europe's Social Reality* (Liddle and Lérais, 2007) argues that a 'timeless European model' has never existed, so could not be subjected to a 'globalization shock'. Instead, there has been adaptation over the years to succeeding pressures. Some are different; some, like crime and mass migration, are familiar. All might have threatened the cohesion of European societies. The outstanding example of a threat turned into an opportunity is Europe's development of a welfare state after the Second World War. The authors argue that there are contemporary opportunities in Europe's trajectory to a dominantly post-industrial knowledge and service economy which need to be taken if societies are not to be split by generational gaps, child poverty in particular, and other serious risks of polarization.

The measure of post-industrialization in Europe is that in the entire EU-25, manufacturing accounted for less than a fifth of all jobs, whilst service jobs accounted for almost two-thirds. Over eight million new jobs in the service sector were created between 2000 and 2004 (Liddle and Lérais, 2007). The CEE countries may be especially well-positioned, as they have proved their ability to change in the past decade and generally have high standards of higher education. One conclusion is that higher education holds many of the keys which will make the difference between an active and a passive response.

In this situation, higher education is a topic of strategic European interest. The higher education policy community itself is concerned. Jurgen Enders and Oliver Fulton suggest that academics in general tend to see globalization as a catch-all phrase to catalogue more or less everything that has changed since the 1970s: advances in information technology; greater capital flow across borders; international mobility of labour or of students; new public management and the weakening power of nation states; credit transfers in higher education and the international recognition of degrees (Enders and Fulton, 2002, p. 5).

However, the more operational definitions of globalization, such as Wolf's (2005), suggest that there are other phenomena to which Europe's higher education communities should also be paying attention. The question is whether those in higher education, who want to see globalization turned to a human and social development advantage, are paying enough attention to the uncertainties and options related to knowledge in a context in which universities are ever more conscious of globaliz-

ation: knowledge as exemplified by student mobility, knowledge in terms of production, and knowledge as legitimated by a universal model.

UNCERTAIN GLOBAL FLOWS OF STUDENTS AND ACADEMICS

Policymakers naturally recognize the significance of international or global student flows. The asymmetry of the flows is of cultural and economic importance, a matter of 'brain gain' or 'brain drain'. The main host countries of Europe (the UK, Ireland, France, Norway and Sweden) court overseas students assiduously, especially those from the Asian economies. This represents Europe's new brain gain, countering some of the brain drain to the USA that is traditional in Western Europe. CEE countries now see themselves as suffering brain drain to Western Europe (Sadlak, 2003). Encouraging study within the EU, rather than in other world regions, has been the highest priority of 92% of European universities (Reichert and Tauch, 2003). The economic risks inherent in these flows are huge. The British higher education system would collapse, bringing down a significant part of the research effort, if clever and highly motivated fee-paying overseas students suddenly stopped coming.

There is earlier evidence of flows changing suddenly. Decades back, study abroad reflected colonial or ideological patterns, with Moscow and Washington vying for African and European elite. The phrase was coined that study abroad was the 'fourth dimension of diplomacy'. Some commentators now urge caution about numbers of international students, suggesting that enhanced mobility is unlikely to be a strong force for the globalization of higher education. Even in OECD countries, the number of mobile students does not exceed 10% of the student population (Gibbons, 1998, p. 71). Numbers of international students drop with downturns of the economy. In addition, there are signs that with national economic development and the strengthening of the sending country's system of higher education, there could be less enthusiasm for sending students abroad. However the geographical evidence of flows within Europe shows the potential for greater disparities within nations. The cosmopolitan regions are increasingly attractive, the rest become less so (Rodriguez-Posé and Vilalta-Bufi, 2005).

Such economic analyses need to be complemented by studies which show what mobile students gain from exposure to systems other than their own. It is their active learning which offers hope for exploiting the opportunities of globalization and minimizing the threats.

THE GLOBALIZATION OF KNOWLEDGE PRODUCTION
Another area where globalization appears to be a solidly

anchored fact of life is in the sphere of knowledge production/research. Integral to the knowledge economy is the global flow of information and data. Knowledge production and transmission is widely agreed to have lost a traditional linear character (if it ever existed) (Gibbons et al., 1994; Scott, 1998; Rodrigues, 2002). Accelerated by IT, a growing sector of the economy is dependent for innovation on cycles of creation, destruction, and re-creation. Logically, this means that universities need to adapt to the growing market structure for all kinds of specialized knowledge, rather than the results of basic and scientific research that interested firms in the industrial age. It is evident that globalization has stimulated the expansion of potential producers of knowledge in firms and specialized research organizations outside the universities (Gibbons et al., 1994). This changing supply side is matched by a changing demand side: the requirement for specialized knowledge is also expanding rapidly. This situation typically generates new collaborative structures which are part university, part private sector. Such structures operate under very different rules from that of the traditional faculty (Gibbons, 1998, p. 77).

The notion of knowledge as private property, whose accumulation can be calculated like any good, is an issue that universities in many western European societies have been facing in recent years. This represents a fundamental challenge to the university concept of knowledge as a 'non-rival good' or something that is enhanced by sharing. Globalization makes it ever more urgent that European universities deal with this issue, among others. Are they still, or can they continue to be, institutions exemplifying values which the market does not honour, such as a belief that scholars are not entrepreneurs, and students are apprentices not consumers? In Europe, for example, it is the student body and some governments that have fought for the notion of university teaching and research as a public good that should be embedded in the Bologna Process (European Ministers Responsible for Higher Education, 2001). University leaders are divided. This is a live, fundamental issue, which is highlighted by globalization.

A CHALLENGE TO WESTERN SCIENTIFIC TRADITION?
A third issue which directly affects universities is the challenge to Western scientific traditions. Within Western systems, it is largely taken for granted that science builds on notions of epistemological objectivity, and is firmly rooted in experimental and empirical techniques. However, some voices have claimed that the same legitimacy should be accorded to contextualized knowledge production and local knowledge traditions, which reflect the social and cultural diversity (see Scott, 1998, p. 112).

Globalization increases the tension around this issue. It is not uncommon in developing countries to regard Europe as trying to impose a new form of colonialism through its model of the legitimization of knowledge. The process of peer review in scientific journals is seen by some as a new form of tyranny. The claim is that new contexts need new content. The Zgaga report (2006) quotes the measured opinion of Goolam Mohamedbhai, who was then chairman of the international Universities Association (see Mohamedbhai's paper Chapter II.2, this report), in relation to the Bologna Process in general, including its three-cycle structure. As he put it, universities in developing countries would not welcome the 'imposition' of a European model (Zgaga, 2006, pp. 15, 16, 47). However, neither the report, nor the follow-up strategy, question what sharing knowledge (Zgaga, 2007) actually consists of. Yet this must be a fertile area for the development of knowledge and capabilities amongst the partners concerned.

VISIONS AND STRATEGIES

The GUNI-generated debate on how higher education in Europe might respond to issues of human and social development comes at a propitious time in terms of European policy activity. The EU and the Bologna Process share a 2010 target date. The EU's target is to advance its knowledge strategy, and modernize universities; the Bologna Process's goal is to create a European Higher Education Area. Questions such as the social dimension of European higher education, the nature of the 'public good' and the international role of European universities are among the priority issues for the next meeting of ministers of higher education. There could not be a better time to ask whether governments, universities and employers are expecting higher education to take human and social development seriously. In particular, can we say of Europe that it is not simply looking after itself, as part of the rich Northern hemisphere against the poor South?

All the international institutions that are active in European higher education can argue that the well-being of European citizens underpins all their efforts. The EU can rightly boast of what it has done to expand and strengthen democratic practice in the region, and to improve rights in the social field (Liddle and Lérais, 2007). Jan Figel, the European Commissioner for Education, is on record as saying somewhat defensively: 'I don't want you to think that the EU has a purely instrumental view of universities' (quoted in Olsen, 2007). As the Bologna Process has evolved, it has continued to incorporate the concerns of the higher education stakeholders for 'well-being' issues related to equity. There is a vision of the university anchored in notions of the public good (See Table II.5.6). The Council of Europe vision of democracy and human rights, strengthened by its networking with Magna Charta, UNESCO-CEPES and Bologna members, does help CEE countries in the transition process. These activities ought to provide a healthy incentive for western European countries to reassess their practices.

FILLING A VACUUM

However, I suggest that there is a vacuum at the centre of the European reform movement around the Bologna Process. This gap is not quite filled by the Magna Charta Observatory or the work of UNESCO-CEPES. Olsen and colleagues have called for a new pact within Europe between the university, political authorities and society at large. This pact should recognize the university as an institution with its organizational structures and processes, which need to be taken into consideration at times of change (Gornitzka et al., 2007). More critically, experts with a CEE background have forcefully attacked the Bologna Process as not sufficiently intellectual (Kwiek, 2006, Tomusk, 2006). Generalizing more widely, Brennan suggests that reform strategies do not take into account the multiple roles of universities; roles as both reproductive – of elites, and of knowledge – and transformative agents (Brennan, 2002).

What does seem clear is that much of the Bologna debate has been about the practicalities of devising acceptable policy instruments for recognition and qualification, and rather less about what Bologna and the complementary EU action is for. Thus, there is little general debate as to how universities can contribute to North–South solidarity, sustainable development, climate change and the personal development priorities of the WCHE – though these issues are alive and well in some institutions. More dangerously in a globalized world, such a lack of intellectual debate indicates that Europe might be looking after itself, and that even higher education cooperation is self-interested and takes neo-colonial and/or overtly exploitive forms.

A NEW INTERNATIONALIZATION STRATEGY

Surely, what we ought to be calling for is an explicit link between the Bologna Process and the WCHE agenda. The aim would be to get governments, academics, students and other stakeholders in European universities to discuss how to engage with the issues that make for a more sustainable world. Were there this greater clarity and knowledge of what European universities *are*, as well as what they *do*, universities in the European region would be in

a much better position to implement an internationalization strategy that is much more supportive of human and social development factors. Such a strategy should be based on greater mutual respect and willingness to exchange. There could be an inspiring picture of how many are already contributing through their teaching and their research, but also an awareness of gaps and missed opportunities to learn from the rest of the world and, in the case of a historically fragmented Europe, from the east as well as the west.

Martin Wolf, the globalization enthusiast quoted earlier, maintains that the biggest shortcoming, by far, of the developed countries is the low level transfer of capital and ideas to the developing world (Wolf, 2005, p. 11). Help is undoubtedly needed. Examples put forward in Bologna discussions by Penina Mlama of the Forum for African Women Educationalists include the role of higher education in democratization processes, cross-border provision, finance, enhancing institutional cooperation, brain-drain issues and gender issues (Zgaga, 2006, p. 112).

But collaboration between North and South should not be determined solely on European terms. Much depends on how the collaboration works and whether working together in ways that combine analysis and development can lead to new solutions to global phenomena such as the emergence of new geographic and income inequalities as the fortunes of winners and losers diverge; the consequences of immigration into Europe from less developed countries; terrorism, religious intolerance and climate change (Giddens, 2007).

If the charges of European 'imposition' are to be avoided, it is surely crucial that the transfer, sharing and exchange of capital and ideas are not exclusively commercial transactions, nor essentially driven by post-colonial knowledge-and-power motivations. In a world which is much more interdependent and interconnected, universities are well placed to negotiate and develop ideas and strategies.

AN IMPLEMENTATION STRATEGY FOR A MORE HUMAN AND SOCIAL DEVELOPMENT-ORIENTED APPROACH

The traditions of European higher education collaboration produce some positive policy lessons about how to get support from the corresponding policy sector. Imposition from the top to the bottom has not worked in Europe, any better than imposition from North to South works in development policy or international cooperation.

The Bologna policy trajectory reveals another model. It has been open to agenda setting, as Table II.5.6 reveals. The processes are collaborative. The stakeholders have real influence at all stages of policy formulation. Furthermore, it is expected that the way policies will be interpreted is largely dependent on how national systems interpret the pressures.

The policy aims are not to harmonize systems but to develop a community of practice. This is a novel approach. The fact that so many governments have agreed that they should act at European level to create a European frame is an achievement. Bologna's working methods region-wide to create a European Higher Education Area are bound to draw in ever wider networks. This loosely organized process has been sufficiently stable and sufficiently open to provide a forum in which participants can continue to make the case for policy development. In tackling issues collectively, participants have already introduced new thinking on matters which had not seemed to require choice at national level.

CONCLUSIONS

I believe that we can conclude that such a developmental and cooperative approach to policy change means that the Bologna Process could be a good basis on which to work for a more meaningful commitment to WCHE aims, in association with the EU. However, for WCHE concerns to become integral to the way universities function in the European region, two things are essential. One is that universities develop critical thinking and research in relevant areas, as they judge fit. This is consistent with academic freedom and institutional autonomy. The other is that national governments and the EU should provide more motivating resources to follow such paths. Rather than having formal new charges laid upon them, universities should be allowed to do what they do best through their teaching, their curriculum and their research, in a framework of academic freedom and greater institutional autonomy. This combination of consciousness-raising and solid knowledge accumulation, rather than government or EU order, will encourage new generations of students and academics to think that the WCHE manifesto is crucial in an interdependent world.

NOTES

1   Israel is in the Western Europe group (see Table II.5.1), but is not part of any of the international organizations with a predominantly European focus. This is not to say that contacts with individual universities of Europe do not exist. However, Israel is at the margins of a number of the policy issues discussed here.
2   See the European Commission website: http://ec.europa.eu/ education/policies/educ/html.
3   The OECD has not been included since, although it has been active on some issues relevant to higher education, such as

the development of performance indicators, it has been relatively inactive in the last decade on WCHE issues.
4   Statistics derived from *UIS Global Education Digest 2006*, Table 8 (enrolments).
5   The press reported a British Council survey claiming that in the UK higher education export earnings, at £28 billion, were worth more than those of financial services (£19 billion) or the automotive industry (£20 billion) (*Guardian*, 18 September 2007).
6   In 2006, hostility to globalization and the management of it by the French and Dutch governments defeated the aim of European leaders to create a constitution for the EU.

REFERENCES AND BIBLIOGRAPHY

Bologna Follow-up Group (2007). Berlin, 17–18 April. http://www.ond.vlaanderen.be/hogeronderwijs/bologna/.

Brennan, J. (2002) Transformation or reproduction? Contradictions in the social role of the contemporary university. In: Enders, J. and Fulton, O. (eds). *Higher Education in a Globalizing World. International Trends and Mutual Observations: A Festschrift in Honour of Ulrich Teichler*. Dordrecht: Kluwer.

Corbett, A. (2005) *Universities and the Europe of Knowledge: Ideas, Institutions and Policy Entrepreneurship in European Union Higher Education, 1955–2005*. Basingstoke: Palgrave Macmillan.

Council of Europe Parliamentary Assembly (2006) Academic freedom and university autonomy. Committee on Culture, Science and Education. Rapporteur Josef Jarab. Strasbourg: Council of Europe.

Council of Europe Parliamentary Assembly (2006) Academic freedom and university autonomy. Recommendation 1962 (2006) Strasbourg: Council of Europe.

Crosier, D., Purser, L. and Smidt, H. (2007) *Trends V: Universities Shaping the European Higher Education Area*. Brussels: European University Association.

Enders, J. and Fulton, O. (2002) (eds) *Higher Education in a Globalising World. International Trends and Mutual Observations. A Festschrift in Honour of Ulrich Teichler*. Dordrecht: Kluwer.

European Commission (2005) *Mobilising the Brainpower of Europe: Enabling Universities to Make Their Full Contribution to the Lisbon Strategy*. COM (2005) 152 final.

European Commission (2005) *Working together for growth and jobs: a new start for the Lisbon strategy*. Communication.

European Commission (2005) *The European Charter for Researchers: the code of conduct for the recruitment of researchers*. Brussels: Directorate-General for Research, Human Resources and Mobility.

European Commission (2006a) *Efficiency and Equity in European Education and Training Systems*. Communication from the Commission to the Council and the European Parliament.

European Commission (2006b) *Delivering on the Modernisation Agenda for Universities: Education, Research and Innovation*. COM(2006)208. Brussels.

European Commission (2006c) *Developing a Knowledge Flagship: the European Institute of Technology*. Communication from the Commission to the Council.

European Commission (2006d) *Education and Training 2010: Diverse Systems, Shared Goals – the Education and Training Contribution to the Lisbon Strategy*. Brussels.

European Commission (2007) *From Bergen to London: The Contribution of the European Commission to the Bologna Process.* Brussels.

European Council (2000) *Presidency Conclusions from the European Lisbon Council.* Lisbon, 23–24 March.

Council of Europe (2006) *Academic freedom and university autonomy.* Recommendation 1762(2006) from the Parliamentary Assembly.

European Ministers Responsible for Higher Education (1999) The Bologna Declaration of 19 June 1999, Joint Declaration of European Ministers of Education. Bologna.

European Ministers Responsible for Higher Education (2001) *Towards the European Higher Education Area.* Communiqué of the meeting of European Ministers in Charge of Higher Education. Prague, 19 May.

European Ministers Responsible for Higher Education (2003) *Realising the European Higher Education Area.* Berlin, 19 September.

European Ministers Responsible for Higher Education (2005) *The European Higher Education Area – Achieving the Goals.* Bergen.

European Ministers Responsible for Higher Education (2007) *Towards the European Higher Education Area: Responding to the Challenges in a Globalised World.* London, 18 May.

Gibbons, M. (1998) A Commonwealth perspective on the globalisation of higher education. In: Scott, P. (ed.) *The Globalisation of Higher Education.* Buckingham: Society for Research into Higher Education and Open University Press.

Gibbons, M., Limoges, C., Nowotny, H., Schwartman, S., Scott, P. and Trow, M. (1994) *The New Production of Knowledge.* London: Kogan Page.

Giddens, A. (2007) *Europe in the Global Age.* Cambridge: Polity.

Gornitzka, A., Maassen, P., Olsen, P. and Stensaker, B. (2007) 'Europe of Knowledge': Search for a new pact. In: Maassen, P. and Olsen, J.P. (eds) *University Dynamics and European Integration.* Dordrecht: Springer.

Kwiek, M. (2006) Emergent European educational policies under scrutiny: the Bologna Process from a Central European perspective. In: Tomusk, V. (ed.) *Creating the European Area of Higher Education: Voices from the Periphery.* Dordrecht: Springer.

Liddle, R. and Lérais, F. (2007) *Europe's Social Reality.* A consultation paper from the Bureau of European Policy Advisers. Brussels: European Commission.

Magna Charta Observatory (1988) *Magna Charta Universitatum.* Bologna: Bologna University.

March, J. and Olsen, J.P. (1989) *Rediscovering Institutions: the Organisational Basis of Politics.* New York: Free Press.

Olsen, J. and Maassen, P. (2007) European debates on the knowledge institution: The modernisation of the university at European level. In: Maassen, P. and Olsen, J. (eds) *University Dynamics and European Integration.* Dordrecht: Springer.

Olsen, J. (2007) The institutional dynamics of the European university. In: Maassen, P. and Olsen, J. *University Dynamics and European Integration.* Dordrecht: Springer.

Reichert, S. and Tauch, C. (2003) *Trends III: Progress Towards the European Higher Education Area.* Brussels: European University Association.

Reinalda, B. and Kulesza, E. (2005) *The Bologna Process: Harmonizing Europe's Higher Education.* Barbara Budrick Publishers.

Rodrigues, M.-J. (2002) (ed.) *The New Knowledge Economy in Europe, a Strategy for International Competitiveness and Social Cohesion.* Cheltenham: Edward Elgar.

Rodriguez-Posé, A. and Vilalta-Bufi, M. (2005) Education, migration and job satisfaction: the regional returns of human capital in the EU. *Journal of Economic Geography* **5**(5): 545–66.

Sadlak, J. (2003) *Report on Trends and Developments in Higher Education in Europe in the Context of the WCHE +5 (1998–2003).* Paris: European Centre for Higher Education (UNESCO-CEPES)

Scott, P., (1998) (ed.) *The Globalisation of Higher Education.* Buckingham: Open University Press for Society for Research in Higher Education.

Tomusk, V. (2006) (ed.) *Creating the European Area of Higher Education.* Dordrecht: Springer.

United Nations Development Programme (UNDP) www.undp.org

Wolf, M. (2005) *Why Globalisation Works: the Case for the Global Market Economy.* New Haven: Yale University Press.

World Conference on Higher Education (1998) World Declaration on Higher Education for the Twenty-first Century: Vision and Action and Framework for Priority Action for Change and Development in Higher Education. Paris: UNESCO.

Zgaga, P. (2006) *Looking Out: The Bologna Process in a Global Setting: On the 'External Dimension' of the Bologna Process.* Oslo: Norwegian Ministry of Education and Research.

Higher education for human and social development in Portugal[1]

António Fragoso

INTRODUCTION

Higher education (HE) in Portugal is currently being reformed due to multidimensional factors that will bring about major changes in the short term. It is important to analyse these ongoing changes in order to understand what is likely to happen to the Portuguese HE system. The specific forms that higher education institutions (HEIs) take to deal with these hurried changes will determine the potentialities and limitations of their activities in the area of human and social development.

THE CURRENT SITUATION

In 2006/07[1] there were 152 HEIs in Portugal, unevenly distributed between public (56) and private (96) institutions. However, student numbers clearly show that private HEIs do not dominate in Portugal. Out of a total of 366,729 students (46% men and 54% women) studying HE in academic year 2006–2007 in Portugal, 275,321 (75%) are registered in public HEIs, whereas only 91,408 (25%) are enrolled in private HEIs. If we analyse trends since 1997, the number of students in public HEIs has increased whilst the number in private HEIs has decreased.

The percentage of students who finish their degrees is 65% in public HEIs and 68% in private HEIs. The student/teacher ratio in public HEIs in 2005 was 13.2 (one teacher for each 13 students). However, this ratio will increase rapidly, due to financial cuts. In 2007, the total amount of money that public HEIs received from the state budget (€295,233,492) covered 71% of their total expenses (€414,465,316). The political situation leads us to forecast that this percentage will be lower in years to come.

Public provision for HE has been decreasing over the years, and the 2006 cut was a dramatic one. This is clearly coherent with the hegemonic vision of a shrinking, non-providing, neo-liberal state, which desperately tries to lower public expenses to adjust its finances.

HEIs have been unable to increase their income by the same proportion as their losses, and their main solution for survival has been to reduce staff numbers.

Past mistakes have led to a situation that is equally unsustainable. In fact, the 1980s marked a sudden increase in new HEIs in Portugal for two reasons: the pressure to democratize HE and produce qualified professionals to feed the labour market; and the neo-liberal trend in education, which has created an incredible number of private HEIs. Both have led to a staggered HE system that benefits no one. In response, the opposite trend has appeared: an eagerness to excessively control both the number and the nature of professional profiles, which will shrink the Portuguese HE system and force peripheral HEIs to merge or work in networks to survive.

The contribution of HE to social and human development in this scenario is ambiguous. Our system is clearly not effective and reforms are needed. However, a certain lack of central control has allowed interesting and essential practices to develop.

In 2007, legislation will be announced to reform HE in accordance with OCED recommendations.

THE ECONOMY TAKES OVER

The main trends for HE and HEIs in Portugal can be summarized as follows:

- Hegemonic economic and political paradigms are shaping HE and clearly pushing HEIs towards roles that have to be fully assumed, as their survival depends on them.
- New models of professional management of universities will appear in the near future. These will eliminate the huge amount of time that teachers spend on management tasks, liberating them for research or community services. However, there is the risk that management will control the scientific priorities of HEIs.

- There is growing pressure for HEIs to focus on training professionals to feed the labour market more efficiently, to coordinate with companies and to give priority to technologies.
- There is growing pressure to reduce costs and increase income, leading to the perception that every project in HEIs should be profitable. The value given to activities is proportional to the institutional income they produce.

THE CRITICAL CONCEPT OF HUMAN AND SOCIAL DEVELOPMENT

The aforementioned trends are promoting the emergence of a certain version of human and social development in HEIs, based on the following assumptions:

1. HEIs promote regional and national economic growth by supplying well-trained professionals to the labour market.
2. HEIs promote regional and national economic growth by contributing to the hegemonic paradigms that insist on public disinvestment and on placing management at the top of their priorities.
3. HEIs promote regional and national economic growth while shaping their main scientific areas of action (like technology) according to the market needs.

I have no doubt that these premises are correct. However, I strongly oppose a cause–effect correlation between them and the path to human and social development. The oldest mistake of all is confounding economic growth with development.

Planned development over the past 50 years has involved a number of paradigms (modernization, dependency, neo-liberalism and so on). However, the initial dreams of peace and prosperity for all have been transformed into a nightmare (Escobar, 1995) that includes new forms of poverty, ecological degradation and violence, which is especially serious in the most unprotected societal groups (women, children and elderly people). The growing speed of globalization has reduced the power of the nation-state, as new forms of regulation and control do not apply within the geographic borders of nations. The multiplicity of social circles and relations, communication networks or market relations – none of which are rooted in a determined space (Beck, 2000) – are gradually annihilating space. This has had serious impacts on local communities, where space is still an important locus for norms and value building (Bauman, 1998), and has created new sources of inequalities.

For some, the biggest problem with development is development itself. Nevertheless, none of the development paradigms represent the end of history, not even neo-liberalism. In addition, despite all the difficulties, countries still have space to manoeuvre and make policy (Griffin, 1999). The development I believe in lies in the concepts of human development and in the search for radical alternatives. Such alternatives should be focused on people's emancipation but within the hegemonic paradigms. In the 1990s, we learned from experiences that pointed towards new forms of participative democracy, such as the participative budget in Porto Alegre (Santos, 2003), and the participative democracy in Kerala (Heller and Isaac, 2003). These forms of democracy are now spreading all over the world, and HEIs have a role to play in this context.

HEI STRATEGIES FOR ACHIEVING HUMAN AND SOCIAL DEVELOPMENT

- The mainstream culture of HEIs is increasingly characterized by their contributions to economic growth and their role in training competent professionals, in accordance with changing market needs. If HEIs passively agree to be positioned in society with this type of reduced role, their ability to guide (or even to follow) social and human development will be increasingly weakened.
- The future management changes in Portuguese HEIs could be positive if they result in a more balanced workload. Thus, teachers would have more time for research and for engaging in community action.
- HEI must not abandon community projects and experiences simply because profits may be hard or impossible to obtain. HEIs should assume responsibilities for social change that is targeted at the more deprived communities and their interests.
- In HEI development, projects are sometimes exclusively related to the 'expertise' of HEI staff. Experts in this context are mainly consultants that civil society organizations (CSOs) use within a very narrow scope. This detachment, rather than engagement, reduces the number of HEI responsibilities. Therefore, experts should work closely with CSOs. They should become radical and reflexive partners committed to social change that is linked to the characteristics of regional and national contexts rather than the particular interests of either HEIs or CSOs.
- Methodologies used in development projects should highlight the growing autonomy of the social actors involved. Innovative knowledge should be transferred to people and priority should be given to sustained activities that can solve problems in communities. Participatory research, for instance, as defined by Hall (1997) or Tandon (1988), could be implemented.

The Portuguese HE system will face major changes in coming years, which will question the capacity of HEIs for reform. Although the challenges that lie before us seem hard, it is time to decide whether our values are strong enough to fight back: to creatively rebuild structures so that human and social development can be promoted to benefit the Portuguese population.

REFERENCES

Bauman, Z. (1998) *Globalisation. The human consequences.* Cambridge: Polity Press.

Beck, U. (2000) *What is Globalization?* Cambridge: Polity Press.

Escobar, A. (1995) *Encountering Development. The Making and Unmaking of the Third World.* New Jersey: Princeton University Press.

Griffin, K. (1999) *Alternative Strategies for Economic Development.* London: Macmillan – now Palgrave Macmillan.

Hall, B.L. (1997) Participatory research. In: John P. Keeves (ed.) *Educational Research, Methodology, and Measurement: An International Handbook* (pp. 198–204). Cambridge: Pergamon.

Heller, P., and Isaac, T. (2003) O perfil político e institucional da democracia participativa: lições de Kerala, Índia. In: Boaventura de Sousa Santos (org.), *Democratizar a Democracia: Os Caminhos da Democracia Participativa* (pp. 499–535). Porto: Edições Afrontamento.

Santos, B. de S. (2003) Orçamento participativo em Porto Alegre: para uma democracia redistributiva. In: Boaventura de Sousa Santos (org.), *Democratizar a Democracia: Os Caminhos da Democracia Participativa* (pp. 377–465). Porto: Edições Afrontamento.

Tandon, R. (1988) Social transformation and participatory research, *Convergence*, **XXI**(2/3), pp. 5–18.

NOTE

1   All the statistics presented in this paper came from the Observatory of Science and Higher Education, http://www.estatisticas.gpeari.mctes.pt/

The National System of Recognition, Validation and Certification of Competences: a description of the Lagoa centre (University of the Algarve, Portugal)

António Fragoso

CONTEXT

A series of statistics and research has focused on the level of qualifications of the Portuguese workforce. As Duarte (2004) clearly states, the 2004 forecasts for Portugal show that a high percentage of the population has low qualifications (68.4%). The forecasts also reveal that Portugal has the lowest capacity for recovery of all European countries. According to the National Institute of Statistics, in 2000 more than three million active adults had not completed their nine years of basic schooling.

In 2001, a national system of Recognition, Validation and Certification of Competences (RVCC) was created for adults in Portugal. The main assumption of this system was that a high number of adults were quite competent at their jobs, but did not have formal diplomas. The main source of their learning was therefore not school education, but a multitude of informal contexts and experiences. The idea was that this experiential learning could be certified.

The main instrument of the RVCC process is a national framework of key competences. These competences are divided into four areas: language and communication; mathematics for life; citizenship and employability; and information and communication technologies. Adults who wish to have their competences certified can register in one of the centres that have gradually been established for this purpose in Portugal. With the help of pedagogical teams, people are able to demonstrate that they have the competences stated in the framework.

DESCRIPTION

In 2005, the University of the Algarve was allowed to open an RVCC centre. Until the end of 2006, this university was the only higher education institution (HEI) that had an RVCC centre. The main stages of the RVCC process in our centre are:

1. *Recognition*

This involves identifying the competences that individuals have acquired throughout their lives in different contexts, for example social, family, workplace learning and so on.

An RVCC professional conducts two biographical interviews with each adult to form a first impression of her/his life path and to ascertain whether other types of educational paths are more suited to the adult's present situation. Adults are then divided into small groups. Over the following six weeks, they participate in working sessions, in which they share their life experiences. They try to understand the types of life situations that could demonstrate the particular competences they might have. Some of these sessions are thematically oriented, according to the framework of key competences. After this period, our team has a clearer view of each individual. This enables the team to negotiate with each adult, in order to decide which level they want to reach and what training they need to achieve their goals.

2. *Validation*

Training is essential to this phase. It is conducted either by the centre's trainers or by other external programmes, if necessary. This training enables adults to build up a portfolio that contains the evidence of their competences. Since experiential learning is central to this process, the portfolios vary in structure and, more particularly, in their content. The logical end of the process is validation by a jury that assesses the adults' portfolios. An external evaluator sits on the jury.

3. *Certification*

This is the official confirmation of the validation. Adults receive a formal diploma. When the process has been completed, adults have guided working sessions in which our team helps them with their future projects. Such projects may range from continuing their studies to starting a new micro-enterprise.

OBJECTIVES

- To certify experiential learning by means of formal educational diplomas.
- To give adults a second opportunity to enter the world of education and training.
- To increase the academic level of the Portuguese population.

APPLICATION

- The RVCC process has been applied in Portugal from 2001.

RESULTS

The RVCC process targets the most deprived communities, where it has been shown to be effective in many ways. The majority of people who go through this process undergo clearly visible transformations. They usually enter the centre with extremely low levels of self-confidence and self-esteem, convinced that their professions are worthless and that their social significance is null. They are not used to being listened to or to being the centre of attention. Biographical approaches are partially responsible for the transformations. Adults review their lives by looking at events or phenomena with the help of professionals who show them their value. Gradually, they discover new meanings and values that give them a sense of worthiness.

A number of professions have very low social value. However, in the RVCC process, every profession involves some competences. The surprise that some people feel on discovering this simple fact is also helpful in the 'conscientization' (Freire, 1987) processes that form part of all the activities in the centre.

Some adults report immediate advantages on finishing the RVCC process (for instance, a better salary). Most adults who finish the RVCC process continue with their studies, search for training in very different areas, and come back to the centre to seek information and personalized help.

RECOMMENDATIONS

Until 2006, there was a network of 90 RVCC centres in Portugal. Many of these centres were run by civil society organizations that had done prior work in adult education and informal education in particular. This network has earned a strong reputation. It bases its work on the fundamental principles and values of adult education.

The new Portuguese government had concerns about the low levels of qualifications held by the active Portuguese population. Therefore, it decided to rapidly increase the size of the network. In less than a year, more than 170 new centres were opened, mainly in secondary schools. This has turned a stable network into a very confusing one, in which it is impossible to control pedagogical methodologies. Although we have no room to put forward an argument, the RVCC system is now in a very precarious situation. It risks being transformed into a certification factory, where diplomas are handed out sim-

ply because Portugal needs to change its statistics. And certification does not necessarily mean qualification.

REFERENCES

Duarte, I. M. (2004) The value of experiential learning in the centres of Recognition, Validation and Certification of Competences. In: Licínio Lima and Paula Guimarães (eds) *Perspectives of Adult Education in Portugal*. Braga: University of Minho.

Freire, P. (1987) *Acção Cultural para a Liberdade*. São Paulo: Editora Paz e Terra.

GOOD PRACTICE II.5

The Dutch National Network for Sustainable Development in Higher Education Curricula (Netherlands)

GUNI Observatory[1]

BACKGROUND

In 1987 the concept of sustainable development was introduced by the World Commission on Environment and Development (the WCED) in the Brundtland Report, *Our Common Future*. The Report defines sustainable development as:

> Development that meets the needs of the present without compromising the ability of future generations to meet their own needs.

In 1992 the United Nations Conference on Environment and Development (UNCED), known as the 'Earth Summit', brought together representatives from 179 governments in Rio de Janeiro, Brazil. At this conference, the main sustainability and natural resources conservation issues were considered. In addition, an action plan was drawn up for a global sustainable future. This plan has specific objectives and is called Agenda 21. Agenda 21 recognizes that the participation of all social agents is essential to sustainable development.

Chapter 36 states that education is fundamental to achieving sustainable development. This means that universities, NGOs, governments and companies

need to establish partnerships and develop new methods and strategies that enable them to share knowledge and engage in common activities. This has led to the creation of several higher education initiatives to achieve these objectives. One notable initiative involves the work of the Dutch National Network for Sustainable Development in Higher Education Curricula (DHO).

OBJECTIVES

Within the framework of higher education, the DHO aims to create opportunities, as well as innovative learning environments and methodologies, to enable individuals to develop sustainable development skills. Specifically, the DHO aims to boost such opportunities for all students in higher education institutions (HEIs) in the Netherlands.

Thus, students can acquire the following:

- New insight about the concept of sustainable development
- New insight about what their discipline can contribute to sustainable development

- Skills for working with representatives from other disciplines
- Skills for developing strategies to work on sustainable development in their future professional careers.

DESCRIPTION

The DHO was created in 1998. It is an independent, government-funded foundation. Currently, active Network participants include over a thousand HEI lecturers and managers as well as key representatives of NGOs, companies and governments. In addition to members in the Netherlands, the DHO has international partners in the North and the South. The institution's annual budget is approximately US$800,000.

Most of the working groups are coordinated by the Expertise Centre for Sustainable Development (ECDO) at the University of Amsterdam. The ECDO also coordinates communication between the different DHO organizations and acts as an information clearing house.

The DHO has six main projects:

1. North–South student projects
2. Motivating experts

3. Auditing Instrument for Sustainability in Higher Education (AISHE)
4. Charter for sustainable development in vocational training
5. Interdisciplinary education
6. Past, present and future.

PROCESS

1. *North–South student projects on sustainable development in Asia, Africa and Latin America*

   The North–South project was created in January 2001. The idea was that students need both practical experience and theoretical knowledge to gain the aforementioned skills. Thus, students form part of an interdisciplinary and intercultural team that researches sustainable development in Africa, Asia or Latin America, in collaboration with a local organization and a local university.

2. *Motivating experts*

   The best way to motivate lecturers and researchers is to refer to their field of specialization and present sustainable development as an intellectual challenge within that field. Thus, lecturers in specific disciplines were invited to write a review describing the challenges of incorporating sustainable development into teaching practice in their field. The review also had to contain recommendations for improving education. Once the reviews had been written, seminars were organized for lecturers from the same university and from other universities. The reviews were presented in these seminars and the recommendations were discussed.

3. *Auditing Instrument for Sustainability in Higher Education (AISHE)*

   Although many universities want sustainable development to be part of education, they often do not know how to integrate it into their courses. Thus, AISHE audits are used to assess syllabuses and to identify at least 20 targets that will help to introduce the topic of sustainable development. A second audit of a syllabus is recommended

after one or two years, to assess the results and design the next steps.

The AISHE team also offers other services. These include organizing sessions on the basic principles of sustainable development before the first AISHE audit. After the audit, the AISHE team can offer additional instruments that help to implement the plan.

4. *Charter for sustainable development in vocational training*

   The objectives of the charter for sustainable development in vocational training are:

   - To improve the way in which universities deal with and promote the concept of sustainable development in their operations and educational activities
   - To increase involvement in and financial aid for the charter for sustainable development in vocational training
   - To increase the number of joint projects involving vocational training institutes, companies and scientific research institutions
     To improve and increase cooperation between vocational training schools and universities.

5. *Interdisciplinary education*

   The project offers master's students the opportunity to participate in an interdisciplinary research programme related to sustainable development. This research project is situated in a real-life setting. The aim is to train students in the skills needed to work on complex problems. Therefore, the project needs the involvement of different social agents and individuals from different disciplines.

   The educational model is developed by the participating lecturers. The research team is made up of students from different disciplines and different HEIs. A basic document is drawn up that contains general information pertaining to the case. The students use this document to formu-

late their own research proposal, with the consensus of the other participating students. The lecturer's role is to provide support for the research team.

The students should persuade several relevant agents to participate in the research activities. Such agents may include companies, citizen organizations, NGOs and national or regional governments. During the project, the students identify possible conflicts of interests and values that might emerge when working on sustainable development in a real-life situation. All the participating agents are invited to a final presentation and their comments on the report are taken into account in the students' final assessments.

6. *Past, present and future*

   This project group was established in 2002 to work on education in sustainable development with a view to the future.
   The aims of the project are to:

   - Define the relationship between sustainable development and plans for the future
   - Devise possible courses for the future
   - Link cognitive and creative areas
   - Offer the best methods and the best practices
   - Encourage and help DHO Network members to implement educational methods for the future
   - Exchange methods and reports with national and international partners.

RESULTS

1. *North–South student projects on sustainable development in Asia, Africa and Latin America*

   In general, students and other participating agents have found the North–South initiative rewarding. This experience revealed that students learn more effectively in intercultural settings if there is a balance between the abilities and ages of the participants. However, these practices are still very new. The experience gained after two years of interdisciplinary and intercultural projects could be used to improve the method and devise similar projects with interested parties.

2. *Motivating experts*
Many individuals were involved in the seminars and in the process of writing the disciplinary reviews. Meetings with specialist colleagues from other institutions often provide the basis for the reviews. In addition to the documents produced, the master classes that were given as part of this project were of great strategic value.

3. *Action Plan*
The experiences gained led to a series of recommendations that have been incorporated into the Action Plan for the Motivation of Experts. This Action Plan is a practical method for institutions and lecturers who want to work on incorporating the concept of sustainable development into education by means of disciplinary reviews.

4. *Auditing Instrument for Sustainability in Higher Education (AISHE)*
Some of the quantitative results are as follows:

- Over 100 AISHE assessments were carried out between 2002 and 2006
- By the end of 2006, approximately 40 certificates had been awarded in the Netherlands and in Belgium.

5. *The charter for sustainable development in vocational training*
This has been signed by 170 departments of 31 different higher education schools and by the Ministry of Agriculture, Nature and Food Quality; the Ministry of Education, Culture and Science; the Ministry of Housing, Spatial Planning and the Environment; the Ministry of Finance; and the Council of Vocational Training Schools.

Every six years, the vocational training schools need to be recognized by private accreditation organizations. In addition to this kind of recognition, the schools can opt for a special quality mark. Recently, sustainable development has become one of these quality marks. The DHO and the five accreditation organizations operating in the Netherlands have agreed that a vocational training school or a university awarded two stars for the quality of sustainable development in higher education can also use the special quality mark in sustainable development.

6. *Interdisciplinary education*
The results to date show that this educational model is an excellent method for students to learn about sustainable development. However, this project does not only benefit the students. In addition, recommendations for real improvements emerge that can be applied in society. It is highly rewarding to motivate, involve and educate students in sustainable development so that they can use this experience in their future roles in society.

RECOMMENDATIONS

The following factors are important when one is developing a project with these characteristics:

- Cooperation between universities
- The involvement of ministries and the private sector.

The formation of networks like the DHO in other countries or regions is advisable, as this represents another step towards attaining sustainable human development.

NOTE

1   Text written by the Universities and Social Commitment Observatory with information provided by Niko Roorda.

Abstract

Higher education in Canada and the USA responds to and is part of the powerful tides of globalization, which, as the saying goes, 'do not float all boats'. Globalization has created new forms of global markets. Knowledge flows instantly throughout the world in wired and unwired ways. But profoundly disturbing gaps between the rich and the poor increase, unsustainable energy uses are proliferating, particularly in North America, and the proportion of national resources devoted to military expenditure and security in the USA is troubling. At the same time, one of the most creative and transformative innovations ever seen in higher education circles is emerging from this contradictory region of the world. The tensions between market forces as the drivers of higher education and its perception as a public good are dramatically evident in this region of the world. Given that 25% of all international students in the world study in the USA, what happens with higher education here ripples throughout the world. Our review draws particular attention to current contexts, challenges of globalization, the role of higher education in addressing human and social concerns, civic engagement, community-based research, the 'greening of universities' and suggestions for new directions for the future.

INTRODUCTION

North America, for purposes of this study, consists of Canada and the USA. Within UNESCO regional groupings, these two countries are linked by the European region. In many ways, a North American overview of higher education is difficult given the differences in scale and jurisdictional traditions in the two countries. Canada claims over one million university students in what the Association of Universities and Colleges of Canada (AUCC) claims as 93 institutions. The vast majority of Canadian universities are public institutions supported by provincial governments. They collectively spend US$9 billion per year on research. In contrast, there are about 4200 universities in the USA (with a significant percent-

II.6
THE ROLE OF HIGHER EDUCATION FOR HUMAN AND SOCIAL DEVELOPMENT IN THE USA AND CANADA

Budd L. Hall and Cornelia Dragne

age of private universities) with some 18 million students, accounting for over US$30 billion in research.

It is estimated, for example, that there are nearly 600 for-profit higher education institutions (HFIs) in the USA. The University of Phoenix is the largest, with 100,000 full-time students, and it grows by 20% per year. In addition, there are now an estimated 6000 'corporate universities' or in-house training and educational facilities run directly by companies. The Humboldtian idea of the research university accounts for about 125 universities in the USA and as few as 20 in Canada.

HIGHER EDUCATION IN CANADA AND THE USA TEN YEARS AFTER THE 1998 REGIONAL MEETING HELD IN TORONTO IN PREPARATION FOR THE UNESCO WORLD CONFERENCE ON HIGHER EDUCATION (WCHE)

OVERVIEW OF HIGHER EDUCATION IN CANADA AND THE USA

Canada is a confederation of ten provinces and three territories stretching across North America, from the Atlantic Ocean to the Pacific Ocean and north to the Arctic Ocean, with a population estimate of approximately 32 million (Statistics Canada, 2007). The country has two major linguistic groups and two official languages – English and French. English is the primary language for approximately three-quarters of the population, while French is the primary language for the remainder. Most French speakers (Francophones) live in the province of Quebec, where they form a majority. Another major factor that contributes to cultural diversity is immigration. In 2001, 18.4% of the total population was born outside the country. The immigration programme is coupled with a national policy of multiculturalism, which encourages the development of educational programmes that reflect the country's cultural diversity. Minority language education is guaranteed wherever numbers warrant (Council of Ministers of Education, 2006).

Higher education (HE) in Canada dates

from 1663 with the establishment of Le Grand Séminaire de Québec, a forerunner to Laval University. At the time the Confederation of Canadian Provinces was formed in 1867, there were 18 universities across Canada. Early in the 20th century, the newly formed four Western provinces began to set up provincially chartered universities, but most of them came onto the scene in the 1960s. In Canada, the provinces and territories are responsible for elementary, secondary and post-secondary education (PSE). As a result, Canada has no national or federal department of education. Although primary responsibility for education rests with the provinces and territories, in PSE the Government of Canada plays an important support role through fiscal transfers to the provinces and by funding university research and student assistance.

The US higher education system started to emerge around 1636, with the establishment of Harvard College, followed by what are now known as the 'colonial colleges' – nine institutions were chartered before the American Revolution. From its very beginnings, the system has been shaped by the emerging values of the North American society: social and physical mobility and high adaptability to changing social and economic needs. In order to ease and encourage the transfer between institutions, the US higher education authorities invented the course and credit hour system in the 1890s. At the beginning of the post-Second-World-War era, the USA claimed a well-developed system of higher education, with around 1.5 million students enrolled on approximately 1700 campuses, some of which rivalled the best older European universities. Overall, they were elitist, male, white and relatively aloof from society. Education matters were reserved to the states by the US Constitution whereby the federal government had more of a data-gathering role. However, in the late 1950s federal support for university research started to increase, and in 1965 and 1972 federal higher education acts created a system of student financial aid directed towards students in order to increase access and promote competitiveness between institutions (Marchese, 1997). Since the war, the USA has greatly expanded its participation in its HE system by a stunning factor of more than ten. In the 1960s, the US higher education system underwent intense expansion and development in order to accommodate the 'baby boom' generation born in the aftermath of the Second World War. As a result, college enrolment jumped from 3.6 to 8 million students. Today, the US higher education system enrols around 18 million students. While provincial governments in Canada were mainly involved in increasing the demand for PSE, in the USA the market played a greater role. Thanks to the proliferation of information technologies (IT), more than 90% of US institutions with more than 10,000 students now offer courses online, and 'virtual' universities now exist (Marchese, 1997).

STRUCTURE

In Canada, there are four types of post-secondary degree-granting institutions: universities, university-colleges, Cégeps and community colleges. Universities offer bachelor's degrees, master's degrees and doctorates. University-college is a nomenclature used to differentiate this type of institution from the community college. University-colleges offer both degree programmes and college diplomas and certificates. In Alberta, they operate at the level of university studies and are accredited by the Private Colleges Accreditation Board. According to data from 2006, there are 121 degree-granting institutions in Canada: 73 public institutions and 48 private, not-for-profit institutions (Canadian Association of University Teachers (CAUT), 2007). Cégep stands for Collèges d'Enseignement Général et Professionnel (College of General and Vocational Education) and is a two- to three-year general or technical education that Quebec offers between high school and university; it provides education and training programmes directly related to the workplace. The 175 Canadian community-colleges offer diplomas for vocationally oriented programmes.

During the 1997–2007 decade, some public colleges were given applied degree-granting authority by their provincial governments and a small number of private institutions also obtained permission to offer degree programmes. IT increasingly blended with more traditional delivery mechanisms. As internet access became ubiquitous in Canada, e-learning replaced mail-based distance learning and became the de facto form of delivery in distance education and distributed learning. In addition to the distance education programmes offered by conventional universities, three Canadian provinces – British Columbia, Alberta and Quebec – each developed an 'open university', whose programmes are designed to help students pursue a university degree in a format, place and time frame that accommodate people employed in the workforce. According to 2005 Carnegie Classification data, the USA has a total of 4,388 institutions that offer graduate and undergraduate degrees (1734 public and 2654 private) (Carnegie Foundation, 2006).

FINANCE AND MANAGEMENT

Although there is no pan-Canadian accreditation body, the AUCC is generally deemed the equivalent. The AUCC was formed in 1911 and now comprises 93 public and private not-for-profit universities and university-degree level colleges (AUCC, 2007a).

In the USA, state support for public colleges and universities began to decline nationwide in 1978. During the past decade, this has continued, and the decline in state appropriations has reached 40%. Between 2001 and 2004, state appropriations per student declined by US$650. The causes may be found in economic recession, but also in the fact that the federal government has transferred partial or full responsibility for many programmes to the state and local level. This shift in philosophy, known as 'new federalism', has resulted in a significant squeeze in higher education appropriations for most states. The budget shortfall has been picked up by rising tuition fees and by private support, with fundraising becoming an increasingly important activity for US colleges and universities (Weerts and Ronca, 2006).

In Canada, while the actual figures of provincial expenditures on PSE might have increased in some provinces over the past decade, as a share of the provincial gross domestic product (GDP) they decreased, with the notable exception of Saskatchewan. Provincial funding for full-time equivalent (FTE) student enrolment increased by 2% in British Columbia (BC) and by 24% in Saskatchewan and decreased by between 1% and 60% in the rest of the country (CAUT, 2007).

ACCESS AND PARTICIPATION

Canada and the USA have one of the highest PSE participation rates in the world. In 2004–2005, more than 1.2 million Canadians were enrolled in full-time or part-time post-secondary programmes at universities and colleges. Among those, 830,556 were full-time university students (CAUT, 2007). According to the National Center for Education Statistics (NCES, 2007), the HE system in the USA enrolled approximately 18 million students in autumn 2005 at some 6500 PSE institutions, around 4200 of which were universities. The majority of students (61%) were enrolled at four-year institutions, while the rest were enrolled at two-year or less-than-two-year institutions.

According to UNESCO Institute for Statistics data from 2005, Canada's educational attainment indicator (highest level of education attained by population aged 25 to 64) for the tertiary education and advanced research programmes is 22, while the US indicator is 29, the world mean is 9.6 and the OECD mean is 16 (UNESCO Institute for Statistics, 2007). In Canada this translates to approximately 39% of the above age group having a post-secondary credential. In the USA, according to data from 2006, 36.7% of persons aged 25 and over hold a post-secondary degree and another 17% have some kind of college qualification (Snyder et al., 2007). For the 18–24 age group, the university participation rate increased continuously from 17.7% in 1996–1997 to 21.1% in 2004–2005 (CAUT, 2007).

In 2004, Canadian universities awarded an estimated

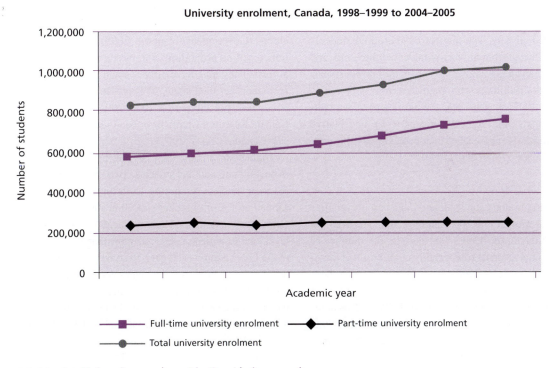

University enrolment, Canada, 1998–1999 to 2004–2005

FIGURE II.6.1 University enrolment in Canada increased

Source: Statistics Canada, 2007.

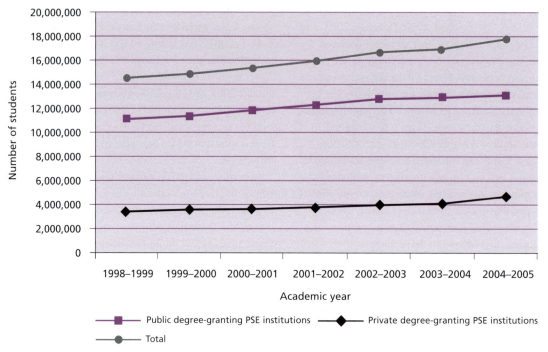

Post-secondary enrolment, USA, 1998–1999 to 2004–2005

FIGURE II.6.2 **Participation in post-secondary education in the USA increased**
Source: US Department of Education, 2006.

150,000 bachelor's degrees, 30,000 master's degrees and close to 4000 doctoral degrees (AUCC, 2007b). During the 1997–2007 decade, full-time university enrolment increased by almost a third, while part-time enrolment decreased slightly. The number of aboriginal students who graduated from university increased threefold, and there was an almost similar increase in the number of persons with disabilities who graduated from universities (CAUT, 2007). In the USA, the enrolment of African-Americans (7%), Asian-Americans (6%), and Native Americans (1%) approached their percentages in the general population (Marchese, 1997).

INTERNATIONALIZATION

In addition to domestic students, Canadian universities enrolled around 66,700 international students in 2004–2005. In the 1994–2004 decade, the number of international students rose steadily at all levels of education. At bachelor's degree level, international student enrolment for the decade soared from around 15,000 in 1994 to around 40,000 in 2004 (CAUT, 2007). This number represents approximately 7.4% of the total enrolments and this figure is on an upward trend. While each province implements its own strategy with regard to internationalization, what happens in Ontario (the most populated province, which alone accounts for 42% of full-time uni-

versity enrolment) serves as a model, and in Ontario the recent McGuinty Government Plan for Postsecondary Education specifies the goal to attract more international students and to encourage students from Ontario to study abroad (Government of Ontario, 2005). Due to immigration, a certain proportion of domestic students are born abroad. They may have either Canadian citizenship or permanent resident status. This is also true of the academic staff. For the period 2000–2005, around 30% of Canada Research Chairs have been recruited from outside Canada (CAUT, 2007).

Higher education in the USA now has a long tradition in hosting international students. Two thirds of these pay for their studies. According to Philip Altbach (2004), Monan professor of higher education and director of the Center for International Higher Education at Boston College, foreign students contribute more than US$12 billion to the US economy each year. In some graduate specialties, such as engineering, computer sciences and a few others, foreign students constitute the majority of students at the doctoral level (Altbach, 2004). Data from 2003 indicates that, with its 586,000 international students, the USA is currently by far the largest host country and home to more than a quarter of the world's foreign students. According to Altbach and to OECD data from 2003, the USA attracts more foreign students than its three largest competitors (UK, Germany and France) combined. Although it is the top attractor, as a percentage of all students enrolled on higher education programmes, foreign students in the USA constitute only 3.5%, much smaller than in the UK (10.9%) or in Germany (9.6%). The large majority of foreign students in the USA come from developing and newly industrialized countries, with 55% from Asia. The top five countries sending scholars to study in the USA are India, China, South Korea, Japan and Taiwan.

THE ROLE PLAYED BY THE USA AND CANADA IN THE 1998 UNESCO WORLD CONFERENCE ON HIGHER EDUCATION

The delegation consisted of Canadians from the government, non-governmental organizations (NGOs), HEIs, and associations representing a wide range of actors and decision-makers in the field. In his intervention, the Honourable Andrew Petter stressed that Canada feels that economic concerns should be balanced with civil and social concerns. He used as an illustration the value inherent in learning to live together, a value that a society based on immigration such as the Canadian society particularly cherishes.

The second speaker was the Honourable Pauline Marois, the Minister of Education for Quebec and Deputy Head of the Canadian delegation. Ms Marois (1998) stressed that the final declaration and the action plan should acknowledge that HE passes through a transitional phase due to ongoing transformations in technology and society. She also stressed the importance of:

- Adopting a lifelong learning approach
- Recognizing non-formal and non-traditional education
- Giving greater attention to the mobility of individuals and the dissemination of knowledge through IT
- Implementing a learner-centred approach, according to the vision of the Delors Report and the Hamburg Conference on Adult Education
- Promoting differentiation and diversity.

ACTIONS UNDERTAKEN IN THE NORTH AMERICAN REGION AS A RESPONSE TO THE RECOMMENDATIONS OF THE 1998 REGIONAL MEETING IN TORONTO

The meeting adopted clear guidelines in support of a humanist perspective of higher education, where ecolog-

ical, cultural and ethical dimensions of human and social development are given as much attention as the economic dimension. It reiterated the crucial role of HE in knowledge creation and dissemination and the increasing role of IT in HE. Knowledge is perceived as a new indicator of power in an increasingly information-based economy. The report of the meeting is explicit about the need for HE to make its research, teaching and decision-making more relevant to communities and to recognize the community sector as a partner in an atmosphere of mutual respect and credibility. It also calls for interdisciplinary approaches that would combine social and natural sciences in the search for ecological and sustainable solutions to development. The report recommends the creation of local expertise rather than taking advantage of the brain-drain phenomenon. The report also speaks about the need for diversifying forms of delivery, and the need to reach out to non-traditional and disadvantaged groups, with respect for different kinds of knowledge and different ways of knowing (Canadian Commission for UNESCO, 1998).

- In the USA, the Education for Innovation Initiative aims to double the number of science, technology, engineering and mathematics graduates with bachelor's degrees by 2015, rather than attract them from other areas (Business Roundtable, 2005)
- Some community-colleges in the USA and university-colleges in Canada were granted the right to award baccalaureate/bachelor's degrees
- There is increased access for underprivileged and non-traditional students, such as aboriginals, people with disabilities and minority groups
- Programmes are offered in minority languages such as French, Spanish and Inuit
- IT capabilities are used, with some universities collaborating to offer common programmes. An example is the Certificate in Adult and Continuing Education offered by four Canadian universities: the University of Victoria, the University of Alberta, the University of Saskatchewan and the University of Manitoba
- The National Science and Engineering Research Council (NSERC) instituted the Brockhouse Canada Prize for Interdisciplinary Research in Science and Engineering.

Box II.6.1 The knowledge to live together

A society can respect human rights, foster a culture of peace and function as a democracy by promoting education for a viable future only if its citizens have acquired the ability, and here we stress the importance of attitudes and skills as well as knowledge, for living in their local, national and global communities.

Source: Petter, 1998.

QUESTIONS RELATED TO THE IMPLICATIONS OF TECHNOLOGY FOR HIGHER EDUCATION IN THE REGION

STRUCTURAL AND OPERATING CHANGES ATTRIBUTABLE TO TECHNOLOGY

There are so many implications for technology in HE that the difficulty of our task is more to synthesize than to find them. Below we have selected several aspects which we consider constitute the most important changes induced by technology in the ways HEIs operate.

THE 'COMPRESSION' OF TIME AND SPACE

During the decade following the 1998 WCHE, computers with high-speed (broadband) internet/intranet connections became ubiquitous in North American HEIs. Over the past five years, the vast majority of North American campuses have developed wireless capabilities, which allow users to roam within the campus. Email, voice mail, instant messaging, and teleconferencing have become the way people communicate. Online conferences are not regarded as an innovation anymore. Today the standard computer services offered to a registered student in a North American university may be summarized as email, web hosting and research account.

ACCESS TO INFORMATION AND TRANSPARENCY

This aspect is perhaps the most important contribution of ICT to education and learning. The internet not only gives access to huge amounts of information and revolutionizes access to library resources, but also allows HEIs to make their activity public and more transparent. In North America at least, all recognized/accredited/licensed HEIs serving more than 10,000 students have a website that provides information about the institution. Likewise, it is the norm for academic staff to have web pages to offer professional contact details and information about their research interests and activities.

TOOLS FOR DEVELOPING AND TEACHING COURSES

Specialized web server platforms that provide online interactive environments for students and teachers – such as WebCT, Blackboard or WebBoard – became very popular among teaching staff in North America, not only for distance-learning courses but also for face-to-face instruction. The results of a survey of almost 1200 Canadian and 700 US faculties conducted in 2001 on technology and student success suggest that using IT to develop and manage courses is no longer innovative, but has become everyday practice (Hamilton, 2003).

NETWORKING

Another major implication of ICT is that it eases and enhances connectivity between people with common academic interests, regardless of physical location. Numerous research projects and publishing collaborations would be impossible without employing ICT. More or less formal networks create professional communities that are fertile terrains for the advancement of their field of study. In Canada, the federal government gave special attention to facilitating networking between people with similar research interests, and in 1997 established a permanent programme called the Networks of Centres of Excellence (NCE), whose mission is to bring together researchers and partners from the academic, private, public and non-profit sectors.

DISTANCE EDUCATION

- Since 1998 the ability to offer distance courses has been exploited by more and more universities, for various reasons: to enhance off-campus outreach, to support lifelong learning, to expand access to university education for non-traditional students, or for profit. According to a survey carried out on members of the National Association of State Universities and Land Grant Colleges (NASULGC) members, two thirds participate in a virtual university or employ IT to deliver distance education (Olien, 2002)

- There are around 60 online universities in the USA, many being members of the United States Distance Learning Association (USDLA). In Canada there are only three universities that can be named online universities: Athabasca University, Thompson Rivers University and the Saskatchewan Institute of Applied Science and Technology. In addition, there is a consortium of accredited Canadian universities that

---

Box II.6.2 Globalization changes our communicative culture

Most fundamentally, globalization is producing a revolution in 'communicative culture'. Universities have developed a particular communicative culture – cerebral, objective, codified and symbolic – a culture summed up in single word *logos*, which embraces mathematics and the natural sciences just as much as, and perhaps more than, the traditional humanities. Yet globalization promotes a different kind of 'communicative culture' – visual, intuitive, volatile, and subjective – in which the distinctions between the intimate and the domestic and the official, the public and the corporate have been eroded.

Source: Scott, 2005, pp. 53–4.

Box II.6.3 Economic inequalities translate into academic inequalities

Deep inequalities undergird many of the current trends in globalization and internationalization in higher education, and they too need to be understood as part of the picture. A few countries dominate global scientific systems, primarily multinational corporations or academic institutions in the major Western industrialized nations own the new technologies, and the domination of English creates advantages for the countries that use English as the medium of instruction and research. All this means that developing countries find themselves dependent on the major academic superpowers.

Source: Altbach, 2002.

offers over 2,500 online courses, named the Canadian Virtual University.

IMPLICATIONS OF GLOBALIZATION IN HIGHER EDUCATION IN THE REGION

CHALLENGES OF GLOBALIZATION

To survive in the global marketplace, institutions must adapt to the demands of the knowledge-based economy for more people to acquire a higher level of professional qualification, which translates into more students for HEIs. The globalized, knowledge-based economy leads to lifetime fluidity between school and work (Beebe, 2001). HEIs are in the best position to tap into the life-long need to learn. Research conducted in the USA and Canada suggests that globalization also brings about major challenges:

- Instruction tends to be valued for and carried out with economic ends in mind ('economizing')
- Education is more sensitive to the needs of business and industry ('the new vocationalism')
- In a more competitive environment, HEIs tend to emulate corporation's behaviour ('corporatism')
- With the diminution in state funding, universities may seek and favour research contracts that lead to substantial revenue ('academic capitalism') (Levin, 2002).

INTERNATIONALIZATION OF HIGHER EDUCATION AND IMPLICATIONS FOR NORTH–SOUTH COOPERATION

Internationalization is a major trend in higher education (Altbach, 2002). In North America, it mainly takes the forms of:

- International students and Canadian and US citizens studying abroad
- Curricula providing international perspectives and cross-cultural skills
- Universities operating offshore
- Distance learning offered to international students
- Collaboration with academic and non-academic institutions in other countries
- Policies related to foreign students, international research and so on.

ISSUES OF DIVERSITY: RACE, GENDER, DISABILITY AND SEXUAL ORIENTATION

A definition of diversity includes race, gender, age, sexual orientation, socioeconomic class and disability, with the additional considerations of religion, education and family/marital status. Diversity is understood as more than a set of categories to which people belong or identify themselves with and extends to the principles of inclusion, the recognition and valuing of difference, and the ability to participate equitably in society (Ministry of Multiculturalism and Immigration, 2000). Over the past decade, both Canada and the USA have experienced demographic shifts that have led to the increase in the number of domestic students that belong to minorities, especially Asians and Hispanics. This shift has raised the issue of culture in an educational system that has been largely mono-cultural and mono-linguistic.

In Canada, the terms 'first nation', 'aboriginal' and 'indigenous' are preferred to describe the pre-contact populations, while in the USA the preferred terms are 'native American' and 'American Indian'. During the 1970s, native people in the USA began a movement to create their own colleges and universities, which led to the creation of 32 tribally controlled community-colleges in the USA and one in Canada. The Canadian aboriginal movement led to the creation of an Institute of Indigenous Governance in British Columbia in 1995. There has also been also an increase in advocacy for improving enrolment and completion rates for aboriginal students in non-aboriginal universities.

These developments led to diversity being raised as an issue in post-secondary institutions, with attention being paid to exclusion, discrimination, inequities and harassment. While in Canada there are no explicit 'diversity policies' at the state level, diversity policy statements are included in the Multiculturalism Act, the Charter of Rights and Freedoms, the Employment Equity Act, and the Canadian Human Rights Act. The Federal Government of Canada has no direct jurisdiction over post-secondary institutions. However, federal legislation has implications for policy and practices within provincial educational institutions. In the context of globalization and interna-

Box II.6.4 HEIs seek increased participation of minorities both as students and as teachers

The participation of First Nations and Aboriginal students has improved, but it is still well below the provincial average. I am particularly convinced of the importance of increasing the number of Aboriginal teachers and health professionals. We cannot allow another generation to grow up in the Province without strong support of higher education ... If we chart a different course, we shall all be the beneficiaries.

Source: Rae, 2005, p. 11.

---

tionalization, when universities are searching for students willing to pay them tuition fees, diversity policies found an unexpected ally in the fact that being inclusive has become good business. Recent studies suggest that in the USA, HEIs have been roused to action to provide organizational responses to diversity by demands, pressures and normative expectations originating in their external world, especially in industry (Siegel, 2006).

DIVERSIFYING FUNDING SOURCES AND THE CORPORATIZATION OF HIGHER EDUCATION

In *The University in a Corporate Culture*, Eric Gould (2003) speaks about 'the consumerist university culture' and about a growing corporate ethos and process of corporatization apparent on modern university campuses. According to Gould, students become more cost opportunistic, non-traditional in expectations and impatient to receive graduate credentials. They also become more interested in practical training to succeed in the new economy. Industry is happy to help; hence students and industry alike are shaping academic programmes to promote their economic potential.

Private universities in particular contemplate imitating the business world as a safe strategy that has done well in the marketplace, and thus introduce criteria of competitiveness, marketability and profitability. In an essay review of five recent books (2003 and 2004) about the relationship between universities and the marketplace, Daniel Levy (2006) asks whether we are moving towards a 'market university' and speaks about the 'marketization' of universities.

The growing tendency of universities to depend increasingly on private financial support, which has been noted in the literature, raises questions about the impact on the autonomy and management of universities. While autonomy from the state increases, the question is what types of dependencies are nascent.

KEY ISSUES RELATED TO THE CONTRIBUTION OF HIGHER EDUCATION TO HUMAN AND SOCIAL DEVELOPMENT IN CANADA AND THE USA

TABLE II.6.1
Current trends in HE and democracy

More democratic	Less democratic
Civic engagement	Dominance of market orientation
Curricular reform	Increased corporate influence
Multiculturalism	Dependence on private funds
Increased continuing education access	Decline of public support
Internationalization	Linguistic uniformity

COMMUNITY ENGAGEMENT AND HIGHER EDUCATION

Since this Declaration was issued in 1999, 542 presidents of US HEIs have signed it. Students at Campus Compact member schools have contributed US$4.45 billion of value to the community. Jeanne Shaheen, Director of the Institute of Politics, Harvard University, said, 'Over the past 20 years, we've seen an increase in community service and civic engagement thanks in large part to Campus Compact' (Shaheen, 2007, p. 1). There has been a strong increase in the scope, range and depth of community engagement strategies in recent years in both the USA and Canada. Discussions in the USA focus on the risk of losing what some call the 'social charter' between higher education and the public (Kezar et al., 2005, p. xiii). The

---

Box II.6.5 Knowledge transfer and community involvement – part of a university's mission

A university's contribution to the community consists in the main of knowledge creation, knowledge preservation, and knowledge transfer and knowledge application. These activities occur across a broad spectrum, ranging from the direct benefits of our teaching and research, our adult and continuing education programs, through community engagement in our fine and performing arts and athletics programs, through technology transfer and the development of spin-off companies. Our role in supporting knowledge transfer and contributing to the intellectual, social, cultural and economic development of this region and country is central to our mission.

Source: University of Victoria, 2007, p. 12.

Box II.6.6 University presidents about civic engagement

As presidents of colleges and universities, both private and public ... we challenge higher education to re-examine its public purposes and its commitments to the democratic ideal. ...This country cannot afford to educate a generation that acquires knowledge without ever understanding how that knowledge can benefit society.

Source: Campus Compact, 1999.

concept of the social charter includes such commitments as developing research to improve society, training leaders for public service, educating citizens to serve the democracy, increasing economic development and critiquing public policy. Highly respected scholars such as Bok (2003) and Kennedy (1997) have written about the shift in the USA, away from what is referred to as the public good. At the same time, perhaps in response to concerns about privatization and market influences, we are witnessing a strong emergence of diverse programmes that share the purpose of supporting higher education engaging or re-engaging with communities. The range of programmatic activities includes: community-based service learning, community-based research, the K-16 movement, community HE partnerships, continuing education, neighbourhood linkage programmes and more. The Ernest Boyer (1990) (former Carnegie Foundation President) articulation of the value and need for 'engaged scholarship' is often quoted in the studies on community engagement. The Kellogg Foundation has supported a mission to reinvigorate the original spirit of the land-grant colleges and universities with its Commission on the Future of State and Land-Grant Universities. The statement of Portland State University (PSU) President Daniel O. Bernstine is illustrative of the spirit of engagement now being called for (Office of Marketing and Communications at PSU, 2003).

Canada has also seen substantial increases of interest in community engagement by senior leadership, as the extract from the 2007 Strategic Plan for the University of Victoria illustrates (Box II.6.8).

There has been a strong growth in what is referred to in Canada as community-based research, that is, research undertaken as part of a collaborative partnership between university lecturers and students and community agencies and organizations. Community-based research has been stimulated by funding from several of the Federal Canadian Government funding agencies such as the Social Sciences and Humanities Research Council (SSHRC) and the Canadian Institutes for Health Research (CIHR). Community and university research partners have been meeting periodically at Community-University Expositions.

There has also been a growing interest in the topic of community service-learning (CSL) in Canadian higher education institutions. A scan of CSL in Canada reveals that, while it is national in scope, there is still much groundwork needed to educate lecturers, students, professionals and community agencies on what CSL is (Hayes, 2006).

Box II.6.7 'Our' university

Portland State has been called 'The university of the future' because of our focus on community-based learning, our belief in the benefits of collaboration, and our understanding that, while some forms of higher education must be altered to adapt to changing educational needs, we cannot change the tradition of excellence in academic, research and service programs. So when I look to the future of Portland State I see a university that is even more integrated with its community, so integrated, in fact, that the community automatically recognizes that the University is part of the solution for civic issues and problems. My vision is of a university so thoroughly engaged in its community that people throughout the region refer to it as 'our university.' I see a university that is well known for the quality of education our students receive, for the importance of the research we perform, and for the positive impact we've had on quality of life and the economy of our region and our state.

Source: Daniel O. Bernstine, interview with the Office of Marketing and Communications at Portland State University, 2003.

Box II.6.8 Community engagement

Objective 26: To engage the community by taking our activities off campus.

26b) Enhance civic literacy and promote the value of community engagement among our students, faculty and staff.

26c) Further support community-based research initiatives and links with community groups.

26e) Promote opportunities for community engagement in UVic research, teaching and program design.

26g) Promote opportunities for knowledge transfer in addition to those associated with technology transfer.

Source: University of Victoria Planning and Priorities Committee, 2007.

Adrianna Kezar (Kezar, 2005) notes:

In summary, several public, social and community-oriented movements have emerged that counter the private and economic orientation that has been so forceful in the last two decades … It is important to understand that these movements alone cannot transform the current climate and mould a new social charter. (pp. 51–2)

THE GREENING OF HIGHER EDUCATION

The *Framework for Priority Action for Change and Development of Higher Education* of the WCHE calls for HEIs to 'use their autonomy and high academic standards to contribute to the sustainable development of society' (UNESCO, 1998, paragraph 6a). The increased attention to climate change at a global level stimulated by the Kyoto agreement has had a profound impact on social and political agendas in North America. While at national levels contestation between oil and gas industry cries of caution and environmental movement calls for action now is unresolved, many other jurisdictions have made a decision to act on their own. HEIs are responding in diverse ways.

The American College and University Presidents Climate Commitments is a high visibility effort to address global warming through joint commitment to achieve climate neutrality for their campuses and develop the capability of society to do the same. This initiative sought commitment from 200 college and university presidents by June 2007 and 1000 by the end of 2009. The commitment, to be signed by the president or chancellor of the college or university, calls for the implementation of plans for specific actions to reduce greenhouse gases. Among the actions recommended are: constructing all new buildings in accordance with the Leadership in Energy and Environmental Design (LEED) Green Building Council standard; adopting an energy-efficient purchasing policy; off-setting all greenhouse gas emissions due to air travel; encouraging public transport; purchasing electricity from renewable sources; and reviewing investment portfolios vis-à-vis climate and sustainability issues (Dautremont-Smith et al., 2007).

Colleges and universities in the USA are responding to the calls for action on climate change in a variety of creative ways. The ten-campus University of California system has pledged to provide 20% of its electricity needs from renewable resources by 2017. Nine colleges and universities are working to make their campuses completely energy independent by 2012. More than 18 American colleges and universities have adopted LEED policies. In 2004, Carleton College used money from its endowment to build a 1.65 MW wind turbine which produces 40% of the college's electricity. Arizona State University established the first School of Sustainability with academic work in law, business, engineering, architecture, planning and education.

Michael M'Gonigle and Justine Starke (2006) from the University of Victoria in Canada have written a book which is on the 'must read' list of most of the charitable foundations and most of the university presidents in Canada. *Planet U* is a call to place institutions of higher education at the core of sustaining the world. They note that the rise of higher education is one of the most important, and most overlooked, trends of the past half century. The university – they point out – is an 'industry' in the new knowledge economy, and more. Given that the specialists in all other industries are trained at colleges and universities, higher education is literally 'the mother of all industries' (p. 36).

With over a million students, the combined contribution of Canadian universities to the GDP of Canada is larger than that of the pulp and paper industry or the automotive industry. The contribution was as big as the arts, entertainment and recreation industries combined (AUCC, 2002). The task is to begin where one stands. One begins with a focus on place. From knowing the history and ecology of the land where the institution now stands, an entire range of possibilities exists for leadership by universities as institutions. From transport choices, to types of student engagement, and from watershed strategies to building codes, *Planet U* puts a name to a way of looking at Canadian HEI in the 21st century.

Box II.6.9 University goes green

Higher education is a $317 billion industry that employs millions and spends billions of dollars on fuel, energy, and infrastructure. If every U.S. campus used 100% clean energy, it would nearly quadruple our current renewable electricity demand, create thousands of new jobs, support emerging 'green' industries, and speed the availability of innovative financing options.

Source: American College & University Presidents Climate Commitment, 2007.

Box II.6.10 Sombre self-assessment

We remained so far ahead of our competitors for so long, however, that we began to take our postsecondary superiority for granted. The results of this inattention, though little known to many of our fellow citizens, are sobering.

Source: US Department of Education, 2006, Preamble, p. vi.

VISIONS FOR THE FUTURE

THE US GOVERNMENT PERSPECTIVE

The report of the US Department of Education's Commission on the Future of Higher Education quoted above is arguably the broadest assessment of the current state of higher education in the USA. The conclusions are that, in spite of past successes and an increasingly vital link to the future of the country, Americans are just not getting the education that they need or deserve:

- We are losing some students in our high schools, which do not yet see preparing all pupils for post-secondary education and training as their responsibility
- Others do not enter post-secondary educational institutions because of inadequate information and rising costs, combined with a confusing financial aid system
- Among high school graduates who do make it ... a troubling number waste time mastering English and math skills, which they should have learned in high school
- There are disturbing signs that many students who earn degrees have not actually mastered the reading, writing and thinking skills expected
- The consequences of these problems are most severe for students from low-income families and for racial and ethnic minorities
- Compounding all of these difficulties is a lack of clear, reliable information about cost and quality of post-secondary institutions. (US Department of Education, 2006, p. vii).

The Commission on the Future of US Higher Education has expressed a set of goals, which are expected of US higher education:

- We want a world-class higher education system that creates new knowledge, contributes to economic prosperity and global competitiveness and empowers citizens
- We want a system that is accessible to all Americans, throughout their lives
- We want post-secondary institutions to provide high-quality instruction while improving efficiency in order to be more affordable
- We want a higher education system that gives Americans the workplace skills they need to adapt to a rapidly changing economy

- We want post-secondary institutions to adapt to a world altered by technology, changing demographics and globalization, in which the higher education landscape includes new providers and new paradigms, from for-profit universities to distance learning. (US Department of Education, 2006, p. viii)

A DEMOCRATIC DEFICIT?

It is important to note that this influential government report on higher education in the USA does not concern human and social development in the USA in a way that many of the higher education leaders themselves address them. The overarching concerns of this report are access, costs (but with solutions coming from cost-cutting from within the HEIs themselves), competitiveness (the slip to 9th among OECD countries in the number of students attending HEIs is noted) and the quality of teaching and learning. Sorting out the financial aid systems, increasing accountability and providing better comparative data for students and parents to make their market decisions are seen as part of the vision for the future. The clear message is that for the US Government of 2007, the market will sort things out.

A vision for higher education in the USA will need to deal with the very real contestation at play. Poor people, blacks, Hispanics, Native Americans and others will continue to struggle for the kinds of access and support that others take for granted. Public higher education bodies will be increasingly challenged not only by the corporate sectors for partnerships, but by the people and organizations in the very communities where the institutions of higher education are located. Issues of climate change, civic engagement, global harmony, inclusion, and the reduction of violence in the lives of people everywhere are also finding their place in the policy debates about the role of HEIs in the human and social development of the USA.

However, as Clark Kerr (2002), one of the most respected scholars on higher education issues in the US notes, 'it is increasingly difficult to talk about a future of higher education. Many different segments each have their own future ... Institutions in different sectors will not know or care much about each other.' (p. 10).

Box II.6.11 In Canada, PSE is recognized as crucial to social cohesion

There is also broad agreement that PSE plays a crucial role in improving social cohesion and inclusion. Given the changing face of Canada, post-secondary education is much more essential to society than at any time in the past.

Source: CCL, 2006, p. 3.

A VIEW FROM THE NORTH

As we have noted, Canada's PSE system is largely a public one, without a federal ministry of education. The AUCC and the newly created Canadian Council on Learning (CCL) provide some elements of a common vision. In 2006, the CCL published its first Canadian PSE report.

Analysis of the findings available at the time of this report led to the following conclusions:

- There are anticipated labour-market shortages in key professions and occupations in Canada
- Canada ranks in the top three OECD countries in participation rates, educational attainment and investment as a percentage of GDP
- Canada's overall R&D intensity continues to rank 15th among OECD member countries. The role of PSE institutions in R&D is greater than in other countries
- Access to and benefits of PSE are not equally distributed among Canadians
- Despite high levels of educational attainment, two out of every five Canadians have literacy levels below the minimum needed in today's economy
- Canada lacks mechanisms at the national level to ensure coherence or to effectively support a distinctively Canadian culture and identity.

Similarly to the US national report, the CCL overview deals mainly with structural issues. It is worth noting, however, that from a human and social development perspective, the report does mention the crucial role of higher education in improving social cohesion and inclusion. The report also draws attention to the need to give priority to under-represented groups, including aboriginal peoples. The Council of Ministers of Education also identified the learning needs of aboriginal peoples as one of its top three priorities in 2004.

Additional insights are provided by documents either commissioned or written by the AUCC. The AUCC (2005, 2006a, 2006b) recommends:

- That the federal government work with the university community to build upon the current outreach efforts of universities. Universities are prepared to expand their outreach efforts to contribute to developing a research and science culture
- That a flagship programme of international graduate scholarships be created
- That the federal government maintain or augment investment in research funding councils, infrastructure support and graduate scholarships.

TOWARDS A NEW SOCIAL CONTRACT

Bob Rae (2005), a former premier of Canada's largest and richest province, Ontario, was asked to undertake a study on the future of higher education in that province. His report, *Ontario, a Leader in Learning* was published in February 2005. He says that we ignore our institutions of higher education at our peril. He notes:

> Education matters. It matters for each of us as individuals. It matters for our society and our economy. Yet higher education has not been the public priority that it should be. The picture that the public has of our colleges and universities is a relatively benign one. The result has been benign neglect. (p. 5)

Martha Piper is the highly respected former president of the University of British Columbia (UBC). She was asked to give the 2002 Killam Annual Lecture in the human and social sciences (http://www.killamtrusts.ca/docs/Killam_Lec_02.pdf). Her remarks in the Killam Lecture have been taken as the most articulate expres-

Box II.6.12 An evolving and transparent social contract

The social contract with universities is formulated over time and shaped by history ... The social contract requires continuous reflection and dialogue between the university and society, as each era renews the social contract according to its needs ... The university must permit public scrutiny of its affairs, be transparent in how choices are made to achieve its academic mission and be accountable to government and to the public about how public funds have been spent ... In order to maintain its autonomy, the university must make a commitment to dialogue about these tasks and the role of university in society. The social contract implies an obligation on the university to reflect upon these tasks, to think and to write about them publicly, to articulate their value in society, to defend them when they are threatened but also to reconsider them in light of criticism and evolving social needs.

Source: Fallis, 2004, p. 35.

Box II.6.13 HE for a vibrant civil society

<table>
<tr>
<td>But even as we pride ourselves on such achievements, there are those who argue our influence on the world stage is waning. And a walk down to Hastings and Main in Vancou-</td>
<td>ver provides a sober reminder that poverty, and homelessness and drug abuse, and mental illness are only a five-minute walk away from the up-scale souvenir shops and restaurants of</td>
<td>Gaston. That in the heart of one of the most affluent cities in the world is a dreadful reminder that something is wrong.

Source: Piper, 2003, p. 122.</td>
</tr>
</table>

sion of the emerging mandate of Higher Education institutions in Canada.

HIGHER EDUCATION INSTITUTIONS: SOME TRANSFORMATIVE IDEAS

In locations where HEIs exist, the collective resources of universities and other institutions of HE (students, academic staff, facilities, research funding, knowledge, skills) are arguably the largest single underutilized resource for the improvement of community well-being and change anywhere.

As in the case for environmental change made so cogently by Michael M'Gonigle and Justine Starke in *Planet U*, universities, in an era of knowledge strategies, represent an extraordinary and as yet underutilized resource for making a direct difference in our communities, regions and nations. With a relatively modest adjustment of curricular, merit and promotion criteria, and ideas of service and engagement, the visibility and practical contributions of our HEIs to our immediate communities could be greatly enhanced. Here are some ideas that are already in place, that could be tried out on a larger scale and that would respond to the challenges of globalization facing all our institutions.

CIVIC/COMMUNITY ENGAGEMENT

a. Incorporate robust language on civic engagement into the *strategic plans* of all HEIs in North America drawing on ideas from Campus Compact in the USA, the University of Victoria, St. Francis Xavier University and the University of British Columbia in Canada

b. Create university-wide *offices*, programmes or centres *for community or civic engagement*, as at Portland State University and many others

c. Create institutional and national working groups on the *implications for merit, tenure and promotion* of community-engaged programming

d. Create chairs of community-engaged scholarship

e. Support journals, performance standards and knowledge exchange in community-engaged scholarship through inclusion of community peers

f. Consolidate a Canadian network of community-engaged university practices

g. Support the creation of places for community scholars-in-residence

h. Support open-source databases for community-based knowledge

i. Select a number of strategic goals for action such as language revitalization and recovery of aboriginal/First Nations/Native American languages.

INTERNATIONALIZATION

a. Promote curriculum reforms that focus on the inclusion of a truly global base of theorizing and reflection of practice

b. Link HEIs in North America with institutions in the global South with the idea of mutual strengthening.

REFERENCES

Altbach, P.G. (2002) Perspectives on internationalizing higher education (electronic version). *International Higher Education* **27**(Spring). Retrieved 3 May 2007, from http://www.bc.edu/bc_org/avp/soe/cihe/newsletter/News27/text004.htm.

Altbach, P.G. (2004) Higher education crosses borders: Can the United States remain the top destination for foreign students? *Change* **36**(2), March/April, pp. 18–24.

American College & University Presidents Climate Commitment (2007) *A Call for Climate Leadership*. http://www.presidentsclimatecommitment.org/.

AUCC (2002) A strong foundation for innovation (electronic document). *AUCC Publications and Resources*. Ottawa, ON: AUCC. Retrieved 3 May 2007, from http://www.aucc.ca/_pdf/english/reports/2002/innovation/intro_context_e.pdf.

AUCC (2005) *Momentum: The 2005 Report on University Research and Knowledge Transfer* (electronic document). Ottawa, ON: AUCC. Retrieved 11 March 2007, from http://www.aucc.ca/momentum/en/_pdf/momentum_report.pdf.

AUCC (2006a) University research: Canada's strength in a changing world (electronic document). *AUCC Publications and Resources*. Ottawa, ON: AUCC. Retrieved 3 May 2007, from http://www.aucc.ca/momentum/en/_pdf/university_research_dec1206_e.pdf.

AUCC (2006b) Canada's universities. Our strength. Our future (electronic document). *Advocacy and Research*. Ottawa, ON: AUCC. Retrieved 11 March 2007, from http://www.aucc.ca/policy/priorities/can_univ_fact_sheet_02_23_e.html.

AUCC (2007a) *Information and Overview about the Association of Universities and Colleges of Canada*. Ottawa, ON:

AUCC. Retrieved 2 May 2007, from http://www.aucc.ca/about_us/index_e.html.

AUCC (2007b) *AUCC Research Report. Trends in Higher Education. Vol. 1 Enrolment* (electronic document). Ottawa, ON: AUCC. Retrieved 11 March 2007, from http://www.aucc.ca/publications/auccpubs/research/trends/trends_e.html.

Beebe, M.A. (2001) Learning partnerships in Africa: Commercial transactions or reciprocal exchanges. In: L.C. Barrows (ed.), *Transnational Education and the New Economy: Delivery and Quality*, Bucharest: UNESCO-CEPES, pp. 107–20.

Bok, D.C. (2003) *Universities in the Marketplace: The Commercialization of Higher Education*. Princeton, NJ: Princeton University Press.

Boyer, E.L. and Carnegie Foundation (1990) *Campus Life: In Search of Community*. Lawrenceville, NJ: Princeton University Press.

Business Roundtable (2005) *Tapping America's Potential. The Education for Innovation Initiative* (electronic document). Washington, DC: Business Roundtable. Retrieved 4 May 2007, from http://www.businessroundtable.org/pdf/20050727002TAPStatement.pdf.

Campus Compact (1999) *Presidents' Declaration on the Civic Responsibility of Higher Education* (electronic document). Providence, RI: Brown University. Retrieved 10 March 2007, from http://www.compact.org/resources/declaration/.

Canadian Commission for UNESCO (1998) *Report of the North American Preparatory Meeting for the 1998 UNESCO World Conference on Higher Education*. Ottawa, ON: Canadian Commission for UNESCO.

Canadian Council on Learning (2006) *Report on Learning in Canada 2006, Canadian Post-secondary Education: A Positive Record – An Uncertain Future* (electronic version). Ottawa, ON: Canadian Council on Learning. Retrieved 2 May 2007, from http://www.ccl-cca.ca/NR/rdonlyres/BD46F091-D856-4EEB-B361-D83780BFE78C/0/PSEReport2006EN.pdf.

Carnegie Foundation (2006) *The Carnegie Classification of Institutions of Higher Education*. Retrieved 2 May 2007, from http://www.carnegiefoundation.org/classifications/.

CAUT (2007) *CAUT Almanac of Postsecondary Education in Canada* (electronic version). Ottawa, ON: Canadian Association of University Teachers. Retrieved 12 March 2007, from http://www.caut.ca/en/publications/almanac/default.asp.

Chan, A. (2005) Policy discourses and changing practices: Diversity and the university-college. *Higher Education*, **50**(1), pp. 129–57.

Council of Ministers of Education (2006) *Education@Canada. International Gateway to Education in Canada*. Overview. Retrieved 2 May 2007, from http://www.educationcanada.cmec.ca/.

Dautremont-Smith, J., Gamble, N., Perkowitz, R.M. and Rosenfeld, D. (2007) *A Call for Climate Leadership. Progress and Opportunities in Addressing the Defining Challenge of Our Time*. American College & University Presidents Climate Commitment (electronic version). Retrieved 2 May 2007, from http://www.presidentsclimatecommitment.org/pdf/climate_leadership.pdf.

Fallis, G. (2004) The mission of the university. Submission to the Rae Commission. In: Government of Ontario *Postsecondary Review: Higher Expectations for Higher Education*. Toronto, ON: York University.

Gould, E. (2003) *The University in a Corporate Culture*. New Haven, CT: Yale University Press.

Government of Ontario (2005) Reaching higher: The McGuinty government plan for postsecondary education (electronic article) *Backgrounder*. Ottawa, ON: Ontario Government, Ministry of Finance, 11 May, pp. 1–3. Retrieved 4 May 2007, from http://www.fin.gov.on.ca/english/budget/ontariobudgets/2005/pdf/bke1.pdf.

Hamilton, J. (2003) Technology affects student success (electronic article). *University News*. Retrieved 2 May 2007, from http://www.universityaffairs.ca/issues/2003/jan/en30.pdf.

Hayes, E. (2006) *Community Service Learning in Canada: A Scan of the Field*. Guelph, ON: Canadian Association for Community-Service Learning.

Kennedy, D. (1997) *Academic Duty*. Cambridge, MA: Harvard University Press.

Kerr, C. (2002) Shock wave II: An introduction to the 21st century. In: Brint, S. (ed.), *The Future of the City of Intellect: The Changing American University*. Stanford, CA: Stanford University Press.

Kezar, A.J. (2005) Creating a Metamovement. A Vision Toward Regaining the Public Social Charter. In: Kezar, A.J., Chambers, T.C. and Burkhardt, J. (eds) *Higher Education for the Public Good: Emerging Voices from a National Movement* (1st edn). San Francisco, CA: Jossey-Bass, pp. 43–53.

Levin, J.S. (2002) In education and in work: The globalized community college. *The Canadian Journal of Higher Education*, **32**(2), pp. 47–77.

Levy, D.C. (2006) Market university? *Comparative Education Review*, **50**(1), pp. 113–24.

Marchese, T.J. (1997) U.S. higher education in the post-war era: Expansion and growth. *U.S. Society & Values*, **2**(5), pp. 10–15.

Marois, P. (1998) Canadian Intervention on the occasion of the UNESCO World Conference on Higher Education (electronic document). Paris: Council of Ministers of Education, Canada. Retrieved 5 May 2007, from http://www.cmec.ca/international/SPKNTS-E.PDF.

M'Gonigle, M. and Starke, J. (2006) *Planet U. Sustaining the World, Reinventing the University*. Gabriola Island, BC: New Society Publishers.

Ministry of Multiculturalism and Immigration (2000) *Framework for Diversity: Multiculturalism, Human Rights, Employment Equity and Social Justice*. Vancouver, BC: Ministry of Multiculturalism and Immigration.

NCES (National Center for Education Statistics) (2007) *Enrolment in Postsecondary Institutions, Fall 2005; Graduation Rates, 1999 and 2002 Cohorts; and Financial Statistics, Fiscal Year 2005* (electronic document). Washington, DC: NCES Institute of Education Sciences. Retrieved 12 March 2007, from http://nces.ed.gov/pubsearch/pubsinfo.asp?pubid=2007154.

Olien, D.W. (2002) Back to earth: Expectations for using technology to improve the university experience. In: Alexander, F. K. and Alexander, K. (eds) *The University: International Expectations*. Montreal: McGill-Queen's University Press, pp. 124–38.

Petter, A. (1998) Canadian Intervention on the occasion of the UNESCO World Conference on Higher Education (electronic document). Paris: Council of Ministers of Education, Canada. Retrieved 5 May 2007, from http://www.cmec.ca/international/SPKNTS-E.PDF.

Piper, M.C. (2003) Building a civil society: A new role for the human sciences. *The Canadian Journal of Higher Education* **33**(1), pp. 113–30.

Portland State University, Office of Marketing and Communication at PSU (2003) Interview with President Daniel O. Bernstine (electronic article). *News*, January. Retrieved 3 May 2007, from http://www.pdx.edu/news/3892.

Rae, B. (2005) *Ontario, a Leader in Learning. Report & Recommendations* (electronic version). Toronto, ON: Government of Ontario. Retrieved 2 March 2007, from http://www.uwo.ca/pvp/president_reports/documents/RaeFinalReport.pdf.

Scott, P. (2005) The opportunities and the threats of globalization. In: Jones, G.A., McCarney, P.L. and Skolnik, M.L. (eds) *Creating Knowledge, Strengthening Nations: The Changing Role of Higher Education*. Toronto, ON: University of Toronto Press, pp. 53–4.

Shaheen, J. (2007) *Campus Compact* (electronic document). Providence, RI: Brown University. Retrieved 10 May 2007, from http://www.compact.org/about/Why_Campus_Compact 07 pdf.

Siegel, D.J. (2006) Organizational response to the demand and expectation for diversity. *Higher Education* **52**(3), pp. 465–86.

Snyder, T.D., Dillow, S.A. and Hoffman, C.M. (2007) *Digest of Education Statistics 2006* (electronic version). National Center for Education Statistics, Institute of Education Sciences, U.S. Department of Education. Washington, DC: U.S. Government Printing Office. Retrieved 6 May 2007, from http://nces.ed.gov/pubsearch/pubsinfo.asp?pubid=2007017.

Statistics Canada (2007) Population estimate. Retrieved 2 May 2007, from http://www.statcan.ca/menu-en.htm.

UNESCO (1998) *Framework for Priority Action for Change and Development of Higher Education*. Retrieved 11 March 2007, from http://portal.unesco.org/education/en/ev.php-URL_ID=19193&URL_DO=DO_TOPIC&URL_SECTION=201.html.

UNESCO Institute for Statistics (2007) Table 1.01 Educational attainment of the adult population. Montreal, QC: UNESCO Institute for Statistics. Retrieved 25 March 2007, from http://www.uis.unesco.org/ev.php?ID=6206_201&ID2=DO_TOPIC.

University of Victoria Planning and Priorities Committee (2007) *A Vision for the Future – Building on Strength. A Strategic Plan for the University of Victoria* (electronic document). Victoria, BC: University of Victoria. Retrieved 5 May 2007, from http://web.uvic.ca/strategicplan/.

US Department of Education (2006) *A Test of Leadership: Charting the Future of U.S. Higher Education* (electronic version). Washington, D.C. Retrieved 5 April 2007, from http://www.ed.gov/about/bdscomm/list/hiedfuture/reports/pre-pub-report.pdf.

Weerts, D.J. and Ronca, J.M. (2006) Examining differences in state support for higher education: A comparative study of state appropriations for research I universities. *Journal of Higher Education* **77**(6), pp. 935–67.

SPECIAL CONTRIBUTION II.3

Higher education for human and social development in the USA

Sylvia Hurtado

The purpose of educating citizens to carry out public work has roots as old as the establishment of the first college in America. More importantly, the notion of intentionally educating citizens in higher education for the complexity of a pluralistic democracy and a world that is economically, socially and culturally interdependent has received renewed emphasis in recent years. However, given the new challenges that American higher education currently faces, it is appropriate to reflect on how institutions are integral in promoting social transformation and are contributing to human and social development. The purpose of this paper is to discuss how the contributions of American higher education have been documented, to reflect on new challenges, and to highlight new developments in institutional activity that further both student learning and societal progress. In light of the need for continuing social change to resolve issues of inequality, I conclude by indicating how social transformation is

interconnected with higher education's role in the development of individuals who have the capacity to serve the public and take leadership for a diverse democracy in the future.

First, it is important to note some facts about the US higher education context. Higher education in the USA historically began with a strong private sector and subsequently developed a strong public sector. These sectors share similar goals and are committed to advancing human and social development. However, unlike other countries across the globe, education in the USA is the responsibility of state governments. Federal government assistance in higher education is limited to awards for specific research projects (mostly granted to teaching staff affiliated with institutions) and for federal financial aid programmes that provide grants for students from low-income families and loans for both low- and middle-income families. That is, no direct federal aid is provided for institutional operating expenses, except in special circumstances

for educational programmes deemed to be of national interest (for example funds approved by Congress to institutions that serve large numbers of students from populations under-represented in higher education). This has allowed one of the unique roles of the American system of higher education to emerge: institutions operate with a great deal of autonomy, and may serve as critics of society and government for the purpose of advancing knowledge, ideas and discovery independently of governmental or political control. Therefore, the stability of American higher education is due to the normative pressures institutions exert on one another, acting under similar rationale and constraints. The federal government may encourage institutions to move towards meeting national goals by means of incentives and minimal regulation tied to funding. State governments may dictate priorities with their own funding resources to public institutions. However, they have no control over private institutions. Over time, the 'power of the purse' has declined. This is because state financial support for public higher education has declined and public institutions have exercised their autonomy in adopting the strategies of private institutions to increase their funding base through private resources and increases in tuition fees.

However, increasing public scrutiny of higher education in the USA has come as a result of increases in the cost of attending both private and public institutions. Concerns about access to post-secondary education have arisen at the same time that increasing numbers of students seek a place in higher education. Over two-thirds of high school graduates in the USA now enrol in some type of post-secondary education immediately after completing secondary school (NCES, 2006). With more students seeking access and variations in student preparation for college, policymakers are asking post-secondary institutions to become more accountable in demonstrating their value for the significant investment that individuals make (US Department of Education, 2006). I will return to this issue of institutional assessment and accountability at the end of this paper.

ADVANCING HUMAN DEVELOPMENT: THE MULTIPLE OUTCOMES OF COLLEGE

Fortunately, for more than 30 years scholars have been concerned with the contributions made by American higher education. They have used empirical studies to establish its value to both individuals and society. Economist Howen Bowen published *Investment in Learning* in 1977, a landmark book that describes the broad range of benefits of higher education to individual development and to the progress of American society. Basing his work on available empirical evidence, he outlined the value of higher education and clearly described its intended goals. Higher education aims to benefit individuals across a wide range of economic, social and personal spheres. He reviewed evidence on the gains for individual college students in cognitive learning (using multiple measures),

changes in values and aspirations, achievement of personal identity, reduction of prejudice and increasing liberalism of religious thought. He concluded that college also has documented effects on practical competencies, including measures of citizenship participation and individual economic productivity. It was acknowledged then, as it is now, that college has multiple and wide-ranging outcomes. Students grow, learn and develop cognitive, social and democratic capacities. In addition, they benefit economically from having a college education. Bowen's work was among the first empirical syntheses of the contribution of higher education to both individual and social development.

Since the 1970s, two more volumes of research on college students have been produced. These volumes synthesize the effect of college on individual change and development (Pascarella and Terenzini, 1991; Pascarella and Terenzini, 2005). They critically evaluate thousands of studies conducted over several decades, many of which used multiple-institutional and longitudinal research designs appropriate for determining the impact of college on individuals. The authors conclude that students make significant first year to senior year gains in: learning skills and cognitive/intellectual skills, psychosocial dimensions (for example self and relational systems), attitudes and values (for example becoming less doctrinaire in religious beliefs and more tolerant of political, social and religious views), and moral development. In their evaluation of the long-term effects of college attendance in socioeconomic terms, the authors conclude that a bachelor's degree compared with a high school degree confers a net advantage in earnings of 37% for men and 39% for women. Individuals with a bachelor's degree will earn nearly twice as much as those with secondary school diplomas. In their lifetime, bachelor degree holders will earn an average of US$2.1 million (Day and Newburger, 2002). The long-term advantages of obtaining a baccalaureate degree were

evident on other economic indicators (occupational status, employment stability) as well as a personal disposition for life-long learning, and quality of life indices (for example health, child welfare and subjective well-being). Pascarella and Terenzini (2005) conclude:

> Even after adjusting for other forces, and even if the exposure lasts for only a year or two, college changes students to a degree unattributable to normal maturation or other influences outside of the academy. (p. 628)

Further, they conclude that:

> What happens to students after they enrol at a college or university has more impact on learning and change than the structural characteristics of the institutions these students attend. (p. 642)

That is, after taking into account that different types of colleges educate different types of students (in terms of ability, income and preparation), the '*degree of net change* that students experience at the various categories of institutions is essentially the same' (p. 641). Traditional measures of college quality (selectivity of the freshmen class, prestige/reputation) have little consistent effect on learning and psychosocial development outcomes, with the exception of career and socioeconomic attainments. Differences in students' interactions and encounters with peers and teaching staff within colleges, however, play a significant role in learning and development. These conclusions are based on many studies in which large numbers of students were surveyed and tested at college entry into many colleges and universities, and at subsequent time points that include post-graduate or alumni results. The continual involvement of institutions in national studies or collaborative research efforts ensures that we will have several more volumes of research documenting the contributions of American higher education to individual development.[1]

CHANGING CONTEXTS AND INSTITUTIONAL RESPONSES

However, evidence of student outcomes in higher education is not sufficient when it comes to a society that is still stratified by race and income disparities in access to quality education. In this new context, in which more students from a variety of backgrounds are seeking admission to colleges and universities, the American Association of Colleges and Universities (AAC&U) has strongly articulated the aims of college level learning for the 21st century. It is important for all students to achieve these aims. The AAC&U is a non-governmental membership organization consisting of higher education institutions across the USA. The organization is focused on curricular issues and educational practices that foster the values, skills and dispositions associated with a liberal education, with an increasing emphasis on education for global issues and the challenges of uncertainty and change. The AAC&U (2007) states that the essential learning outcomes for the 21st century should include gains in:

1. Knowledge of human cultures and the natural and physical world, through studying the sciences, social sciences and humanities.
2. Intellectual and practical skills, including critical and creative thinking, quantitative literacy, information literacy, teamwork and problem-solving.
3. Personal and social responsibility, including local and global civic knowledge and engagement, inter-cultural knowledge and competence, ethical reasoning and action, and skills for lifelong learning.
4. Integrative learning, involving synthesis and accomplishment across general and specialized studies.

They note that personal and social responsibility should be acquired through active involvement with diverse communities and real-world challenges, advocating that campuses facilitate student engagement with a variety of communities and the ill-structured problems of today's society. The AAC&U has reformulated the notion of a liberal education as one that is accessible to all types of students; results not only from reading and interpreting classic texts but is also built from knowledge and engagement with the changing conditions of our society; and is practical in the sense that it provides essential skills for changing job and economic conditions. This stance is a departure from previous definitions of what constitutes a liberal education. The association's approach is nothing short of a national advocacy campaign to reinvigorate goals for individual development in higher education that are more fitting for a diverse and changing world. They are actively engaged in helping campuses to reform undergraduate education, implement successful practices, and assess the outcomes of student learning and development.

Many may think that institutions are slow to change. However, I offer one example of how a national crisis precipitated institutional responses. These responses reveal a willingness to actively engage in global issues that result in individual development. The September 11 terrorist attacks on two US buildings that were symbols of American economic power (the World Trade Center) and military power (the Pentagon) significantly changed how many Americans came to view world events. The attacks made 2001 a turning point in concerns about national security and relations with specific countries. However, the immediate response on college campuses was to provide an open forum for discussion and use knowledge to empower students during a difficult time. Many of the campuses responded immediately after the terrorist attacks with opportunities to discuss events in freshman seminars and engage in collective demonstrations of sentiment (for example campus vigils), special expert panels, and classes where guidelines were provided for teaching staff to constructively lead discussions on political and cultural issues during an emotional time. Research conducted on college students at ten public universities prior to the event and a few months afterwards indicated that students who actively engaged in these campus activities increased their capacity for functioning in a diverse and complex world (Hurtado, 2003). That is, growth from initial predispositions was evident in students' capacity to adopt a pluralist perspective in terms of negotiating different perspectives and willingness to have their own views challenged. They were more skilled than their peers who did not engage in any collective or campus-organized educational activities. In fact, those students who experienced a negative effect (for example experienced fear, became more wary of individuals who appeared to be Middle Eastern) were least likely to have demonstrated growth in their skills for participation in a diverse society. Clearly, the level of engagement afforded students in American colleges in terms of advancing knowledge and experience with diversity and global issues has an impact on students' capacity to develop as citizens of a global society. The 'post 9/11' context requires even more effort by US colleges to prepare students to negotiate racial/ethnic, religious and political differences, as institutions are responsible for the development of the next generation of 'office holders' (Gutmann, 1987) – diplomats and elected officials who set policy – as well as leaders of businesses that increasingly involve both constituents and workers throughout the world (Friedman, 2005).

ADVANCING SOCIETY: MULTIPLE OUTCOMES

While there is much focus on individual development, one cannot ignore the multiple social goals and outcomes of higher education that are the result of teaching and the aggregate of human development (for example citizenship, economic productivity); research and related partnerships that benefit communities (for example scientific advances, social welfare experiments); or direct services to the public (for example campus museums, artistic and musical events). A recent survey of chief academic officers at four-year colleges and universities revealed that over 85% stated public service aims were addressed in their institutional mission statement, which guides institutional policy (Hurtado, forthcoming). This indicates that social goals are integral to each institution's stated function. Bowen (1977) noted multiple outcomes of higher education that were intended to benefit society. These societal goals included the *advancement of knowledge*, its 'preservation and dissemination of cultural heritage' as well as the discovery and dissemination of new knowledge (p. 58). American higher education has traditionally been the place for the production of new knowledge – this role is undisputed – though some changes are evident in the number of private organizations outside academia that undertake research in science, technology and policy areas. Some campuses summarize and aggregate many individual discoveries, the engagement of teaching staff and students in public service, and the accumulation of awards (for example Nobel prizes) as evidence for the public about their contributions to society and commitment to excellence.

Other social goals of higher education were included in Bowen's catalogue: the *discovery and encouragement of talent*, with broad representation from every community, and the *advancement of social welfare* (including economic growth, enhancement of national prestige, progress towards the identification and solution of social problems, improvements in values and attitudes in individuals that result in an improved quality of life (aggregated change in culture), and progress in human equality, justice, health and security, to name a few. At the time of his writing, the evidence on social contributions was not highly developed and there is still some debate on how these social or public goods can be measured.

Many of these public service goals are embedded in our evaluation and reward structure for tenure and promotion, in which employees must demonstrate how

their work in institutions has an impact in terms of teaching, research and service. Recent developments have allowed teaching staff at some institutions to give more emphasis to one of the above categories in promotion decisions. Some teaching staff opt to demonstrate excellence in service and moderate achievements in the other areas (see for example the Indiana University Promotion and Tenure Criteria for the School of Education http://site.educ.indiana.edu/Portals/28/Policy%20Council/2001-2002/02.30R.pdf). In short, these changes in the flexibility of the promotion criteria help to encourage and reward those who can demonstrate not only an impact on their field of study (the advancement of knowledge) but also on the communities that are the sites for their activities (the advancement of social welfare).

Recent developments also indicate that institutions are becoming more intentional about public service goals and activities. Although American education has always implemented some form of civic education in schools, activities at the post-secondary level became more explicit when a civic engagement/public service movement started to emerge. This brought about an increase in campus-based initiatives and multi-campus organizations. For example, on a national level, an organization of college presidents (both private and public) dedicated to public service initiatives emerged called Campus Compact, and the American Association of State Colleges and Universities (AASCU) developed the American Democracy project as an initiative to renew their commitment to serving the public good. Over this time, new administrative units and positions emerged on campuses. These units were devoted to coordinating public service activities and community outreach/partnerships. Courses that incorporated service learning (or a community service component) were introduced into the college curriculum. In short, campuses have explicitly developed strong links with communities that can benefit

greatly from an exchange of expertise and problem-solving capacities with dedicated teaching staff and students.

Aside from these changes in practice and the emphasis on public service, there is still some debate and disagreement as to how one goes about documenting and measuring the societal contributions of higher education. These are most readily identified in economic analyses (taking into account the costs as well as the returns on investment). Most work in this area is conducted in response to reductions in spending for public institutions (Lewis and Hearn, 2003), or in the interest of promoting investments to improve education in the different states. State governments, for example, have begun to make the connection between baccalaureate attainments in the population and the ability to attract employers in science and technology. They are moving their economy from a manufacturing emphasis to a more sophisticated service economy powered by educated workers. In addition, economists have calculated that achieving equity in baccalaureate attainments across racial ethnic groups in various states (particularly for African Americans and Hispanics) could not only help attract employers seeking skilled workers, but also bring in billions of additional dollars in tax revenues. According to Carnevale and Fry (2000), 'Increasing minority participation to a level equal to non-Hispanic Whites would add $231 billion in increased GDP, an amount that would generate at least $80 billion in new tax revenues' (p. 11). Everyone stands to gain when institutions of higher education achieve significant progress in creating diverse learning environments that result in more equitable degree attainments across the population.

Public non-monetary benefits of higher education have also been documented and summarized in the literature (Rowley and Hurtado, 2003). In regions that have more individuals with college degrees and/or the presence of higher education institutions, researchers have identified a reduction in unemployment, crime rates, poverty rates and income inequality. Improvements have also been documented in environmental quality and the population's ability to use and adapt to new technology. Increases have also been noted in charitable giving, community service, democratic institutions, attention to human rights and political stability. Greater social cohesion and appreciation of diversity have also been noted in such communities. Substantial progress has been made in documenting the contributions of higher education in advancing societal goals. The question is whether this evidence is substantial enough to garner sufficient public support for institutions and stave off criticisms of higher education. Even with increasingly sophisticated economic studies, however, most contend that financial support for higher education will not return to previous levels (Brandl and Holdsworth, 2003).

CONCLUSION

With substantial research on the contributions to individuals and society, and the added value that higher education provides (as summarized in brief here), why is American higher education confronted with pressure to assess institutional productivity (degree outputs) and student learning outcomes? There is continuing concern about access and affordability for the population, variations in retention rates through college graduation that persist across and within institutions, and international competitiveness in terms of the skills of college graduates. These are important concerns that are widely shared, both inside and outside higher education. However, the Department of Education recommends a method of controlling costs, assessing institutional productivity, and using accountability measures to develop a way for the public to assess the quality of higher education institutions (US Department of Education, 2006). It is important to continually monitor the multiple outcomes of higher education and become more transparent about institutional processes and accomplishments. However, this consumer-oriented approach is problematic because it

will limit the outcomes of higher education or focus on a single set of measures that exclude results such as citizenship, moral development, intercultural competency, and the flexibility in thinking necessary to lead in a diverse and complex world. It will most likely result in yet another ranking of institutions with no regard for the types of students they educate or the available resources of an institution. This 'outcome-based' approach will only highlight the disparities. It will not eliminate disparities or lead to significant investment in institutional programmes and educational innovation that promote a broad array of outcomes.

If we were to place nations on a 'continuum between individualist and collectivistic extremes of educational philosophy' (Bowen, 1977, p. 47), we would conclude that American higher education has always leaned towards an individualist philosophy, with periods throughout our history in which we have made significant public investments for matters of national import. Unfortunately, most of these matters of import have been rationalized by policymakers as necessary for our 'national defence' (as in the National Defence and Education Act, and National Defence Student Loan programmes that made higher education accessible to war veterans and subsequently to students from low-income families). Other matters of public good have been given lower priority than these concerns. The underlying funding for American higher education is largely based on the assumption that higher education is a private good in which individuals must make an investment, This may be the source of the problem. Some dramatic effort is needed to reverse this frame, to reinvest in American higher education, to consider more completely its contributions to the public good and its multiple outcomes.

This current push towards assessment and greater accountability is not the first effort to gain greater control over the autonomy of higher education. Howard Bowen's 1977 book was clearly a response to such pressures, and it is likely that campuses will continually be questioned on

how they are making a difference to the lives of individuals and to macro-levels of social development. It will be hard to maintain higher education's role as an independent critic of society when society has become critical of its higher education institutions. Campuses that regularly engage with local communities and widely publicize their activities stand a better chance of retaining public confidence. Assessment of students and documentation of contributions to society will continue in the future. Institutions would do well to define their multiple goals for advancing human and social development, implement innovations to achieve them and document their accomplishments.

One of the greatest contributions of higher education institutions has been in advancing the social transformation process. In times when our institutions were not moving fast enough, our own students became critics who invested in the transformation of our institutions to meet the needs of a changing society. Higher education is the place to foster a critical consciousness and commitment to social change. Institutions have been actively engaged in the production of citizens who are not simply technically skilled. They also possess the values, skills, and knowledge to close the growing social gaps that exist in our society. Intentional education with the aim of fostering concern for the public good reflects a belief that our students represent our best investment for a more just, equitable and democratic society. What institutions collectively do to strive for a new vision of society and to educate students to attain this will be of key importance to our future.

REFERENCES

AAC&U (2007) *College Learning for the New Global Century*. A report from the National Leadership Council for Liberal Education and America's Promise (http://www.aacu.org/advocacy/leap/documents/GlobalCentury_final.pdf).
Bowen, H.R. (1977) *Investment in Learning: The Individual and Social Value of American Higher Education*. San Francisco: Jossey-Bass Publishers.

Brandl, J.E. and Holdsworth, J.M. (2003) On measuring what universities do: A reprise. In: Lewis, D.R. and Hearn, J. (eds). *The Public Research University: Serving the Public Good in New Times*. Lanham, MD: University Press of America.

Carnevale, A.P. and Fry, R.A. (2000) *Crossing the Great Divide: Can We Achieve Equity When Generation Y Goes to College?* Princeton, NJ: Educational Testing Service.

Day, J.C. and Newburger, E.C. (2002) *The Big Payoff: Educational Attainment and Synthetic Estimates of Work–Life Earnings*. Washington, DC: US Census Bureau.

Friedman, T. (2005) *The World is Flat: A Brief History of the 21st Century*. New York: Farrar, Straus and Giroux.

Gutmann, A. (1987) *Democratic Education*. Princeton, NJ: Princeton University Press.

Hurtado, S. (in press) The sociology of the study of college impact. In: Gumport, P.J. (ed.) *Sociology of Higher Education*. Baltimore, MA: Johns Hopkins University Press.

Hurtado, S. (2003) *Preparing college students for a diverse democracy*. Final report to the US Department of Education, Office of Educational Research and Improvement, Field Initiated Studies Program. (see website www.umich.edu/~divdemo/presentations.htm for pdf copy).

Lewis, D.R. and Hearn, J. (eds) (2003) *The Public Research University: Serving the Public Good in New Times*. Lanham, MD: University Press of America.

NCES (National Center for Education Statistics) (2006) *The Condition of Education, 2006*. US Department of Education. Washington, DC: US Government Printing Office. Retrieved

from http://www.nces.ed.gov/programs/coe/index.asp.

Pascarella, E.T. and Terenzini, P.T. (1991) *How College Affects Students: Findings and Insights from Twenty Years of Research*. San Francisco: Jossey-Bass.

Pascarella, E.T. and Terenzini, P.T. (2005) *How College Affects Students: A Third Decade of Research*. San Francisco: Jossey-Bass.

Rowley, L. and Hurtado, S. (2003) The non-monetary benefits of undergraduate education. In: Lewis, D.R. and Hearn, J. (eds) *The Public Research University: Serving the Public Good in New Times*. Lanham, MD: University Press of America.

US Department of Education (2006) *A Test of Leadership: Charting the Future of US Higher Education*. Washington, DC. Retrieved from: http://www.ed.gov/about/bdscomm/list/hiedfuture/index.htlm.

NOTE

1   For example, more than 200 institutions have participated in data collection efforts for over 40 years as part of the Cooperative Institutional Research Programme (administered by the Higher Education Research Institute at the University of California at Los Angeles) that offers student surveys at college entry and subsequent follow-ups at the end of the first year, fourth year and occasionally 10 years after college entry. In any one year, 600–700 institutions participate and this collaborative effort is independent of government investment in student and teaching staff surveys.

GOOD PRACTICE II.6

Training and research for community-based development (Coady International Institute, Canada)

GUNI Observatory[1]

CONTEXT

The Millennium Development Goals are a blueprint agreed to by all the world's countries and leading development institutions.

Civil society organizations, local governments and NGOs play a crucial role in working towards these global goals. These entities work to improve living conditions at the local level in a way that respects the unique characteristics of each locale and supports community-based development processes.

Today's major development organizations and their leaders must be prepared to respond creatively and dynamically to rap-

idly changing contexts. Knowledge, training and the ability to transfer development experiences are therefore essential to the success of civil society organizations, especially in today's world, where rapid global transformations can have a profound impact on the organization and mobilization of people and communities around the world.

The Coady International Institute is dedicated to supporting and strengthening associations that work at the local and/or national levels to achieve the Millennium Development Goals through local, community-based development.

DESCRIPTION

The Coady International Institute is an independent unit of Saint Francis Xavier University. Founded in 1959, the Institute is dedicated to training the leaders of community organizations, NGOs, local governments and institutions to improve the living conditions of poor communities, especially in developing countries.

The Institute's perspective is essentially defined by its training method, its parallel activities in research and development of training materials, and its involvement in international networks.

The Institute works with an annual

budget of US$3,700,000. It receives funding from the Canadian federal government through the Canadian International Development Agency (CIDA), from public and private donors, and through its own activities (registration fees, projects and consulting services).

The activity of the Coady International Institute is based on a tradition that dates back to the 1920s, when Moses Coady began pioneering a practice of popular education and community organizing in the area surrounding Saint Francis Xavier University (Canada). In 1928, the university's Extension Department was founded on the six guiding principles of the Antigonish Movement:

- The primacy of the individual.
- Social reform must come through education.
- Education must begin with the economic.
- Education must be through group action.
- Effective social reform involves fundamental changes in social and economic institutions.
- The ultimate objective of the movement is a full and abundant life for everyone in the community.

GOALS

The following are the main goals of the Coady International Institute:

- To provide education for action.
- To provide local leaders with a transformative learning experience that equips them with new knowledge and practical skills that they can use to help develop their communities.
- To deepen knowledge of local community development proposals.
- To develop materials to train grassroots organizations and communities in community organization methods and microcredits.

PROCESS

Due to its extensive experience in the field of adult education, the Coady International Institute initially focused its efforts on training the leaders of grassroots community organizations, NGOs and institutions dedicated to the struggle against poverty. The Institute eventually began to see the need to complement the education of graduate students and to carry out training and research activities tailored to each local context. As a result, it defined two major areas of activity: (1) training, and (2) research and cooperation.

TRAINING PROGRAMMES

The Institute currently offers four educational programmes:

1. *Diploma programme:* This 23-week, face-to-face educational programme is designed for experienced leaders of civil society organizations and social movements.
2. *Certificate programme:* The Institute offers nine three-week courses that focus on specific topics.
3. *Master of Adult Education – Community Development Stream:* This programme, created in 2005, relies mostly on distance-learning methods, including professional internships at international institutions or foundations.
4. *Distance learning:* Since 2006, the Institute has offered a distance-learning course on community-based microcredits.

Women and aboriginal people are given priority in the student selection process. The Institute only accepts applications from active members of civil society organizations with demonstrable experience. With the exception of the master's programme, a formal university education is not a prerequisite for admission to the Institute's programmes. However, applicants are expected to demonstrate a minimum level of studies and, most importantly, competence in the English language.

The Institute offers a scholarship programme, which also gives priority to women and aboriginal people. In awarding scholarships, the Institute does not consider income levels, since it is assumed that all participants will use their training for social purposes and therefore improve the general living conditions of their communities.

RESEARCH AND COOPERATION PROJECTS

1. *Asset-based community development*
   The main activities of this international area of research are as follows:
   - Documenting and analysing existing international examples of community-driven and asset-based development.
   - Exploring ways in which an asset-based community development approach can be successfully applied in various international contexts.
   - Assessing the implications of an asset-based approach for the role of NGOs, local governments and other intermediaries.
   - Identifying the optimal policy and regulatory environment for the successful application of asset-based community development projects.

2. *Microfinance*
   In 2005, the Ford Foundation entrusted the Institute with assessing the implementation of a rural microcredit programme over the course of three years. In 2006, the Institute formed a permanent microcredit group that works on cooperation projects with microfinance organizations in India, participates in international conferences and publishes academic papers and books. The Institute has published three training manuals that focus on microcredits.

3. *Peace-building and conflict transformation*
   The following are some of the Institute's most important projects in this area:
   - A five-year project to develop a culture of peace in post-war Sierra Leone. Three local organizations and two conflict-management organizations are also involved in this project.

- Collaboration with the Talaat Harb Center for Training and Consultancy and the Coptic Evangelical Organization for Social Services in Cairo, Egypt, to develop peace-building training materials.

4. *First Nations fisheries*
The Institute collaborates with fishery organizations in three Canadian provinces to promote traditional fishing practices that are sustainable and environmentally friendly. Through hands-on training programmes, professional fishermen are taught traditional fishing techniques.

5. *Advocacy and networking*
Civil society organizations and social movements need to be engaged in influencing political programmes and national legislation. Their participation encourages the development of social policies focused on community development and guarantees the transparency of the processes and the commitment of political actors.

Civil society organizations and social movements is currently involved in training and support programmes in Namibia, Egypt and India that aim to prepare civil society to participate in the development of social policies.

6. *Global partnership programme*
The Institute provides support and trained personnel to local develop- ment organizations in various regions of the world. Through these activities, the Institute has formed an international network of local collaborators and partners that provides mechanisms for disseminating best practices and debating issues related to community development.

RESULTS

The overall results of the Coady International Institute can be summarized as follows:

- Over the years, 5000 local leaders from 130 countries have graduated from the Institute, which represents an average of over 100 participants per year in the various training courses.
- The Institute engages in an ongoing learning process to refine its educational methods. In order to offer a truly practical education, the Institute continually works to develop innovative curricular content, cooperative techniques and a wide range of focused methods.
- The Institute's research – and especially its action research – involves participatory techniques.

The following are some of the Institute's quantitative results for 2007:

- Creation of ten community-based development training manuals, which can be used to offer training programmes suited to specific local needs.
- Publication of five scientific articles documenting learning processes and innovative practices in various local contexts.
- Preparation of five case studies using community-based research techniques.
- Support provided to ten local institutions.

RECOMMENDATIONS

To offer training in community-based development, we recommend the following:

- Respect the experience, knowledge and skills of the students.
- Link the activity of learning to the learning of the activity.
- Provide spaces for dialogue and reflection.

When carrying out community-based cooperation and research projects, it is essential to select partner organizations carefully. As a rule, they should be deeply rooted in the community and have transparent management and planning principles. The proper selection of partner organizations ensures that the key activities of the project – planning and execution – can be carried out correctly. The organization's knowledge of the local area is essential to the success of the project.

NOTE

1   Text written by the Universities and Social Commitment Observatory with information provided by Jim Marlon, Olga Gladkikh and Nanci Lee, Coady International Institute.

GOOD PRACTICE II.7
Research and service-learning model (Duke University, USA)

GUNI Observatory[1]

CONTEXT

The USA is one of the countries where service-learning is most widespread among higher education institutions. Indeed, over 900 US universities have service-learning departments. Service-learning in the USA is mainly voluntary. It aims to give students a sense of responsibility towards social problems in their community.

Various institutional organizations promote this form of learning, which is linked to voluntary work and civic programmes (such as Learn and Serve America). In addition, various networks formed by universities and public organizations (such as Campus Compact) promote voluntary service for students and service-learning. Finally, some universities have centres for researching and promoting service-learning. An interesting example is the Service-Learning Research and Development Center at the University of California at Berkeley.

Duke University is one of the 900 universities with a service-learning department. Over ten years' experience in running service-learning programmes have helped the University to identify some of the challenges it must face in order to improve its services to the community. For example, experience shows that the voluntary activities carried out by students do not require high qualifications. If the skills of students – professionals in training – were used, a greater contribution would be made to the community. Another challenge involves encouraging students to reflect more on the impact of their work on the community. The University's Kenan Institute for Ethics has proposed a model that links research with service-learning. This aims to help students make greater use of the specific concepts and skills of their discipline, thus increasing the value of their contribution to society.

DESCRIPTION

The Kenan Institute for Ethics at Duke University, and various other university departments, launched the Research Service-Learning (RSL) programme in 1997. In 2002, the programme received Federal Government funding through the Scholarship with a Civic Mission programme (http://rslduke.mc.duke.edu/). By the end of 2006, a total of US$250,000 had been allocated to the programme.

The RSL method is an educational initiative that establishes a link between service-learning programmes and university research. It consists of training courses for students taking part in service-learning. These students acquire the necessary skills to combine academic research with their voluntary work.

The programme is currently supported by the student association Learning through Experience, Action, Partnership, and Service (LEAPS) and the University's own Office of Service-Learning.

GOALS

The programme aims to promote a service-learning model that:

- Adds value to the students' learning process
- Provides greater benefits to the community by improving students' academic skills and capacities
- Helps the University promote a socially relevant research model.

PROCESS

The RSL programme uses a three-stage model. This model prepares undergraduates and graduates to conduct a research project during their service-learning. The aim of the three-stage approach is for students to gain skills and a deep understanding of research methods as well as ethical principles and civic engagement. The programme modules are titled Scholarship with a Civic Mission. They provide students with a higher level of specialization.

The stages are:

1. *The Gateway Course*: introduces key aspects of service-learning, basic research development skills and reflection on certain ethical issues. At the end of this stage, students present a research project based on their service-learning experience.
2. *The Community Based Research Opportunity*: includes field research as part of students' service-learning. This requires students to keep a research journal that addresses academic, ethical and civic issues of their work.
3. *The Capstone Course*: part of the Scholarship with a Civic Mission programme, in which all students must choose a research project and develop it in collaboration with the communities in which they are working.

Students who complete all three stages will be named 'Duke Civic Scholars'.

PATHWAYS THROUGH RSL

In addition to the training modules, RSL is divided into pathways. This enables students to choose training that either has an interdisciplinary perspective or is related to a specific academic discipline.

Three interdisciplinary pathways are currently under development:

1. Human development and education
2. Human rights and humanitarian issues
3. Public health inequalities.

Two disciplinary pathways are under development:

1. Political science
2. Public policy.

The division of the course into stages and pathways enables students to achieve all the objectives of the RSL method. In addition, students are encouraged to discuss new stages and develop their own pathways according to their interests. They receive the full support of the RSL staff in this process.

RESULTS

- Twenty-one faculties, 9 departments and 48 community partners participate in the programme.
- In the 2005–2006 academic year, 18 gateway courses and 7 community-based research opportunities were completed.
- Since the launch of the programme, 437 students have taken the gateway course, 111 students have taken the second stage, and 3 students are currently taking the final stage. These students will be professionally trained in issues related to community-based research and social action. The RSL training will add value to the theoretic and professional training obtained during their undergraduate studies.

RECOMMENDATIONS

To redefine a service-learning programme, one must:

- Identify areas that need improving.

- Obtain the support of different sectors and departments in the university, especially those that are able to provide specialist knowledge on specific areas that can be improved.

- Include the experience and proposals of students who have taken or are taking the service-learning programme.
- Make sure the number of students is appropriate, in order for each one to receive the necessary support. This is particularly important in the third stage, which requires individual tutoring.

NOTE

1   Text written by the Universities and Social Commitment Observatory with information provided by Betsy Alden and Lauren Hunt, Duke University.

Abstract

The first part of the paper analyses the need to achieve sustainable human development in Latin America and the Caribbean in the context of globalization, the implications of this phenomenon, and its effects on higher education.

The paper argues that higher education is vital in achieving sustainable human development in the region, as a mechanism of equality, justice and modernization. It also analyses the challenges facing universities in the region, such as redefining their social relevance, ensuring equity and addressing the deep inequalities that exist.

The paper emphasizes the need for reform and a radical change in higher education institutions (HEIs) that comprises the range of programmes offered, the syllabus, the range of available qualifications, the scientific method, the different technological perspectives and their fundamental niche markets, the priorities in distributing resources and the social relevance of the education provided, which must be aimed at constructing social and economic platforms for sustainability and responsible human development.

Finally, the paper proposes ideas for achieving a positive transformation of higher education, and underlines that this task must involve all sectors of political and civil society.

INTRODUCTION

The pressing need to establish a new model of sustainable development in Latin America and the Caribbean may not be globally necessary, but nevertheless should not be considered futile. The problems in resolving this need are already apparent and either could be transformed into opportunities to leave behind decades of underdevelopment and widening inequalities or they may become virtually insurmountable obstacles.

The environment in which the core of the higher education system is based consists of the public universities of the region, which survive in the most challenging conditions of inequality and financial hardship. They suffer from pronounced deficits at all levels of their organ-ization, a high degree of obsolescence and traditionalism, scarce investment in infrastructure and only minimal support for innovation and the organization of learning platforms for knowledge areas.

Poverty in the region continues to affect more than 200 million people, of whom 88 million live in abject poverty. This number represents more than a quarter of the total population. During the final decades of the 20th century, now considered the 'lost decades', the entire region was affected by one of the most acute economic crises in its history. The situation persisted until the end of the century and, although slight variations were observed, a full recovery was never made.[1]

Dominant globalization, which serves the interests of a small number of powers and countries, imposed new imbalances and conditions that, rather than contribute to the development of local capabilities for creating and disseminating knowledge and increasing the possibilities of equitable development, placed further constraints on and weakened those capabilities.

This was the price paid by Latin America and the Caribbean for joining the globalization market, which stalled further development in higher education and scientific research – two areas that could have worked together to disseminate knowledge and learning as beneficial public assets used to fight poverty and inequality, to improve competitiveness and to underline the transition towards a consolidated democratic society. Thus, questions were asked of the region's ability to reach desirable sustainability goals; failure to do so would relegate it to the turbulent group of societies with environmental problems, ongoing structural divides, growing imbalances in science and technology and increasing inequality. A number of international commitments have been signed by different governments in Latin America and the Caribbean, such as the Millennium Development Goals, Education for All, cooperation agreements for attaining development with equality and justice, and agreements related to human rights, peace, gender equality and overcoming poverty.

Education in general, and particularly higher

Axel Didriksson

education, has become a common concern for all social agents and sectors and is considered pivotal in development as a mechanism for equality, justice and modernization. However, the dominant strategies of the past three decades have not been capable of translating this conception into effective indicators of fundamental social impact.

Nevertheless, the new political atmosphere of the 21st century has created new expectations, with the emergence of democratic governments in leading countries such as Argentina, Chile, Uruguay, Brazil and Ecuador, and in the administrations of major cities such as Mexico City. These expectations concern the possibility of linking higher education to sustainability and creating platforms for new, socially relevant knowledge areas.

CONTEXT

The great challenge that faces the universities of Latin America and the Caribbean is to redefine their social coverage, to reach greater levels of equality and to overcome the profound backwardness that exists. These initiatives should be related to the reform and radical change of the range of programmes offered, the syllabus, the range of available qualifications, the scientific method, the different technological perspectives and their fundamental niche markets, the priorities for resource distribution and the social relevance of the education, which is related to the pressures of the unequal and exclusionist scenario in which it operates.

Consequently, the priority for universities in the region is to combine strategies that focus on broadening education and changing its organizational foundations and teaching content. This will require enormous effort during the coming years, as it will be necessary not only to extend secondary and higher education to a broader social base (given the growth of school-age groups), but also to create new learning opportunities, social skills, knowledge and abilities that break the traditional vicious circle of one-dimensional, hierarchical teaching, which is representative of a structured liberal organization.

The conditions in which this task must be performed are far from ideal and the challenges enormous, but they cannot be approached from an impractical, local perspective. However, neither is it possible to raise them to a broader social level without introducing a new structure of *regional* integration linked to the new international division between work and knowledge. We cannot resort to a nationalistic mentality, yet neither can we adopt a narrow, regionalist stance, since isolated institutions are not capable of tackling the major challenges of the future. However, the conditions do not yet exist in which the current international consensus can be incorporated and extended in a new type of interconnected, cooperative educational model.

The logic of globalization today acts against itself by eroding institutions' capacity to integrate and collaborate. It imposes a single discourse, one of a global threat and a unique power that determines the commercialization of knowledge, rather than providing a path of solidarity and convergence towards addressing the problems of survival and human risk.

These divergences are best illustrated in the field of education because, whereas the development of human capital depends directly on its maximum expansion and quality in those countries with the greatest potential for expansion through educated youngsters, the conditions in which this phenomenon acts are extremely poor, as is the case in Latin America and the Caribbean.

The situation described above indicates that globalization has been unable to create a suitable and socially relevant alternative to the joining of international powers in support of a new and diverse knowledge society based on a culture of egalitarianism. This is illustrated through a crisis of transition in which the conditions for the eventual emergence and expansion of this society are not yet fully adapted or even properly configured. The most important issue that must be tackled by public policy in the region is therefore how to overturn this long-standing, fundamental situation.

The current state of higher education in the region demonstrates the conditions in which it operates, its inequalities[2] and complexity, but there is also evidence of possible solutions, provided that these will be based on rediscovering the essence of universities in terms of education, social responsibility and as catalysts for development.

The combined responsibility implicit in these considerations forms the basis of the present paper, which has two aims: first, it will analyse the continuity of the present scenario, in which slow development and lack of active participation of public universities as the key agents in a process of change will ultimately restrict them; second, it will suggest within the context of a regional and international discussion that the effect of this action could be profoundly negative. In light of this, an explicit alternative scenario is proposed in which knowledge and innovation within universities are considered public assets and strategic instruments for fighting poverty and inequality, raising the educational level of the population and encouraging democratization and the greater participation of civil society through national financial policies that benefit society as a whole.

These options are presented in a framework of urgent

need, since there is not much time for the governments and principal agents and sectors involved to carry out the tasks required. The cost of ignorance, of slow technological and scientific development and inequality will soon be reflected in a high-risk situation and a socioeconomic catastrophe in our countries. This is, therefore, a task that must be tackled responsibly by the current generation: the subsequent generation will face different problems.

THE CHALLENGES OF GLOBALIZATION IN THE REGION

The region has a specific profile of social development and potential for sustainability, which is, of course, different to that of other regions due to its characteristics and its historical structures and diversity. Based on its attractive, realistic connotations[3] and on the perspective of the principal indicators of human development proposed and maintained by the United Nations Development Programme (UNDP), the region maintains:

- a high rate of population growth and a greater proportion of young people and young adults, which will become more pronounced in the next 20 years[4]
- sustained growth of urbanization and the macrocephalic concentration of the population in large cities
- a risk of replicating traditional inequalities and inequities, where the social debt in education gains particular importance as a factor in some of the greatest difficulties for transforming education and endowing it with social relevance.

If we consider the situation from the point of view of long-term trends, this scenario of regional social inequality becomes extremely complicated in terms of its effect on sustainable human development.

From a different perspective, an absolute priority in the coming decades will be to overcome and overturn social debt in the region, given its current magnitude. This task will have to address the problem of 110 million people living in abject poverty and in conditions of overpowering inequality, in which the income of the richest 20% of the population is 19 times greater than that of the poorest 20%.

In addition, poverty is being shifted to and concentrated in large cities, affecting a mixed population who move from the country to settle in urban centres, migrate to other countries in the worst possible conditions, return when possible to survive in rural areas and re-enter the cycles of poverty of cities in the region or the rest of the world.

Consequently, Latin America is one of the world's largest exporters of its young population, but also of young people with secondary and higher education, which should not be a source of pride in the region.

The extreme inequality in the region can be seen in recruitment to the labour market, in unemployment (more than a quarter of the economically active population) and in informal employment (more than 55% of the population).

The problem has become more acute at a time when the demographic curve of the region could be used as an opportunity, given its potential impact on the labour markets, on unemployment and underemployment, on overcoming levels of poverty and forced migration. This demographic trend could also have an effect on the continued existence of low-quality education that has little impact on the dominating, exclusionist structures of international science and technology markets, which has been the case until now.[5] This demographic situation could also be beneficial to the conditions in which the knowledge society operates and the emergence of new areas of production, which are based on national and regional systems of scientific and technological research and innovation that rely on the flow of young researchers.

Education and human development must therefore move forward together to avoid a pattern of greater dependence on traditional divides and power structures, which are obsolete from the perspective of constructing not only shared interests in the region, but also unique interests specific to certain areas, without which it will be impossible to ensure the desired social and cultural survival. Consequently, the relationships between education and sustainable development should be the areas in which the region works to overcome models that associate education indiscriminately with productivity or with the concept of training as human capital, considered only from a technical or economic perspective. This central relationship must be focused on constructing an alternative in which the values of a new citizenship are interwoven with full participation in a new context of social richness and greater well-being with equality and equity.

THE IMPLICATIONS OF HIGHER EDUCATION FOR HUMAN AND SOCIAL DEVELOPMENT

The definition of governmental policies, both at national and regional level, is crucial to understanding this point. The development scenario is becoming increasingly global in terms of its commercial, financial, technological and economic values and the general perspective of information. However, it also depends on local political forces, which determine courses of action and take decisions. On a global level this situation is creating a dual society of increasing inequality between nations as a whole and large sectors of their populations. Globalization is characterized by its asymmetry: it concentrates wealth in very small sectors and drives increasingly broad sections of the population into poverty. The prevailing globalization is neither inclusive nor liberating but exclusive and dominating. It is based more on the accumulation of wealth by a small minority than on human solidarity. For example, 20% of the world's population control 83% of global income and the poorest 20% receive only 1.4%. And while 24% of the global population currently live in poverty and earn less than one dollar per day, a further 46% earn less than two dollars per day. A UN report from January 2005 states that more than one billion people (a fifth of the world population) try to survive on incomes of less than one dollar per day and a further 2.7 billion receive only two dollars. The report also states that 840 million people go hungry and one thousand million do not have access to drinking water. As a result, human development linked to higher education, which is a lever for fundamental change in the region, is inconsistent and unequal between different countries, since it is controlled by the decisions of prominent governments and agents. Although this heterogeneity is understandable and necessary, given the characteristics of Latin America and the Caribbean, it is more pronounced in some countries and more *restricted* and apparently modernizing in others.

Consequently, there is no sense in defining a model to represent the automatic and acritical insertion (if indeed this is possible) into an irresponsible globalization and a process of unintelligent knowledge societies in which islands of prosperity with high standards of quality of life contrast with widespread poverty that affects millions and millions of people. As stated by the United Nations report *Understanding Knowledge Societies* (2005):

> To be a Smart Knowledge Society (as distinct from a Nominal or Warped Knowledge Society), it is not enough to be rich in main assets and to take care of their development. A new sense of direction in development and a commitment to this new direction must assure high levels of quality and safety of life. Mass production of the knowledge 'to do', piling up technological innovation, and converting them into products and services in the framework of the Knowledge Economy managed by the currently existing market does not by itself assure high levels of quality and safety of life for all people everywhere. The new direction in development can be formulated on the basis of using the techniques and means to mass-produce knowledge to turn out and apply the knowledge 'to be', to 'co-exist' and to maintain developmental equilibrium. (p. xii)

If the tendency prevails, in which emphasis is placed on developing knowledge societies with no social benefits and subjected to a market dominated by transnational companies, as part of a process in which abundant wealth and abundant poverty become concentrated, the scenario for countries in Latin America and the Caribbean will continue to be one of great vulnerability. Changing this situation will call on the ability of these countries to establish strategies focused on internal decisions and governability, of a new type of society that is necessarily different from the preferred model of subordinating globalization and that will depend on making use of technology, expertise, knowledge, education and capital in the framework of an accelerated learning process of cultural and intellectual development.

The possibility of overcoming the inherent vulnerability of the region will depend on different factors, the most influential of which include the prevention of mass migration of the workforce, the ability to successfully combat the destructive effects of global warming and the alteration of the biosphere, drug-related terrorism and violence, corruption and political manipulation, natural disasters and those caused by foreseeable and unforeseeable diseases.[6] Water is another variable that must be considered a significant element in the destabilization of countries in the region, not simply in terms of supply, health or quantity, but because of its relationship with development and education. The UNDP Human Development Report 2006 states: 'Some 1.1 billion people in the developing world do not have access to a minimal amount of clean water [and] some 2.6 billion people – half the developing world's population – do not have access to basic sanitation [...] The time burden of collecting and carrying water is one explanation for the very large gender gaps in school attendance in many countries. In Tanzania school attendance levels are 12% higher for girls in homes 15 minutes or less from a water source than in homes an hour or more away. [...] For millions of poor households, there is a straight trade-off between time spent in school and time spent collecting water'.

In addition to the destabilizing variables mentioned above, which impede the creation of a new scenario of human development in the region, we should also consider those related to knowledge, science and technology. We are, of course, referring to the digital divide, the delay in incorporating new learning models and generally available computer facilities, and the illiteracy of this new era. In cases such as this, rampant globalization for transnational benefit works against progress. The costs of computerization measured in user tariffs and distribution of connectivity are higher in Latin America than North America, Europe and even Asia: from 40 dollars to more than 100 dollars. In addition, 80% of all websites are in English, even though only one in ten people on the planet speak this language.

The trend towards trade and commercialization in higher education should also be considered in this series of difficulties.[7]

The arguments given above present a scenario in which the region is actually moving away from the Millennium Development Goals, from the patterns of a new type of development and the perspectives of an intelligent knowledge society. It is therefore necessary to work according to a different, original plan of action and to embark on new regional and international discussion that aims not to be an extension of previous work or models but to take on the challenge of an alternative strategy.

The key may be found in the way higher education, science and technology are changed and carried out and in the impact of this new scenario on income distribution, which is a strong, multidimensional relationship. Latin America and the Caribbean is the region with the most unequal distribution of wealth in the world, which is a cause of the low proportion of young people with secondary and higher education (it has an average education rate of approximately 19%). This is much lower than the rates in developed countries, which are around 60%. These vast differences are reflected in the expenditure per student and in the investment aimed at overcoming severe structural deficiencies.

This is reflected in the poor performance of the regional population in average indicators of educational performance, above all in the 18 to 30 age group. This is the age group that could have the greatest impact on the dynamics of the labour markets and produce changes aimed at creating a generalized information society for the benefit of society as a whole. This also means that the relationship between people with education related to modern knowledge, people with a critical civic conscience and people with a broad relationship with science and technology is reflected in a lack of cutting edge research at the regional or national level, which means that networks for creating and disseminating new technology emerge in companies and are therefore subject to the transnational chains that dominate the world market.

The inequalities in access to education and the lack of opportunities to move into the contemporary labour markets represent the most acute problem in the region. This is witnessed above all in the indigenous population, in mothers and daughters who are excluded from education, in marginalized young people and in the adult population with a high degree of educational deficit (that is, who have not completed basic education). Consequently, inequality is found in the region for reasons of gender, colour, ethnic origin and social class, which already exist in basic education and become more acute in secondary and higher education.

Therefore, the solutions to this huge problem should be related to governmental public and social policies to offer wider and more secure access at all levels of education. They must overcome the obsolescence of the discriminatory curricular system and the lack of substance in modern methods and content by providing programmes of equity and equality that can play a direct role in improving the chances of admission and career prospects.

CHALLENGES TO HIGHER EDUCATION IN THE REGION

Higher education is at the centre of discussions on the possibility of creating a knowledge society. This is illustrated in the scale of expansion of higher education and in the dramatic increase in the number of students across the world.[8] In Latin America and the Caribbean this expansion is apparent in the wider variety of HEIs and in the growth of private and transnational companies. This forms part of a contradictory process in which inequalities continue to deny access to higher education to vast majorities of the population and the services provided by universities are excessively privatized and commercialized. Due to the combination of a rigid syllabus, principally organized across hermetic disciplines, and the inequalities discussed above, access to higher education remains limited and the plan to achieve widespread access and, ultimately, universal access is failing, at a time when there should be generalized access to *socially significant knowledge*.[9]

This reveals an extremely complex variable that will continue to affect educational and human development in Latin America and the Caribbean as long as the mass generalization of knowledge production and transfer is not accompanied by necessary changes in the access to information and communication technologies, in the creation of new learning platforms related to new, interdisciplinary knowledge areas and the transformation of excessively traditional and obsolete management, funding and leadership models. The initiatives for a new type of higher education for human development in the region continue to be based on the same approach that was used at least two decades ago.

This can be seen in the level of investment in scientific and technological research during the first decade of the 21st century, which is between three and five times lower than in developed countries. In addition, this investment is concentrated in four or five leading countries, as are the majority of postgraduate students, particularly at doctoral level. Needless to say, this destroys the possibility of linking the knowledge gained from research to the needs of companies across the region and generates underemployment and unemployment among university graduates, even those with high levels of specialization. On the whole, innovation that is both original and adapted to the region is extremely limited, despite the significant advances in this area in the past decade.[10] The widespread creation of assessment and accreditation bodies has done little to bring about this change, since these organizations have focused on assessing existing models and introducing quality standards, rather than proposing innovative prospective models.

This process of imitation focused on models of assessment and accreditation that incorporated performance indicators common to developed countries, rather than using indicators that are relevant to developing countries and determine whether standards of social profile and equality are being met. The outcome of this process has been spread across the entire region.[11] These results have been the cause of much celebration and a sense of complacency, despite the fact they are generally poor and repeated year after year, albeit with some exceptions.

Simultaneously to the introduction of these unchanged assessment models based on quality indicators for other, predominantly developed, countries, the commercialization of higher education services and national and transnational privatization began to take greater hold of the region, as discussed above. The influence of the private sector in higher education in the region has been growing steadily since the 1990s. By 2005, private higher education accounted for 37% of the total enrolment,[12] and had increased to 47.5% by 2006. These increasingly high average values for the region are a consequence of values as high as approximately 70% being returned from countries such as Brazil and Colombia.[13]

The global assessment made by UNESCO in 1998 did not envisage commercialization of higher education on this scale, but it must now be paid special attention given the rapid expansion of private universities even into the less developed countries in the region. This expansion fuels inequality, creates a false sense of social progress and saturates the market with graduates qualified in law, marketing, IT, administration and other similar profiles, as well as perpetuating the obsolescence of the system and levels of underemployment. The privatization of higher education in the area has not led to advances in human development but has, in reality, had the opposite effect. It is, however, just another element of a business that operates on a global scale.[14]

IDEAS FOR CHANGE

Around the turn of the century, the agenda of public universities began to change considerably: over a period of two decades, the traditional focus on social demands, growth, decentralization or planning gave way to an insistence on issues such as assessment and accreditation, the handling and management of the recession, and programmes for extraordinary funding linked to competition, tuition fees, the generation of resources, commercialization and the intervention of international financial bodies.

Consequently, the traditional agents of change in universities (students and unions) have adopted a less direct role in university reform (concentrating instead on union demands), whereas researchers, lecturers and academic heads gained prominence and become the principal agents in defining the internal and external changes of HEIs.

Changes have also been made to the traditional systems for granting government subsidies and assigning resources. Policies of diversification have introduced a greater degree of competition between institutions and it has been suggested that public universities should gradually give way to private institutions as the most representative higher education organizations at the national level.

Nevertheless, in terms of numbers of researchers, numbers of projects, scientific production and the cultural impact of institutional initiatives at undergraduate and particularly postgraduate level, public universities have clearly maintained their leading role within the higher education system, nationally and even regionally. The concentration of researchers and postgraduate programmes in the public universities of Latin America and the Caribbean has significantly overtaken the regional average.

At the same time, regional cooperation in higher education and by HEIs has increased noticeably. Issues such as university mobility, recognition of credits and equivalence of degrees, combined programmes in different areas and at different levels, the extensive use of new technologies, shared degree programmes and the creation of multilateral networks and programmes have been addressed in a number of initiatives, with relative success, and have become part of the priority agenda for change in HEIs at the regional level.

In practice, with the exception of lower quality, less representative universities, the vast majority of public universities in Latin America and the Caribbean are now involved in bilateral and trilateral relationships, in some cases at the sub-regional or regional levels.

We may have moved into a new century, but the general panorama of higher education shows signs of stagnation. While the fragmentation of the traditional model –

which we have discussed for public universities – has been consolidated by a series of new institutions of different types and levels (private and public, university and non-university, polytechnic, technological, short-cycle and commercial, among others), and a new wave of demand for higher education has spread across the region, the same inequalities and injustices based on gender, race, ethnicity and socioeconomic level have simply been replicated on a larger scale. In addition, the new model espouses the notion that market logic is one of the most important indicators of educational quality, while transnational companies and firms dedicated to the commercialization of educational services have found substantial room for expansion. As stated in the following report:

> Higher education in Latin America has recorded increases since the second half of the 20th century. The number of universities has grown from 75 in 1950 to more than 1500 in the present day, most of which are private. The number of students has increased from 276,000 in 1950 to almost 12 million; in other words, enrolment increased by a factor of 45 in 50 years … The annual enrolment growth rate has been 6% since 1990. This rate has been much higher for private universities (8%) than public institutions (2.5%). This has led to a situation in which more than 50% of university enrolment in Latin America now takes place at private universities, unlike the situation in 1980, in which Latin American universities were predominantly state-run … The increase in enrolment has led to a considerable increase in the overall tertiary education participation rate: from 2% in 1950 to 19% in 2000 (a tenfold increase in 50 years). However, this rate is much lower than the corresponding value in developed countries: 51.6% in 1997.[15]

Yet despite the impact of this increasingly unequal situation, we also find substantial advances in different types of programme, institution and policy, but above all in the emphasis on change in the (mainly public) universities themselves to promote influential new initiatives and innovations. For example, we should note that there are already structures, associations, networks and organizations at different levels and different stages of development that are working to support the construction of a new period of autonomy and improvement by laying the essential foundations for tasks related to a Latin American knowledge society. Examples of this are the work of organizations such as the Union of Universities of Latin America and the Caribbean (UDUAL), the Network of Public Macrouniversities of Latin America and the

Caribbean, the Montevideo Group University Association, the Higher Council of Latin American Universities (CSUCA), which is the principal sub-regional association, the Association of Caribbean Universities and Research Institutes (UNICA) and the Andrés Bello Agreement for Andean and non-Andean countries. There are also several other associations responsible for the changes that are appearing in Latin American universities as a move towards new development.

A large number of European and international cooperation agencies also carry out beneficial work in the region, the most important of which are the International Association of Universities and the Spanish Agency for International Cooperation (AECI). The AECI currently administers funds provided by the Spanish government, the UNDP, the EU, the Latin American and Caribbean Economic System (SELA) and the United Nations Conference on Trade and Development (UNCTAD). These funds are directed toward cooperation programmes such as Intercampus (which promotes mobility among students and academics) MEC-MER (scientific cooperation), Ibercue (university-company cooperation) and specific support initiatives.

By a resolution adopted on 10 March 1994, the European Union offers the ALFA programme for academic training in Latin America, which is inspired by similar programmes in Europe (such as Erasmus, Tempus and Comett. The ALFA programme aims to: 'encourage cooperation between higher education institutions of the European Union and Latin America' and to promote cooperation programmes on two levels: institutional management and scientific and technological training. Banco Santander also carries out important cooperation work through its Universia initiative, which has provided support to numerous local, regional and national programmes.

The developments considered above show that the region is entering a new era in which higher education will acquire greater status and become more internationalized. As such, it will be important to continue to promote initiatives that contribute to university mobility, processes of integration and shared teaching. Likewise, universities should work towards achieving horizontal inter-institutional cooperation, which should form the basis of policies explicitly aimed at internationalizing courses and reaching higher levels of academic achievement.

Finally, universities should break with the traditional cooperation structure that operates primarily via bilateral agreements promoted by the academic exchange offices that exist in most of the universities across Latin America and the Caribbean. In recent years, universities have tried to focus this policy on obtaining official recognition for the quality of degree and postgraduate programmes, which has become fundamental in facilitating cooperation within the region.

CONSTRUCTING A DIFFERENT SCENARIO

It has become necessary and is now possible to set up a new strategy of inter-university cooperation and mobility, which aims to develop and strengthen the abilities of countries in Latin America to produce and disseminate scientific and technical knowledge at the regional, national and international levels.

The strategic perspectives of these initiatives should be based on the notion that structural change in higher education is imperative and that the new expression of regional and international cooperation plays a highly relevant role in this process. The fundamental aim of this cooperation should be to strengthen the key components in integrating and linking the individuals, institutions, agencies and resources involved to guarantee a flexible structure of academic networks and mobility that does not replace, alter or overrule local initiatives.

The central objective of the new forms of cooperation should be for participants to develop their own knowledge production and transfer capabilities or to develop this capacity at the local, sub-regional and regional levels. This means that the local agents have the greatest responsibility for designing and formulating the proposals, programmes and projects and are the principal agents in the transformation.

Thus, the scenario of change based on cooperation and regional integration to attain a new social status for the importance of knowledge can be considered a new and alternative approach; it places emphasis on meeting the new demands and requirements of HEIs, which must now begin to plan new organizational structures that facilitate access to knowledge with a social value and new teaching procedures that will be responsible for creating the new regional and global workforce.

In this new scenario of university reform, the academic community is able to integrate with different networks, have an input into public life and the process of democratization, and use widely available learning environments to provide permanent education. This is based on a teaching and organizational model which considers that education is upheld by maintaining the uniqueness of difference, by the creation of new objects of knowledge, by reflection on the role of the other and of totality, by the promotion of self-learning models and by recognition of diversity.

This conception of university reform is based on identifying institutional and regional strengths, understanding the original developments and looking to reshape the abilities of individuals and sectors, rather than drawing distinctions between or reproducing existing inequalities. In terms of higher education policy, this means a model of change that encourages institutions to share their experiences, combine functions and foster relationships, rather than compete with one another.

Above all, this alternative conception requires us to consider educational quality not in terms of products and goals, but in terms of the real conditions of general development and the social value of the knowledge that is produced and distributed and that is linked to national priorities.

This implies a *paradigm shift* in the meaning of university reform in the present era: a shift towards the conception of an open, flexible and self-regulating organizational structure with a strong regional focus and multiple agents operating at different levels.

Knowledge production implies that the knowledge gained from research and from new learning systems is defined by the context in which it is applied and by its public usefulness.

Consequently, knowledge production and transfer refers to an articulated process from existing knowledge to new and recreated knowledge. This definition includes a series of elements and components of know-how, expertise, varied techniques and abilities, mechanisms, programmes, institutions, agencies and agents in the process. An institution that is designed to produce knowledge and transfer it to society must therefore be complex, dynamic and uniquely different.

Organizing innovation requires increased efficiency in the decision-making process, in the decentralization of the institution and in greater horizontal participation, a higher degree of delegation of responsibilities and authorities, and broad integration of autonomous units.

This new role of collective responsibility may be capable of driving progress towards a sustainable knowledge society and is closely related to the nature of the subject we are discussing and the work being carried out in the region by UNESCO-IESALC.

This approach is widely supported. The work of public universities in the region is directly related, to a greater or lesser extent, to the funding systems in place and the well-documented recession, and to the redefined nationwide policies of current regional governments that promote a relationship between equality and knowledge and foster sustainability and human development through the vision of a responsible, equal, just and democratic society.

Given the above considerations, we understand prospective action not as an isolated policy, but as a series of diverse, coherent and coordinated tasks in the short, medium and long term. These tasks will be carried out by public bodies, society in general and the international community to implement changes that will facilitate the introduction of a new, high-level management structure for higher education to construct new knowledge areas, expand social coverage and contribute to the education of new citizens. This new higher education will be a universal right, conceived as a continuous process of academic and personal trajectories linked to other levels of education and aimed at making a tangible contribution to all areas of human development.

As has been stressed throughout this paper, the term human development has specific connotations for the region in question, which are obviously different to those of other contexts. We will consider three of these connotations and study them in context.

As pointed out in the previous chapters, the scenario in this region is immeasurably complex, but also dynamic and full of opportunities. These opportunities depend heavily on the changes introduced by HEIs, above all by public universities, to align their work with the efforts of an active, emerging society with new social agents and leadership structures, which characterizes the current period.

However, the paths to change and progress are different and contradictory, since higher education in Latin America and the Caribbean presents myriad possibilities for creativity and innovation based on two fundamental areas: first, change as a means of bridging the divides of an unequal society; and second, knowledge production and transfer.

Some believe that HEIs should play a market-determined role by training technicians and professionals to meet demands for production, competitiveness and productivity.

Others, such as ourselves, support the transformation of existing institutions and universities to formulate new structures for management and innovation, a new syllabus to serve a new society, and skills related to the free use of knowledge as a public asset intended to lay the economic and social foundations of sustainability and responsible human development. The numerous perspectives converge at this point and produce numerous dynamic combinations, but we will endeavour to outline the principal differences and options and present our own position regarding a fundamental change.

The following points are some of the central ideas, proposals and approaches that should be discussed at the regional level (not in order of priority):

1. Higher education must be predominantly public and free, with a high degree of social relevance in terms of assuming regional and national cooperation and solidarity responsibilities. This will make it possible to set up dynamic networks that share material and human resources, establish creative links, share courses and credits and facilitate mobility in higher education.

2. The knowledge produced and transferred by universities should be aimed at fighting poverty, inequality and inequity and at reducing the gulf between developed and less developed countries. This knowledge should also strengthen the competitiveness and productivity of the region and individual countries on the basis of a new horizontal cooperation and policies of shared responsibility with all social and educational agents and sectors. These commitments should include the training of critical, free citizens with high-level abilities and skills who can assume leading roles in strengthening the democracy and institutions of the region.

3. The universities must strengthen, update and introduce innovations into their research capabilities, in particular by strengthening their scientific foundations and postgraduate programmes and by extending the benefits of this work to society. Above all, they must combat brain drain and the commercial policies that establish knowledge as a private, commercial asset.

4. It is important to diversify funding, but above all to increase budgetary resources as part of a governmental policy that directly favours using resources to support national and even regional priorities through cooperation organizations (regional, national and international), as mentioned above.

5. The region needs an educational policy that acts from a prospective, national vision to establish the transformation of the national education system as its fundamental line of action. This will entail implementing measures that make it possible to design and construct the new teaching, scientific and technological models that underpin a knowledge society for sustainable human development, characterized by equity and equality. It will be necessary to prioritize tasks that have a strong impact on eliminating the traditional educational divides, for example by increasing the levels of coverage and quality of the education and scientific system, and by planning a platform upon which to build a new system for the long term.

6. Support should be provided to the two defined population groups without education – the group aged under 14 and the group aged 15 and over – using teaching approaches that combine formal education with non-formal and open education in a curricular model that combines multiple learning environments supported by the extensive use of information systems, telecommunications, television, radio and all available mass communication media to marshal and stimulate the educational abilities of these population groups.

7. Comprehensive, vocational education should be promoted for the group aged 15 and over.

8. The region must plan to increase and pay closer attention to continuity in the education system, taking into account the annual demographic growth rates for each age group. In particular, priority should be given to increasing coverage of and attention to the groups in upper secondary and higher education.

9. Governments should declare a mandatory schooling period of 12 years.

10. The current goal should be the 'universalization' of upper secondary and higher education.

11. Formal and informal education should be expanded and performance standards and permanence in higher education should be raised to the national average. It will be important to understand that this task is not merely educational but is also related to the social and economic order. Consequently, remedial programmes should be set up in areas such as self-employment, social organization and governability.

12. It is vital to instigate a process of reform and change in upper secondary education, which should be considered a common space for vocational training, high intelligence and scientific and technological development. Institutions at this level should not be nuclei for disseminating knowledge. Instead, they must be transformed into centres for knowledge production and transfer, for a high level of cultural dissemination and for relevance to and connection with the wider social context. The central element in assessing the quality of service offered should be the relevance of the academic work.

13. Science and technology should be considered the strategic components that underpin a knowledge society.

GLOBAL SCENARIO OF THE IMPACT OF THE STRATEGY[16]

If these policies and priorities are implemented, the results will become visible in the period between 2007 and 2012, above all in the educational conditions for young people and young adults, in their ability to meet the demands of complex sectors of the labour market, in the transfer of high-technology, added value components, in the disappearance of imbalance in educational level and in the growth of cultural expression. The results will not be complete or definitive, but they will be dramatic.

A very important advance will be seen in the growth of higher education, in the general average of regular school attendance and in the fact that by 2012, eight of every ten people over the age of 18 will possess twelve years of full-time education. By the same year, the region should have reached the world literacy rate and vocational training will be offered to the whole population.

Between 2012 and 2020 the potential for educational, scientific and technological development will be defined as the foundations of a knowledge society in the region. The change in the education system will be the motor behind this period, which will be characterized by a new dynamism and the break with models that defined almost a century of educational life and development.

The method for overturning the previous model of 'how things are done' will be based on five broad areas of organizing human development, all of which depend on the direction of the proposed educational change:

1. The sense and interconnection of people in their daily lives: that is, how they work and consume, how they move between different areas of social interrelation, how they talk and communicate, how they interact with other people, how they organize their homes, how they relax, how they intervene in political and personal life, how they think and love, and how they fall ill and recover. All these elements depend on the way in which people use the knowledge, information and technology at their disposal.

2. The working population will have to interact increasingly with new technologies, innovations, symbols, languages and abstract concepts that will require them to design unique solutions to unique problems.

3. The organization of this new development, productivity and social welfare will be related to some of the following areas: biotechnology, computing, microelectronics, new materials, space sciences, telecommunications and energy. None of these areas will depend directly on available natural resources, cheap labour or capital. Instead, they will all depend on the building blocks of the new model of production and social relationships: knowledge and learning.

4. The importance of these factors will acquire a market value: in other words, the rewards for the level of knowledge and education reached will increase.

5. The traditional model that remained in place for a century will be replaced quickly and intensively. People will discover that there are thousands of different ways of living, working, maintaining human relationships and producing ideas.

This new society, built on educational and cultural change, will relate local factors directly to the global context, technological factors to the social context, and information to everyday life. This change will be made against the clock as it will be presented as a challenge to society and governments in the region, where equal opportunities and the greater well-being of the population increasingly depend on wider and more egalitarian access to knowledge. The task of governing during this period will be synonymous with educating, and living will be understood as constant access to multiple, varied and permanent forms of learning.

Therefore, the very concept of education will be different and based on a learning model that will have overturned and transformed the most fundamental concepts of the previous model, which was based on the outmoded knowledge criteria of memorization and repetition.

Education will be understood as a series of social or institutional practices that will offer all types of opportunities and stimuli for learning and for knowledge and technology production and transfer. The new system of education for everyone will be presented as an open, flexible lifelong system that will not use sex, economic level, race or age as a criterion governing admission or graduation. This lifelong education will be imparted in a number of forms (formal, informal, open, distance, network-based and so on), although the principal axis will continue to be formal schooling, principally because this type of education will be designed to teach multiple abilities and skills with which to develop 'social culture and intelligence'.

Establishing this new, permanent and lifelong educational system will form part of a new educational policy, understood as a series of common principles, goals and objectives shared between the public and private sectors, the national government, society as a whole, social groups and individuals. This new educational policy will call on a strong public commitment, built upon a broad social consensus that will act as a popular mandate for the short, medium and long term.

The responsibility for reaching these objectives will fall to all sectors of political and civil society. The keys to transforming learning models and establishing a permanent and lifelong education system are the participation and cooperation of HEIs and the support and supervision of the community and the national government. Education becomes a right, but also a duty, for all citizens.

NOTES

1 'Indeed, following the failure of the Structural Adjustment Programmes promoted by the IMF and the World Bank in the 1980s, the 1990s were the backdrop to a certain economic recovery that was not capable, however, of modifying the upward trend of absolute poverty, while relative poverty only decreased by 5 percentage points in the period 1990–1997, affecting around 43 per cent of the population at the end of this period. At the same time, Latin America remains the most unequal region in the world, with levels in the upper income quintile that are between 10 and 16 times higher than those in the lower quintile.' See: Xavier Bonal (2006) 'Globalisation, Education and Poverty in Latin America: toward a new political agenda?' In: Xavier Bonal (ed.) *Globalisation, Education and Poverty in Latin America*. Barcelona: CIDOB Foundation, p. 11.

2 Among many other works on this subject, see the following: 'Latin America is noted for being the developing region with the greatest income inequality. And as has been pointed out by Psacharopoulos et al. (1992): education is the variable with the greatest impact on income inequality … According to the report by the Inter-American Development Bank (IDB) entitled "Education: the Gordian knot", if we want to find the fundamental cause of income inequality in Latin America, we need look no further than its unbalanced education system … Instead of contributing to progress, schooling is reinforcing poverty, perpetuating inequality and slowing economic growth. The problem is not the access, but the permanence indices …'. Robert F. Arnove (2006) 'Education in Latin America: Dependency, Underdevelopment, and Inequality'. In: Xavier Bonal (ed.) *Globalisation, Education and Poverty in Latin America*. Barcelona: CIDOB Foundation, p. 50.

3 Of the many descriptions that have been given of Latin America and the Caribbean, the one I like most and which I consider to be the most accurate was written by the Colombian essayist William Ospina: 'Called Hispanic by the Spanish, Iberian by the Portuguese, Latin by the French, equinoctial, isthmic, insular and meridional by Baron von Humboldt and the Creoles, our America has spent centuries trying to define itself, and this largely fruitless search reveals, at least symbolically, the complexity of its composition and the magnitude of its difficulties. Neither the Spanish language, nor its extension to the Iberian languages, nor even its extension to languages of Latin origin can fully account for this complexity. This America is branded with the stigma of always tending to be defined by something exterior or by only a part of its composition and historical legacy. Perhaps this is why it has never gained complete recognition of itself, since the designations it finds usually exclude some element of its complexity. It is like a creature that will never find its name, a being that, in order to designate itself, had to renounce the evidence of its eyes, its dreams, its wings. This exciting characteristic is gradually becoming a substantive part of its identity and has marked many serious episodes in its history … However, it could be said that of all the names it has sought for itself, the most appropriate could be Mestizo America, which at least attempts to define it by the diversity of its mixtures, and not by the predominance of one of its elements. The term "mestizo" should be understood not only as the mixture of Iberian and indigenous ethnic and cultural elements, but as the multiple convergence of African elements, elements from other European nations and the growing incorporation of traditions from the rest of the world. Our America is less a homogeneous geographical entity than a historical and cultural conjunction, but the common destiny of its inhabitants eventually converted it into a world that must be thought of and approached as a whole, in the same way that, when one thinks of Europe the mind automatically includes Scandinavia and Iceland because shared history ultimately influences geography'. *América Mestiza, el país del futuro*. Ed. Aguilar, Colombia, 2004, pp. 11–12.

4 'Through 2020, an increasing percentage of the population will be in the labor force, and dependency ratios and the

population aged 6 to 18 will decline. This demographic window of opportunity could lead to greater savings and growth and should make it easier for the region to raise education expenditure, increasing coverage and performance'. IDB (2005) *Expanding the Knowledge Capital of Latin America and the Caribbean: An IDB Strategy for Education and Training*. Washington, DC: IDB, p. 19.

5 'In the period that begins after the Second World War, Latin America develops its technological capabilities in the context of the expansion phase of the mass production model of developed countries … Latin American companies also benefited from this system: from the new techniques incorporated in machinery and equipment, from the knowledge obtained by the management staff and workers from their experience in transnational companies … The system was complemented by the learning process derived from adapting plants, the efforts to improve production organization, the vertical articulation between companies linked to production activities and the creation of private and state institutions for the adaptation and dissemination of knowledge and technology … [However] economic reforms begin to take shape in Latin America when the mass production system of developed countries reached maturity and the new technologies linked to the IT and microelectronics revolution and to a new type of industrial and management organization began to develop rapidly … While there is some technology transfer and diffusion in the region incorporated into imported machinery and equipment and through direct foreign investment – that is, from the *know how* imported from the subsidiaries of transnational companies – it is not at the technological forefront and does not develop in the sense of constantly creating new demand for products in continuous diversification … Indeed, transnational companies opened their subsidiaries in search of greater efficiency (cost reduction) and raw materials, also seeking certain technical skills – such as a sufficiently qualified workforce – to carry out their activities. But in most cases, as shown by the studies of Patel and Pavit (1991), Cantwell (1997) and Cimoli (2001), these companies have kept research and development in their own countries, without establishing links with local technological centres or universities. Similarly, the materials, machinery and equipment required come from companies and suppliers belonging to integrated international production systems, which leave no room for local suppliers'. Fernando Calderón (2003) *¿Es sostenible la globalización en América Latina?, Conversations with Manuel Castells*. UNDP, Vol. I, Economic Culture Fund, Chile, pp. 70–7.

6 'The poorest households show a greater tendency to be affected by infectious diseases, as a result of which the life expectancy of the children in these households is lower. A study carried out in different countries shows that transmissible diseases are responsible for 56 per cent of the deaths in the poorest 20 per cent of the population compared with 8 per cent of the deaths recorded in the 20 per cent of the population with the highest income. Similarly, the under-five mortality rates in the poorest 20 per cent of the population mortality are usually twice as high as those in the wealthiest 20 per cent of households (in Bolivia and Peru, the mortality rates are between four and five times higher). And the mortality rates in the poorest 20 per cent of households are falling at almost less than half the average rate of decrease in many countries, a problem identified in the Human Development Report 2005 as a serious threat to achieving the Millennium Development Goals.' UNDP. 2006 Human Development Report. Chapter 1, p. 51.

7 The subject has been developed extensively by a number of authors. See, for example: Hebe Vessuri (ed.) et al., *Perfiles Educativos, Ediciones de Perfiles*, Vol. XXVIII, 2006.

8 The Global Education Digest (2006) of the UNESCO Institute for Statistics provides the latest statistical data on enrolment in different regions and countries. The gross international enrolment index increased from approximately 72 million in 1994 to 132 million in 2004. The gross enrolment rate (GER) for 2004 was 24%. Therefore, the enrolment rate increased by 83% in the space of a decade. This increase was extremely imbalanced. The greatest increase was recorded in the Arab States, which showed an average annual growth rate of approximately 12.83%. This was followed by South and Western Asia, with an average annual growth rate of 9%. Eastern Asia and the Pacific and Sub-Saharan Africa registered an average annual growth rate of 8.9%. Central and Eastern Europe showed an average annual growth rate of 6.6%. This was followed by Latin America and the Caribbean, with 6.1%. The regions of North America, Western Europe and Central Asia experienced the slowest growth, recording rates of 1.68% and 1.10% respectively'. Francisco López Segrera (2007) Educación Superior Internacional Comparada, February, pp. 95–106.

9 See: Carmen García Guadilla (2005) 'Complejidades de la globalización e internacionalización de la educación superior'. *Cuadernos del Centro de Estudios del Desarrollo* (CENDES), 22(58), Tercera Epoca, January–April, p. 5.

10 'The growth of postgraduate programmes is one of the most notable transformations to have occurred in the 1990s in the higher education system: Between 1994 and 1999 postgraduate programmes increased by 168 per cent.' Ernesto Villanueva (2004) 'La Acreditación en América Latina: el caso de Argentina en la RIACES y en el MERCOSUR'. *Revista Iberoamericana de Educación*, **35**, p. 102.

11 See: Ernesto Villanueva (op. cit.). See also Francisco López Segrera (op. cit., pp. 115–7). For a critical reference readers should consult the work of the Brazilian journal *Evaluaçao*, edited by Dr. José Dias Sobrinho.

12 See IDB (2005) *Expanding the Knowledge Capital of Latin America and the Caribbean: An IDB Strategy for Education and Training*. Washington, DC: IDB, pp. 54–5.

13 See López Segrera (op. cit., p. 25).

14 'Global data indicate that international commerce in higher education is 3% greater than the total for all commercial services, and in several countries educational services are situated in the top five are ranked among the top five export sectors (OECD, 2002). The principal recipient country is the United States, which received US$10.29 million from foreign students in 2000, an amount that is greater than the total public budget for higher education in Latin America. According to the OECD (2002) the higher education market in its member countries is worth approximately US$30 billion a year'. Carmen García Guadilla(op. cit.), p. 14.

15 Norberto Fernández Lamarra (2004) 'La Convergencia de los sistemas de educación superior en América Latina. Situación y Desafíos'. Mimeo, Tres De Febrero University, Buenos Aires, Argentina, November, 2004, pp. 2–3.

16 The references for this part of the study are taken from the book published under the United Nations Development Programme (UNDP) and coordinated by Hernando Gómez Buendía. *Educación: la Agenda del Siglo XXI*. UNDP, TM Editores, Colombia, 1998; and from a series of documents released by UNESCO and UNESCO-IESALC.

The social responsibility of universities in Latin America

The social responsibility of universities (SRU) is what links scientific, technological, humanistic and artistic knowledge produced in the context of its application to local, national and global needs. Its primary objective is to promote the social utility of knowledge, thus contributing to improved quality of life. This objective creates the need for an exchange of views between universities and society and entails a sharp expansion in the critical uses of knowledge in society and the economy.

Not all Latin American universities have completely changed their profile to what Gibbons (1997) calls Mode 2 of generating socially useful knowledge. However, in nearly all such institutions, small islands of innovation exist. They contain the seeds of change in the sense that is currently underpinned by the SRU. In this context, there is no doubt that it is important to take stock of the new ideas that foster the relationship between university and society. They are based on knowledge production in specific contexts of application with the aim of contributing to higher levels of social welfare and sustainable human development for Latin American and Caribbean societies.

There follows some examples of the changes brought about by the SRU in Latin American universities, which could provide the basis for an agenda for social commitment in the region.

The National Autonomous University of Honduras has begun a gradual process of bringing the university and social issues closer together through various programmes designed to draw attention to orphans living in extreme poverty, people with very scant financial resources, and teenagers and women in vulnerable situations.

This same project to bring universities closer to marginal sectors of society has been carried out by various universities in Mexico, including the Benemerita Autonomous University of Puebla, the Autonomous University of Sinaloa, the University of Guadalajara and the National Autonomous University of Mexico. These universities organize research, professional training and scientific dissemination programmes directly with marginal communities, which helps them to achieve the following goals:

1. To extend the institutional role of the universities and the results of their academic work into society.
2. To set up programmes to provide services and access to the results of academic research that help to meet the needs of society.
3. To play an important part in recovering popular knowledge and defending national identity in a globalized context.
4. To contribute towards educating citizens to understand local, national and global identities.
5. To become a channel for promoting sustainable development.
6. To bring about the necessary changes to improve the quality of life in their society.
7. To identify problems and demands in society.
8. To carry out research to improve the quality of life for people and society as a whole.

The reduction of the social divides in developing countries must be based on the critical, systematic work of universities. Innovation has a vital role to play both in conventional professional training and where continuing university education is linked to formal curricular structures. For example, the University of Costa Rica opens up its academic facilities to people over the age of 50 who wish to satisfy their intellectual interests, make use of their free time, and exchange experience and knowledge with ordinary students and lecturers through the Dr Alfonso Trejos Willis comprehensive programme for senior citizens.

The SRU is also expressed in the educational innovations designed and developed by universities to operate in emerging situations. The main feature of these programmes is that the sectors of society that are to benefit most from them, along with local communities, local authorities and NGOs, all participate in requesting, designing, implementing and assessing them. Here are just a few examples of these programmes:

1. Legal clinics at the University of Costa Rica provide free legal advice in various parts of the country for people with limited resources who require the services of a lawyer. Advice is given by students with a high average grade nearing the end of their law degrees. These students can themselves obtain advice from the manager of the centre and a legal assistant.
2. The University of Costa Rica's University Community Work project is made up of interdisciplinary programmes that vary according to the academic profile of the faculties, schools and university chairs. The project coordinates teaching, research and service to society. Those who benefit from its services participate in designing, planning and implementing the programme. This means that lecturers and students work together with members of the Costa Rican community to find solutions to the country's problems.
3. Demand from society for more law and order has led to the development of intervention programmes aimed at citizenship training for people who have committed some kind of crime. For example, the University of Buenos Aires has set up the UBA XXII programme, a multidisciplinary project providing training in seven prisons. This takes the University into prisons and provides all inmates with university access, thus enabling them to acquire a general education and contributing to their reintegration into

society. The programme, which is funded out of the University's own budget, provides extracurricular courses and university training in prisons. The extracurricular courses in computing aim to facilitate the general education of the entire prison population. The University training programme makes it possible for around 1,000 inmates to become university students. Many of these graduate while in prison or on being released. The undergraduate courses offered are in law, economics, social sciences and psychology. The extension activities provided help to develop awareness of social responsibility and citizenship among prisoners.

4. The comprehensive healthcare programmes at the University of Costa Rica, the Benemerita Autonomous University of Puebla, the University of Guadalajara and the National Autonomous University of Mexico take place on the university premises. They aim to contribute to comprehensive healthcare in the entire catchment area. The objective of these programmes is to provide professional training using various comprehensive healthcare models based on multidimensional perspectives, teamwork and cross-sectoral participation. The programmes cover comprehensive healthcare, teaching, research, social work and social participation, the goal being to reduce the health divide.

5. At the National University of La Plata and the National University of Colombia, the Inter-American Development Bank set up the Support Programme for Initiatives Involving the Social Responsibility of Universities, Ethics and Development with the aim of facilitating and overseeing the implementation of SRU, ethics and development initiatives in Latin American universities by producing models, strategies and tools in the areas of management, teaching, research and university extension; creating greater synergy and increased communication between university stakeholders in Latin America; and ensuring the local sustainability and global impact of the initiatives proposed.

6. The intensive participation of universities in strengthening sustainable development in the region is exemplified by the botanical gardens at various universities, including the University of Costa Rica, the University of Havana and the National Autonomous University of Mexico. These gardens have contributed to professional training, research, the dissemination of knowledge and the sustainable use of biodiversity. The nature reserves at the Autonomous University of Sinaloa and the National Autonomous University of Mexico have a fundamental social purpose: to preserve biodiversity and natural heritage. At these nature reserves, research is carried out and strategies are designed for the sustainable use of natural resources in the region.

7. Both the Benemerita Autonomous University of Puebla and the National Autonomous University of Mexico run support programmes for indigenous peoples to provide them with comprehensive academic training and help them finish their studies in conditions of equal opportunity and full respect for their cultural identities. Along the same lines, the Central University of Venezuela's Delta programme provides advice on general and specific problems in the region, thus promoting the overall development of the state of Delta Amacuro and especially that of the indigenous population.

Over the past five years, great efforts have been made to promote, strengthen and assess all activities connected with the SRU. Various activities have been organized in which students can propose solutions to complex social, environmental and scientific problems through professional training programmes, research projects and university extension activities.

To complete this brief summary, it is worth highlighting the international call for a high level of SRU made at the World Conference on Higher Education (1998), where the following guidelines were agreed on:

- Relevance in higher education should be assessed in terms of the fit between what society expects of institutions and what they do. This requires ethical standards, political impartiality, critical abilities and, at the same time, closer coordination with the problems of society and the world of work, by basing long-term policies on societal aims and needs, including respect for cultures and environmental protection
- Higher education should reinforce its role of service to society, especially its activities aimed at eliminating poverty, intolerance, violence, illiteracy, hunger, environmental degradation and disease, mainly through an interdisciplinary and transdisciplinary approach
- Higher education should enhance its contribution to the development of the whole education system, notably through improved teacher training, curriculum development and educational research
- Ultimately, higher education should aim to create a new non-violent and non-exploitative society consisting of highly educated, motivated and integrated individuals, inspired by love for humanity and guided by wisdom.

All of the above guidelines are a call to HEIs to participate in building a fairer, more cooperative society. This implies carrying out various tasks, including the following:

1. Encouraging the conversion of existing structures into networks that foster knowledge production in specific contexts and make transdisciplinary training possible.
2. Strengthening interaction between the various stakeholders and sectors in society, at both the national and regional levels.
3. Professionalizing the academic structures intended to create ties with the community.

4. Designing indicators to evaluate the level and direction of social responsibility at the macro-universities.
5. Creating institutional links between university extension activities and everyday university life.
6. Incorporating activities designed to instil social responsibility into undergraduate and postgraduate syllabuses.
7. Improving academic quality by promoting social responsibility, values and commitment.
8. Carrying out comprehensive institutional analyses based on an understanding of social problems in their context at the local, national and international levels.
9. Strengthening the identity of universities as institutions that have strong principles with regard to social responsibility.
10. Coordinating information systems to monitor programmes for the SRU.
11. Maintaining and consolidating SRU forums and ethics seminars aimed at analysing the impact of university-designed solutions to the urgent problems of the region.
12. Creating mechanisms to break down barriers around universities so that society can influence educational processes by providing real information about the world.
13. Designing new learning experiences that foster the critical appropriation
of knowledge and the production of new conceptual and methodological models with regard to problems in the real world.
14. Expressing the SRU in the form of a quest for general welfare, sustainable human development and sustainability.

REFERENCES

Gibbons, A. (1997) *Innovation and the Developing System of Knowledge Production*. Brighton, UK: University of Sussex.

SPECIAL CONTRIBUTION II.5

Marcela Mollis

Higher education in Argentina: taking stock at the turn of the millennium

ARGENTINE HIGHER EDUCATION IN NUMBERS

In Argentina, the so-called higher education 'system' is a complex, heterogeneous institutional conglomerate made up of more than 1700 non-university tertiary level institutions and 102 universities.

The non-university education system is made up of teacher training institutes for the various educational levels and specialized technical schools and institutes. In terms of management and funding, public institutions depend on the provincial governments or on the municipal government of Buenos Aires. Private institutions are funded through tuition fees. However, private teacher training institutions that offer reduced fees also receive public subsidies.

In 2007, the country had 102 officially recognized university institutions: 38 national universities, 41 private universities, 6 national university institutes created under the legal system for provincial universities, 14 private university institutes, one provincial university, one foreign university and one international university. This range of institutions is characterized by its complexity, diversity and heterogeneous multifunctionality, meaning that a single university may carry out several missions or functions, such as teaching, providing professional training, conducting research, developing the local culture and selling services.

According to the *Anuario 2005 de Estadísticas Universitarias* of the Argentine Secretariat of University Policies (SPU, 2005), the 1990s saw a trend towards institutional expansion and privatization, which involved the creation of a large number of national and private institutions. The past 16 years have seen the creation of 24% of the country's national universities, 44% of its private universities, 83% of its national university institutes, 93% of its private university institutes, and 100% of its provincial and foreign universities.

This growth has produced a highly heterogeneous and diverse framework that includes universities of many types: new and traditional, public and private, Catholic and secular, elite and popular, those focused on professional training and those focused on research.

It is true that private universities have been expanding. However, Table 1 shows that of the new students who accessed a university in 2005, less than 21% enrolled in the private sector, while 79% enrolled in public universities. In university institutes, these figures are more even: 59% of new students enrolled in

TABLE 1
New students by management sector, 2005

Institution	State managed 2005		Privately managed 2005		Total new students	
	Number	%	Number	%	Number	%
Universities	289,708	80	73,265	20	362,973	100
University institutes	4,249	59.4	2,907	40.6	7,156	100
Total	293,957		76,172		370,129	

Source: SPU, Anuario 2005 de Estadísticas Universitarias, p. 173. Drawn up by the author.

state-managed institutes, while 41% enrolled in privately managed institutes.

With 73.5% of students, universities continue to dominate the overall higher education system, while non-university tertiary institutions account for 26.5% of students. These quantitative trends are the opposite of those observed in Brazil and Mexico, where public universities offer elite academic postgraduate programmes and a huge number of private tertiary institutions offer programmes for the majority of the population.

Table 2 shows that the private university institutes had the highest annual growth rate from 2001 to 2005 (43.63%), even though they only account for 16.50% of the total number of students. In contrast, the state-managed and private universities account for 83.50%, as shown in Table 3.

GLOBALIZATION AND THE NEW COSMOPOLITANISM: BUSINESS CULTURE IN HIGHER EDUCATION

Throughout the past two decades, higher education systems have been in transition across almost the entire world (Forest and Altbach, 2006). This transition from one model to another can be summed up with a widely used phrase: *from state to market*. The economic power of the North can be seen in the dominance of a higher education model oriented towards satisfying the global labour market. This model is advancing throughout the region and in the post-socialist countries.

Market-oriented policies are replacing the visions of social democracy; this is the empire of marketing (Marginson and Mollis, 2001). The role of government is being reinvented, 'new technologies have replaced previous perceptions', and globalization and internationalism have accelerated the dissemination of the new values of business culture, which has spread to social and cultural institutions (De Sousa Santos, 2005). The following quote exemplifies the basic global *economic imperative* that justifies transforming higher education systems in developing countries:

> There are notable exceptions, but currently, across most of the developing world, the potential of higher education to promote development is being realized only marginally. (World Bank, 2000, p. 10.)

THE GLOBALIZATION AGENDA AND ITS IMPACT ON ARGENTINE HIGHER EDUCATION

In 1999, Argentina's unemployment, poverty and social-marginalization indicators reached their all-time worst values. The local response to the global logic manifested itself in social exclusion[1] derived from the applied economic model. Without a doubt, the 'crisis of the welfare state' was the main factor in the economic transformation of Argentina and Latin America as a whole. The consequences of the crisis worsened throughout the 1980s, and were accompanied by rising foreign debt, the stagnation of economic growth rates, the impoverishment and marginalization of large sectors of the population, and, as a result, a widening social-inequality gap.

For these and other reasons, I believe that the crisis that has dramatically affected university education in the third millennium is an identity crisis. As a doctor might say, a 'global' diagnosis of a distant disease has been made, and a treatment consisting of financial credits applied to internationally designed public policies has been prescribed. The reforms advocated by the World Bank in Latin America and the post-socialist countries were based on a universal, homogeneous diagnosis at the global level. The subsequent reports (World Bank, 2000) were economy-centred, ahistoric, neglectful of cultural plurality, oriented towards the privatization of public universities, and premised on the pragmatic recognition of the market as the only source of 'innovation and quality'. The promotion of degrees oriented towards the service sector further strengthened the predominance of a globalized business profile.[2]

TRENDS AND CHALLENGES IN ARGENTINE HIGHER EDUCATION

In the 1990s, the strategies promoted by the 'new modernization agenda' as a means of achieving financial rationalization included deregulation, administrative simplification, privatization and the reduction of the central government's responsibility for providing public services. The tables presented above show the difference between the growth dynamic of the institutional market, with its tendency towards privatization, and the dynamic represented by students' preference for public universities.

Institutional privatization has become more widespread throughout Latin

TABLE 2
Number of students: average annual growth rate (AAGR) by management sector, 2005

Institution	State managed			Privately managed		
	2001	2005	AAGR	2001	2005	AAGR
Universities	1,200,215	1,273,554	1.49	196,357	244,844	5.67
University institutes	9,423	12,071	6.39	2,179	9,273	43.63
Totals	1,209,638	1,285,625	1.53	198,536	254,117	6.36

Source: SPU, *Anuario 2005 de Estadísticas Universitarias*, p. 173. Drawn up by the author.

TABLE 3
Distribution of students by management sector, 2005

Type of institution	Year 2005		
	National	Private	Total
Number of students	1,285,625	254,117	1,539,742
Percentage	83.50	16.50	100.00

Source: SPU, *Anuario 2005 de Estadísticas Universitarias*, p. 174. Drawn up by the author.

America. Nevertheless, as shown by the above tables, public institutions remain predominant. Latin American students have also demonstrated a preference for public higher education systems, despite the expansion of the private market in response to restricted state funding.

Whether because it is free or because the labour market prefers it – certain multinational corporations recruit graduates from public higher education programmes in Business Administration, Systems Engineering and Computer Science (*Revista Mercado*, 1998, p. 38) – the public university system remains the dominant choice in Argentina.

Over the past ten years, worldwide higher education reforms have tended to decrease the state's regulation of public rights while they have increased the regulation of areas of private interest – that is, companies that represent the public interest have been privatized and deregulated, while the interests of the governing political class have been commercialized in the pursuit of private profits (Mollis, 2006). This has resulted in a contradictory formula: deregulation and control in both spheres, with 'altered' interests. Today, the public's interest in higher education is demonstrated by the choices of the various stakeholders, most of whom opt for the public educational sector. Although private institutions have grown and developed, their enrolment figures still represent a minority of all students in higher education programmes. In Argentina, unlike in Mexico and Brazil, public higher education remains the option in greatest demand. Nevertheless, the governing classes, which used to receive their education in the public universities, are nowadays perpetuating their hold on power by taking postgraduate courses at prestigious universities in the USA.

Indeed, the mentality of many public policymakers and other individuals responsible for the fate of public education institutions is oriented towards satisfying corporate interests, which are not always in line with the general welfare of society.

A PROPOSAL FOR CHANGE

Fascinated by the dream of a homogeneous global identity, public universities in Argentina and throughout Latin America have strayed from their historical social functions. The medieval communitarian tradition of academia has faded as ultra-individualism has taken root among the scholarly community. At Argentine universities, the teaching staff tend to be highly heterogeneous, ranging from researchers working on an incentive basis (who make up 18% of the university teaching staff nationwide) to lecturers who are recent graduates themselves (who make up a significant majority of the overall university teaching staff). The identity of public university lecturers is also in transition – from *scholar to international consultant* – due to the fact that their 'prestige and income' come from other sources of funding, such as national or international banks and the central government.

Faced with the transformations caused by globalization, Argentina's public universities are now taking on the greatest challenge in their history: *the struggle for survival*.

In order to survive and recover the meaning upon which they were founded, it is imperative that public universities set themselves new priorities.

Where should they begin? To change, they must recognize certain things about themselves. They must recognize the educational deficiencies of the syllabuses that train teachers for other levels of the education system. They must recognize the need to reconstruct their institutional missions and the value of knowledge. They must recognize the representativity crisis of decision-making bodies and the dysfunctionality of the administrative structure. They must focus their research on the satisfaction of urgent cultural and social needs at the local level, and train political leaders with public sensibilities and social ethics. Finally, they must educate the public on the problems universities face, and then politicize and departisanize these problems. They must reflect on the meaning, mission and practices of the universities in order to develop *a comprehensive project that is sustained by the social epistemology of local knowledge*. This epistemology must in turn be sustained by a liberating scientific paradigm in order to discover, innovate and produce knowledge that is original, useful and technological, and apply it to local problems. This means posing questions according to unsatisfied social needs and finding appropriate answers to unresolved local problems. We must create universities that are sensitive to society's urgent needs and guided by public, productive ethics of knowledge that can help us overcome the geopolitical inequality between the 'consumer' countries of the North and the 'producing' countries of the South.

REFERENCES

De Sousa Santos, B. (2005) *La Universidad en el Siglo XXI*, Laboratorio de Políticas Públicas (LPP) y Miño y Dávila, Buenos Aires.

Forest, J. and Altbach, P. (eds) (2006) *International Handbook of Education*, Vol. 18, Springer, Berlin, Heidelberg, New York.

Marginson, S. and Mollis, M. (2001), The door opens and the tiger leaps: theories and reflexivities of comparative education for a global millennium, *Comparative Education Review*, University of Chicago Press, **45**(4), Nov. pp. 581–615.

Mollis, M. (2006) Geopolítica del saber: biografías recientes de las universidades latinoamericanas. In: Teichler, U. (ed.) (2006), *Reformas de los modelos de la educación superior en Europa, Japón y América Latina: Análisis Comparados*, Vol. 2. Serie Educación Superior, Educación Comparada y Trabajo, University of Kassel and the Faculty of Arts and Letters, University of Buenos Aires. Miño y Dávila Editores, Buenos Aires.

Revista Mercado (1998) '¿Qué egresados

prefieren las top 10 del mercado?',
Oct.–Dec., Buenos Aires, pp. 36–40.
SPU (2005) Argentine Secretariat of University Policies, Ministry of Education,

Science and Technology, *Anuario 2005 de Estadísticas Universitarias* [PDF document].
World Bank (2000) *Higher Education in*

Developing Countries: Peril and Perish, WB and the Task Force, Ford Foundation, Washington, DC.

NOTES

1   In May 1995, Argentina's unemployment rate reached a record high (18.4%), while underemployment reached 11.3% (Ministry of Finance and National Institute of Statistics and Censuses, 1999).

2   The most popular degrees among young people in Argentina and Hungary are Administration, Marketing, Computer Science and Communications Science.

SPECIAL CONTRIBUTION II.6

Higher education for human and social development in the Caribbean

Claudia Harvey and Christine Marrett

INTRODUCTION

The concept of development is imprecise. Esman generalizes that:

> Development connotes steady progress toward improvement in the human condition; reduction and eventual elimination of poverty, ignorance, and disease; and expansion of well-being and opportunity for all. It implies modernization – secularization, industrialization and urbanization – but not necessarily Westernization. (Esman, 1991, p. 5)

The human development index (HDI) used by the United Nations Development Programme (UNDP) includes long and healthy lives, knowledge and a decent standard of living as indicators of development, rather than using income to measure human well-being (UNDP, 2005, p. 214).

Information and communication technologies (ICTs) are impacting and, in some ways, driving changes in many spheres of life and have contributed to the 'knowledge economy' and 'globalization', fuelling a demand for higher-level education.

Defining the Caribbean region is not straightforward. Some political definitions include countries that are not in or contiguous to the Caribbean Sea, such as the Bahamas, Guyana and Suriname. There tends to be a divide along linguistic lines, based on the experience of col-

onization by various European powers. While most Caribbean territories are now independent countries, some remain dependencies or colonies of Britain, France, the Netherlands and the United USA. The comments here are mainly – although not exclusively – concerned with those countries that are members of the Caribbean Community (CARICOM, www.caricom.org).

THE PRESENT SITUATION

The CARICOM countries can be generally described as small in terms of population (all have populations of less than 1 million, except Haiti, with over 8 million, Jamaica with about 2.6 million, and Trinidad and Tobago with about 1.3 million) and geographical size (all are small islands, except Belize, Guyana and Suriname).

The region is described as 'developing' and the countries share problems generally ascribed to small developing countries, including a small domestic market, a limited private sector, reliance on foreign capital and very few primary export products, as well as openness and therefore vulnerability to external events, poverty, and proneness to natural disasters (UNCTAD, 1990; Commonwealth Secretariat/World Bank, 2000).

Anthony identifies as a challenge the lack of confidence or the mindset of insufficiency, especially among policymakers in the Caribbean, who 'enter the development arena with the foregone conclusion

that we are too insignificant to change the world' (Anthony, 2002, p. 1).

To overcome this mindset, he recommends that 'the tremendous accomplishments that Caribbean people have wrought' be studied and validated. The international accomplishments of Caribbean people in various fields (academia, art and sports, for example) paradoxically highlight another challenge for the region: the 'brain drain' caused by emigration.

In addition to these traditional challenges, new challenges have emerged for the region, such as:

● the impact of HIV/AIDS, with the region having the second-highest prevalence rate in the world, especially among people aged 15–25 (CARICOM, 2006)
● the increase in deaths caused by non-communicable, lifestyle-related diseases such as heart disease, hypertension and obesity, which account for 35,000 deaths per year in the region (CARICOM, 2006)
● the impact of globalization
● increasing rates of crime and violence in many of the countries.

Austin and Marrett (2002, p. xii) identify close to 30 non-Spanish-speaking Caribbean universities, including the regional University of the West Indies (UWI), which now serves 16 English-speaking countries. Since 2002, the region has seen a trend towards the establishment (actual or planned) of other universities, both public and private, largely through the amalgamation of existing tertiary institutions. Another trend over the past 20 or so years is the establishment of offshore universities in a number of Caribbean countries, some of which are accessible to Caribbean citizens. The region is also served by a wide range of other tertiary institutions, such as community colleges, teachers' colleges, other professional schools, and technical and vocational training institutions.

Without attempting to assess the quality of the tertiary education provided, Roberts (2004) reviews the performance of 15 countries in respect of the CARICOM target set in 1997 to increase tertiary enrolment among the relevant age group (17–24) from 7.5% to 15% by 2005. Using a simple head count of Caribbean citizens enrolled full- or part-time in face-to-face or distance programmes at local, regional and extra-regional tertiary institutions, she finds that eight countries reached or exceeded the target, as shown in Table 1.

Although there may be some satisfaction that the 15% target was met or exceeded in many instances, Roberts (2004, p. 4) points out that this percentage is way below tertiary enrolment for the United Kingdom (over 50%), the USA and France (over 80%), and Singapore (35%).She notes:

In a changing world, targets are only milestones which keep changing. Although Barbados, for example, has surpassed the 15 per cent target, there is now a new target of one university graduate in each household by 2020. This translates to an enrolment rate well in excess of the current situation and particularly so, if the target is based on a minimum of bachelor's degrees. Trinidad and Tobago has also set a goal of becoming a developed country by 2020, which has tertiary education enrolment implications. (Roberts, 2004, p. 4)

TABLE 1
Performance of CARICOM countries in respect of the 15% tertiary enrolment target for 2005

Country	2004–2005 enrolment percentage
Anguilla	4
Antigua	16
Bahamas	21
Barbados	29
British Virgin Islands	20
Cayman Islands	8
Dominica	14
Grenada	18
Guyana	9
Montserrat	6
Saint Kitts/Nevis	16
Saint Lucia	8
Saint Vincent and the Grenadines	12
Trinidad and Tobago	15
Turks and Caicos Islands	20

Source: Roberts (2004, p. 3).

MAIN TRENDS FOR THE FUTURE ROLE OF HIGHER EDUCATION IN HUMAN AND SOCIAL DEVELOPMENT IN THE CARIBBEAN

Traditional universities face the threat of large corporate institutions, such as Disney, Time Warner and Microsoft, which link with major research universities to package and deliver courses for which the universities create and validate materials (ibid., p. 142). The indigenous universities in the Caribbean are already feeling the impact of these developments. Rather than give in to the onslaught, Clayton suggests:

We will have to cede ground in areas where we have no comparative advantage, but we may be able to gain increasing market share in areas where we can develop a role at the cutting edge. (Clayton, 2000, p. 144)

For the small countries of the Caribbean, there is the tension between the establishment of national universities to safeguard national identity and pride, on the one hand, and the international trend towards developing an electronic world market with far more 'globalized values', on the other. The risk is that these values are not so much globalized as they are the values of the dominant culture. Thus, the regional university, UWI, has been grappling with the concept of foundation courses, which seek to examine history, literature and languages and so ground students from all areas of study in the cultural ethos of their region and provide a sense of 'Caribbeanness', despite the onslaught of globalization.

Therefore, the major challenges for Caribbean tertiary education are as follows:

- To address the particular conditions and needs of the small states of the Caribbean in critical areas of knowledge generation, such as culture, economy and sustainability. This includes, for example, coming to grips with the threat to small island states in a period of global warming and remaining viable in the face of major economic blocks.

- To apply such knowledge to produce international high-flyers in various spheres but at the same time improve the quality of life and life choices of the majority of the population.

- To overcome the exclusion of many from tertiary education by harnessing resources, and to benefit from the partnerships, concentration of efforts and dissemination initiated by centres of excellence.

- To generate and apply the latest knowledge to the persistent problems of unemployment and underperformance, as well as to new issues such as environmental threats and HIV/AIDS.

STRATEGIES AND ACTIONS

One overarching role of universities is to contribute to the debate on the meaning of development and to help define the path(s) that lead to such development. For example, an ongoing examination of the Millennium Development Goals needs to be conducted in the Caribbean context.

Within this context, universities should:

- Conduct research and subsequently develop curricula that address the particular circumstances (problems and achievements) of the region.
- Look inwards to the region, but also outwards to incorporate the academic and professional skills among and beyond the Caribbean diaspora, and seek to attract international students.
- Harness information and communication technologies to empower all other areas. A small but growing number of universities offer distance education courses. However, collaboration among them is limited, which may lead to duplication of effort (Marrett, 2006).

In the context of globalization, the role of the education sector and universities in particular is integral, not only in training a skilled professional labour force, but also in grappling with the issues of social change, inclusion and improving the life choices of the most marginalized (see UNDP, 2005, for more on the inclusion of improved life choices as an indicator of human development).

GOOD PRACTICES AND EXAMPLES

The aforementioned suggestions for strategies and actions are not new. Below are a few examples of how universities are contributing to human and social development in the Caribbean.

COMMUNITY DEVELOPMENT

Universities are helping to integrate the marginalized. For example, in Jamaica, the University of Technology and the Mona Campus of UWI are in close proximity to a low-income community known as August Town (population 15,000), which has a high level of crime and social dysfunction. The two universities have proposed a project that would apply the wealth of expertise that resides within the institutions to the integrated and participatory development of August Town and transform this troubled community into one that provides a model for the application of the knowledge gained to similar areas. The project, which is still in its infancy, could be applied to the development of Haiti, the only country in the region with a low HDI rating.

PARTNERING WITH REGIONAL AGENCIES

Through partnering with regional agencies, the role of the universities in knowledge generation is enhanced. In 1999, UWI and CARICOM signed a Memorandum of Understanding that established a collaborative relationship 'designed to focus the energies and know-how of both entities into providing regional leadership with the sort of vital information that such an alliance could provide'. This university research could be applied to regional policymaking. The Memorandum envisions higher education institutions participating in development by widening the context of policy dialogue with political decision-makers (CARICOM: www.caricom.org/jsp/projects/uwi_caricom.jsp?menu=projects).

EDUCATION SECTOR HIV AND AIDS CAPACITY-BUILDING PROGRAMME

The universities play a role in improving regional health that goes beyond simply providing medical education. The Caribbean Education Sector HIV and AIDS Capacity-Building Programme aims 'to improve the response of the education sector as a partner in a multi-sectoral strategy for the prevention and mitigation of the HIV and AIDS epidemic in CARICOM Member States' (CARICOM, 2006). Addressing this pandemic, which potentially threatens both individual lives and Caribbean civilization itself, is a new role for higher education. This programme is one of the key initiatives of CARICOM and the Pan-Caribbean Partnership Against HIV and AIDS (PANCAP) in response to the problem.

CONCLUSIONS AND FINAL COMMENTS

Higher education faces undeniable challenges in its quest to serve development. Part of the problem is that academic institutions are by their very nature contemplative and therefore slow-moving, while the pace of change is exponential. Yet these slow-moving entities are expected to generate knowledge to lead change! Moreover, one aspect of globalization is the focus on competition and personal rewards. Therefore, academia may not offer the quick returns and prestige required to attract the upwardly mobile.

Nevertheless, examples of collaboration among policymakers and institutions, and academics and communities, show that the institutions are dealing with fundamental issues such as including the marginalized and generating knowledge to inform policymaking, as well as issues that affect our very ability to survive, such as environmental sustainability and HIV/AIDS. It is clear that the Caribbean institutions are attempting to address urgent development challenges, and in some cases they are in fact succeeding.

REFERENCES

Anthony, K. (2002) Rethinking fundamental relationships in Caribbean human resource development. In: Cowell, N. and Branche, C. (eds) *Human Resource Development and Workplace Governance in the Caribbean*, pp. 1–7. Kingston: Ian Randle Publishers.

Austin, I. and Marrett, C. (eds) (2002) *Adult Education in Caribbean Universities*. Kingston: UNESCO.

CARICOM (2006) *Communiqué of the Fifteenth Meeting of the Council for Human and Social Development of the Caribbean Community, 19–21 October 2006, Georgetown, Guyana*. CARICOM: www.caricom.org/jsp/pressreleases/pres200_06.jsp.

CARICOM. *UWI-CARICOM Project: Strategic Alliance for Institutional Cooperation*. CARICOM: www.caricom.org/jsp/projects/uwi_caricom.jsp?menu=projects.

Clayton, A. (2000) Current trends in higher education and the implications for the UWI. In: Hall, K. and Benn, D. (eds) *Contending with Destiny: The Caribbean in the 21st Century*, pp. 137–46. Kingston: Ian Randle Publishers.

Commonwealth Secretariat/World Bank

(2000) *Small States: Meeting Challenges in the Global Economy*. London: Commonwealth Secretariat.

Esman, M.J. (1991) *Management Dimensions of Development: Perspectives and Strategies*. Bloomfield, CT: Kumarian Press.

Marrett, C. (2006) *Institutional collaboration in distance education at the terti-ary level in the small, developing countries of the Commonwealth Caribbean: To what extent does it enhance human resource development?* Ph.D. thesis. University of the West Indies, Mona.

Roberts, V. (2004) Widening access to tertiary education: Re-visiting the fifteen per cent target. Unpublished.

UNCTAD (1990) *Problems of Island Developing Countries and Proposals for Concrete Action*. New York: UNCTAD.

UNDP (2005) *Human Development Report 2005. International Cooperation at a Crossroads: Aid, Trade and Security in an Unequal World*. UNDP: http://hdr.undp.org/reports/global/2005/.

GOOD PRACTICE II.8

Description of the Mexico Multicultural Nation University Programme (UNAM, Mexico)

José de Val

Multiculturality and inter-culturality, seen as essential traits of contemporary societies and of Mexico in particular, have been recurring subjects in research studies and academic programmes at the National Autonomous University of Mexico (UNAM). However, in the past, no coordinating body was dedicated specifically to this important social and historical phenomenon, even though it has been recognized in the Political Constitution of the United Mexican States since 1992.

The Mexico Multicultural Nation University Programme (PMUC-UNAM) has the following founding mandate:

1. To link the intellectual, methodological and technical efforts of individuals and groups inside and outside UNAM working on matters related to the multicultural and indigenous composition of the Mexican nation.
2. To foster the highest academic quality in studies on the subject.
3. To plan and support the development of research, training, extension and documentation activities on cultural aspects of the indigenous peoples of Mexico.
4. To support and promote educational activities that convey knowledge about the relations between the different cultures of Mexico and constructive ways of transforming those relations, and that spread knowledge derived from research and diffuse experiences from other studies carried out in the area of multiculturality.[1]

Many UNAM departments deal with the problems associated with cultural pluralism. Each department has its own approach. The following objectives have been behind all the PUMC–UNAM activities in the areas of teaching, research, dissemination, administration and social relations:

- boost the potential social impact of projects
- identify modes of interdisciplinary coordination
- formalize new areas of thought and creativity
- open up university departments to strategic matters that are not sufficiently explicit
- consolidate access for sectors of the population that have suffered social discrimination in general and educational discrimination in particular.

In other words, the objective is to 'inter-culturalize' our own educational establishment and project the results onto the whole of society.

One of the PUMC–UNAM's main components, the Teaching Programme, designed a new subject: 'Mexico, multicultural nation'. This was adopted as an optional subject at UNAM in the faculties of Law, Arts, Social and Political Sciences, Architecture, Economics, Science, Medicine, Veterinary Medicine and Zootechnics; in the UNAM's National School of Social Work; and in its science and humanities colleges. It was also adopted at the National School of Anthropology and History at the Autonomous University of Mexico City, at the National Pedagogic University, at the Ibero-American University and at the General Directorate of Popular and Indigenous Cultures. From 2003 to 2007, a total of 6,090 students took this subject. The theoretical and educational objectives were:

- to systematically develop the theme of inter-culturality in UNAM and other educational establishments that expressed an interest
- to do so in a transdisciplinary way, by promoting teaching in the social sciences and in the exact and natural sciences
- to concentrate most of the activities on degree courses, without excluding postgraduate students
- to employ specialists for teaching each of the 14 subjects in the programme in order to guarantee high quality
- to develop a range of activities related to the subject, both inside and outside the university.

Another initiative of great academic and social importance was the creation of the Grant System for Indigenous Students. Its main objective is to give financial support to students from indigenous peoples and to ensure that they stay in the classrooms and finish their higher education. It also aims to promote intercultural relations, to help narrow the gap created by the lack of understanding between the indigenous peoples and the rest of Mexican society, and to interest other sectors of society that could give financial or social support to the project, broaden it or consolidate it. As a result of the grant awards of 2005, 2006 and 2007, the grant system currently supports 220 grant holders (94 women and 126 men) from 29 different ethnic groups and 13 Mexican states. These grant holders are enrolled in 30 UNAM degree courses. The grant system also organizes a monitoring and tutorial plan that includes support to help underachieving students reach the right academic level, a register of life histories, advice on how to deal with disadvantages, underdevelopment and discrimination, and encouragement to participate in the cultural and recreational activities that complement higher education studies.

In the area of research, the PUMC–UNAM included two new subjects in the list of studies on inter-culturality: 'Afro-America: the third root' and, more recently, 'Immigration and cultural diversity: the Mexicans the world gave us'. Thus, it expanded the scope of its research work, which had previously concentrated on the indigenous peoples, and began to systematically support research on immigrant groups in Mexico, such as Africans and their descendants, Spaniards, other Europeans, Jews, Lebanese, Asians, North Americans, Central Americans, Mennonites and Gypsies. As the result of an inter-institutional agreement, the Programme agreed to carry out a research project entitled 'State of the economic and social development of the indigenous peoples of Guerrero'. The project concentrates on four main peoples of this Mexican state (the Nahuas, Mixtecos, Tlapanecos and Amuzgos). Its first extensive report is currently in its final stages. Other interesting research projects are 'Half a century of indigenous movements and organizat-

ions in Latin America'; 'Model of socio-environmental development in Costa Chica de Oaxaca'; 'Silent colonization: megaprojects and indigenous regions in Latin America' and 'Diagnosis of audience rates for the indigenous radio stations run by the National Committee for the Development of the Indigenous Peoples (CNDPI)'.

The Programme's cultural diversity information system deserves special attention. It copies and systematizes a large quantity of information, and has an electronic portal and information banks specializing in the following subjects:

- indigenous peoples of America
- indicators of the well-being and development of indigenous peoples
- mega-projects and indigenous territories
- migration, languages and aboriginal peoples of America
- traditional medicine.

At the request of 25 of the most representative indigenous leaders of the continent, PUMC–UNAM drew up an evaluation of the International Decade of the World's Indigenous Peoples entitled *Evaluation Report for the First International Decade of the World's Indigenous Peoples*.[2]

The results were presented at the 6th Session of the United Nations Permanent Forum on Indigenous Issues, held in New York, thus ratifying the alliance established between the University and the indigenous peoples of the Americas. The Forum itself commissioned PUMC–UNAM to set up a monitoring system for the second decade established by the UN (2005–2014), using culturally suitable indicators. The relation with the indigenous peoples at a national level has taken different forms, including regular meetings at the PUMC on 'The future of the indigenous peoples of Mexico'. These meetings bring together a large

number of representatives of communities and organizations.

As part of the Network of Public Macro-universities of Latin America and the Caribbean, UNAM heads the coordination of two of the network's ten 'areas of knowledge'. The second of them, 'Multicultural studies and national identities', is coordinated by PUMC–UNAM', which has already started work on an ambitious continental project entitled 'Social processes and inter-cultural relations in Latin America'.

In its short life, PUMC–UNAM has carried out extensive publishing activity, producing about 20 books in three collections: 'Cultural Plurality in Mexico', 'Reports and Studies', and 'Indigenous Voices'. In coordination with the Mexico City Government, it is currently publishing the Nahuatl dictionary *El náhuatl que todos hablamos*, drawn up by a group of leading specialists on the subject. This dictionary will be widely available. In addition, it is working alongside UNAM's department of information technology and Microsoft Mexico in producing a version of the Windows Vista operating system in Náhuatl, an indigenous language spoken by two million people in Mexico.

The Arturo Warman Inter-institutional Chair and the Arturo Warman Prize (both created in honour of the outstanding Mexican anthropologist) promote specialized research projects and regularly bring experts together on courses, conferences and seminars about social science subjects, the study of agricultural problems, indigenous studies and ethnomusicology.

It is worth noting that PUMC–UNAM has a small nucleus of research scientists and a much larger group of young graduates and students (thesis writers and social service assistants) who have the opportunity to make academic and professional progress.

NOTES

1 *Acuerdo por el que se crea el Programa Universitario México, Nación Multicultural* (2004). In: *Gaceta UNAM*, 2 December.

2 *Evaluation Report for the First International Decade of the World's Indigenous Peoples (1995–2004)* (2007) *Pedregal Accord*. Mexico: UNAM-Rigoberta Menchú Foundation.

PART III
DELPHI POLL

III.1
DELPHI POLL – HIGHER EDUCATION FOR HUMAN AND SOCIAL DEVELOPMENT

Josep Lobera and GUNI Secretariat[1]

INTRODUCTION

A Delphi poll has been included in this report to gauge the emerging trends in opinions and perspectives of experts on the role of higher education (HE) in social and human development. This objective and the social research method chosen to achieve it are the same as those previously used in the GUNI series on the Social Commitment of Universities.

The experts who were invited to participate in this poll include HE specialists; rectors and other positions in higher education management; public policymakers; and members of civil society involved in various areas of development. This sample was selected on the basis of two variables: the profile of the individual; and the region about which the individual has specialized knowledge. The poll aims to gather the diverse opinions that could arise from each participant's approach to the subject of the report, according to their professional or regional area of specialization. Thus, it combines an overall perspective with the views of experts with different profiles and from different regions.

The higher education specialists were asked to provide opinions based on their academic work in teaching and research. This group included UNESCO experts, authors of this GUNI report and other specialists. In total, this group comprised 49% of the participants in the Delphi poll.

In approaching rectors and other higher education management positions we sought their valuable experience in managing universities and other HE institutions. This group made up 19% of all participants.

Public policymakers were expected to have views derived from their experience of education issues in public administrations and 15% of all participants fell into this group.

Finally, we wished to include the opinions of civil society members, particularly those involved in non-governmental organizations linked to different development areas. Their opinions are particularly relevant to the topic of this report. This group represented 17% of all poll participants.

The 'region' variable included the five UNESCO regions. However, the USA was separated from Europe, as HE has different characteristics in these two regions. This second variable in our sample allowed us to compare the opinions of participants from different areas of the world and to complement the overall picture with participants' regional perspectives.

METHOD

The Delphi method was chosen for this study. This is a social research method that uses expert opinions to make forecasts on complex topics. It incorporates aspects of both qualitative and quantitative research and can be applied in qualitative and quantitative stages without the need for statistical representation to measure the weight of the different trends and opinions given by the experts.

In this study, a web-based survey was carried out in *two rounds* in real time. This facilitated the participation of experts from different geographical areas. The first round was a qualitative phase, based on a questionnaire containing six questions. Both open and closed questions were included. The second round was quantitative. In a questionnaire made up of five closed questions, participants were given the opportunity to review their opinions and either strengthen them or alter them. The questions aimed to reveal the degree of participants' agreement with the different categorized items. These items were drawn from an analysis of the results of the first round.

In analysing the results of the Delphi poll, different phenomena that could affect prospective social studies, such as this one, have to be taken into account: the halo effect (Thorndike, 1920);[2] the spiral of silence (Anderson, 1996, p. 214; Miller, 2005, p. 277);[3] and the social desirability effect (Bradburn et al., 2004, p. 363).[4] In short, reflections on the Delphi poll do not aim to describe the actual situation or provide a single conclusion. Instead, they identify emerging trends in opinions, drawn from the experts' statements.

TECHNICAL SPECIFICATIONS AND STATISTICAL DATA

A sample of 1,218 people was initially invited to participate in the study whose profiles and regional areas are shown in Table III.1.1.

In the first round, 214 people participated, that is 18% of the invited experts. Table III.1.2 shows the distribution of participants per region and profile, as well as the percentages of regional participation with respect to the initial sample.

The highest response rates to the invitation to participate were found in the Latin America and the Caribbean region. The other region with above-average participation was Asia-Pacific (Table III.1.2). The highest response rate was from HE specialists and was almost twice that of individuals from the other profiles.

A list of participants in the poll can be found at the end of this Report. In the first round, participants came from 80 countries (Table III.1.3). The region with the highest participation was Europe, followed by Latin America and the Caribbean, Asia-Pacific and Africa, all with similar percentages. North America and the Arab States were the least represented regions (Figure III.1.1).

Almost half the responses in the first round came from HE specialists (48%). The other half of the responses came in equal numbers from rectors and other university employees, public policymakers and civil society experts (Figure III.1.2).

The second round of the poll was based on questions drawn up from the responses, opinions and reflections of the experts who had completed the first questionnaire. *Over two-thirds of the experts who participated in the first round (69%) also took part in the second round.* In the second round, they reflected on their initial opinions in light of the contributions of the other participants. In general, the trends in opinions observed in the previous round were validated in the second round.

The percentages and total numbers of participants in the second round, by region and by profile, can be found in Table III.1.4 and Figures III.1.3 and III.1.4.

QUESTIONNAIRE

The design of the questionnaire was based on several premises; firstly the subject matter which was which new challenges and emerging roles in social and human development were foreseen for HE in the different

---

TABLE III.1.1
The initial sample of people invited to participate

Profile	Region						Total
	Africa	Latin America and the Caribbean	Asia-Pacific	Arab States	Europe	North America	
HE specialists	43	53	47	23	88	46	300
Rectors and other university employees	64	40	98	55	29	57	343
Public policymakers	85	25	23	32	45	24	234
Civil society	50	40	33	8	180	30	341
Total	242	158	201	118	342	157	1218

TABLE III.1.2
Participants in the first round by region and profile

Profile	Region						Total	% profile from sample
	Africa	Latin America and the Caribbean	Asia-Pacific	Arab States	Europe	North America		
HE specialists	12	23	20	8	27	14	104	34
Rectors and other university employees	6	9	10	4	8	1	38	11
Public policymakers	10	6	4	5	5	2	32	9
Civil society	8	7	6		19		40	17
Total	36	45	40	17	59	17	214	18
% region from sample	15	28	20	14	17	11	18	

TABLE III.1.3
Home country of the participants

Africa	Latin America and the Caribbean	Asia-Pacific	Arab States	Europe	North America
Burundi	Argentina	Australia	Algeria	Bulgaria	Canada
Ghana	Bolivia	Bangladesh	Egypt	Croatia	USA
Kenya	Brazil	China	Jordan	Czech Republic	
Mali	Chile	Fiji	Kuwait	Denmark	
Mauritius	Colombia	India	Lebanon	Estonia	
Nigeria	Costa Rica	Indonesia	Oman	France	
Senegal	Cuba	Iran	Sudan	Germany	
Sierra Leone	Dominican Republic	Japan	Syria	Greece	
South Africa	El Salvador	Korea	Tunisia	Ireland	
Uganda	Jamaica	Malaysia	Yemen	Israel	
United Republic of Tanzania	Mexico	Mongolia		Italy	
Zambia	Nicaragua	Nepal		Lithuania	
Zimbabwe	Peru	New Zealand		Malta	
	Puerto Rico	Sri Lanka		Montenegro	
	Venezuela	Thailand		Netherlands	
		The Philippines		Norway	
				Poland	
				Portugal	
				Romania	
				Russia	
				Spain	
				Sweden	
				Switzerland	
				UK	

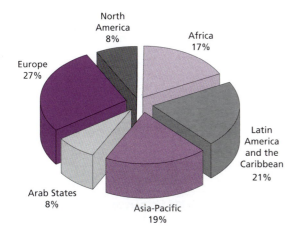

FIGURE III.1.1 **Participants in the first round by region (%)**

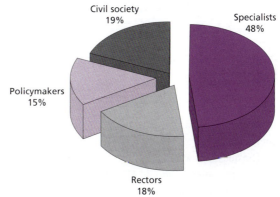

FIGURE III.1.2 **Participants in the first round by profile (%)**

regions. From this starting point, work was carried out to identify the elements that the questionnaire should contain to ensure that its content was relevant and – without being exhaustive – it set out key topics in the role of HE in the face of human and social development challenges. Second, it was important for the questionnaire to be brief. Therefore, it was stipulated that it should con-

tain no more than six questions. Using these guidelines, we selected the questions for the survey. Once analysed and systematized, the responses to these questions would serve to draw up the second round questionnaire.

The study described below is the result of an analysis of the entire poll process. The results of this Delphi poll revealed significant trends in the issues considered and

TABLE III.1.4
Participants in the second round by region and profile

Profile	Region							
	Africa	Latin America and the Caribbean	Asia-Pacific	Arab States	Europe	North America	Total	% profile in the 2nd round, compared to the 1st round
HE specialists	8	17	14	6	19	8	72	70
Rectors	3	8	7	4	6		28	74
Public policymakers	6	5	3	3	4	1	22	69
Civil society	5	6	4		11		26	65
Total	22	36	28	13	40	9	148	69
% region in the 2nd round, compared to the 1st round	61	80	70	76	69	53	69	

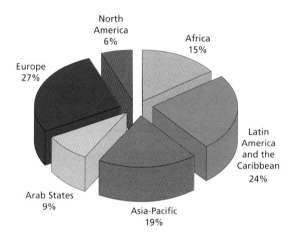

FIGURE III.1.3 Participants in the second round by region (%)

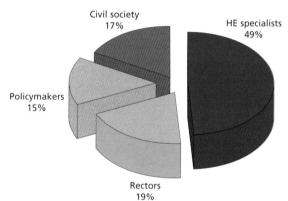

FIGURE III.1.4 Participants in the second round by profile (%)

facilitated the comparison of these trends in the different regions.

The questions were:

1. In your opinion, should HE play an active role in human and social development? Why?
2. Which of the challenges relating to human and social development should be given maximum priority for HE in your region or country?
3. What measures should be taken to encourage the contribution of HE institutions in human and social development?
4. What do you think are, will be and should be the main attributes and characteristics of university graduates at the end of their educational process?
5. What is your opinion of the following statement: 'Universities are the central institution in the knowledge society, and therefore in our society'?

REPORT QUESTION 1: THE ROLE OF HIGHER EDUCATION

In your opinion, should HE play an active role in social and human development? Why?

The experts clearly indicated that HE should play an active role in addressing human and social development. However, the reasons they gave reflected different approaches (Table III.1.5).

The two most frequently given reasons why HE should play an active role in human and social development were: that training citizens who are capable of participating actively in the different spheres of society; and that contributing to human and social development is an obligation that HE should carry out 'through relevant and committed interaction with its surrounding environment'.

When justifying the active role that HE should play in

TABLE III.1.5	
Reasons why higher education should contribute to human and social development	
In addition to training good professionals, higher education should also train people to become citizens who participate actively in the different spheres of society (social, economic, cultural, political and so on)	83%
Higher education has the obligation, as one of its main aims, to contribute to human and social development through a relevant and committed interaction with its environment	82%
Higher education is fundamental for the creation, dissemination and use of knowledge that is essential for human and social development, through research that is not based on financial reward	63%
Higher education provides a capacity for research that is fundamental in assuring the competitiveness of countries or regions and helps increase their productivity	26%
Higher education offers the opportunity of facing the challenges of globalization due to the important role that it can play in adapting to the rapid delocalization of economies, bringing greater competitiveness to the industrial sector	12%
Higher education should prepare the leaders, agents of change and technicians who will carry out the policies of development in the country.	10%
Higher education has the capacity to contribute to the development of the state, as it is through higher education that the leaders of the future are trained and given the knowledge to be able to run a society's administrations	9%
Higher education should above all provide human resources that are adapted to the needs of the market and highly qualified	9%
Higher education is the main source of research and analysis of programmes of human and social development to be implemented by public administrations	1%

human and social development, educational and research functions were linked to a broad conception of human and social development associated with developing citizenship, democracy and equity. However, this association was weaker in the case of research. More of the justifications in this area were related to increasing competitiveness and productivity.

This analysis of the results is based on the open responses given by participants. These have been complemented by the responses obtained in the second round, which are shown in Table III.1.5. The reasons given by the participants in the two rounds of the poll can be grouped in the following way:

Many of the responses fit more than one box, though generally they can be situated within the same column. Column I responses refer to boosting democracy, equity, active citizenship and the broader concept of human and social development. Responses categorized in column II are focused more on the contribution of HE to local economic activity in a global context, and on boosting productivity and competitiveness. The third column, which represents the responses of fewer participants,

refers to the contribution of HE to national development, public policies and state planning. Most of the experts' opinions fall into column I (75%), followed by column II (15%). These results were corroborated by those of the second round.

AN ANALYSIS BY REGION

An analysis of the open responses indicates that the experts believe HE should contribute to human and social development either as part of a specific society, reflecting that society's opportunities and weaknesses; or as a means for attaining a certain development model.

Participants from the Asia-Pacific, European and North American regions (Tables III.1.7, III.1.8 and III.1.9) had a response profile similar to that of the consolidated response. Most responses could be classified in column I. Of these, around 80% were in the educational and institutional category, and around 60% to 70% in the HE research category. There was a slight deviation towards HE's contribution to economic development and competitiveness.

In the responses of the Arab States, Latin America and the Caribbean and African participants, there was greater

TABLE III.1.6			
Why should higher education play an active role in human and social development (open response)?			
Because HEIs should or could ...	I	II	III
Education	Educate active citizens (socially, economically, culturally and politically)	Provide competitive human resources	Train experts and leaders for development policies
Research	Carry out research that is not financially motivated	Increase the productivity of the region or country	Contribute knowledge to development policies
Institutional mission	Make human and social development the central aim of the institution	Meet the demands of globalization and increased competitiveness	Contribute to the development of the state

TABLE III.1.7 **Main arguments of the Asia-Pacific participants**	
In addition to training good professionals, higher education should also train people to become citizens who participate actively in the different spheres of society (social, economic, cultural, political and so on)	90%
Higher education has the obligation, as one of its main aims, to contribute to human and social development through a relevant and committed interaction with its environment	83%
Higher education is fundamental for the creation, dissemination and use of knowledge that is essential for human and social development, through research that is not based on financial reward	69%

TABLE III.1.8 **Main arguments of the European participants**	
In addition to training good professionals, higher education should also train people to become citizens who participate actively in the different spheres of society (social, economic, cultural, political and so on)	84%
Higher education has the obligation, as one of its main aims, to contribute to human and social development through a relevant and committed interaction with its environment	79%
Higher education is fundamental for the creation, dissemination and use of knowledge that is essential for human and social development, through research that is not based on financial reward	63%

TABLE III.1.9 **Main arguments of the North American participants**	
Higher education has the obligation, as one of its main aims, to contribute to human and social development through a relevant and committed interaction with its environment	90%
In addition to training good professionals, higher education should also train people to become citizens who participate actively in the different spheres of society (social, economic, cultural, political and so on)	90%
Higher education is fundamental for the creation, dissemination and use of knowledge that is essential for human and social development, through research that is not based on financial reward	70%

emphasis on the link between the research function and increasing productivity and competitiveness. The rectors and other university employees were the group that most strongly associated research with this category (45%).

AFRICA
Africa is one of the regions in which experts most frequently stated that HE should contribute to increasing competitiveness, in order to confront the challenges of globalization (27%). Likewise, although most of the

experts' responses fell into column I (65%), Africa is the region that put most stress on the need for education to train future leaders and provide knowledge for managing public administrations (27%).

ARAB STATES
The Arab States participants were those who most frequently stated that research is a means of boosting competitiveness and increasing productivity (44%). Likewise, along with Africa, more participants from this region con-

TABLE III.1.10 **Main arguments of the African participants**	
Higher education has the obligation, as one of its main aims, to contribute to human and social development through a relevant and committed interaction with its environment	77%
In addition to training good professionals, higher education should also train people to become citizens who participate actively in the different spheres of society (social, economic, cultural, political and so on)	69%
Higher education is fundamental for the creation, dissemination and use of knowledge that is essential for human and social development, through research that is not based on financial reward	61%

TABLE III.1.11 **Main arguments of the Arab States participants**	
Higher education has the obligation, as one of its main aims, to contribute to human and social development through a relevant and committed interaction with its environment	78%
In addition to training good professionals, higher education should also train people to become citizens who participate actively in the different spheres of society (social, economic, cultural, political and so on)	78%
Higher education is fundamental for the creation, dissemination and use of knowledge that is essential for human and social development, through research that is not based on financial reward	56%
Higher education provides a capacity for research that is fundamental in assuring the competitiveness of countries or regions and helps increase their productivity	44%

TABLE III.1.12	
Main arguments of the Latin American and Caribbean participants	
In addition to training good professionals, higher education should also train people to become citizens who participate actively in the different spheres of society (social, economic, cultural, political and so on)	86%
Higher education is fundamental for the creation, dissemination and use of knowledge that is essential for human and social development, through research that is not based on financial reward	61%
Higher education provides a capacity for research that is fundamental in assuring the competitiveness of countries or regions and helps increase their productivity	36%

sidered that universities should educate leaders, agents of change and experts to implement development policies in the country.

LATIN AMERICA AND THE CARIBBEAN

- Latin American and Caribbean participants gave a slightly higher than average (86%) response to the opinion that HE should contribute to human and social development through relevant and committed interaction with its surrounding environment, and educate citizens who are able to participate actively in the different spheres of society. In addition, they stressed more frequently than in other regions the 'obligation' that HE has in these issues, as one of the main objectives of its educational and institutional activity.
- Furthermore, along with the Arab States, it is the region that most frequently identified the research activity of HE as fundamental to ensuring the competitiveness and increasing the productivity of the countries and regions (36%).

REPORT QUESTION 2: MAIN CHALLENGES

Which of the challenges relating to human and social development should be given maximum priority for HE in your region or country?

The results show noticeable *agreement* on which challenges for human and social development should be the highest priority for HE, particularly within each region.

The participants highlighted the following social challenges to which HE should contribute:

1. Poverty reduction, leading to greater social equity.
2. The changes required for sustainable development (in its social, environmental and economic aspects).
3. The inclusion of critical thinking and ethical values in the globalization process.
4. An improvement in governability and participative democracy in society.

Other HE priorities that appeared with significant frequency in the responses (from 20% to 40%) were as follows: improve access to education; train human resources that are adapted to the needs of the local economy; improve access to the knowledge society and to new technologies; and improve multicultural relations.

Similar results were found for the different profiles. The four most frequently chosen challenges were highlighted by all the profiles, although with varying emphasis. Public policymakers put most weight on training human resources adapted to the local economy (50%). Of all the participants, this group gave least importance to incorporating critical thinking and ethical values into the globalization process (30%). In contrast, the rectors expressed this opinion most frequently (60%).

A noticeable concentration of proposals was found in the open responses, particularly within each region. As we will see, there was greater agreement on the identification of problems than on the identification of solutions (question 3). The percentage of participants who chose each priority in the second round was similar to that in

TABLE III.1.13	
Most frequently identified challenges for human and social development	
Reduce poverty and achieve greater *social* equity	60%
Change attitudes to bring about *sustainable development*, in its social, environmental and economic aspects	58%
Incorporate *critical thinking* and *ethical values* into the globalization process	50%
Improve governability and participative *democracy*	44%
Improve the population's *access to education*	38%
Train *qualified human resources* that are adapted to the needs of the local economy	35%
Improve access to *the knowledge society* and to new technologies	28%
Improve *multicultural* relations through mutual understanding	25%
Defend *human rights*	12%
Increase the *competitiveness* and productivity of companies	10%

the first round, except in the case of two priorities: incorporating critical thinking and ethical values into the globalization process, with an increase from 20% to 50%; improving access to the knowledge society and new technologies, with an increase from 6% to nearly 30%. These are the only two proposals that received more support in the second round than in the first round.

AN ANALYSIS BY REGIONS

AFRICA

- Contributing to *poverty reduction* stood out as the human and social development challenge that is the highest priority for HE (selected by 77% of African participants).
- A higher percentage of African participants than those of other regions considered that it was a priority to train human resources adapted to the needs of the local economy (61%).
- In addition, improving governability and participative democracy (54%) and contributing to the change required for sustainable development (46%) appeared among the main concerns that should be tackled by HE.
- In the open responses, most of the participants who stressed the challenge of poverty reduction also highlighted that of improving governability. In addition, a similar – though slightly weaker – relation was observed between the challenge of poverty reduction and that of sustainable development. Nevertheless, this parallelism was not found among the responses of those who highlighted the challenge of training human resources and economic growth. This may be because poverty reduction is considered to be implicit in these challenges.
- Similar results were found for the different profiles. In both rounds, public policymakers selected the training of human resources that are adapted to the local economy with greater frequency than the other groups. In contrast, the rectors indicated with greater frequency than the other groups their preference for improving the population's access to education and incorporating critical thinking and ethics into the globalization process.

LATIN AMERICA AND THE CARIBBEAN

- Latin American participants considered that incorporating *critical thinking* and *ethical values* into the globalization process was the human and social development challenge that should be the greatest priority for HE systems (69%).
- The priorities of poverty reduction (67%) and sustainable development (64%) emerged with a similar frequency. The open responses given by participants from this region show a clear link between the challenge of poverty reduction and a more balanced distribution of resources between the different social sectors.
- Half the participants in this region considered that one HE priority should be to improve the population's access to education. The frequency of this response was higher among the civil society and public policy-maker groups.

ASIA-PACIFIC

- The three most frequently expressed priorities were poverty reduction, sustainable development and improving governability and participative democracy.
- This region, and Europe, showed the most concern for improving multicultural relations through mutual understanding (41%). This is markedly different from Latin America and the Caribbean, the region that least expressed this preference (6%).
- Four priorities received a similar number of responses in this region (30%): training qualified human resources; improving access to the knowledge society and new technologies; incorporating critical thinking and ethical values into the globalization process; and improving the population's access to education.

TABLE III.1.14 Priority challenges for African participants	
Reduce poverty and achieve greater *social* equity	77%
Train *qualified human resources* that are adapted to the needs of the local economy	61%
Improve governability and participative *democracy*	54%

TABLE III.1.15 Priority challenges for Latin American and Caribbean participants	
Incorporate *critical thinking* and *ethical values* into the globalization process	69%
Reduce poverty and achieve greater *social* equity	67%
Change attitudes to bring about *sustainable development*, in its social, environmental and economic aspects	64%

TABLE III.1.16 **Priority challenges for Asia-Pacific participants**	
Reduce poverty and achieve greater *social* equity	62%
Change attitudes to bring about *sustainable development*, in its social, environmental and economic aspects	55%
Improve governability and participative *democracy*	51%

TABLE III.1.17 **Priority challenges for Arab States participants**	
Change attitudes to bring about *sustainable development*, in its social, environmental and economic aspects	67%
Reduce poverty and achieve greater *social* equity	56%
Improve governability and participative *democracy*	56%
Train *qualified human resources* that are adapted to the needs of the local economy	56%

TABLE III.1.18 **Priority challenges for European participants**	
Incorporate *critical thinking* and *ethical values* into the globalization process	66%
Change attitudes to bring about *sustainable development*, in its social, environmental and economic aspects	55%
Improve governability and participative *democracy*	47%

TABLE III.1.19 **Priority challenges for North American participants**	
Reduce poverty and achieve greater *social* equity	80%
Change attitudes to bring about *sustainable development*, in its social, environmental and economic aspects	80%
Improve the population's *access to education*	70%

ARAB STATES

- After Africa, the Arab States is the region that put most emphasis on the priority of training human resources that are adapted to the needs of the local economy (56%). The priorities of poverty reduction, improving governability and democracy appeared with the same frequency.

- The challenge of contributing to change for sustainable development (67%) was selected with slightly more frequency, particularly in the responses given by HE experts.

- A relation between the challenges of governability and improving human rights was observed in the responses of experts from this region.

EUROPE

- The incorporation of critical thinking and ethical values into the globalization process is the challenge that was most frequently identified by the European participants (66%). In second place, emerged concerns to contribute to the changes needed for sustainable development, in its social, environmental and economic aspects (55%).

- Improving governability was the other aspect highlighted by the participants (47%). This challenge appeared to be linked to developing mechanisms of active civil society participation. Different opinions converged in expressing the challenge of contributing to the development of an active citizen, committed to public affairs.

- To a lesser extent, participants highlighted the challenges of contributing to improving multicultural relations (43%); poverty reduction (35%); and training human resources that are adapted to the needs of the local economy (35%). Concern for multicultural relations was mainly associated with the social changes produced by migration and, in second place, with international conflicts.

NORTH AMERICA

- The challenges expressed with the greatest frequency were contributing to sustainable development and to poverty reduction. These were frequently linked to greater equity between social and ethnic groups.

- The need to contribute to improving multicultural relations was given less importance in North America than in other regions, such as Asia-Pacific and Europe, where this concern was frequently expressed.

- Improving access to education was expressed as one of the priorities in this region (70%), as was the incorporation of critical thinking and ethical values into the globalization process.

REPORT QUESTION 3: MEASURES TO ADOPT

What measures should be taken to encourage the contribution of HE institutions in human and social development?

There was a certain degree of unanimity in the responses to question 2, which identified the problems to be tackled. However, there was greater divergence in participants' opinions when defining what measures should be adopted. Participants mentioned a wide variety of measures. In addition, proposals in similar fields were dealt with in very different ways, as we will see below. This gap between the degree of agreement when identifying challenges and that found when defining measures to be taken suggests that there is much room for research. In addition, it indicates that alternative models are needed to group the different proposals for HE policy changes that contribute to human and social development.

One initial proposal, with which the highest number of experts agreed, is that *more dialogue with the rest of society is needed*. Most of the proposals were related to social dialogue about what kind of university is required, how this should be adapted locally, and what is understood by its social relevance. In some cases, the experts had different opinions on who the interlocutors should be. Proposals included social movements, employers' organizations and public administrations. Most of the proposals either indicated that social dialogue should involve all of society, or did not specify which actors should be involved.

The following measures were most frequently mentioned by the participants:

- *Curricular reform*. There were different approaches to this topic: introducing different kinds of human and social development values; increasing the link with the needs of the social or productive sector; multidisciplinary knowledge; and so on.
- *Improving the training of teaching staff*, in accordance with the different curricular reform proposals.
- *Increasing funding for HEIs*, although there were different ideas about the source of funding (public–private).[5]
- *Improving university governance*. There were different ideas about how to achieve this: increasing university autonomy; increasing the role of stakeholders; increasing dialogue with those responsible for public policies; and so on.
- *Accreditation*[6] *and quality improvements*; with differences in the criteria of relevance and efficiency.
- *Improving the mechanisms for accessing HE.*
- *Increasing the volume of research*, whether on social problems, in interdisciplinary areas, or involving

increasing the competitiveness of local companies and so on.

In the second round of the poll, in which participants were given feedback on their colleagues' responses, some convergence was seen in the measures expressed. Three measures were expressed by almost 50% of the experts:

- Include the environmental, economic and social aspects of sustainability in the curricula of all students, in research, and in the institutional activity of universities (curricular reform).
- Improve the training of teaching staff, both in contents and pedagogy, so that human and social development challenges are included in academic activity.
- Increase public funding for HE.

Other measures that had a high number of responses (approximately 40%) were the following:

- Improve the quality of HE systems.
- Boost education and research that contributes to critical thinking.

The experts' proposals varied according to the different profiles. Public policymakers put great emphasis on training teaching staff (70%) and improving the quality of the HE system (60%). University rectors more frequently selected the proposal: participate in coordinated international networks that give opinions on and influence global and regional problems, thus increasing the involvement of university specialists in political decisions related to their area of knowledge (55%). The opinion of HE specialists was close to the overall average, with a slight leaning towards increasing public funding for HE. Civil society participants selected the following proposals with above-average frequency: include sustainability in all areas of HE institutions (60%); provide institutional spaces for democratic participation in society; and participate actively in civil society networks (60%).

AN ANALYSIS BY REGION

AFRICA

- Improve the training of teaching staff, both in content and pedagogy, so that human and social development challenges are included in academic activity (the measure most frequently selected by participants from this region (69%)). Along with the Arab States, this is the region that put most emphasis on training teaching staff. This measure tallies with the challenge to train human resources that are adapted to the needs of the local economy. This challenge was identified in the previous question by participants from both these regions.
- Public policymakers and civil society members

TABLE III.1.20.	
Priority action lines	
Include environmental, economic and social aspects of *sustainability* in the *curricula* of all students, in *research* and in the *institutional* activity of universities	51%
Improve *the training of teaching staff*, both in content and pedagogy, so that human and social development challenges are included in academic activity	49%
Increase *public funding* in HE	47%
Improve the *quality* of HE systems	44%
Boost education and research that contribute to *critical thinking*	41%
Participate in coordinated *international networks* that *provide opinions* on and influence global and regional problems, thus boosting the *involvement* of university specialists in *policy decisions* linked to their area of knowledge	36%
Increase the *relevance* of programmes, bringing them in line with the needs of the social environment	35%
Provide institutional spaces for *democratic participation* in society and participate actively in *civil society networks* (NGOs, local communities, social movements, social platforms and so on) that work for social and human development	35%

TABLE III.1.21.	
Priority action lines for African experts	
Improve *the training of teaching staff*, both in content and pedagogy, so that human and social development challenges are included in academic activity	69%
Increase *public funding* in HE	54%
Boost education and research that contribute to *critical thinking*	54%

TABLE III.1.22	
Priority action lines for Latin American and Caribbean experts	
Include environmental, economic and social aspects of *sustainability* in the *curricula* of all students, in *research* and in the *institutional* activity of universities	64%
Increase *public funding* in HE	50%
Improve the *quality* of HE systems	47%

TABLE III.1.23	
Priority action lines for Asia-Pacific experts	
Include environmental, economic and social aspects of *sustainability* in the *curricula* of all students, in *research* and in the *institutional* activity of universities	59%
Improve the *training of teaching staff*, both in content and pedagogy, so that human and social development challenges are included in academic activity Provide people with an undergraduate *education that is holistic, multidisciplinary and generalist*	52%
Improve the *quality* of HE systems	45%

favoured this measure more than participants from other profiles.

- Two other measures stood out: increase public funding for HE; and boost education and research that contribute to critical thinking.

LATIN AMERICA AND THE CARIBBEAN

- The measure selected with most frequency by Latin America and the Caribbean participants was the inclusion of sustainability in all aspects of universities (64%). Public policymakers and civil society members favoured this measure more than participants from other profiles.
- The second most frequently selected measures were

increasing public funding for HE (50%) and improving HE quality (47%).

ASIA-PACIFIC

- In this region, the most frequently proposed measure was also including sustainability in all areas of universities (59%). This is consistent with the responses to the previous question, in which sustainability was identified as a challenge by 55% of the experts in this region.
- Other measures proposed were training teaching staff (50%) and giving people a degree education that is holistic, multidisciplinary and generalist (50%).

- This region's experts were those that most frequently proposed improving the training of teaching staff (78%). In second place, they highlighted increasing public funding (55%) as one of the measures that would contribute to improving HEIs.

EUROPE

- There was a greater diversity of proposals in this region than in other regions. Most of the experts stated that the quality of HE needed to be improved (53%). This region put more emphasis on this measure than the other regions.

- Likewise, boosting education and research that contributes to critical thinking was proposed by many participants (50%). In the previous question, this topic had been identified as a challenge by 66% of the experts in this region.

- A second group of proposals received slightly less support: increasing public funding of HE; including sustainability in universities; improving the training of teaching staff, both in content and in teaching methodology.

NORTH AMERICA

- This region is among those that put most emphasis on the need for communication and interaction with other actors outside universities.

- The following measures were highlighted: including sustainability in universities (70%); increasing the relevance of programmes, by putting them in the context of their social setting (50%); participating in international networks that give opinions on global and regional problems (50%); providing spaces for democratic participation within society, participating in civil society networks (50%).

REPORT QUESTION 4: MAIN ATTRIBUTES ACQUIRED BY UNIVERSITY GRADUATES

What do you think are, will be and should be the main attributes and characteristics of university graduates at the end of their educational process?

The results show interesting differences among the experts' opinions of the main attributes that university graduates have *now*; their proposals for *desirable attributes in the future*; and their perspectives on the most likely *future attributes* (Table III.1.27).

The experts highlighted the following *main attributes* that are currently acquired: an orientation towards *competitiveness* in carrying out professional activities (cho-

TABLE III.1.24 **Priority action lines for Arab States experts**	
Improve the *training of teaching staff*, both in content and pedagogy, so that human and social development challenges are included in academic activity	78%
Increase *public funding* in HE	55%
Boost education and research that contribute to *critical thinking* Provide people with an undergraduate *education that is holistic, multidisciplinary and generalist* Improve the *quality* of HE systems Increase *university autonomy*	44%

TABLE III.1.25 **Priority action lines for European experts**	
Improve the *quality* of HE systems	53%
Boost education and research that contribute to *critical thinking*	50%
Increase *public funding* in HE	45%

TABLE III.1.26 **Priority action lines for North American experts**	
Include environmental, economic and social aspects of *sustainability* in the *curricula* of all students, in *research* and in the *institutional* activity of universities	70%
Increase the *relevance* of programmes, bringing them in line with the needs of the social environment	50%
Provide institutional spaces for *democratic participation* in society and participate actively in *civil society networks* (NGOs, local communities, social movements, social platforms and so on) that work for social and human development	50%
Participate in coordinated *international networks* that *provide opinions* on and influence global and regional problems, thus boosting the *involvement* of university specialists in *policy decisions* linked to their area of knowledge	50%

TABLE III.1.27	
A general selection of the attributes that are, will be and should be acquired in HEI (second round)	
Current attributes	
An orientation towards *competitiveness* in future professional activities	56%
An ability to *adapt and utilize* constantly changing technological environments	41%
The ability to develop *critical thinking* and to confront *complex and uncertain situations*	40%
An orientation towards *active participation in social and cultural life*	23%
An understanding of the *human and social problems* of our time, regardless of profession	19%
The ability to respect and/or accept as valid *non-scientific forms of knowledge*	5%
Most likely future attributes	
An ability to *adapt and utilize* constantly changing technological environments	52%
The ability to lead and/or fit into *multicultural* teams, to be at ease and respectful when working in them, and to have *practical knowledge of different cultural environments*	40%
An orientation towards *creativity, innovation and research practice*	36%
The ability to develop *critical thinking* and to confront *complex and uncertain situations*	27%
An understanding of, assessment of, and assumption of responsibility for, the *ethical implications and wider consequences* (cultural, political, social, environmental and so on) of their *professional activity*, in both a local and global context	21%
An understanding of the relationship between their area of knowledge and other knowledge about human life, from an *interdisciplinary and holistic perspective*	13%
Most desirable attributes	
The ability to develop *critical thinking* and to confront *complex and uncertain situations*	59%
An understanding of the relationship between their area of knowledge and other knowledge about human life, from an *interdisciplinary and holistic perspective*	48%
An understanding of the *human and social problems* of our time, regardless of profession	35%
Education in *ethical and human values and citizenship*, which prepares graduates to undertake their professional activity in accordance with *universal ethical criteria*	24%
An understanding of, assessment of, and assumption of responsibility for the *ethical implications and wider consequences* (cultural, political, social, environmental and so on) *for their professional activity*, in both a local and global context	21%
The ability to lead and/or fit into *multicultural* teams, to be at ease and respectful when working in them, and to have practical knowledge of different cultural environments	9%

sen by over half the participants); the ability to adapt and *utilize constantly changing technological environments*; the ability to develop *critical thinking*; and the ability to face complex, uncertain situations. Each of these options was selected by around 40% of the participants.

This consolidates the trend observed in the responses to the first questionnaire. However, in the second round, participants focused particularly on an orientation towards competitiveness, rather than on attributes such as an orientation towards active participation in social and cultural life or an understanding of the social and human problems of our time. Such responses were observed less than in the previous round.

There was also noticeable agreement in the participants' opinions on the *main attributes that will be acquired in the future*. One of the most frequently stressed abilities was adapting and *utilizing* constantly changing technological environments. This was selected by over half the participants. Other options that stood out were the ability to lead and/or fit into *multicultural* teams and be at ease and respectful when working in them, having *practical knowledge of different cultural environments*;

and an orientation towards *creativity, innovation and research practice*.

Thus, three of the attributes that had been emphasized in the first round were confirmed in the second round. However, the experts' perspectives of the future were more narrowly defined in the second round, in which they focused on abilities related to managing new technologies. Attributes of a less practical nature were chosen less frequently in the second round, for example the ability to develop critical thinking; an understanding of, assessment of, and assumption of responsibility for the ethical implications and wider consequences of their professional activity; and an understanding of the relation between the different areas of human knowledge.

If we compare the forecasts of the experts with their descriptions of the current situation, we can see that *the importance of* attributes related to utilizing *new technologies* and adapting to the *multiculturality* of an increasingly globalized world are consolidated. Likewise, the importance of the ability to develop *critical thinking will be maintained in the future*, and *attributes such as an orientation towards innovation and research* will be boosted.

Such attributes can be considered as neglected or under-valued at present.

Nevertheless, participants *did not consider that attributes such as understanding and assuming responsibility for the ethical implications and wider consequences of professional activity* would have a prominent role. Only a minority of participants predicted that this would be important in the future. This *prospective view* of the participants *differed in some ways with their views of which graduate attributes are desirable*.

From a *prescriptive perspective*, the experts consider that the acquisition of the following three attributes *should be boosted*: the ability to develop *critical thinking* (selected by almost two-thirds of participants); an understanding of the relation between their area of knowledge and other knowledge from an *interdisciplinary and holistic* perspective (chosen by almost half the experts); and an *understanding of the human and social* problems of our time, which was mentioned by over a third of participants. In all regions, an orientation towards *competitiveness* was *the least-valued of the desirable future attributes*. Only a minority of experts – mainly in Africa – indicated the importance of an orientation towards competitiveness in the future.

Thus, the attributes that were highlighted in the second round were in accord with those of the first round. However, many participants selected the ability to develop critical thinking above attributes such as education in universal ethical values; an understanding of human and social problems; the ethical implications of professional activity; and taking responsibility for the wider consequences of professional actions. All these attributes were selected less frequently in the second round than in the first round.

AN ANALYSIS BY REGION

AFRICA

- In the analysis of the *current situation*, the ability to develop *critical thinking* (54%) was the attribute most frequently selected in this region. This was followed by an understanding of *human and social problems* (39%), with an orientation towards competitiveness (31%). Africa is one of the few regions in which *accepting non-scientific forms of knowledge* was selected as a current attribute. However, it was selected by the lowest number of African participants (8%). African *public policymakers'* choice of competitiveness as an attribute that is currently acquired in the region differed from the selection of other profiles, and particularly from that of HE specialists.

- In terms of predictions about *the most likely future situation*, over a third of African experts selected: *an understanding of, and assumption of responsibility for the ethical implications and consequences of professional activity*. African participants stressed the future relevance of this attribute more frequently than participants from other regions. Abilities related to multiculturality – one of the main attributes in the general selection – were seen as least important for the future in this region.

- With respect to the *most desirable future situation*, the experts in this region most strongly emphasized the importance of *understanding the relationship between different areas of human knowledge*. This attribute was supported by 80% of participants. African participants were those that least emphasized (barely 8%) the importance of attributes such as education in values; or an understanding of and assumption of responsibility for the ethical implications and consequences of pro-

TABLE III.1.28 African participants' selection of attributes	
Current attributes	
The ability to develop *critical thinking* and to confront *complex and uncertain situations*	54%
An understanding of the *human and social problems* of our time, regardless of profession	38%
An ability to *adapt and utilize* constantly changing technological environments	35%
Most likely attributes	
An ability to *adapt and utilize* constantly changing technological environments	50%
An orientation towards *creativity, innovation and research practice*	38%
The ability to develop *critical thinking* and to confront *complex and uncertain situations*	35%
Most desirable attributes	
An understanding of the relationship between their area of knowledge and other knowledge about human life, from an *interdisciplinary and holistic perspective*	81%
The ability to develop *critical thinking* and to confront *complex and uncertain situations*	65%
An understanding of the *human and social problems* of our time, regardless of profession	19%

TABLE III.1.29

Latin American and Caribbean participants' selection of attributes

Current attributes	
An orientation towards *competitiveness* in future professional activities	61%
An ability to *adapt and utilize* constantly changing technological environments	44%
The ability to develop *critical thinking* and to confront *complex and uncertain situations*	33%
Most likely attributes	
An ability to *adapt and utilize* constantly changing technological environments	44%
The ability to lead and/or fit into *multicultural* teams, to be at ease and respectful when working in them, and to have *practical knowledge* of different cultural environments	42%
An orientation towards *creativity, innovation and research practice*	39%
Most desirable attributes	
The ability to develop *critical thinking* and to confront *complex and uncertain situations*	72%
An understanding of the relationship between their area of knowledge and other knowledge about human life, from an *interdisciplinary and holistic perspective*	42%
Education in *ethical and human values and citizenship*, which prepares graduates to undertake their professional activity in accordance with *universal ethical criteria*	33%

fessional activity. These attributes were the least selected in the region, below abilities related to multiculturality. In addition, African participants were those that least stressed an understanding of human and social problems as a priority attribute for the future.

LATIN AMERICA AND THE CARIBBEAN

- This is one of the regions that most frequently selected an orientation towards *competitiveness and the utilization of new technologies* as attributes acquired in current higher education institutions. In particular, *higher education specialists and civil society participants* are those who most frequently selected competitiveness as the main current attributes, while rectors and public policymakers mostly chose abilities related to new technologies.

- The selection of the *attributes that would be most likely to be acquired in the future* was in agreement with general opinion. Abilities related to new technologies, multiculturality and an orientation towards research were selected. However, the emphasis varied with the profile of the participants. *HE specialists* most frequently attributed an important future role to abilities related to multiculturality. In contrast, *rectors* and other university employees mainly chose abilities related to new technologies. *Public policymakers* opted for an orientation towards creativity.

- With respect to *the most desirable attributes for the future*, the Latin America and the Caribbean experts were – together with the more economically developed regions – those who showed most concern for the importance of *education in ethical values and an understanding of human and social problems*. These attributes were selected by over a third of experts in

this region. However, this is one of the regions that least valued abilities related to multiculturality.

ASIA-PACIFIC

- This is the region that most strongly identified *an orientation towards competitiveness* as a current attribute. This attribute was selected by almost three quarters of this region's experts (72%). This, and abilities related to new technologies were the only attributes that received more support in the second round (almost double the percentage in the first round) in this region.

- After North America, this region is the one that most frequently chose *abilities related to new technologies* as an attribute that would probably be acquired in the future. The percentage of participants who selected this attribute doubled in the second round (from 27% to 62%).

- Over half the participants indicated that *an understanding of the relationship between different areas of human knowledge* was a desirable attribute for the future. Other attributes that appeared with significant frequency in the responses were an *understanding of human and social problems and education in ethical values*. These attributes were highlighted by over a third of experts in the region, particularly by rectors and other HE specialists.

ARAB STATES

- This is the *region that most diverged from the general selection of current attributes*, as the acceptance of *non-scientific forms of knowledge* was on the same level as an orientation towards competitiveness. These attributes were selected by almost half the par-

TABLE III.1.30
Asia-Pacific participants' selection of attributes

Current attributes	
An orientation towards *competitiveness* in future professional activities	72%
An ability to *adapt and utilize* constantly changing technological environments	41%
The ability to develop *critical thinking* and to confront *complex and uncertain situations* An orientation towards *active participation in social and cultural life*	24%
Most likely attributes	
An ability to *adapt and utilize* constantly changing technological environments	62%
The ability to lead and/or fit into *multicultural* teams, to be at ease and respectful when working in them, and to have *practical knowledge of different cultural environments*	48%
An orientation towards *creativity, innovation and research practice*	31%
Most desirable attributes	
An understanding of the relation between their area of knowledge and other knowledge about human life, from an *interdisciplinary and holistic perspective*	55%
The ability to develop *critical thinking* and to confront *complex and uncertain situations*	48%
An understanding of the *human and social problems* of our time, regardless of profession Education in *ethical and human values and citizenship*, which prepares graduates to undertake their professional activity in accordance with *universal ethical criteria*	34%

ticipants in this region. In addition, this is the only region that included an orientation towards *participation in social and cultural life* as one of the three main currently acquired attributes.

- From a *prospective perspective*, this is the region that gave most importance to an *understanding of the relations between the different areas of human knowledge* and least importance to abilities related to new technologies. However, according to two-thirds of the participants from this region, an *orientation towards creativity and research* is the attribute that will most probably be boosted in the future.
- The participants in this region, after the North Amer-

ican participants, are those that put most emphasis (almost 50%) on *an understanding of human and social problems* as a desirable and necessary future attribute. Over a third of experts in this region, expressed their concerns for increasing an *understanding of and the assumption of responsibility for the ethical implications and wider consequences of professional activity*.

EUROPE

- In terms of the *current situation*, the selection of the European experts in the second round was focused on the same attributes as those highlighted in the general

TABLE III.1.31
Arab States participants' selection of attributes

Current attributes	
An orientation towards *competitiveness* in future professional activities The ability to respect and/or accept as valid *non-scientific forms of knowledge*	44%
An orientation towards *active participation in social and cultural life*	33%
The ability to develop *critical thinking* and to confront *complex and uncertain situations* An ability to *adapt and utilize* constantly changing technological environments	22%
Most likely attributes	
An orientation towards *creativity, innovation and research practice*	67%
The ability to lead and/or fit into *multicultural* teams, to be at ease and respectful when working in them, and to have *practical knowledge of different cultural environments*	44%
An understanding of the relationship between their area of knowledge and other knowledge about human life, from an *interdisciplinary and holistic perspective*	33%
Most desirable attributes	
The ability to develop *critical thinking* and to confront *complex and uncertain situations*	78%
An understanding of the *human and social problems* of our time, regardless of profession	44%
An understanding of, assessment of, and assumption of responsibility for the *ethical implications and wider consequences* (cultural, political, social, environmental and so on) *of their professional activity*, in both a global and local context	33%

TABLE III.1.32

European participants' selection of attributes

Current attributes	
An orientation towards *competitiveness* in future professional activities	57%
The ability to develop *critical thinking* and to confront *complex and uncertain situations*	51%
An ability to *adapt and utilize* constantly changing technological environments	43%
Most likely attributes	
An ability to *adapt and utilize* constantly changing technological environments	54%
The ability to lead and/or fit into *multicultural* teams, to be at ease and respectful when working in them, and to have *practical knowledge of different cultural environments*	51%
The ability to develop *critical thinking* and to confront *complex and uncertain situations*	32%
Most desirable attributes	
The ability to develop *critical thinking* and to confront *complex and uncertain situations*	51%
An understanding of the relationship between their area of knowledge and other knowledge about human life, from an *interdisciplinary and holistic perspective*	
An understanding of, assessment of, and assumption of responsibility for *the ethical implications and wider consequences* (cultural, political, social, environmental and so on) *of their professional activity*, in both a global and local context	38%
An understanding of the *human and social problems* of our time, regardless of profession	35%

analysis. However, the selection was more balanced and critical thinking was given more precedence than abilities related to new technologies.

- With respect to the most realistic *perspectives for the future*, the opinion of European experts was divided between the importance of abilities related to *multiculturality* and those linked to *new technologies*. Each of these was selected by over half the European participants as attributes that would probably be acquired in the near future. The *ability to develop critical thinking* emerged as one of the three main attributes, above an orientation towards creativity and research.
- From a *prescriptive perspective*, many European participants (almost 40%) considered that *understand-

ing the ethical implications of one's profession was as important as understanding the *relationship between different areas of human knowledge*, which was notable in the general selection. *European civil society participants* were those who most emphasized the priority of this attribute for the future. However, *rectors* and other university employees also showed their concern for attributes related to an understanding of human and social problems and education in ethical values.

NORTH AMERICA

- In the analysis of *current* attributes, apart from those from Latin America, North American participants

TABLE III.1.33

North American participants' selection of attributes

Current attributes	
An orientation towards *competitiveness* in future professional activities	70%
An ability to *adapt and utilize* constantly changing technological environments	50%
The ability to develop *critical thinking* and to confront *complex and uncertain situations*	40%
Most likely attributes	
An ability to *adapt and utilize* constantly changing technological environments	70%
The ability to lead and/or fit into *multicultural* teams, to be at ease and respectful when working in them, and to have *practical knowledge of different cultural environments*	
An orientation towards *creativity, innovation and research practice*	
The ability to develop *critical thinking* and to confront *complex and uncertain situations*	30%
Most desirable attributes	
An understanding of the *human and social problems* or our time, regardless of profession	90%
An understanding of the relationship between their area of knowledge and other knowledge about human life, from an *interdisciplinary and holistic perspective*	
The ability to develop *critical thinking* and to confront *complex and uncertain situations*	
Education in *ethical and human values and citizenship*, which prepares graduates to undertake their professional activity in accordance with *universal ethical criteria*	30%

were those that put most emphasis on an orientation towards *competitiveness* in HE institutions. Although only chosen by a minority and given less importance in the second round, North America is another of the regions that *identified accepting non-scientific forms of knowledge* as an attribute that is currently acquired.

- With respect to *the most likely future situation*, this is the region that most strongly indicated (70%) that utilizing *new technologies* was the main attribute that would be boosted in the medium-term.
- In terms of the *most desirable future attributes, an understanding of human and social problems was given the most support*. This attribute was selected almost unanimously by this region's participants (90%).

If we look in more detail at regional selections, we find that an orientation towards *competitiveness* was the most frequently selected current attribute, particularly in *Europe, Asia-Pacific* and *North America*. This was also considered to be a currently acquired attribute by between one- and two-thirds of participants in regions such as *Africa, the Arab States* and *Latin America and the Caribbean*.

In contrast, attributes that were practically absent from the overall analysis, were particularly highlighted by participants from some regions. *Africa*, for example, was the only region that highlighted an *understanding of human and social problems* among the three attributes that are currently acquired. The *ability to accept non-scientific forms of knowledge* – which had the most dramatic drop in interest in the second round, from one in five participants to barely five in a hundred – had a specific weight in the *Arab States*.

In terms of the *dominant view of the future*, there was agreement between the opinions of experts from *Latin America, Asia-Pacific, Europe and North America* on the medium-term importance of abilities related to technologies, multiculturality and research. Most experts from *Africa* agreed in their belief that the ability to utilize new technologies would be one of the attributes acquired in the future. However, their choice of the other main attributes differed from the general opinion. The *opinions of Arab States participants differed most from the* average. They highlighted other attributes above those related to new technologies – to which they gave the same importance as an understanding of, and assumption of responsibility for the consequences of professional activity.

With respect to *the ideal future situation*, the results reveal *the participants' concern for attributes that are essential to human and social development*, such as education in universal ethical values and an understanding of the ethical implications of professional activity or the assumption of responsibility for the wider consequences of actions. *The acquisition of these attributes is not considered to be likely in the near future, even though they were identified as desirable qualities by experts from all the regions. Nevertheless, only a minority of African participants* selected these attributes.

This concern is in *agreement with the views expressed by the participants in response to the first question on the role that HE should play in relation to human and social development*. As the report on this question highlights, most experts associate the teaching function of universities with educating socially, economically, culturally and politically active citizens. The attributes that were selected with least frequency by the African participants are in accordance with the greater importance that they give to improving competitiveness to boost economic development in the region.

In the selection of currently acquired attributes, the *HE specialists, rectors* and other university employees are the groups that most emphasized an orientation towards *competitiveness* (over two-thirds), compared with only a third of public policymakers who stressed this option. *Civil society participants* opted equally for an orientation towards competitiveness and the ability to develop critical thinking. Together with *public policymakers*, they were the group that put most emphasis on an understanding of *human and social problems* as a current attribute.

There were certain similarities and differences *in the future perspective of the different profiles*. The forecasts of most of the *HE specialists and rectors* basically coincided with the overall view. However, *civil society* participants gave particular importance to an understanding of and assumption of responsibility for the ethical implications of professional activities. They consider that this attribute will be boosted in the near future, even more than an orientation towards creativity and research. In contrast, the *public policymakers* believe that HE institutions will mainly promote an orientation towards creativity, innovation and research practice.

The opinions of *HE specialists* and *public policymakers* on *the ideal future attributes* coincide with the overall assessment. However, most *rectors* indicated the importance of understanding the relationship between the different areas of human knowledge from a *holistic and interdisciplinary perspective*. They put equal emphasis on education in ethical values and the ability to develop critical thinking. In addition, *civil society* participants stressed the importance of introducing a holistic educational perspective more frequently than the other profiles. Education in ethical values received quite low support in this group.

In short, the participants' responses indicated that the current HE systems focus on ensuring the competitiveness of university graduates in their future professions, particularly by developing their ability to adapt and utilize new technologies. However, important values for social and human development – such as assuming responsibility for the ethical implications and cultural, political, social and environmental consequences of professional activity, or understanding the human and social problems of our time – were not among the attributes that are most frequently found in HE institutions. In addition, although they are considered desirable attributes, few professionals predicted that they would play an important role in the future. This contrast between the selection of desirable attributes and those that are most likely in the future suggests that the experts have a certain lack of control over changes in HE systems.

REPORT QUESTION 5: UNIVERSITIES' ROLE IN SOCIETY

What is your opinion of the following statement: 'Universities are the central institution in the knowledge society, and therefore in our society'?

Almost 90% of participants affirmed that universities are a *central institution in the knowledge society*. They mentioned their historic function and that it is essential to knowledge production, preservation and transfer. In addition, many participants showed their *concerns about the future role of universities* in a society in which an increasing number of agents have the ability to influence knowledge creation and dissemination. Thus, the results show the experts' concerns about *ensuring that essential knowledge for human and social development remains in the public domain*.

The *vast majority* of experts *recognize that universities have a central position* in the knowledge society. However, these experts can be divided into two groups: those who consider that universities are the most important institution; and those who consider that this centrality is shared with other agents. Within the majority opinion, many express reservations about the central position of universities. Some experts cite the non-universal nature of the knowledge society, indicating that it is not a reality in many parts of the planet. Others draw attention to the challenges universities are facing to maintain their central position in the current knowledge society, and to the emergence of non-university agents who manage information and knowledge in the private sector.

In the open responses, the participants expressed a certain degree of preoccupation about the production and dissemination of knowledge as a public good. This function was assumed by universities when no other institu-

tions were capable of taking it on. However, this university function may now be threatened. In addition, there are concerns about the impact that this new situation could have on teaching and research which are not linked to the economic goals of the private sector.

According to the experts who expressed these concerns, universities must *overcome a crisis of legitimacy* by ensuring equal access; improving the quantity and quality of an education that guarantees individual and social development; and by becoming more receptive to social needs. In addition, universities should turn the threat to their hegemony into an opportunity, by opening themselves up and interacting with emerging knowledge production and dissemination agents, such as companies, non-university research centres, the media and civil society, among others.

The centrality of universities was affirmed by the majority of participants. This was followed by the opinion that universities share their central role in the knowledge society. Just over 10% of the participants considered that universities do not have a central position in the knowledge society, either because they disagreed with the existence of the knowledge society, or because they believed that other agents (companies, the media, non-governmental organizations or public and private research centres that are independent from universities) play the central role in this society.

The majority opinion was the same in all the regions, although with different emphases. The regions that most clearly stressed the *centrality* of universities were the *Arab States, Asia-Pacific, Europe and Latin America and the Caribbean*. In these regions, this stance was supported by between 55% and 67% of the participants. In the same regions, around a third of the experts considered that the central role of universities is shared with other institutions.

This was also the opinion of the majority of *North American participants*. Here, 70% of participants considered that the role of universities in the knowledge society is effectively *central, but shared with other agents*. Only 30% of the North American experts attributed a central role to universities alone (Table III.1.34).

The view that the knowledge society is not currently a reality in certain regions, or that the central role in the knowledge society is played by institutions other than universities was held by only a minority of participants. Even so, this opinion was significant in *Africa and the Arab States*, where around 20% of experts indicated that the knowledge society is not a current reality. In the other regions, this opinion was found in around 5% to 10% of responses, except in North America, where it was not expressed at all.

If we look at the profile of the participants, the central-

TABLE III.1.34
Universities in the knowledge society

	Universities are the central institution	Universities share their central role with other agents	Other institutions play the central role	The knowledge society does not exist in the region
Africa	38%	35%	8%	19%
Latin America and the Caribbean	56%	39%	6%	–
Asia-Pacific	62%	31%	3%	3%
Arab States	67%	11%	–	22%
Europe	57%	38%	5%	–
North America	30%	70%	–	–

ity of universities was the option that was most highlighted by experts from all fields, except the *public policymakers*, who mainly opted (55%) for a *shared central role*. The *opinions that differ most from the* general stance are *mainly found among the HE specialists* and the *civil society participants* from *Africa and the Arab States*.

The civil society experts were those who most frequently (around 20%) stated that the central role in the knowledge society is played by agents other than universities. *HE specialists* were those who most frequently indicated that the knowledge society has not developed in all of the regions. Some participants indicated that it is not only in Africa but in all developing countries that the knowledge society has not yet developed, while others highlighted that there are several knowledge societies with very different degrees of development according to the region.

In short, the experts *are concerned about the future role of HE institutions* in a society in which an increasing number of actors are in a position to play an important role in knowledge production and dissemination. These concerns can be observed among those who affirm the central role of universities and those who consider that such a role does not currently exist but is desirable for the future. This opinion was expressed by participants from all regions and profiles. Therefore, universities should *facilitate dialogue and collaboration with other sectors of society* – particularly with the new agents linked to information and knowledge management – instead of isolating themselves and delegating these historic university tasks to the new agents.

CONCLUSIONS

The results of the Delphi poll show that the majority of experts worldwide agree *that higher education should play an active role in human and social development*. The attribution of this role to HE is based on different arguments that reveal different visions of society and development. The majority opinion of the experts indicates that HE should contribute towards developing active citizenship, democracy and equity by means of relevant interaction with and commitment to the universities' surrounding environments.

The results show noticeable agreement on the *priority challenges* that human and social development poses for HE, particularly within each region. The main challenges identified as priorities include *poverty reduction, sustainable development*, the inclusion of *critical thinking and ethical values* in the globalization process, and the improvement of *governability and participative democracy*.

Nevertheless, there were major disagreements on the most appropriate measures for confronting these challenges. Most of the proposals indicate that *more dialogue is needed* with the rest of society to discover what kind of universities it wants. Thus, universities can be adapted locally; that is, become more socially relevant. The measures that emerged with the most frequency included *curricular reform*, improving the *training of teaching staff*, improving *funding mechanisms, improving* the *management* of HEIs, and improving the *quality* and equity of *access to* HE.

The poll gathered the opinions expressed by the experts about which are, which will be and which should be the main attributes and characteristics of university graduates at the end of their educational process. The experts coincided in identifying an *orientation towards competitiveness in professions* as *the main attribute that is currently acquired by university students*. Other attributes were also identified, such as the ability to adapt and utilize constantly changing technological environments, and the ability to confront complex, uncertain situations. With respect to which should be the main attributes of the graduates at the end of their educational process, most experts recognized the importance of students developing *critical thinking* abilities and an *understanding of the relationship* between the different branches of human knowledge and human and social problems, as well as education *in values* and an understanding of the ethical and social *implications* of their professional activity. However, the experts forecast that the main attribute that will be acquired in the future will be the ability to *adapt* and *utilize changing technological environments. The ability to work in different cultural environments and an orientation towards innovation* were also among the most likely attributes to be boosted in the near future.

The majority of experts consider that universities are *central to the knowledge society*. They refer to their historic function of creating, preserving and disseminating knowledge. Likewise, the experts show their concern for the future role of universities in a society where an increasing number of agents are in a position to influence the production and dissemination of knowledge. The experts suggest that universities should *facilitate dialogue and collaboration with other sectors of society*, particularly with the new agents that are linked with information and knowledge management. This will *ensure the public access to the knowledge that is essential for human and social development.*

NOTES

1   We wish to thank Nuria Crespo for processing the raw information from the Delphi Poll responses.
2   The 'halo effect' refers to possible bias or prejudice in the responses that could occur as a result of identifying or explicitly associating a specific institution, such as GUNI, with some of the opinions under consideration. This identification could involve an emotional charge, which may lead to participants expressing their agreement or disagreement with this particular institution rather than their specific stance on the issue in question. Cf. Thorndike, E. (1920) A constant error on psychological rating, *Journal of Applied Psychology*, **4**, pp. 25–9.
3   In any survey, the participants' perceptions of the effects that a certain response will have on their image – and their desire to preserve this image – can determine their opinions according to whether they consider that their opinion is more or less socially desirable. Likewise, participants are expected to be less prone to openly state opinions if they consider that they are in the minority. This is known as the 'spiral of silence' effect. Cf. Anderson, J.A. (1996) *Communication Theory: Epistemological Foundations*. New York: The Guilford Press; Miller, K. (2005) *Communication Theories: Perspectives, Processes, and Contexts* (2nd edn). New York: McGraw-Hill.
4   Bradburn, N., Sudman, S. and Wansink, B. (2004) *Asking Questions: A Practical Guide to Questionnaire Design*. New York: Jossey-Bass Social and Behavioral Science Series.
5   For an in-depth analysis of opinions on financing models, see the Delphi Poll on Financing, *Higher Education in the World 2006*.
6   For an in-depth analysis of opinions on accreditation, see the Delphi Poll on Accreditation. *Higher Education in the World 2007*.

PARTICIPANTS IN THE DELPHI POLL

Gbemisola Aderemi Adeoti
Professor
Obafemi Awolowo University
Nigeria

John Aitchison
Director
School of Adult and Higher
Education
University of KwaZulu-Natal
South Africa

Hassan Al-Haj Ibrahim
Professor and Director of Quality
Assurance
Al-Baath University
Syria

Amin Al-Hakimi
Director
Yemeni Genetic Resources Centre
Sana'a University
Yemen

**Muneer bin Mohammed
Al-Maskery**
Under-Secretary for Vocational
Training
Ministry of Manpower
Oman

Said Hamad Alrabiey
Director General
Private Universities and Colleges
Ministry of Higher Education
Oman

Philip G. Altbach
Director
Centre for International Higher
Education
Boston College
USA

King-David Amoah
National Coordinator Ecumenical
Association for Sustainable
Agriculture and Rural
Development
Ghana

Kwesi A. Andam
Vice-Chancellor
Kwame Nkrumah University of
Science and Technology
Ghana

Yuichiro Anzai
President
Keio University
Japan

Eduardo Aponte
Adviser
Puerto Rico Council on Higher
Education
Puerto Rico

Akira Arimoto
Professor
Research Institute for Higher
Education
Hiroshima University
Japan

Luis Arza Valdés
President
Continental Organization of
Latin American and Caribbean
Students
Cuba

Abdelbagi O. Azhari
Director General
Training Directorate
Ministry of Higher Education and
Scientific Research
Sudan

Abdel Bagi A.G. Babiker
Dean
Faculty of Education Studies
President
GUNI Regional Network of Arab
States
Sudan

Carlos Alonso Bedoya
General Coordinator
Jubilee Peru Network
Peru

Hamed Ben Dhia
President
Sfax University
Tunisia

Nouria Benghabrit-Remaoun
Director
National Research Centre in
Social and Cultural
Anthropology
Algeria

Ivar Bleiklie
Director
Research Centre in Organization
and Management
University of Bergen
Norway

Peter Boothroyd
Professor
Centre for Human Settlements
University of British Columbia
Canada

Colin Brock
UNESCO Chair of Education as a
Humanitarian Response
University of Oxford
UK

L. David Brown
Professor of Public Policy
Kennedy School of Government
Harvard University
USA

Enric I. Canela
Professor
University of Barcelona
Spain

René Chamussy
Rector
Saint Joseph University of Beirut
Lebanon

Karuna Chanana
Professor
Centre for Educational Studies
Jawaharlal Nehru University
India

Xin Chen
Vice-Principal
Shanghai TV University
China

Peter P.T. Cheung
Executive Director
Hong Kong Council for
Academic Accreditation
China

Kiran B. Chhokar
Programme Coordinator
Centre for Environment Education
India

Thomas W. Clawson
President and CEO
National Board for Certified
Counselors
USA

Beedeeanun Conhye
Adviser
Association for the Development
of Education in Africa
France

Joan Cortadellas
Technical Director
UNESCO Chair of Higher
Education Management
Technical University of Catalonia
Spain

Arabinda Kumar Das
Vice-Chancellor
Kalyani University
India

**Juan Ramón de la Fuente
Ramírez**
Rector
National Autonomous University
of Mexico
Mexico

Gertjan de Werk
President
Osiris Communication Platform
for Sustainable Development
The Netherlands

Carlo di Benedetta
Coordinator
Community of Mediterranean
Universities
Italy

Mohamed Cherif Diarra
Coordinator
Working Group on Finance and
Education
Council for the Development of
Social Science Research in Africa
Senegal

José Dias Sobrinho
Professor
University of Sorocaba
Brazil

Axel Didriksson Takayanagui
Education Secretary
Mexico City
Mexico

David K. Dorkenoo
Head of the International
Department
Trade Union Congress
Ghana

Irina Dragan
International Coordinator
Cooperation and Development
Network Federation of Young
European Greens
Romania

Edwin Durán Zurita
Principal Adviser on University
Advancement
Bolivian Private University
Bolivia

Marit Egner
Adviser
Norwegian Agency for Quality
Assurance in Education
Norway

Toufic El-Houri
President
Administration Council Imam
Ouzai College of Islamic Studies
Lebanon

Nora Espí Lacomba
Executive Secretary National
Board of Accreditation
Cuba

Marise Espineli
International Institute of Rural
Reconstruction
Philippines

Norberto Fernández Lamarra
Director of Postgraduate Studies
Tres de Febrero University
Argentina

Eugenia M. Flores Vindas
Minister for Science and
Technology
Costa Rica

Annalize Fourie
Consultant
Irish Aid Education and Health
Programme
Embassy of Ireland
South Africa

Antonio Fragoso
Professor
School of Education
University of the Algarve
Portugal

Atanu Ghosh
Professor
Shailesh J. Mehta School of
Management
Indian Institute of Technology
India

Antoni Giró Roca
Rector
Technical University of Catalonia
President
Global University Network for
Innovation
Spain

Luis Eduardo González
Director
University Policies and
Management Programme
Interuniversity Development
Centre
Chile

Józef Górniewicz
UNESCO Chair on Quality
Teaching and Learning in Higher
Education under the Conditions
of Systemic Social and Economic
Transformations
University of Warmia and
Mazury
Poland

Corbin Michel Guedegbe
Education Specialist
African Development Bank
Tunisia

Sarah Guri-Rosenblit
Head of Education Studies
Open University of Israel
Israel

Lovemore C.K. Gwati
Executive Secretary
Zimbabwe Council for Higher
Education
Zimbabwe

Budd Lionel Hall
Director
Office of Community-Based
Research
Senior Fellow
Center for Global Studies
University of Victoria
Canada

Lee Harvey
Director
Centre for Research and
Evaluation
Sheffield Hallam University
UK

José Fabio Hernández Díaz
Head of the Academic Division
Higher Education Planning Office
National Council of Rectors
Costa Rica

Alma Herrera Márquez
Coordinator
Observatory of the Network of
Public Macro-Universities of Latin
America
Mexico

Paul Heywood
Director
Malta Equivalence Information
Centre
University of Malta
Malta

Edwin de Jesús Horta Vásquez
Rector
Catholic University of Colombia
Colombia

Johnson M. Ishengoma
Professor and Researcher
Saint Augustine University
of Tanzania
Tanzania

Ana Izvorska
Bulgarian Red Cross Youth
Bulgaria

Ezequiel Jaimes Figueroa
Technical Secretary
Mexican Continuing Education
and Distance Learning
Association
Mexico

Leo Jansen
Professor
Delft University of Technology
The Netherlands

Saran Kaur Gill
Professor
National University of Malaysia
Malaysia

Fayez E. Khasawneh
Former President
Yarmouk University
Member of the Board of
Directors
International Centre for Soil
Fertility and Agricultural
Development
Jordan

Laetitia J. King
Director of Advanced Nursing
Studies
Aga Khan University
Kenya

Jane Knight
Professor
Comparative, International and
Development Education Centre
Canada

André G. Komenan
Director
Education Department
African Development Bank
Tunisia

Jajah Koswara
Professor
Bogor Agriculture University
Indonesia

Marek Kwiek
Director
Centre for Public Policy
Adam Mickiewicz University
Poland

Maria Alice Lahorgue
Professor
Federal University of Rio Grande
do Sul
Brazil

Philippe Laredo
Professor
National School of Bridges and
Roads
France

Iván Lavados Montes
Executive Director
Interuniversity Development
Centre
Chile

Patricia B. Licuanan
Director
Miriam College
Philippines

Ethley D. London
Executive Director
University Council of Jamaica
Jamaica

Altagracia López
Director
Centre for Innovation in Higher
Education
Technological College of Santo
Domingo
Dominican Republic

María López de Asiain
Editorial Consultant
Idea Sostenible
Spain

Francisco López Segrera
Academic Adviser
Global University Network for
Innovation
Cuba

Carlos Losada
Director General
ESADE
Spain

Dietrich Marek
Vice-President
National General Accreditation
Commission
Poland

Francisco Marmolejo
Executive Director
Consortium for North American
Higher Education Collaboration
USA

Elvira Martín Sabina
UNESCO Chair of Higher
Education Management
School of Studies for the
Perfection of Higher Education
University of Havana
Cuba

Sonia Martínez Vives
Manager
Knowledge and Development
Foundation
Spain

Richard Mawditt
UNESCO Chair of Higher
Education Management
University of Bath
UK

Lynn Meek
Director
Centre for Higher Education
Management and Policy
University of New England
Australia

Praveen Mohadeb
Director
Tertiary Education Commission
Mauritius

Goolam Mohamedbhai
President
International Association of
Universities
Mauritius

Teboho Moja
Professor
New York University
USA

Karel F. Mulder
Professor
Delft University of Technology
Project Leader
Education for Sustainable
Development
The Netherlands

Lauren Müller de Pacheco
Rector
Private University of Santa Cruz
de la Sierra
Bolivia

Manuel Ramiro Muñoz
Consultant
International Institute for Higher
Education in Latin America and
the Caribbean
Colombia

Alice Museri
Adviser
University of Burundi
Burundi

Yadmaa Narantsetseg
Professor
Mongolian University of Science
and Technology
Mongolia

John W. Odhiambo
Vice-Chancellor
Strathmore University
Kenya

Ninnat Olanvoravuth
Secretary-General
Association of Southeast Asian
Institutions of Higher Learning
Thailand

Manuel Olave Sarmiento
Rector
Bolivian Private University
Bolivia

Fred Opio
Executive Director
Uganda Debt Network
Uganda

Víctor Ordóñez
Senior Education Fellow
East-West Center
USA

Luis Enrique Orozco Silva
UNESCO Chair of Higher
Education
University of the Andes
Member
Latin American Institute of
Education for Development
Colombia

Humberto Ortiz Roca
Economist
Episcopal Social Action
Conference
Member
Working Group: Debt and
Development, and
Jubilee Peru Network
Peru

Ifeanyi Oyeonoru
Professor
Sociology Department University
of Ibadan
Nigeria

Jaume Pagès
Chief Executive Officer
Universia
Spain

Angélica Paniagua Fuentes
Director
Foundation for Popular
Education
El Salvador

Evangelia Papoutsaki
Professor
Unitec
New Zealand

María Cristina Parra Sandoval
Professor
University of Zulia
Venezuela

Fananidzo B. Pesanai
Member
Technical Committee on
Certification and Accreditation
Southern African Development
Community
Zimbabwe

Muriel Poisson
Programme Specialist
International Institute for
Educational Planning
France

Jan Prusik
UNESCO Chair in Quality
Teaching and Learning in Higher
Education under the Conditions
of Systemic Social and Economic
Transformations
University of Warmia and
Mazury
Poland

Seimus Puirseil
Director
Higher Education and Training
Awards Council
Ireland

Alvydas Pumputis
Rector
Mykolas Romeris University
Lithuania

Gerardo Remolina Vargas
Rector
Pontifical Xavierian University
Colombia

Luciano Rodrigues de
Almeida
President
Polytechnic Institute of Leiria
Portugal

Mohsen Elmahdy Said
Director
Project Management Unit
Ministry of Higher Education
Egypt

Marcelo P. Salazar
Chancellor
Iligan Institute of Technology
Mindanao State University
Philippines

Manuel Sánchez
Researcher
Institute of Administrative
Research
University of Buenos Aires
Argentina

Bikas C. Sanyal
Special Adviser
International Institute of
Educational Planning
France

Astrid Schwietering
Policy Officer
Action Aid
Germany

Peter Scott
Vice-Chancellor
Kingston University
UK

Francisco K. Seddoh
Adviser to the Rector on African
Issues
United Nations University
Chargé de mission
UNESCO Office
Kinshasa
Democratic Republic of Congo

Juan José Sevilla García
Professor and Researcher
Autonomous University of Baja
California
Mexico

Sharifah Hapsah Syed Hasan
Shahabudin
Vice-Chancellor
National University of Malaysia
Malaysia

Sean Si-Heung Park
Director
Office of International Affairs
Korea University
Korea

Jiri Silny
Director
Ecumenical Academy Prague
Czech Republic

Alexander Slepukhin
Vice-Rector of Academic Affairs
Saratov State Technical University
Russia

Paulo Solari Alliende
Academic Sub-director DuocUC
Pontifical Catholic University of
Chile
Chile

Sofia Sountousko
Association for European
Expression
Greece

Adolfo Stubrin
Coordinator
International Affairs Sub-
committee
National Committee of
University Assessment and
Accreditation
Argentina

Eugenijus Stumbrys
Director
Centre for Quality Assessment in
Higher Education
Lithuania

Mohsen Tawfik
Director
UNESCO Asia-Pacific Office
India

Peter Taylor
Research Fellow and Head of
Graduate Programmes
Institute of Development Studies
University of Sussex
UK

Patrick T. Terenzini
Professor and Senior Scientist
Centre for the Study of Higher
Education
UK

Svoboda Tosheva
Development Research Centre
Bulgaria

Carlos Tünnermann Bernheim
President
Central American Council on
Higher Education
Costa Rica

Rosamaría Valle
Director General Educational
Assessment
National Autonomous University
of Mexico
Mexico

Juan Antonio Vázquez
Rector
University of Oviedo
President
Conference of Rectors of
Spanish Universities
Spain

Vlasta Vizek Vidovic
UNESCO Chair in Governance
and Management of Higher
Education
University of Zagreb
Croatia

H.M. Nissanka Warakaulle
Executive Secretary
Committee of Vice-Chancellors
and Directors
Sri Lanka

Ian Whitman
Head of the Programme for
Cooperation with Non-Member
Economies
Organization for Economic
Cooperation and Development
France

Tennyson Williams
Country Director
ActionAid International
Sierra Leone

Wai Sum Wong
Executive Director
Hong Kong Council for
Academic Accreditation
China

Li Yawan
Director
International Cooperation and
Exchange Office
China Central Radio and TV
University
China

Wang Yibing
Professor
Zhejiang University
Adviser
GUNI Asia-Pacific
China

Shuangxu Yin
Research Fellow
Institute of Distance Education
and Learning
China Central Radio and TV
University
China

Rubén Zardoya Loureda
Rector
University of Havana
Cuba

Aminudin Zuhairi
Director
Quality Assurance Centre
Open University of Indonesia
Indonesia

PART IV
STATISTICAL
APPENDIX

DEFINITIONS

Current expenditure on education. Expenditure for goods and services consumed within the current year and which would be renewed if needed in the following year. It includes expenditure on: staff salaries, pensions and benefits; contracted or purchased services; other resources including books and teaching materials; welfare services; and other current expenditure, such as subsidies to students and households, furniture and minor equipment, minor repairs, fuel, telecommunications, travel, insurance and rents.

Enrolment. Number of pupils or students officially enrolled in a given grade or level of education, regardless of age. Typically, this data is collected at the beginning of the school year.

Gender Parity Index (GPI). Ratio of the female-to-male values of a given indicator. A GPI of 1 indicates parity between sexes.

Gross Domestic Product (GDP). The sum of gross value added by all resident producers in the economy, including distributive trades and transport, plus any product taxes and minus any subsidies not included in the value of the products.

Gross Enrolment Ratio (GER). Number of pupils enrolled in a given level of education, regardless of age, expressed as a percentage of the population in the theoretical age group for the same level of education. For the tertiary level, the population used is the five-year age group following on from the secondary school leaving age.

Human development index (HDI). Is a summary composite index that measures the average achievements in a country in three basic dimensions of human development: a long and healthy life; knowledge; and a decent standard of living. It is calculated for 177 countries and areas for which data is available. In addition human development indicators are presented for another 17 UN member countries for which complete data was not available.

Literacy. The ability to read and write, with understanding, a simple statement related to one's daily life. It involves a continuum of reading and writing skills, and often includes basic arithmetic skills (numeracy).

Regional average. Regional averages are calculated on the basis of the published data and using the best possible non-publishable estimates where no data exists. Countries are weighted with the appropriate national school-age populations.

Total public expenditure on education. The sum of the expenditure on education and education administration made by local, regional and national/central governments, including municipalities. Household contributions and inter-governmental transfers are excluded.

BIBLIOGRAPHY

UNESCO Institute for Statistics, *Global Education Digest 2006*. Annex B. Available at: http://www.uis.unesco.org/TEMPLATE/pdf/ged/2006/GED 2006.pdf

http://hdr.undp.org/en/reports/global/hdr2006

Table IV.1.1	Adult and youth literacy (2004)
Table IV.1.2	Education expenditure, spending as a percentage of gross domestic product/financial year ending in 2004
Table IV.1.3	Education expenditure, sources as a percentage of gross domestic product/financial year ending in 2004
Table IV.1.4	Tertiary education enrolment and teaching staff
Table IV.1.5	Research and development expenditures as a percentage of the GDP and researchers in R&D per million people
Table IV.1.6	Human development rank, index, total population and GDP per capita

The following symbols are used in the Statistical Tables:

...	No data available
*	National estimation
**	UIS estimation
-	Magnitude nil or negligible
(.)	Not applicable
(p)	Data for the reference year or more recent years is provisional
x	Data included in another category or column
+n	Data refers to the school or financial year (or period) n years or periods after the reference year or period
-n	Data refers to the school or financial year (or period) n years or periods before the reference year or period

TABLE IV.1.1
Adult and youth literacy (2004)

Region	Adults (aged 15 and over)						Youth (aged 15 to 24)					
	Literacy rate (%)				Illiterate population		Literacy rate (%)				Illiterate population	
Country or territory	MF	M	F	GPI	MF	%F	MF	M	F	GPI	MF	%F
Arab States												
Algeria	70	80	60	0.76	6,422,833	66	90	94	86	0.92	704,848	69
Bahrain	87	89	84	0.94	66,385	49	97	97	97	1.00	3,359	43
Djibouti	...	...	...	...	...	...	...	...	...	...	...	...
Egypt	71	83	59	0.71	14,210,331	71	85	90	79	0.88	2,381,708	67
Iraq	74	84	64	0.76	3,706,566	69	85	89	80	0.91	764,749	63
Jordan	90	95	85	0.89	330,010	74	99	99	99	1.00	9,592	61
Kuwait	93 +1	94 +1	91 +1	0.96 +1	138,641 +1	49 +1	100 +1	100 +1	100 +1	1.00 +1	1,094 +1	38 +1
Lebanon	...	...	...	...	...	...	...	...	...	...	...	...
Libyan Arab Jamahiriya	...	...	...	...	...	...	...	...	...	...	...	...
Mauritania	51	60	43	0.73	731,505	60	61	68	55	0.82	198,964	58
Morocco	52	66	40	0.60	10,106,367	65	70	81	60	0.75	1,888,486	67
Oman	81	87	74	0.85	300,192	57	97	98	97	0.99	14,356	59
Palestinian Autonomous Territories	92	97	88	0.91	153,266	78	99	99	99	1.00	7,300	57
Qatar	89	89	89	0.99	66,686	29	96	95	98	1.03	4,373	24
Saudi Arabia	79	87	69	0.80	2,680,976	65	96	98	94	0.96	157,422	75
Sudan[1]	61	71	52	0.73	7,557,205	63	77	85	71	0.84	1,467,517	64
Syrian Arab Republic	80	86	74	0.86	2,347,875	65	92	94	90	0.96	332,577	62
Tunisia	74	83	65	0.78	1,878,110	68	94	96	92	0.96	117,660	67
United Arab Emirates	...	...	...	...	...	...	...	...	...	...	...	...
Yemen	...	...	...	...	...	...	...	...	...	...	...	...

TABLE IV.1.1
cont'd

Region / Country or territory	Adults (aged 15 and over)						Youth (aged 15 to 24)					
	Literacy rate (%)				Illiterate population		Literacy rate (%)				Illiterate population	
	MF	M	F	GPI	MF	%F	MF	M	F	GPI	MF	%F
Central and Eastern Europe												
Albania	99	99	98	0.99	27,879	69	99	99	99	1.00	2,996	46
Belarus	100 [-1]	100 [-1]	99 [-1]	1.00 [-1]	33,236 [-1]	77 [-1]	100 [-1]	100 [-1]	100 [-1]	1.00 [-1]	3,132 [-1]	40 [-1]
Bosnia and Herzegovina	97	99	94	0.95	105,717	86	100	100	100	1.00	1,144	38
Bulgaria	98	99	98	0.99	120,973	66	98	98	98	1.00	20,262	52
Croatia	98	99	97	0.98	69,429	83	100	100	100	1.00	2,172	48
Czech Republic	...	...	...	...	...	...	...	...	...	...	...	...
Estonia	100	100	100	1.00	2,609	57	100	100	100	1.00	456	40
Hungary	...	...	...	...	...	...	...	...	...	...	...	...
Latvia	100	100	100	1.00	4,927	64	100	100	100	1.00	846	43
Lithuania	100	100	100	1.00	9,955	54	100	100	100	1.00	1,486	43
Poland	...	...	...	...	...	...	...	...	...	...	...	...
Republic of Moldova	98	99	98	0.99	56,036	75	100	99	100	1.00	3,851	47
Romania	97	98	96	0.98	491,304	71	98	98	98	1.00	77,500	49
Russian Federation	99	100	99	1.00	675,976	75	100	100	100	1.00	66,675	41
Serbia and Montenegro[2]	96	99	94	0.95	245,734	85	99	99	99	1.00	7,237	52
Slovakia	...	...	...	...	...	...	...	...	...	...	...	...
Slovenia	...	...	...	...	...	...	...	...	...	...	...	...
The Former Yugoslav Rep. of Macedonia	96	98	94	0.96	62,018	77	99	99	98	0.99	4,164	59
Turkey	87	95	80	0.84	6,388,706	81	96	98	93	0.95	583,143	77
Ukraine	99	100	99	0.99	229,306	80	100	100	100	1.00	14,255	42
Central Asia												
Armenia	99	100	99	0.99	13,979	76	100	100	100	1.00	1,061	37
Azerbaijan	99 [-1]	99 [-1]	98 [-1]	0.99 [-1]	66,594 [-1]	79 [-1]	100 [-1]	100 [-1]	100 [-1]	1.00 [-1]	1,632 [-1]	43 [-1]
Georgia	...	...	...	...	...	...	...	...	...	...	...	...
Kazakhstan	100 [-1]	100 [-1]	99 [-1]	1.00 [-1]	53,049 [-1]	77 [-1]	100 [-1]	100 [-1]	100 [-1]	1.00 [-1]	4,111 [-1]	40 [-1]
Kyrgyzstan	99 [-1]	99 [-1]	98 [-1]	0.99 [-1]	40,935 [-1]	74 [-1]	100 [-1]	100 [-1]	100 [-1]	1.00 [-1]	2,873 [-1]	42 [-1]
Mongolia	98	98	98	1.00	36,105	56	98	97	98	1.01	12,142	34
Tajikistan	99	100	99	1.00	19,488	71	100	100	100	1.00	1,876	49
Turkmenistan	99 [-1]	99 [-1]	98 [-1]	0.99 [-1]	30,999 [-1]	73 [-1]	100 [-1]	100 [-1]	100 [-1]	1.00 [-1]	1,522 [-1]	49 [1]
Uzbekistan	...	...	...	...	...	...	...	...	...	...	...	...
East Asia and the Pacific												
Australia	...	...	...	...	...	...	...	...	...	...	...	...
Brunei Darussalam	93	95	90	0.95	17,079	65	99	99	99	1.00	695	49
Cambodia	74	85	64	0.76	2,262,169	73	83	88	79	0.90	543,225	63
China	91	95	87	0.91	87,018,720	73	99	99	99	0.99	2,259,650	63
Cook Islands	...	...	...	...	...	...	...	...	...	...	...	...
Democratic People's Republic of Korea	...	...	...	...	...	...	...	...	...	...	...	...
Fiji	...	...	...	...	...	...	...	...	...	...	...	...
Hong Kong (China), SAR	...	...	...	...	...	...	...	...	...	...	...	...
Indonesia	90	94	87	0.92	15,100,434	69	99	99	99	1.00	548,979	56
Japan	...	...	...	...	...	...	...	...	...	...	...	...
Kiribati	...	...	...	...	...	...	...	...	...	...	...	...
Lao People's Democratic Republic	69	77	61	0.79	969,644	64	78	83	75	0.90	225,347	59

TABLE IV.1.1
cont'd

Region	Adults (aged 15 and over)						Youth (aged 15 to 24)					
	Literacy rate (%)				Illiterate population		Literacy rate (%)				Illiterate population	
Country or territory	MF	M	F	GPI	MF	%F	MF	M	F	GPI	MF	%F
East Asia and the Pacific cont'd												
Macao, China	91	95	88	0.92	30,602	74	100	99	100	1.00	247	26
Malaysia	89	92	85	0.93	1,722,457	64	97	97	97	1.00	119,521	48
Marshall Islands	...	...	...	...	...	...	...	...	...	...	...	...
Micronesia (Federated States of)	...	...	...	...	...	...	...	...	...	...	...	...
Myanmar	90	94	86	0.92	3,200,837	70	95	96	93	0.98	523,886	60
Nauru	...	...	...	...	...	...	...	...	...	...	...	...
New Zealand	...	...	...	...	...	...	...	...	...	...	...	...
Niue	...	...	...	...	...	...	...	...	...	...	...	...
Palau	...	...	...	...	...	...	...	...	...	...	...	...
Papua New Guinea	57	63	51	0.80	1,320,694	56	67	69	64	0.93	341,826	52
Philippines	93	93	93	1.00	3,502,959	50	95	94	96	1.01	759,097	43
Republic of Korea	...	...	...	...	...	...	...	...	...	...	...	...
Samoa	...	...	...	...	...	...	...	...	...	...	...	...
Singapore	93	97	89	0.92	232,450	77	100	99	100	1.00	2,484	38
Solomon Islands	...	...	...	...	...	...	...	...	...	...	...	...
Thailand	93	95	91	0.95	3,354,254	66	98	98	98	1.00	222,736	53
Timor-Leste	...	...	...	...	...	...	...	...	...	...	...	...
Tokelau	...	...	...	...	...	...	...	...	...	...	...	...
Tonga	99 [-1]	99 [-1]	99 [-1]	1.00 [-1]	644 [-1]	47 [-1]	99 [-1]	99 [-1]	99 [-1]	1.00 [-1]	134 [-1]	46 [-1]
Tuvalu	...	...	...	...	...	...	...	...	...	...	...	...
Vanuatu	74 [-1]	...	...	...	28,083 [-1]	...	...	...	...	...	...	...
Viet Nam	90 [-1]	94 [-1]	87 [-1]	0.93 [-1]	4,909,406 [-1]	69 [-1]	94 [-1]	94 [-1]	94 [-1]	0.99 [-1]	956,135 [-1]	52 [-1]
Latin America and the Caribbean												
Anguilla	...	...	...	...	...	...	...	...	...	...	...	...
Antigua and Barbuda	...	...	...	...	...	...	...	...	...	...	...	...
Argentina	97	97	97	1.00	756,287	52	99	99	99	1.00	71,379	40
Aruba	97	98	97	1.00	1,890	57	99	99	99	1.00	110	43
Bahamas	...	...	...	...	...	...	...	...	...	...	...	...
Barbados	...	...	...	...	...	...	...	...	...	...	...	...
Belize	...	...	...	...	...	...	...	...	...	...	...	...
Bermuda	...	...	...	...	...	...	...	...	...	...	...	...
Bolivia	87	93	81	0.87	683,049	74	97	99	96	0.98	43,188	72
Brazil	89	88	89	1.00	15,051,896	50	97	96	98	1.02	1,122,581	33
British Virgin Islands	...	...	...	...	...	...	...	...	...	...	...	...
Cayman Islands	...	...	...	...	...	...	...	...	...	...	...	...
Chile	96	96	96	1.00	495,479	52	99	99	99	1.00	26,253	40
Colombia	93	93	93	1.00	2,216,528	52	98	98	98	1.01	167,407	39
Costa Rica	95	95	95	1.00	137,754	47	98	97	98	1.01	17,969	40
Cuba	100	100	100	1.00	17,911	52	100	100	100	1.00	668	51
Dominica	...	...	...	...	...	...	...	...	...	...	...	...
Dominican Republic	87	87	87	1.00	730,625	49	94	93	95	1.03	102,120	39
Ecuador	91	92	90	0.97	740,511	57	96	96	96	1.00	88,240	49
El Salvador	...	...	...	...	...	...	...	...	...	...	...	...
Grenada	...	...	...	...	...	...	...	...	...	...	...	...
Guatemala	69	75	63	0.84	2,034,504	62	82	86	78	0.91	420,916	62
Guyana	...	...	...	...	...	...	...	...	...	...	...	...

TABLE IV.1.1
cont'd

Region	Adults (aged 15 and over)						Youth (aged 15 to 24)					
	Literacy rate (%)				Illiterate population		Literacy rate (%)				Illiterate population	
Country or territory	MF	M	F	GPI	MF	%F	MF	M	F	GPI	MF	%F
Latin America and the Caribbean cont'd												
Haiti	...	...	...	...	...	...	...	...	...	...	...	...
Honduras	80	80	80	1.01	773,274	49	89	87	91	1.05	152,497	40
Jamaica	80 −1	74 −1	86 −1	1.16 −1	339,800 −1	37 −1	...	...	...	...	...	...
Mexico	91	92	90	0.97	6,521,245	60	98	98	98	1.00	492,439	49
Montserrat	...	...	...	...	...	...	...	...	...	...	...	...
Netherlands Antilles	...	...	...	...	...	...	...	...	...	...	...	...
Nicaragua	77	77	77	1.00	691,266	51	86	84	89	1.06	153,687	40
Panama	92	93	91	0.99	162,819	54	96	97	96	0.99	21,353	55
Paraguay	...	...	...	...	...	...	...	...	...	...	...	...
Peru	88	93	82	0.88	2,270,534	73	97	98	96	0.98	173,989	66
Saint Kitts and Nevis	...	...	...	...	...	...	...	...	...	...	...	...
Saint Lucia	...	...	...	...	...	...	...	...	...	...	...	...
Saint Vincent and the Grenadines	...	...	...	...	...	...	...	...	...	...	...	...
Suriname	90	92	87	0.95	32,401	62	95	96	94	0.98	4,539	57
Trinidad and Tobago	...	...	...	...	...	...	...	...	...	...	...	...
Turks and Caicos Islands	...	...	...	...	...	...	...	...	...	...	...	...
Uruguay	...	...	...	...	...	...	...	...	...	...	...	...
Venezuela	93	93	93	0.99	1,166,409	52	97	96	98	1.02	136,634	34
North America and Western Europe												
Andorra	...	...	...	...	...	...	...	...	...	...	...	...
Austria	...	...	...	...	...	...	...	...	...	...	...	...
Belgium	...	...	...	...	...	...	...	...	...	...	...	...
Canada	...	...	...	...	...	...	...	...	...	...	...	...
Cyprus	97	99	95	0.96	17,719	79	100	100	100	1.00	246	40
Denmark	...	...	...	...	...	...	...	...	...	...	...	...
Finland	...	...	...	...	...	...	...	...	...	...	...	...
France	...	...	...	...	...	...	...	...	...	...	...	...
Germany	...	...	...	...	...	...	...	...	...	...	...	...
Gibraltar	...	...	...	...	...	...	...	...	...	...	...	...
Greece	96	98	94	0.96	375,492	73	99	99	99	1.00	16,446	45
Holy See	...	...	...	...	...	...	...	...	...	...	...	...
Iceland	...	...	...	...	...	...	...	...	...	...	...	...
Ireland	...	...	...	...	...	...	...	...	...	...	...	...
Israel	97	98	96	0.97	135,669	74	100	100	100	1.00	2,311	100
Italy	98	99	98	0.99	784,588	64	100	100	100	1.00	12,165	47
Liechtenstein	...	...	...	...	...	...	...	...	...	...	...	...
Luxembourg	...	...	...	...	...	...	...	...	...	...	...	...
Malta	88 −1	86 −1	89 −1	1.03 −1	35,735 −1	45 −1	96 −1	94 −1	98 −1	1.04 −1	2,222 −1	27 −1
Monaco	...	...	...	...	...	...	...	...	...	...	...	...
Netherlands	...	...	...	...	...	...	...	...	...	...	...	...
Norway	...	...	...	...	...	...	...	...	...	...	...	...
Portugal	...	...	...	...	...	...	...	...	...	...	...	...
San Marino	...	...	...	...	...	...	...	...	...	...	...	...
Spain	...	...	...	...	...	...	...	...	...	...	...	...
Sweden	...	...	...	...	...	...	...	...	...	...	...	...

TABLE IV.1.1
cont'd

| Region | Adults (aged 15 and over) | | | | | | Youth (aged 15 to 24) | | | | | |
| | Literacy rate (%) | | | | Illiterate population | | Literacy rate (%) | | | | Illiterate population | |
Country or territory	MF	M	F	GPI	MF	%F	MF	M	F	GPI	MF	%F
North America and Western Europe cont'd												
Switzerland	…	…	…	…	…	…	…	…	…	…	…	…
United Kingdom	…	…	…	…	…	…	…	…	…	…	…	…
United States	…	…	…	…	…	…	…	…	…	…	…	…
South and West Asia												
Afghanistan	28	43	13	0.29	9,048,359	59	34	51	18	0.36	2,888,550	61
Bangladesh	…	…	…	…	…	…	…	…	…	…	…	…
Bhutan	…	…	…	…	…	…	…	…	…	…	…	…
India	61	73	48	0.65	268,426,053	65	76	84	68	0.80	46,290,248	66
Iran, Islamic Republic of	77	84	70	0.84	10,508,505	64	…	…	…	…	…	…
Maldives	96	96	96	1.00	5,992	47	98	98	98	1.00	1,088	46
Nepal	49	63	35	0.56	7,661,416	65	70	81	60	0.75	1,436,836	66
Pakistan	50 +1	63 +1	36 +1	0.57 +1	48,818,411 +1	62 +1	65 +1	76 +1	55 +1	0.72 +1	11,612,414 +1	64 +1
Sri Lanka	91	92	89	0.97	1,379,793	57	96	95	96	1.01	168,230	43
Sub-Saharan Africa												
Angola	67	83	54	0.65	2,400,678	74	72	84	63	0.75	749,460	70
Benin	35	48	23	0.49	2,717,916	60	45	59	33	0.56	828,346	61
Botswana	81	80	82	1.02	206,497	50	94	92	96	1.04	26,027	36
Burkina Faso	22	29	15	0.52	5,052,131	55	31	38	25	0.65	1,725,397	54
Burundi	59	67	52	0.78	13,727	62	73	77	70	0.92	347,541	57
Cameroon	68	77	60	0.78	2,764,066	64	…	…	…	…	…	…
Cape Verde	…	…	…	…	…	…	…	…	…	…	…	…
Central African Republic	49	65	33	0.52	1,107,082	67	59	70	47	0.67	314,764	65
Chad	26	41	13	0.31	3,206,486	61	38	56	23	0.42	954,855	64
Comoros	…	…	…	…	…	…	…	…	…	…	…	…
Congo	…	…	…	…	…	…	…	…	…	…	…	…
Côte d'Ivoire	49	61	39	0.63	4,732,544	59	61	71	52	0.74	1,349,261	62
Democratic Rep. of the Congo	67	81	54	0.67	8,901,036	71	70	78	63	0.81	3,013,058	63
Equatorial Guinea	87	93	80	0.86	33,426	76	95	95	95	1.00	4,286	49
Eritrea	…	…	…	…	…	…	…	…	…	…	…	…
Ethiopia	…	…	…	…	…	…	…	…	…	…	…	…
Gabon	…	…	…	…	…	…	…	…	…	…	…	…
Gambia	…	…	…	…	…	…	…	…	…	…	…	…
Ghana	58	66	50	0.75	4,893,831	60	71	76	65	0.86	1,200,166	58
Guinea	29	43	18	0.43	3,507,031	58	47	59	34	0.57	908,034	60
Guinea-Bissau	…	…	…	…	…	…	…	…	…	…	…	…
Kenya	74	78	70	0.90	4,480,121	58	80	80	81	1.01	1,348,536	49
Lesotho	82	74	90	1.23	182,194	32	…	…	…	…	…	…
Liberia	…	…	…	…	…	…	…	…	…	…	…	…
Madagascar	71	77	65	0.85	2,609,275	60	70	73	68	0.94	923,361	54
Malawi	64 −1	75 −1	54 −1	0.72 −1	2,132,718 −1	66 −1	76 −1	82 −1	71 −1	0.86 −1	525,039 −1	62 −1
Mali	19 −1	27 −1	12 −1	0.44 −1	4,601,325 −1	56 −1	24 −1	32 −1	17 −1	0.52 −1	1,692,328 −1	54 −1
Mauritius	84	88	81	0.91	137,596	63	95	94	95	1.02	11,727	42
Mozambique	…	…	…	…	…	…	…	…	…	…	…	…
Namibia	85	87	83	0.96	163,152	57	92	91	93	1.03	28,819	42

TABLE IV.1.1
cont'd

| Region | Adults (aged 15 and over) | | | | | | Youth (aged 15 to 24) | | | | | |
| | Literacy rate (%) | | | | Illiterate population | | Literacy rate (%) | | | | Illiterate population | |
Country or territory	MF	M	F	GPI	MF	%F	MF	M	F	GPI	MF	%F
Sub-Saharan Africa cont'd												
Niger	29 +1	43 +1	15 +1	0.35 +1	5,032,652 +1	59 +1	37 +1	52 +1	23 +1	0.44 +1	1,666,738 +1	60 +1
Nigeria	...	...	...	...	...	...	...	...	...	...	...	...
Rwanda	65	71	60	0.84	1,470,747	61	78	79	77	0.98	381,968	53
São Tomé and Principe	...	...	...	...	...	...	...	...	...	...	...	...
Senegal	39	51	29	0.57	3,672,238	61	49	58	41	0.70	1,142,354	59
Seychelles	92	91	92	1.01	4,875	50	99	99	99	1.01	128	35
Sierra Leone	35	47	24	0.52	1,971,765	60	48	59	37	0.63	522,448	61
Somalia	...	...	...	...	...	...	...	...	...	...	...	...
South Africa	82 -1	84 -1	81 -1	0.96 -1	4,867,391 -1	56 -1	94 -1	93 -1	94 -1	1.01 -1	530,755 -1	47 -1
Swaziland	80	81	78	0.97	117,598	57	88	87	90	1.03	26,399	45
Togo	53	69	38	0.56	1,390,844	67	74	84	64	0.76	288,190	69
Uganda	67	77	58	0.75	4,230,012	65	77	83	71	0.86	1,215,880	62
United Republic of Tanzania	69	78	62	0.80	6,194,268	63	78	81	76	0.94	1,627,813	55
Zambia	68 -1	76 -1	60 -1	0.78 -1	1,797,093 -1	63 -1	69 -1	73 -1	66 -1	0.91 -1	662,687 -1	55 -1
Zimbabwe	...	...	...	...	...	...	...	...	...	...	...	...
REGIONAL AVERAGES												
World	82	87	77	0.89	780,925,967	64	87	90	84	0.93	139,013,662	62
Arab States	70	80	59	0.73	57,812,284	66	85	90	79	0.88	9,426,079	67
Central and Eastern Europe	97	99	96	0.97	9,319,847	79	99	99	98	0.99	822,859	68
Central Asia	99	100	99	0.99	381,909	72	100	100	100	1.00	46,550	48
East Asia and the Pacific	92	95	88	0.93	125,627,228	71	98	98	98	0.99	6,807,345	57
Latin America and the Caribbean	90	91	89	0.98	38,571,952	55	96	96	96	1.01	4,109,432	45
North America and Western Europe	99	99	99	1.00	6,312,007	62	99	100	99	1.00	493,146	50
South and West Asia	59	71	46	0.66	399,015,544	63	72	80	63	0.79	80,414,646	63
Sub-Saharan Africa	61	70	54	0.77	143,885,197	61	73	78	68	0.88	36,893,605	59

Notes: 1: Sudan: data is for North Sudan only

2: Serbia and Montenegro: data excludes Kosovo and Metohia

Source: UIS. Excel sheets taken from UIS website. *Global Education Digest 2006,* Table 15.

TABLE IV.1.2
Education expenditure, spending as a percentage of gross domestic product/financial year ending in 2004

Region Country or territory	Public expenditure per student as a % of GDP per capita			Total public expenditure on education	
	Primary	Secondary	Tertiary	as a % of GDP	as a % of total government expenditure
Arab States					
Algeria	11.3 **,+1	17.1 **,-1	...	...	...
Bahrain	15.8 **,-2	17.7 **,-2	...	...	...
Djibouti	55.5 **,+1	79.9 **,+1	504.8 **,+1	7.9 **,+1	27.3 **,+1
Egypt (p)	...	...	...	...	...
Iraq	...	...	...	...	...
Jordan (p)	15.2 -2	18.0 -2	...	...	...
Kuwait	12.2 +1	18.1 +1	104.9 +1	5.1 +1	12.7 +1
Lebanon	7.2 **,+1	7.6 **,+1	15.9 +1	2.6 +1	11.0 +1
Libyan Arab Jamahiriya	...	...	...	...	...
Mauritania	9.8 **,+1	24.7 **,+1	39.9 **,+1	2.3 +1	8.3 +1
Morocco	22.9 +1	39.6 **,+1	93.0 +1	6.7 +1	27.2 +1
Oman	15.7 +1	13.2 +1	14.6 +1	3.6 +1	24.2 +1
Palestinian Autonomous Territories	...	...	...	...	...
Qatar	...	...	...	...	...
Saudi Arabia	...	...	...	...	...
Sudan	...	...	...	...	...
Syrian Arab Republic	14.5 -2	26.8 -2	...	...	...
Tunisia (p)	21.1 **,+1	24.4 **,+1	56.4 +1	7.3 +1	20.8 +1
United Arab Emirates	...	...	...	1.3 **,+1	27.4 **,+1
Yemen	...	...	...	...	...
Central and Eastern Europe					
Albania	7.7 **,-2	11.9 **,-2	36.3 **,-2	2.8 **,-2	...
Belarus	14.1 **,+1	25.3 **,+1	28.3 +1	6.0 +1	11.3 +1
Bosnia and Herzegovina	...	...	...	...	...
Bulgaria (p)	16.2 -2	19.0 -2	18.7 -2	3.6 -2	...
Croatia	24.0 **,-2	23.5 **,-2	34.5 -2	4.5 -2	10.0 -2
Czech Republic (p)	12.0 -2	23.0 -2	31.8 -2	4.4 -2	...
Estonia	19.8 -2	25.5 -2	24.9 -2	5.7 -2	...
Hungary (p)	20.8 -2	21.4 -2	36.1 -2	5.5 -2	...
Latvia	22.4 -2	25.9 -2	19.0 -2	5.8 -2	...
Lithuania	...	...	32.9 -2	5.9 -2	...
Poland (p)	23.5 -2	20.8 -2	22.1 -2	5.6 -2	12.8 -2
Republic of Moldova	16.6 **,+1	24.1 **,+1	12.9 +1	4.3 +1	21.1 +1
Romania	9.9 **,-2	15.1 **,-2	26.5 -2	3.5 -2	...
Russian Federation (p)	...	...	...	3.8 **,-2	10.7 **,-2
Serbia and Montenegro	...	...	...	...	...
Slovakia (p)	11.3 -2	18.8 -2	31.1 -2	4.3 -2	...
Slovenia	...	...	26.3 -2	6.0 -2	...
The Former Yugoslav Rep. of Macedonia	23.6 **,-2	7.7 -2	23.7 -2	3.5 -2	...
Turkey (p)	13.9 **,-2	9.4 **,-2	50.3 -2	3.6 -2	...
Ukraine	14.8 **,+1	23.9 **,+1	34.1 +1	6.4 +1	18.9 +1

TABLE IV.1.2
cont'd

Region Country or territory	Public expenditure per student as a % of GDP per capita			Total public expenditure on education	
	Primary	Secondary	Tertiary	as a % of GDP	as a % of total government expenditure
Central Asia					
Armenia	8.9 **,-2	11.1 **,-2	38.3 **,-2	3.2 **,-2	...
Azerbaijan	6.3 **,+1	10.2 **,+1	10.4 +1	2.5 +1	19.6 +1
Georgia	...	...	...	2.9	13.1
Kazakhstan	10.0 **,+1	7.9 **,+1	5.7 +1	2.3 +1	...
Kyrgyzstan	7.7 **,-2	14.5 **,-2	21.2 -2	4.4 **,-1	...
Mongolia	15.7	14.6	25.0	5.6	...
Tajikistan	8.7 **,+1	11.3 **,+1	14.1 +1	3.5 +1	18.0 +1
Turkmenistan	...	...	...	...	...
Uzbekistan	...	...	...	...	...
East Asia and the Pacific					
Australia (p)	16.4 -2	14.6 -2	22.6 -2	4.9 -2	...
Brunei Darussalam	...	...	...	...	...
Cambodia	6.5 **	...	...	2.0	...
China (p)	...	...	...	...	...
Cook Islands	...	...	...	...	...
Democratic People's Republic of Korea	...	...	...	...	...
Fiji	18.5	17.2	66.9	6.4	20.0 -2
Hong Kong (China), SAR	14.9 +1	19.9 +1	60.6 +1	4.2 +1	23.0 +1
Indonesia (p)	2.9 -2	5.6 -2	15.6 -2	1.1 -2	9.0 **,-2
Japan (p)	22.1 -2	21.6 -2	17.1 -2	3.6 -2	...
Kiribati	...	...	...	16.0 **,-2	...
Lao People's Democratic Republic	9.7 +1	4.9 +1	26.8 +1	2.3 +1	11.7 +1
Macao, China	7.8 **,-1	...	...	2.9 -1	16.1 -2
Malaysia (p)	20.2 -2	28.3 -2	102.4 -2	8.1 -2	20.3 -2
Marshall Islands	28.7 **,-2	33.8 **,-2	89.9 **,-2	14.8 **	15.8 -1
Micronesia (Federated States of)	...	...	...	...	...
Myanmar	...	...	...	...	...
Nauru	...	...	...	...	...
New Zealand (p)	19.2 +1	22.4 +1	25.1 +1	6.5 +1	...
Niue	...	...	...	...	10.1 -2
Palau	...	...	...	10.1 **,-2	...
Papua New Guinea	...	...	...	...	...
Philippines (p)	11.1 -2	9.2 -2	14.5 -2	3.2 -2	17.8 -2
Republic of Korea (p)	16.3 -2	23.7 -2	...	4.2 -2	15.5 -2
Samoa	12.1 **,-2	...	...	4.3 **,-2	13.7 **,-2
Singapore	...	...	...	...	...
Solomon Islands	...	...	...	...	...
Thailand (p)	...	...	24.9 +1	4.2 +1	25.0 +1
Timor-Leste	...	...	...	...	...
Tokelau	...	...	...	...	14.5 -1
Tonga	12.2	9.4	...	4.8	13.5 -1
Tuvalu	...	...	...	...	44.0 -2
Vanuatu	...	...	...	9.6 -1	...
Viet Nam	...	...	...	...	...

TABLE IV.1.2
cont'd

Region Country or territory	Public expenditure per student as a % of GDP per capita			Total public expenditure on education	
	Primary	Secondary	Tertiary	as a % of GDP	as a % of total government expenditure
Latin America and the Caribbean					
Anguilla	12.2 [**,–1]	35.6 [**,–1]	...	7.4 [–1]	...
Antigua and Barbuda	...	...	...	3.8 [–2]	...
Argentina (p)	10.9 [–2]	14.9 [–2]	13.1 [–2]	4.0 [–2]	13.8 [–2]
Aruba	13.3 [*,+1]	19.5 [*,+1]	34.2 [*,+1]	5.1 [+1]	15.4 [+1]
Bahamas	...	...	...	...	...
Barbados	23.4 [**,+1]	27.6 [+1]	...	6.9 [+1]	16.4 [+1]
Belize	15.4	10.6	198.0	5.1	18.1 [–1]
Bermuda	...	...	...	...	...
Bolivia	16.4 [**]	13.0 [**]	35.9 [**]	6.4 [**]	18.1 [–1]
Brazil	...	...	...	...	...
British Virgin Islands	...	...	...	...	12.4 [+1]
Cayman Islands	...	...	...	...	...
Chile (p)	12.3 [+1]	13.6 [+1]	11.9 [+1]	3.5 [+1]	...
Colombia	19.5 [+1]	18.4 [+1]	24.6 [+1]	4.8 [+1]	11.1 [+1]
Costa Rica	17.1	19.7	...	4.9	18.5
Cuba	37.3 [+1]	44.2 [+1]	51.5 [+1]	9.8 [+1]	16.6 [+1]
Dominica	...	...	...	...	...
Dominican Republic	8.1 [**,+1]	5.8 [**,+1]	...	1.8 [+1]	9.7 [+1]
Ecuador	...	...	...	...	...
El Salvador	9.2 [**,+1]	10.5 [**,+1]	17.2 [**,+1]	2.8 [+1]	...
Grenada	11.9 [*,–1]	13.1 [*,–1]	...	5.2 [–1]	12.9 [–1]
Guatemala	4.9 [+1]	3.7 [+1]	...	...	...
Guyana	17.1 [+1]	16.2 [+1]	37.2 [+1]	8.5 [+1]	14.5 [+1]
Haiti	...	...	...	...	...
Honduras	...	...	...	...	...
Jamaica (p)	15.4 [–1]	24.7 [–1]	44.4 [**,–1]	5.3 [–1]	9.5 [–1]
Mexico (p)	14.4 [–2]	16.2 [–2]	49.8 [–2]	5.3 [–2]	...
Montserrat	10.0 [**,–2]	...	...	4.9 [**,–2]	...
Netherlands Antilles	...	...	...	...	...
Nicaragua	9.1	10.7	...	3.1 [**,–1]	15.0 [–2]
Panama	9.9	12.6	27.0 [**]	3.9 [**]	8.9 [**]
Paraguay (p)	12.3 [–2]	13.7 [–2]	28.2 [**,–2]	4.4 [–2]	11.4 [–2]
Peru (p)	6.7 [+1]	8.9 [**,+1]	9.0 [**,+1]	2.4 [+1]	13.7 [+1]
Saint Kitts and Nevis	...	...	...	9.3 [+1]	...
Saint Lucia	14.8 [+1]	19.1 [+1]	–	5.8 [+1]	16.9 [+1]
Saint Vincent and the Grenadines	22.7 [+1]	29.7 [+1]	...	8.2 [+1]	16.1 [+1]
Suriname	...	...	...	...	...
Trinidad and Tobago	16.0 [**,–2]	...	...	4.3 [**,–2]	...
Turks and Caicos Islands	...	...	...	...	16.5 [–2]
Uruguay (p)	7.9 [–2]	9.0 [–2]	19.0 [**,–2]	2.6 [–2]	9.6 [–2]
Venezuela	...	...	...	...	...

TABLE IV.1.2
cont'd

Region Country or territory	Public expenditure per student as a % of GDP per capita			Total public expenditure on education	
	Primary	Secondary	Tertiary	as a % of GDP	as a % of total government expenditure
North America and Western Europe					
Andorra	...	...	...	...	...
Austria (p)	23.9 ⁻²	28.2 ⁻²	47.0 ⁻²	5.7 ⁻²	...
Belgium (p)	19.0 ⁻²	25.2 ⁻²	38.6 ⁻²	6.3 ⁻²	...
Canada	...	...	...	...	...
Cyprus	20.3 *,⁻²	34.1 *,⁻²	45.1 *,⁻²	6.1 ⁻²	...
Denmark (p)	24.9 ⁻²	36.1 ⁻²	74.6 ⁻²	8.5 ⁻²	...
Finland (p)	18.3 ⁻²	27.4 ⁻²	38.1 ⁻²	6.4 ⁻²	...
France (p)	17.8 ⁻²	28.6 ⁻²	29.3 ⁻²	5.6 ⁻²	...
Germany (p)	16.7 ⁻²	22.6 ⁻²	...	4.8 ⁻²	...
Gibraltar	...	...	...	...	...
Greece (p)	15.6 **,⁻²	...	26.8 ⁻²	4.0 ⁻²	...
Holy See	...	...	...	...	...
Iceland (p)	25.3 ⁻²	23.3 ⁻²	32.5 ⁻²	7.6 **,⁻²	...
Ireland (p)	12.4 ⁻²	18.1 ⁻²	26.6 ⁻²	4.3 ⁻²	...
Israel (p)	23.0 ⁻²	23.5 ⁻²	26.6 ⁻²	7.5 ⁻²	13.7 ⁻²
Italy (p)	25.4 ⁻²	28.1 ⁻²	27.4 ⁻²	4.7 ⁻²	...
Liechtenstein	...	...	...	...	...
Luxembourg	...	...	...	...	...
Malta	14.0 ⁻²	23.6 ⁻²	51.8 ⁻²	4.6 ⁻²	...
Monaco	...	...	...	...	...
Netherlands (p)	18.0 ⁻²	22.9 ⁻²	39.8 ⁻²	5.1 ⁻²	...
Norway (p)	20.5 **,⁻²	30.7 **,⁻²	48.5 ⁻²	7.6 ⁻²	...
Portugal (p)	24.0 ⁻²	31.6 ⁻²	26.0 ⁻²	5.8 ⁻²	...
San Marino	...	...	...	...	...
Spain (p)	19.2 ⁻²	24.7 ⁻²	23.1 ⁻²	4.5 ⁻²	...
Sweden (p)	24.4 ⁻²	26.7 ⁻²	50.6 ⁻²	7.7 ⁻²	...
Switzerland (p)	24.3 ⁻²	29.2 ⁻²	59.9 ⁻²	5.8 ⁻²	...
United Kingdom (p)	16.3 ⁻²	15.4 ⁻²	28.8 ⁻²	5.3 ⁻²	11.5 **,⁻²
United States (p)	21.6 ⁻²	24.9 ⁻²	25.9 ⁻²	5.7 ⁻²	...
South and West Asia					
Afghanistan	...	...	...	...	...
Bangladesh	7.7 **,⁺¹	14.7 ⁺¹	49.7 ⁺¹	2.5 ⁺¹	14.2 ⁺¹
Bhutan	...	...	...	...	...
India	...	...	...	...	...
Iran, Islamic Republic of	9.7 ⁺¹	11.0 ⁺¹	22.8 ⁺¹	4.7 ⁺¹	22.8 ⁺¹
Maldives	22.0 ⁺¹	... ⁺¹	... ⁺¹	7.1 ⁺¹	15.0 ⁺¹
Nepal	12.4 **,⁻¹	10.5 ⁻¹	71.2 ⁻¹	3.4 ⁻¹	14.9 ⁻¹
Pakistan	...	...	...	2.3 ⁺¹	10.9 ⁺¹
Sri Lanka	...	...	...	...	...
Sub-Saharan Africa					
Angola	...	...	...	...	...
Benin	11.5 **,⁺¹	...	...	3.5 **,⁺¹	14.1 **,⁺¹
Botswana	17.2 ⁺¹	44.0 **,⁺¹	479.9 ⁺¹	10.7 ⁺¹	21.5 ⁺¹
Burkina Faso	34.7 ⁺¹	21.6 ⁺¹	212.3 ⁺¹	4.7 ⁺¹	16.6 ⁺¹

TABLE IV.1.2
cont'd

Region	Public expenditure per student as a % of GDP per capita			Total public expenditure on education	
Country or territory	Primary	Secondary	Tertiary	as a % of GDP	as a % of total government expenditure
Sub-Saharan Africa cont'd					
Burundi	19.1 +1	73.3 **,+1	348.8 **,+1	5.1 +1	17.7 +1
Cameroon	6.1 *,+1	2.6 *,+1	66.6 *,+1	1.8 *,+1	8.6 *,+1
Cape Verde	19.8 +1	25.7 +1	72.7 +1	6.6 +1	25.4 +1
Central African Republic	11.8 **,+1	...	...	...	...
Chad	7.3 +1	30.1 **,+1	359.9 **,+1	2.1 +1	10.1 +1
Comoros	12.4 **,−2	33.9 **,−2	...	3.9 −2	24.1 −2
Congo	4.0 **,+1	...	...	2.2 +1	8.1 +1
Côte d'Ivoire	...	...	...	...	...
Democratic Rep. of the Congo	...	...	...	...	...
Equatorial Guinea	...	...	...	0.6 **,−1	...
Eritrea	11.3 +1	15.4 +1	...	5.4 +1	...
Ethiopia	...	...	...	4.6 **,−2	...
Gabon	...	...	...	...	...
Gambia	7.1 **	8.7 **	229.7 **	1.9 **	8.9 −2
Ghana	...	...	...	...	...
Guinea	...	...	...	...	...
Guinea-Bissau	...	...	...	...	...
Kenya	24.7	23.8	274.7	7.0	29.2
Lesotho	24.2 **,+1	49.0 **,+1	1104.8 **,+1	13.4 +1	29.8 +1
Liberia	...	...	...	...	...
Madagascar	8.4 +1	...	175.0 +1	3.2 +1	25.3 +1
Malawi	14.0 −1	29.7 **,−1	...	6.0 −1	...
Mali	...	...	...	4.3 +1	14.8 +1
Mauritius	11.8 +1	19.8 +1	37.1 +1	4.5 +1	14.3 +1
Mozambique	...	...	...	...	...
Namibia	21.0 −1	25.2 −1	111.1 −1	7.2 −1	...
Niger	19.0 **,−2	64.3 **,−2	...	2.3	...
Nigeria	...	...	...	...	...
Rwanda	11.3 **,+1	18.6 **,+1	408.8 **,+1	3.8 +1	12.2 +1
São Tomé and Principe	...	...	...	...	...
Senegal	20.8 **,+1	39.8 **,+1	267.6 **,+1	5.4 +1	18.9 +1
Seychelles	15.9 **	17.4 **	(.)	5.4 **	...
Sierra Leone	...	...	...	...	...
Somalia	...	...	...	...	...
South Africa	14.2 +1	17.6 +1	49.6 +1	5.4 +1	17.9 +1
Swaziland	11.7 **	29.0 **	260.7	6.2	...
Togo	6.7 **,−2	...	...	2.6 −2	13.6 −2
Uganda	11.2 **	33.7 **	187.5	5.2 **	18.3 **
United Republic of Tanzania	...	...	...	...	...
Zambia	5.4 +1	8.2 +1	...	2.0 +1	...
Zimbabwe	...	...	...	...	...

Source: UIS. Excel sheets taken from UIS website.

TABLE IV.1.3
Education expenditure, sources as a percentage of gross domestic product/financial year ending in 2004

Region Country or territory	Expenditure on educational institutions and educational administration as a % of GDP						
	All sources of funds (public, private, international)		Public sources		Private sources		International sources
	Total	Tertiary	Total	Tertiary	Total	Tertiary	Total
Arab States							
Algeria	...	...	...	...	...	...	...
Bahrain	...	...	...	...	...	...	...
Djibouti	...	...	7.5 +1	0.8 **,+1	...	...	...
Egypt	...	...	...	...	...	...	...
Iraq	...	...	...	...	...	...	...
Jordan	...	...	...	...	...	...	...
Kuwait	6.2 +1	2.1 +1	5.1 +1	1.6 +1	1.2 +1	0.4 +1	(.)
Lebanon	...	...	2.6 +1	0.7 +1	...	...	...
Libyan Arab Jamahiriya	...	...	...	...	...	...	...
Mauritania	...	...	2.3 **,+1	0.1 **,+1	...	...	...
Morocco	...	...	6.7	1.1	...	...	...
Oman	...	...	3.6 **,+1	0.3 **,+1	...	...	...
Palestinian Autonomous Territories	...	...	...	...	...	...	...
Qatar	...	...	...	...	...	...	...
Saudi Arabia	...	...	...	...	...	...	...
Sudan	...	...	...	...	...	...	...
Syrian Arab Republic	...	...	...	...	...	...	...
Tunisia (p)	...	...	7.3 +1	1.8 +1	...	...	...
United Arab Emirates	...	...	...	...	...	...	...
Yemen	...	...	...	...	...	...	...
Central and Eastern Europe							
Albania	...	...	2.8 **,-2	0.5 **,-2	...	...	...
Belarus	...	...	6.0 +1	1.5 +1	...	...	...
Bosnia and Herzegovina	...	...	...	...	...	...	...
Bulgaria (p)	4.2 -2	1.1 -2	3.4 -2	0.5 -2	0.7 -2	0.6 -2	0.02 -2
Croatia	...	...	4.3 -2	0.7 -2	...	...	0.01 -2
Czech Republic (p)	4.4 -2	0.9 -2	4.2 -2	0.8 -2	0.2 -2	0.1 -2	– -2
Estonia	...	...	5.2 -2	0.9 -2	...	...	...
Hungary (p)	...	...	5.0 -2	1.0 -2	...	...	– -2
Latvia	6.1 -2	1.3 -2	5.4 -2	0.7 -2	0.7 -2	0.6 -2	0.04 -2
Lithuania	...	...	5.5 -2	1.2 -2	...	...	...
Poland (p)	...	...	5.5 -2	1.1 -2	...	...	...
Republic of Moldova	6.0 **,+1	1.8 **,+1	4.3 +1	0.4 +1	1.7 **,+1	1.4 **,+1	–
Romania	3.8 -2	0.9 -2	3.4 -2	0.6 -2	0.2 -2	0.1 -2	0.13 -2
Russian Federation (p)	...	...	3.8 **,-2	0.7 **,-2	...	...	...
Serbia and Montenegro	...	...	...	...	...	...	...
Slovakia (p)	...	...	4.0 -2	0.7 -2	...	...	...
Slovenia	6.3 -2	1.3 -2	5.4 -2	1.0 -2	0.9 -2	0.3 -2	0.01 -2
The Former Yugoslav Rep. of Macedonia	...	...	3.3 -2	0.5 -2	...	...	...
Turkey (p)	3.8 -2	1.1 -2	3.4 -2	1.0 -2	0.4 -2	0.1 -2	...
Ukraine	...	...	6.4 **,+1	1.9 **,+1	...	...	...

TABLE IV.1.3
cont'd

Region / Country or territory	All sources of funds (public, private, international)		Public sources		Private sources		International sources
	Total	Tertiary	Total	Tertiary	Total	Tertiary	Total
Central Asia							
Armenia	...	...	...	...	...	...	...
Azerbaijan	...	...	2.5 **,+1	0.2 **,+1	...	...	...
Georgia	...	...	...	...	...	...	...
Kazakhstan	3.0 **,+1	0.7 **,+1	2.3 +1	0.3 +1	0.6 +1	0.5 +1	...
Kyrgyzstan	...	...	4.4 −2	x	...	...	...
Mongolia	5.6	1.0	5.6	1.0	(.)	(.)	(.)
Tajikistan	...	...	3.5 +1	0.3 +1	...	...	...
Turkmenistan	...	...	...	...	...	...	...
Uzbekistan	...	...	...	...	...	...	...
East Asia and the Pacific							
Australia (p)	5.8 −2	1.6 −2	4.3 −2	0.8 −2	1.5 −2	0.8 −2	–
Brunei Darussalam	...	...	...	...	...	...	...
Cambodia	...	...	1.8 −2	x	...	...	...
China	...	...	...	...	...	...	...
Cook Islands	...	...	...	...	...	...	...
Democratic People's Republic of Korea	...	...	...	...	...	...	...
Fiji	...	...	6.4	x	...	...	...
Hong Kong (China), SAR	...	...	3.9 +1	1.1 +1	...	...	...
Indonesia (p)	...	...	1.0 −2	0.3 −2	...	...	...
Japan (p)	4.7 −2	x	3.5 −2	x	1.2 −2	0.6 −2	– −2
Kiribati	...	...	...	...	...	...	...
Lao People's Democratic Republic	2.3 +1	0.2 +1	2.3 +1	0.2 +1	1.1 +1	0.1 +1	1.21 +1
Macao, China	...	...	...	...	...	...	...
Malaysia (p)	...	...	8.0 −2	2.6 −2	...	...	...
Marshall Islands	15.1 −2	3.1 −2	9.2 −2	0.8 −2	2.8 −2	2.4 −2	3.18 −2
Micronesia (Federated States of)	...	...	...	...	...	...	...
Myanmar	...	...	...	...	...	...	...
Nauru	...	...	...	...	...	...	...
New Zealand	6.8 +1	1.4 +1	5.5 +1	0.9 +1	1.3 +1	0.6 +1	– −1
Niue	...	...	...	...	...	...	...
Palau	...	...	...	...	...	...	...
Papua New Guinea	...	...	...	...	...	...	...
Philippines (p)	5.2 −2	x	3.1 −2	0.4 −2	2.1 −2	x	(.) −2
Republic of Korea (p)	7.1 −2	x	4.1 −2	x	2.9 −2	1.9 −2	(.) −2
Samoa	...	...	...	...	...	...	...
Singapore	...	...	...	...	...	...	...
Solomon Islands	...	...	...	...	...	...	...
Thailand	...	...	3.8 +1	0.6 +1	...	...	...
Timor-Leste	...	...	...	...	...	...	...
Tokelau	...	...	...	...	...	...	...
Tonga	...	...	...	...	...	...	...
Tuvalu	...	...	...	...	...	...	...
Vanuatu	...	...	...	...	...	...	...
Viet Nam	...	...	...	...	...	...	...

TABLE IV.1.3
cont'd

Region / Country or territory	Expenditure on educational institutions and educational administration as a % of GDP						
	All sources of funds (public, private, international)		Public sources		Private sources		International sources
	Total	Tertiary	Total	Tertiary	Total	Tertiary	Total
Latin America and the Caribbean							
Anguilla	...	...	7.4 [-1]	x	...	...	...
Antigua and Barbuda	3.5 [-2]	x	3.5 [-2]	...	(.) [-2]	(.) [-2]	(.) [-2]
Argentina	...	...	...	...	...	...	...
Aruba	...	...	4.5 [+1]	0.6 [+1]	...	...	0.39 [+1]
Bahamas	...	...	...	...	...	...	...
Barbados	6.6 [+1]	1.8 [+1]	6.1 [+1]	1.8 [+1]	0.1 [+1]	–	0.44 [+1]
Belize	...	...	5.1	0.6	...	...	...
Bermuda	...	...	...	...	...	...	...
Bolivia	...	...	...	...	...	...	– [-1]
Brazil	...	...	...	...	...	...	...
British Virgin Islands	...	...	4.3	2.3	...	...	...
Cayman Islands	...	...	...	...	...	...	...
Chile	6.4 [+1]	2.0 [+1]	3.3 [+1]	0.3 [+1]	3.1 [+1]	1.7 [+1]	(.)
Colombia	7.6 [+1]	1.6 [+1]	4.8 [+1]	0.7 [+1]	...	...	(.)
Costa Rica	4.8	0.9	4.7	0.9	(.)	(.)	0.05
Cuba	9.9 [+1]	2.2 [+1]	9.8 [+1]	2.2 [+1]	0.2 [+1]	–	–
Dominica	...	...	...	...	...	...	...
Dominican Republic	...	...	1.8 [+1]	–	...	...	0.09 [+1]
Ecuador	...	...	...	...	...	...	...
El Salvador	...	...	2.8 [+1]	0.3 [+1]	...	...	0.20 [+1]
Grenada	6.4 [-1]	x	5.2 [-1]	x	0.3 [-1]	– [-1]	0.88 [-1]
Guatemala	...	–	1.2 [+1]	...	...	–	–
Guyana	10.1 [+1]	0.9 [+1]	8.4 [+1]	0.4 [+1]	0.5 [+1]	0.5 [+1]	1.12 [+1]
Haiti	...	...	...	...	...	...	...
Honduras	...	...	...	...	...	...	...
Jamaica	...	...	5.1 [+1]	1.2 [+1]	...	...	...
Mexico (p)	6.2 [-2]	1.4 [-2]	5.1 [-2]	1.0 [-2]	1.2 [-2]	0.4 [-2]	– [-2]
Montserrat	...	...	...	...	...	...	...
Netherlands Antilles	...	...	...	...	...	...	...
Nicaragua	...	–	...	...	2.7 [+1]	–	...
Panama	...	...	...	...	(.)	(.)	...
Paraguay (p)	6.5 [-2]	1.6 [-2]	4.4 [-2]	0.7 [-2]	2.1 [-2]	0.9 [-2]	– [-2]
Peru	3.2 [+1]	0.7 [+1]	2.4 [+1]	0.3 [+1]	0.7 [+1]	0.4 [+1]	–
Saint Kitts and Nevis	...	...	9.3 [+1]	...	...	...	...
Saint Lucia	...	...	5.8 [+1]	–	...	...	0.23 [+1]
Saint Vincent and the Grenadines	...	(.)	7.6 [+1]	(.)	...	(.)	0.91 [+1]
Suriname	...	...	...	...	...	...	...
Trinidad and Tobago	...	...	...	...	...	...	...
Turks and Caicos Islands	...	...	...	...	...	...	...
Uruguay (p)	2.8 [-2]	0.6 [-2]	2.6 [-2]	0.6 [-2]	0.2 [-2]	– [-2]	0.06 [-2]
Venezuela	...	...	...	...	...	...	...

TABLE IV.1.3
cont'd

Region / Country or territory	Expenditure on educational institutions and educational administration as a % of GDP						
	All sources of funds (public, private, international)		Public sources		Private sources		International sources
	Total	Tertiary	Total	Tertiary	Total	Tertiary	Total
North America and Western Europe							
Andorra	...	...	...	...	...	...	...
Austria (p)	5.7 ⁻²	1.1 ⁻²	5.4 ⁻²	1.0 ⁻²	0.4 ⁻²	0.1 ⁻²	(.) ⁻²
Belgium (p)	...	...	6.0 ⁻²	1.2 ⁻²	...	...	– ⁻²
Canada	...	...	...	...	...	...	...
Cyprus	6.8 ⁻²	1.0 ⁻²	5.9 ⁻²	0.7 ⁻²	0.8 ⁻²	0.3 ⁻²	0.09 ⁻²
Denmark (p)	7.1 ⁻²	1.9 ⁻²	6.8 ⁻²	1.9 ⁻²	0.3 ⁻²	– ⁻²	– ⁻²
Finland (p)	6.0 ⁻²	1.8 ⁻²	5.9 ⁻²	1.7 ⁻²	0.1 ⁻²	0.1 ⁻²	– ⁻²
France (p)	5.9 ⁻²	1.1 ⁻²	5.4 ⁻²	0.9 ⁻²	0.5 ⁻²	0.2 ⁻²	– ⁻²
Germany (p)	5.3 ⁻²	1.1 ⁻²	4.4 ⁻²	1.0 ⁻²	0.9 ⁻²	0.1 ⁻²	0.01 ⁻²
Gibraltar	...	...	...	...	...	...	...
Greece (p)	...	...	3.9 ⁻²	x	...	...	...
Holy See	...	...	...	...	...	...	...
Iceland (p)	...	...	7.2 **,⁻²	1.0 ⁻²	...	...	– ⁻²
Ireland (p)	...	...	4.0 ⁻²	1.0 ⁻²	...	...	0.02 ⁻²
Israel (p)	9.2 ⁻²	x	7.3 ⁻²	x	1.9 ⁻²	x	– ⁻²
Italy (p)	4.9 ⁻²	0.9 ⁻²	4.5 ⁻²	0.7 ⁻²	0.4 ⁻²	0.2 ⁻²	– ⁻²
Liechtenstein	...	...	...	...	...	...	...
Luxembourg	...	...	...	...	...	...	...
Malta	4.8 ⁻²	0.8 ⁻²	4.2 ⁻²	0.7 ⁻²	0.6 ⁻²	0.0 ⁻²	0.05 ⁻²
Monaco	...	...	...	...	...	...	...
Netherlands (p)	5.1 ⁻²	1.3 ⁻²	4.6 ⁻²	1.0 ⁻²	0.5 ⁻²	0.3 ⁻²	– ⁻²
Norway (p)	...	...	6.7 ⁻²	1.4 ⁻²	...	...	– ⁻²
Portugal (p)	5.8 ⁻²	x	5.7 ⁻²	x	0.1 ⁻²	0.1 ⁻²	– ⁻²
San Marino	...	...	...	...	...	...	...
Spain (p)	...	...	4.3 ⁻²	0.9 ⁻²	...	...	– ⁻²
Sweden (p)	6.9 ⁻²	1.8 ⁻²	6.6 ⁻²	1.5 ⁻²	0.2 ⁻²	0.2 ⁻²	0.05 ⁻²
Switzerland (p)	...	...	5.7 ⁻²	1.4 ⁻²	...	...	...
United Kingdom (p)	6.0 ⁻²	1.2 ⁻²	5.0 ⁻²	0.8 ⁻²	0.9 ⁻²	0.3 ⁻²	– ⁻²
United States (p)	7.4 ⁻²	2.7 ⁻²	5.5 ⁻²	1.2 ⁻²	1.9 ⁻²	1.5 ⁻²	(.) ⁻²
South and West Asia							
Afghanistan	...	...	...	...	...	...	...
Bangladesh	...	...	2.3 ⁺¹	0.3 ⁺¹	...	...	...
Bhutan	...	...	...	...	...	...	...
India	...	...	...	...	...	...	...
Iran, Islamic Republic of	...	...	4.7 ⁺¹	0.7 ⁺¹	...	...	(.)
Maldives	...	...	7.1 **,⁺¹	...	...	...	...
Nepal	...	...	3.4 ⁻¹	x	...	...	...
Pakistan	...	...	...	...	...	...	...
Sri Lanka	...	...	...	...	...	...	...

| TABLE IV.1.3 |
| cont'd |

Region	Expenditure on educational institutions and educational administration as a % of GDP						
	All sources of funds (public, private, international)		Public sources		Private sources		International sources
Country or territory	Total	Tertiary	Total	Tertiary	Total	Tertiary	Total
Sub-Saharan Africa							
Angola	...	...	...	...	...	...	...
Benin	...	...	...	...	...	...	...
Botswana	...	...	8.8 +1	1.1 +1	...	...	...
Burkina Faso	...	...	4.6 +1	0.3 +1	...	...	...
Burundi	...	...	5.1 **,+1	0.8 **,+1	...	...	...
Cameroon	...	...	1.8 **,+1	0.4 **,+1	...	...	...
Cape Verde	...	...	6.3	0.2 **,+1	...	...	1.02 +1
Central African Republic	...	...	...	...	...	...	...
Chad	...	...	2.1 +1	0.4 +1	...	...	...
Comoros	...	...	3.9 **,−2	0.3 **,−2	...	...	...
Congo	...	...	2.2 +1	0.6 **,+1	...	...	...
Côte d'Ivoire	...	...	...	...	...	...	...
Democratic Rep. of the Congo	...	...	...	...	...	...	...
Equatorial Guinea	0.6 −2	x	0.6 −2	0.2 −2	− −2	− −2	− −2
Eritrea	...	...	5.4 +1	3.0 +1	...	...	...
Ethiopia	...	...	...	...	...	...	...
Gabon	...	...	...	...	...	...	...
Gambia	...	...	1.8 **	0.1	...	...	...
Ghana	...	...	5.4 +1	1.1 +1	...	...	...
Guinea	...	...	2.0 +1	0.6 +1	...	...	...
Guinea-Bissau	...	...	...	...	...	...	...
Kenya	...	...	7.0	0.9	...	...	...
Lesotho	...	...	10.1 +1	1.8 **,+1	...	...	...
Liberia	...	...	...	...	...	...	...
Madagascar	...	...	3.0 +1	0.4 +1	...	...	0.67 +1
Malawi	...	...	5.9 −1	x	...	...	...
Mali	...	...	...	...	...	...	0.96 +1
Mauritius	...	...	4.5 +1	0.5	...	...	...
Mozambique	...	...	...	...	...	...	...
Namibia	...	...	7.2 −1	0.6 −1	...	...	...
Niger	...	...	...	...	...	...	...
Nigeria	...	...	...	0.6 −1	...	...	...
Rwanda	...	...	3.2 +1	0.7	...	...	...
São Tomé and Principe	...	...	...	...	...	...	...
Senegal	...	...	5.4 **,+1	1.4 **,+1	...	...	...
Seychelles	...	...	4.5 −1	0.1 −1	...	...	− −2
Sierra Leone	...	...	...	...	...	...	...
Somalia	...	...	...	...	...	...	...
South Africa	...	...	5.3 +1	0.8 +1	...	...	−
Swaziland	...	...	4.2 −2	...	...	...	...
Togo	...	...	2.4 −2	0.3 −2	...	...	...
Uganda	...	...	...	...	...	...	0.52
United Republic of Tanzania	...	...	...	...	...	...	...
Zambia	...	...	1.8 **,+1	0.3 **,+1	...	...	...
Zimbabwe	...	...	...	...	...	...	...

Source: UIS. Excel sheets taken from UIS website.

TABLE IV.1.4
Tertiary education enrolment and teaching staff

Region	Total enrolment 2005		Gross enrolment ratio 2005				Teaching staff 2005	
Country or territory	MF	%F	MF	M	F	GPI	MF	% F
Arab States								
Algeria	755,463	57	20	17	24	1.37	269,938	34
Bahrain	18,841 **	68 **	36	22	50	2.23	756 **	41 **
Djibouti	1,696	42	2	3	2	0.73	96	21
Egypt	2,594,186	...	34 **	...	...	...	...	...
Iraq	424,908	36	15 **	19 **	11 **	0.59 **	19,231 **	35 **
Jordan	217,823	50	39	38	40	1.06	8,251	21
Kuwait	38,630 **	70 **	20	11	29	2.66	2,045 **	27 **
Lebanon	165,730	53	51	47	54	1.15	20,764	37
Libyan Arab Jamahiriya	... **	... **	...	...	...	...	... **	... **
Mauritania	8,758	25	3	5	2	0.33	356	4
Morocco	366,879	45	11	12	10	0.85	19,374	24
Oman	48,483	51	18	18	19	1.09	2,991	29
Palestinian Autonomous Territories	127,214	50	38 **	37 **	39 **	1.04 **	4,526 **	15 **
Qatar	9,760 **	68 **	19	10	33	3.45	664	32
Saudi Arabia	603,671	58	28	23	34	1.47	26,836	33
Sudan	...	...	...	...	...	...	...	...
Syrian Arab Republic	...	...	...	...	...	...	...	...
Tunisia	311,569	57	30	25	35	1.40	16,671	40
United Arab Emirates	... **	... **	...	...	...	...	...	...
Yemen	201,043	26	9	14	5	0.37	6,062 **	16 **
Central and Eastern Europe								
Albania	...	...	...	...	...	...	...	...
Belarus	528,508	57	62	53	72	1.37	41,715	56
Bosnia and Herzegovina	...	...	...	...	...	...	...	...
Bulgaria	237,909	52	44	41	47	1.14	21,102	45
Croatia	...	...	...	...	...	...	...	...
Czech Republic	336,307	53	48	44	52	1.16	24,298	40
Estonia	67,760	62	66	50	82	1.66	6,842 **	49 **
Hungary	436,012	58	65	53	78	1.46	25,413	39
Latvia	130,706	63	74	54	96	1.79	6,268	58
Lithuania	195,405	60	76	59	93	1.57	13,157	53
Poland	2,118,081	58	63	53	74	1.41	95,143	41
Republic of Moldova	118,528	59	34 *	27 *	41 *	1.48 *	5,909	54
Romania	738,806	55	45	40	50	1.26	30,857	43
Russian Federation	9,019,556 **	57 **	71 **	60 **	82 **	1.36 **	624,916	54
Serbia and Montenegro	...	...	...	...	...	...	...	...
Slovakia	181,419	55	41	36	46	1.29	12,709	42
Slovenia	112,228	58	81	67	96	1.43	4,475	33
The Former Yugoslav Rep. of Macedonia	49,364	57	30	25	35	1.38	2,922	44
Turkey	2,106,351	42	31	36	26	0.74	82,096	38
Ukraine	2,604,875	54 *	69	63	75	1.20	187,402	...

TABLE IV.1.4
cont'd

Region	Total enrolment		Gross enrolment ratio				Teaching staff	
	2005		2005				2005	
Country or territory	MF	%F	MF	M	F	GPI	MF	% F
Central Asia								
Armenia	86,629	55	28	25	31	1.22	12,459	46
Azerbaijan	128,634	47	15	16	14	0.90	15,145	42
Georgia	174,255	50	46	45	47	1.04	12,651	46
Kazakhstan	753,181	58	53	44	62	1.42	42,333	61
Kyrgyzstan	220,460	55	41	37	46	1.25	13,337	54
Mongolia	123,824	61	43	33	54	1.62	8,018	55
Tajikistan	119,317	26	17	26	9	0.35	7,303	32
Turkmenistan	...	...	...	...	...	...	...	...
Uzbekistan	... **	... **	...	...	...	...	...	...
East Asia and the Pacific								
Australia	1,015,060	54	72	64	80	1.25	...	...
Brunei Darussalam	5,023	67	15	10	20	2.02	590	39
Cambodia	56,810	31	3	5	2	0.46	2,498	16
China	21,335,646	47	20	21	20	0.95	1,223,374 **	43 **
Cook Islands	(.)	(.)	(.)	(.)	(.)	(.)	(.)	(.)
Democratic People's Republic of Korea	...	...	...	...	...	...	...	...
Fiji	12,717	53	15 **	14 **	17 **	1.20 **	...	...
Hong Kong (China), SAR	152,294	51	31	32	31	0.95	...	...
Indonesia	3,640,270	44	17 **	19 **	15 **	0.79 **	271,891	39
Japan	4,038,302	46	55	59	52	0.89	496,528	17
Kiribati	(.)	(.)	(.)	(.)	(.)	(.)	(.)	(.)
Lao People's Democratic Republic	47,424	41	8	9	7	0.72	2,287	31
Macao, China	23,420	43	61	71	52	0.73	1,521	32
Malaysia	...	...	...	...	...	...	...	...
Marshall Islands	...	...	...	...	...	...	...	...
Micronesia (Federated States of)	...	...	...	...	...	...	...	...
Myanmar	...	...	...	...	...	...	...	...
Nauru	(.)	(.)	(.)	(.)	(.)	(.)	(.)	(.)
New Zealand	239,983	59	82	66	99	1.50	15,053	50
Niue	(.)	(.)	(.)	(.)	(.)	(.)	(.)	(.)
Palau	...	...	...	...	...	...	...	...
Papua New Guinea	...	...	...	...	...	...	...	...
Philippines	2,402,649	54	28	25	31	1.23	112,941 **	56 **
Republic of Korea	3,224,875	37	90	110	69	0.62	176,147	29
Samoa	...	...	...	...	...	...	...	...
Singapore	...	...	...	...	...	...	...	...
Solomon Islands	(.)	(.)	(.)	(.)	(.)	(.)	(.)	(.)
Thailand	2,359,127	52	43	41	45	1.11	...	...
Timor-Leste	...	...	...	...	...	...	...	...
Tokelau	(.)	(.)	(.)	(.)	(.)	(.)	(.)	(.)
Tonga	...	...	...	...	...	...	...	...
Tuvalu	(.)	(.)	(.)	(.)	(.)	(.)	(.)	(.)
Vanuatu	...	...	...	...	...	...	...	...
Viet Nam	1,354,543	41 **	16	19	13	0.71	47,646 **	40 **

TABLE IV.1.4
cont'd

Region	Total enrolment		Gross enrolment ratio				Teaching staff	
	2005		2005				2005	
Country or territory	MF	%F	MF	M	F	GPI	MF	% F
Latin America and the Caribbean								
Anguilla	33	76	3 **	2 **	5 **	3.11 **	24	54
Antigua and Barbuda	...	...	...	...	...	...	...	...
Argentina	...	...	...	...	...	...	...	...
Aruba	2,106	60	34 *	27	40	1.49 *	228	45
Bahamas	(.)	(.)	(.)	(.)	(.)	(.)	(.)	(.)
Barbados	...	...	...	...	...	...	...	...
Belize	...	...	...	...	...	...	97	49
Bermuda	...	...	...	...	...	...	...	...
Bolivia	... **	...	...	...	...	...	...	...
Brazil	...	...	...	...	...	...	...	...
British Virgin Islands	1,200	69	75 **	46 **	106 **	2.28 **	110 **	55
Cayman Islands	...	...	...	...	...	...	...	...
Chile	663,694	48	48	49	47	0.96	...	...
Colombia	1,223,594	51	29	28	31	1.09	93,673	34
Costa Rica	110,717	54	25 **	23 **	28 **	1.26 **	...	...
Cuba	471,858	62	61	46 *	78 *	1.72 *	91,087	59
Dominica	(.)	(.)	(.)	(.)	(.)	(.)	(.)	(.)
Dominican Republic	... **	... **	...	...	...	...	...	...
Ecuador	...	...	...	...	...	...	...	...
El Salvador	122,431	55	19	17	21	1.23	8,070	34
Grenada	(.)	(.)	(.)	(.)	(.)	(.)	(.)	(.)
Guatemala	...	...	...	...	...	...	...	...
Guyana	7,278	68	10	6	13	2.13	578	44
Haiti	...	...	...	...	...	...	...	...
Honduras	...	...	...	...	...	...	...	...
Jamaica	...	...	...	...	...	...	...	...
Mexico	2,384,858	50	24	24	24	0.99	251,253	...
Montserrat	(.)	(.)	(.)	(.)	(.)	(.)	(.)	(.)
Netherlands Antilles	...	...	...	...	...	...	...	...
Nicaragua	...	...	...	...	...	...	...	...
Panama	126,242	61	44	34	55	1.63	11,431	47
Paraguay	...	...	...	...	...	...	...	...
Peru	909,315	50	33 **	33 **	34 **	1.03 **	...	...
Saint Kitts and Nevis	(.)	(.)	(.)	(.)	(.)	(.)	(.)	(.)
Saint Lucia	2,197	74	14	7	20	2.80	174	48
Saint Vincent and the Grenadines	(.)	(.)	(.)	(.)	(.)	(.)	(.)	(.)
Suriname	...	...	...	...	...	...	...	...
Trinidad and Tobago	16,920	56	12 **	11 **	14 **	1.27	1,800 **	33 **
Turks and Caicos Islands	(.)	(.)	(.)	(.)	(.)	(.)	(.)	(.)
Uruguay	...	...	...	...	...	...	...	...
Venezuela	...	...	...	...	...	...	...	..

TABLE IV.1.4
cont'd

Region	Total enrolment		Gross enrolment ratio				Teaching staff	
	2005		2005				2005	
Country or territory	MF	%F	MF	M	F	GPI	MF	% F
North America and Western Europe								
Andorra	342	51	8 *	8 *	9 *	1.06 *	88 **	47 **
Austria	244,410	54	50	46	55	1.20	...	...
Belgium	389,547	54	63	56	70	1.24	25,774	41
Canada	...	...	...	...	...	...	...	...
Cyprus	20,078	52	33 *	31 *	35 *	1.13 *	1,406 **	42 **
Denmark	232,255	57	80	67	94	1.39	...	...
Finland	305,996	54	92	83	101	1.21	18,605	46
France	2,187,383	55	56	49	64	1.29	...	...
Germany	...	...	...	...	...	...	287,251	34
Gibraltar	(.)	(.)	(.)	(.)	(.)	(.)	(.)	(.)
Greece	646,587	51	89	83	95	1.14	27,161	36
Holy See	...	...	...	...	...	...	...	...
Iceland	15,529	65	71 **	50 **	93 **	1.85 **	1,782	45
Ireland	186,561	55	59	52	67	1.27	11,628	39
Israel	310,937	56	58	50	66	1.34	...	...
Italy	2,014,998	57	66	56	76	1.36	94,371	34
Liechtenstein	...	...	...	...	...	...	...	...
Luxembourg	...	...	...	...	...	...	...	...
Malta	9,441	56	32	27	37	1.36	825	23
Monaco	(.)	(.)	(.)	(.)	(.)	(.)	(.)	(.)
Netherlands	564,983	51	61	58	63	1.08	44,656	35
Norway	213,940	60	80	63	97	1.54	...	...
Portugal	380,937	56	56	49	64	1.30	36,773	42
San Marino	...	...	...	...	...	...	...	...
Spain	1,809,353	54	67	60	74	1.22	144,973	39
Sweden	426,723	60	82	64	100	1.55	37,684	43
Switzerland	199,696	46	47	52	43	0.84	34,076	32
United Kingdom	2,287,541	57	60	50	70	1.39	122,305	40
United States	17,272,044	57	83	69	97	1.40	1,208,213	43
South and West Asia								
Afghanistan	...	...	...	...	...	...	...	...
Bangladesh	911,600	33	6	8	4	0.53	52,297	15
Bhutan	...	...	...	...	...	...	...	...
India	11,777,296	39	11	13	9	0.70	...	...
Iran, Islamic Republic of	2,126,274	51	24	23	25	1.09	115,340	19
Maldives	...	...	...	...	...	...	...	...
Nepal	...	...	...	...	...	...	...	...
Pakistan	782,621	45	5	5	4	0.88	69,298 *	17 *
Sri Lanka	...	...	...	...	...	...	...	...

TABLE IV.1.4
cont'd

Region	Total enrolment		Gross enrolment ratio				Teaching staff	
	2005		2005				2005	
Country or territory	MF	%F	MF	M	F	GPI	MF	% F
Sub-Saharan Africa								
Angola	48,184	...	3	...	...	...	...	...
Benin	...	...	...	...	...	...	...	...
Botswana	10,950	50	5	5	5	1.00	529	37
Burkina Faso	27,942	31	2	3	1	0.45	1,984	6
Burundi	16,889	28	2 **	3 **	1 **	0.38 **	719 **	14 **
Cameroon	99,864	40	6 *	7 *	5 *	0.66 *	3,173	...
Cape Verde	3,910	51	7	7	7	1.04	485	41
Central African Republic	6,270	...	2 **	... **	... **	...	...	...
Chad	10,468	13	1 **	2 **	– **	0.14 **	1,100 **	3 **
Comoros	...	...	...	...	...	...	...	...
Congo	...	...	...	...	...	...	...	...
Côte d'Ivoire	...	...	...	...	...	...	...	...
Democratic Rep. of the Congo	...	...	...	...	...	...	...	...
Equatorial Guinea	...	...	...	...	...	...	...	...
Eritrea	...	...	...	...	...	...	...	...
Ethiopia	191,165	24	3	4	1	0.32	4,847	10
Gabon	...	...	...	...	...	...	...	...
Gambia	...	...	...	...	...	...	...	...
Ghana	119,559	35	5	7	4	0.56	3,142	13
Guinea	23,788	19	3	5	1	0.24	1,069	4
Guinea-Bissau	...	...	...	...	...	...	...	...
Kenya	...	...	...	...	...	...	...	...
Lesotho	7,918	57	3	3	4	1.27	558	...
Liberia	...	...	...	...	...	...	...	...
Madagascar	44,948	47	3	3	2	0.89	1,763	31
Malawi	...	...	...	...	...	...	...	...
Mali	32,609	31	3	3	2	0.47	1,112 **	...
Mauritius	16,852	55	17	15	19	1.26	...	...
Mozambique	28,298	33	1	2	1	0.49	3,009	21
Namibia	...	...	...	...	...	...	...	...
Niger	10,799	30	1	1	1	0.45	726	6
Nigeria	...	...	...	...	...	...	...	...
Rwanda	26,378	39	3 **	3 **	2 **	0.62 **	1,817 **	12
São Tomé and Principe	(.)	(.)	(.)	(.)	(.)	(.)	(.)	(.)
Senegal	59,127	...	5	...	...	...	...	...
Seychelles	(.)	(.)	(.)	(.)	(.)	(.)	(.)	(.)
Sierra Leone	...	...	...	...	...	...	...	...
Somalia	...	...	–	–	–	–	...	...
South Africa	735,073	55	15	14	17	1.22	43,336	50
Swaziland	5,897	52	4	4	5	1.06	432	36
Togo	...	...	...	...	...	...	...	...
Uganda	...	...	...	...	...	...	...	...
United Republic of Tanzania	51,080	32	1 **	2 **	1 **	0.48 **	2,735	17
Zambia	...	...	...	...	...	...	...	...
Zimbabwe	...	...	...	...	...	...	...	...

TABLE IV.1.4
cont'd

Region	Total enrolment		Gross enrolment ratio				Teaching staff	
	2005		2005				2005	
Country or territory	MF	%F	MF	M	F	GPI	MF	% F
REGIONAL AVERAGES								
World	137,930,727	...	...	...	...	...	8,822,576 **	... **
Arab States	6,782,849	49 **	21	21 **	21 **	1.01 **	269,938 **	34 **
Central and Eastern Europe	19,413,835	55	57	51	63	1.25	1,211,111	50
Central Asia	2,060,035	51 **	27 **	26 **	28 **	1.08 **	140,817 **	49 **
East Asia and the Pacific	41,576,196	47	24	25	23	0.93	2,566,174	37
Latin America and the Caribbean	15,293,181 **	54 **	29 **	27 **	32 **	1.17 **	1,207,957 **	...
North America and Western Europe	33,422,094	56	70	60	80	1.33	2,493,489	40
South and West Asia	15,842,175	41	11	12	9	0.74	784,334 **	33 **
Sub-Saharan Africa	3,540,362 **	38 **	5 **	6 **	4 **	0.62 **	148,756 **	28 **

Source: UIS. Excel sheets taken from UIS website.

TABLE IV.1.5
Research and development expenditures as a percentage of the GDP and researchers in R&D per million people

HDI Rank		Research and development (R&D) expenditures (% of GDP) 2000–03[a]	Researchers in R&D (per million people) 1990–2003[a]
1	Norway	1.7	4,587
2	Iceland	3.1	6,807
3	Australia	1.6	3,670
4	Ireland	1.1	2,674
5	Sweden	4.0	5,416
6	Canada	1.9	3,597
7	Japan	3.1	5,287
8	United States	2.6	4,484
9	Switzerland	2.6	3,601
10	Netherlands	1.8	2,482
11	Finland	3.5	7,992
12	Luxembourg	1.8	4,301
13	Belgium	2.3	3,478
14	Austria	2.2	2,968
15	Denmark	2.5	5,016
16	France	2.2	3,213
17	Italy	1.2	1,213
18	United Kingdom	1.9	2,706
19	Spain	1.1	2,195
20	New Zealand	1.2	3,405
21	Germany	2.5	3,261
22	Hong Kong, China (SAR)	0.6	1,564
23	Israel	4.9	1,613

TABLE IV.1.5
cont'd

HDI Rank		Research and development (R&D) expenditures (% of GDP) 2000–03[a]	Researchers in R&D (per million people) 1990–2003[a]
24	Greece	0.6	1,413
25	Singapore	2.2	4,745
26	Republic of Korea	2.6	3,187
27	Slovenia	1.5	2,543
28	Portugal	0.9	1,949
29	Cyprus	0.3	563
30	Czech Republic	1.3	1,594
31	Barbados	...	...
32	Malta	0.3	694
33	Kuwait	0.2	69
34	Brunei Darussalam	...	274
35	Hungary	0.9	1,472
36	Argentina	0.4	720
37	Poland	0.6	1,581
38	Chile	0.6	444
39	Bahrain	...	...
40	Estonia	0.8	2,523
41	Lithuania	0.7	2,136
42	Slovakia	0.6	1,984
43	Uruguay	0.3	366
44	Croatia	1.1	1,296
45	Latvia	0.4	1,434
46	Qatar	...	...
47	Seychelles	...	19

TABLE IV.1.5
cont'd

HDI Rank		Research and development (R&D) expenditures (% of GDP) 2000–03[a]	Researchers in R&D (per million people) 1990–2003[a]
48	Costa Rica	0.4	368
49	United Arab Emirates	...	...
50	Cuba	0.6	537
51	Saint Kitts and Nevis	...	...
52	Bahamas	...	...
53	Mexico	0.4	268
54	Bulgaria	0.5	1,263
55	Tonga	...	...
56	Oman	...	...
57	Trinidad and Tobago	0.1	399
58	Panama	0.3	97
59	Antigua and Barbuda	...	...
60	Romania	0.4	976
61	Malaysia	0.7	299
62	Bosnia and Herzegovina	...	...
63	Mauritius	0.4	201
64	Libyan Arab Jamahiriya	...	361
65	Russian Federation	1.3	3,319
66	Macedonia, TFYR	0.3	...
67	Belarus	0.6	1,871
68	Dominica	...	...
69	Brazil	1.0	344
70	Colombia	0.2	109
71	Saint Lucia	...	483
72	Venezuela	0.3	236
73	Albania	...	...
74	Thailand	0.2	286
75	Samoa (Western)	...	...
76	Saudi Arabia	...	...
77	Ukraine	1.2	1,774
78	Lebanon	...	...
79	Kazakhstan	0.2	629
80	Armenia	0.3	1,537
81	China	1.3	663
82	Peru	0.1	226
83	Ecuador	0.1	50
84	Philippines	...	...
85	Grenada	...	...
86	Jordan	...	1,927
87	Tunisia	0.6	1,013
88	Saint Vincent and the Grenadines	0.2	179
89	Suriname	...	...
90	Fiji	...	...
91	Paraguay	0.1	79
92	Turkey	0.7	341

TABLE IV.1.5
cont'd

HDI Rank		Research and development (R&D) expenditures (% of GDP) 2000–03[a]	Researchers in R&D (per million people) 1990–2003[a]
93	Sri Lanka	...	...
94	Dominican Republic	...	...
95	Belize	...	...
96	Iran, Islamic Rep. of	...	467
97	Georgia	0.3	2,600
98	Maldives	...	...
99	Azerbaijan	0.3	1,236
100	Occupied Palestinian Territories	...	...
101	El Salvador	...	47
102	Algeria	...	...
103	Guyana	...	...
104	Jamaica	0.1	...
105	Turkmenistan	...	...
106	Cape Verde	...	127
107	Syrian Arab Republic	...	29
108	Indonesia	...	...
109	Viet Nam	...	...
110	Kyrgyzstan	0.2	406
111	Egypt	0.2	...
112	Nicaragua	...	44
113	Uzbekistan	...	...
114	Moldova, Rep. of	...	172
115	Bolivia	0.3	120
116	Mongolia	0.3	681
117	Honduras	...	78
118	Guatemala	...	...
119	Vanuatu	...	...
120	Equatorial Guinea	...	...
121	South Africa	0.8	307
122	Tajikistan	...	...
123	Morocco	0.6	782
124	Gabon	...	...
125	Namibia	...	...
126	India	0.8	119
127	São Tomé and Principe	...	...
128	Solomon Islands	...	...
129	Cambodia	...	...
130	Myanmar	...	...
131	Botswana	...	...
132	Comoros	...	...
133	Lao People's Dem. Rep.	...	...
134	Pakistan	0.2	86
135	Bhutan	...	...
136	Ghana	...	...
137	Bangladesh	...	...

TABLE IV.1.5
cont'd

HDI Rank		Research and development (R&D) expenditures (% of GDP) 2000–03[a]	Researchers in R&D (per million people) 1990–2003[a]
138	Nepal	0.7	59
139	Papua New Guinea	...	...
140	Congo	...	30
141	Sudan	0.3	263
142	Timor-Leste	...	...
143	Madagascar	0.1	15
144	Cameroon	...	...
145	Uganda	0.8	24
146	Swaziland	...	...
147	Togo	...	...
148	Djibouti	...	...
149	Lesotho	...	42
150	Yemen	...	...
151	Zimbabwe	...	...
152	Kenya	...	...
153	Mauritania	...	...
154	Haiti	...	...
155	Gambia	...	...
156	Senegal	...	...
157	Eritrea	...	...
158	Rwanda	...	...
159	Nigeria	...	...
160	Guinea	...	251
161	Angola	...	...
162	Tanzania, U. Rep. of	...	...
163	Benin	...	...
164	Côte d'Ivoire	...	...
165	Zambia	...	51
166	Malawi	...	...
167	Congo, Dem. Rep. of the	...	...
168	Mozambique	...	...
169	Burundi	...	...

TABLE IV.1.5
cont'd

HDI Rank		Research and development (R&D) expenditures (% of GDP) 2000–03[a]	Researchers in R&D (per million people) 1990–2003[a]
170	Ethiopia	...	...
171	Chad	...	...
172	Central African Republic	...	...
173	Guinea-Bissau	...	...
174	Burkina Faso	...	17
175	Mali	...	...
176	Sierra Leone	...	...
177	Niger	...	...

Without HDI Rank			
	Afghanistan	...	...
	Andorra	...	...
	Iraq	...	...
	Kiribati	...	...
	Korea, Dem. Rep.	...	...
	Liberia	...	...
	Liechtenstein	...	...
	Marshall Islands	...	...
	Micronesia, Fed. Sts.	...	...
	Monaco	...	676
	Nauru	...	...
	Palau	...	...
	San Marino	...	...
	Somalia	...	...
	Tuvalu	...	...
	Serbia and Montenegro	....	1,031

Note: a.Data refers to the most recent year available during the period specified.

Source: UNDP. Excel sheets taken from UNDP website.

column 1: World Bank (2006) *World Development Indicators 2006.* CD-ROM, Washington, DC; aggregates calculated for the Human Development Report Office by the World Bank.

column 2: World Bank (2006) *World Development Indicators 2006.* CD-ROM. Washington, DC; aggregates calculated for the Human Development Report Office by the World Bank.

TABLE IV.1.6
Human development rank, index, total population and GDP per capita

HDI Rank		Human development index (HDI) value 2004	GDP per capita (PPP US$) (HDI) 2004	Total population (millions) 2004	2015ᵃ
1	Norway	0.965	38,454	4.6	4.8
2	Iceland	0.960	33,051	0.3	0.3
3	Australia	0.957	30,331	19.9	22.2
4	Ireland	0.956	38,827	4.1	4.7
5	Sweden	0.951	29,541	9.0	9.3
6	Canada	0.950	31,263	32.0	35.1
7	Japan	0.949	29,251	127.9	128.0
8	United States	0.948	39,676	295.4	325.7
9	Switzerland	0.947	33,040	7.2	7.3
10	Netherlands	0.947	31,789	16.2	16.8
11	Finland	0.947	29,951	5.2	5.4
12	Luxembourg	0.945	69,961 c	0.5	0.5
13	Belgium	0.945	31,096	10.4	10.5
14	Austria	0.944	32,276	8.2	8.3
15	Denmark	0.943	31,914	5.4	5.6
16	France	0.942	29,300	60.3	62.3
17	Italy	0.940	28,180	58.0	57.8
18	United Kingdom	0.940	30,821	59.5	61.4
19	Spain	0.938	25,047	42.6	44.4
20	New Zealand	0.936	23,413	4.0	4.3
21	Germany	0.932	28,303	82.6	82.5
22	Hong Kong, China (SAR)	0.927	30,822	7.0	7.8
23	Israel	0.927	24,382	6.6	7.8
24	Greece	0.921	22,205	11.1	11.2
25	Singapore	0.916	28,077	4.3	4.8
26	Korea, Rep. of	0.912	20,499	47.6	49.1
27	Slovenia	0.910	20,939	2.0	1.9
28	Portugal	0.904	19,629	10.4	10.8
29	Cyprus	0.903	22,805	0.8	0.9
30	Czech Republic	0.885	19,408	10.2	10.1
31	Barbados	0.879	15,720 d,e	0.3	0.3
32	Malta	0.875	18,879	0.4	0.4
33	Kuwait	0.871	19,384 f	2.6	3.4
34	Brunei Darussalam	0.871	19,210 d,g	0.4	0.5
35	Hungary	0.869	16,814	10.1	9.8
36	Argentina	0.863	13,298	38.4	42.7
37	Poland	0.862	12,974	38.6	38.1
38	Chile	0.859	10,874	16.1	17.9
39	Bahrain	0.859	20,758	0.7	0.9
40	Estonia	0.858	14,555	1.3	1.3
41	Lithuania	0.857	13,107	3.4	3.3
42	Slovakia	0.856	14,623	5.4	5.4
43	Uruguay	0.851	9,421	3.4	3.7
44	Croatia	0.846	12,191	4.5	4.5
45	Latvia	0.845	11,653	2.3	2.2
46	Qatar	0.844	19,844 d,h	0.8	1.0

TABLE IV.1.6
cont'd

HDI Rank		Human development index (HDI) value	GDP per capita (PPP US$) (HDI)	Total population (millions)	
		2004	2004	2004	2015[a]
47	Seychelles	0.842	16,652	0.1	0.1
48	Costa Rica	0.841	9,481 f	4.3	5.0
49	United Arab Emirates	0.839	24,056 f	4.3	5.6
50	Cuba	0.826	...	11.2	11.4
51	Saint Kitts and Nevis	0.825	12,702 d	(.)	(.)
52	Bahamas	0.825	17,843 d	0.3	0.4
53	Mexico	0.821	9,803	105.7	119.1
54	Bulgaria	0.816	8,078	7.8	7.2
55	Tonga	0.815	7,870 f	0.1	0.1
56	Oman	0.810	15,259	2.5	3.2
57	Trinidad and Tobago	0.809	12,182	1.3	1.3
58	Panama	0.809	7,278	3.2	3.8
59	Antigua and Barbuda	0.808	12,586	0.1	0.1
60	Romania	0.805	8,480	21.8	20.9
61	Malaysia	0.805	10,276	24.9	29.6
62	Bosnia and Herzegovina	0.800	7,032	3.9	3.9
63	Mauritius	0.800	12,027	1.2	1.3
64	Libyan Arab Jamahiriya	0.798	... d,j	5.7	7.0
65	Russian Federation	0.797	9,902	143.9	136.7
66	Macedonia, TFYR	0.796	6,610	2.0	2.1
67	Belarus	0.794	6,970	9.8	9.2
68	Dominica	0.793	5,643	0.1	0.1
69	Brazil	0.792	8,195	183.9	209.4
70	Colombia	0.790	7,256 f	44.9	52.1
71	Saint Lucia	0.790	6,324	0.2	0.2
72	Venezuela	0.784	6,043	26.3	31.3
73	Albania	0.784	4,978	3.1	3.3
74	Thailand	0.784	8,090	63.7	69.1
75	Samoa (Western)	0.778	5,613	0.2	0.2
76	Saudi Arabia	0.777	13,825 f	24.0	30.8
77	Ukraine	0.774	6,394	47.0	41.8
78	Lebanon	0.774	5,837	3.5	4.0
79	Kazakhstan	0.774	7,440	14.8	14.9
80	Armenia	0.768	4,101	3.0	3.0
81	China	0.768	5,896 k	1,308.0	1,393.0[l]
82	Peru	0.767	5,678	27.6	32.2
83	Ecuador	0.765	3,963	13.0	15.1
84	Philippines	0.763	4,614	81.6	96.8
85	Grenada	0.762	8,021	0.1	0.1
86	Jordan	0.760	4,688	5.6	7.0
87	Tunisia	0.760	7,768	10.0	11.1
88	Saint Vincent and the Grenadines	0.759	6,398	0.1	0.1
89	Suriname	0.759	... f,m	0.4	0.5
90	Fiji	0.758	6,066	0.8	0.9
91	Paraguay	0.757	4,813 f	6.0	7.6
92	Turkey	0.757	7,753	72.2	82.6

TABLE IV.1.6
cont'd

HDI Rank		Human development index (HDI) value 2004	GDP per capita (PPP US$) (HDI) 2004	Total population (millions)	
				2004	2015[a]
93	Sri Lanka	0.755	4,390	20.6	22.3
94	Dominican Republic	0.751	7,449 f	8.8	10.1
95	Belize	0.751	6,747	0.3	0.3
96	Iran, Islamic Rep. of	0.746	7,525	68.8	79.9
97	Georgia	0.743	2,844	4.5	4.2
98	Maldives	0.739	... d,f,m	0.3	0.4
99	Azerbaijan	0.736	4,153	8.4	9.1
100	Occupied Palestinian Territories	0.736	...	3.6	5.0
101	El Salvador	0.729	5,041 f	6.8	8.0
102	Algeria	0.728	6,603 f	32.4	38.1
103	Guyana	0.725	4,439 f	0.8	0.7
104	Jamaica	0.724	4,163	2.6	2.7
105	Turkmenistan	0.724	4,584 d	4.8	5.5
106	Cape Verde	0.722	5,727 f	0.5	0.6
107	Syrian Arab Republic	0.716	3,610	18.6	23.8
108	Indonesia	0.711	3,609	220.1	246.8
109	Viet Nam	0.709	2,745	83.1	95.0
110	Kyrgyzstan	0.705	1,935	5.2	5.9
111	Egypt	0.702	4,211	72.6	88.2
112	Nicaragua	0.698	3,634 f	5.4	6.6
113	Uzbekistan	0.696	1,869	26.2	30.7
114	Moldova, Rep. of	0.694	1,729	4.2	4.1
115	Bolivia	0.692	2,720	9.0	10.9
116	Mongolia	0.691	2,056	2.6	3.0
117	Honduras	0.683	2,876 f	7.0	8.8
118	Guatemala	0.673	4,313 f	12.3	15.9
119	Vanuatu	0.670	3,051 f	0.2	0.3
120	Equatorial Guinea	0.653	20,510 d,f	0.5	0.6
121	South Africa	0.653	11,192 f	47.2	47.9
122	Tajikistan	0.652	1,202	6.4	7.6
123	Morocco	0.640	4,309	31.0	36.2
124	Gabon	0.633	6,623	1.4	1.6
125	Namibia	0.626	7,418 f	2.0	2.2
126	India	0.611	3,139 f	1,087.1	1,260.4
127	São Tomé and Principe	0.607	1,231 d,h	0.2	0.2
128	Solomon Islands	0.592	1,814 f	0.5	0.6
129	Cambodia	0.583	2,423 f	13.8	17.1
130	Myanmar	0.581	1,027 d,j	50.0	55.0
131	Botswana	0.570	9,945	1.8	1.7
132	Comoros	0.556	1,943 f	0.8	1.0
133	Lao People's Dem. Rep.	0.553	1,954	5.8	7.3
134	Pakistan	0.539	2,225	154.8	193.4
135	Bhutan	0.538	1,969 d,h	2.1	2.7
136	Ghana	0.532	2,240 f	21.7	26.6
137	Bangladesh	0.530	1,870	139.2	168.2
138	Nepal	0.527	1,490	26.6	32.7

TABLE IV.1.6
cont'd

HDI Rank		Human development index (HDI) value 2004	GDP per capita (PPP US$) (HDI) 2004	Total population (millions) 2004	2015[a]
139	Papua New Guinea	0.523	2,543 f	5.8	7.0
140	Congo	0.520	978	3.9	5.4
141	Sudan	0.516	1,949 f	35.5	44.0
142	Timor-Leste	0.512	... o	0.9	1.5
143	Madagascar	0.509	857	18.1	23.8
144	Cameroon	0.506	2,174	16.0	19.0
145	Uganda	0.502	1,478 f	27.8	41.9
146	Swaziland	0.500	5,638	1.0	1.0
147	Togo	0.495	1,536 f	6.0	7.8
148	Djibouti	0.494	1,993 f	0.8	0.9
149	Lesotho	0.494	2,619 f	1.8	1.7
150	Yemen	0.492	879	20.3	28.5
151	Zimbabwe	0.491	2,065	12.9	13.8
152	Kenya	0.491	1,140	33.5	44.2
153	Mauritania	0.486	1,940 f	3.0	4.0
154	Haiti	0.482	1,892 d,f	8.4	9.8
155	Gambia	0.479	1,991 f	1.5	1.9
156	Senegal	0.460	1,713	11.4	14.5
157	Eritrea	0.454	977 f	4.2	5.8
158	Rwanda	0.450	1,263 f	8.9	11.3
159	Nigeria	0.448	1,154	128.7	160.9
160	Guinea	0.445	2,180	9.2	11.9
161	Angola	0.439	2,180 f	15.5	20.9
162	Tanzania, U. Rep. of	0.430	674	37.6	45.6
163	Benin	0.428	1,091	8.2	11.2
164	Côte d'Ivoire	0.421	1,551	17.9	21.6
165	Zambia	0.407	943	11.5	13.8
166	Malawi	0.400	646	12.6	16.0
167	Congo, Dem. Rep. of the	0.391	705 f	55.9	78.0
168	Mozambique	0.390	1,237 f	19.4	23.5
169	Burundi	0.384	677 f	7.3	10.6
170	Ethiopia	0.371	756 f	75.6	97.2
171	Chad	0.368	2,090 f	9.4	12.8
172	Central African Republic	0.353	1,094 f	4.0	4.6
173	Guinea-Bissau	0.349	722 f	1.5	2.1
174	Burkina Faso	0.342	1,169 f	12.8	17.7
175	Mali	0.338	998	13.1	18.1
176	Sierra Leone	0.335	561	5.3	6.9
177	Niger	0.311	779 f	13.5	19.3

Without HDI Rank					
	Afghanistan	...	...	28.6	41.4
	Andorra	...	...	0.1	0.1
	Iraq	...	...	28.1	36.5
	Kiribati	...	...	0.1	0.1
	Korea, Dem. Rep.	...	...	22.4	23.3

TABLE IV.1.6
cont'd

HDI Rank		Human development index (HDI) value 2004	GDP per capita (PPP US$) (HDI) 2004	Total population (millions) 2004	2015[a]
Without HDI Rank *cont'd*					
	Liberia	...	...	3.2	4.4
	Liechtenstein	...	...	(.)	(.)
	Marshall Islands	...	...	0.1	0.1
	Micronesia, Fed. Sts.	...	...	0.1	0.1
	Monaco	...	...	(.)	(.)
	Nauru	...	...	(.)	(.)
	Palau	...	...	(.)	(.)
	San Marino	...	...	(.)	(.)
	Somalia	...	...	8.0	11.0
	Tuvalu	...	...	(.)	(.)
	Serbia and Montenegro	...	...	10.5	10.4

Notes:

a. Data refers to medium-variant projections.

c. For purposes of calculating the HDI, a value of $40,000 (PPP US$) was applied.

d. Data refers to year other than that specified.

e. World Bank (2005) *World Development Indicators 2005*. CD-ROM. Washington, DC.

f. Estimate is based on regression.

g. World Bank (2003) *World Development Indicators 2003*. CD-ROM. Washington, DC.

h. Heston, Alan, Robert Summers and Bettina Aten (2002) 'Penn World Tables Version 6.1.' University of Pennsylvania, Center for International Comparisons, Philadelphia. [http://pwt.econ.upenn.edu/.]. Accessed March 2005. Data differs from the standard definition.

i. Efforts to produce a more accurate and recent estimate are ongoing (see Readers' guide and note to tables in *Human Development Report 2006*). A preliminary estimate of $5,700 (PPP US$) was used.

j. Heston, Alan, Robert Summers and Bettina Aten (2001) Correspondence on data from the Penn World Tables 6.0. (March) Philadelphia, PA. Data differs from the standard definition.

k. Estimate based on a bilateral comparison between China and the United States (Ruoen, Ren and Chen Kai (1995) 'China's GDP in U.S. Dollars Based on Purchasing Power Parity.' Policy Research Working Paper 1415. World Bank, Washington, DC).

l. Population estimates include Taiwan, province of China.

m. In the absence of an official estimate of GDP per capita (PPP US$), the following preliminary World Bank estimates, subject to further revision, were used: Maldives $4,798; and Suriname $6,552.

o. A national estimate of $1,033 (PPP US$) was used.

Source: UNDP. Excel sheets taken from UNDP website.

column 1: calculated on the basis of data in columns 6–8; see technical note 1 for details (should be linked).

column 2: World Bank (2006) *World Development Indicators 2006*. CD-ROM. Washington, DC, unless otherwise noted; aggregates calculated for the Human Development Report Office by the World Bank.

column 3: UN (United Nations) (2005b) *World Population Prospects 1950–2050: The 2004 Revision*. Database. Department of Economic and Social Affairs, Population Division. New York.

column 4: UN (United Nations) (2005b) *World Population Prospects 1950–2050: The 2004 Revision*. Database. Department of Economic and Social Affairs, Population Division. New York.

Sonia Fernández Lauro[1]

INTRODUCTION

This bibliography contains a selection of available reference literature on the role of higher education, its institutions, and their contribution to human and social development in the context of globalization.

The aim of higher education institutions is not just to transfer knowledge or produce highly specialized technicians who are able to face the challenges and new opportunities arising from technological innovations; they should also aim to actively participate in the search for innovative answers that foresee the needs of today's complex societies.

The different publications are a reflection of how higher education institutions are being called upon to deepen ties with society, by means of analysis, research, a study of society's problems and a raising of possible solutions, to strengthen their functions in the service of society.

The degradation of the environment (contamination of water, the energy crisis, global warming, and so on); the fight against poverty, hunger, violence and intolerance, the difficulty of accessing public goods, the study of progressive contraction of the job market and its consequences, the serious crisis of values that societies face, and the speed of the changes affecting societies – these are subjects that are more and more present and unavoidable in the university debate.

The challenges faced by higher education differ according to regions, but it can be noted that although technology has facilitated the strengthening of international cooperation, and increased the exchange of knowledge, which has in turn enabled some of society's needs to be anticipated, it is still far from fulfilling the objectives stated in the World Declaration on Higher Education for the XXI Century: Vision and Action approved by UNESCO at the 1998 worldwide conference.

As a study of these texts reveals, although some progress has been made, higher education institutions still have a greater role to play in generating a more equitable and fairer society in a bid to reduce the disparity between developing and industrialized countries.

For most of the authors, in spite of the difficulties, it is vital to pursue this goal and to continue to promote by all means of knowledge a suitable local and global action, the respect for human rights, sustainable development, democracy and peace.

GENERAL

Alliance for Global Sustainability (AGS) (2006) The Observatory: Status of Engineering Education for SD in European Higher Education. Barcelona (Spain): Technical University of Catalonia.

Altbach, P.G. (2003) *The Decline of the Guru. The Academic Profession in Developing and Middle-Income Countries*. New York: Palgrave Macmillan.

Altbach, P.G. (2007) *Tradition and Transition. The International Imperative in Higher Education*. Boston College (USA), Center for International Higher Education. Rotterdam: Sense Publishers.

Altbach, P.G. and P. McGill Peterson (eds) (1999) *Higher Education in the 21st Century: Global Challenge and National Response*. Published in cooperation with the Institute of International Education, New York (USA). (Spanish-language translation published by Editorial Biblios, Buenos Aires)

Association of College and Research Libraries (2000) *Information Literacy Competency Standards for Higher Education*. Chicago, USA. Last revised May 2007. Accessed from: http://www.ala.org/ala/acrl/acrlstandards/informationliteracycompetency.htm

Attali, J. (1998) *Pour un modèle d'enseignement supérieur*. Paris: Stock.

Berchem, T. (2004) *Tradition et progrès. La mission de l'université*. Paper presented at the Conference 'Leçon inaugurale au Collège de France'. Paris, 15 January.

Brown, L., D.G. Bammer, S. Batliwala et al. (2003) Framing practice-research engagement for democratizing knowledge. *Action Research*, **1**(1): 85–102.

Brundtland, G.H. (1987) *Our Common Future. World Commission on Environment and Development*. Oxford (UK): Oxford University Press. (also available in French and Spanish)

Brunner, J.J. (2001) Globalization, education and technical revolution. *Prospects, Quarterly Review of Comparative Education*, **XXXI**(2).

Burton R.C. (1998) *Creating Entrepreneurial Universities: Organizational Pathways of Transformation*. London: Pergamon.

Castells, M. (2006) *Nuevas Perspectivas Críticas en Educación*. Madrid: Paidos, Ibérica.

Castells, M. (2006) *La Era de la Información: Economía, sociedad y cultura*, 3 vols. Madrid: Alianza Editorial S.A.

Chitoran, D. and M.A. Días (1998) The relevance of international co-operation in higher education for graduate employment. In: Anne Holden Ronning and Mary-Louise Kearney (eds) *Graduate Prospects in a Changing Society*. Paris: UNESCO, pp. 63–76.

Clark, B.R. (1998) *Creating Entrepreneurial Universities: Organization Paths of Transformation*. Oxford (UK): Pergamon.

Clark, B.R. (2004) *Sustaining Change in Universities: Continuities in Case Studies and Concepts*. Maidenhead (UK): Open University Press.

Coraggio, J.L. and R.M. Torres (1997) *La Educación Según el Banco Mundial: Un Análisis de sus Propuestas y Métodos* (1st edn). Buenos Aires: Centro de estudios multidisciplinarios Miño y Dávila editores.

Delanty, G. (2001) *Challenging Knowledge: The University in the Knowledge Society*. Buckingham (UK): Open University Press.

Delanty, G. (2000) *Citizenship in the Global Age: Culture, Society and Politics.* Buckingham (UK): Open University Press.

De Sousa Santos, B.A. (2004) *Universidade no século XXI. Para uma reforma democrática e emancipatória da Universidade*. Cortez, Sao Paulo (Brazil).

De Sousa Santos, B.A. (2005) *La Universidad en el Siglo XXI. Para una Reforma Democrática y Emancipadora de la Universidad.* Ciudad de México: Universidad Nacional Autónoma de México.

Dolence, M.G. and D.M. Norris (1997) *Transforming Higher Education: A Vision for Learning in the 21st Century.* Ann Arbor, MI (USA): Society for College and University Planning.

Duderstadt, J.J. (2000) *A University for the 21st Century*. Ann Arbor, MI (USA): University of Michigan Press.

Dutch Network for Sustainable Higher Education (2006) *Disciplinary reviews SD*. Amsterdam. Some in English, e.g. Egbert Tellegen, *Sociology and SD*.

Ederer, P. (2006) *Innovation at Work: The European Human Capital Index*. Brussels: The Lisbon Council Policy Brief. Accessed from http://www.lisboncouncil.net/media/lisbon_council_european_human_capital_index.pdf

Ehrlich, T. (2000) *Civic Responsibility and Higher Education*. Phoenix, AZ: American Council on Education/ Oryx Press.

Factor 10 Club (2004) *Towards Sustainable Futures – Tools and Strategies*. International Conference Tampere, Finland, 14/15 June 2004.

Fadeeva, Z. (2007) From centre of excellence to centre of expertise: Regional centres of expertise on education for SD. In: Wals, Arjen E.J. (ed.) *Social Learning Towards a Sustainable World: Principles, Perspectives, and Praxis*, pp. 245–64. Netherlands: Wageningen Academic Publishers.

Fischer, S. (2003) Globalization and its challenges. *American Economic Review*, **93**(2).

Fransworth, K.A. (2007) *Leadership as Service: A New Model for Higher Education in a New Century*. Westport, CT (USA): Praeger.

Geiger, R.L. (2004) *Knowledge and Money: Research Universities and the Paradox of the Marketplace*. Stanford (USA): Stanford University Press.

Gibbons, M., C. Limoges, H. Nowotny et al. (1994) *New Production of Knowledge: The Dynamics of Science and Research in Contemporary Societies*. London, (UK): Sage.

Ginkel, H. van (2003) What does globalization mean of higher education? In: Gilles Breton and Michel Lambert (eds) *Universities and Globalization: Private Linkages, Public Trust*. Paris: UNESCO/Université Laval/Economica.

Kenneth, K., S. McGrath, D. Stone et al. (2002) The Globalisation of development knowledge and comparative education: dossier. *Compare, A Journal of Comparative Education*, **32**(3/10).

Hayward, F. (2002) *An Overview of Higher Education and GATS*. Document prepared for the American Council on Education in July.

Inayatullah, S. and J. Gidley (2000) *The University in Transformation: Global Perspectives on the Futures of the University*. Westport, (USA): Bergin and Garvey.

Innovation at Work: *The European Human Capital Index* (Lisbon Council Policy Brief) *see* Ederer, P. (2006)

Jasanoff, Sheila (2006) Technology as a site and object of politics. In: Charles Tilly and Robert E. Goodin (eds) *The Oxford Handbook of Contextual Political Analysis*. Oxford: Oxford University Press, pp. 745–63.

Jasanoff, Sheila and M. Long Martello (eds) (2004) *Earthly Politics: Local and Global in Environmental Governance*. Massachusetts (USA): MIT Press.

Jones, G.A., P.L. McCarney and M.L. Skolnik (eds) (2005) *Creating Knowledge, Strengthening Nations: The Changing Role of Higher Education*. Toronto (Canada): University of Toronto Press.

Khan, A.W. (2006) *Distance Education for Development*. Paper presented at ICDE SCOP Conference, Norway: Revoir.

Martens, P. and J. Rotmans (2002) *Transitions in a Globalising World*. Lisse, (Netherlands): Swets and Zeitlinger B.V.

Mayor, F. (2001) *The World Ahead: Our Future in the Making*. Paris: UNESCO (also published in Spanish).

Mayor, F. (1995) *Science and Power Today and Tomorrow*. Paris: UNESCO (Science and Power series).

Morin, E. *La Méthode*, 6 vols.
La Nature de la nature (vol. 1) (1981) (1st edn 1977). Paris: Seuil. (Also available in Chinese, English, Italian, Korean, Japanese, Portuguese, Rumanian, Russian, Spanish and Turkish.)
La Vie de la vie (vol. 2) (1985) (1st edn 1980). Paris: Seuil. (Also available in Italian, Japanese, Portuguese and Spanish.)
Connaissance de la Connaissance (vol. 3) (1st edn 1986) (1990). Paris: Seuil, collection 'Points'. (Also available in Greek, Italian, Japanese, Portuguese and Spanish.)
Les Idées. Leur habitat, leur vie, leurs moeurs, leur organisation (vol. 4) (1991). Paris: Seuil. (Also available in Chinese, Greek, Italian, Japanese, Portuguese and Spanish.)
L'identité humaine (vol. 5) (2003) (1st edn 2001). Paris: Seuil. (Also available in Greek, Italian, Iranian, Japanese, Portuguese and Spanish.)
Ethique (vol. 6) (2006) (1st edn 2004). Paris: Seuil (coll. 'Points Essais').

Morin, E. (2005) *Introduction à la Pensée Complexe* (2nd edn) Paris: Seuil (coll. 'Points').

Morin, E. (2003) *Les sept savoirs nécessaires à l'éducation du futur* (first published 2000) Paris: Seuil. (Also available in Croatian, Deutsch, English, Greek, Indonesian, Italian, Korean, Portuguese, Spanish and Turkish.)

Morin, E., R. Motta and E.R. Ciurana (2003) *Éduquer pour l'ère planétaire, la pensée complexe comme méthode d'apprentissage dans l'erreur e l'incertitudes humaines*. Paris: Balland.

Mulder, K. and L. Jansen (2005) Evaluating the sustainability of research of a University of Technology: Towards a general methodology. In: *Proceedings 'Committing Universities to SD, RNS TU*. Graz (Austria), pp. 249–56.

Ndebele, N. (2001) *The Way Forward for the University of Cape Town. Introduction to Vision 2001 and Beyond. Cape Town (South Africa): University of Cape Town*. Accessed from: www.uct.ac.za/downloads/uct.ac.za/about/management/vcvision2001andbeyond.pdf

Neave, G. (ed.) (2000) *The Universities' Responsibilities to Society: International Perspectives*. Amsterdam: Elsevier Science.

Neave, G. (2001) *Educación Superior: Historia y Política*. Barcelona: Editorial Gedisa.

Northouse, P.J. (2001) *Leadership Theory and Practice*. New York: Sage.

Nowotny, H., Scott, P. and Gibbons, M. (2002) *Rethinking Science: Knowledge and the Public*. Cambridge (UK): Polity Press.

Ordonez, V. (2005) Tertiary education and Education for All: Establishing policy linkages. *Higher education in Europe*, **XXX**(30), 3–4, pp. 267–75.

Peet, D.J., Mulder, K.F. and Bijma, A. (2004) Integrating SD into engineering courses at the Delft University of Technology: the individual interaction method. *International Journal of Sustainability in Higher Education*, 5(3), pp. 278–88.

Perkin, H. (2006) History of universities. In: Forest, James and P. Altbach (eds) *International Handbook of Higher Education*. Dordrecht, Netherlands: Springer, pp. 159–206.

Phillips, N., T.B. Lawrence and C. Hardy (2004) Discourse and institutions. *Academy of Management Review*, **29**(4), pp. 635–52.

Pusser, B. (2006) Reconsidering higher education and the public good: the role of public spheres. In: W. G. Tierney (ed.) *Governance and the Public Good*. Albany: State University of New York Press.

Reason, P. and Bradbury, H. (eds) (2001) *Handbook of Action Research: Participative Inquiry and Practice*. London: Sage.

Rodríguez Días, M.A. (2003) Ensino superior, ciência e tecnologia:bases para a utopia da construçao de uma sociedad mais justa. *Estudo & Debate*, **10**(1).

Rodrígues Días, M.A. (1998) Higher education: vision and action for the coming century. *Prospects*, **XXVIII**(4), December, Issue Number 10.

Roorda, N. (2004) Policy development for sustainability in higher education – results of AISHE audits. In: Peter Blaze Corcoran and Arjen E.J. Wals (eds) *Higher Education and the Challenge of Sustainability*. Dordrecht: Kluwer, pp. 305–18.

Sachs, J.D. (2005) *The End of Poverty. Economic Possibilities for Our Time*. New York (USA): Penguin.

Sadlak, J. (2000) Globalization versus the universal role of the university. La globalization contre le rôle universel de l'université; UNESCO European Centre for Higher Education (Romania). *Higher Education in Europe/Enseignement supérieur en Europe* 25(2) pp. 243–9.

Sanyal, B.C. (2005) *The role of higher education in obtaining EFA goals with particular focus on developing countries*. Paper prepared for UNESCO Forum on Higher Education, Research and Knowledge. Paris: UNESCO.

Shapiro, B. (2000) The role of universities in a changing culture. In: S.E. Khan and D. Pavlich (eds) *Academic Freedom and the Inclusive University*. Vancouver and Toronto: University of British Columbia Press.

Siegel, D.J. (2006) Organizational response to the demand and expectation for diversity. *Higher Education*, **52**(3), pp. 465–86.

Sörlin, S. and H. Vessuri (eds) (2007) *Knowledge Society vs. Knowledge Economy: Knowledge, Power and Politics*. New York: Palgrave Macmillan.

Spies, Ph. (2000) University Traditions and the Challenge of Global Transformation. In: S. Inayatullah and J. Gidley (eds) *The University in Transformation: Global Perspectives on the Futures of the University*. Westport, CT (USA): Bergin and Garvey.

Stiglitz, J. (2006) *Making Globalization Work*. New York (USA): Penguin.

Stiglitz, J. (2002) *Globalization and its Discontents*. New York (USA): W. W. Norton.

Stokes, D.E. (1997) *Pasteur's Quadrant: Basic Science and Technological Innovation*. Washington, DC (USA): Brookings Institution Press.

Stuart, M. (2002) *Collaborating for Change? Managing Widening Participation in Further and Higher Education*. Leicester (UK): The National Institute of Adult Continuing Education – England and Wales (NIACE).

Tandon, R. (2005) *Reinventing the Wheel. Whither Community Development?* INTRAC's Civil Society and Community Development Conference. Amman, April, 18–20. New Delhi: PRIA.

Talloires *Declaration on the civic roles and social responsibilities of higher education (The)* (2005) Accessed from: http://www.tufts.edu/talloiresnetwork/downloads/Talloires-Declaration2005.pdf

Taylor, P. (2003) Making learning relevant: principles and evidence from recent experiences. Chapter III in: *Education for Rural Development. Towards New Policy Responses*, Paris: FAO-UNESCO.

Taylor, P. and S. Boser (2006) Power and transformation in higher education institutions – challenges for change. *IDS Bulletin* 37(6), Brighton (UK): Institute of Development Studies.

Taylor, P., J. Pettit and A. Deak (2006) *Learning for social change. Exploring concepts, theory and practice*. Brighton (UK): Institute of Development Studies.

Teichler, U. (2003) *Hochschule und Arbeitswelt: Konzepte, Diskussionen, Trends* (Higher Education and the World of Work: Concepts, Discussions, Trends). Frankfurt, (Germany) and New York: Campus Verlag.

UNESCO (2003) *General Report by Mr Jacques Proulx. The Meeting of Higher Education Partners*. Paris: UNESCO Headquarters, 23–25 June 2003. Accessed from: http://portal.unesco.org/education/en/file_download.php/9dd8eff2c6e82b9d5b829484e0d22f32final-repE.pdf

University in Transformation: Global Perspectives on the Futures of the University (The) see Inayatullah, S. and J. Gidley (eds) (2000).

Van Damme, D. (2002) *Outlooks for the International Higher Education Community in Constructing the Global Knowledge Society*. Paper presented at the First Global Forum on International Quality Assurance, Accreditation and the Recognition of Qualifications in Higher Education. Paris: UNESCO, 17–18 October.

Wallerstein, I. (2004) *The Uncertainties of Knowledge*. Philadelphia, PA: Temple University Press.

Wallerstein, I. (2003) *Decline of American Power: The U.S. in a Chaotic World*. New York: New Press.

Wals, Arjen E.J. (2007) *Social Learning Towards a Sustainable World, Principles, Perspectives, and Praxis*. Netherlands: Wageningen Academic Publishers.

Weaver, P., L. Jansen, G. von Grootveld et al. (2000) *Sustainable Technology Development*. Sheffield (UK): Greenleaf Publishing.

Wilkinson, D. (1994) Transforming the social order: The role of the university in social change. *Sociological Forum*, **9**(3) September.

REGIONAL STUDIES

AFRICA

ADEA Working Group on Higher Education/AAU (2006) *Toolkit for Mainstreaming Gender in Higher Education in Africa*. Accra (Ghana): ADEA Working Group on Higher Education/Association of African Universities. Accessed from: http://www.adeanet.org/downloadcenter/WGHE/Tooltik-complete.pdf

ADEA (2007) *Working Group on Higher Education (The)*. Paris: Association for the Development of Education in Africa (ADEA). Accessed from: http://www.adeanet.org/publications/en_pubs_wghe.html

African Development Fund (ADF) (2006) *Multinational Support for Higher Education in The West African Economic and Monetary Union Countries (WAEMU)*. Appraisal report. Department of Social Development, African Development Fund.

African Union (AU) (2006) *Second Decade of Education for Africa (2006–2015)*. Draft Plan of Action. Addis Ababa (Ethiopia).

Ajayi, J.F.A., L.K.H. Goma and A.G. Johnson (1996) *The African Experience with Higher Education*. Accra: Association of African Universities (AFU).

Ajayi, S. Ibi (2003) *Globalization and Equity in Sub-Saharan Africa*. Paper presented at the Fourth Annual Global Development Conference. Cairo. Ibadan (Nigeria): University of Ibadan. http://www.gdnet.org/pdf/Fourth_Annual_Conference/Parallels1/SubSaharanAfrica/ajayi_paper.pdf

Assié-Lumumba, N.T. (2003) *Recent Higher Education Innovations in Sub-Saharan Africa: Universities in Francophone Countries*. Accra (Ghana): ADEA Working Group on Higher Education/Association of African Universities (AAU).

Association of African Universities (AAU) (2004) *The Implication of WTO/GATS for Higher Education in Africa*. Proceedings of Accra Workshop on GATS. Accra: Association of African Universities.

Association of African Universities (AAU) (2006) *Planning Consultation Report. Regional Capacity Mobilisation Initiative (RCMI) for Revitalizing Higher Education in Africa*. Accra (Ghana): AAU.

Bentley, K., A. Habib and S. Morrow (2006) *Academic Freedom, Institutional Autonomy and the Corporatised University in Contemporary South Africa*. Pretoria: Council on Higher Education.

Bloom, D., D. Canning and K. Chan (2006) *Higher Education and Economic Development in Africa*. Washington, DC (USA): Harvard University.

Doulo, D. (2004) The brain drain in Africa. *JHEA/RESA* **2**(3), pp. 1–18.

Faria, Fernanda (2004) *Crisis Management in Sub-Saharan Africa – The Role of the European Union*. Paris: European Union Institute for Security Studies. Occasional Paper 51. (also available in French)

Harvey, C. (2004) *The Role of Universities in Contributing to Education for All in the Windhoek Office Cluster Countries*. Windhoek (Namimbia): UNESCO Windhoek Office Cluster Countries.

Holtland, G. and A. Boeren (2006) *Achieving the Millennium Goals in Sub-Saharan Africa: The Role of International Capacity Building Programmes for Higher Education and Research*. The Hague: Nuffic. Accessed from: http://www.nuffic.nl/pdf/os/Achieving-millennium-goals.

Jonathan, R. (2006) *Academic Freedom, Institutional Autonomy and Public Accountability in Higher Education: a Framework for Analysis of the 'State-Sector' Relationship in a Democratic South Africa*. Cape Town (South Africa): Council on Higher Education.

Kibwika, P. (2006) *Learning to Make Change: Developing Innovation Competence for Recreating the African University of the 21st Century*. Netherlands: Wageningen Academic Publishers.

Kagisano Issue Number 4 (2006) *Ten Years of Higher Education Under Democracy*. Cape Town (South Africa): Council on Higher Education.

Kraak, A. (ed.) (2000) *Changing Modes: New Knowledge Production and its Implications for Higher Education in South Africa*. Pretoria (South Africa): HSRC.

Mbaya, M. (2001) Le rôle de l'université dans une société africaine en mutation. *Afrique et développement*. **XXVI**(3 et 4), pp. 27–42.

Ministry of Education, Republic of South Africa (2001) *National Plan for Higher Education in South Africa*. Accessed from: http://aafaq.kfupm.edu.sa/features/npafrica.pdf

Moja, Teboho (2002) *Globalisation Apartheid – The Role of Higher Education in Development*. Montréal: Université Laval, Québec Canada.

Saint, W.S. (1992) *Universities in Africa: Strategies for Stabilization and Revitalization*. World Bank Technical Paper, 194. Washington, DC (USA).

Samoff, J. and Carrol, B. (2004) *From Manpower Planning to the Knowledge Era: World Bank Policies on Higher Education in Africa*, pp. 19–28. ED.04/Conf. 611/06. Paris: UNESCO.

Sen, A. (2001) *Development as Freedom*. London, Oxford University Press. (Also available in French, German, Italian, Spanish.)

UNESCO (2003) *Recent Developments and Future Prospects of Higher Education in Sub-Saharan Africa in the 21st Century*. Meeting of higher education partners, Paris, 23–25 June 2003, UNESCO Headquarters.

UNESCO (2006) *High-Level Experts' Meeting on the UNESCO Teacher Training Initiative for Sub-Saharan Africa. Final Report*. Paris: UNESCO Headquarters, 9–21 October 2005. (ED/HED/TED/2005/ME/7/REV). (Also available in French.) Accessed from: http://unesdoc.unesco.org/images/0014/001437/143738E.pdf; http://unesdoc.unesco.org/images/0014/001437/143738f.pdf

Zeleza Tiyambe, P. (2006) *The Study of Africa*. Volume 1: *Disciplinary and Interdisciplinary Encounters*; Volume 2: *Transnational and Global Engagements*. Dakar: Codesria Book Series, 2006–7.

Zeleza Tiyambe, P. (2004) *African Universities in the Twenty-First Century*. Volume 1: *Liberalization and Internationalization*; Volume 2: *Knowledge and Society*. Dakar: Codesria Book Series, 2004.

ARAB STATES

Badrawi, N. (2006) *Cross Border – Higher Education for Capacity Development*. Paper presented to The World Bank, OECD and Nuffic International workshop on cross-border higher education for capacity development. The Hague, Netherlands.

Bashshur, M. (2004) *Higher Education in the Arab States*. Beirut: UNESCO Regional Bureau for Education in the Arab States.

Mazawi, André Elias (1999) *Gender and higher education in the Arab States*. Boston: Center for International Higher Education, *International Higher Education*, Fall issue.

Mekouar, H. (1996) University autonomy and academic freedom in Morocco: Elements for a current debate. *Higher Education Policy*, **9**(4), pp. 303–8.

UNESCO Regional Office, Arab States (UNEDBAS) (2003) *Higher Education in the Arab Region 1998–2003*. Meeting of Higher Education Partners. Paris, 23–25 June. Document prepared by UNESCO Regional Bureau for Education in the Arab States.

ASIA AND THE PACIFIC

Alam, M., M.S. Haque, and S.F. Siddique (2004) *Private Higher Education in Bangladesh*. N.V. Varghese (ed.) Paper presented at the Policy Forum on Private Higher Education in Africa, held on 2–3 November in Accra, Ghana. Accessed from: http://unesdoc.unesco.org/images/0015/001501/150151e.pdf

Altbach, P.G. and T. Umakoshi (2004) *Asian Universities – Historical Perspectives and Contemporary Challenges*. Baltimore, MD: Johns Hopkins University Press.

Chen, David Y. (2002) The amalgamation of Chinese higher education institutions. In: *Education Policy Analysis Archives*. **10**(20), April.

Jason, T. (1999) Recent developments in higher education in Singapore. *International Higher Education*, **14**, winter.

Kaneko, M. (2004) Japanese higher education: Contemporary reform and the influence of tradition. In: P.G. Altbach and T. Umakoshi (eds) *Asian Universities: Historical Perspectives and Contemporary Challenges* (pp. 115–43). Baltimore, MD: Johns Hopkins University Press.

Lee, Molly N. (2004) *Restructuring Higher Education in Malaysia. School of Educational Studies*. Penang, Malaysia: Universiti Sains Malaysia (USM).

Meek, V. Lynn and C. Suwanwela (eds) (2007) *Higher Education, Research, and Knowledge in the Asia-Pacific Region*. International Association of Universities (IAU). Basingstoke (UK): Palgrave Macmillan.

Mohanty, R. and R. Tandon (2006) *Participatory Citizenship. Identity, Exclusion, Inclusion*. New Delhi: Society for Participatory Research in Asia.

Mok, K.H. (2007) *When Neo-Liberalism Colonizes Higher Education in Asia: Bringing the 'Public' Back in the Contemporary University*. Paper submitted at International Conference held at Zhejiang University, 2–4 April.

Oba, J. (2005) *Japanese Higher Education. Incorporation of National Universities and the Development of Private Universities*. Paper prepared for seminars on higher education, held in Istanbul and Ankara,Turkey, February. Accessed from: http://www.tr.emb-japan.go.jp/T_04/Education.pdf

Postiglione, G.A. and C.L. Grace (1997) *Asian Higher Education: An International Handbook and Reference Guide*. London: Greenwood Press.

SEAMEO-RIHED (2006) *Proceedings of Regional Seminar on Higher Education in Southeast Asian Countries: A Current Update*. Bangkok: SEAMEO-RIHED. Accessed from: http://www.rihed.seameo.org/Publication/HECurrentreport.pdf

Tilak, J.G.G. (2002) Privatization in India, International Higher Education. *International Higher Education*, Fall issue.

UNESCO (2005) *Implications of WTO/GATS on Higher Education in Asia and the Pacific*. Part I. Papers presented at the Regional Seminar for Asia Pacific 27–29 April, Seoul, The Republic of Korea (UNESCO Forum occasional paper series 8). ED.2006/WS/46; ED.06/GATS Seminar. Asia-Pacific/1- Accessed from: http://unesdoc.unesco.org/images/0014/001467/146737e.pdf; Part II. (UNESCO Forum occasional paper series 9). ED.2006/WS/48; ED.06/GATS Seminar.Asia-Pacific/1 – Accessed from: http://unesdoc.unesco.org/images/0014/001467/146742e.pdf

UNESCO (2005) *University industry partnership in China: present scenario and future strategy; project report*. CN/2005/PI/H/2. (Also available in Chinese.)

UNESCO/IIEP (2001) *Impact of the Economic Crisis on Higher Education in East Asia: Country Experiences*. N. V. Varghese (ed.). (Policy Forum,12) Paris: UNESCO-IIEP.

Varghese, N.V. (2004) *Institutional Restructuring in Higher Education in Asia: Trends and Patterns*. Paper prepared for the Policy Forum held in Asia, 23–24 August, Hue City (Vietnam). Paris: UNESCO-IIEP. Accessed from: http://www.unesco.org/iiep/PDF/pubs/PolForum_Asia04.pdf

Yibling, Wang (2006) Chinese Higher Education on an Overpass of Four-fold Transitions. *Higher Education Research*, No.11.

EUROPE

Bologna Process (2007) *Stocktaking Report 2007*. Report from a working group appointed by the Bologna Follow-up Group to the Ministerial Conference in London, May. PPAPG/D16(6909)/0507.

Bridges, D. et al. (eds) (2007) *Higher Education and National Development: Universities and Societies in Transition*. Abingdon (UK): Routledge.

Corbett, A. (2003) Ideas, institutions and policy entrepreneurs: towards a new history of higher education in the European Community. *European Journal of Education* **38**(3), pp. 315–30.

Education International Study (2007) *Constructing Paths to Staff Mobility in the European Higher Education Area*. Prepared by Conor Cradden for the Bologna Process Official Seminar 'Making Bologna a Reality – Mobility of Staff and Students'. Brussels: E.I.

Fägerlind, I. and G. Strömqvist (2004) *Reforming Higher Education in the Nordic Countries: Studies of Change in Denmark, Finland, Iceland, Norway and Sweden. Higher Education and Specialized Training. (New Trends in Higher Education)*. Paris: UNESCO-IIEP.

Graz Declaration 2003. *Forward from Berlin: the Role of the Universities*. Geneva: EUA. Accessed from: http//www.unige.ch/be (multilingual version).

Harkavy, I. (2006) The role of universities in advancing citizenship and social justice in the 21st century. *Education, Citizenship and Social Justice* **1**(1), pp. 5–37.

Kehm, B. and U. Lanzendorf (eds) (2006) *Reforming University Governance: Changing Conditions for Research in Four European Countries*. Bonn (Germany): Lemmens Verlags.

LATIN AMERICA AND THE CARIBBEAN

Arocena, R. and J. Sutz (2005) Latin American universities: from an original revolution to an uncertain transition. *Higher Education*, **50**(4), pp. 573–92.

Arocena, R. and J. Sutz (2001) *La Universidad Latinoamericana del Futuro Tendencias – Escenarios – Alternativas*.

Montevideo: Universidad de la República Oriental del Uruguay, Colección UDUAL 11.

Barrow, C.W. and S. Didou-Aupetit (2003) *Globalisation, Trade Liberalisation, and Higher Education in North America. The Emergence of a New Market under NAFTA?* Pays-Bas, Dordrecht: Kluwer Academic Publishers.

Brunner, J.J. (2007) *Tendencias Internacionales y transformaciones en la Enseñanza Superior.* Yucatán (Mexico): Universidad Autónoma de Yucatán.

Centro Interuniversitario de Desarrollo (Cinda) (2007) *Educación Superior en Iberoamérica.* Informe. Santiago, Santiago de Chile: Cinda.

Declaración de Caracas en el Marco del II Encuentro de Consejos de Rectores, Redes Universitarias y Entidades vinculadas a la Educación Superior de América Latina y el Caribe (2007). Caracas, 4 May. Accessed from: http://www.iesalc. unesco.org.ve/sid/Declaracion_CcsEEF.pdf (bilingual, Spanish/English).

Didriksson, A. (2006) *Universidad, sociedad del conocimiento y nueva economía.* Ciudad de México, Red de Investigadores Sobre Educación Superior (RISEU).

Education policy and social change *see* Morales-Gomez and Torres (1992).

García Guadilla, C. (2002) ACGS (GATS) *Educación Superior y América Latina.* Accessed from: www.google.es/search?q=escenarios

García Guadilla, C. (2003) *Tensiones y Transiciones. Educación Superior Latinoamericana en los Albores del Tercer Milenio.* Caracas: Nueva Sociedad y Centro de Estudios del Desarrollo (CENDES).

Gorostiaga, X. (2000) En busca del eslabón perdido entre educación y desarrollo: desafíos y retos para la Universidad en América Latina y el Caribe. In: Tünnermann, Bernheim, C. and López Segrera, F. (eds) *La educación en el horizonte del siglo XXI*, Colección Respuestas, No. 12. Caracas: IESALC-UNESCO.

López Segrera, F. (2006) *Escenarios Mundiales de la Educación Superior.* Buenos Aires: Consejo Latinoamericano de Ciencias Sociales (CLACSO).

López Segrera, F., J.L. Grosso and M.R. Muñoz (2004) *América Latina y el Caribe en el Siglo XX. Perspectiva y Prospectiva de la Globalización.* México: Universidad Autónoma de Zacatecas.

Mollis, M. (2003) Las Universidades en América Latina: ¿Reformadas o Alteradas? In: Marcela Mollis (ed.) *La Cosmética del Poder Financiero.* Buenos Aires: Consejo Latinoamericano de Ciencias Sociales (CLACSO).

Morales-Gómez, D.A. and C.A. Torres (1992) *Education, Policy, and Social Change, Experiences from Latin America.* London: Praeger/Greenwood.

Ordorika, I. (1995) Organización, Gobierno y Liderazgo Universitario: una base conceptual para el análisis del cambio en la educación superior. *Revista Universidades*, ANUIES, México, No. 10, July–December.

Programa Politicas da Cor na Educaçao Brasileira (PPCOR) (2007) Políticas de ação afirmativa no ensino superior: avaliação e perspectivas. *Boletim*, **32**, June.

Rivoir, A.L. (2005) *Latin American Perspectives in the Information and Knowledge Society: Different Approaches and their Implications for Policies.* Montevideo: Instituto del Tercer Mundo (IteM). (World Summit on the Information Society. Tunis, 16–18 November 2005) Accessed from: http://wsis-papers.choike.org/ (also available in French and Spanish).

Peters, F. (1998) An overview of Caribbean higher education. In: *Higher Education in the Caribbea*n. Caracas: IESALC/UNESCO.

Rodríguez Días, M.A. (2004) *Cooperación Internacional: Cuestión de Necesidad.* Accessed from: http://www.crue.org/prdias.htm.

Torres, Carlos Alberto (ed.) (1995) *Education and Social Change in Latin America.* Albert Park (Australia): James Nicholas Publishers.

Tünnermann, Bernheim C. and de Souza Chaui, M. (2004) *Challenges of the University in the Knowledge Society, Five Years after the World Conference on Higher Education.* (UNESCO Forum Occasional Paper Series, 4) Paris, UNESCO (ED-2004/WS/11).

Vessuri, H. (2006) (ed.) *Conocimiento y Necesidades de las Sociedades Latinoamericanas.* Caracas: Ediciones IVIC.

Vessuri, H., M. Mollis and L. Lomnitz (eds) (2006) *Ciencia, Tecnología y Educación Superior en América Latina: Convergencias y Tensiones.* Buenos Aires: CLACSO.

Williams, G. and C. Harvey (1996) Universidad de las Indias Occidentales: el desarrollo de personal y la igualdad de los sexos en las universidades caribeñas del Commonwealth: la experiencia de la Universidad de las Indias Occidentales In: *La Mujer en la Gestión de la Enseñanza Superior*, series pp. 185–99. Caracas: UNESCO-CRESALC.

NORTH AMERICA

Association of Universities and Colleges of Canada (AUCC) (2001) *Canadian Higher Education and the GATS.* AUCC Background Paper. Ottawa (Canada): Association of Universities and Colleges of Canada.

Association of Universities and Colleges of Canada (AUCC) (2003) *Globalization of higher education and research: a Canadian priority for engagement in the Americas.* A brief presented to the Department of Foreign Affairs and International Trade (DFAIT) in preparation for the Special Summit of the Americas. Accessed from: http://socrates.aucc.ca/_pdf/english/reports/2003/special_summit_americas_e.pdf

Eckel, P. and J.E. King (2004) *Overview of Higher Education in the United States: Diversity, Access, and the Role of the Marketplace.* Washington, DC: American Council on Education.

Farrell, G., S. Johnstone, and P. Lopez del Puerto (1996) *The Role of Technology in Higher Education in North America. Policy Implication. Understanding the Differences.* Working Paper No. 5, Series on Higher Education in Canada, Mexico, and the United States. Boulder, CO (USA): Western Interstate Commission for Higher Education.

Jones, G.A., T. Shanahan and P. Goyan (2004) The Academic Senate and university governance in Canada. *The Canadian Journal of Higher Education*, **34**(2), pp. 35–68.

Kezar, A., Chambers, A. and Burkhardt, J. (eds) (2005) *Higher Education for the Public Good: Emerging Voices from a National Movement.* San Francisco (USA): Jossey Bass.

Marois, P. (1998) *Canadian Intervention on the Occasion of the UNESCO World Conference on Higher Education.* Paris: UNESCO.

Program for North American Mobility in Higher Education. Call for proposals 2007. *Neighbouring in the global village: North American cooperation and collaboration in Higher Education. A context for the program for North American Mobility in Higher Education: Past, Present, and Future Consortium for North American Higher Education Collaboration.* http://www.hrsdc.gc.ca/en/hip/lld/lssd/iam/CFP/NA-Guidelines-2007.pdf

Pusser, B. and I. Ordorika (2001) Bringing political theory to university governance: The University of California and the Universidad Nacional Autónoma de México. In: *Higher Education, Handbook of Theory and Research*. Vol. XVI, pp. 147–94.

INTERNATIONAL AND MULTILATERAL ORGANIZATIONS

Council of Europe (2006) *Academic Freedom and University Autonomy*. Report. Committee on Culture, Science and Education. Strasbourg, Parliamentary Assembly. Doc.10943.

Commission of the European Communities (2005). *Mobilising the Brainpower of Europe: Enabling Universities to Make their Full Contribution to the Lisbon Strategy*. Brussels, Communication from the Commission to the Council and the European Parliament. COM (2005) 152 final. Brussels.

Commission of the European Communities (2006) *Delivering on the Modernisation Agenda for Universities: Education, Research and Innovation*. Communication from the Commission to the Council and the European Parliament. COM (2006) 208 final. Brussels. Accessed from: http://www.kowi.de/en/Portaldata/2/Resources/fp/comuniv2006_en.pdf

European Commission (2006) *Education and Training 2010. Diverse Systems, Shared Goals. Higher Education in the Lisbon Strategy*. Accessed from: http://ec.europa.eu/education/policies/2010/lisbon_en.htm

European Commission (2007) Directorate-General for Education and Culture. *Focus on the structure of higher education in Europe. National trends in the Bologna Process*, 2006/07 Edition. Brussels: Eurydice. Accessed from: http://www.eurydice.org

Organisation for Economic Co-operation and Development (2005) What is a University in the 21st Century? (By B. Denman) *Higher Education Management and Policy*, **17**(2), December 5, pp. 1–156.

Organisation for Economic Co-operation and Development (OECD) (2006) *Education at a Glance. OECD Indicators*. Accessed from: http://www.oecd.org/dataoecd/31/52/37393677.pdf

Organisation for Economic Co-operation and Development (2006) Higher education management and policy. *Institutional Management in Higher Education*. **18**(2). (also available in French).

Organisation for Economic Co-operation and Development (2006) *Lessons Learned from an OECD Review of 14 Regions Throughout 12 Countries. Supporting the Contribution of Higher Education to Regional Development*. (By F. Marmolejo and J. Puukka). Contribution to UNESCO Forum on Higher Education, Research and Knowledge. Colloquium on Research and Higher Education Policy.

Organisation for Economic Co-operation and Development (2006) *The Economics of Knowledge: Why Education is Key for Europe's Success*. (By Andreas Schleicher) Programme for International Student Assessment (PISA). Accessed from: http://www.pisa.oecd.org

Organisation for Economic Co-operation and Development (2006) *Society at a Glance*. OECD Social indicators 2006. Multilingual summaries. Accessed from: www.sourceoecd.org/societyatglance

Organisation for Economic Co-operation and Development (2007) *Evidence in Education. Linking Research and Policy*. Paris: Centre for Educational Research and Innovation.

Organisation for Economic Co-operation and Development (2007) Globalisation, the 'idea of a university' and its ethical regimes. (By Marginson, S.) *Higher Education Management and Policy*, **19**(1). (IMHE Programme) (also available in French).

Organisation for Economic Co-operation and Development (2007) *Human Capital. How What you Know Shapes your Life*. (By B. Keeley) OECD Insights Series. (also available in French).

UN – The United Nations (2007) *The Millennium Development Goals. Report 2007*. New York. Accessed from: http://www.un.org/millenniumgoals/pdf/mdg2007.pdf; http://www.onu.org.pe/upload/documentos/MDG_Report_2007-r2.pdf

UNDP – United Nations Development Programme (2006) *Human Development Report 2006. Beyond Scarcity: Power, Poverty and the Global Water Crisis*. New York. Accessed from: http://hdr.undp.org/hdr2006/pdfs/report/HDR06-complete.pdf; http://www.undp.org/spanish/publicaciones/informeanual2006/IAR06_SP.pdf.

UNESCO (1998) *Higher Education in the Twenty-first century: Vision and Action. Final Report*. Paris: World Conference on Higher Education (WCHE), UNESCO Headquarters, 5–9 October 1998. Accessed from: http://unesdoc.unesco.org/images/0011/001163/116345e.pdf; http://unesdoc.unesco.org/images/0011/001163/116345s.pdf; http://unesdoc.unesco.org/images/0011/001163/116345f.pdf

UNESCO (1998) *Higher Education and Research: Challenges and Opportunities: Thematic Debate*. Paris: World Conference on Higher Education (WCHE), UNESCO Headquarters, 5–9 October 1998.

UNESCO (1998) *Requirements of the World of Work. Thematic Debate*. Paris: World Conference on Higher Education (WCHE), UNESCO Headquarters, 5–9 October 1998.

UNESCO – United Nations Educational, Scientific and Cultural Organization (2003) *Challenges of the University in the Knowledge Society, Five Years After the World Conference on Higher Education*. By C.Tünnermann Bernheim and M. de Souza Chaui. (UNESCO Forum Occasional Paper Series, No. 4).

UNESCO (2003) *Universities and Globalization: Private Linkages, Public Trust*. P. Breton, G. and M. Lambert (eds) Paris: UNESCO/Université Laval/Economica.

UNESCO (2003) Globalization and its implications for universities in developing countries. (By G. Mohamedbhai) In: Breton, G. and Lambert, M. (eds) *Universities and Globalization: Private Linkages, Public Trust*. Paris: UNESCO/Universite Laval/Economica.

UNESCO (2003) Higher education and rural development: a new perspective. (By Macguire, C. and D. Atchoarena) In: Atchoarena, D. and L. Gasperini (eds) *Education for Rural Development: Towards New Policy Resources*. Joint study conducted by FAO and UNESCO-IIEP.

UNESCO (2004) *Towards Knowledge Societies: UNESCO World Report*. (By J. Bindé) World Summit on the Information Society. (also available in Arabic, Chinese, French, Russian and Spanish).

UNESCO (2004) *Higher education in a globalized society: position paper*. Prepared by S. Uvalic-Trumbic (also available in Arabic, Chinese, French Russian and Spanish). Accessed from: http://unesdoc.unesco.org/images/0013/001362/136247e.pdf; http://unesdoc.unesco.org/images/0013/001362/136247a.pdf; http://unesdoc.unesco.org/images/0013/001362/136247cb.pdf; http://unesdoc.unesco.org/images/0013/001362/136247f.pdf; http://unesdoc.unesco.org/images/0013/001362/136247r.pdf; http://unesdoc.unesco.org/images/0013/001362/136247s.pdf

UNESCO (2005) Developmental dialogues in the context of education for all and quality assurance in higher education. *Higher Education in Europe*, **XXX** (3–4), pp. 247–463.

UNESCO (2005) *Globalization and Education for Sustainable Development – Sustaining the Future*. International conference: Nagoya, Japan, 28–29 June 2005. UNU-UNESCO-ACU. Accessed from: http://www.ias.unu.edu/research/Nagoyaconference.cfm.

UNESCO (2005) *Guidelines and recommendations for reorienting teacher education to address sustainability.* Education for sustainable development in action: technical paper, no. 2. Paris (ED.2005/WS/66). (also available in Arabic, French, and Spanish)

UNESCO (2006) *Challenges and opportunities of re-inventing higher education institutions as centres of research capacity building*. Presentation by M. Mammo at UNESCO Forum on Higher Education, Research and Knowledge, November 29 – December 1.

UNESCO (2006) *Drivers and barriers for implementing sustainable development in higher education*. Education for sustainable development in action: technical paper, no. 3. Prepared by J. Holmberg and B.E. Samuelson. (ED.2006/WS/63) (Workshop on Drivers and Barriers for Implementing Sustainable Development in Higher Education, Göteborg, Sweden, 2005).

UNESCO (2006) *Globalization and Education for Sustainable Development: Sustaining the Future*. Laura Wong (ed.). International Conference on Globalization and Education for Sustainable Development: Sustaining the Future. Nagoya (Japan). (BSP/DIR/2006/RP/H/1). Accessed from: http://unesdoc.unesco.org/images/0014/001492/149295e.pdf

UNESCO (2006) *Universities as Centres of Research and Knowledge Creation: An Endangered Species?* UNESCO Forum on Higher Education, Research and Knowledge. Colloquium on Research and Higher Education Policy. Paris, 29 November to 1 December 2006. (also available in French).

UNESCO (2006) *Round Table on the Role of UNESCO in the Construction of Knowledge Societies through the UNITWIN/UNESCO Chairs Programme* Proceedings. Tunis, World Summit on the Information Society. ED.2006/WS/51.

UNESCO (2007) *Educational Equity and Public Policy*. Prepared by J. Sherman and J.M. Poirier. Montréal: UNESCO-Institute for Statistics (UIS).

UNESCO (2007) *Ethical Implications of Emerging Technologies: a Survey*. Prepared by Mary Rundle and Chris Conley. Paris (CI.2007/WS/2). Accessed from: http://unesdoc.unesco.org/images/0014/001499/149992E.pdf

UNESCO (2007) *Knowledge, Power and Dissent. Critical Perspectives on Higher Education and Research in the Knowledge Society*. G. Neave (ed.). (Education on the Move series), Paris.

UNESCO/AGFUND (2005) *UNESCO/AGFUND Cooperation: a Joint Force Serving Human Development*. ODG/HGA/05/3. (also available in French).

World Bank (1988) *Education in Sub-Saharan Africa: Policies for Adjustment, Revitalization and Expansion*. A World Bank Policy Study. Washington, DC (USA).

World Bank (2000) *Higher Education in Developing Countries: Peril and Promise*. Washington, DC (USA).

World Bank (2002) *Constructing Knowledge Societies: New Challenges for Tertiary Education*. Report. Washington, DC (USA). http://www.kowi.de/en/Portaldata/2/Resources/fp/comuniv2006_en.pdf

World Bank (2007) *Atlas of Global Development: A Visual Guide to the World's Greatest Challenges*. (By H. Collins) Washington, DC (USA).

World Bank (2007) *Global Monitoring Report 2007: Confronting the Challenges of Gender Equality and Fragile States*. Washington, DC (USA).

World Bank (2007) *World Development Report 2007: Development and the Next Generation*. Washington, DC (USA).

USEFUL WEBSITES

INTERNATIONAL AND MULTILATERAL ORGANIZATIONS

Comisión Económica para América Latina (CEPAL)
http://cepal.org

Economic Commission for Latin America and the Caribbean (ECLA)
http://www.eclac.cl

Information Network of Education in Europe – EURYDICE –
www.euridyce.org

Inter-American Development Bank
http://www.iadb.org/

Banco Interamericano de Desarrollo
http://www.iadb.org/index.cfm?language=spanish

Organisation for Economic Co-operation and Development (OECD)
www.ocde.org

UNESCO
http://www.unesco.org http://unesdoc.unesco.org

UNESCO-CEPES
http://www.cepes.es

UNESCO-FORUM
http://portal.unesco.org/education/en/ev

UNESCO-IBE
http://www.ibe.unesco.org

UNESCO-IESALC
http://www.iesalc.unesco.org.ve

UNESCO-IIEP
http://www.unesco.org/iiep

UNESCO-UIS
http://www.uis.unesco.org

WORLD BANK
http://www.worldbank.org

UNDP
http://www.undp.org

UNU United Nations University
http://www.unu.edu

UNU Institute of Advanced Studies
http://www.ias.unu.edu

UNESCO Asia and the Pacific Regional Bureau for Education
www.unescobkk.org

ASSOCIATIONS AND RESEARCH CENTRES IN THE FIELD OF HIGHER EDUCATION

American Council on Education (ACE)
http://www.acenet.edu

Asociación de Universidades Grupo Montevideo
http://www.grupomontevideo.edu.uy/

Association des Universités Africaines (AAU)
http://www.aau.org

Association of Arab Universities (AARU)
http://www.aaru.edu.jo
http://www.kowi.de/en/Portaldata/2/Resources/fp/comuniv2006_en.pdf

Association of Commonwealth Universities (ACU)
http://www.acu.ac.uk/
Association of Universities of Asia and the Pacific (AUAP)
http://sut2.sut.ac.th/auap
Association of Universities and Colleges of Canada (AUCC)
http://www.aucc.ca
Boston College Center for International Higher Education
http://www.bc.edu/cihe/
Cátedra UNESCO de Dirección Universitaria (CUDU)
http://www.upc.es/cudu
Cátedra UNESCO en Gestión de la Educación Superior
http://www.unq.edu.ar/
Centro Interuniversitario de Desarrollo (CINDA)
http://www.cinda.cl
Commonwealth of Learning (COL)
http://www.col.org
Conférence des Présidents d'Université (CPU)
http://www.cpu.fr/
Conferencia de Rectores de las Universidades Españolas (CRUE)
http://www.crue.org
Consejo latinoamericano de ciencias sociales (CLACSO)
http://www.clacso.org
Consortium for North American Higher Education Collaboration (CONAHEC)
http://www.conahec.org
Council for the Development of Social Science Research in Africa
http://www.codesria.org
Council on Higher Education
http://www.che.ac.za
Dutch Network for Sustainable Higher Education
http://www.dho21.nl
Education International/International de l'éducation/ Internacional de la Educación
http://www.ei-ie.org
European Association for International Education
http://www.eaie.org
European Association for Quality Assurance in Higher Education (ENQA)
http://www.enqa.eu
European Centre for Strategic Management of Universities (ESMU)
http://www.esmu.be
European Higher Education in a Worldwide Perspective
http://ec.europa.eu/education/policies/2010/
European University Association (EUA)
http://www.eua.be
Global University Network for Innovation (GUNI)
http://www.guni-rmies.net
Higher Education Authority
http://www.hea.ie
Higher Education Research Institute (HERI)
http://www.gseis.ucla.edu/heri/heri.html
Inter-American Organization for Higher Education (OUI-IOHE)
http://www.oui-iohe.qc.ca
International Association of Universities (AIU)
http://www.unesco.org/aiu
International Association of University Presidents (IAUP)
http://www.iaups.org/
International Education Association of South Africa (IEASA)
http://www.nu.ac.za/ieasa
International Network for Quality Assurance Agencies in

Higher Education (INQAAHE)
http://www.inqaahe.org/
National Center for Higher Education Management Systems NCHEMS
http://www.nchems.org
National Forum on Higher Education for the Public Good AAUP
http://www.thenationalforum.org
National Information Center for Higher Education Policymaking and Analysis
http://www.nchems.org
Network for Curriculum Integration and Academic Mobility (RIMA)
http://www.rima.pucsp.br/
Network of Universities from the Capitals of Europe (UNICA)
http://www.ulb.ac.be/unica
Observatoire International des Reformes Universitaires (ORUS)
http://www.orus-int.org
Organizacion Universitaria Interamericana
http://www.oui-iohe.qc.ca
Programme Palestinian–European–American Cooperation in Education (PEACE)
http://portal.unesco.org/education/en/ev.php-URL_ ID=52853&URL_DO=DO_TOPIC&URL_ SECTION=201.html
Research Institute for Higher Education, Hiroshima University (RIHE)
http://en.rihe.hiroshima-u.ac.jp
Red de investigadores en educación superior (RISEU)
http://www.unam.mx/coordum/riseu
Society for research into Higher Education (SRHE)
http://www.srhe.ac.uk
UNAMAZ Amazonian Universities Association
http://www.campus-oei.org/guiauniv/red011.htm
UNESCO Chair in Applied Research in Education
http://www.unesco.ntu-kpi.kiev.ua/
UNESCO Chair in comparative higher education
http://www.upr.clu.edu/home1200.html
UNESCO Chair in Education for Sustainable Development
http://www.chalmers.se/en/
UNESCO Chair in Education Planning and Management
http://www.aniedu.am/ENG/indexeng.html
UNESCO Chair in Education sciences
http://www.iplac.rimed.cu/
UNESCO Chair in Education Sciences in Latin America and the Caribbean
http://www2.uah.es/educiencias/
UNESCO Chair in Educational Policy, Planning, Management and Research Development
http://mak.ac.ug/makerere/
UNESCO Chair in Educational Technologies
http://dec.uwi.edu/
UNESCO Chair in Evaluation of Higher Education in Algeria
http://portal.unesco.org/education/en/ev.php- URL_ID=40371&URL_DO=DO_TOPIC&URL_SEC- TION=201.html
UNESCO Chair in Evaluation of Institutions and public policies
http://portal.unesco.org/education/en/ev.php- URL_ID=54036&URL_DO=DO_TOPIC&URL_SEC- TION=201.html
UNESCO Chair in Governance and Management of Higher Education
http://www.aaen.edu.yu/english/mainpages-en/ unesco.html

UNESCO Chair in Governance and Management of Higher
  Education
  http://rektorat.unizg.hr/kontakt/kon_engl.htm
UNESCO Chair in Governance and Management of Higher
  Education
  http://unescochair.ubbcluj.ro/
UNESCO Chair in Higher Education
  http://www.mieonline.org/home/
UNESCO Chair in Higher Education
  http://www.pku.edu.cn/eindex.html
UNESCO Chair in Higher Education
  http://www.uniandes.edu.co/
UNESCO Chair in Higher Education for Sustainable
  Development
  http://www.uni-lueneburg.de/infu/
UNESCO Chair in Higher Education Management
  http://www.bath.ac.uk/
UNESCO Chair in Higher Education Management
  http://www.uh.cu/
UNESCO Chair in Higher Education Management and
  Policy
  http://www.gampi.upm.es/
UNESCO Chair in innovation and management of the
  entrepreneurial culture within the university framework
  http://www.usc.es/
UNESCO Chair in Open Distance Learning
  http://www.unisa.ac.za/
UNESCO Chair in Policies of Higher Education
  http://www.pfu.edu.ru/
UNESCO Chair in Political Economy of Education
  http://www.nottingham.ac.uk/
UNESCO Chair in Quality Assurance of Transnational Higher
  Education
  http://www.cinvestav.mx/
UNESCO Chair in Quality Teaching and Learning in Higher
  Education under the Conditions of Systemic Social and

Economic Transformations
  http://www.uwm.edu.pl/
UNESCO Chair in Technical Higher Education, Applied
  Systems Analysis and Informatics
  http://www.unesco.ntu-kpi.kiev.ua/
UNESCO Chair in University Management and Planning
  http://www.usu.ru/
UNESCO Chair of Higher Education
  http://dec.uwi.edu/
UNESCO Chair on Regional Integration and University
  http://catedras.ucol.mx/integra/index.html
UNESCO-EOLSS Chair in Intellectual Entrepreneurship in
  the World of Work for Sustainable Development
  http://www.wspiz.edu.pl/index.php/en/
UNESCO-UNU Chair in Leadership
  http://www.ju.edu.jo/
  http://www.unesco.org/unuoe/unufr/centres/ila.htm
UNESCO-UNU Mobile Chair in University History and
  Future
  http://portal.unesco.org/education/en/ev.php-
  URL_ID=4224&URL_DO=DO_TOPIC&URL_SEC-
  TION=201.html
UNIVERSIA
  http://www.universia.net
Universities Worldwide
  http://univ.cc
Virtual University and e-learning
  http://www.unesco.org/iiep/virtualuniversity/home.php

NOTE

1   The author is responsible for the choice and presentation of
    the facts contained in this work and for the opinions
    expressed therein.